ECONOMICS TODAY

First Canadian Edition

THE MICRO VIEW

Roger LeRoy Miller

Institute for University Studies, Arlington, Texas

Nancy W. Clegg

Kwantlen University College, B.C.

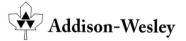 Addison-Wesley

An imprint of Addison Wesley Longman Ltd.

Don Mills, Ontario • Reading, Massachusetts • Harlow, England
Melbourne, Australia • Amsterdam, The Netherlands • Bonn, Germany

To David, Chris, Gillian, and Alex,
for their support and endless patience over my 'booking.'

N.W.C.

Photo Credits
Page 3, J. L. Pelaez/First Light; page 20, First Light; page 50, L.Redkoles/B. Bennett Studios; page 81, Jean-Marc Biboux/Gamma Liaison; page 105, courtesy of H&R Block Inc.; page 135, Martin Rogers/Stock, Boston; page 163, © Corel Corporation; page 191, © Corel Corporation; page 215, © Corel Corporation; page 235, First Light; page 264, courtesy of Future Shop Ltd.; page 291, Peter Menzel/ Stock, Boston; page 318, Addison-Wesley/N.S. Ranadive; page 348, courtesy of the *National Post*; page 369, *The Toronto Star*; page 394, CP Picture Archive (Moe Doiron); page 415, Addison-Wesley/M. Ranadive; page 435, Jon Murray/*The Province*; page 457, © David Witbeck/The Picture Cube; page 477, Sanguinetti/Monkmeyer; page 497, Andy Hernandez/Gamma Liaison.

The publishers will gladly receive information enabling them to rectify any errors in references or credits.

Publisher: Ron Doleman
Managing Editor: Linda Scott
Editor: Muriel Fiona Napier
Proofreader: Gail Copeland
Cover Design: Anthony Leung
Page Design and Layout: Anthony Leung
Production Coordinator: Alexandra Odulak
Manufacturing Coordinator: Sharon Latta Paterson
Printing and Binding: Bryant Press

Canadian Cataloguing in Publication Data

Miller, Roger LeRoy
        Economics today: the micro view

1st Canadian ed.
Includes index.
ISBN 0-201-38935-5

1. Microeconomics. 2. Economics. I. Clegg, Nancy W., 1949-   . II. Title.

HB172.M63 1999   338.5   C99-930527-1

ISBN 0-201-38935-5

Printed and bound in Canada.

A B C D E -BP - 03 02 01 00 99

CONTENTS IN BRIEF

CONTENTS IN DETAIL

Part 3   Market Structure, Resource Allocation, and Regulation   233

Part 4 Productive Factors, Poverty, the Environment, and Development   367

PREFACE

FROM THE AUTHOR

When Addison-Wesley asked if I would be interested in adapting Roger LeRoy Miller's *Economics Today* for use in Canada, I was hesitant. I thought, "Why add another principles book to a market that already has several suitable texts?" But when I looked through Miller's ninth edition, I saw immediately why it had survived so long, and been so popular in the American market. *Economics Today* presents economic principles in a straightforward, intuitive manner which is both relevant to, and readily accessible by, introductory economics students.

In this first Canadian edition of *Economics Today*, I have combined the proven approach of the US text with a thorough Canadianization of the material. Issues and applications are the strength of this text. Each chapter begins with an issue that requires a knowledge of certain economic principles to understand; those principles are presented throughout the chapter, and at the end of the chapter an "Issues and Applications" section appears. Two "For Critical Analysis" questions follow, which help reinforce the theory at hand and encourage students to reflect on economics in the "real" world—their world. In addition, each chapter contains several examples, or "mini-issues," which illustrate the points being made in the text. And I have not ignored the effect of the media on our thinking. "Thinking Critically About the Media" boxes in each chapter look carefully at media reports, and what the real economics of the reportage suggest.

At the same time, I have been mindful of Canada's reliance on global events for our economic well-being. I have therefore used many examples and issues which connect Canada with the rest of the world. In keeping with today's "wired world," I have added a chapter on cybernomics, the economics of the Internet. I have also incorporated Internet applications into many of the chapters and have provided problems for students to solve using the Internet.

Over the years I have found that more of my principles students are heading for degrees in business than in economics. In recognition of this trend, the accompanying Study Guide includes a "Business Section" in each chapter, providing Business Applications and problems that apply economic theory to accounting,

marketing, finance, management, small business, and entrepreneurship.

The complete *Economics Today* package makes economics interesting and relevant to principles students. Whether those students are headed for the more academic world of economics or the practical world of business, or are just interested in the way our economy works, *Economics Today* helps them to see today's economics as a part of their lives.

ECONOMIC PRINCIPLES IN PRACTICE

Chapter Opening Issues. Each opening issue motivates student interest in the key chapter concepts. The issue presented is revisited in the "Issues and Applications" section at the culmination of the chapter.

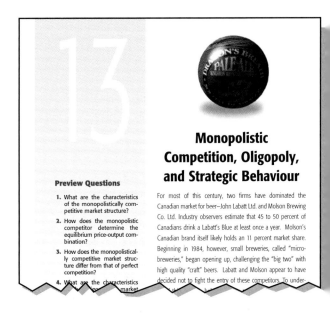

Preview Questions

1. What are the characteristics of the monopolistically competitive market structure?
2. How does the monopolistic competitor determine the equilibrium price-output combination?
3. How does the monopolistically competitive market structure differ from that of perfect competition?
4. What are the characteristics of the oligopoly market

Monopolistic Competition, Oligopoly, and Strategic Behaviour

For most of this century, two firms have dominated the Canadian market for beer—John Labatt Ltd. and Molson Brewing Co. Ltd. Industry observers estimate that 45 to 50 percent of Canadians drink a Labatt's Blue at least once a year. Molson's Canadian brand itself likely holds an 11 percent market share. Beginning in 1984, however, small breweries, called "micro-breweries," began opening up, challenging the "big two" with high quality "craft" beers. Labatt and Molson appear to have decided not to fight the entry of these competitors. To under-

Issues and Applications. The "Issues and Applications" feature is designed to encourage students not just to apply economic concepts, but also to think critically about them. Each begins with the concepts being applied in this instance, and is followed by two "For Critical Analysis" questions that could be used to

Issues and Applications

Game Theory: Opening Up the Brewing Industry

Concepts Applied: Game theory, strategic behaviour, entry deterrence

Craft beers with exotic names like Dragon's Breath Pale Ale and Warthog Lager are slowly gaining a share of the beer market. Labatt and Molson beer companies have found it too expensive to fight their entry.

prompt in-class discussions. Suggested answers to these questions are given at the back of the text (p. 527), as well as in the Instructor's Manual along with the relevant chapter.

Thinking Critically About the Media.
These boxed items keep students abreast of recent newsmaking issues, while at the same time offering a "twist" on typical media coverage. They encourage students to think critically about, rather than simply accept, what they hear and read in the news.

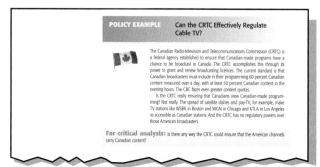

Thinking Critically About the Media | **It's Priceless!**

Museums around the world are filled with one-of-a-kind art objects. In particular, many museums have items that were crafted by humans thousands of years ago. Occasionally, one of these unique artifacts is stolen. The media are quick to point out that because of the unique nature of the stolen object, it is "priceless." The implication is that the utility humans receive from the stolen object is in fact without limits, or infinite. In a world of scarcity, however, nothing can be truly "priceless." If, rather than being stolen, the art object were put up for sale at auction, it would fetch some price below infinity.

Policy Examples.
Many of the economic debates reported in the media involve important policy issues. Here, students are presented with various key policy questions on both the domestic and international fronts. Each "Policy Example" and "International Policy Example" is followed by a "For Critical Analysis" question that encourages students to consider exactly what is involved in the discussion, and what the further ramifications might be. Suggested solutions to these questions are provided in the Instructor's Manual, at the end

of the appropriate chapter. In addition, students will find hints and suggested answers with each chapter in the Study Guide.

A World of Global Examples.
International examples emphasize today's global economy. The issues presented in them, and the "For Critical Analysis" question which follows each, help students to understand the worldwide economy and Canada's place in it. Suggested answers to the questions are given in the Instructor's Manual and in the Study Guide.

406
PART 4 · PRODUCTIVE FACTORS, POVERTY, THE ENVIRONMENT, AND DEVELOPMENT

INTERNATIONAL EXAMPLE
Monopsony in College Sports

How many times have you read stories about American colleges and universities violating National Collegiate Athletic Association (NCAA) rules? If you keep up with the sports press, these stories about alleged violations occur every year. About 600 four-year colleges and universities in the United States belong to the NCAA, which controls more than 20 sports. In effect, the NCAA operates an intercollegiate cartel that is dominated by universities which operate big-time athletic programs. It operates as a cartel with monopsony (and monopoly) power in four ways:

1. It regulates the number of student athletes that universities can recruit.
2. It often fixes the prices that the university charges for tickets to important intercollegiate sporting events.
3. It sets the prices (wages) and the conditions under which the universities can recruit these student athletes.
4. It enforces its regulations and rules with sanctions and penalties.

The NCAA rules and regulations expressly prohibit bidding for college athletes in an overt manner. Rather, the NCAA requires that all athletes be paid the same for tuition, fees, room, board, and books. Moreover, the NCAA limits the number of athletic scholarships that can be given by a particular university. These rules are ostensibly to prevent the richest universities from "hiring" the best student athletes.

Not surprisingly, from the very beginning of the NCAA, individual universities and colleges have attempted to cheat on the rules in order to attract better athletes. The original agreement among the colleges was to pay no wages. Almost immediately after this agreement was put into effect, colleges switched to offering athletic scholarships, jobs, free room and board, travel expenses, and other enticements. It was not unusual for athletes to be paid $10 an hour to rake leaves ... the going wage rate for such workers was only $5 an hour ...

Examples Closer to Home.
Many thought-provoking and relevant examples highlight Canadian events and demonstrate economic principles. "For Critical Analysis" questions with each encourage students to apply the knowledge and information gained from the example. Possible answers to the questions are provided in the Instructor's Manual and in the Study Guide.

57
CHAPTER 3 DEMAND AND SUPPLY

EXAMPLE | **New Car Sales, Automobile Leases, and the Law of Demand**

New car prices have risen steadily since the 1960s as increasingly sophisticated consumers demand additional special features in their vehicles. But comprehensive warranties, catalytic converters, air bags, and the like all push up the price of the basic automobile. Monthly car-loan repayments are becoming beyond the means of many Canadian car buyers. In 1996, new car dealers found that sales fell by 10 percent over those in 1995, and they expect further declines over time.

The dealers, however, understand the law of demand. They are offering to lease–rent–new vehicles for monthly payments that are often far below the loan repayments that would be required if the car was actually purchased. As a result, more than 20 percent of all new car deals in Canada in 1996 were leases. Another benefit to the dealers is that the vehicles returned at the end of the lease make a good supply of late-model used cars for those customers still looking to buy an automobile.

For critical analysis: What do you think will happen in the market for used cars over the course of the next five years?

POLICY EXAMPLE | **Can the CRTC Effectively Regulate Cable TV?**

The Canadian Radio-television and Telecommunications Commission (CRTC) is a federal agency established to ensure that Canadian-made programs have a chance to be broadcast in Canada. The CRTC accomplishes this through its power to grant and renew broadcasting licences. The current standard is that Canadian broadcasters must include in their programming 60 percent Canadian content measured over a day, with at least 50 percent Canadian content in the evening hours. The CBC faces even greater content quotas.

Is the CRTC really ensuring that Canadians view Canadian-made programming? Not really. The spread of satellite dishes and pay-TV, for example, make TV stations like WSBK in Boston and WGN in Chicago and KTLA in Los Angeles as accessible as Canadian stations. And the CRTC has no regulatory powers over those American broadcasters.

For critical analysis: Is there any way the CRTC could ensure that the American channels carry Canadian content?

Interacting with the Internet.   At the end of many chapters, World Wide Web sites where students can find further information are given.

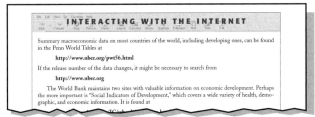

As well, an Internet-related exercise is included in the end-of-chapter problem set, requiring students to use the Internet to find economic information.

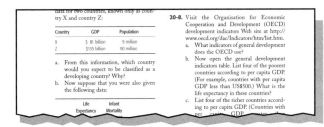

www.econtoday.com.   The *Economics Today* Web site provides on-line access to innovative teaching and learning tools.

PEDAGOGY WITH A PURPOSE

This first Canadian edition of *Economics Today* is loaded with the same time-tested pedagogy of Roger LeRoy Miller's successful US text. It helps students apply what they learn.

For Critical Analysis.   At the end of each example, students are asked to reflect on real-world problems by answering "For Critical Analysis" questions. The answers to the questions are found as follows:
- Issues and Applications—at the end of the student text (p. 527)
- Examples, International Examples, Cyberspace Examples, Policy Examples, International Policy Examples—in the student Study Guide, at the end of the relevant chapter
- All "For Critical Analysis" questions (i.e., all of the above)—in the Instructor's Manual, along with the appropriate chapter

Did You Know That ...?   Each chapter starts with a provocative question to engage students' interest and lead them into the content of the chapter.

Preview Questions.   On the first page of each chapter, several questions are posed, giving purpose and focus for the chapter. These are then fully answered at the end of the chapter. Students are also directed to try answering the preview questions as the topic of each is covered in the text.

Graphs.   Articulate and precise, the four-colour graphs illustrate key concepts.

Key Terms.   Key terms are printed in bold type, and are defined in the margin of the text the first time they appear. These terms are also reproduced alphabetically in the Glossary at the end of the text (p. 533).

Concepts in Brief.   At the end of each major section in each chapter, "Concepts in Brief" summarizes the main points, thus reinforcing students' knowledge as well as testing their learning.

Chapter Summary.   Every chapter ends with a concise but thorough summary of the important ideas of the chapter.

Problems.   A variety of problems support each chapter, and answers for all odd-numbered problems are provided at the back of the textbook. The complete set of problem answers (both even- and odd-numbered) appears in the Instructor's Manual.

TEACHING/LEARNING PACKAGE

For the Instructor

Instructor's Manual.   The Instructor's Manual has been adapted by author Nancy Clegg for this first Canadian edition of *Economics Today*. Features include:
- Chapter overviews, objectives, and outlines
- Points to emphasize, including more theoretical issues for those who wish to stress theory
- Suggested questions for further class discussion
- Answers to the "For Critical Analysis" questions

that follow each example in the chapter
- Answers, with detailed step-by-step solutions, to all end-of-chapter problems
- Selected references

www.econtoday.com. The *Economics Today* Web site provides on-line access to innovative teaching and learning tools.

Test Bank. The test bank contains over 1300 multiple-choice questions with answers. The test bank has been adapted by Brenda Abbott.

For the Student

Study Guide. Available in Micro and Macro versions, the Study Guides have been adapted by Sam Fefferman and Brenda Abbott of the Northern Alberta Institute of Technology in Edmonton. Each includes the following:
- Putting the chapter into perspective
- Learning objectives

- Chapter outlines
- Key terms
- Key concepts
- Completion questions
- True-or-false questions
- Multiple-choice questions
- Matching questions
- Problems
- A Business Section, giving applications and problems that relate to economic theory in accounting, marketing, finance, management, small business, and entrepreneurship
- Answers to the problems and questions that are included in the Study Guide
- Hints or answers to the "For Critical Analysis" questions that follow examples in the textbook
- Glossary of terms, defined exactly as in the textbook

www.econtoday.com. The *Economics Today* Web site is designed for the US edition of the text, but contains many features that are of interest and use to Canadian students.

ACKNOWLEDGEMENTS

No author can adapt a principles text without the assistance of others. I have been helped by a hard-working and supportive group at Addison-Wesley. Linda Scott, my Managing Editor, provided assistance in all aspects of this project. My Publisher, Ron Doleman, helped me make decisions about the direction the text should take and provided unending encouragement and confidence in my abilities throughout. My Copy Editor, Muriel Fiona Napier, kept me on task and worked miracles with my prose, and became a good friend in the process. To all these Addison-Wesley team members—including Brian Henderson who initiated the project originally—thank you, and I look forward to working with you again.

I would also like to thank the following professors who helped with the development of this text by offering me their insightful comments and constructive criticisms.

Terri Anderson, *Fanshawe College*
Walter Behnke, *Vancouver Community College*
Tom Chambers, *Canadore College*
Wendy Cornwall, *Mount St. Vincent University*
Victoria Digby, *Fanshawe College*
Peter Fortura, *Algonquin College*

Bill Gallivan, *University College of Cape Breton*
Kevin Gillis, *Mount Royal College*
Carl Graham, *Assiniboine Community College*
James Hnatchuk, *Champlain-Ste. Lambert College*
Lionel Ifill, *Algonquin College*
Ernie Jacobson, *Northern Alberta Institute of Technology*
Robert L. Jeacock, *Malaspina University College*
Cheryl Jenkins, *John Abbott College*
Susan Kamp, *University of Alberta*
Joe Luchetti, *Sault College*
Bill Luxton, *Southern Alberta Institute of Technology*
John Newark, *Athabasca University*
Victor Olshevski, *University of Winnipeg*
David R. Sabiston, *Laurentian University*
Lance Shandler, *Kwantlen University College*
William Sinkevitch, *St. Clair College*
Judith Skuce, *Georgian College*
Campion Swartout, *SIAST-Palliser Institute*

In keeping with the cyberage, and because I would appreciate suggestions about what to do in future editions, you and your students can contact me via the *Economics Today* Web site at: **www.econtoday.com**.

Nancy W. Clegg

PART 1

Introduction

Chapter 1

The Nature of Economics

Chapter 3

Demand and Supply

Chapter 5

The Public Sector

Chapter 2

Scarcity and the World of Trade-Offs

Appendix A

Reading and Working with Graphs

Chapter 4

Extensions of Demand and Supply Analysis

Chapter 6

Economies in Transition

The Nature of Economics

For most people, choosing a spouse has never been an inexpensive or easy activity. Not long ago, some people were arguing that the institution of marriage was dying. Nevertheless, over 85 percent of Canadians making up family units are legally married. Spouse selection is clearly an activity that most people eventually choose to engage in. A variety of considerations are involved. For example, the ease or difficulty of obtaining a divorce may have an effect on how spouses are chosen; so may the factor called love. Is there a rational, economic reason why individuals prefer a marriage in which there is mutual love? To answer this question, you need to know about the nature of economics.

Preview Questions

1. What is the difference between microeconomics and macroeconomics?

2. What role does rational self-interest play in economic analysis?

3. Why is the study of economics a science?

4. What is the difference between positive and normative economics?

Did You Know That... between 1987 and 1997, the number of fax machines in Canadian offices and homes increased by over 10,000 percent? During the same time period, the number of bike messengers in downtown Toronto *decreased* by over 50 percent. The world around us is definitely changing. Much of that change is due to the dramatically falling cost of communications and information technology. In the late 1990s, the computers inside video games cost only a few hundred dollars, yet had 50 times the processing power that a US$10 million IBM mainframe had in 1975. It's not surprising that since the start of the 1990s, Canadian firms have been spending more on communications equipment and computers than on new construction and heavy machinery.

Cyberspace, the information superhighway—call it what you want, but your next home (if not your current one) will almost certainly have an address on it. Close to 100 percent of Canadian households have at least one telephone, and more than 80 percent have video recorders. Almost 30 percent of homes have personal computers, and about half of those machines are set up to send and receive information via phone lines. Your decisions about such things as when and what type of computer to buy, whether to accept a collect call from a friend travelling in Europe, and how much time you should invest in learning to use a new multimedia system involve an untold number of variables: where you live, the work your parents do, what your friends think, and so on. But, as you will see, there are economic underpinnings for nearly all the decisions you make.

THE POWER OF ECONOMIC ANALYSIS

Knowing that an economic problem exists every time you make a decision is not enough. You also have to develop a framework that will allow you to analyse solutions to each economic problem—whether you are trying to decide how much to study, which courses to take, if you should finish school, or if Canada should send peacekeeping troops abroad or raise tariffs. The framework that you will learn in this text is based on the *economic way of thinking*.

This framework gives you power—the power to reach informed conclusions about what is happening in the world. You can, of course, live your life without the power of economic analysis as part of your analytical framework. Indeed, many people do. But economists believe that economic analysis can help you make better decisions concerning your career, your education, financing your home, and other important issues. In the business world, the power of economic analysis can help you increase your competitive edge as an employee or as the owner of a business. As a voter, for the rest of your life you will be asked to make judgments about the policies advocated by a particular political party. Many of these policies will deal with questions related to international economics, such as whether the Canadian government should encourage or discourage immigration, prevent foreigners from investing in domestic TV stations and newspapers, or restrict other countries from selling their goods here. Finally, just as taking an art, music, or literature appreciation class increases the pleasure you receive when you view paintings, listen to concerts, or read novels, taking an economics course will increase your understanding when watching the news on TV, listening to it on radio, or reading the newspapers.

DEFINING ECONOMICS

What is economics exactly? Some cynics have defined *economics* as "common sense made difficult." But common sense, by definition, is within everyone's grasp. In the following pages you will encounter numerous examples which show that economics is, in fact, pure and simple common sense.

Economics is one of the social sciences, and as such seeks explanations of real events. All social sciences analyse human behaviour. The physical sciences, on the other hand, generally analyse the behaviour of electrons, atoms, and other nonhuman phenomena.

> Economics is the study of how people allocate their limited resources in an attempt to satisfy their unlimited wants. As such, economics is the study of how people make choices.

To understand this definition fully, two other words need explaining: *resources* and *wants*. **Resources** are things that have value and, more specifically, are used to produce other things that satisfy people's wants. **Wants** are all of the things that people would consume if they had unlimited income.

Whenever an individual, a business, or a nation faces alternatives, a choice must be made, and economics helps us study how those choices are made. For example, you have to choose how to spend your limited income. You also have to choose how to spend your limited time. You may have to choose how much of your company's limited funds to spend on advertising and how much to spend on new-product research. In economics, we examine situations in which individuals choose how to do things, when to do things, and with whom to do them. Ultimately, the purpose of economics is to explain choices.

▶ **Economics**
The study of how people allocate their limited resources to satisfy their unlimited wants.

▶ **Resources**
Things used to produce other things to satisfy people's wants.

▶ **Wants**
What people would buy if their incomes were unlimited.

MICROECONOMICS VERSUS MACROECONOMICS

Economics is typically divided into two types of analysis: **microeconomics** and **macroeconomics**.

> Microeconomics is the part of economic analysis that studies decision making undertaken by individuals (or households) and by firms. It is like looking through a microscope to focus on the small parts of our economy.

> Macroeconomics is the part of economic analysis that studies the behaviour of the economy as a whole. It deals with economy-wide phenomena such as changes in unemployment, the general price level, and national income.

▶ **Microeconomics**
The study of decision making undertaken by individuals (or households) and by firms.

▶ **Macroeconomics**
The study of the behaviour of the economy as a whole, including such economy-wide phenomena as changes in unemployment, the general price level, and national income.

Try Preview Question 1:

What is the difference between microeconomics and macroeconomics?

Microeconomic analysis, for example, is concerned with the effects of changes in the price of gasoline relative to that of other energy sources. It examines the effects of new taxes on a specific product or industry. If price controls were to be re-instituted in Canada, how individual firms and consumers would react to them would be in the realm of microeconomics. The raising of wages by an effective union strike would also be analysed using the tools of microeconomics.

By contrast, issues such as the rate of inflation, the amount of economy-wide unemployment, and the yearly growth in the output of goods and services in the nation all fall into the domain of macroeconomic analysis. In other words, macroeconomics deals with **aggregates**, or totals—such as total output in an economy.

▶ **Aggregates**

Total amounts or quantities; aggregate demand, for example, is total planned expenditures throughout a nation.

Be aware, however, of the blending of microeconomics and macroeconomics in modern economic theory. Modern economists are increasingly using microeconomic analysis—the study of decision making by individuals and by firms—as the basis of macroeconomic analysis. They do this because even though in macroeconomic analysis aggregates are being examined, those aggregates are made up of individuals and firms.

THE ECONOMIC PERSON: RATIONAL SELF-INTEREST

Economists assume that individuals act as *if* motivated by self-interest and respond predictably to opportunities for gain. This central insight of economics was first clearly articulated by Adam Smith in 1776. Smith wrote in his most famous book, *An Inquiry into the Nature and Causes of the Wealth of Nations*, that "it is not from the benevolence of the butcher, the brewer, or the baker that we expect our dinner, but from their regard to their own interest." Otherwise stated, the typical person about whom economists make behavioural predictions is assumed to look out for his or her own self-interest in a rational manner. Because monetary benefits and costs of actions are often the most easily measured, economists most often make behavioural predictions about individuals' responses to ways to increase their wealth, measured in money terms. Let's see if we can apply the theory of rational self-interest to explain an anomaly concerning the makeup of a small town in northeastern British Columbia.

Try Preview Question 2:

What role does rational self-interest play in economic analysis?

EXAMPLE	Atlantic Migration to British Columbia

Fort Nelson is a small town in northern British Columbia, near the Alberta border. In recent years the proportion of residents who were born in Atlantic Canada has grown to around 40 percent. Can we use Adam Smith's ideas to understand why so many people from Atlantic Canada have decided to move west? Perhaps.

Consider the economic conditions in Newfoundland and the other Atlantic provinces. Unemployment is high and hopes for a rapid recovery of the cod fishery are low. Look at Figure 1.1 to see the rate of migration to and from Newfoundland since 1972. Notice that the rate of outmigration has increased rapidly since closure of the cod fishery. Now also consider the economic conditions in Fort Nelson. The town is booming with jobs in forestry, mining, and the service sector. While many people from southern British Columbia are reluctant to

Figure 1.1
Net Migration to and from Newfoundland, 1972–1996

Newfoundland has had more people leave than enter in all but four of the past 24 years. This would suggest that there is something pulling people away to other parts of Canada or the world.

Source: CANSIM University Base. Statistics Canada Series C103456

move to the north, the prospect of steady work in a mill at a starting wage of $12 per hour provides a strong incentive for an unemployed Newfoundlander to move 6,000 kilometres west. The drive for economic well-being explains the Atlantic migration to northern British Columbia.

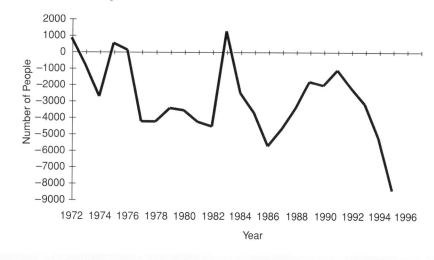

For critical analysis: What nonmonetary reasons are there for people from the Atlantic provinces to move to Fort Nelson?

The Rationality Assumption

▶ **Rationality assumption**
The assumption that people do not intentionally make decisions that would leave them worse off.

The **rationality assumption** of economics, simply stated, is as follows:

We assume that individuals do not intentionally make decisions that would leave them worse off.

The distinction here is between what people may think—the realm of psychology and psychiatry and perhaps sociology—and what they do. Economics does *not* involve itself in analysing individual or group thought processes. Economics looks at what people actually do in life with their limited resources. It does little good to criticize the rationality assumption by stating, "Nobody thinks that way" or "I never think that way" or "How unrealistic! That's as irrational as anyone can get!"

Take the example of driving. When you consider passing another car on a two-lane highway with oncoming traffic, you have to make very quick decisions: You must estimate the speed of the car you are going to pass, the speed of the oncoming cars, the distance between your car and the oncoming cars, and your car's potential rate of acceleration. If we were to apply a model to your behaviour, we would use the laws of calculus. In actual fact, you and most other drivers in such a situation do not actually think of using the laws of calculus, but we could predict your behaviour *as if* you understood the laws of calculus.

In any event, when you observe behaviour around you, what may seem irrational often has its basis in the rationality assumption, as you can see by the following example.

EXAMPLE   When It Is Rational *Not* to Learn New Technology

The standard young person's view of older people is that they're reluctant to learn new things. The saying "You can't teach an old dog new tricks" seems to apply. Young people, in contrast, seem eager to learn about new technology—mastering computers and multimedia, playing interactive games, cruising the information superhighway. But there is a rational reason for older people's reduced willingness to learn new technologies. If you are 20 years old and learn a new skill, you will be able to gain returns from your investment in learning over the course of many decades. If you are 60, however, and invest the same amount of time and effort learning the same skill, you will almost certainly not be able to reap those returns for as long a time period. Hence it is perfectly rational for "old dogs" not to want to learn new tricks.

For critical analysis: Some older people do learn to use new technologies as they emerge. What might explain this behaviour?

Responding to Incentives

If it can be assumed that individuals never intentionally make decisions that would leave them worse off, then almost by definition they will respond to different incentives. We define **incentives** as the potential rewards available if a particular activity is undertaken. Indeed, much of human behaviour can be explained in terms of how individuals respond to changing incentives over time.

▶ **Incentives**

Things that encourage us to engage in a particular activity.

School students are motivated to do better by a variety of incentive systems, ranging from gold stars and certificates of achievement when they are young, to bet-

INTERNATIONAL EXAMPLE
Why Are There So Many Brush Fires in Corsica?

Corsica is a Mediterranean French island about 1.5 times the size of Prince Edward Island. Every summer, 10,000 to 40,000 acres of Corsican brush go up in flames. As many as 37 brush fires have been reported on a single day. One might attribute the prevalence of brush fires to the island's physical differences from other European locations, but that is not the explanation. Rather, the European Union (EU) has provided an incentive for some Corsicans to set brush fires deliberately. Most Corsican cattle are left to roam freely on common land, and when brush is burned, more grazing land becomes available. Corsicans who claim that they tend at least 100 head of cattle receive a "suckling cow premium" from the EU, equal to more than US$2,000 a month. The large number of brush fires on the island of Corsica is no accident.

For critical analysis: The average cow in Europe is three years old before she gives birth, whereas in Corsica the average age is a year and a half. Why do you think Corsicans breed their cows earlier than other Europeans?

ter grades with accompanying promises of a "better life" as they get older. There are, of course, negative incentives that affect our behaviour, too. Students who disrupt the class are given after-school detentions or sent to the vice-principal for other punishment.

Implicitly, people react to changing incentives after they have done some sort of rough comparison of the costs and benefits of various courses of action. In fact, making rational choices invariably involves balancing costs and benefits.

The linked concepts of incentive and costs and benefits can be used to explain seeming anomalies in the world around us.

Defining Self-Interest

Self-interest does not always mean increasing one's wealth as measured in dollars and cents. We assume that individuals seek many goals, not just increased monetary wealth. Thus the self-interest part of our economic-person assumption includes goals relating to prestige, friendship, love, power, helping others, creating works of art, and many other matters. We can also think in terms of enlightened self-interest, whereby individuals in the pursuit of what makes them better off also achieve the betterment of others around them. In brief, individuals are assumed to want the right to further their goals by making decisions about how things around them are used.

Otherwise stated, charitable acts are not ruled out by self-interest. The giving of gifts can be considered a form of charity that is nonetheless in the self-interest of the giver. But how efficient is such gift giving?

EXAMPLE   *Katimavik*—Combining Self-Interest and Charity

Katimavik, Inuit for "meeting place," is a community service agency which operated from 1977 until 1986, and has recently been revived. The agency sends young people between the ages of 17 and 21 out into communities across Canada to work in locally sponsored jobs. These may take various forms: clearing trails in municipal parks, helping out in daycare centres, assisting seniors as required, and so on. The pay is low: Human Resources Development Canada pays for travel, lodgings, and food, and in addition volunteers are paid $3 per day. At the end of their seven-and-a-half month tour, they receive a further $1,000.

So why did 230 young Canadians choose to volunteer in 1995? Because they wanted to gain practical skills and job experience which would benefit them later. The volunteers, in following their own self-interest, nevertheless gave to the communities in which they worked. Self-interest and charity combine forces in *Katimavik.*

For critical analysis: What do you think would happen to the number of volunteers for *Katimavik* if the daily allowance and final remuneration were eliminated?

Concepts in Brief

- Economics is a social science that involves the study of how individuals choose among alternatives to satisfy their wants.
- Wants are what people would buy if their incomes were unlimited.
- Microeconomics, the study of the decision-making processes of individuals (or households) and firms, and macroeconomics, the study of the performance of the economy as a whole, are the two main branches into which the study of economics is divided.
- In economics, we assume that people do not intentionally make decisions that will leave them worse off. This is known as the rationality assumption.
- Self-interest is not confined to material well-being but also involves any action that makes a person feel better off, such as having more friends, love, power, affection, or providing more help to others.

ECONOMICS AS A SCIENCE

Economics is a social science that makes use of the same kinds of methods used in other sciences such as biology, physics, and chemistry. Similar to these other sciences, economics uses **models**, or **theories**. Economic models, or theories, are simplified representations of the real world that we use to help us understand, explain, and predict economic phenomena in the real world. There are, of course, differences between sciences. The social sciences—especially economics—make little use of laboratory methods in which changes in variables can be explained under controlled conditions. Rather, social scientists, and especially economists, usually have to examine what has already happened in the real world in order to test their models, or theories.

▶ **Models, or theories**
Simplified representations of the real world used as the basis for predictions or explanations.

Models and Realism

At the outset it must be emphasized that no model in *any* science, and therefore no economic model, is complete in the sense that it captures *every* detail or interrelationship that exists. Indeed, a model, by definition, is an abstraction from reality. It is conceptually impossible to construct a perfectly complete realistic model. For example, in physics we cannot account for every molecule and its position, nor for every atom and subparticle. Not only would such a model be prohibitively expensive to build, but also working with it would be impossibly complex.

The nature of scientific model building is such that the model should capture only the essential relationships that are sufficient to analyse the particular problem or answer the particular question with which we are concerned. *An economic model cannot be faulted as unrealistic simply because it does not represent every detail of the real world.* A map of a city that shows only major streets is not necessarily unrealistic if, in fact, all you need to know is how to pass through the city using major streets. As long as a model is realistic in terms of shedding light on the *central* issue at hand or forces at work, it may be useful.

Try Preview Question 3:

Why is the study of economics a science?

A map is the basic model. It is always a simplified representation, always unrealistic. But it is also useful in making (refutable) predictions about the world. If the model—the map—predicts that when you take Campus Avenue to the north, you always reach the campus, that is a (refutable) prediction. If our goal is to explain observed behaviour, the simplicity or complexity of the model we use is irrelevant. If a simple model can explain observed behaviour in repeated settings just as well as a complex one, the simple model has some value and is probably easier to use.

Assumptions

Every model, or theory, must be based on a set of assumptions. Assumptions define the set of circumstances in which our model is most likely to be applicable. When scientists predicted that sailing ships would fall off the edge of the earth, they used the *assumption* that the earth was flat. Columbus did not accept the implications of such a model. He assumed that the world was round. The real-world test of his own model refuted the flat-earth model. Indirectly, then, it was a test of the assumption of the flat-earth model.

Thinking Critically About the Media **Cancer and Smoking**

You read it in the newspaper and hear about it on TV—smoking imposes higher costs on all Canadians. The Canadian Cancer Society has convinced the media that smoking is costly due to patients' lengthy hospital stays for treatment of lung cancer and other smoking-related diseases. As a result, life insurance premiums go up. But we also have to look at the other side of the ledger. Premature death due to smoking saves Canadians millions of dollars in pension and medical payments, as well as millions of dollars in nursing home expenses. All things considered, according to economist Jean-Pierre Vidal, smoking does not impose higher costs on all Canadians. (That does not, to be sure, mean that we should encourage more smoking!)

EXAMPLE **Getting Directions**

Assumptions are a shorthand for reality. Imagine that you have decided to drive from your home in Windsor to downtown Toronto. Because you have never driven this route, you decide to get directions from the local office of the Canadian Automobile Association (CAA).

When you ask for directions, the travel planner could give you a set of detailed maps showing each city on the way—London, Woodstock, Kitchener, Cambridge, Mississauga, and so on—and then, opening each map, show you exactly how the freeway threads by each of these cities. You would get a nearly complete description of reality because the CAA travel planner will not have used many simplifying assumptions. It is more likely, however, that the travel planner will simply say, "Get on Highway 401 going east. Stay on it for about 400 kilometres. Follow the signs for Toronto. Take any exit marked 'Downtown.'" By omitting all of the trivial details, the travel planner has told you all that you really need and want to know. The models you will be using in this text are similar to the simplified directions on how to drive from Windsor to Toronto—they focus on what is relevant to the problem at hand and omit what is not.

For critical analysis: In what way do small talk and gossip represent the use of simplifying assumptions?

▶ **Ceteris paribus
[KAY-ter-us PEAR-uh-bus]
assumption**

The assumption that nothing
changes except the factor or factors being studied.

The Ceteris Paribus Assumption: All Other Things Being Equal.
Everything in the world seems to relate in some way to everything else in the world.
It would be impossible to isolate the effects of changes in one variable on another
variable if we always had to worry about the many additional variables that might
also enter the analysis. As in other sciences, economics uses the ***ceteris paribus
assumption***. *Ceteris paribus* means "other things constant" or "other things equal."

Consider an example taken from economics. One of the most important determinants of how much of a particular product a family buys is how expensive that
product is relative to other products. We know that in addition to relative prices,
other factors influence decisions about making purchases. Some of them have to do
with income, others with tastes, and yet others with custom and religious beliefs.
Whatever these other factors are, we hold them constant when we look at the relationship between changes in prices and changes in how much of a given product
people will purchase.

Deciding on the Usefulness of a Model

We generally do not attempt to determine the usefulness, or "goodness," of a model
merely by evaluating how realistic its assumptions are. Rather, we consider a model
good if it yields usable predictions and implications for the real world. In other
words, can we use the model to predict what will happen in the world around us?
Does the model provide useful implications as to how things happen in our world?

Once we have determined that the model does predict real-world phenomena,
the scientific approach to the analysis of the world around us requires that we consider evidence. Evidence is used to test the usefulness of a model. This is why we call
economics an **empirical** science, *empirical* meaning that evidence (data) is looked at
to see whether we are right. Economists are often engaged in empirically testing
their models.

▶ **Empirical**

Relying on real-world data in
evaluating the usefulness of a
model.

Consider two competing models for the way students act when doing complicated probability problems to choose the best gambles. One model predicts that,
based on the assumption of rational self-interest, students who are paid more for
better performance will in fact perform better on average during the experiment. A
competing model might be that students whose last names start with the letters A
through L will do better than students with last names starting with M through Z,
irrespective of how much they are paid. The model that consistently predicts more
accurately is the model that we would normally choose. In this example, the "alpha-
bet" model did not work well: The first letter of the last name of the students who
actually did the experiment was irrelevant in predicting how well they would perform the mathematical calculations necessary to choose the correct gambles. The
model based on rational self-interest predicted well, in contrast.

Models of Behaviour, Not Thought Processes

Take special note of the fact that economists' models do not relate to the way people *think*; they relate to the way people *act*, to what they do in life with their limited
resources. Models tend to generalize human behaviour. Normally, the economist
does not attempt to predict how people will think about a particular topic, such as a

higher price of oil products, accelerated inflation, or higher taxes. Rather, the task at hand is to predict how people will act, which may be quite different from what they say they will do (much to the consternation of poll takers and market researchers). The people involved in examining thought processes are psychologists and psychiatrists, who are not usually economists.

An Economic Model: The Circular Flow of Income

A simple model economists use to explain the workings of the economy is the Circular Flow of Income. Figure 1.2 shows the basic form of the Circular Flow model.

Figure 1.2
The Circular Flow of Income

Firms go to the labour market to hire workers for production. They pay workers a wage, represented by the flow of income from the firms through the labour market to the households. The households spend part of their income purchasing goods and services in the product market. The money they pay for the goods and services flows back to the firms in the form of revenues. If households save any of their income, they put it in the financial market where firms go to borrow money for production purposes. This flow is represented by the arrow from the households through the financial market to the firms.

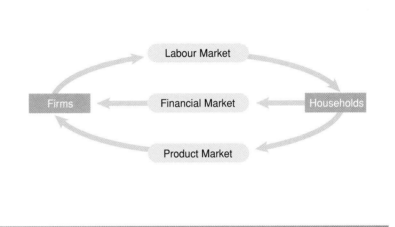

When using the Circular Flow model, we make two main assumptions. The first is that households—people like you and me—produce nothing, but *own* everything in the economy. This makes sense when you think that we own our own labour, and we also own all the firms—whether as shareholders or as entrepreneurs. Firms own nothing, since the shareholders own it all, but they *produce* everything in the economy. As soon as someone produces a good or a service to be sold in the economy, we call that producer a firm.

A good place to start thinking about this model is with the firms. The firms go to the labour market and hire workers to produce their output. In exchange, the firms pay the workers a wage, and income flows *from* the firms *to* the households. Households need food, shelter, and clothing, so they go to the product (or output) market to purchase goods and services. In exchange for the goods and services, the households give the firms a part of their incomes, and income flows *from* the households *to* the firms. So the flow of income in the economy is circular; it flows from firms to households and back to firms again.

We can complicate our model to make it a little more realistic. Most households wish to save part of their income. That part therefore does not flow through the product market, but instead flows to the financial market—to savings accounts with banks, credit unions, and trust companies. These financial institutions hold the households' savings, which they lend to firms that need funds for investment. Thus the income paid out by firms to workers still returns to them via the product market and the financial market.

Whether this is a useful model depends on how well it predicts real-world events. For example, what would happen to the economy if the government decided to put a tax (or an additional tax) on household incomes? Households would have less money to spend and/or save. The Circular Flow model predicts that households would purchase less and save less, and the flows to the firms would diminish. If the flows to the firms diminished, the firms would produce less, and hire fewer workers—thus compounding the problem of shrinking incomes. We could test this prediction by looking at Canada's, and other similar countries', experiences when taxes have risen. We would almost certainly find a slowing in the growth of the economy; our model would represent this as a slowing of the flows between the households and the firms.

If we ask what would happen to our economy if the Americans asked Canadian firms to produce twice as many automobile parts for them than in the past, what will our model predict? We have not included the foreign sector in our simple model, but we could look at the opportunity to increase our sales to the United States as a large injection of income into the firms. The firms would go to the labour market and hire more workers to produce the extra output. Increased income would flow from the firms to the households, and, *ceteris paribus*, back to the firms again. The economy would grow with the increased economic activity.

POSITIVE VERSUS NORMATIVE ECONOMICS

Economics uses *positive analysis*, a value-free approach to inquiry. No subjective or moral judgments enter into the analysis. Positive analysis relates to statements such as "If *A*, then *B*." For example, "If the price of gasoline goes up relative to all other prices, then the amount of it that people will buy will fall." That is a positive economic statement. It is a statement of *what is*. It is not a statement of anyone's value judgment or subjective feelings. For many problems analysed in the hard sciences such as physics and chemistry, the analyses are considered to be virtually value-free. After all, how can someone's values enter into a theory of molecular behaviour? But economists face a different problem. They deal with the behaviour of individuals, not molecules. That makes it more difficult to stick to what we consider to be value-free or **positive economics** without reference to our feelings.

When our values are interjected into the analysis, we enter the realm of **normative economics**, involving *normative analysis*. A positive economic statement is "If the price of gas rises, people will buy less." If we add to that analysis the statement "so we should not allow the price to go up," we have entered the realm of normative economics—we have expressed a value judgment. In fact, any time you see the word *should*, you will know that values are entering into the discussion. Just remember that positive statements are concerned with *what is*, whereas normative statements are concerned with *what ought to be*.

Each of us has a desire for different things. This fact means that we have different values. When we express a value judgment, we are simply saying what we prefer, like, or desire. Because individual values are diverse, we expect—and indeed observe—people expressing widely varying value judgments about how the world ought to be.

▶ **Positive economics**
Analysis that is strictly limited to making either purely descriptive statements or scientific predictions; for example, "If *A*, then *B*." A statement of *what is*.

▶ **Normative economics**
Analysis involving value judgments about economic policies; relates to whether things are good or bad. A statement of *what ought to be*.

Try Preview Question 4:

What is the difference between positive and normative economics?

A Warning: Recognize Normative Analysis

It is easy to define positive economics. It is quite another matter to catch all unlabelled normative statements in a textbook such as this one (or any other), even though authors go over the manuscript many times before it is printed. Therefore, do not get the impression that a textbook's authors will be able to keep all personal values out of the book. They will slip through. In fact, the very choice of which topics to include in an introductory textbook involves normative economics. There is no value-free, or objective, way to decide which topics to use in a textbook. The authors' values ultimately make a difference when choices have to be made. But from your own standpoint, you might want to be able to recognize when you are engaging in normative as opposed to positive economic analysis. Reading this text will help equip you for that task.

Economic Policy

As we noted above, economic models will enhance your ability to understand and predict behaviour. In chapters to come, we'll illustrate how these models prove useful in evaluating, assessing, and reacting to government policies that affect you as a consumer, an employee, an investor, a business owner, and a concerned citizen.

Most government economic policies are action plans designed to achieve commonly accepted socio-economic goals. The major goals are listed here. We discuss them in more detail in Chapter 5.

1. Full Employment: an economy in which people looking for work find jobs reasonably quickly.
2. Efficiency: an economy in which resources are allocated and goods and services are distributed to achieve the maximum benefit for society.
3. Economic Growth: an economy with the ability to increase its rate of production over time to enhance society's well-being.
4. Price Stability: an economy in which prices remain relatively stable over time.
5. Distribution of Income: an economy in which no particular group of people lives below or near the poverty level.

Concepts in Brief

- A model, or theory, uses assumptions and is by nature a simplification of the real world. The usefulness of a model can be evaluated by bringing empirical evidence to bear on its predictions.
- Models are not necessarily deficient simply because they are unrealistic and use simplifying assumptions. Every model in every science requires simplification compared to the real world.
- Most models use the *ceteris paribus* assumption, that all other things are held constant, or equal.
- Positive economics is value-free and relates to statements that can be refuted, such as "If *A*, then *B*." Normative economics involves people's values, and normative statements typically contain the word *should*.

How Relevant Is Love in a Marriage Contract?

Concepts Applied:
Rationality assumption, costs, benefits

Economist Gary Becker argues that dating can be understood in terms of the rationality assumption. For instance, the better off an individual thinks he or she may be in a marriage, the more that individual is willing to invest in finding the right mate.

Looking for a mate can be analysed from a sociological, psychological, or anthropological point of view. Here we want to examine this activity in terms of the rationality assumption developed in this chapter. We present an economic analysis based in part on the work of Nobel Prize–winning economist Gary Becker.

Minimizing Costs

According to the rationality assumption, individuals will not knowingly engage in activities that will make them worse off. Consequently, we predict that in choosing a spouse, individuals will naturally want to marry someone with whom they get along. So we predict that likes will attract more often than not: Individuals will tend to marry others with similar values. Dating and "courting" can be viewed as resource-using activities designed to determine with more certainty the values that each potential marriage partner has.

The more benefits one believes can be derived from the marriage contract, the more costs one will incur in searching for a spouse. The longer one searches, the more costs are incurred due to dating and courtship activities. The more durable the marriage contract, the greater the investment people will be willing to make in trying to find the "right" spouse.

Divorce and Wrong Partner Choices

The most durable marriage contract occurs in a legal setting in which divorce is impossible. One benefit is that a spouse cannot later leave because he or she prefers someone else. In many societies, the tendency has been towards fewer restrictions on divorce.

As divorces have become easier (that is to say, less costly), the durability of the marriage contract has seemed to decline. This result follows, at least in part, from economic analysis: As the expected durability of marriage declines, individuals implicitly have less incentive to incur longer searches for the "right" partner. The result: more wrong choices about a partner and hence more frequent divorces.

Why Love Matters

One aspect of love is that the level of happiness of the person loved affects the well-being of the other person. The more one loves another person, the more one is motivated to help that other person. Within a marriage, each spouse is dependent on the other.

When one spouse fails to uphold his or her end of the bargain, this tends to reduce the well-being of the other. Within a marriage, there is no actual iron-clad agreement about who provides what, how, and when. Therefore, it is relatively easy for one spouse not to do what he or she is supposed to do or at least not do it very well. The more love is involved, however, the more each spouse wants to make the other spouse better off. So we predict that marriages work out better the more spouses love each other. Hence individuals generally want to be in a marriage environment in which there is mutual love.

For Critical Analysis

1. Is there any difference between what economics predicts about a "good" marriage and what most people believe anyway?
2. If divorce is impossible, how does this affect spouse selection?

CHAPTER SUMMARY

1. Economics as a social science is the study of how individuals make choices to satisfy wants. Wants are defined as what people would buy if their incomes were unlimited.

2. Economics is usually divided into microeconomic analysis, which is the study of individual decision making by households and firms, and macroeconomics, which is the study of nation-wide phenomena, such as inflation and unemployment.

3. The rationality assumption is that individuals never intentionally make decisions that would leave them worse off.

4. We use models, or theories, to explain and predict behaviour. Models, or theories, are never completely realistic because by definition they are simplifications using assumptions that are not directly testable. The usefulness of a theory, or model, is determined not by the realism of its assumptions but by how well it predicts real-world phenomena.

5. An important simplifying assumption is that all other things are held equal, or constant. This is sometimes known as the *ceteris paribus* assumption.

6. No model in economics relates to individuals' thought processes; all models relate to what people do, not to what they think or say they will do.

7. Much economic analysis involves positive economics; that is, it is value-free. Whenever statements embodying values are made, we enter the realm of normative economics, or how individuals and groups think things ought to be.

DISCUSSION OF PREVIEW QUESTIONS

1. What is the difference between microeconomics and macroeconomics?

Microeconomics is concerned with the choice-making processes of individuals, households, and firms, whereas macroeconomics focuses on the performance of the economy as a whole.

2. What role does rational self-interest play in economic analysis?

Rational self-interest is the assumption that individuals behave in a reasonable (rational) way in making choices to further their interests. In other words, we assume that individuals' actions are motivated primarily by their self-interest, keeping in mind that self-interest can relate to monetary and nonmonetary objectives, such as love, prestige, and helping others.

3. Why is the study of economics a science?

Economics is a science in that it uses models, or theories, that are simplified representations of the real world to analyse and make predictions about the real world. These predictions are then subjected to empirical tests in which real-world data are used to decide whether to accept or reject the predictions.

4. What is the difference between positive and normative economics?

Positive economics deals with what is, whereas normative economics deals with what ought to be. Positive economic statements are of the "if ... then" variety; they are descriptive and predictive and are not related to what "should" happen. Normative economics, by contrast, is concerned with what ought to be and is intimately tied to value judgments.

PROBLEMS

(Answers to the odd-numbered problems appear at the back of the book.)

1-1. Construct four separate models to predict the probability that a person will die within the next five years. Include only one determining factor in each of your models.

1-2. Does it matter whether all of a model's assumptions are "realistic"? Why or why not?

1-3. Give a refutable implication (one that can be disproved by evidence from the real world) for each of the following models:

a. The accident rate of drivers is inversely related to their age.

b. The rate of inflation is directly related to the rate of change in the nation's money supply.

c. The wages of professional basketball players are directly related to their high school grade point averages.

d. The rate at which bank employees are promoted is inversely related to their frequency of absenteeism.

1-4. Is gambling an example of rational or irrational behaviour? What is the difference between gambling and insurance?

1-5. Over the past 20 years, first-class mail rates have increased more than five times over, while prices of long-distance phone calls, televisions, and sound systems have decreased. Over a similar period, it has been reported that there has been a steady decline in the ability of high school graduates to communicate effectively in writing. Do you feel that this increase in the relative price of written communication (first-class mail rates) is related to the alleged decline in writing ability? If so, what do you feel is the direction of causation? Which is causing which?

1-6. If there is no way to test a theory with real-world data, can we determine if it is a good theory? Why is empirical evidence used to validate a theory?

1-7. Identify which of the following statements use positive economic analysis and which use normative economic analysis.

a. Recent increases in college tuition fees are unfair to students.

b. The elimination of barriers to the free movement of individuals across European borders has caused wages to become more equal in many industries.

c. Paying Members of Parliament more provides them with less incentive to commit wrongful acts.

d. We need more restrictions on companies that pollute because air pollution is destroying our way of life.

1-8. Visit the Mining Co. Web site at http://economics.miningco.com/ and click on "Features." Then select "1998 Features" and click on "Economics and Happiness." Read about the Misery Index and answer the following questions.

a. Does the Misery Index qualify as an economic model? If yes, how?

b. What role does positive economics play in devising the Misery Index?

c. What role does normative economics play in the construction of the Misery Index?

d. Do you think that the use of normative economics in the construction of the Misery Index invalidates the usefulness of the Index as a model?

INTERACTING WITH THE INTERNET

The Internet is a web of educational, corporate, and research computer networks around the world. Today, over 40 million people are using it, and more than 60,000 networks are connected to it. Perhaps the most interesting part of the Internet is the World Wide Web, commonly called the Web, which is a vast interlinked network of computer files all over the world. You can use the Internet to find discussion groups, news groups, and electronic publications. The most common use of the Internet is for electronic mail (e-mail).

At many colleges and universities, you can get an e-mail address and a password. Your address is like a mailbox at which you will receive electronic information. Many of the chapters in this edition of *Economics Today* end with Internet addresses and activities that you will find helpful in your study of the principles of economics. In any event, if you don't already have one you should get an Internet address now. Pick up a copy of the new user's handbook and start using e-mail.

If you want to "surf" (browse) economics resources immediately, go directly to Resources for Economists on the Internet by typing in

http://econwpa.wustl.edu/EconFAQ/EconFAQ.html

This site is maintained by Professor William Goffe of the University of Southern Mississippi. This is his "home page," the table of contents for a particular Web site. On this page you will find a catalogue of "hypertext" pointers, which are highlighted words or phrases that you can click on to connect to places around the Web.

To get in the last laugh, you might want to look up some economist jokes at

http://netec.mcc.ac.uk/JokEc.html

Happy surfing!

2

Scarcity and the World of Trade-Offs

Preview Questions

1. Do affluent people face the problem of scarcity?

2. Fresh air may be consumed at no charge, but is it free of cost to society?

3. Why does the scarcity problem force individuals to consider opportunity costs?

4. Can a "free" college education ever be truly free?

Is there anything more frightening than being the victim of a crime? Most people would say no, though frequently we behave as if we were looking for trouble. We routinely act in ways that increase our chances of becoming crime victims, including leaving valuables in clear view in our cars, or walking to clubs or bars on dark evenings, or wearing expensive clothing and jewellery. Government policymakers pass laws to protect citizens from crime, but they cannot eliminate every risk that exists. They can, however, force society to spend resources to reduce risk to life and property. When they do, a trade-off is involved because risk reduction involves the use of things that are scarce.

▶ **Scarcity**
A situation in which the ingredients for producing the things that people desire are insufficient to satisfy all wants.

Did You Know That... some people make a profit out of standing in line? Prior to a recent *Tragically Hip* concert in Toronto, several "professional line waiters" set up camp at the ticket booth the night before tickets went on sale. When the box office opened the next morning, they bought tickets, not for themselves, but for the many young people who paid them $20 in addition to the price of the ticket to stand in line for them. What were those young people doing? They were working at jobs that paid them more than $20 for the day. They did not want to miss the opportunity to make that income. After all, those young people do not have an unlimited amount of time to work and to stand in line. Time is scarce to them.

SCARCITY

Whenever individuals or communities cannot obtain everything they desire simultaneously, choices occur. Choices occur because of *scarcity*. **Scarcity** is the most basic concept in all of economics. Scarcity means that we do not and cannot have enough income or wealth to satisfy our *every* desire. Scarcity exists because human wants always exceed what can be produced with the limited resources and time that nature makes available.

What Scarcity Is Not

Scarcity is not a shortage. When flooding forced many people in southern Manitoba to leave their homes, TV newscasts showed those evacuated crowding into the local high school gymnasium or community centre common room for the night. A news commentator noted that this crowding was caused by a scarcity of short-term housing. But housing is always scarce—we cannot obtain all we want at a zero price. The flood victims were not facing a scarcity of short-term housing, rather there was a shortage of it. Do not confuse the concept of scarcity, which is general and all-encompassing, with the concept of shortages as evidenced by people standing in line to obtain a particular product.

Scarcity is not the same thing as poverty. Scarcity occurs among the rich as well as the poor. Even the richest person on earth faces scarcity because available time is limited. Low income levels do not create more scarcity. High income levels do not create less scarcity.

Scarcity is a fact of life, like gravity. And just as physicists did not invent gravity, economists did not invent scarcity—it existed well before the first economist ever lived. It exists even when we are not using all of our resources.

▶ **Try Preview Question 1**:
Do affluent people face the problem of scarcity?

Scarcity and Resources

The scarcity concept arises from the fact that resources are insufficient to satisfy our

▶ **Production**
Any activity that results in the conversion of resources into products that can be used in consumption.

▶ **Land**
The natural resources that are available from nature. Land as a resource includes location, original fertility and mineral deposits, topography, climate, water, and vegetation.

▶ **Labour**
Productive contributions of humans who work, involving both mental and physical activities.

▶ **Physical capital**
All manufactured resources, including buildings, equipment, machines, and improvements to land that is used for production.

▶ **Human capital**
The accumulated training and education of workers.

▶ **Entrepreneurship**
The factor of production involving human resources that perform the functions of raising capital, organizing, managing, assembling other factors of production, and making basic business policy decisions. The entrepreneur is a risk taker.

▶ **Goods**
All things from which individuals derive satisfaction or happiness.

▶ **Economic goods**
Goods that are scarce.

every desire. Resources are the inputs used in the production of the things that we want. **Production** can be defined as virtually any activity that results in the conversion of resources into products that can be used in consumption. Production includes delivering things from one part of the country to another. It includes taking ice from an ice tray to put in your soft-drink glass. The resources used in production are called *factors of production,* and some economists use the terms *resources* and *factors of production* interchangeably. The total quantity of all resources that an economy has at any one time determines what that economy can produce.

Factors of production can be classified in many ways. Here is one such classification:

1. **Land** encompasses all the nonhuman gifts of nature, including timber, water, fish, minerals, and the original fertility of the land. It is often called the *natural resource.*

2. **Labour** is the human resource, which includes all productive contributions made by individuals who work, such as steelworkers, ballet dancers, and professional baseball players.

3. **Physical capital** consists of the factories and equipment used in production. It also includes improvements to natural resources, such as irrigation ditches.

4. **Human capital** is the economic characterization of the education and training of workers. How much the nation produces depends not only on how many hours people work but also on how productive they are, and that, in turn, depends in part on education and training. To become more educated, individuals have to devote time and resources, just as a business has to devote resources if it wants to increase its physical capital. Whenever a worker's skills increase, human capital has been improved.

5. **Entrepreneurship** is actually a subdivision of labour and involves human resources that perform the functions of organizing, managing, and assembling the other factors of production to make business ventures. Entrepreneurship also encompasses taking risks that involve the possibility of losing large sums of wealth on new ventures. It includes new methods of doing common things, and generally experimenting with any type of new thinking that could lead to making more money income. Without entrepreneurship, virtually no business organization could operate.

Goods Versus Economic Goods

Goods are defined as all things from which individuals derive satisfaction or happiness. Goods therefore include air to breathe and the beauty of a sunset, as well as food, cars, and CD players.

Economic goods are a subset of all goods—they are goods derived from scarce resources about which we must constantly make decisions regarding their best use. By definition, the desired quantity of an economic good exceeds the amount that is directly available from nature at a zero price. Virtually every example we use in economics concerns economic goods—cars, CD players, computers, socks, baseball bats, and so on. Weeds are a good example of *bads*—goods for which the desired quantity is much *less* than what nature provides at a zero price.

▶ **Services**
Mental or physical labour or help purchased by consumers. Examples are the assistance of doctors, lawyers, dentists, repair personnel, housecleaners, educators, retailers, and wholesalers; things purchased or used by consumers that do not have physical characteristics.

Sometimes you will see references to "goods and services." **Services** are tasks that are performed for someone else, such as laundry, cleaning, hospital care, restaurant meal preparation, car polishing, psychological counselling, and teaching. One way of looking at services is to think of them as *intangible goods.*

WANTS AND NEEDS

Wants are not the same as needs. Indeed, from the economist's point of view, the term *needs* is objectively indefinable. When someone says, "I need some new clothes," there is no way of knowing whether that person is stating a vague wish, a want, or a life-saving necessity. If the individual making the statement were dying of exposure in northern Quebec during the winter, we might argue that indeed the person does need clothes—perhaps not new ones, but at least some articles of warm clothing. Typically, however, the term *need* is used very casually in most conversations. What people usually mean is that they want something that they do not currently have.

Humans have unlimited wants. Just imagine if every single material want that you might have were satisfied. You can have all of the clothes, cars, houses, CDs, tickets to concerts, and other things that you want. Does that mean that nothing else could add to your total level of happiness? Probably not, because you might think of new goods and services that you could obtain, particularly as they came to market. You would also still be lacking in fulfilling all of your wants for compassion, friendship, love, affection, prestige, musical abilities, sports abilities, and so on.

In reality, every individual has competing wants but cannot satisfy all of them, given limited resources. This is the reality of scarcity. Each person must therefore make choices. Whenever a choice is made to do or buy something, something else that is also desired is not done or not purchased. In other words, in a world of scarcity, every want that ends up being satisfied causes one or more other wants to remain unsatisfied or to be forfeited.

Concepts in Brief

- Scarcity exists because human wants always exceed what can be produced with the limited resources and time that nature makes available.
- We use scarce resources, such as land, labour, physical and human capital, and entrepreneurship, to produce economic goods—goods that are desired but are not directly obtainable from nature to the extent demanded or desired at a zero price.
- Wants are unlimited; they include all material desires and all nonmaterial desires, such as love, affection, power, and prestige.
- The concept of need is difficult to define objectively for every person; consequently, we simply consider that every person's wants are unlimited. In a world of scarcity, satisfaction of one want necessarily means nonsatisfaction of one or more other wants.

SCARCITY, CHOICE, AND OPPORTUNITY COST

The natural fact of scarcity implies that we must make choices. One of the most important results of this fact is that every choice made (or not made, for that matter) means that some opportunity had to be sacrificed. Every choice involves giving up another opportunity to do or use something else.

Consider a practical example. Every choice you make to study one more hour of economics requires that you give up the opportunity to do any of the following activities: study more of another subject, listen to music, sleep, browse at a local store, read a novel, or work out at the gym. Many more opportunities are forgone also if you choose to study economics an additional hour.

Because there were so many alternatives from which to choose, how could you determine the value of what you gave up to engage in that extra hour of studying economics? First of all, no one else can tell you the answer because only you can *subjectively* put a value on each alternative. Only you know the value of another hour of sleep, or of an hour looking for the latest CDs. That means that only you can determine the highest-valued, next-best alternative that you had to sacrifice in order to study economics one more hour. It is you who come up with the *subjective* estimate of the expected value of the next-best alternative.

▶ **Opportunity cost**

The highest-valued, next-best alternative that must be sacrificed to attain something or to satisfy a want.

The value of the next-best alternative is called **opportunity cost**. The opportunity cost of any action is the value of what is given up—the next-highest-ranked alternative—because a choice was made. When you study one more hour, there may be many alternatives available for the use of that hour, but assume that you can do only one thing in that hour—your next-highest-ranked alternative. What is important is the choice that you would have made if you hadn't studied one more hour. Your opportunity cost is the *next-highest-ranked* alternative, not *all* alternatives.

In economics, cost is always a forgone opportunity.

One way to think about opportunity cost is to understand that when you choose to do something, you lose. What you lose is being able to engage in your next-highest-valued alternative. Thus, the cost of your choice is your next-highest-valued alternative. This is your opportunity cost.

Try Preview Question 2:

Fresh air may be consumed at no charge, but is it free of cost to society?

Let's consider the opportunity cost entertainers face when they change bands.

INTERNATIONAL EXAMPLE
The Costs and Benefits of de-Spicing

In June, 1998, in the middle of the World Spice Tour, Geri Halliwell, better known as "Ginger Spice," announced that she was leaving the pop group Spice Girls. She cited differences with Sporty, Scary, Baby, and Posh (the remaining Spice Girls) as the reason. What was Ginger giving up because of her decision to quit the band?

It is estimated that the Spice Girls earn collectively in excess of 50 million pounds sterling (about $120 million) per year from their CD sales and movie revenues. In addition, the World Spice Tour is estimated to have earned them another $50 million. Ginger's share, after expenses, is about 10 percent of the gross. So her opportunity cost of quitting would be in the range of $17 million during the first year alone.

Why would Ginger elect to quit when the opportunity cost is so great? We know from the last chapter that she will choose to quit when she will make herself better off by doing so. It appears that this is the case: Ginger is not only discussing having her own television show with the British Broadcasting Corporation (BBC), but she will also probably receive a buy-out from the Spice Girls of about $25 million.

For critical analysis: Do you think that by quitting the Spice Girls Ginger is giving up more than the money she would have earned as a member of the group?

THE WORLD OF TRADE-OFFS

Whenever you engage in any activity using any resource, even time, you are *trading off* the use of that resource for one or more alternative uses. The value of the trade-off is represented by the opportunity cost. The opportunity cost of studying economics has already been mentioned—it is the value of the next-best alternative. When you think of any alternative, you are thinking of trade-offs.

Let's consider a hypothetical example of a one-for-one trade-off between the results of spending time studying economics and accounting. For the sake of this argument, we will assume that additional time studying either economics or accounting will lead to a higher grade in the subject studied more. One of the best ways to examine this trade-off is with a graph. (If you would like a refresher on graphical techniques, study Appendix A at the end of this chapter before going on.)

Graphical Analysis

In Figure 2.1, the expected grade in accounting is measured on the vertical axis of the graph, and the expected grade in economics is measured on the horizontal axis. We simplify the world and assume that you have a maximum of 10 hours per week to spend studying these two subjects, and that if you spend all 10 hours on economics, you will get an A in the course. You will, however, fail accounting. Conversely, if you spend all of your 10 hours studying accounting, you will get an A in that subject, but you will flunk economics. Here the trade-off is a special case: one-to-one. A one-to-one trade-off means that the opportunity cost of receiving one grade higher in economics (for example, improving from a C to a B) is one grade lower in accounting (falling from a C to a D).

The Production Possibilities Curve (PPC)

The graph in Figure 2.1 illustrates the relationship between the possible results that can be produced in each of two activities, depending on how much time you choose

Figure 2.1

Production Possibilities Curve for Grades in Accounting and Economics (Trade-offs)

We assume that only 10 hours can be spent per week on studying. If the student is at point *x*, equal time (5 hours a week) is spent on both courses and equal grades of C will be received. If a higher grade in economics is desired, the student may go to point *y*, thereby receiving a B in economics but a D in accounting. At point *y*, 2.5 hours are spent on accounting and 7.5 hours on economics.

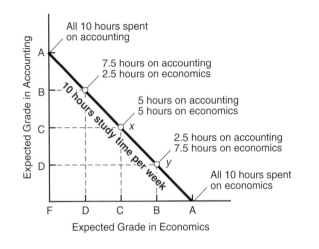

▶ **Production possibilities curve (PPC)**

A curve representing all possible combinations of total output that could be produced assuming (1) a fixed amount of productive resources of a given quality, and (2) the efficient use of those resources.

to devote to each. This graph is a representation of a **production possibilities curve (PPC)**.

Consider that you are producing a grade in economics when you study economics and a grade in accounting when you study accounting. Then the graph in Figure 2.1 can be related to the production possibilities you face. The line that goes from A on one axis to A on the other axis therefore becomes a production possibilities curve. It is defined as the maximum quantity of one good or service that can be produced, given that a specific quantity of another is produced. It is a curve that shows the possibilities available for increasing the output of one good or service by reducing the amount of another. In the example in Figure 2.1, your time for studying was limited to 10 hours per week. The two possible outputs were grades in accounting and grades in economics. The particular production possibilities curve presented in Figure 2.1 is a graphical representation of the opportunity cost of studying one more hour in one subject. It is a *straight-line production possibilities curve*, which is a special case. (The more general case is discussed next.) If you decide to be at point *x* in Figure 2.1, five hours of study time will be spent on accounting and five hours will be spent on economics. The expected grade in each course will be a C. If you are more interested in getting a B in economics, you will go to point *y* on the production possibilities curve, spending only two-and-a-half hours on accounting but seven-and-a-half hours on economics. Your expected grade in accounting will then drop from a C to a D.

Note that these trade-offs between expected grades in accounting and economics are the result of *holding constant* total study time as well as all other factors that might influence a student's ability to learn, such as computerized study aids. Quite clearly, if you wished to spend more total time studying, it would be possible to have higher grades in both economics and accounting. In that case, however, we would no longer be on the specific production possibilities curve illustrated in Figure 2.1. We would have to draw a new curve, farther to the right, to show the greater total study time and a different set of possible trade-offs.

Concepts in Brief

- Scarcity requires us to choose. When we choose, we lose the next-highest-valued alternative.
- Cost is always a forgone opportunity.
- Another way to look at opportunity cost is as the trade-off that occurs when one activity is undertaken rather than the next-best alternative activity.
- A production possibilities curve (PPC) graphically shows the trade-off that occurs when more of one output is obtained at the sacrifice of another. The PPC is a graphical representation of, among other things, opportunity cost.

THE CHOICES SOCIETY FACES

The straight-line production possibilities curve presented in Figure 2.1 can be generalized to demonstrate the related concepts of scarcity, choice, and trade-offs that Canada faces. As you will see, the production possibilities curve is a simple but powerful economic model because it can demonstrate these related concepts. The example we will use is the choice between the production of automobiles and newsprint. We assume for the moment that these are the only two goods that can be produced in Canada. Part (a) of Figure 2.2 gives the various possible combinations of automobiles and newsprint. If all resources are devoted to auto production, 3 million per year can be produced. If all resources are devoted to newsprint production, 12 mil-

Figure 2.2
Society's Trade-Off Between Automobiles and Newsprint
The production of automobiles is measured in millions of units per year, while the production of newsprint is measured in millions of tonnes per year. The various combinations are given in part (a) and plotted in part (b). Connecting the points A–G with a relatively smooth line gives the production possibilities curve for automobiles and newsprint. Point R lies outside the production possibilities curve and is therefore unattainable at the point in time for which the graph is drawn. Point S lies inside the production possibilities curve and therefore represents an inefficient use of available resources.

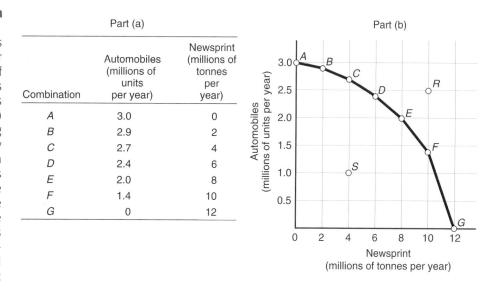

Part (a)

Combination	Automobiles (millions of units per year)	Newsprint (millions of tonnes per year)
A	3.0	0
B	2.9	2
C	2.7	4
D	2.4	6
E	2.0	8
F	1.4	10
G	0	12

Try Preview Question 3:
Why does the scarcity problem force individuals to consider opportunity costs?

lion tonnes per year can be produced. In between are various possible combinations. These combinations are plotted as points *A*, *B*, *C*, *D*, *E*, *F*, and *G* in part (b) of Figure 2.2. If these points are connected with a smooth curve, Canada's production possibilities curve is shown, demonstrating the trade-off between the production of automobiles and newsprint. These trade-offs occur *on* the production possibilities curve.

Notice the major difference in the shape of the production possibilities curves in Figures 2.1 and 2.2. In Figure 2.1, there is a one-to-one trade-off between grades in economics and in accounting. In Figure 2.2, the trade-off between newsprint production and automobile production is not constant, and therefore the production possibilities curve is a *bowed* line. To understand why the production possibilities curve for a society is typically bowed outward, you must understand the assumptions underlying the PPC.

Assumptions Underlying the Production Possibilities Curve

When we draw the curve that is shown in Figure 2.2, we make the following assumptions:

1. That resources are fully employed.
2. That we are looking at production over a specific time period—for example, one year.
3. That the resource inputs, in both quantity and quality, used to produce automobiles or newsprint are fixed over this time period.
4. That technology does not change over this time period.

▶ **Technology**
Society's pool of applied knowledge concerning how goods and services can be produced.

Technology is defined as society's pool of applied knowledge concerning how goods and services can be produced by managers, workers, engineers, scientists, and craftspeople, using land and capital. You can think of technology as the formula (or recipe) used to combine factors of production. (When better formulas are developed, more production can be obtained from the same amount of resources.) The level of technology sets the limit on the amount and types of goods and services that we can derive from any given amount of resources. The production possibilities curve is drawn under the assumption that we use the best technology that we currently have available, and that this technology doesn't change over the time period under study.

Being off the Production Possibilities Curve

Look again at part (b) of Figure 2.2. Point *R* lies *outside* the production possibilities curve and is *impossible* to achieve during the time period assumed. By definition, the production possibilities curve indicates the *maximum* quantity of one good given some quantity of the other.

It is possible, however, to be at point *S* in Figure 2.2. That point lies beneath the production possibilities curve. If the nation is at point *S*, it means that its resources are not being fully utilized. This occurs, for example, during periods of unemployment. Point *S* and all such points within the production possibilities curve are always attainable but are usually not desirable.

Efficiency

The production possibilities curve can be used to define the notion of efficiency. Whenever the economy is operating on the PPC at points such as *A*, *B*, *C*, or *D*, we say that its production is efficient. Points such as *S* in Figure 2.2, which lie beneath the production possibilities curve, are said to represent production situations that are not efficient.

▶ **Efficiency**
The case in which a given level of inputs is used to produce the maximum output possible. Alternatively, the situation in which a given output is produced at minimum cost.

Efficiency can mean many things to many people. Even within economics, there are different types of efficiency. Here we are discussing efficiency in production, or productive efficiency. An economy is productively efficient whenever it is producing the maximum output with given technology and resources.

A simple commonsense definition of efficiency is getting the most out of what we have as an economy. Clearly, we are not getting the most that we have if we are at point *S* in part (b) of Figure 2.2. We can move from point *S* to, say, point *C*, thereby increasing the total quantity of automobiles produced without any decrease in the total quantity of newsprint produced. We can move from point *S* to point *E*, for example, and have both more automobiles and more newsprint. Point *S* is called an **inefficient point**, which is defined as any point below the production possibilities curve.

▶ **Inefficient point**
Any point below the production possibilities curve at which resources are being used ineffi-

The concept of economic efficiency relates to how goods are distributed among different individuals and entities. An efficient economy is one in which people who place relatively the most value on specific goods end up with those goods. If you own a vintage electric Fender guitar, but I value it more than you, I can buy it from you. Such trading benefits both of us. In the process, the economy becomes more efficient. The maximum efficiency an economy can reach is when all such mutual benefits through trade have been exhausted.

The Law of Increasing Relative Cost

In the example in Figure 2.1, the trade-off between a grade in accounting and a grade in economics is one-to-one. The trade-off ratio was fixed. That is to say, the production possibilities curve was a straight line. The curve in Figure 2.2 is a more general case. We have re-created the curve in Figure 2.2 as Figure 2.3. Each combination, *A* through *G*, of automobiles and newsprint is represented on the production possibilities curve. Starting with the production of zero newsprint, Canada could produce 3 million automobiles with its available resources and technology. When we increase production of newsprint from zero to 2 million tonnes per year, we have to give up the automobile production represented by that first vertical arrow, *Aa*. From part (a) of Figure 2.2 you can see that this is 0.1 million autos a year (3.0 million − 2.9 million). Again, if we increase production of newsprint by 2 million tonnes per year, we go from *B* to *C*. In order to do so, we have to give up the vertical distance *Bb*, or 0.2 million automobiles a year. By the time we go from 10 million to 12 million tonnes of newsprint, to obtain that 2 million tonne increase we have to forgo the vertical distance *Ff*, or 1.4 million automobiles. In other words, the opportunity cost of the last 2 million tonnes of newsprint is 1.4 million autos, compared with 0.1 million autos, the opportunity cost for the first 2 million tonnes of newsprint (starting at zero production).

Figure 2.3
The Law of Increasing Relative Cost

Consider equal increments of newsprint production, as measured on the horizontal axis. All of the horizontal arrows—*aB, bC,* and so on—are of equal length (2 million tonnes). The opportunity cost of going from 10 million tonnes of newsprint per year to 12 million *(Ff)* is much greater than going from zero tonnes to 2 million tonnes *(Aa)*. The opportunity cost of each additional equal increase in newsprint production rises.

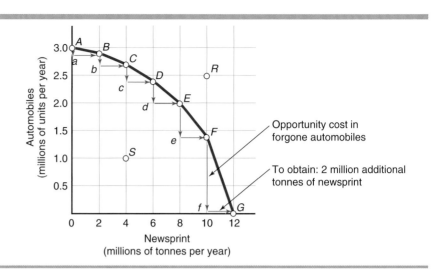

▶ **Law of increasing relative cost**

The observation that the opportunity cost of additional units of a good generally increases as society attempts to produce more of that good. This accounts for the bowed-out shape of the production possibilities curve.

What we are observing is called the **law of increasing relative cost**. When society takes more resources and applies them to the production of any specific good, the opportunity cost increases for each additional unit produced. The reason that, as a country, we face the law of increasing relative cost (which causes the production possibilities curve to bow outward) is that certain resources are better suited for producing some goods than they are for others. Resources are generally not *perfectly* adaptable for alternative uses. When increasing the output of a particular good, producers must use less efficient resources than those already used in order to produce the additional output. Hence the cost of producing the additional units increases. In our hypothetical example here, at first the mechanical technicians in the automobile industry would shift over to producing newsprint. After a while, though, upholstery specialists and windshield installers would also be asked to help. Clearly, they would be less effective in making newsprint.

As a rule of thumb, the more *specialized the resources, the more bowed the production possibilities curve.* At the other extreme, if all resources are equally suitable for newsprint production or automobile production, the curves in Figures 2.2 and 2.3 would approach the straight line shown in our first example in Figure 2.1.

Concepts in Brief

- Trade-offs are represented graphically by a production possibilities curve (PPC) showing the maximum quantity of one good or service that can be produced, given a specific quantity of another, from a given set of resources over a specified period of time—for example, one year.
- A PPC is drawn holding the quantity and quality of all resources fixed over the time period under study.
- Points outside the production possibilities curve are unattainable; points inside are attainable but represent an inefficient use or under-use of available resources.
- Because many resources are better suited for certain productive tasks than for others, society's production possibilities curve is bowed outward, following the law of increasing relative cost.

ECONOMIC GROWTH AND THE PRODUCTION POSSIBILITIES CURVE

Over any particular time period, a society cannot be outside the production possibilities curve. Over time, however, it is possible to have more of everything. This occurs through economic growth. Figure 2.4 shows the production possibilities curve for automobiles and newsprint shifting outward. The two additional curves represent new choices open to an economy that has experienced economic growth. Such economic growth occurs because of many things, including increases in the number of workers and productive investment in equipment.

Scarcity still exists, however, no matter how much economic growth there is. At any point in time, we will always be on some production possibilities curve; thus we will always face trade-offs. The more we want of one thing, the less we can have of others.

If a nation experiences economic growth, the production possibilities curve between automobiles and newsprint will move outward, as is shown in Figure 2.4. This takes time and does not occur automatically. One reason it will occur involves the choice about how much to consume today.

Figure 2.4
Economic Growth Allows for More of Everything

If the nation experiences economic growth, the production possibilities curve between automobiles and newsprint will shift out, as shown. This takes time, however, and it does not occur automatically. This means, therefore, that we can have more automobiles and more newsprint only after a period of time during which we have experienced economic growth.

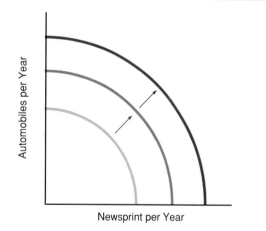

THE TRADE-OFF BETWEEN THE PRESENT AND THE FUTURE

The production possibilities curve and economic growth can be used to examine the trade-off between present **consumption** and future consumption. When we consume today, we are using up what we call consumption or consumer goods—food and clothes, for example. And we have already defined physical capital as the manufactured goods, such as machines and factories, used to make other goods and services.

▶ **Consumption**
The use of goods and services for personal satisfaction.

Why We Make Capital Goods

Why would we be willing to use productive resources to make things—capital goods—that we cannot consume directly? For one thing, capital goods enable us to produce larger quantities of consumer goods or to produce them less expensively than we otherwise could. Before fish are "produced" for the market, equipment such as fishing boats, nets, and poles are produced first. Imagine how expensive it would be to obtain fish for market without using these capital goods. Catching fish with one's hands is not an easy task. The price per fish would be very high if capital goods weren't used.

Forgoing Current Consumption

Whenever we use productive resources to make capital goods, we are implicitly forgoing current consumption. We are waiting until some time in the future to consume the fruits that will be reaped from the use of capital goods. In effect, when we forgo current consumption to invest in capital goods, we are engaging in an economic activity that is forward-looking—we do not get instant utility or satisfaction from our activity. Indeed, if we were to produce only consumer goods now and no capital goods, our capacity to produce consumer goods in the future would suffer. Here we see a trade-off situation.

The Trade-Off Between Consumption Goods and Capital Goods

To have more consumer goods in the future, we must accept fewer consumer goods today. In other words, an opportunity cost is involved here. Every time we make a choice for more goods today, we incur an opportunity cost of fewer goods tomorrow, and every time we make a choice of more goods in the future, we incur an opportunity cost of fewer goods today. With the resources that we don't use to produce consumer goods for today, we invest in capital goods that will produce more consumer goods for us later. The trade-off is shown in Figure 2.5. On the left in part (a), you can see this trade-off depicted as a production possibilities curve between capital goods and consumption goods.

Assume that we are willing to give up $1 billion worth of consumption today. We will be at point A in the left-hand diagram of part (a). This will allow the economy to grow. We will have more future consumption because we invested in more capital goods today. In the right-hand diagram of part (a), we see two goods represented, food and recreation. The production possibilities curve will move outward if we collectively decide to restrict consumption each year and invest in capital goods.

In part (b), we show the results of our willingness to forgo more current consumption. We move to point *C*, where we have many fewer consumer goods today, but produce a lot more capital goods. This leads to more future growth in this simplified model, and thus the production possibilities curve in the right-hand side of part (b) shifts outward more than it did in the right-hand side of part (a).

Figure 2.5
Capital Goods and Growth

In part (a), the nation chooses not to consume $1 billion, so it invests that amount in capital goods. In part (b), it chooses even more capital goods. The PPC moves even further to the right on the right-hand diagram in part (b) as a result.

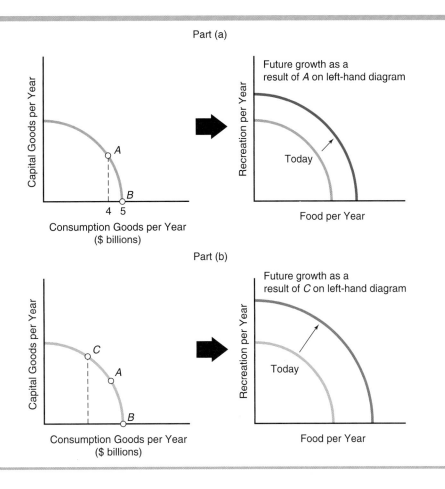

Part (a)

Part (b)

Try Preview Question 4:
Can a "free" college education ever be truly free?

In other words, the more we give up today, the more we can have tomorrow, provided, of course, that the capital goods are productive in future periods and that society desires the consumer goods produced by this additional capital.

INTERNATIONAL EXAMPLE
Consumption Versus Capital Goods in the United States and in Japan

The trade-off of capital versus consumption goods (shown in the production possibilities curves of Figure 2.5) can be observed in real life when we compare different countries. The Japanese, for example, have chosen to devote more than twice the amount of resources each year to the production of capital goods than have the Americans. Not surprisingly, the Japanese have, until recently, experienced a much higher rate of economic growth than the United States. In effect, then, Japan is represented by part (b) in Figure 2.5—choosing more capital goods—and the United States by part (a)—choosing fewer capital goods.

For critical analysis: Does this analysis apply to the trade-off between consumption and human capital for you as an individual? If so, how?

Concepts in Brief

- The use of capital requires using productive resources to produce capital goods that will later be used to produce consumer goods.
- A trade-off is involved between current consumption and capital goods or, alternatively, between current consumption and future consumption. This is because the more we invest in capital goods today, the greater the amount of consumer goods we can produce in the future, and the smaller the amount of consumer goods we can produce today.

SPECIALIZATION AND GREATER PRODUCTIVITY

▶ **Specialization**
The division of productive activities among persons and regions so that no one individual or area is totally self-sufficient. An individual may specialize, for example, in law or medicine. A nation may specialize in the production of lobsters, computers, or cameras.

Specialization involves working at a relatively well-defined, limited endeavour, such as accounting or teaching. It involves a division of labour among different individuals and regions. Most people, in fact, do specialize. For example, you could probably change the oil in your car if you wanted to. Typically, though, you take your car to a garage and let the mechanic do it. You benefit by letting the garage mechanic specialize in changing the oil and in completing other repairs on your car. The specialist has all the proper equipment to do the work, and will likely get the job finished sooner than you could. Specialization usually leads to greater productivity, not only for each individual but also for the country.

Absolute Advantage

▶ **Absolute advantage**
The ability to produce a good or service at an "absolutely" lower cost, usually measured in units of labour or resource input required to produce one unit of the good or service.

Specialization occurs because different individuals and different nations have different skills. Sometimes it seems that some individuals are better at doing everything than anyone else. A president of a large company might be able to type better than any of the typists, file better than any of the file clerks, and wash windows better than any of the window washers. The president has an **absolute advantage** in all of these endeavours— by using fewer labour hours for each task than anyone else in the company. The president does not, however, spend time doing those other activities. Why not? Because a president is paid the most for undertaking managerial duties and specializes in that one particular task despite having an absolute advantage in all tasks. Indeed, absolute advantage is irrelevant in predicting how the president's time is spent; only *comparative advantage* matters.

Comparative Advantage

▶ **Comparative advantage**
The ability to produce a good or service at a lower opportunity cost compared to other producers.

Comparative advantage is the ability to perform an activity at the lowest opportunity cost. You have a comparative advantage in one activity whenever you have the lowest opportunity cost of performing that activity. Comparative advantage is always a *relative* concept. You may be able to change the oil in your car; you might even be able to change it faster than the local mechanic. But if the opportunity cost you face by changing the oil exceeds the mechanic's opportunity cost, the mechanic has a comparative advantage in changing the oil. The mechanic faces a lower opportunity cost for that activity.

You may be convinced that everybody can do everything better than you. In this extreme situation, do you still have a comparative advantage? The answer is yes. To discover your comparative advantage you need to find a job in which your *disadvantage* relative to others is the smallest. You do not have to be a mathematical genius to figure this out. The market tells you very clearly by offering you the highest income for the job for which you have the smallest disadvantage compared to others. Stated differently, to find your comparative advantage no matter how much better everybody else can do the jobs that you want to do, you simply find which job maximizes your income.

The coaches of sports teams are constantly faced with determining each player's comparative advantage. Former Blue Jay Dave Winfield was originally one of the best pitchers in college baseball, winning the most valuable player award for pitching for the University of Minnesota Golden Bears in the 1973 College World Series. After he was drafted by the San Diego Padres, the coach decided to make him an outfielder even though he was one of the best pitchers on the roster. The coach wanted Winfield to concentrate on his hitting. Good pitchers do not bring in as many fans as home-run kings. Dave Winfield's comparative advantage was clearly in hitting homers rather than practising and developing his pitching game.

Scarcity, Self-Interest, and Specialization

In Chapter 1, you learned about the assumption of rational self-interest. It says that for the purposes of our analyses we assume that individuals are rational in that they will do what is in their own self-interest. They will not consciously carry out actions that will make them worse off. In this chapter, you learned that scarcity requires people to make choices. We assume that they make choices based on their self-interest, and attempt to maximize benefits net of opportunity cost. In so doing, individuals choose their comparative advantage and end up specializing. Ultimately, when people specialize, they increase the money income they make and therefore become richer. When all individuals and businesses specialize simultaneously, the gains are seen in greater material well-being. With any given set of resources, specialization will result in higher output.

EXAMPLE	How Specialization Can Lead to Career Changes

 Most of you will make several career changes during your working lives. Some of these may be forced upon you by circumstance, but others will be because of a comparative advantage you can exploit. Someone who has developed his comparative advantage is William Deverell, author of five novels including *Kill All the Lawyers* and *Platinum Blues*, and the non-fiction work *Fatal Cruise*. He also wrote the pilot for *Street Legal*, a CBC television series.

Deverell started his working life as a journalist in Saskatoon, Montreal, and Vancouver. After attending law school, he began his practice of law in 1964. For 15 years he specialized in criminal law and civil rights, and began writing fiction in his spare time. In 1979 his first novel *Needles*, which won the Seal First Novel award, was published.

In recent years Deverell has not practised law but has specialized in his career as a writer. Fortunately, he recognized his comparative advantage in writing crime fiction, an art few can master.

For critical analysis: What is William Deverell's opportunity cost of choosing to be a full-time writer?

THE DIVISION OF LABOUR

▶ **Division of labour**
The segregation of a resource into different specific tasks; for example, one automobile worker puts on bumpers, another doors, and so on.

In any firm that includes specialized human and nonhuman resources, there is a **division of labour** among those resources. The best-known example of all time comes from one of the earliest and perhaps most famous economists, Adam Smith, who in *The Wealth of Nations* (1776) illustrated the benefits of a division of labour in the making of pins: "One man draws out the wire, another straightens it, a third cuts it, a fourth points it, a fifth grinds it at the top for receiving the head; to make the head requires two or three distinct operations; to put it on is a peculiar business, to whiten the pins is another; it is even a trade by itself to put them into the paper."

Making pins this way allowed 10 workers without very much skill to make almost 48,000 pins "of a middling size" in a day. One worker, toiling alone, could have made perhaps 20 pins a day; therefore, 10 workers could have produced 200. Division of labour allowed for an increase in the daily output of the pin factory from 200 to 48,000! (Smith did not attribute all of the gain to the division of labour according to talent, but credited also the use of machinery and the fact that less time was spent shifting from task to task.)

What we are discussing here involves a division of the resource called labour into different kinds of labour. The different kinds of labour are organized in such a way as to increase the amount of output possible from the fixed resources available. We can therefore talk about an organized division of labour within a firm leading to increased output.

Thinking Critically About the Media | International Trade

If you watch enough news on TV or frequently read the popular press, you get a distinct impression that international trade is somehow different from trade within our borders. At any given time, Canada is either at economic war with the United States over our exports of softwood lumber, or we are fighting with the European Union over whether Canadian furs caught using leg-hold traps should be allowed into the EU. International economics is just like any other type of economics; trade is just another economic activity. Indeed, one can think of international trade as a production process that transforms goods that we sell to other countries (exports) into what we buy from other countries (imports). International trade is a mutually beneficial exchange that occurs across political borders. If you imagine a world that was just one country, trade would still exist worldwide, but it would not be called international trade.

COMPARATIVE ADVANTAGE AND TRADE AMONG NATIONS

Though most of our analysis of absolute advantage, comparative advantage, and specialization has dealt with individuals, it is equally applicable to countries. First consider Canada. The Prairie provinces have a comparative advantage in the production of grains and other agricultural goods. Ontario and Quebec in Central Canada tend to specialize in industrialized production, such as automobiles and newsprint. Not surprisingly, grains are shipped from the Prairies to Central Canada, and automobiles are shipped in the reverse direction. Such specialization and trade allow for higher incomes and standards of living. If both the Prairies and Central Canada were politically defined as separate countries, the same analysis would still hold, but we would call it international trade. Indeed, Europe is smaller than Canada in area, but instead of one nation, Europe has 15. What in Canada we call *interprovincial trade*, in Europe is called *international trade*. There is no difference, however, in the economic results—both yield greater economic efficiency and higher average incomes.

Political problems that do not normally arise within a particular nation often do between nations. For example, if Nova Scotia crab fishers develop a cheaper method of harvesting crabs than fishers in British Columbia, British Columbia fishers will lose out. They cannot do much about the situation except try to lower their own costs of production. If crab fishers in Alaska, however, develop a cheaper method, both Nova Scotia and British Columbia fishers can (and likely will) try to raise political barriers to prevent Alaskan fishers from freely selling their product in Canada. Canadian crab fishers will use such arguments as "unfair" competition and loss of Canadian jobs. In so doing, they are only partly right: Crab-fishing jobs may decline in Canada, but jobs will not necessarily decline overall. If the argument of Canadian crab fishers had any validity, every time a region in Canada developed a better way to produce a product manufactured somewhere else in the country, employment in Canada would decline. That has never happened and never will.

When countries specialize where they have a comparative advantage and then trade with the rest of the world, the average standard of living in the world rises. In effect, international trade allows the world to move from inside the global production possibilities curve towards the curve itself, thereby improving worldwide economic efficiency.

Concepts in Brief

* With a given set of resources, specialization results in higher output; in other words, there are gains to specialization in terms of greater material well-being.
* Individuals and nations specialize in their areas of comparative advantage in order to reap the gains of specialization.
* Comparative advantages are found by determining which activities have the lowest opportunity cost—that is, which activities yield the highest return for the time and resources used.
* A division of labour occurs when different workers are assigned different tasks. Together, the workers produce a desired product.

Issues and Applications

The Cost of Crime

Concepts Applied:
Scarcity, opportunity costs, trade-offs

While the cost of crime is high, the cost of eliminating crime is much higher.

I t is impossible today to pick up a newspaper or watch a television newscast without reading or hearing about crime. Reports of murders, assaults, thefts, prostitution, and drug-trafficking are frequent. Not surprisingly, Canadians often express concern about crime rates, and support the notion of increasing the number of police in order to fight crime. But how many more police officers would we require, and what would be the cost?

More than 160,000 automobiles are stolen every year in Canada, many to be sold to eastern European or South American countries. Some studies suggest that each extra police officer hired would reduce automobile thefts by up to seven per year. At that rate, we would have to hire about 23,000 officers to wipe out car theft altogether.

The Cost of Crime

A study by economist Stephen Easton and criminologist Paul Brantingham tried to calculate the cost of crime in Canada for the year 1993. They found that Canada had a relatively low murder rate (53rd out of 83 countries studied) but a relatively high property crime rate (7th out of 83). Property crime includes theft, motor vehicle theft, vandalism, and fraud. This ranking is typical of western developed countries. (The United States is the exception with high rates of both murder and property crime.) Table 2.1 shows a rough breakdown of property crime in Canada for 1993.

Easton and Brantingham estimated the cost to victims of nonviolent property crime to be about $2,000 per incident, for a total of $4 billion per year. When we add to the victims' costs the cost of the courts, the police, and the prisons, the total begins to soar. It continues to climb as we add on the social cost of crime: the emotional trauma and the days of lost or reduced productivity as the victims deal with the shock of being victims.

The Cost of Preventing Crime

Perhaps it would be less costly to prevent crime than to deal with its effects. But how much are we prepared to spend? Currently, one in eight Canadian families owns some sort of burglar alarm, while one in fifty owns a monitored security device. Altogether we spend about $195 million on private security. This amount grew substantially between 1971 and 1991. The number of police officers per capita has also grown since 1971, but more slowly than the number of security guards.

What would it cost to wipe out property crime? We know it would take roughly 23,000 more police officers to stop motor vehicle thefts. At an average salary of $50,000, that would cost taxpayers about $1.15 billion per year. And what about preventing robberies and fraud, to say nothing of violent crime? It is clear that the price tag attached to a "crime-less" society is a high one indeed.

Table 2.1. **Cost to Victims of Property Crime**

Losses	Theft	Vandalism	Break and Enter	Automobile Theft	Robbery	Fraud
Number of reported incidents	888,617	415,645	406,582	156,811	29,961	113,054
Average loss (1993 dollars)	2,054	615	2,225	3,500	2,754	3,403
Total losses (millions of 1993 dollars)	1,821	255	905	549	83	385
Total loss from all sources (millions of 1993 dollars)	3,998					

Source: Paul Brantingham and Stephen T. Easton, *The Crime Bill: Who Pays and How Much?* Vancouver: The Fraser Institute, 1996.

The Trade-Offs That Are Really Involved

Let's assume that the rate of property crime prevention per police officer is the same for the other categories as it is for car theft. We would have to hire about 265,000 more police officers, in addition those mentioned above. The total bill for their salaries would be around $14.5 billion per year, roughly the same amount that Canadians collected in employment insurance in 1997. This sum is $3 billion more than the federal government transferred to the provinces collectively for health, education, and welfare in 1998.

So trade-offs are clearly involved here. With $14.5 billion, Canada could build 20 fixed links like the one between New Brunswick and Prince Edward Island, or 100 new universities like the University of Northern British Columbia. Is the total absence of property crime worth this much to you?

Actually the Risk Is Falling

Violent crime and property crime are everywhere in the news today. Does that mean that Canada is becoming a more dangerous place to live? Fortunately, no. While the property crime rate was three times higher in 1992 than in 1962, it has taken a 20 percent dip in the past six years. So while a larger number of people are the victims of property crime because our population has grown, the proportion of our population that is victimized is falling.

For Critical Analysis

1. Why is opportunity cost such an important concept in analysing government programs to prevent crime?
2. What would happen to the opportunity cost of policing if we allocated more and more of our resources to crime prevention?

CHAPTER SUMMARY

1. All societies at all times face the universal problem of scarcity because we cannot obtain everything we want from nature without sacrifice. Thus scarcity and poverty are not synonymous. Even the richest persons face scarcity because they also have to make choices among alternatives.

2. The resources we use to produce desired goods and services can be classified into land, labour, physical and human capital, and entrepreneurship.

3. Goods are all things from which individuals derive satisfaction. Economic goods are those for which the desired quantity exceeds the amount that is directly available from nature at a zero price. The goods that we want are not necessarily those that we need. The term *need* is indefinable in economics, whereas humans have unlimited *wants*, which are defined as the goods and services on which we place a positive value.

4. We measure the cost of anything by what has to be given up in order to have it. This cost is called opportunity cost.

5. The trade-offs we face as individuals and those we face as a society can be represented graphically by a production possibilities curve (PPC). This curve shows the maximum quantity of one good or service that can be produced, given a specific quantity of another, from a given set of resources over a

specified period of time, usually one year.

6. Because resources are specialized, production possibilities curves bow outward. This means that each additional increment of one good can be obtained only by giving up more and more of the other goods. This is called the law of increasing relative cost.

7. It is impossible to be outside the production possibilities curve, but we can be inside it. When we are, we are in a situation of unemployment, inefficiently organized resources, or some combination of the two.

8. There is a trade-off between consumption goods and capital goods. The more resources we devote to capital goods, the more consumption goods we can normally have in the future (and less currently). This is because more capital goods allow the economy to grow, thereby moving the production possibilities curve outward.

9. You find your comparative advantage by looking at the activity that has the lowest opportunity cost. That is, your comparative advantage lies in the activity that generates the highest income. By specializing in that comparative advantage, you are assured of reaping the gains of specialization.

10. Division of labour occurs when workers are assigned different tasks.

DISCUSSION OF PREVIEW QUESTIONS

1. **Do affluent people face the problem of scarcity?**

   Scarcity is a relative concept and exists because wants are great, relative to the means of satisfying those wants (wealth or income). Even though affluent people have relatively and absolutely high levels of income or wealth, they nevertheless typically want more than they can have (in luxury goods, power, prestige, and so on).

2. **Fresh air may be consumed at no charge, but is it free of cost to society?**

   Individuals are not charged a price for the use of air. Yet truly fresh air is not free to society. If a good were free to society, every person would be able to use all that he or she wanted to use; no one would have to sacrifice anything in order to use that good, and people would not have to compete for it. In Canada, different groups compete for air; for example, environmentalists and concerned citizens compete with automobile drivers and factories for clean air.

3. **Why does the scarcity problem force people to consider opportunity costs?**

   Individuals have limited incomes; as a consequence, an expenditure on an automobile necessarily precludes expenditures on other goods and services. The same is true for society, which also faces the scarcity problem; if society allocates specific resources to the production of a steel mill, those same resources cannot be allocated elsewhere. Because resources are limited, society is forced to decide how to allocate its available resources; scarcity means that the cost of allocating resources to produce specific goods is ultimately assessed in terms of other goods that are necessarily sacrificed. Because there are millions of ways in which the resources allocated to a steel mill might otherwise be allocated, we are forced to consider the *highest-valued* alternative. We define the opportunity cost of a good as its highest-valued alternative; the opportunity cost of the steel mill to society is the highest-valued output that those same resources could otherwise have produced.

4. **Can a "free" college education ever be truly free?**

   Suppose that you were given a college education without having to pay any fees whatsoever. You could say that you were receiving a free education. But someone is paying for your education because you are using scarce resources—buildings, professors' time, electricity for lighting, etc. The opportunity cost of your education is certainly not zero, so in that sense it is not free. Furthermore, by going to college, you are giving up the ability to earn income during that time period. Therefore, there is an opportunity cost to your attending classes and studying. You can approximate that opportunity cost by estimating what your current after-tax income would be if you were working instead of going to school.

PROBLEMS

(Answers to the odd-numbered problems appear at the back of the book.)

2-1. The following sets of numbers represent hypothetical production possibilities for a country in 1998. Plot these points on graph paper.

Cheese	Apples
4	0
3	1.6
2	2.4
1	2.8
0	3.0

Does the law of increasing relative cost seem to hold? Why? On the same graph, plot and draw the production possibilities curve that will represent 10 percent economic growth.

2-2. If, by going to college, you give up the chance to work in your mother's business for 35 hours per week at $7.00 per hour, what would be your opportunity cost of earning a two-year college diploma? What incentives exist to make you incur that opportunity cost? What resources are you giving up today in order to have more in the future?

2-3. Answer the questions using the following information.

Employee	Daily Work Effort	Production
Ann Jones	4 hours	8 jackets
	4 hours	12 ties
Ned Chapman	4 hours	8 jackets
	4 hours	12 ties
		16 jackets
Total daily output		24 ties

a. Who has an absolute advantage in jacket production?
b. Who has a comparative advantage in tie production?
c. Will Jones and Chapman specialize?
d. If they specialize, what will total output equal?

2-4. Two countries, Workland and Playland, have similar populations and identical production possibilities curves but different preferences. The production possibilities combinations are as follows:

Point	Capital Goods	Consumption Goods
A	0	20
B	1	19
C	2	17
D	3	14
E	4	10
F	5	5

Playland is located at point *B* on the PPC, and Workland is located at point *E*. Assume that this situation continues into the future and that all other things remain the same.

a. What is Workland's opportunity cost of capital goods in terms of consumption goods?
b. What is Playland's opportunity cost of capital goods in terms of consumption goods?
c. How would the PPCs of Workland and Playland be expected to compare to each other 50 years in the future?

2-5. Which of the following are part of the opportunity cost of going to a football game in town instead of watching it on TV at home? Explain why.

a. The expense of lunch in a restaurant prior to the football game.
b. The value of one hour of sleep lost because of a traffic jam after the game.
c. The expense of a babysitter for your children if they are too young to go to a football game.

2-6. Assume that your economics and English exams are scheduled for the same day. How would you determine how much time you should spend studying for each exam? Does the grade you are currently receiving in each course affect your decision? Why or why not?

2-7. Some people argue that air is not an economic good. If you agree with this statement, explain why. If you disagree, explain why. (Hint: Is all air the same?)

PPENDIX A

READING AND WORKING WITH GRAPHS

▶ **Independent variable**
A variable whose value is determined independently of, or outside, the equation under study.

▶ **Dependent variable**
A variable whose value changes according to changes in the value of one or more independent variables.

Table A-1
Gas Consumption as a Function of Driving Speed

Kilometres per Hour	Kilometres per Litre
70	11
80	10
90	9
100	8
110	7
120	6
130	5

▶ **Direct relationship**
A relationship between two variables that is positive, meaning that an increase in one variable is associated with an increase in the other and a decrease in one variable is associated with a decrease in the other.

▶ **Inverse relationship**
A relationship between two variables that is negative, meaning that an increase in one variable is associated with a decrease in the other and a decrease in one variable is associated with an increase in the other.

A graph is a visual representation of the relationship between variables. In this appendix, we'll stick to just two variables: an **independent variable,** which can change freely in value, and a **dependent variable,** which changes only as a result of changes in the value of the independent variable. For example, if nothing else is changing in your life, your weight depends on the amount of food you eat. Food is the independent variable and weight the dependent variable.

A table is a list of numerical values showing the relationship between two (or more) variables. Any table can be converted into a graph, which is a visual representation of that list. Once you understand how a table can be converted to a graph, you will understand what graphs are and how to construct and use them.

Consider a practical example. A conservationist may try to convince you that driving at lower highway speeds will help you conserve gas. Table A-1 shows the relationship between speed—the independent variable—and the distance you can go on a litre of gas at that speed—the dependent variable. This table does show a pattern of sorts. As the data in the first column get larger in value, the data in the second column get smaller.

Now let's take a look at the different ways in which variables can be related.

DIRECT AND INVERSE RELATIONSHIPS

Two variables can be related in different ways, some simple, others more complex. For example, a person's weight and height are often related. If we measured the height and weight of thousands of people, we would surely find that taller people tend to weigh more than shorter people. That is, we would discover that there is a **direct relationship** between height and weight. By this we simply mean that an increase in one variable is usually associated with an increase in the related variable. This can easily be seen in part (a) of Figure A-1.

Let's look at another simple way in which two variables can be related. Much evidence indicates that as the price of a specific commodity rises, the amount purchased decreases—there is an **inverse relationship** between the variable's price per unit and quantity purchased. A table listing the data for this relationship would indicate that for higher and higher prices, smaller and smaller quantities would be purchased. We see this relationship in part (b) of Figure A-1.

Figure A-1
Relationships

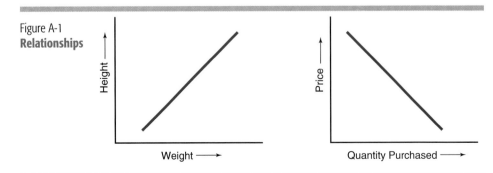

Figure A-2
Horizontal Number Line

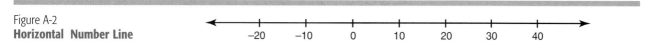

▷ **Number line**
A line that can be divided into segments of equal length, each associated with a number.

Figure A-3
Vertical Number Line

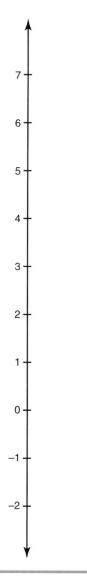

CONSTRUCTING A GRAPH

Let us now examine how to construct a graph to illustrate a relationship between two variables.

A Number Line

The first step is to become familiar with what is called a **number line.** One is shown in Figure A-2. There are two things that you should know about it.

1. The points on the line divide the line into equal segments.
2. The numbers associated with the points on the line increase in value from left to right; saying it the other way around, the numbers decrease in value from right to left. However you say it, what we're describing is formally called an *ordered set of points.*

On the number line, we have shown the line segments—that is, the distance from 0 to 10 or the distance between 30 and 40. They all appear to be equal and, indeed, are equal to 13 mm. When we use a distance to represent a quantity, such as barrels of oil, graphically, we are scaling the number line. In the example shown, the distance between 0 and 10 might represent 10 barrels of oil, or the distance from 0 to 40 might represent 40 barrels. Of course, the scale may differ on different number lines. For example, a distance of 1 cm could represent 10 units on one number line but 5,000 units on another. Notice that on our number line, points to the left of 0 correspond to negative numbers and points to the right of 0 correspond to positive numbers.

Of course, we can also construct a vertical number line. Consider the one in Figure A-3. As we move up this vertical number line, the numbers increase in value; conversely, as we descend, they decrease in value. Below 0 the numbers are negative, and above 0 the numbers are positive. And as on the horizontal number line, all the line segments are equal. This line is divided into segments such that the distance between −2 and −1 is the same as the distance between 0 and 1.

Combining Vertical and Horizontal Number Lines

By drawing the horizontal and vertical lines on the same sheet of paper, we are able to express the relationships between variables graphically. We do this in Figure A-4.

We draw them (1) so that they intersect at each other's 0 point and (2) so that they are perpendicular to each other. The result is a set of coordinate axes, where each line is called an axis. When we have two axes, they span a plane.

For one number line, you need only one number to specify any point on the line; equivalently, when you see a point on the line, you know that it represents one number or one value. With a coordinate value system, you need two numbers to specify a single point in the plane; when you see a single point on a graph, you know that it represents two numbers or two values.

Figure A-4
A Set of Coordinate Axes

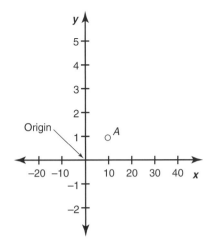

▶ **y axis**
The vertical axis in a graph.

▶ **x axis**
The horizontal axis in a graph.

▶ **Origin**
The intersection of the y axis and the x axis in a graph.

The basic things that you should know about a coordinate number system are that the vertical number line is referred to as the **y axis,** the horizontal number line is referred to as the **x axis,** and the point of intersection of the two lines is referred to as the **origin.**

Any point such as A in Figure A-4 represents two numbers—a value of x and a value of y. But we know more than that; we also know that point A represents a positive value of y because it is above the x axis, and we know that it represents a positive value of x because it is to the right of the y axis.

Point A represents a "paired observation" of the variables x and y; in particular, in Figure A-4, A represents an observation of the pair of values $x = 10$ and $y = 1$. Every point in the coordinate system corresponds to a paired observation of x and y, which can be simply written (x, y)—the x value is always specified first, then the y value. When we give the values associated with the position of point A in the coordinate number system, we are in effect giving the coordinates of that point. A's coordinates are $x = 10$, $y = 1$, or $(10, 1)$.

Table A-2
T-Shirts Purchased

(1) Price of T-Shirts	(2) Number of T-Shirts Purchased per Week
$10	20
9	30
8	40
7	50
6	60
5	70

GRAPHING NUMBERS IN A TABLE

Consider Table A-2. Column 1 shows different prices for T-shirts, and column 2 gives the number of T-shirts purchased per week at these prices. Notice the pattern of these numbers. As the price of T-shirts falls, the number of T-shirts purchased per week increases. Therefore, an inverse relationship exists between these two variables, and as soon as we represent it on a graph, you will be able to see the relationship. We can graph this relationship using a coordinate number system—a vertical and horizontal number line for each of these two variables. Such a graph is shown in part (b) of Figure A-5.

In economics, it is conventional to put dollar values on the y axis. We therefore construct a vertical number line for price and a horizontal number line, the x axis, for quantity of T-shirts purchased per week. The resulting coordinate system allows the

Figure A-5
Graphing the Relationship Between T-Shirts Purchased and Price

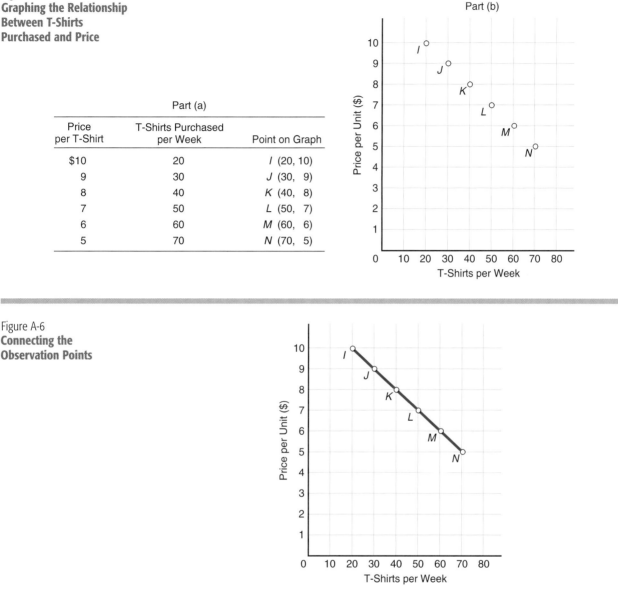

Part (a)

Price per T-Shirt	T-Shirts Purchased per Week	Point on Graph
$10	20	I (20, 10)
9	30	J (30, 9)
8	40	K (40, 8)
7	50	L (50, 7)
6	60	M (60, 6)
5	70	N (70, 5)

Figure A-6
Connecting the Observation Points

plotting of each of the paired observation points; in part (a), we repeat Table A-2, with a column added expressing these points in paired-data (x, y) form. For example, point *J* is the paired observation (30, 9). It indicates that when the price of a T-shirt is $9, 30 will be purchased per week.

If it were possible to sell parts of a T-shirt ($\frac{1}{2}$ or $\frac{1}{20}$ shirt), we would have observations at every possible price. That is, we would be able to connect our paired observations, represented as lettered points. Let's assume that we can make T-shirts perfectly divisible. We would then have a line that connects these points, as shown in the graph in Figure A-6.

In short, we have now represented the data from the table in the form of a graph. Note that an inverse relationship between two variables shows up on a graph as a line or curve that slopes downward from left to right. (You might as well get used to the idea that economists call a straight line a "curve" even though it may not curve at all. Much of economists' data turn out to be curves, so they refer to everything represented graphically, even straight lines, as curves.)

THE SLOPE OF A LINE (A LINEAR CURVE)

An important property of a curve represented on a graph is its *slope*. Consider Figure A-7, which represents the quantities of shoes per week that a seller is willing to offer at different prices. Note that in part (a) of Figure A-7, as in Figure A-5, we have expressed the coordinates of the points in parentheses in paired-data form.

The **slope** of a line is defined as the change in the *y* values divided by the corresponding change in the *x* values as we move along the line. Let's move from point *E* to point *D* in part (b) of Figure A-7. As we move, we note that the change in the *y* values, which is the change in price, is +$20, because we have moved from a price of $20 to a price of $40 per pair. As we move from *E* to *D*, the change in the *x* values is +80; the number of pairs of shoes willingly offered per week rises from 80 to 160 pairs. The slope calculated as a change in the *y* values divided by the change in the *x* values is therefore

$$\frac{20}{80} = \frac{1}{4}$$

It may be helpful for you to think of slope as a "rise" (movement in the vertical direction) over a "run" (movement in the horizontal direction). We show this abstractly in Figure A-8. The slope is measured by the amount of rise divided by the amount of run. In the example in Figure A-8, and of course in Figure A-7, the

Figure A-7
A Positively Sloped Curve

Part (a)

Price per Pair	Pairs of Shoes Offered per Week	Point on Graph
$100	400	A (400, 100)
80	320	B (320, 80)
60	240	C (240, 60)
40	160	D (160, 40)
20	80	E (80, 20)

Part (b)

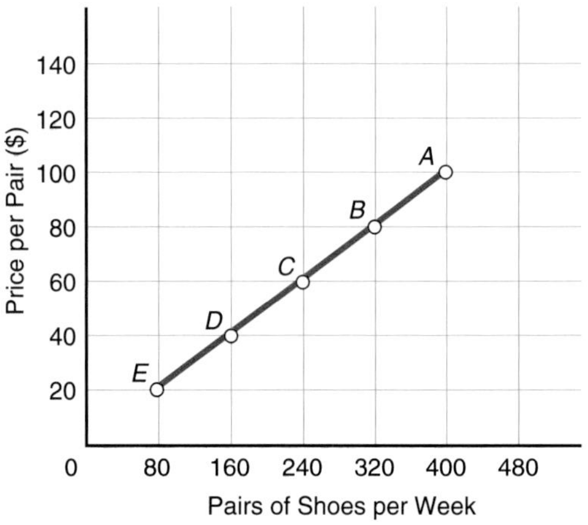

Figure A-8
Figuring Positive Slope

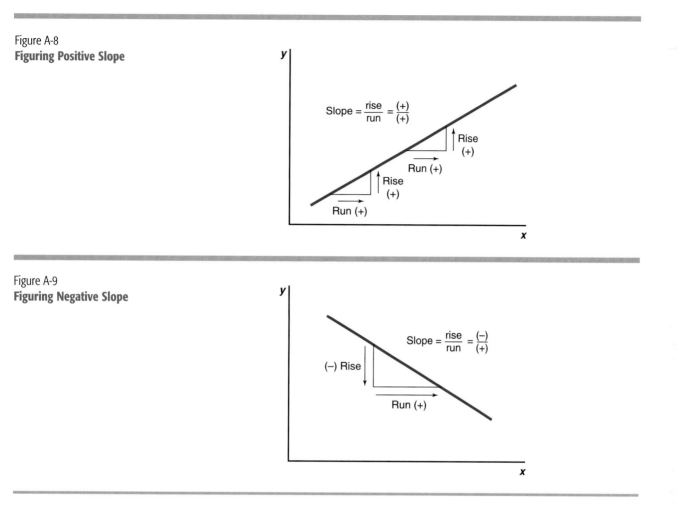

Figure A-9
Figuring Negative Slope

amount of rise is positive and so is the amount of run. That's because it's a direct relationship. We show an inverse relationship in Figure A-9. The slope is still equal to the rise divided by the run, but in this case the rise and the run have opposite signs because the curve slopes downward. That means that the slope will have to be negative and that we are dealing with an inverse relationship.

Now let's calculate the slope for a different part of the curve in part (b) of Figure A-7. We will find the slope as we move from point B to point A. Again, we note that the slope, or rise over run, from B to A equals

$$\frac{20}{80} = \frac{1}{4}$$

A specific property of a straight line is that its slope is the same between any two points; in other words, the slope is constant at all points on a straight line in a graph.

We conclude that for our example in Figure A-7, the relationship between the price of a pair of shoes and the number of pairs of shoes willingly offered per week is linear, which simply means "in a straight line," and our calculations indicate a constant slope. Moreover, we calculate a direct relationship between these two variables, which turns out to be an upward-sloping (from left to right) curve. Upward-sloping curves have positive slopes—in this case, it is $+\frac{1}{4}$.

We know that an inverse relationship between two variables shows up as a downward-sloping curve—rise over run will be a negative slope because the rise and run have opposite signs as shown in Figure A-9. When we see a negative slope, we know that increases in one variable are associated with decreases in the other. Therefore, we say that downward-sloping curves have negative slopes. Can you verify that the slope of the graph representing the relationship between T-shirt prices and the quantity of T-shirts purchased per week in Figure A-6 is $-\frac{1}{10}$?

Slopes of Nonlinear Curves

The graph presented in Figure A-10 indicates a *nonlinear* relationship between two variables, total profits and output per unit of time. Inspection of this graph indicates that at first, increases in output lead to increases in total profits; that is, total profits rise as output increases. But beyond some output level, further increases in output cause decreases in total profits.

Can you see how this curve rises at first, reaches a peak at point *C*, and then falls? This curve relating total profits to output levels appears mountain-shaped.

Considering that this curve is nonlinear (it is obviously not a straight line), should we expect a constant slope when we compute changes in *y* divided by corresponding changes in *x* in moving from one point to another? A quick inspection, even without specific numbers, should lead us to conclude that the slopes of lines joining different points in this curve, such as between *A* and *B*, *B* and *C*, or *C* and *D*, will *not* be the same. The curve slopes upward (in a positive direction) for some values and downward (in a negative direction) for other values. In fact, the slope of the line between any two points on this curve will be different from the slope of the line between any two other points. Each slope will be different as we move along the curve.

Instead of using a line between two points to discuss slope, mathematicians and economists prefer to discuss the slope *at a particular point*. The slope at a point on the curve, such as point *B* in the graph in Figure A-10, is the slope of a line *tangent*

Figure A-10
The Slope of a Nonlinear Curve

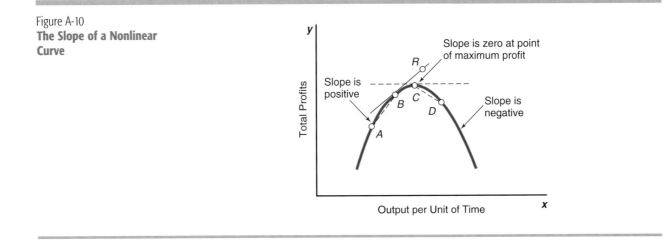

to that point. A tangent line is a straight line that touches a curve at only one point. For example, it might be helpful to think of the tangent at B as the straight line that just "kisses" the curve at point B.

To calculate the slope of a tangent line, you need to have some additional information besides the two values of the point of tangency. For example, in Figure A-10, if we knew that the point R also lay on the tangent line and we knew the two values of that point, we could calculate the slope of the tangent line. We could calculate rise over run between points B and R, and the result would be the slope of the line tangent to the one point B on the curve.

APPENDIX SUMMARY

1. Direct relationships involve a dependent variable changing in the same direction as the change in the independent variable.

2. Inverse relationships involve the dependent variable changing in the opposite direction of the change in the independent variable.

3. When we draw a graph showing the relationship between two economic variables, we are holding all other things constant (the Latin term for which is *ceteris paribus*).

4. We obtain a set of coordinates by putting vertical and horizontal number lines together. The vertical line is called the y axis; the horizontal line, the x axis.

5. The slope of any linear (straight-line) curve is the change in the y values divided by the corresponding change in the x values as we move along the line. Otherwise stated, the slope is calculated as the amount of rise over the amount of run, where rise is movement in the vertical direction and run is movement in the horizontal direction.

6. The slope of a nonlinear curve changes; it is positive when the curve is rising and negative when the curve is falling. At a maximum or minimum point, the slope of the nonlinear curve is zero.

APPENDIX PROBLEMS

(The answer to Problem A-1 appears at the back of the book.)

A-1. Complete the schedule and plot the following function:

$y = 3x$

y	x
	4
	3
	2
	1
	0
	−1
	−2
	−3
	−4

A-2. Complete the schedule and plot the following function:

$y = x^2$

y	x
	4
	3
	2
	1
	0
	−1
	−2
	−3
	−4

3

Demand and Supply

Between 1990 and 1996, the number of suppliers of sports trading cards increased by almost 5,000 percent. You might predict that more suppliers would mean that more cards would be put on the market and the price of cards would fall. In general you would be correct. However, what actually happened was that the prices of some sports cards fell while the prices of others rose. To understand how these seemingly contradictory results are actually quite logical, you will need the tools of supply and demand analysis.

Did You Know That... more than 20 million people worldwide currently own portable cellular phones? Two million Canadians have purchased them since their introduction in 1985. Over the last decade, sales outside Canada have grown between 45 to 50 percent every year. Marketing consultants expect cell phone ownership to increase by 10 to 15 percent per year for the next several years. There are many reasons for the growth in ownership of cellular phones, not least being the dramatic reduction in both price and size thanks to improved and cheaper computer chips used in making them. There is something else at work, though. It has to do with security. In a recent survey, 46 percent of new cellular phone users said that personal safety was the main reason they bought a portable phone. In the case of an automobile breakdown, for example, they would be able to call a garage or tow truck for help.

We could attempt to explain the phenomenon simply by saying that more people like to use portable phones. But that explanation is neither satisfying nor entirely accurate. If we use the economist's primary set of tools, *demand and supply*, we will have a better understanding of the cellular phone's explosion in popularity, as well as many other phenomena in our world. Demand and supply are two ways of categorizing the influences on the price of goods that you buy, and the quantities available. As such, demand and supply form the basis of virtually all economic analysis of the world around us.

As you will see throughout this text, the operation of the forces of demand and supply take place in *markets*. A **market** is an abstract concept referring to all the arrangements individuals have for exchanging with one another. Goods and services are sold in markets, such as the automobile market, the health food market, and the compact disc market. Workers offer their services in the labour market. Companies, or firms, buy workers' labour services in the labour market. Firms also buy other inputs in order to produce the goods and services that you buy as a consumer. They purchase machines, buildings, and land. These markets are in operation at all times. One of the most important activities in them is the setting of the prices of all of the inputs and outputs that are bought and sold in our complicated economy. To understand the determination of prices, you first need to look at the law of demand.

▶ **Market**

All of the arrangements that individuals have for exchanging with one another. Thus we can speak of the labour market, the automobile market, and the credit market.

THE LAW OF DEMAND

▶ **Demand**

A schedule of how much of a good or service people will purchase at any price during a specified time period, other things being constant.

Demand has a special meaning in economics. It refers to the quantities of specific goods or services that individuals, either singly or as a group, will purchase at various possible prices, other things being constant. We can therefore talk about the demand for microprocessor chips, French fries, compact disc players, and children.

Associated with the concept of demand is the **law of demand**, which can be stated as follows:

▶ **Law of demand**

The observation that there is a negative, or inverse, relationship between the price of any good or service and the quantity demanded, holding other factors constant.

When the price of a good goes up, people buy less of it, other things being equal. When the price of a good goes down, people buy more of it, other things being equal.

The law of demand tells us that the quantity demanded of any commodity is inversely related to its price, other things being equal. In an inverse relationship, one variable moves up in value when the other moves down. The law of demand states that a change in price causes the quantity demanded to change in the *opposite* direction.

Notice that we tacked onto the end of the law of demand the statement "other things being equal." We referred to this in Chapter 1 as the *ceteris paribus* assumption. It means, for example, that when we predict that people will buy fewer CD players if their price goes up, we are holding constant the price of all other goods in the economy as well as people's incomes. Implicitly, therefore, if we are assuming that no other prices change when we examine the price behaviour of CD players, we are looking at the *relative* price of CD players.

The law of demand is supported by millions of observations of how people behave in the marketplace. Theoretically, it can be derived from an economic model based on rational behaviour, as was discussed in Chapter 1. Basically, if nothing else changes and the price of a good falls, the lower price induces us to buy more over a certain period of time. This is because we can enjoy additional net gains that were unavailable at the higher price. For the most part, if you examine your own purchasing behaviour, you will see that it generally follows the law of demand.

Relative Prices Versus Money Prices

▶ **Relative price**

The price of a commodity expressed in terms of another commodity.

▶ **Money price**

The price that we observe today, expressed in today's dollars. Also called the *absolute, nominal,* or *current price.*

The **relative price** of any commodity is its price in terms of another commodity. The actual price that you pay in dollars and cents for any good or service at any point in time is called its **money price**. Consider an example that you might hear quite often around older friends or relatives. "When I bought my first new car, it cost only $1500." The implication, of course, is that the price of cars today is outrageously high because the average new car might cost $20,000. But that is not an accurate comparison. What was the price of the average house during that same year? Perhaps it was only $12,000. By comparison, then, given that houses today average about $150,000, the current price of a new car doesn't sound so far out of line, does it?

The point is that money prices during different time periods don't tell you much. You have to find out relative prices. Consider an example of the price of CDs versus the price of cassettes from last year and this year. In Table 3.1, we show the money price of CDs and cassettes for two years during which both have gone up. That means that we have to pay out more for each in today's dollars and cents. If we look, though, at the relative prices of CDs and cassettes, we find that last year, CDs were twice as expensive as cassettes, whereas this year they are only 1.81 times as expensive. Conversely, if we compare cassettes to CDs, last year they cost only half as much as CDs, but today they cost about 55 percent as much. In the one-year period, while both prices have gone up in money terms, the relative price of CDs has fallen (and, equivalently, the relative price of cassettes has risen).

Try Preview Question 1:

Why are relative prices important in understanding the law of demand?

Table 3.1
**Money Price Versus
Relative Price**

The money price of both compact discs (CDs) and cassettes has risen. But the relative price of CDs has fallen (or conversely, the relative price of cassettes has risen).

	Money Price		Relative Price	
	Last Year	This Year	Last Year	This Year
CDs	$18	$20	$18 / $9 = 2.0	$20 / $11 = 1.81
Cassettes	$ 9	$ 11	$9 / $18 = 0.5	$11 / $20 = 0.55

Thinking Critically About the Media　The Real Price of Stamps

The press is fond of pointing out the rise in the price of a particular good, such as a stamp for first-class mail. In the 1940s, a first-class stamp in Canada cost only 4 cents, but by the mid-1990s, it had climbed to 45 cents. That is the absolute price of postage, however. What about the relative price, the price relative to the average of all other prices? The relative price of postage is actually lower today than when it reached its peak in 1975. Many other relative prices have fallen over the years, ranging from gasoline prices to the prime minister's salary. Indeed, relatively speaking, the prime minister's current $155,000-a-year salary is peanuts compared to what Prime Minister William Lyon Mackenzie King earned in 1946. In relative terms (dollars in 1947), the current prime minister earns only about 78 percent of Mr. King's salary, even though in absolute terms, the current prime minister makes more. Remember, everything is relative.

INTERNATIONAL EXAMPLE
Cross-Border Shopping in Europe

The increase in cross-border shopping is a good example of how individuals respond to relative prices rather than absolute, or money, prices. Several times a week, bargain-conscious Basques from Bilbao, Spain, cross the French border (which is without customs or immigration control because it is part of the European Union) to shop for food. At current exchange rates, similar-quality food costs about 40 percent less on the French side of the border. Similarly, for cost-conscious consumers in Switzerland who live along the border with France, such trips are frequent. Professor Stephen Stearns, of Basel, Switzerland, claims that shopping in France saves a typical family more than 30 percent on its weekly food bill. At current exchange rates, pork and beef cost only half as much in France as they do in Switzerland, and cheese is 40 percent less expensive. Germans and Belgians who live on the border with Luxembourg and the Netherlands often travel to those countries to buy food and consumer products such as shampoo. All this border crossing bears out the fact that relative prices, not absolute (money) prices, determine people's shopping habits.

For critical analysis: How would we calculate the net benefit to cross-border shopping for the people who engage in it? (Hint: What are some of the costs of such shopping?)

Concepts in Brief

- The law of demand states that there is an inverse relationship between the quantity demanded of a good and its price, other things being equal.
- The law of demand applies when other things, such as income and the prices of all other goods and services, are held constant.

THE DEMAND SCHEDULE

Let's take a hypothetical demand situation to see how the inverse relationship between the price and the quantity demanded looks (holding other things equal). We will consider the quantity of computer diskettes demanded *per year* by one person. Without stating the *time dimension*, we could not make sense out of this demand relationship because the numbers would be different if we were talking about the quantity demanded per month, or the quantity demanded per decade.

In addition to implicitly or explicitly stating a time dimension for a demand relationship, we are also implicitly referring to *constant-quality* units of the good or service in question. Prices are always expressed in constant-quality units in order to avoid the problem of comparing commodities that are in fact not truly comparable.

In part (a) of Figure 3.1, we see that if the price were $1 per diskette, 50 of them would be bought each year by our representative individual, but if the price were $5 per diskette, only 10 would be bought each year. This reflects the law of demand. Part (a) is also called simply demand, or a *demand schedule*, because it gives a schedule of alternative quantities demanded per year at different possible prices.

The Demand Curve

▶ **Demand curve**

A graphical representation of the demand schedule; a negatively sloped line showing the inverse relationship between the price and the quantity demanded (other things being equal).

Tables expressing relationships between two variables can be represented in graphical terms. To do this, we need only construct a graph that has the price per constant-quality diskette on the vertical axis, and the quantity measured in constant-quality diskettes per year on the horizontal axis. All we have to do is take combinations *A* through *E* from part (a) of Figure 3.1 and plot those points in part (b). Now we connect the points with a smooth line, and *voilà*, we have a **demand curve**[1]. It is downward-sloping (from left to right) to indicate the inverse relationship between the price of diskettes and the quantity demanded per year. Our presentation of demand schedules and curves applies equally well to all commodities, including toothpicks, hamburgers, textbooks, credit, and labour services. Remember, the demand curve is simply a graphical representation of the law of demand.

---

[1] Even though we call them "curves," for the purposes of exposition we often draw straight lines. In many real-world situations, demand and supply curves will in fact be lines that do curve. To connect the points in part (b) with a line, we assume that for all prices in between the ones shown, the quantities demanded will be found along that line.

Figure 3.1
The Individual Demand Schedule and the Individual Demand Curve

In part (a), we show combinations A through E of the quantities of diskettes demanded, measured in constant-quality units at prices ranging from $5 down to $1 per disk. In part (b), we plot combinations A through E on a grid. The result is the individual demand curve for diskettes.

Part (a)

Combination	Price per Constant-Quality Diskette	Quantity of Constant-Quality Diskettes per Year
A	$5	10
B	4	20
C	3	30
D	2	40
E	1	50

Part (b)

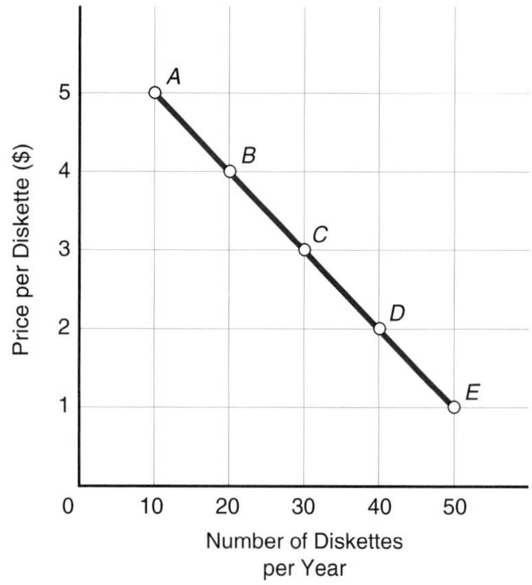

Individual Versus Market Demand Curves

The demand schedule shown in part (a) of Figure 3.1 and the resulting demand curve shown in part (b) are both given for one individual. As we shall see, determining price in the marketplace depends on, among other things, the **market demand** for a particular commodity. The way in which we measure a market demand schedule and derive a market demand curve for diskettes or any other commodity is by adding the individual demand at each price for all those in the market. Suppose that the market for diskettes consists of only two buyers: buyer 1, for whom we've already shown the demand schedule in Figure 3.1, and buyer 2, whose demand schedule is displayed in Figure 3.2, part (a), column 3. Column 1 of Figure 3.2, part (a) shows the price, and column 2 gives the quantity demanded by buyer 1 (data taken directly from Figure 3.1). Column 4 states the total quantity demanded at each price, obtained by adding columns 2 and 3. Graphically, in part (d) of Figure 3.2, we add the demand curves of buyer 1 [part (b)] and buyer 2 [part (c)] to derive the market demand curve.

There are, of course, literally millions of potential consumers for diskettes. We'll assume that the summation of all of the consumers in the market results in a demand schedule, given in part (a) of Figure 3.3, and a demand curve, given in part (b). The quantity demanded is now measured in millions of units per year. Remember, part (b) in Figure 3.3 shows the market demand curve for the millions of users of diskettes. The "market" demand curve that we derived in Figure 3.2 assumed that there were only two buyers in the entire market. This is why that demand curve is not a smooth line, whereas the true market demand curve in part (b) of Figure 3.3 is, and has no kinks.

Now consider some special aspects of the market demand curve for new cars.

▶ **Market demand**
The demand of all consumers in the marketplace for a particular good or service. The summing at each price of the quantity demanded by each individual.

Figure 3.2
The Horizontal Summation of Two Demand Schedules

Part (a) shows how to sum the demand schedule for one buyer with that of another buyer. Column 2 shows the quantity demanded by buyer 1, taken from part (a) of Figure 3.1. Column 4 is the sum of columns 2 and 3. We plot the demand curve for buyer 1 in part (b) and the demand curve for buyer 2 in part (c). When we add those two demand curves horizontally, we get the market demand curve for two buyers, shown in part (d).

Part (a)

(1) Price per Diskette	(2) Buyer 1 Quantity Demanded	(3) Buyer 2 Quantity Demanded	(4) = (2) + (3) Combined Quantity Demanded per Year
$5	10	10	20
4	20	20	40
3	30	40	70
2	40	50	90
1	50	60	110

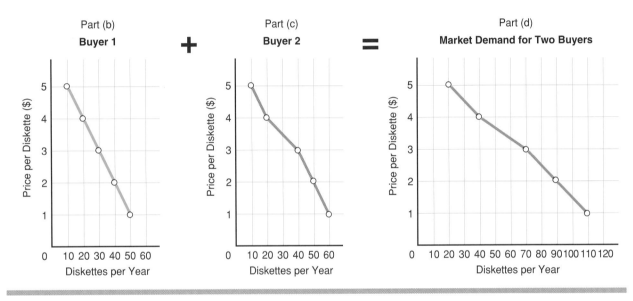

Figure 3.3
The Market Demand Schedule for Diskettes

In part (a), we add up the millions of existing demand schedules for diskettes. In part (b), we plot the quantities from part (a) on a grid; connecting them produces the market demand curve for diskettes

Part (a)

Price per Constant-Quality Diskette	Total Quantity Demanded of Constant-Quality Diskettes per Year (millions)
$5	2
4	4
3	6
2	8
1	10

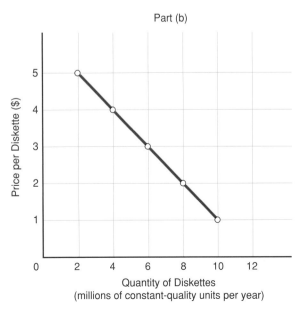

| **EXAMPLE** | New Car Sales, Automobile Leases, and the Law of Demand |

New car prices have risen steadily since the 1960s as increasingly sophisticated consumers demand additional special features in their vehicles. But comprehensive warranties, catalytic converters, air bags, and the like all push up the price of the basic automobile. Monthly car-loan repayments are becoming beyond the means of many Canadian car buyers. In 1996, new car dealers found that sales fell by 10 percent over those in 1995, and they expect further declines over time.

The dealers, however, understand the law of demand. They are offering to lease—rent—new vehicles for monthly payments that are often far below the loan repayments that would be required if the car was actually purchased. As a result, more than 20 percent of all new car deals in Canada in 1996 were leases. Another benefit to the dealers is that the vehicles returned at the end of the lease make a good supply of late-model used cars for those customers still looking to buy an automobile.

For critical analysis: What do you think will happen in the market for used cars over the course of the next five years?

Concepts in Brief

- We measure the demand schedule both in terms of a time dimension and in constant-quality units.
- The market demand curve is derived by summing the quantity demanded by individuals at each price. Graphically, we add the individual demand curves horizontally to derive the total, or market, demand curve.

SHIFTS IN DEMAND

Assume that the federal government gives every student registered in a Canadian college, university, or technical school a personal computer that uses diskettes. The demand curve shown in part (b) of Figure 3.3 is no longer an accurate representation of the total market demand for diskettes. There will now be an increase in the number of diskettes demanded *at each and every possible price*. What we have to do is shift the curve outward, or to the right, to represent the rise in demand. The demand curve in Figure 3.4 will shift from D_1 to D_2. Take any price, say, $3 per diskette. Originally, before the federal government giveaway of personal computers, the amount demanded at $3 was 60 million diskettes per year. After the government giveaway, however, the quantity demanded at $3 is 100 million diskettes per year. What we have seen is a shift in the demand for diskettes.

The shift can also go in the opposite direction. What if colleges uniformly outlawed the use of personal computers by students? Such a regulation would cause a shift inward—to the left—of the demand curve for diskettes. In Figure 3.4, the

Figure 3.4
A Shift in the Demand Curve

If some factor other than price changes, the only way we can show its effect is by moving the entire demand curve, say, from D_1 to D_2. We have assumed in our example that the move was precipitated by the government's giving a free personal computer to every registered college student in Canada. That meant that at all prices, a larger number of diskettes would be demanded than before. Curve D_3 represents reduced demand compared to curve D_1, caused by a law prohibiting computers on campus.

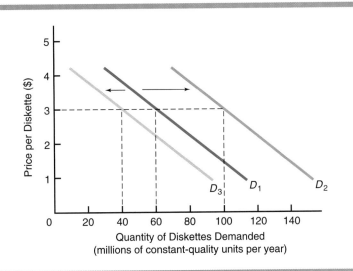

demand curve would shift to D_3; the amount demanded would now be less at each and every possible price.

The Other Determinants of Demand

The demand curve in part (b) of Figure 3.3 is drawn with other things held constant, specifically all of the other factors that determine how much will be bought. There are many such determinants. The major ones are income; tastes and preferences; the prices of related goods; expectations regarding future prices, future incomes, and future product availability; and population (market size). Let's examine each determinant more closely.

Income.   For most goods, an increase in income will lead to an increase in demand. The phrase *increase in demand* always refers to a comparison between two different demand curves. Thus for most goods, an increase in income will lead to a rightward shift in the position of the demand curve from, say, D_1 to D_2 in Figure 3.4. You can avoid confusion about shifts in curves by always relating a rise in demand to a rightward shift in the demand curve, and a fall in demand to a leftward shift in the demand curve. Goods for which the demand rises when income rises are called **normal goods**. Most goods, such as shoes, computers, and CDs, are "normal goods." For some goods, however, demand *falls* as income rises. These are called **inferior goods**. Beans might be an example. As households get richer, they tend to spend less and less on beans and more and more on meat. (The terms *normal* and *inferior* are merely part of the economist's terminology; no value judgments are implied by or associated with them.)

Remember, a shift to the left in the demand curve represents a fall in demand, and a shift to the right represents a rise, or increase, in demand.

▶ **Normal goods**

Goods for which demand rises as income rises. Most goods are considered normal.

▶ **Inferior goods**

Goods for which demand falls as income rises.

Tastes and Preferences.   A change in consumer tastes in favour of a good can shift its demand curve outward to the right. When Frisbees® became the rage, the demand curve for them shifted outward to the right; when the rage died out, the demand curve shifted inward to the left. Fashions depend to a large extent on people's tastes and preferences. Economists have little to say about the determination of tastes; they have no "good" theories of taste determination or why people buy one brand of a product rather than others. Advertisers, however, do have various theories that they use in trying to make consumers prefer their products to those of competitors.

EXAMPLE   ## The Boom in Specialty Coffees

Specialty coffee bars are finding out what happens to their demand when there is a shift in consumer tastes for their product. Where less than 5 percent of coffee drinkers drank specialty coffees in 1995, over 10 percent do now, and industry experts predict that by the year 2000, a full 20 percent of coffee served will be specialty coffee.

Does this increase represent an increase in demand for all coffee? No, says the Coffee Association of Canada. About 51 percent of Canadians, as always, drink on average just under three cups of coffee per day. The total amount of coffee served has not changed appreciably since 1995; it remains at about 51 billion cups per year. What has changed is the drinkers' tastes. Instead of ordering plain coffee, more and more coffee drinkers are ordering espressos, lattes, and cappuccinos.

There is no consensus in the coffee industry about why this change is taking place. The Coffee Association of Canada thinks that coffee is replacing alcohol as a social drink because there are fewer health risks associated with drinking coffee. Industry insiders suggest that drinking specialty coffee has become "cool" and imbues the drinkers with a kind of chic and sophistication. What is clear is that no one really knows why Canadian coffee drinkers are changing their minds.

For critical analysis: From the above, what do you think will be happening to the demand for alcohol?

Prices of Related Goods: Substitutes and Complements.   Demand schedules are always drawn with the prices of all other commodities held constant. In other words, when deriving a given demand curve, we assume that only the price of the good under study changes. For example, when we draw the demand curve for butter, we assume that the price of margarine is held constant. When we draw the demand curve for stereo speakers, we assume that the price of stereo amplifiers is held constant. When we refer to *related goods*, we are talking about goods for which demand is interdependent. If a change in the price of one good shifts the demand for another good, those two goods are related. There are two types of related goods: *substitutes* and *complements*. We can define and distinguish between substitutes and complements in terms of how the change in price of one commodity affects the demand for its related commodity.

▶ **Substitutes**
Two goods are substitutes when either one can be used to satisfy a similar want—for example, coffee and tea. The more you buy of one, the less you buy of the other. For substitutes, the change in the price of one causes demand for the other to shift in the same direction as the price change.

Butter and margarine are **substitutes**. Let's assume that each originally cost $4 per kilogram. If the price of butter remains the same and the price of margarine falls from $4 to $2 per kilogram, people will buy more margarine and less butter. The demand curve for butter will shift inward to the left. If, conversely, the price of margarine rises from $4 to $6 per kilogram, people will buy more butter and less margarine. The demand curve for butter will shift outward to the right. An increase in the price of margarine will lead to an increase in the demand for butter, and an increase in the price of butter will lead to an increase in the demand for margarine. For substitutes, a price change in the substitute will cause a change in demand *in the same direction*.

For **complements**, the situation is reversed. Consider stereo speakers and stereo amplifiers. We draw the demand curve for speakers with the price of amplifiers held constant. If the price per constant-quality unit of stereo amplifiers decreases from, say, $500 to $200, that will encourage more people to purchase component stereo systems. They will now buy more speakers than before at any given price. The demand curve for speakers will shift outward to the right. If, by contrast, the price of amplifiers increases from $200 to $500, fewer people will purchase component stereo systems. The demand curve for speakers will shift inward to the left. To summarize, a decrease in the price of amplifiers leads to an increase in the demand for speakers. An increase in the price of amplifiers leads to a decrease in the demand for speakers. Thus for complements, a price change in a product will cause a change in demand *in the opposite direction*.

Are new learning technologies complements or substitutes for college instructors? Read on.

▶**Complements**

Two goods are complements if both are used together for consumption or enjoyment—for example, coffee and cream. The more you buy of one, the more you buy of the other. For complements, a change in the price of one causes an opposite shift in the demand for the other.

EXAMPLE   ## The Future of College Teaching

In this class and in others, you've probably been exposed to some of the new (and old) instructional technologies such as films and videos, interactive computer software, and interactive CD-ROM learning systems. Your professors have used these as a complement to their teaching, but in the future those technologies may in fact become a substitute for what your professors do in the classroom.

Televised and audio-taped lectures mean that more and more Canadian institutions can offer distance education courses, thus allowing a given number of professors to teach a greater number of students. Athabasca University in Alberta and Simon Fraser University in British Columbia offer enough distance education courses that a student can earn a university degree in business administration, history, or education without ever attending a class. Mount Saint Vincent University in Nova Scotia and CJRT Open College in Ontario offer diplomas entirely through distance education. Now consider interactive CD-ROM learning systems. In theory, virtually every college course could be put on CD-ROM, thereby entirely eliminating the need for instructors. Going one step further, institutions of higher learning are now using the Internet to provide instruction. The University of Western Ontario and Queen's University currently bring their programs to western Canada, offering an executive MBA through a combination of interactive video classroom instruction, high-speed Internet connections, e-mail, and shared application computing.

For critical analysis: What do you predict will happen to the demand curve for college professors in the next decade?

Expectations.   Consumers' expectations regarding future prices, future incomes, and future availability may prompt them to buy more or less of a particular good without a change in its current money price. For example, consumers getting wind of a scheduled 100 percent price increase in diskettes next month may buy more of them today, at today's prices. Today's demand curve for diskettes will shift from D_1 to D_2 in Figure 3.4 on page 58. The opposite would occur if a decrease in the price of diskettes were scheduled for next month.

Expectations of a rise in income may cause consumers to want to purchase more of everything today, at today's prices. Again, such a change in expectations of higher future income will cause a shift in the demand curve from D_1 to D_2 in Figure 3.4. Finally, expectations that goods will not be available at any price will induce consumers to stock up now, increasing current demand.

Population.   An increase in the population in an economy (holding per capita income constant) often shifts the market demand outward for most products. This is because an increase in population means an increase in the number of buyers in the market. Conversely, a reduction in the population will shift most market demand curves inward because of the reduction in the number of buyers in the market.

Changes in Demand Versus Changes in Quantity Demanded

We have made repeated references to demand and to quantity demanded. It is important to realize that there is a difference between a *change in demand* and a *change in quantity demanded*.

Demand refers to a schedule of planned rates of purchase, and depends on a great many nonprice determinants. Whenever there is a change in a nonprice determinant, there will be a change in demand—a shift in the entire demand curve to the right or to the left.

A quantity demanded is a specific quantity at a specific price, represented by a single point on a demand curve. When price changes, quantity demanded changes according to the law of demand, and there will be a movement from one point to another along the same demand curve. Look at Figure 3.5 on page 62. At a price of $3 per diskette, 60 million diskettes per year are demanded. If the price falls to $1, quantity demanded increases to 100 million per year. This movement occurs because the current market price for the product changes. In Figure 3.5, you can see the arrow pointing down the given demand curve D.

When you think of demand, think of the entire curve. Quantity demanded, in contrast, is represented by a single point on the demand curve.

> A change or shift in demand causes the *entire* curve to move. The *only* thing that can cause the entire curve to move is a change in a determinant *other than its own price*.

Try Preview Question 2:

How can we distinguish between a change in demand and a change in quantity demanded?

In economic analysis, we cannot emphasize too much the following distinction that must constantly be made:

A change in a good's own price leads to a change in quantity demanded, for any given demand curve, other things held constant. This is a movement *along* the curve.

A change in any other determinant of demand leads to a change in demand. This causes a shift *of* the curve.

Figure 3.5
Movement Along a Given Demand Curve

A change in price changes the quantity of a good demanded. This can be represented as movement along a given demand schedule. If, in our example, the price of diskettes falls from $3 to $1 apiece, the quantity demanded will increase from 60 million to 100 million units per year.

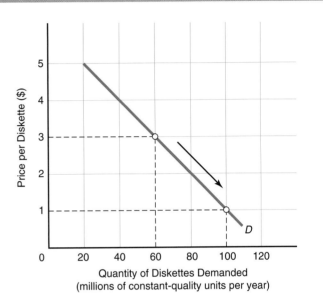

Concepts in Brief

- Demand curves are drawn with determinants other than the price of the good held constant. These other determinants are (1) income; (2) tastes and preferences; (3) prices of related goods; (4) expectations about future prices, future incomes, and future availability of goods; and (5) population (number of buyers in the market). If any one of these determinants changes, the demand schedule will shift to the right or to the left.
- A change in demand happens only when there is a change in the other determinants of demand. This change in demand shifts the demand curve to the left or to the right.
- A change in the quantity demanded occurs when there is a change in the price of the good (other things held constant). Such a change in quantity demanded involves a movement along a given demand curve.

THE LAW OF SUPPLY

▶ **Supply**

A schedule showing the relationship between price and quantity supplied for a specified period of time, other things being equal.

The other side of the basic model in economics involves the quantities of goods and services that firms are prepared to *supply* to the market. The **supply** of any good or service is the amount that firms are prepared to sell under certain conditions during a specified time period. The relationship between price and quantity supplied, called the **law of supply**, can be summarized as follows:

> At higher prices, a larger quantity will generally be supplied than at lower prices, all other things held constant. At lower prices, a smaller quantity will generally be supplied than at higher prices, all other things held constant.

▶ **Law of supply**

The observation that the higher the price of a good, the more of that good sellers will make available over a specified time period, other things being equal.

There is generally a direct relationship between quantity supplied and price. For supply, as the price rises, the quantity supplied rises; as the price falls, the quantity supplied also falls. Producers are normally willing to produce and sell more of their product at a higher price than at a lower price, other things being constant. At $5 per diskette, 3M, Sony, Maxell, Fuji, and other manufacturers would almost certainly be willing to supply a larger quantity than at $1 per unit, assuming, of course, that no other prices in the economy had changed.

As with the law of demand, millions of instances in the real world have given us confidence in the law of supply. On a theoretical level, the law of supply is based on a model in which producers and sellers seek to make the most gain possible from their activities. For example, as a diskette manufacturer attempts to produce more and more diskettes over the same time period, it will eventually have to hire more workers and overutilize its machines. Only if offered a higher price per diskette will the manufacturer be willing to incur these extra costs. That is why the law of supply implies a direct relationship between price and quantity supplied.

THE SUPPLY SCHEDULE

Just as we were able to construct a demand schedule, we can construct a *supply schedule*, which is a table relating prices to the quantity supplied at each price. A supply schedule can also be referred to simply as *supply*. It is a set of planned production rates that depends on the price of the product. We show the individual supply schedule for a hypothetical producer in part (a) of Figure 3.6. At $1 per diskette, for example, this producer will supply 200,000 diskettes per year; at $5, it will supply 550,000 diskettes per year.

The Supply Curve

▶ **Supply curve**

The graphical representation of the supply schedule; a line (curve) showing the supply schedule, which generally slopes upward (has a positive slope), other things being equal.

We can convert the supply schedule in part (a) of Figure 3.6 into a **supply curve**, just as we created a demand curve in Figure 3.1. All we do is take the price-quantity combinations from part (a) of Figure 3.6 and plot them in part (b). We have labelled these combinations *F* through *J*. Connecting these points, we obtain an upward-sloping curve that shows the typically direct relationship between price and quantity supplied. Again, we have to remember that we are talking about quantity supplied *per year*, measured in constant-quality units.

Figure 3.6

The Individual Producer's Supply Schedule and Supply Curve for Diskettes

Part (a) shows that at higher prices, a hypothetical supplier will be willing to provide a greater quantity of diskettes. We plot the various price-quantity combinations in part (a) on the grid in part (b). When we connect these points, we find the individual supply curve for diskettes. It is positively sloped.

Part (a)

Combination	Price per Constant-Quality Diskette	Quantity of Diskettes Supplied (thousands of constant-quality units per year)
F	$5	550
G	4	400
H	3	350
I	2	250
J	1	200

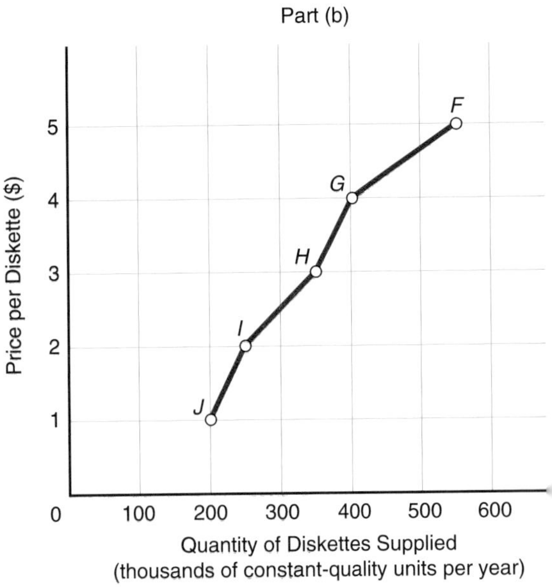

Part (b)

The Market Supply Curve

Just as we had to add the individual demand curves to get the market demand curve, we need to add the individual producers' supply curves to get the market supply curve. Look at Figure 3.7, in which we horizontally sum two typical diskette manufacturers' supply curves. Supplier 1's data are taken from Figure 3.6; supplier 2 is added. The numbers are presented in part (a). The graphical representation of supplier 1 is in part (b), of supplier 2 in part (c), and of the summation in part (d). The result, then, is the supply curve for diskettes for suppliers 1 and 2. There are many more suppliers of diskettes, however. The total market supply schedule and total market supply curve for diskettes are represented in Figure 3.8, with the curve in part (b) obtained by adding all of the supply curves such as those shown in parts (b) and (c) of Figure 3.7. Notice the difference between the market supply curve with only two suppliers in Figure 3.7 and the one with a large number of suppliers—the entire true market—in part (b) of Figure 3.8. There are no kinks in the true total market supply curve because there are so many suppliers.

Observe what happens at the market level when price changes. If the price is $3, the quantity supplied is 60 million diskettes. If the price goes up to $4, the quantity supplied increases to 80 million per year. If the price falls to $2, the quantity supplied decreases to 40 million diskettes per year. Changes in quantity supplied are represented by movements along the supply curve in part (b) of Figure 3.8.

Try Preview Question 3:

Why is there normally a direct relationship between price and quantity supplied (other things being equal)?

Figure 3.7
Horizontal Summation of Supply Curves

In part (a), we show the data for two individual suppliers of diskettes. Adding how much each is willing to supply at different prices, we arrive at the combined quantities supplied in column 4. When we plot the values in columns 2 and 3 on grids in parts (b) and (c) and add them horizontally, we obtain the combined supply curve for the two suppliers in question, shown in part (d).

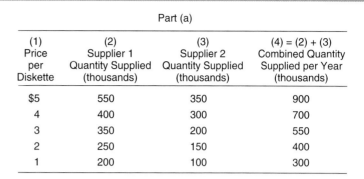

Part (a)

(1) Price per Diskette	(2) Supplier 1 Quantity Supplied (thousands)	(3) Supplier 2 Quantity Supplied (thousands)	(4) = (2) + (3) Combined Quantity Supplied per Year (thousands)
$5	550	350	900
4	400	300	700
3	350	200	550
2	250	150	400
1	200	100	300

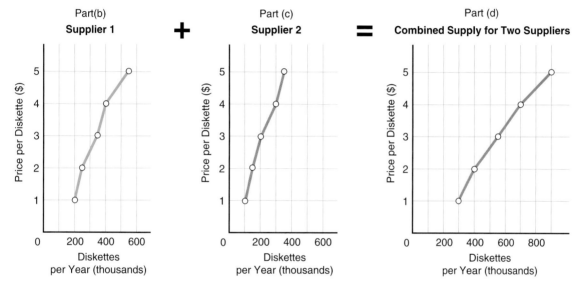

Part(b)
Supplier 1

+

Part (c)
Supplier 2

=

Part (d)
Combined Supply for Two Suppliers

Figure 3.8
The Market Supply Schedule and the Market Supply Curve for Diskettes

In part (a), we show the summation of all the individual producers' supply schedules; in part (b), we graph the resulting supply curve. It represents the market supply curve for diskettes and is upward-sloping.

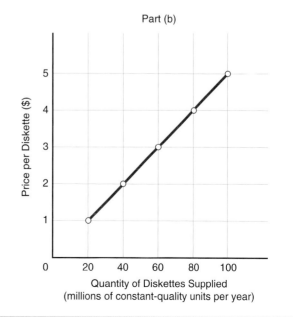

Part (b)

Part (a)

Price per Constant-Quality Diskette	Quantity of Diskettes Supplied (millions of constant-quality units per year)
$5	100
4	80
3	60
2	40
1	20

Concepts in Brief

- There is normally a direct, or positive, relationship between price and the quantity of a good supplied, other things held constant.
- The supply curve normally shows a direct relationship between price and quantity supplied. The market supply curve is obtained by horizontally adding individual supply curves in the market.

SHIFTS IN SUPPLY

When we looked at demand, we found out that any change in anything relevant other than the price of the good or service caused the demand curve to shift inward or outward. The same is true for the supply curve. If something relevant changes apart from the price of the product or service being supplied, we will see the entire supply curve shift.

Consider an example. A new method of putting magnetic material on diskettes has been invented. It reduces the cost of producing a diskette by 50 percent. In this situation, diskette producers will supply more product at all prices because their cost of so doing has fallen dramatically. Competition among diskette manufacturers to produce more at every price will shift the supply schedule of diskettes outward to the right from S_1 to S_2 in Figure 3.9. At a price of $3, the quantity supplied was originally 60 million diskettes per year, but now the quantity supplied (after the reduction in the costs of production) at $3 a diskette will be 90 million diskettes a year. (This is similar to what has happened to the supply curve of personal computers and fax machines in recent years as computer memory chip prices have fallen.)

Now consider the opposite case. If the cost of the magnetic material needed for making diskettes doubles, the supply curve in Figure 3.9 will shift from S_1 to S_3. At each price, the number of diskettes supplied will fall due to the increase in the price of raw materials.

Figure 3.9
A Shift in the Supply Schedule

If the cost of producing diskettes were to fall dramatically, the supply schedule would shift rightward from S_1 to S_2 such that at all prices, a larger quantity would be forthcoming from suppliers. Conversely, if the cost of production rose, the supply curve would shift leftward to S_3.

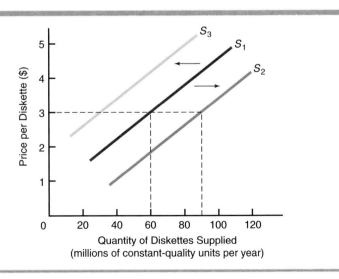

The Other Determinants of Supply

When supply curves are drawn, only the price of the good in question changes, and it is assumed that other things remain constant. The other things assumed constant are the costs of resources (inputs) used to produce the product, technology and productivity, taxes and subsidies, producers' price expectations, and the number of firms in the industry. These are the major nonprice determinants of supply. If any of them changes, there will be a shift in the supply curve.

Cost of Inputs Used to Produce the Product.

If one or more input price falls, the supply curve will shift outward to the right; that is, more will be supplied at each price. The opposite will be true if one or more inputs becomes more expensive. For example, when we draw the supply curve of new cars, we are holding the cost of steel (and other inputs) constant. When we draw the supply curve of blue jeans, we are holding the cost of cotton fixed.

Technology and Productivity.

Supply curves are drawn by assuming a given technology, or "state of the art." When the available production techniques change, the supply curve will shift. For example, when a better, cheaper, production technique for diskettes becomes available, the supply curve will shift to the right. A larger quantity will be forthcoming at every price because the cost of production is lower.

Taxes and Subsidies.

Certain taxes, such as a per-unit tax, are effectively an addition to production costs and therefore reduce the supply. If the supply curve were S_1 in Figure 3.9, a per-unit tax increase would shift it to S_3. A **subsidy** would do the opposite; it would shift the curve to S_2. Every producer would get a "gift" from the government of a few cents for each unit produced.

▶ **Subsidy**
A negative tax; a payment to a producer from the government, usually in the form of a cash grant.

Price Expectations.

A change in the expectation of a future relative price of a product can affect a producer's current willingness to supply, just as price expectations affect a consumer's current willingness to purchase. For example, diskette suppliers may withhold part of their current supply from the market if they anticipate higher prices in the future. The current amount supplied at all prices will decrease.

Number of Firms in the Industry.

In the short run, when firms can only change the number of employees they use, we hold the number of firms in the industry constant. In the long run, the number of firms (or the size of some existing firms) may change. If the number of firms increases, the supply curve will shift outward to the right. If the number of firms decreases, it will shift inward to the left.

Changes in Supply Versus Changes in Quantity Supplied

We cannot overstress the importance of distinguishing between a movement along the supply curve—which occurs only when the price changes for a given supply curve—and a shift in the supply curve—which occurs only with changes in other nonprice factors. A change in price always brings about a change in quantity sup-

INTERNATIONAL EXAMPLE
Changing Technology and the Supply of Salmon

One example of how changes in technology can shift the supply curve out to the right involves salmon. In 1980, the total worldwide catch of salmon (wild and farmed) was just over 10,000 metric tonnes. Since 1980, new technology has been developed in what is called aquaculture, or the farm-raising of fish and related products. Aquaculture currently generates over US$30 billion in worldwide revenues and is one of the world's fastest-growing industries. Farmed salmon from Canada, Chile, Scotland, Norway, and Iceland now exceeds 240,000 metric tonnes a year. Thus it is not surprising that despite a depletion of many wild salmon fishing grounds and a worldwide increase in consumer demand for salmon, the retail price of salmon today (corrected for inflation) is about 50 percent of what it was in 1980.

For critical analysis: What might slow down the growth in salmon farming throughout the world?

plied along a given supply curve. We move to a different coordinate on the existing supply curve. This is specifically called a *change in quantity supplied*. When price changes, quantity supplied changes, and there will be a movement from one point to another along the same supply curve.

When you think of *supply*, think of the entire curve. Quantity supplied is represented by a single point on the curve.

> A change in supply causes the entire curve to shift. The *only* thing that can cause the entire curve to shift is a change in a determinant *other than price*.

Consequently,

> A change in the price leads to a change in the quantity supplied, other things being constant. This is a movement *along* the curve.

> A change in any other determinant of supply leads to a change in supply. This causes a shift *of* the curve.

Concepts in Brief

- If the price changes, we *move along* a curve—there is a change in quantity demanded or supplied. If some other determinant changes, we *shift* a curve—there is a change in demand or supply.
- The supply curve is drawn with other things held constant. If other determinants of supply change, the supply curve will shift. The other major determinants are (1) input costs, (2) technology and productivity, (3) taxes and subsidies, (4) expectations of future relative prices, and (5) the number of firms in the industry.

PUTTING DEMAND AND SUPPLY TOGETHER

In the sections on supply and demand, we tried to confine each discussion to supply or demand only. But you have probably already realized that we can't view the world just from the supply side or just from the demand side. There is an interaction between the two. In this section, we will discuss how they interact and how that interaction determines the prices that prevail in our economy. Understanding how demand and supply interact is essential to understanding how prices are determined in our economy and other economies in which the forces of supply and demand are allowed to work.

Let's first combine the demand and supply schedules and then combine the curves.

Demand and Supply Schedules Combined

Let's place part (a) from Figure 3.3 (the market demand schedule) and part (a) from Figure 3.8 (the market supply schedule) together in part (a) of Figure 3.10. Column 1 shows the price; column 2, the quantity supplied per year at any given price; and column 3, the quantity demanded. Column 4 is merely the difference between columns 2 and 3, or the difference between the quantity supplied and the quantity demanded. In column 5, we label those differences as either excess quantity supplied (a surplus), or excess quantity demanded (a shortage). For example, at a price of $2, only 40 million diskettes would be supplied, but the quantity demanded would be 80 million. The difference is 40 million, which we label as excess quantity demanded (a shortage). At the other end of the scale, a price of $5 per diskette would elicit 100 million in quantity supplied, but quantity demanded would drop to 20 million. This leaves a difference of 80 million units, which we call excess quantity supplied (a surplus).

What do you notice about the price of $3? At that price, the quantity supplied and the quantity demanded per year are both 60 million. The difference, then, is zero. There is neither excess quantity demanded (shortage) nor excess quantity supplied (surplus). Hence the price of $3 is very special. It is called the **market clearing price**— it clears the market of all excess supply or excess demand. There are no willing consumers who want to pay $3 per diskette but are turned away by sellers, and there are no willing suppliers who want to sell diskettes at $3 who cannot sell all they want at that price. Another term for the market clearing price is the **equilibrium price**, the price at which there is no tendency for change. At that price, consumers are able to buy all they want and suppliers are able to sell the quantity that they desire.

Equilibrium

We can define **equilibrium** in general as a point from which there tends to be no movement unless demand or supply changes. Any movement away from this point will set in motion certain forces that will cause movement back to it. Therefore, equilibrium is a stable point. Any point that is not at equilibrium is unstable and cannot be maintained.

▶ **Market clearing, or equilibrium, price**
The price that clears the market, at which quantity demanded equals quantity supplied; the price where the demand curve intersects the supply curve.

▶ **Equilibrium**
The situation when quantity supplied equals quantity demanded at a particular price.

Figure 3.10
Putting Demand and Supply Together

In part (a), we see that at the price of $3, the quantity supplied and the quantity demanded are equal, resulting in neither an excess in the quantity demanded nor an excess in the quantity supplied. We call this price the equilibrium, or market clearing, price. In part (b), the intersection of the supply and demand curves is at E, at a price of $3 per constant-quality diskette and a quantity of 60 million per year. At point E, there is neither an excess in the quantity demanded nor an excess in the quantity supplied. At a price of $2, the quantity supplied will be only 40 million diskettes per year, but the quantity demand-

ed will be 80 million. The difference is excess quantity demanded at a price of $2. The price will rise, so we will move from point A up the supply curve and point B up the demand curve to point E. At the other extreme, $5 elicits a quantity supplied of 100 million but a quantity demanded of only 20 million. The difference is excess quantity supplied at a price of $5. The price will fall, so we will move down the demand curve and the supply curve to the equilibrium price, $3 per diskette.

Part (a)

(1)	(2)	(3)	(4)	(5)
			Difference	
Price per Constant-Quality Diskette	Quantity Supplied (diskettes per year)	Quantity Demanded (diskettes per year)	(2) – (3) (diskettes per year)	Condition
$5	100 million	20 million	80 million	Excess quantity supplied (surplus)
4	80 million	40 million	40 million	Excess quantity supplied (surplus)
3	60 million	60 million	0	Market clearing price—equilibrium (no surplus, no shortage)
2	40 million	80 million	– 40 million	Excess quantity demanded (shortage)
1	20 million	100 million	– 80 million	Excess quantity demanded (shortage)

Part (b)

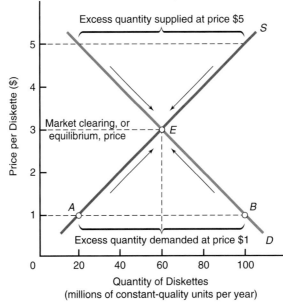

Price per Diskette ($)

Quantity of Diskettes
(millions of constant-quality units per year)

Try Preview Question 4:
Why will the market clearing price occur at the intersection of the supply and demand curves rather than at a higher or lower price?

The equilibrium point occurs where the supply and demand curves intersect. The equilibrium price is given on the vertical axis directly to the left of where the supply and demand curves cross. The equilibrium quantity demanded and supplied is given on the horizontal axis directly underneath the intersection of the demand and supply curves. Equilibrium can change whenever there is a *shock*.

A shock to the supply-and-demand system can be represented by a shift in the supply curve, a shift in the demand curve, or a shift in both. Any shock to the system will result in a new set of supply-and-demand relationships and a new equilibrium; forces will come into play to move the system from the old price-quantity equilibrium (now a disequilibrium situation) to the new equilibrium, where the new demand and supply curves intersect.

Part (b) from Figure 3.3 and part (b) from Figure 3.8 are combined as part (b) in Figure 3.10 on page 70. The only difference now is that the horizontal axis measures both the quantity supplied and the quantity demanded per year. Everything else is the same. The demand curve is labelled *D*, the supply curve *S*. We have labelled the intersection of the two curves as point *E*, for equilibrium. That corresponds to a market clearing price of $3, at which both the quantity supplied and the quantity demanded are 60 million units per year. There is neither a surplus nor a shortage. Point *E*, the equilibrium point, always occurs at the intersection of the supply and demand curves. This is the price towards which the market price will automatically tend to gravitate.

EXAMPLE   **Dinosaurs and the Price of Amber**

When there is a shift in either supply or demand, there is a movement towards equilibrium that usually involves a change in the equilibrium quantity and the equilibrium price. A good example is found in the market for amber, a semi-precious stone in which fossilized insects or plants from millions of years ago are sometimes discovered. In Figure 3.11 (page 72), you see the original supply and demand curves for amber, labelled S and D_1. The equilibrium price is P_1, and the equilibrium quantity is Q_1. Then along came a book, and later a movie, called *Jurassic Park*, written by Michael Crichton. In the story mosquitoes that had feasted on dinosaurs a million years ago were trapped in amber. Scientists were able to clone various dinosaurs by removing the DNA from the dinosaur blood inside the fossilized mosquitoes. (The technique remains in the realm of science fiction.) The success of the book and the movie in the early 1990s made amber suddenly popular; in economic terms, the demand curve for amber shifted outward to D_2. Very quickly, the price rose to P_2 and the equilibrium quantity increased to Q_2.

For critical analysis: It has been a few years since the dinosaur craze peaked in Canada. How would you represent what is now occurring in the market in amber, using supply and demand curves?

Figure 3.11
The Changing Price of Amber

With stable supply, a shift in the demand curve for amber from D_1 to D_2 will cause the equilibrium price to rise from P_1 to P_2 and the equilibrium quantity to increase from Q_1 to Q_2.

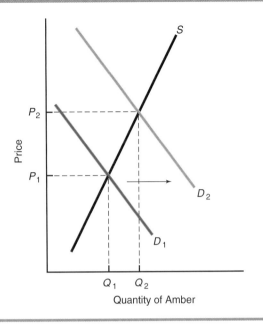

Shortages

The demand and supply curves in Figure 3.10 represent a situation of equilibrium. But a non-market-clearing, or disequilibrium, price will bring into play forces that cause the price to change, and move towards the market clearing price. Then, equilibrium is again sustained. Look once more at part (b) in Figure 3.10 on page 70. Suppose that instead of being at the market clearing price of $3 per diskette, for some reason the market price is $1 per diskette. At this price, the quantity demanded (100 million), exceeds the quantity supplied (20 million). We have a situation of excess quantity demanded at the price of $1. This is usually called a **shortage**. Consumers of diskettes would find that they could not buy all that they wished at $1 apiece. But forces will cause the price to rise: Competing consumers will bid up the price, and suppliers will raise the price and increase output, whether explicitly or implicitly. (Remember, some buyers would pay $5 or more rather than do without diskettes. They do not want to be left out.) We would move from points *A* and *B* towards point *E*. The process would stop when the price again reached $3 per diskette.

▶ **Shortage**

A situation in which quantity demanded is greater than quantity supplied at a price below the market clearing price.

At this point, it is important to recall a distinction made in Chapter 2:

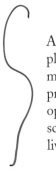

Shortages and scarcity are not the same thing.

A shortage is a situation in which the quantity demanded exceeds the quantity supplied at a price *below* the market clearing price. Our definition of scarcity was much more general and all-encompassing: a situation in which the resources available for producing output are insufficient to satisfy all wants. Any choice necessarily costs an opportunity, and the opportunity is lost. Hence we will always live in a world of scarcity because we must constantly make choices, but we do not necessarily have to live in a world of shortages.

Surpluses

Now let's repeat the experiment with the market price at $5 per diskette rather than at the market clearing price of $3. Clearly, the quantity supplied will exceed the quantity demanded at that price. The result will be an excess quantity supplied at $5 per unit. This excess quantity supplied is often called a **surplus**. Given the curves in part (b) in Figure 3.10, however, there will be forces pushing the price back down towards $3 per diskette: Competing suppliers will attempt to reduce their inventories by cutting prices and reducing output, and consumers will offer to purchase more at lower prices. Suppliers will want to reduce inventories, which will be above their optimal level; that is, there will be an excess over what each seller believes to be the most profitable stock of diskettes. After all, inventories are costly to hold. But consumers may find out about such excess inventories and see the possibility of obtaining increased quantities of diskettes at a decreased price. It benefits consumers to attempt to obtain a good at a lower price, and they will therefore try to do so. If the two forces of supply and demand are unrestricted, they will bring the price back to $3 per diskette.

Shortages and surpluses are resolved in unfettered markets—markets in which price changes are free to occur. The forces that resolve them are those of competition: In the case of shortages, consumers competing for a limited quantity supplied drive up the price; in the case of surpluses, sellers compete for the limited quantity demanded, thus driving prices down to equilibrium. The equilibrium price is the only stable price, and all (unrestricted) market prices tend to gravitate towards it.

What happens when the price is set below the equilibrium price? Here come the scalpers.

▶ **Surplus**
A situation in which quantity supplied is greater than quantity demanded at a price above the market clearing price.

EXAMPLE   Should Shortages in the Ticket Market Be Solved by Scalpers?

If you have ever tried to get tickets to a playoff game in sports, a popular play, or a superstar's rock concert, you know about "shortages." The standard ticket situation for a Stanley Cup hockey game is shown in Figure 3.12 (page 74). At the face-value price of Stanley Cup tickets (P_1), the quantity demanded (Q_2) greatly exceeds the quantity supplied (Q_1). Because shortages last only so long as prices and quantities do not change, markets tend to exhibit a movement out of this disequilibrium towards equilibrium. Obviously, the quantity of Stanley Cup tickets cannot change, but the price can go as high as P_2.

Enter the scalper. This colourful term is used because when you purchase a ticket that is being resold at a price that is higher than face value, the seller is skimming an extra profit off the top. Every time an event sells out, ticket prices by definition have been lower than market clearing prices. Sellouts indicate that the event is very popular, and that there may be people without tickets willing to buy high-priced tickets because they place a greater value on the entertainment event than the actual face value of the ticket. Without scalpers,

Figure 3.12
Shortage of Stanley Cup Tickets

The quantity of tickets for any one Stanley Cup is fixed at Q_1. At the price per ticket of P_1, the quantity demanded is Q_2, which is greater than Q_1. Consequently, there is an excess quantity demanded at the below–market clearing price. Prices can go as high as P_2 in the scalpers' market.

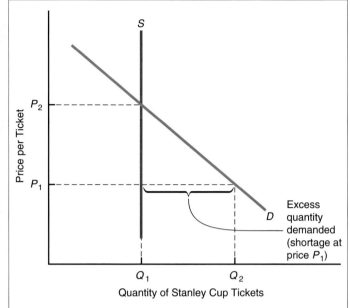

those individuals would not be able to attend the event. In the case of the 1994 Stanley Cup, various forms of scalping occurred nationwide. Tickets have been sold for more than $225 a piece, almost four times their face value. In front of every Stanley Cup game arena, you can find ticket scalpers hawking their wares.

In most provinces, scalping is illegal. In Ontario, convicted scalpers are fined around $500 for each infraction. For an economist, such legislation seems strange. As one Toronto ticket broker said, "I look at scalping like working as a stockbroker, buying low and selling high. If people are willing to pay me the money, what kind of problem is that?"

For critical analysis: What happens to ticket scalpers who are still holding tickets after an event has started?

Concepts in Brief

- The market clearing price occurs at the intersection of the market demand curve and the market supply curve. It is also called the equilibrium price, the price from which there is no tendency to change unless there is a change in demand or supply.
- Whenever the price is greater than the equilibrium price, there is an excess quantity supplied (a surplus).
- Whenever the price is less than the equilibrium price, there is an excess quantity demanded (a shortage).

Issues and Applications

How the Prices of Hockey Cards Have Responded to Changes in Supply and Demand

Concepts Applied: Demand and supply, shifts in demand and supply, relative prices

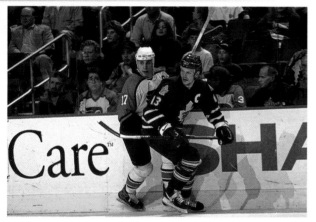

The price of hockey cards depends on their demand and supply. If supply is restricted by acquisitive collectors, prices will rise.

A few years ago, one of the hottest trends in Canada was collecting sporting cards. Baseball cards and hockey cards were no longer sold only as part of chewing gum packs, but were also sold in packages by themselves. The effect of this on the price of sporting cards depends on which card you are talking about: a 1951-52 Maurice Richard card will sell for as much as $2,100 and Gordie Howe's rookie card from the same year now sells for at least $2,800.

However, not all hockey cards have become more valuable over time. For example, the price of a 1979-80 Wayne Gretzky O-Pee-Chee card rose more than 40 percent from $840 to $1,190 between 1990 and 1996, but the price of Gretzky's 1989-90 card fell from $3.50 to $2.10, a change of 40 percent in the opposite direction over the same period. How can the relative prices of these cards change in such different ways?

Increasing Demand for Hockey Cards

The market for hockey cards is shown in parts (a) and (b) of Figure 3.13. Notice that the demand curve, D_1, refers to the year 1990 in both parts, and the demand curve D_2 refers to the year 1996. Part (a), however, is the market for 1979-80 hockey cards, while part (b) is the market for 1989-90 cards.

During the 1979-80 hockey season, only two companies, O-Pee-Chee and Topps, produced trading cards. Therefore the supply

Figure 3.13
The Market for Hockey Cards

In part (a), the market for 1970–80 hockey cards is shown. The demand in 1990 is illustrated by D_1, while the demand in 1996 is shown by D_2. The supply in both years is shown by curve S. When demand increases for 1979–80 cards, the price rises from P_1 to P_2. In part (b), both the demand and the supply increases from 1990 to 1996. The price falls from P_3 to P_4 because supply increases more than demand at every price.

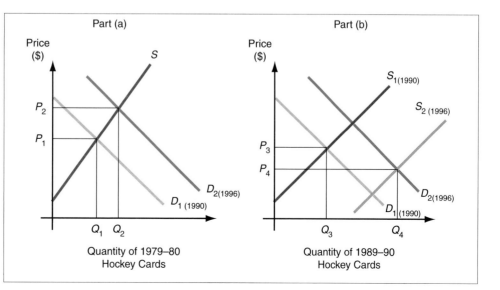

of cards from that year is very limited. This is shown by the supply curve, S, in part (a). When collecting became a fad in North America and the demand for old trading cards increased, something had to give. What happened? The price of Gretzky's 1979-80 trading card rose from P_1 to P_2.

Increasing Supply of Hockey Cards

Over the course of several years, the price rise convinced more firms to supply trading cards. By the 1994-95 hockey season, 106 different companies were listed in the Beckett Hockey Monthly as suppliers! This supply increase is shown in part (b) by the curve S_2. Notice that the price of cards has fallen from P_3 to P_4, since at price P_3 the supply has increased substantially more than demand.

Relatively Rare Cards

If the relative price of hockey cards depends only on supply and demand, why are Maurice Richard's and Gordie Howe's 1951-52

cards worth twice as much as Gretzky's later card? If you said that there must have been an even smaller supply of the earlier cards, you were right. Before 1968, almost all hockey cards were sold in Canada, and Canadians tend to hold onto their valuable collectibles. By contrast, Americans trade their valuables if the market is there, so the supply of post-1968 cards at any given time is relatively greater than that of the earlier years.

For Critical Analysis

1. Some card traders suggest that the hockey players' lockout during the 1994-95 season dampened many collectors' enthusiasm for trading cards. If this is the case, what has happened to the two markets illustrated in parts (a) and (b) of Figure 3.13?

2. What do you think the expansion of the National Hockey League into more American cities is doing to the two markets illustrated in parts (a) and (b) of Figure 3.13?

CHAPTER SUMMARY

1. The law of demand says that at higher prices, individuals will purchase less of a commodity and at lower prices, they will purchase more, other things being equal.

2. Relative prices must be distinguished from absolute, or money, prices. During periods of rising prices, almost all prices go up, but some rise faster than others.

3. All references to the laws of supply and demand refer to constant-quality units of a commodity. A time period for the analysis must also be specified.

4. The demand schedule shows the relationship between various possible prices and their respective quantities purchased per unit time period. Graphically, the demand schedule is a demand curve and is downward-sloping.

5. The nonprice determinants of demand are (a) income, (b) tastes and preferences, (c) the prices of related goods, (d) expectations, and (e) population, or market, size. Whenever any of these determinants of demand changes, the demand curve shifts.

6. The supply curve is generally upward-sloping such that at higher prices, more will be forthcoming than at lower prices. At higher prices, suppliers are willing to incur the increasing costs of higher rates of production.

7. The nonprice determinants of supply are (a) input costs, (b) technology and productivity, (c) taxes and subsidies, (d) price expectations, and (e) entry and exit of firms.

8. A movement along a demand or supply curve is not the same thing as a shift of the curve. A change in price causes movement along the curve. A change in any other determinant of supply or demand shifts the entire curve.

9. The demand and supply curves intersect at the equilibrium point, marking the market clearing price, where quantity demanded just equals quantity supplied. At that point, the plans of buyers and sellers mesh exactly.

10. When the price of a good is greater than its market clearing price, an excess quantity is supplied at that price; it is called a surplus. When the price is below the market clearing price, an excess quantity is demanded at that price; it is called a shortage.

DISCUSSION OF PREVIEW QUESTIONS

1. **Why are relative prices important in understanding the law of demand?**

   People respond to changes in relative prices rather than changes in absolute prices. If the price of CDs rises by 50 percent next year, while at the same time the prices of everything else, including your wages, also increase by 50 percent, the relative price of CDs has not changed. If nothing else has changed in your life, your normal quantity demanded of CDs will remain about the same. In a world of generally rising prices (inflation), you have to compare the price of one good with the average of all other goods in order to decide whether the relative price of that one good has gone up, gone down, or stayed the same.

2. **How can we distinguish between a change in** *demand* **and a change in** *quantity demanded*?

   Use the accompanying graphs to aid you. Because demand is a curve, a change in demand is equivalent to a *shift* of the demand curve. Changes in demand result from changes in the other determinants of demand, such as income, tastes and preferences, expectations, prices of related goods, and population. A change in quantity demanded, given demand, is a movement along a demand curve and results only from a change in the price of the commodity in question.

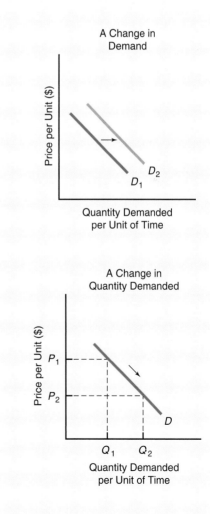

A Change in Demand

A Change in Quantity Demanded

3. **Why is there normally a direct relationship between price and quantity supplied (other things being equal)?**

   In general, businesses experience increasing *extra* costs as they expand output in the short run. This means that additional units of output, which may be quite similar in physical attributes to initial units of output, actually cost the firm more to produce. Consequently, firms often require a higher and higher price as an incentive to produce more in the short run; this "incentive" effect implies that higher prices, other things being constant, lead to increases in quantity supplied.

4. **Why will the market clearing price occur at the intersection of the supply and demand curves rather than at a higher or lower price?**

Consider a price of \$4 per unit, where the quantity demanded exceeds the quantity supplied ($F > C$); a shortage of this commodity exists at a price of \$4 per unit. Buyers will not be able to get all they want at that relatively low price. Because buyers are competing for this good, buyers who are willing to give up more of other goods in order to get this one will offer higher and higher prices. By doing so, they eliminate buyers who are not willing to give up more of other goods. An increase in price encourages sellers to produce and sell more. A shortage exists at *any* price below P_e, and therefore price will rise if it is below P_e.

At P_e, the quantity supplied equals the quantity demanded, Q_e, and both buyers and sellers are able to realize their intentions. Because neither group has an incentive to change its behaviour, equilibrium exists at P_e.

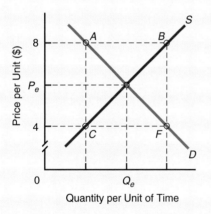

Consider the graph above. To demonstrate that the equilibrium price will be at P_e, we can eliminate all other prices as possibilities. Consider a price above P_e, \$8 per unit. By inspection of the graph, we can see that at that price, the quantity supplied exceeds the quantity demanded for this product ($B > A$). Clearly, sellers cannot sell all they wish at \$8, and they therefore find it profitable to lower price and decrease output. In fact, this surplus situation exists at *all* prices above P_e. Sellers, competing for sales, will reduce prices if a surplus exists.

PROBLEMS

(Answers to the odd-numbered problems appear at the back of the book.)

3-1. Construct a demand curve and a supply curve for skateboards, based on the data provided in the following tables.

Price per Skateboard	Quantity Demanded per Year
$75	300,000
50	600,000
35	900,000
25	1,200,000
15	1,500,000
10	1,800,000

Price per Skateboard	Quantity Supplied per Year
$75	1,800,000
50	1,500,000
35	1,200,000
25	900,000
15	600,000
10	300,000

What is the equilibrium price? What is the equilibrium quantity at that price?

3-2. "Hospitals are obviously complementary to physicians' services." Is this statement always correct?

3-3. Five factors, other than price, that affect the demand for a good were discussed in this chapter. Place each of the following events in its proper category, and state how it would shift the demand curve in parentheses.
a. New information is disclosed that large doses of vitamin C prevent common colds. (Demand for vitamin C)
b. A drop in the price of educational inter-active CD-ROMs occurs. (Demand for teachers)
c. A fall in the price of pretzels occurs. (Demand for beer)

3-4. Examine the following table, and then answer the questions.

	Price per Unit Last Year	Price per Unit Today
Heating oil	$1.00	$2.00
Natural gas	.80	3.20

What has happened to the absolute price of heating oil? Of natural gas? What has happened to the price of heating oil relative to the price of natural gas? What has happened to the relative price of heating oil? Will consumers, through time, change their relative purchases? If so, how?

3-5. Suppose that the demand for oranges remains constant but a frost occurs in Florida that could potentially destroy one-third of the orange crop. What will happen to the equilibrium price and quantity for Florida oranges?

3-6. "The demand has increased so much in response to our offering of a $75 rebate that our inventory of portable laptop computers is now running very low." What is wrong with this assertion?

3-7. Analyse the following statement: "Federal farm price supports can never achieve their goals because the above-equilibrium price floors that are established by the Ministry of Agriculture invariably create surpluses (quantities supplied in excess of quantities demanded), which in turn drive the price right back down towards equilibrium."

3-8. Suppose that an island economy exists in which there is no money. Suppose further that every Sunday morning, at a certain location, hog farmers and cattle ranchers gather to exchange live pigs for cows. Is this a market, and if so, what do the supply and demand diagrams use as a price? Can you imagine any problems arising at the price at which cows and pigs are exchanged?

3-9. Here is a supply and demand schedule for rain in an Amazon jungle settlement where cloud seeding or other scientific techniques can be used to coax rainfall from the skies.

Price (cruzeriros per yearly centimetre of rain)	Quantity Supplied (centimetres of rain per year)	Quantity Demanded (centimetres of rain per year)
0	200	150
10	225	125
20	250	100
30	275	75
40	300	50
50	325	25
60	350	0
70	375	0
80	400	0

What are the equilibrium price and the equilibrium quantity? Explain.

Extensions of Demand and Supply Analysis

It was billed as the battle of grunge against greed. Eddie Vedder and the other members of Seattle grunge band Pearl Jam decided that the service charges required by Ticketmaster, the biggest distributor of tickets in Canada and the United States, were too high. Pearl Jam took the case to court, claiming that Ticketmaster was extracting its "pound of flesh" from poor fans by exploiting its unique position as an intermediary in the live rock concert business. To understand about intermediaries is to understand about markets and exchange and how the forces of supply and demand can be altered by government actions, all topics discussed in this chapter.

Preview Questions

1. Does an increase in demand always lead to a rise in price?

2. Can there ever be shortages in a market with no restrictions?

3. How are goods rationed?

4. When would you expect to encounter black markets?

Did You Know That... hundreds of thousands of cigarettes are being illegally imported into Manitoba from Ontario every year? Why does a black market in cigarettes exist? Because Ontario, Quebec, and the Atlantic provinces collect substantially less sales tax on each packet of cigarettes than Manitoba, Saskatchewan, and Alberta. Since 1994, over 200 people have been caught smuggling cigarettes for resale into Manitoba, so there must be a continuing demand for these illegal goods. Illegal markets such as the one for cigarettes can be analysed using the supply and demand analysis you learned in Chapter 3. Similarly, you can use this analysis to examine purported shortages of apartments in Toronto, and many other similar phenomena. All of these examples are part of our economy, which we can characterize as a price system.

THE PRICE SYSTEM

▶ **Price system**
An economic system in which relative prices are constantly changing to reflect changes in supply and demand for different commodities. The prices of those commodities are signals to everyone within the system as to what is relatively scarce and what is relatively abundant.

A **price system,** otherwise known as a *market system,* is one in which relative prices are constantly changing to reflect changes in supply and demand for different commodities. The prices of those commodities are the signals to everyone within the system as to what is relatively scarce and what is relatively abundant. Indeed, it is the *signalling* aspect of the price system that provides the information to buyers and sellers about what should be bought and what should be produced. In a price system, there is a clear-cut chain of events in which any changes in demand and supply cause changes in prices. Those price changes in turn affect the opportunities that businesses and individuals have for profit and personal gain. Such changes influence our use of resources.

EXCHANGE AND MARKETS

▶ **Voluntary exchange**
An act of trading, done on a voluntary basis, in which both parties to the trade are subjectively better off after the exchange.

▶ **Terms of exchange**
The terms under which trading takes place. Usually the terms of exchange are equal to the price at which a good is traded.

The price system features **voluntary exchange,** acts of trading between individuals that make both parties to the trade subjectively better off. The **terms of exchange—** the prices we pay for the desired items—are determined by the interaction of the forces underlying supply and demand. In our economy, the majority of exchanges take place voluntarily in markets. A market encompasses the exchange arrangements of both buyers and sellers that underlie the forces of supply and demand. Indeed, one definition of a market is a low-cost institution for facilitating exchange. A market in essence increases incomes by helping resources move to their highest-valued uses by means of prices. Prices are the providers of information.

Transaction Costs

▶ **Transaction costs**
All of the costs associated with exchanging, including the informational costs of finding out price and quality, service record, and durability of a product, plus the cost of contracting and enforcing that contract.

Individuals turn to markets because markets reduce the cost of exchanges. These costs are sometimes referred to as **transaction costs,** which are broadly defined as the costs associated with finding out exactly what is being transacted as well as the cost of enforcing contracts. If you were Robinson Crusoe and lived alone on an island, you would never incur a transaction cost. For everyone else, transaction costs are just as real as the costs of production. High-speed large-scale computers have allowed us to reduce transaction costs by increasing our ability to process information and keep records.

Consider some simple examples of transaction costs. The supermarket reduces transaction costs relative to your having to go to numerous specialty stores to obtain the items you desire. Organized stock exchanges, such as the Toronto Stock Exchange, have reduced transaction costs of buying and selling stocks and bonds. In general, the more organized the market, the lower the transaction costs. One group of individuals who constantly attempt to lower transaction costs are intermediaries.

good guy the you mean the
dealers or brokers

The Role of the Intermediary

As long as there are costs to bringing together buyers and sellers, there will be an incentive for intermediaries, often called middlemen, to lower those costs. This means that intermediaries specialize in lowering transaction costs. Whenever producers do not sell their products directly to the final consumer, there are, by definition, one or more intermediaries involved. Farmers typically sell their output to distributors, who are usually called wholesalers, who then sell those products to grocery stores.

Recently, technology has reduced the need, and hence the job prospects, for intermediaries.

EXAMPLE   Technology and the Death of Intermediaries

For decades, most airline travellers bought their tickets from a travel agent, not from the airline itself. In 1996, there were more than 2,200 travel agencies in Canada. That year, Air Canada and Canadian Airlines International cut the commissions paid to these intermediaries by capping them at $60 per round-trip domestic flight rather than the 8.25 percent of ticket purchase price which had hitherto been paid. In an effort to reduce the impact of this move on the travel agents, the two carriers raised the base commission rate to 9 percent. Basically, the airlines have realized that there are high-tech alternatives to travel agents for the distribution of their tickets. Each has its own Web site on the World Wide Web and these, along with other on-line services, such as Microsoft's Expedia, allow subscribers to consult airline timetables and to reserve tickets from their homes or office personal computers. As people become more and more familiar with how to use computers, modems, and on-line services, the trend towards cutting out the intermediary, at least in airline travel, will continue.

For critical analysis: How can travel agents more effectively compete with on-line computer services that offer airline reservations?

CHANGES IN DEMAND AND SUPPLY

It is in markets that we see the results of changes in demand and supply. In certain situations, it is possible to predict what will happen to equilibrium price and equilibrium quantity when a change occurs in demand or supply. Specifically, whenever one curve is stable while the other curve shifts, we can tell what will happen to price and quantity. Consider the four possibilities in Figure 4.1. In part (a), the supply curve remains stable but demand increases from D_1 to D_2. Note that the result is both an increase in the market clearing price from P_1 to P_2 and an increase in the equilibrium quantity from Q_1 to Q_2.

In part (b), there is a decrease in demand from D_1 to D_3. This results in a decrease in both the relative price of the good and the equilibrium quantity. Parts (c) and (d) show the effects of a shift in the supply curve while the demand curve is stable. In part (c), the supply curve has shifted to the right. . The relative price of the product falls; the equilibrium quantity increases. In part (d), supply has shifted to the left—there has been a supply decrease. The product's relative price increases; the equilibrium quantity decreases.

Try Preview Question 1:

Does an increase in demand always lead to a rise in price?

Figure 4.1

Shifts in Demand and in Supply: Determinate Results

In part (a), the supply curve is stable at S. The demand curve shifts outward from D_1 to D_2. The equilibrium price and quantity rise from P_1, Q_1 to P_2, Q_2, respectively. In part (b), again the supply curve remains stable at S. The demand curve, however, shifts inward to the left, showing a decrease in demand from D_1 to D_3. Both equilibrium price and equilibrium quantity fall. In part (c), the demand curve now remains stable at D. The supply curve shifts from S_1 to S_2. The equilibrium price falls from P_1 to P_2. The equilibrium quantity increases, however, from Q_1 to Q_2. In part (d), the demand curve is stable at D. Supply decreases as shown by a leftward shift of the supply curve from S_1 to S_3. The market clearing price increases from P_1 to P_3. The equilibrium quantity falls from Q_1 to Q_3.

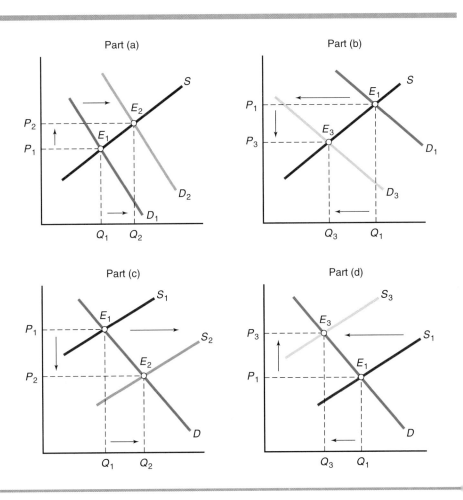

When Both Demand and Supply Shift

The examples given in Figure 4.1 each showed a unique outcome of a shift in either the demand curve holding the supply curve constant, or the supply curve holding the demand curve constant. When both supply and demand curves change, the outcome is indeterminate for either equilibrium price or equilibrium quantity.

When both demand and supply increase, all we can be certain of is that equilibrium quantity will increase. We do not know what will happen to equilibrium price until we determine whether demand increased relative to supply (equilibrium price will rise) or supply increased relative to demand (equilibrium price will fall). The same analysis applies to decreases in both demand and supply, except that in this case equilibrium quantity falls.

We can be certain that when demand decreases and supply increases, the equilibrium price will fall, but we do not know what will happen to the equilibrium quantity unless we actually draw the new curves. If supply decreases and demand increases, we can be sure that equilibrium price will rise, but again we do not know what happens to equilibrium quantity without drawing the curves. In every situation in which both supply and demand change, you should always draw graphs to determine the resulting change in equilibrium price and quantity.

PRICE FLEXIBILITY AND ADJUSTMENT SPEED

We have used a market in which prices are quite flexible as an illustration for our analysis. Some markets are indeed like that. In others, however, price flexibility may take the form of indirect adjustments such as hidden payments or quality changes. For example, although the published price of bouquets of flowers may stay the same, the freshness of the flowers may change, meaning that the price per constant-quality unit changes. The published price of French bread might stay the same, but the quality could go up or down, thereby changing the price per constant-quality unit. There are many ways to change prices without actually changing the published price for a nominal unit of a product or service.

We must also consider the fact that markets do not return to equilibrium immediately. There must be an adjustment time. A shock to the economy in the form of an oil embargo, a drought, or a long strike will not be absorbed overnight. This means that even in free market situations, in which there are no restrictions on changes in prices and quantities, temporary excess quantities supplied and excess quantities demanded may appear. Our analysis simply indicates what the market clearing price ultimately will be, given a demand curve and a supply curve. Nowhere in the analysis is there any indication of the speed with which a market will get to a new equilibrium if there has been a shock. The price may overshoot the equilibrium level. Remember this warning when we examine changes in demand and in supply due to changes in their nonprice determinants.

Now consider how long it takes the world market for gold to adjust to changes in demand and supply.

Try Preview Question 2:

Can there ever be shortages in a market with no restrictions?

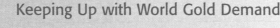

INTERNATIONAL EXAMPLE
Keeping Up with World Gold Demand

Gold prices are watched with great interest by miners, jewellers, and speculators alike. These prices are set, like many other goods, by world supply and world demand. But since new gold supplies have to be located before they are mined and subsequently offered on the market, there is almost always an adjustment lag in the market for raw gold.

Throughout the 1950s and 1960s, the price of gold rose slowly, suggesting that supply was pretty well keeping up with demand. However, as the 1970s progressed, people in many western countries started to buy gold as a hedge against inflation. The price began to rise more rapidly, peaking in 1980. Since then, gold prices have varied within a relatively narrow range. Figure 4.2 shows the historical picture of gold prices.

Figure 4.2
Relative Gold Prices, 1956-1996

The relative price of gold is expressed as a price index, where the price in 1986 is set at 100. The price remained quite low and steady until the 1970s, when the demand increased and prices rose. By the 1980s, new deposits of gold were located and were being mined, satisfying some of the world demand for gold.

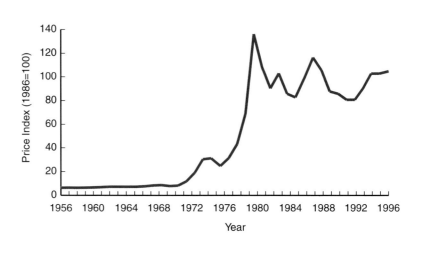

Figure 4.3
Adjustment to Changes in Demand and Supply in the Market for Gold

The world demand for gold in 1960 was D_1 and the supply was S_1. The equilibrium price was P_1. An increase in the demand for gold shifted the demand curve out to D_2; the world price rose to P_2. After some time, new gold deposits were discovered and mined, shifting the supply curve out to S_2. The price fell to P_3, still higher than the original price of P_1.

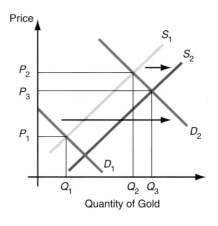

In 1980, 56 percent of world gold production took place in South Africa. China produced 25 percent, North America 6 percent, and Oceania 1 percent The rising prices of the 1970s induced a search for new reserves of gold, with the result that North America now produces 21 percent and Oceania 12 percent of the world supply. South Africa's share has dropped to 28 percent and China's to 18 percent However, there was an adjustment lag of almost 10 years while gold supply caught up with demand.

Figure 4.3 illustrates what happened in the market for gold. The demand for gold in 1960, for example, looked like D_1. The supply was S_1 and price at P_1. Through the 1970s, the demand shifted out in response to general inflation, so that by 1980 it was at D_2. However, it took some time for the supply to catch up, and this adjustment lag allowed prices to rise to P_2. Eventually, as new sources of gold were exploited, the supply increased to S_2, resulting in a long-term price of P_3. Notice that P_3 still exceeds P_1 as world demand for gold is still strong.

For critical analysis: Analysts of the world gold market predict that world demand will stay strong, while 100 gold mines will close in the next three to four years. What will this do to the existing demand and supply of gold, and the equilibrium price? How quickly will it happen?

Concepts in Brief

- The terms of exchange in a voluntary exchange are determined by the interaction of the forces underlying demand and supply. These forces take place in markets, which tend to minimize transaction costs.
- When the demand curve shifts outward or inward with a stable supply curve, equilibrium price and quantity increase or decrease, respectively. When the supply curve shifts outward or inward given a stable demand curve, equilibrium price moves in the opposite direction to equilibrium quantity.
- When there is a shift in demand or supply, the new equilibrium price is not obtained instantaneously. Adjustment takes time.

Thinking Critically About the Media   Water "Rationing"

More and more these days, we hear about the lack of water in some city, province, or country. During the summer, most Canadians are allowed to water their lawns only on certain days and at certain times to restrict water usage. A few years ago, Puerto Rico suffered a drought when rainfall dropped to 35 percent below normal; residents of San Juan were subjected to water cutoffs every other day. These stories about "running out of water" always focus on the supply of water, never on the demand. The demand curve for water slopes downward, just like that for any other good or service. When the supply of strawberries increases in the summer, their prices go down; when the supply decreases, their prices go up. When the supply of water falls because of a drought, one way to ration a smaller supply is to increase the price. For some reason, politicians and media announcers reject this possibility, implying that water is different. Beware when you see the word *rationing* in the media; it typically means that the price of a good or service has not been allowed to reach equilibrium.

THE RATIONING FUNCTION OF PRICES

A shortage creates a situation that forces price to rise towards a market clearing, or equilibrium, level. A surplus brings into play forces that cause price to fall towards its market clearing level. The synchronization of decisions by buyers and sellers that creates a situation of equilibrium is called the *rationing function of prices*. Prices are indicators of relative scarcity. An equilibrium price clears the market. The plans of buyers and sellers, given the price, are not frustrated.[1] It is the free interaction of buyers and sellers which sets the price that eventually clears the market. Price, in effect, rations a commodity to demanders who are willing and able to pay the highest price. Whenever the rationing function of prices is frustrated by government-enforced price ceilings that set prices below the market clearing level, a prolonged shortage situation is not allowed to be corrected by the upward adjustment of the price.

You should note that prices which serve rationing functions need not always be stated in dollars and cents. Admission to universities and colleges is often rationed not by tuition (a dollars and cents price) but by grade point average. The highest "bidders" for admission—those with the highest GPAs—are accepted.

There are other ways to ration goods. *First come, first served* is one method. *Political power* is another. *Physical force* is yet another. Cultural, religious, and physical differences have been and are used as rationing devices throughout the world.

Consider "first come, first served" as a rationing device. In countries that do not allow prices to reflect true relative scarcity, first come, first served has become a way of life. We call this *rationing by queues*, where *queue* means "line." Whoever is willing to wait in line the longest obtains meat that is being sold at less than the market clearing price. All who wait in line are paying a higher *total* price than the money price paid for the meat. Personal time has an opportunity cost. To calculate the total price of the meat, we must add up the money price plus the opportunity cost of the time spent waiting.

Lotteries are another way to ration goods. You may have been involved in a rationing-by-lottery scheme during your first year in college when you were assigned a parking pass for campus lots. Selling raffle tickets for popular college sweatshirts is also a method of rationing by lottery.

Rationing by *coupons* has also been used, particularly during wartime. In Canada during World War II, families were allotted coupons that allowed them to purchase specified quantities of rationed goods, such as meat and gasoline. To purchase these goods, you had to pay a specified price *and* give up a coupon.

Rationing by *waiting* may occur in situations in which entrepreneurs are free to change prices to equate quantity demanded with quantity supplied, but choose not to do so. This results in queues of potential buyers. The most obvious conclusion seems to be that the price in the market is being held below equilibrium by some noncompetitive force. That is not true, however.

Try Preview Question 3:

How are goods rationed?

---

[1] There is a difference between frustration and unhappiness. You may be unhappy because you can't buy a Rolls Royce, but if you had sufficient income, you would not be frustrated in your attempt to purchase one at the current market price. By contrast, you would be frustrated if you went to your local supermarket and could get only two cans of your favourite soft-drink when you had wanted to purchase a dozen and had the necessary income.

The reason is that queuing may also arise when the demand characteristics of a market are subject to large or unpredictable fluctuations, and the additional costs to firms (and ultimately to consumers) of constantly changing prices, or of holding sufficient inventories, or providing sufficient excess capacity to cover these peak demands are greater than the costs to consumers of waiting for the good. This is the usual case of waiting in line to purchase a fast-food lunch, or to purchase a movie ticket a few minutes before the next show.

The Essential Role of Rationing

In a world of scarcity, there is, by definition, competition for what is scarce. After all, any resources that are not scarce can be had by everyone at a zero price in as large a quantity as everyone wants, such as air to burn in internal combustion engines. Once scarcity arises, there has to be some method to ration the available resources, goods, and services. The price system is one form of rationing; the others that we mentioned are alternatives. Economists cannot say which system of rationing is best. They can, however, say that rationing via the price system leads to the most efficient use of available resources. This means that generally in a price system, further trades could not occur without making somebody worse off. In other words, in a freely functioning price system, all of the gains from mutually beneficial trade will be exhausted.

Concepts in Brief

- Prices in a market economy perform a rationing function because they reflect relative scarcity, allowing the market to clear. Other ways to ration goods include first come, first served; political power; physical force; lotteries; and coupons.
- Even when businesses can change prices, some rationing by waiting will occur. Such queuing arises when there are large unexpected changes in demand, coupled with high costs of satisfying those changes immediately.

▶ **Price controls**
Government-mandated minimum or maximum prices that may be charged for goods and services.

▶ **Price ceiling**
A legal maximum price that may be charged for a particular good or service.

▶ **Price floor**
A legal minimum price below which a good or service may not be sold. Legal minimum wages are an example.

THE POLICY OF GOVERNMENT-IMPOSED PRICE CONTROLS

The rationing function of prices is often not allowed to operate when governments impose price controls. **Price controls** typically involve setting a **price ceiling**—the maximum price that may be allowed in an exchange. The world has had a long history of price ceilings applied to some goods, wages, rents, and interest rates, among other things. Occasionally a government will set a **price floor**—a minimum price below which a good or service may not be sold. These have most often been applied to wages and agricultural products. Let's consider price controls in terms of price ceilings.

Price Ceilings and Black Markets

As long as a price ceiling is below the market clearing price, imposing a price ceiling creates a shortage, as can be seen in Figure 4.4. At any price below the market clearing, or equilibrium, price of P_e, there will always be a larger quantity demanded than quantity supplied, that is, a shortage. This was discussed initially in Chapter 3. Normally, whenever a shortage exists, there is a tendency for price and output to rise to equilibrium levels. This is exactly what we pointed out when discussing shortages in the market for gold. But with a price ceiling, this tendency cannot be fully realized because everyone is forbidden to trade at the equilibrium price.

The result is fewer exchanges and **nonprice rationing devices**. In Figure 4.4, at an equilibrium price of P_e, the equilibrium quantity demanded and supplied (or traded) is Q_e. But at the price ceiling of P_1, the equilibrium quantity offered is only Q_s. What happens if there is a shortage? The most obvious nonprice rationing device to help clear the market is queuing, or long lines, which we have already discussed.

Typically, an effective price ceiling leads to a **black market**. A black market is a market in which the price-controlled good is sold at an illegally high price through various methods. For example, if the price of gasoline is controlled at lower than the market clearing price, a gas station attendant may take a cash payment on the side in order to fill up a driver's car. If the price of beef is controlled at below its market clearing price, the butcher may give special service to a customer who offers the butcher great seats at an upcoming football game. Indeed, the number of ways in which the true implicit price of a price-controlled good or service can be increased is infinite, limited only by the imagination. (Black markets also occur when goods are made illegal.)

Whenever a nation attempts to freeze all prices, a variety of problems arise. Many of them occurred a few years ago in Mexico.

▶ **Nonprice rationing devices**

All methods used to ration scarce goods that are price-controlled. Whenever the price system is not allowed to work, nonprice rationing devices will evolve to ration the affected goods and services.

▶ **Black market**

A market in which goods are traded at prices above their legal maximum prices or in which illegal goods are sold.

Try Preview Question 4:
When would you expect to encounter black markets?

Figure 4.4
Black Markets

The demand curve is D. The supply curve is S. The equilibrium price is P_e. The government, however, steps in and imposes a maximum price of P_1. At that lower price, the quantity demanded will be Q_d, but the quantity supplied will only be Q_s. There is a shortage, and black markets develop. The price at which the restricted quantity could sell on the market (the *implicit* price) rises to P_2.

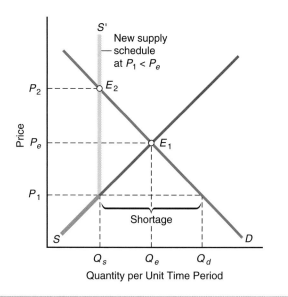

INTERNATIONAL EXAMPLE
Mexico's Price Freeze and the Shopping Cops

The mid-1990s marked a low point for the Mexican economy when its currency, the peso, plunged in value relative to the dollar and other international currencies. In anticipation of rapidly rising domestic prices, the Mexican government imposed a temporary freeze on all prices. Almost immediately, shoppers began complaining about supermarkets, department stores, car dealerships, and mom and pop stores that were illegally raising their prices. In response, the Mexican Consumer Attorney General's Office sent out a small army of "shopping cops" to impose fines as necessary, and temporarily closed hundreds of stores. During one national sample of commercial establishments, 70 percent were found to be cheating on the price freeze.

One way merchants got around government price controls was to place "sold" stickers on merchandise. Consumers then had to agree to pay a higher price in order to obtain the goods. Many automobile dealerships refused to deliver cars bought prior to the dramatic reduction in the value of the Mexican peso. Indeed, the number of ways to evade price controls was limited only by the imagination of buyers and sellers.

For critical analysis: How would you graphically illustrate the situation in Mexico using a supply and demand diagram?

Concepts in Brief

- Government policy can impose price controls in the form of price ceilings and price floors.
- An effective price ceiling is one that sets the legal price below the market clearing price and is enforced. Effective price ceilings lead to nonprice rationing devices and black markets.

THE POLICY OF CONTROLLING RENTS

▶ **Rent control**

The placement of price ceilings on rents.

Most provinces have at some time operated under some form of rent control. **Rent control** is a system under which the provincial government tells building owners how much rent they can charge their tenants. In Canada, rent controls date back to at least World War II. The objective of rent control is to keep rents below levels that would be observed in a freely competitive market.

The Functions of Rental Prices

In any housing market, rental prices serve three functions: (1) to promote the efficient maintenance of existing housing and stimulate the construction of new housing, (2) to allocate existing scarce housing among competing claimants, and (3) to ration the use of existing housing by current demanders.

Rent Controls and Construction. Rent controls have discouraged the construction of new rental units. Rents are the most important long-term determinant of profitability, and rent controls have artificially depressed them. Consider some examples. Halifax, with less than 15 percent of the population of Toronto, built proportionally more rental units than Toronto in 1995. This, in spite of a 7.2 percent vacancy rate in Halifax, compared to a 1.2 percent vacancy rate in Toronto. The major difference? There were no rent controls in Halifax, while rent increases were strictly controlled in Toronto. In the same year, Vancouver, with 70 percent of the population of Toronto, saw the construction of 11,000 rental units; only 4,000 were built in Toronto. Again, the difference was that there were no rent controls in Vancouver.

Effects on the Existing Supply of Housing. When rental rates are held below equilibrium levels, property owners cannot use higher rents to recover the cost of maintenance, repairs, and capital improvements. Hence they curtail these activities. In the extreme situation, taxes, utilities, and the expenses of basic repairs exceed rental receipts. The result is abandoned and/or deteriorating buildings. It is estimated that over 15 percent of the rental housing in Toronto will deteriorate so much by the early 2000s that it will be uninhabitable. In the 1970s, when Vancouver did have a system of rent controls, landlords, unable to increase rents, converted thousands of apartments into condominiums. The landlords then sold the condominiums and recouped their investment that way. This had the effect of severely reducing the supply of rental housing, thus making the housing shortage even worse.

Rationing the Current Use of Housing. Like any other price, rents serve the purpose of rationing output, in this case the allocation of apartments among prospective tenants. When the rent is held at an arbitrarily low level, the number of prospective tenants increases and excess demand develops. Students, for example, who might otherwise live with their families, decide they can afford to live on their own. In this situation, rationing of the available supply of rental housing is achieved through nonprice mechanisms such as queuing or making "under the table" payments to landlords.

Attempts at Evading Rent Controls

The distortions produced by rent controls lead to efforts by both landlords and tenants to evade the rules. This, in turn, leads to the growth of expensive government bureaucracies whose job it is to make sure that those rules are indeed followed. In 1995, the Ontario government spent about $1.8 million administering its *Residential Rent Regulation Act*.

In the 1980s, Ontario landlords had an incentive to speculate on the real estate market. They bought and sold apartment buildings, driving up prices and financing costs. Then they applied for rent increases to cover the rising costs. Tenants, for their part, routinely try to sublet all or part of their rent-controlled apartments at fees substantially above the rent they pay to the owner. They pocket the difference, perhaps to help pay for a more expensive apartment.

Who Gains and Who Loses from Rent Controls?

The big losers from rent controls are clearly landlords. But there is another group of losers—low-income individuals, especially single mothers, trying to find their first apartment. Some observers now believe that rent controls have worsened the problem of homeless people in such cities as Toronto.

Landlords of rent-controlled apartments often charge "key money" before a new tenant is allowed to move in. This is a large up-front cash payment, usually illegal but demanded nonetheless—just one aspect of the black market in rent-controlled apartments. Poor individuals cannot afford a hefty key money payment, nor can they assure the landlord that their rent will be on time or even paid each month. Because controlled rents are usually below market clearing levels, there is little incentive for apartment owners to take any risk on low-income-earning individuals as tenants. This is particularly true when a prospective tenant's chief source of income is a welfare cheque.

INTERNATIONAL EXAMPLE
Rent Controls in Bombay

In the mid-1990s, Bombay, India, had the highest rents of any capital city in the world. The annual rent per square foot for *available* unleased space was estimated at about $200, compared to $30 in downtown Vancouver or Toronto. In addition, most landlords insist on receiving a year's rent in advance, plus an additional security deposit equal to two years' rent. For major businesses, this can add up to millions of dollars, which are usually returned, but in three to five years and without payment of any interest.

One reason Bombay rents are so high is the existence of rent controls and other laws intended to protect tenants. These controls and restrictions have kept out real estate developers, and even scared owners of rentable property out of renting that property, be it commercial or residential. One rent control law makes it almost impossible for a landlord to evict a tenant or to raise rents. Tenants can obtain what is called *statutory tenancy*, which allows them and their descendants to remain without a lease in any property they currently rent. There are situations in Bombay in which renters from 50 years ago still live in the same apartment, paying approximately the same rent as they originally did. Not surprisingly, unleased rental space is hard to find and hence quite expensive.

For critical analysis: What effect do you think Bombay's high rents might have on foreign firms' desire to operate in that city?

Who benefits from rent control? Ample evidence indicates that upper-income professionals benefit the most. These are the people who can use their mastery of the bureaucracy and their large network of friends and connections to exploit the rent control system. These are also the people who can easily afford to pay key money, or to pay an agency to locate an apartment for them.

Because the private sector was unwilling to finance construction of new rental units in an environment of rent controls, the Ontario government has had to spend up to $3.5 billion per year subsidizing the building of non-profit housing. Rents may have been controlled at lower-than-market levels, but renters and homeowners alike paid higher than necessary taxes to fund the government's subsidies.

Concepts in Brief

- Rental prices perform three functions: (1) allocating existing scarce housing among competing claimants, (2) promoting efficient maintenance of existing houses and stimulating new housing construction, and (3) rationing the use of existing houses by current demanders.
- Effective rent controls reduce or alter the three functions of rental prices. Construction of new rental units is discouraged. Rent controls decrease spending on maintenance of existing units and also lead to "housing gridlock."
- There are numerous ways to evade rent controls; key money is one.

PRICE SUPPORTS: THE CASE OF AGRICULTURE

Another way that government can affect markets is by imposing price floors or price supports. In Canada, price supports are most often associated with agricultural products.

Over one-half of Canadian farmers' total sales are regulated by agricultural marketing boards. Chickens, turkeys, eggs, milk, butter, tobacco, and mushrooms are all sold through marketing boards which restrict supply of these products to the marketplace. Consequently, our more than 100 marketing boards are referred to as a *supply-management system*.

In the 1970s, the Canadian government was concerned that farm output prices which fluctuated widely left farmers with good incomes one year, but possibly starvation incomes the next. In an effort to stabilize farm incomes and protect the small family farm, the government legislated marketing boards. The boards then set **quotas** for production for each farm in order to regulate supply. Since the supply was restricted, price rose.

▶ **Quota**
A set amount of output (less than the equilibrium amount) which farmers can supply to marketing boards for sale.

Figure 4.5 shows the effect of a marketing board quota on the market for eggs. The demand curve, D, is the domestic demand for Canadian eggs. The supply curve, S, is the domestic supply of eggs. In the absence of a quota, the equilibrium price and quantity of eggs will be P_e and Q_e. When the marketing board sets a quota on production, it limits the amount that farmers are permitted to produce. A quota which is effective will always be less than the equilibrium quantity, Q_e. The vertical

Figure 4.5
The Regulated Market for Eggs

The market demand and supply curves are D and S, and in an unregulated market equilibrium price and quantity would be P_e and Q_e. The Egg Marketing Board, however, sets a quota at the quantity Q_q. This has the effect of stopping all production past $Q_{q'}$ and raising the price to P_q where the demand curve meets the regulated supply $S_{q'}$.

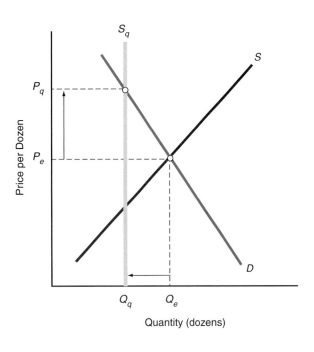

Quantity (dozens)

line S_q represents the quota in the egg market. Notice that the quantity traded falls to Q_q while the price rises to P_q. The marketing board, armed with knowledge of consumer demand for its product, can effectively guarantee a price floor simply by setting quotas.

Who Loses When Marketing Boards Regulate Supply?

The consumer pays more for the regulated goods than necessary and is therefore the biggest loser. One estimate suggests that the average Canadian family pays $200 to $400 per year more than it would if all farm produce were sold at unregulated prices.

Prospective farmers lose too. When quotas were first established, they were given to existing producers. New producers, however, have to purchase quotas from other farmers or from the appropriate marketing board. Some quotas have become prohibitively expensive. To buy a minimum-size quota for a chicken farm today would require $1 million; a minimum-size quota for a dairy farm in the Fraser Valley of British Columbia would take $3 million. And that's not counting the cost of the land or the livestock.

Another loser is the foreign farmer who would like to export farm products to Canada. The government restricts entry of foreign produce, because the additional supply would reduce prices. Canada used to keep out foreign produce with import quotas, but the GATT (General Agreement on Tariffs and Trade) in its latest round of talks banned import quotas on agricultural goods. Thus the federal government now uses import duties (i.e., taxes on imported produce) to restrict supply of foreign goods. The tariff on butter from the United States, for example, is 351 percent.

Who Wins When Marketing Boards Regulate Supply?

Existing farmers are clearly the major winners. The boards do stabilize their incomes, so they can plan from one year to the next. Supporters of marketing boards also point out that by guaranteeing a living for Canadian farmers we are providing ourselves with a made-at-home food supply—something much more valuable than the costs associated with supply management. In addition, we are helping to preserve a way of life which is disappearing elsewhere, and that is the family farm.

Some farmers object to being regulated by marketing boards. They believe that they, as entrepreneurs, will be better salespeople for their products than a government bureaucracy. This is happening most clearly in the wheat industry where a special form of marketing board exists.

EXAMPLE   **Wheat Farmers and the Canadian Wheat Board**

The Canadian government has been involved in guaranteeing prices for wheat farmers since World War I. In 1917, to regulate the supply of wheat to troops in Europe and to Canadians at home, and to guarantee grain farmers a reasonable living, the government set up the Board of Grain Supervisors. After the war, the Board's name was changed to the Canadian Wheat Board. It still operates today. The Canadian Wheat Board buys all the wheat a farmer produces and sells it on world markets. Farmers cannot sell their wheat independently. The Board advances 75 percent of the expected price to farmers in the spring, and then settles up with them after the wheat is sold in the fall. Farmers never receive less than the expected price, so if the world price is lower than predicted , the Wheat Board suffers a loss. But if the price is higher, farmers are paid more. This has the effect of reducing fluctuations in farm income by putting a floor under the price farmers receive.

Recently, some grain growers have been objecting to being forced to sell to the Wheat Board. They claim that by selling directly to the United States, they would earn $2 to $3 per bushel more, a significant price difference. But other farmers want the Wheat Board to remain. They fear as individual farmers they would not have the leverage to stand up against major wheat buyers and demand a high price. In the end they fear their incomes would fall.

For critical analysis: What do you think would happen to the price of Canadian wheat if half the farmers sold independently, while half sold through the Canadian Wheat Board?

PRICE FLOORS IN THE LABOUR MARKET

▶ **Minimum wage**
A wage floor, legislated by government, setting the lowest hourly rate that firms may legally pay workers.

The **minimum wage** is the lowest hourly wage rate that firms may legally pay their workers. Proponents want higher minimum wages to ensure low-income workers a "decent" standard of living. Opponents claim that higher minimum wages cause increased unemployment, particularly among unskilled teenagers.

Every province in Canada has a minimum wage. Figure 4.6 sets out the hourly minimum wage for each province. For many years the federal government had a minimum wage of $4.00 per hour which applied to federal workers. However, this legislated wage was cancelled some time ago, since all workers were already earning more than the minimum anyway.

What happens when the government passes a floor on wages? The effects can be seen in Figure 4.7. We start off in equilibrium with the equilibrium wage rate of

Figure 4.6
Provincial Minimum Wages

In 1996, every province had a legislated minimum wage. The rate varied from a low of $4.75 to a high of $7.00 per hour. The average minimum wage was $5.67.

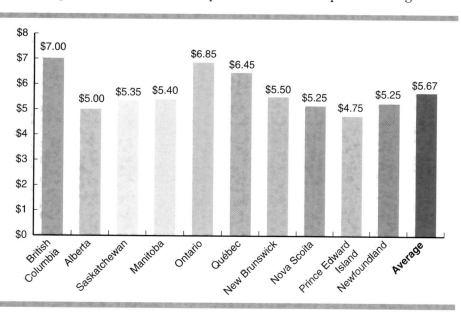

Figure 4.7
The Effect of Minimum Wages

The market clearing wage rate is W_e. The market clearing quantity of employment is Q_e, determined by the intersection of supply and demand at point E. A minimum wage equal to W_m is established. The quantity of labour demanded is reduced to Q_d; the reduction in employment from Q_e to Q_d is equal to the distance between B and A. That distance is smaller than the excess quantity of labour supplied at wage rate W_m. The distance between B and C is the increase in the quantity of labour supplied that results from the higher minimum wage rate.

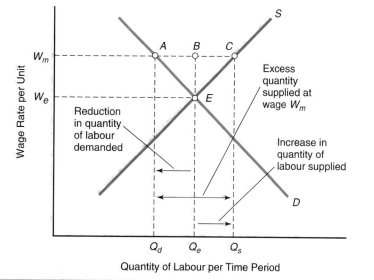

W_e and the equilibrium quantity of labour demanded and supplied equal to Q_e. A minimum wage, W_m, higher than W_e, is imposed. At W_m, the quantity demanded for labour is reduced to Q_d, and some workers now become unemployed. Note that the reduction in employment from Q_e to Q_d, or the distance from B to A, is less than the excess quantity of labour supplied at wage rate W_m. This excess quantity supplied is the distance between A and C, or the distance between Q_d and Q_s. The reason the reduction in employment is smaller than the excess supply of labour at the minimum wage is that the latter also includes a second component, consisting of the additional workers who would like to work more hours at the new, higher minimum wage. Some workers may become unemployed as a result of the minimum wage, but others will move to sectors where minimum wage laws do not apply; wages will be pushed down in these uncovered sectors.

In the long run (a time period that is long enough to allow for adjustment by workers and firms), some of the reduction in labour demanded will result from a reduction in the number of firms, and some will result from changes in the number of workers employed by each firm. Economists estimate that a 10 percent increase in the real minimum wage decreases total employment of those affected by 1 to 2 percent.[2]

QUANTITY RESTRICTIONS

Governments can impose quantity restrictions on a market. The most obvious restriction is an outright ban on the ownership or trading of a good. It is presently illegal to buy and sell human organs. It is also currently illegal to buy and sell certain psychoactive drugs such as cocaine, heroin, and marijuana. It is illegal to open a new chartered bank without obtaining a government charter. This requirement effectively restricts the number of chartered banks in Canada.

Some of the most common quantity restrictions exist in the area of international trade. The Canadian government and many foreign governments impose import quotas on a variety of goods. An **import quota** is a supply restriction that prohibits the importation of more than a specified quantity of a particular good in a one-year period. Canada has had import quotas on cotton textiles, shoes, and immigrant labour. For many years, there were import quotas on dairy products coming into Canada from the United States. These import quotas were recently removed and replaced by tariffs, but the effect is still to limit the amount of dairy products which we import. There are also "voluntary" import quotas on certain goods. Japanese car makers, for example, have agreed since 1981 "voluntarily" to restrict the number of cars they send to Canada.

▶ **Import quota**
A physical supply restriction on imports of a particular good, such as sugar. Foreign exporters are unable to sell in Canada more than the quantity specified in the import quota.

---

[2] Because we are referring to a long-run analysis here, the reduction in labour demanded would be demonstrated by an eventual shift inward to the left of the short-run demand curve, D, in Figure 4.7.

POLICY EXAMPLE

Should the Legal Quantity of Cigarettes Supplied Be Set at Zero?

Nicotine has been used as a psychoactive drug by the Native Peoples of the Americas for approximately 8,000 years. Five hundred years ago, Christopher Columbus introduced tobacco to the Europeans, who discovered that once they overcame the nausea and dizziness produced by chewing, snorting, or smoking the tobacco, they simply could not get along without it. Nicotine quickly joined alcohol and caffeine as one of the world's principal psychoactive drugs of choice. In the century after Columbus returned from the Americas with tobacco, the use of and addiction to nicotine spread quickly around the world. There followed numerous efforts to quash what had become known as the "evil weed." In 1603, the Japanese prohibited the use of tobacco, and repeatedly increased the penalties for violating the ban, which wasn't lifted until 1625. By the middle of the seventeenth century, similar bans on tobacco were in place in Bavaria, Saxony, Zurich, Turkey, and Russia, with punishments ranging from confiscation of property to execution.

What could we predict if tobacco were ever completely prohibited today? Because tobacco is legal, the supply of illegal tobacco is zero. If the use of tobacco were restricted, the supply of illegal tobacco would not remain zero for long. Even if Canadian tobacco growers were forced out of business, the production of tobacco in other countries would increase to meet the demand. Consequently, the supply curve of illegal tobacco products would shift outward to the right as more foreign sources determined they wanted to enter the illegal Canadian tobacco market. The demand curve for illegal tobacco products would emerge almost immediately after the quantity restriction. The price people would pay to satisfy their nicotine addiction would go up.

For critical analysis: What other goods or services follow the same analysis as the one presented here?

Concepts in Brief

- With a price support system, the government sets a quota which limits the amount of output that can be produced. The only way a price support system can survive is for the government to restrict competing imports from adding to domestic supply and thus lowering price.
- When a floor is placed on wages at a rate that is above market equilibrium, the result is an excess quantity of labour supplied at that minimum wage.
- Quantity restrictions may take the form of import quotas, which are limits on the quantity of specific foreign goods that can be brought into Canada for resale purposes.

Issues and Applications

Grunge Meets Greed

Concepts Applied: Markets, exchange, price system, intermediaries, rationing, supply and demand

Pearl Jam's Eddie Vedder refused to sell tickets for the '95–'96 tour through Ticketmaster because the distributor adds on a hefty fee to tickets. Are Ticketmaster's services of convenient ticket purchasing worth the price they charge? Pearl Jam didn't think so.

Arguably, the Seattle grunge band Pearl Jam is one of the most successful rock bands of our time. Not only is it one of the most popular bands in Canada, but it is also the most revolutionary. Pearl Jam refused to make videos for MTV and VH-1 for its second successful album, *Vs.*, and didn't release any singles from that album in Canada. When the band finally decided to tour after an intentionally long hiatus, it demanded a US$20 ceiling on ticket prices, including a top service charge of 10 percent from the leading ticket distributor, Ticketmaster.

Ticketmaster's Position as Intermediary

Ticketmaster uses a highly sophisticated computer system to distribute tickets nationwide for major entertainment events. When asked about Pearl Jam's claims that Ticketmaster was "gouging" fans, a senior company official said that Ticketmaster's investment in that computer system makes it easier for performers to sell large numbers of tickets. Each year, Ticketmaster sells between 50 and 60 million tickets. The official claimed that Ticketmaster has the right to be paid for such services and noted that "if Pearl Jam wants

to play for free, we will be happy to distribute their tickets for free." Ticketmaster currently charges a fee of $5 to $10 per ticket.

The Value That Ticketmaster Adds

Goods have little or no value if consumers cannot obtain them. The value of a good therefore depends on its availability. Intermediaries add value to goods without physically changing them by simply making it easier for consumers to purchase them. As an intermediary, this is what Ticketmaster does. Major entertainment events, such as a Pearl Jam concert, are most profitable and add value to more consumers when they are performed in large venues, such as football stadiums. It would be virtually impossible to service all of the fans desiring to attend a Pearl Jam concert if tickets were sold only at the box office of the venue where the concert was being held. A computerized nationwide system allows popular bands to sell tickets efficiently for concerts at large-capacity venues.

Pearl Jam's Failed Alternative Distribution System

Pearl Jam originally decided to give concerts in the United States without the use of Ticketmaster by distributing tickets through a lottery. Some 175,000 people sent in postcards for the two concerts that were to be held at Constitution Hall in Philadelphia, which seats 3,700 people. Of course, many people who saw those concerts paid extravagant prices by using the services of scalpers. One of the things that Pearl Jam cannot control is the value that fans place on seeing and hearing the band perform live. As long as different fans have different valuations of an activity, there will be some who will willingly give up their tickets at a high enough price, which others will gladly pay.

Neither the lottery nor any other alternatives that Pearl Jam tried to get around the intermediary services of Ticketmaster worked. The band cancelled its 1995–1996 tour. Its spokespersons claimed that "touring without Ticketmaster was too complicated."

Competition for Ticketmaster may be on the horizon, with distributors selling tickets via a high-tech phone system and the Internet.

For Critical Analysis

1. Assume that Ticketmaster distributes 100 percent of all tickets to live entertainment events in Canada. Why wouldn't Ticketmaster charge an even higher service charge per ticket, say, $50?

2. If the government passed a law restricting Ticketmaster to a $2 charge per ticket, what might happen as a result?

CHAPTER SUMMARY

1. A price system, otherwise called a market system, allows prices to respond to changes in supply and demand for different commodities. Consumers' and business managers' decisions on resource use depend on what happens to prices.

2. Exchanges take place in markets. The terms of exchange—prices—are registered in markets that tend to minimize transaction costs.

3. With a stable supply curve, a rise in demand leads to an increase in equilibrium price and quantity; a decrease in demand leads to a reduction in equilibrium price and quantity. With a stable demand curve, a rise in supply leads to a decrease in equilibrium price and an increase in equilibrium quantity; a fall in supply leads to an increase in equilibrium price and a decrease in equilibrium quantity.

4. When both demand and supply shift at the same time, indeterminate results occur. We must know the direction and degree of each shift in order to predict the change in equilibrium price and quantity.

5. When there is a shift in demand or supply, it takes time for markets to adjust to the new equilibrium. During that time, there will be temporary shortages or surpluses.

6. In a market system, prices perform a rationing function—they ration scarce goods and services. Other ways of rationing include first come, first served; political power; physical force; lotteries; and coupons.

7. Government-imposed price controls can take the form of price ceilings, price floors, and quotas. Effective price ceilings—ones that are set below the market clearing price and enforced—lead to nonprice rationing devices and black markets.

8. Rent controls interfere with many of the functions of rental prices. For example, effective rent controls discourage the construction of new rental units. They also encourage "housing gridlock." Landlords lose during effective rent controls. Other losers are typically low-income individuals, especially single mothers, trying to find their first apartments.

9. A quota can take the form of a government-imposed price support for agricultural products. This restricts quantity supplied and drives the price up to the desired level. To maintain that price, the government must restrict competing imports from increasing the domestic supply.

10. A price floor can apply to wages. When the government-imposed minimum wage exceeds the equilibrium wage rate, an excess quantity of labour is supplied. The result is higher unemployment for the affected group of workers.

11. Quantity restrictions can take the form of import quotas, under which there is a limit to the quantity of the affected good that can be brought into Canada and sold.

DISCUSSION OF PREVIEW QUESTIONS

1. Does an increase in demand always lead to a rise in price?

Yes, provided that the supply curve doesn't shift also. If the supply is stable, every rise in demand will cause a shift outward to the right in the demand curve. The new equilibrium price will be higher than the old equilibrium price. If, however, the supply curve shifts at the same time, you have to know in which direction and by how much. If the supply curve shifts outward, indicating a rise in supply, the equilibrium price can rise if the shift is not as great as in demand. If the increase in supply is greater than in demand, the price can actually fall. We can be sure, though, that if demand increases and supply decreases, the equilibrium price will rise. This can be seen in the accompanying graph.

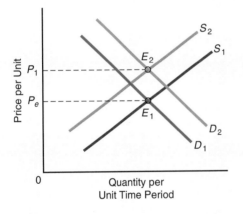

2. Can there ever be shortages in a market with no restrictions?

Yes, there can, because adjustment is never instantaneous. It takes time for the forces of supply and demand to work. In all our graphs, we draw new equilibrium points where a new sup-

ply curve meets a new demand curve. That doesn't mean that in the marketplace buyers and sellers will react immediately to a change in supply or demand. Information is not perfect. Moreover, people are often slow to adapt to higher or lower prices. Suppliers may require months or years to respond to an increase in the demand for their product. Consumers take time to respond to new information about changing relative prices.

3. How are goods rationed?

In a pure price system, prices ration goods. Prices are the indicators of relative scarcity. Prices change so that quantity demanded equals quantity supplied. In the absence of a price system, an alternative way to ration goods is first come, first served. In many systems, political power is another method. In certain cultures, physical force is a way to ration goods. Cultural, religious, and physical differences among individuals can be used as rationing devices. The fact is that given a world of scarcity, there has to be some method to ration goods. The price system is only one alternative.

4. When would you expect to encounter black markets?

Black markets occur in two situations. The first is whenever a good or service is made illegal by legislation. Second, there are black markets whenever a price ceiling (one type of price control) is imposed on any good or service. The price ceiling has to be below the market clearing price and enforced for a black market to exist, however. Price ceilings on rents have created black markets for rental units.

PROBLEMS

(Answers to the odd-numbered problems appear at the back of the book.)

4-1. This is a graph of the supply and demand for oranges.

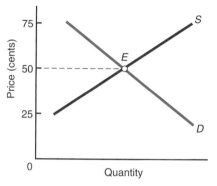

Explain the effect that each of the following events would have on this graph.
   a.   It is discovered that oranges can cure acne.
   b.   A new machine is developed that will automatically pick oranges.
   c.   The government declares a price floor of 25 cents.
   d.   The government declares a price floor of 75 cents.
   e.   The price of grapefruits increases.
   f.   Income decreases.

4-2. What might be the long-run results of price controls that maintained a good's money price below its equilibrium price? Above its equilibrium price?

4-3. Here is a demand schedule and a supply schedule for scientific hand-held calculators.

Price	Quantity Demanded	Quantity Supplied
$10	100,000	0
20	60,000	0
30	20,000	0
40	0	0
50	0	100,000
60	0	300,000
70	0	500,000

What are the equilibrium price and the equilibrium quantity? Explain.

4-4. This is a graph of the supply and demand for raisins.

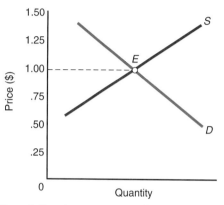

The following series of events occurs. Explain the result of each event.
   a.   An advertising campaign for raisins is successful.
   b.   A fungus wipes out half the grape crop (used to make raisins) in California.
   c.   The price of bran flakes (a complement) increases.
   d.   The price of dried cranberries (a substitute) increases.
   e.   The government declares a price floor of 75 cents.
   f.   The government imposes and enforces a price ceiling of 75 cents.
   g.   Income increases (assume that raisins are an inferior good).

4-5. Below is a demand schedule and a supply schedule for lettuce.

Price per Crate	Quantity Demanded (crates per year)	Quantity Supplied (crates per year)
$1	10 million	0 million
2	9 million	1 million
3	7 million	3 million
4	5 million	5 million
5	2 million	8 million

What are the equilibrium price and the equilibrium quantity? At a price of $2 per crate, what is the quantity demanded? The quantity supplied? What is this disequilibrium situation called? What is the magnitude of the disequilibrium, expressed in terms of quantities? Now answer the same questions for a price of $5 per crate.

4-6. What is wrong with the following statement? "The demand has increased so much in response to our offering of a $500 rebate that our inventory of cars is now running very low."

4-7. Rent control is a price ceiling. There are also legislated price floors. Assume that the equilibrium price for apples is 10 cents each. Draw the supply and demand diagram to show the effect of a government-imposed price floor, or minimum price, of 15 cents per apple. Be sure to label any shortages or surpluses that result. Then show the effect of a price floor of 5 cents per apple.

The Public Sector

In Canada over the course of a year, thousands of tax lawyers and accountants labour alone or with clients to help those clients reduce their tax liabilities and fill out their tax returns. Canadian taxpayers are each estimated to spend approximately 20 hours a year preparing their taxes. The opportunity cost exceeds $4 billion a year. And that is not the end of the story—many individuals spend a lot of valuable time figuring out ways to change their behaviour so as to reduce the taxes they owe. Although there is never any way to avoid the cost of a tax system completely, there are ways to reduce compliance costs to society. One way is to switch to a more simplified tax system. To understand this issue, you need to know more about government and the public sector.

Did You Know That... the average Canadian works from January 1 through June 24 each year to pay for all municipal, provincial, and federal taxes? The average Vancouver resident works approximately one week longer to pay for all of the taxes owed each year. Looked at another way, the average Canadian in a typical eight-hour day works about 3 hours and 50 minutes to pay for government at all levels. The average household with two or more people spends about $26,000 a year in taxes of all kinds. The total amount paid exceeds $270 billion. It would take more than 270,000 millionaires to have as much money as is spent each year by government. So we cannot ignore the presence of government in our society. Government exists, at a minimum, to take care of what the price system does not do well.

WHAT A PRICE SYSTEM CAN AND CANNOT DO

Throughout the book so far, we have alluded to the benefits of a price system. High on that list of benefits is economic efficiency. In its most ideal form, a price system allows resources to move from lower-valued uses to higher-valued uses through voluntary exchange. The supreme point of economic efficiency occurs when all mutually advantageous trades have taken place. In a price system, consumers are sovereign; that is to say, they have the individual freedom to decide what they wish to purchase. Politicians and even business managers do not ultimately decide what is produced; consumers decide. Some supporters of the price system argue that this is its most important characteristic. A market organization of economic activity generally prevents one person from interfering with another in respect to most of that individual's activities. Competition among sellers protects consumers from coercion by one seller, and sellers are protected from coercion by one consumer because other consumers are available.

Sometimes the price system does not generate these results, with too few or too many resources going to specific economic activities. Such situations are called **market failures**. Market failures prevent the price system from attaining economic efficiency and individual freedom, as well as other social goals. Market failures offer one of the strongest arguments in favour of certain economic functions of government, which we now examine.

▶ **Market failure**

A situation in which an unrestrained market economy leads to too few or too many resources going to a specific economic activity.

CORRECTING FOR EXTERNALITIES

In a pure market system, competition generates economic efficiency only when individuals know the true opportunity cost of their actions. In some circumstances, the price that someone actually pays for a resource, good, or service is higher or lower than the opportunity cost that all of society pays for that same resource, good, or service.

Consider a hypothetical world in which there is no government regulation against pollution. You are living in a town that until now has had clean air. A steel

▶ **Externality**

A consequence of an economic activity that spills over to affect third parties. Pollution is an externality.

▶ **Third parties**

Parties who are not directly involved in a given activity or transaction.

mill moves into town. It produces steel and has paid for the inputs—land, labour, capital, and entrepreneurship. The price it charges for the steel reflects, in this example, only the costs that the steel mill incurred. In the course of production, however, the mill gets one input—clean air—by simply taking it. This is indeed an input because in the making of steel, the furnaces emit smoke. The steel mill doesn't have to pay the cost of using the clean air; rather, it is the people in the community who pay that cost in the form of dirtier clothes, dirtier cars and houses, and more respiratory illnesses. The effect is similar to what would happen if the steel mill could take coal or oil or workers' services free. There has been an **externality**, an external cost. Some of the costs associated with the production of the steel have "spilled over" to affect **third parties**, parties other than the buyer and the seller of the steel.

External Costs in Graphical Form

Look at part (a) in Figure 5.1. Here we show the demand curve for steel to be D. The supply curve is S_1. The supply curve includes only the costs that the firms have to pay. The equilibrium, or market clearing, situation will occur at quantity Q_1. Let us take into account the fact that there are externalities—the external costs that you and your neighbours pay in the form of dirtier clothes, cars, and houses, and

Figure 5.1
External Costs and Benefits

In part (a), we show a situation in which the production of steel generates external costs. If the steel mills ignore pollution, at equilibrium the quantity of steel will be Q_1. If the mills had to pay for the additional cost borne by nearby residents that is caused by the steel mill's production, the supply curve would shift inward to the left to S_2. If consumers were forced to pay a price that reflected the spillover costs, the quantity demanded would fall to Q_2. In part (b), we show the situation in which vaccinations against influenza generate external benefits to those individuals who may not be vaccinated but who will benefit because epidemics will not occur. If each individual ignores the external benefit of the flu shot, the market clearing quantity will be Q_1. If external benefits are taken into account by purchasers of flu shots, however, the demand curve would shift rightward to D_2. The new equilibrium quantity would be Q_2 and the price would be higher, P_2.

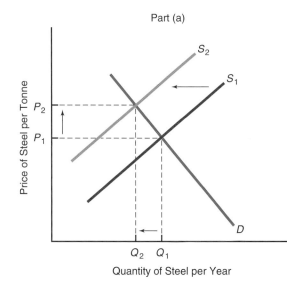

Part (a)

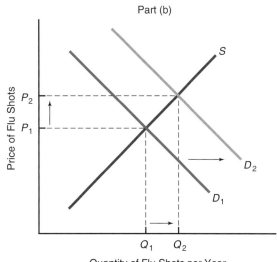

Part (b)

increased respiratory disease due to the air pollution from the steel mill; we also assume that all other suppliers of steel use clean air without having to pay for it. Let's include these external costs in our graph to find out what the full cost of steel production really is. This is equivalent to saying that the price of an input used in steel production increased. Recall from Chapter 3 that an increase in input prices shifts the supply curve inward to the left. Thus in part (a) of the figure, the supply curve shifts from S_1 to S_2. If the external costs were somehow taken into account, the equilibrium quantity would fall to Q_2 and the price would rise to P_2. Otherwise, that price is implicitly being paid, but by two different groups of people. The lower price, P_1, is being explicitly paid for by the purchasers of steel and steel products. The difference between P_2 and P_1 represents the cost that third parties are bearing in the form of dirtier clothes, houses, and cars, and increased respiratory illnesses.

External Benefits in Graphical Form

Externalities can also be positive. To demonstrate external benefits in graphical form, we will use the example of vaccinations against influenza. In part (b) of Figure 5.1, we show the demand curve as D_1 (without taking account of any external benefits) and the supply curve as S. The equilibrium price is P_1, and the equilibrium quantity is Q_1. We assume, however, that flu shots generate external benefits to individuals who may not be vaccinated but will benefit nevertheless because epidemics will not break out. If such external benefits were taken into account, the demand curve would shift outward from D_1 to D_2. The new equilibrium quantity would be Q_2, and the new equilibrium price would be P_2. With no corrective action, this society is not devoting enough resources to flu shots.

When there are external costs, the market will tend to overallocate resources to the production of the good or service in question, for those goods or services will be deceptively low-priced. With the example of steel, too much will be produced because the steel mill owners and managers are not required to take account of the external cost that steel production is imposing on the rest of society. In essence, the full cost of production is unknown to the owners and managers, so the price they charge the public for steel is lower than it would be otherwise. And of course, the lower price means that buyers are willing and able to buy more. More steel is produced and consumed than is socially optimal.

When there are external benefits, the market underallocates resources to the production of that good or service because the good or service is relatively too expensive (because the demand is relatively too low). In a market system, too many of the goods that generate external costs are produced and too few of the goods that generate external benefits are produced.

How the Government Corrects Negative Externalities

The government can in theory correct externality situations in a variety of ways in all cases that warrant such action. In the case of negative externalities, at least two avenues are open to the government: special taxes and legislative regulation or prohibition.

Special Taxes. In our example of the steel mill, the externality problem originates from the fact that the air as a waste disposal place is costless to the firm but not to society. The government could make the steel mill pay a tax for dumping its pollutants into the air. The government could attempt to tax the steel mill commensurate with the cost to third parties from smoke in the air. This, in effect, would be a pollution tax, or an **effluent fee**. The ultimate effect would be to reduce the supply of steel and raise the price to consumers, ideally making the price equal to the full cost of production to society.

> ▶ **Effluent fee**
> A charge to a polluter that gives the right to discharge into the air or water a certain amount of pollution. Also called a pollution tax.

Regulation. To correct a negative externality arising from steel production, the government could specify a maximum allowable rate of pollution. This action would require that the steel mill install pollution abatement equipment within its facilities, that it reduce its rate of output, or some combination of the two. Note that the government's job would not be that simple, for it still would have to determine the level of pollution and then actually measure its output from steel production in order to enforce such regulation.

How the Government Corrects Positive Externalities

What can the government do when the production of one good spills benefits over to third parties? It has several policy options: financing the production of the good or producing the good itself, subsidies (negative taxes), and regulation.

Government Financing and Production. If the positive externalities seem extremely large, the government has the option of financing the desired additional production facilities so that the "right" amount of the good will be produced. Consider again vaccinations against communicable diseases. The government frequently finances campaigns to vaccinate the population. It even operates centres where such vaccinations are free.

Subsidies. A subsidy is a negative tax; it is a payment made either to a business or to a consumer when the business produces, or the consumer buys, a good or a service. In the case of vaccinations against influenza, the government could subsidize everyone who obtains a flu shot by directly reimbursing those vaccinated or by making payments to doctors who provide the shots. If you are attending a university or college, taxpayers are helping to pay the cost of providing your education; you are being subsidized by as much as 80 percent of the total cost. Subsidies reduce the net price to consumers, thereby causing a larger quantity to be demanded.

Regulation. In some cases involving positive externalities, the government can require by law that a certain action be undertaken by individuals in the society. For example, regulations require that all school-aged children be vaccinated before entering public and private schools. Some people believe that a basic school education itself generates positive externalities. Perhaps as a result of this belief, we have regulations—laws—that require all school-aged children to be enrolled in a public or private school.

Concepts in Brief

- External costs lead to an overallocation of resources to the specific economic activity. Two possible ways of correcting these spillovers are taxation and regulation.
- External benefits result in an underallocation of resources to the specific activity. Three possible government corrections are financing the production of the activity, subsidizing private firms or consumers to engage in the activity, and regulation.

THE OTHER ECONOMIC FUNCTIONS OF GOVERNMENT

Besides compensating for externalities, the government performs many other functions that affect the way in which exchange is carried out in the economy. In contrast, the political functions of government have to do with deciding how income should be redistributed among households, and selecting which goods and services have special merits and should therefore be treated differently. The economic and political functions of government can and do overlap.

Let's look at four more economic functions of government.

Providing a Legal System

The courts and the police may not at first seem like economic functions of government (although judges and police personnel must be paid). Their activities nonetheless have important consequences on economic activities in any country. You and I enter into contracts constantly, whether they be oral or written, expressed, or implied. When we believe that we have been wronged, we seek redress of our grievances within our legal institutions. Moreover, consider the legal system that is necessary for the smooth functioning of our system. Our system has defined quite explicitly the legal status of businesses, the rights of private ownership, and a method for the enforcement of contracts. All relationships among consumers and businesses are governed by the legal rules of the game. We might consider the government in its judicial function, then, as the referee when there are disputes in the economic arena.

▶ **Property rights**
The rights of an owner to use and to exchange property.

Much of our legal system is involved with defining and protecting **property rights**. Property rights are the rights of an owner to use and to exchange that property. One might say that property rights are really the rules of our economic game. When property rights are well defined, owners of property have an incentive to use the property efficiently. Any mistakes in their decision about the use of property have negative consequences that the owners suffer. Furthermore, when property rights are well defined, owners of property have an incentive to maintain that property so that if those owners ever desire to sell it, it will fetch a better price.

Establishing and maintaining a well-functioning legal system is not a costless activity, as you can see in the following example.

INTERNATIONAL POLICY EXAMPLE
Who Should Pay the High Cost of a Legal System?

When a huge multinational gets into a lengthy and expensive "shouting match" with its detractors, the public ends up footing part of the legal bill. McDonald's operates worldwide, with annual sales of about $50 billion. It has property rights in the goodwill associated with its name. When two unemployed British social activists published a pamphlet with such chapter headings as "McDollar, McGreedy, McCancer, McMurder, McRipoff, McTorture, and McGarbage," McDonald's was not pleased. The pamphlet accused the American company of torturing animals, corrupting children, and exploiting the Third World. So McDonald's went to court in London. When the case began, there were 26 preliminary hearings spread over a four-year time period, and when it went to trial, 180 witnesses were called. McDonald's itself will end up spending many millions of dollars, but British taxpayers will foot the entire bill for the use of the court system. According to the Lord Chancellor's Department, British taxpayers will pay at least £2.5 million (well over $5.5 million).

Should taxpayers continue to pay for all of the court system? No, according to policymakers in Britain. They have a plan to make litigants pay the full cost of court services, specifically judges' salaries. Such a system that forces litigants to pay for the full opportunity cost of the legal system has yet to be instituted in Canada or elsewhere.

For critical analysis: What other costs, besides judges' salaries, do citizens implicitly pay for in their legal system?

Promoting Competition

▶ **Anticombines legislation**
Laws that restrict the formation of monopolies and regulate certain anti-competitive business practices.

▶ **Monopoly**
A firm that has great control over the price of a good. In the extreme case, a monopoly is the only seller of a good or service.

Many people believe that the only way to attain economic efficiency is through competition. One of the roles of government is to serve as the protector of a competitive economic system. The federal and provincial governments have passed **anticombines legislation**. Such legislation makes illegal certain (but not all) economic activities that might, in legal terms, restrain trade—that is, prevent free competition among actual and potential rival firms in the marketplace. The avowed aim of anticombines legislation is to reduce the power of **monopolies**—firms that have great control over the price of the goods they sell. A number of laws have been passed that prohibit specific anti-competitive business behaviour. The Competition Bureau, which is part of Industry Canada, attempts to enforce these anticombines laws. Various provincial judicial agencies also expend efforts at maintaining competition.

Providing Public Goods

The goods used in our examples up to this point have been **private goods**. When I eat a cheeseburger, you cannot eat the same one. So you and I are rivals for that cheeseburger, just as much as rivals for the title of world champion are. When I use a CD player, you cannot use the same player. When I use the services of an auto mechanic, that person cannot work at the same time for you. That is the distinguishing feature of private goods—their use is exclusive to the people who purchase or rent them. The **principle of rival consumption** applies to all private goods by definition. Rival consumption is easy to understand. With private goods, either you use them or I use them.

There is an entire class of goods that are not private goods. These are called **public goods**. The principle of rival consumption does not apply to them. That is, they can be consumed jointly by many individuals simultaneously. Military defence, police protection, and the legal system, for example, are public goods. If you partake of them, you do not necessarily take away from anyone else's share of those goods.

Characteristics of Public Goods.   Several distinguishing characteristics of public goods set them apart from all other goods.[1]

1. **Public goods are often indivisible.** You can't buy or sell $5 worth of the army's ability to protect you from foreign invasion. Public goods cannot usually be produced or sold very easily in small units.
2. **Public goods can be used by more and more people at no additional cost.** Once money has been spent on the armed forces, the defence protection you receive does not reduce the amount of protection bestowed on anyone else. The opportunity cost of your receiving military protection once it is in place is zero.
3. **Additional users of public goods do not deprive others of any of the services of the goods.** If you turn on your television set, your neighbours don't get weaker reception because of your action.
4. **It is difficult to design a collection system for a public good on the basis of how much individuals use it.** It is nearly impossible to determine how much any person uses or values defence. No one can be denied the benefits of military protection for failing to pay for that public good. This is often called the **exclusion principle**.

One of the problems of public goods is that the private sector has a difficult, if not impossible, time in providing them. There is little or no incentive for individuals in the private sector to offer public goods because it is so difficult to make a profit in so doing. Consequently, a true public good must necessarily be provided by government.

---

[1] Sometimes the distinction is made between pure public goods, which have all the characteristics we have described here, and quasi- or near-public goods, which do not. The major feature of near-public goods is that they are jointly consumed, even though nonpaying customers can be, and often are, excluded—for example, movies, football games, and concerts.

INTERNATIONAL EXAMPLE
Are Lighthouses a Public Good?

 One of the most common examples of a public good is a lighthouse. Arguably, it satisfies all the criteria listed in points 1 through 4. In one instance, however, a lighthouse was not a public good in that a collection system was devised and enforced on the basis of how much individuals used it. In the thirteenth century, the city of Aigues-Mortes, a port in southern France, erected a tower, called the King's Tower, designed to assert the will and power of Louis IX (Saint Louis). The 32 metre high tower served as a lighthouse for ships. More importantly, it served as a lookout so that ships sailing on the open sea, but in its view, did not escape paying for use of the lighthouse. Those payments were then used for the construction of the city walls.

For critical analysis: Explain how a lighthouse satisfies the characteristics of public goods described in points 1, 2, and 3.

▶**Free-rider problem**
A problem that arises when individuals presume that others will pay for public goods so that, individually, they can escape paying for their portion without causing a reduction in production.

Free Riders. The nature of public goods leads to the **free-rider problem**, a situation in which some individuals take advantage of the fact that others will shoulder the burden of paying for public goods such as defence. Free riders will argue that they receive no value from such government services as defence and therefore really should not pay for it. Suppose that citizens were taxed directly in proportion to how much they tell an interviewer that they value military protection. Some people will probably say that they are unwilling to pay for it because they don't want any—it is of no value to them. Many of us may end up being free riders when we assume that others will pay for the desired public good. We may all want to be free riders if we believe that someone else will provide the commodity in question that we actually value.

The free-rider problem is a definite issue among nations with respect to the international burden of defence and how it should be shared. A country may choose to belong to a multilateral defence organization, such as the North Atlantic Treaty Organization (NATO), but then consistently attempt not to contribute funds to the organization. The nation knows it would be defended by others in NATO if it were attacked, but would rather not pay for such defence. In short, it seeks a "free ride."

Ensuring Economywide Stability

The government attempts to stabilize the economy by smoothing out the ups and downs in overall business activity. Our economy sometimes faces the problems of unemployment and oscillating prices. The government, especially the federal government, has made an attempt to solve these problems by trying to stabilize the economy. The notion that the federal government should undertake actions to stabilize business activity is a relatively new idea in Canada, encouraged by high unemployment rates during the Great Depression of the 1930s and subsequent theories about possible ways by which government could reduce unemployment. In 1945, the government formally assumed responsibility for economic performance. It established three goals for government accountability: full employment, price stability, and economic growth. These goals have provided the justification for many government economic programs during the post–World War II period.

Concepts in Brief

- The economic activities of government include (1) correcting for externalities, (2) providing a judicial system, (3) promoting competition, (4) producing public goods, and (5) ensuring economywide stability.
- Public goods can be consumed jointly. The principle of rival consumption does not apply as it does with private goods.
- Public goods have the following characteristics: (1) They are indivisible; (2) once they are produced, there is no opportunity cost when additional consumers use them; (3) your use of a public good does not deprive others of its simultaneous use; and (4) consumers cannot conveniently be charged on the basis of use.

THE POLITICAL FUNCTIONS OF GOVERNMENT

At least two areas of government are in the realm of political, or normative, functions rather than that of the economic ones discussed in the first part of this chapter. These two areas are (1) the regulation and/or provision of merit and demerit goods, and (2) income redistribution.

Merit and Demerit Goods

▶ **Merit good**
A good that has been deemed socially desirable through the political process. Museums are an example.

Certain goods are considered to have special merit. A **merit good** is defined as any good that the political process has deemed socially desirable. (Note that nothing inherent in any particular good makes it a merit good. It is a matter of who chooses.) Some examples of merit goods in our society are museums, ballets, and concerts. In these areas, the government's role is the provision of merit goods to the people in society who would not otherwise purchase them at market clearing prices or who would not purchase an amount of them judged to be sufficient. This provision may take the form of government production and distribution of merit goods. It can also take the form of reimbursement for payment on merit goods or subsidies to producers or consumers for part of the cost of merit goods. Governments do indeed subsidize such merit goods as concerts, ballets, and museums. In most cases, such merit goods would rarely be so numerous without subsidization.

▶ **Demerit good**
A good that has been deemed socially undesirable through the political process. Cigarettes are an example.

    Demerit goods are the opposite of merit goods. They are goods that, through the political process, are deemed socially undesirable. Cigarettes, gambling, and illegal drugs are examples. The government exercises its role in the area of demerit goods by taxing, regulating, or prohibiting their manufacture, sale, and use. Governments justify the relatively high taxes on alcohol and tobacco by declaring them demerit goods. The best-known example of governmental exercise of power in this area is the stance against certain psychoactive drugs. Most psychoactives (except nicotine, caffeine, and alcohol) are either expressly prohibited, as is the case for heroin, cocaine, and opium, or heavily regulated, as in the case of prescription psychoactives.

Income Redistribution

Another relatively recent political function of government has been the explicit redistribution of income. This redistribution uses two systems: the progressive income tax (described later in this chapter) and **transfer payments**. Transfer payments are payments made to individuals for which no services or goods are concurrently rendered in return. The three key money transfer payments in our system are welfare, old age security payments, and employment insurance benefits. Income redistribution also includes a large amount of income **transfers in kind**, as opposed to money transfers. Two income transfers in kind are health care and low-cost public housing.

The government has also engaged in other activities as a form of redistribution of income. For example, the provision of public education is at least in part an attempt to redistribute income by making sure that the very poor have access to education.

▶ **Transfer payments**
Money payments made by governments to individuals for which no services or goods are concurrently rendered in return. Examples are welfare, old age security payments, and Employment Insurance benefits.

▶ **Transfers in kind**
Payments that are in the form of actual goods and services, such as public education, low-cost public housing, and health care, and for which no goods or services are rendered concurrently in return.

EXAMPLE Education Transfer Payments

The federal government has recently increased its transfers in kind to postsecondary students. The 1998 budget contained a number of incentives to encourage more Canadians to continue their education following secondary school. For example, the government is making available 25,000 Canada Study Grants of $3,000 each for needy students with dependants. In addition, the education credit and child care expense deductions for income tax are extended to part-time as well as full-time students.

The federal government is also providing annual Canada Education Savings Grants of 20 percent of the first $2,000 in contributions to your registered education savings plan. You are also now able to make tax-free withdrawals from your RRSP of up to $10,000 per year to a maximum of $20,000 over four years. However, withdrawals must be paid back within 10 years.

Finally, the government has made a number of improvements to the Canada Student Loan program. For example, interest on student loans is now tax deductible. And for students who have problems repaying their student loans, the government provides up to 30 months of interest relief following graduation.

For critical analysis: Why might a tax deduction for post-secondary education expenses be more beneficial to society than an equivalent dollar tax deduction for home mortgage expenses?

Concepts in Brief

- Political, or normative, activities of the government include the provision and regulation of merit and demerit goods and income redistribution.
- Merit and demerit goods do not have any inherent characteristics that qualify them as such; rather, collectively, through the political process, we make judgments about which goods and services are "good" for society and which are "bad."
- Income redistribution can be carried out by a system of progressive taxation, coupled with transfer payments, which can be made in money or in kind, such as health care and public education.

COLLECTIVE DECISION MAKING: THE THEORY OF PUBLIC CHOICE

The public sector has a vast influence on the Canadian economy. Yet the economic model used until now has applied only to the behaviour of the private sector—firms and households. Such a model does not adequately explain the behaviour of the public sector. We shall attempt to do so now.

Governments consist of individuals. No government actually thinks and acts; rather, government actions are the result of decision making by individuals in their roles as elected representatives, appointed officials, and salaried bureaucrats. Therefore, to understand how government works, we must examine the incentives for the people in government as well as those who would like to be in government—avowed candidates or would-be candidates for elected or appointed positions—and special-interest lobbyists attempting to get government to do something. At issue is the analysis of **collective decision making**. Collective decision making involves the actions of voters, politicians, political parties, interest groups, and many other groups and individuals. The analysis of collective decision making is usually called the **theory of public choice**. It has been given this name because it involves hypotheses about how choices are made in the public sector, as opposed to the private sector. The foundation of public-choice theory is the assumption that individuals will act within the political process to maximize their individual (not collective) well-being. In that sense, the theory is similar to our analysis of the market economy, in which we also assume that individuals are motivated by self-interest.

To understand public-choice theory, it is necessary to point out other similarities between the private market sector and the public, or government, sector; then we will look at the differences.

▶ **Collective decision making**
How voters, politicians, and other interested parties act and how these actions influence nonmarket decisions.

▶ **Theory of public choice**
The study of collective decision making.

Similarities in Market and Public-Sector Decision Making

In addition to the similar assumption of self-interest being the motivating force in both sectors, there are other similarities.

Scarcity. At any given moment, the amount of resources is fixed. This means that for the private and the public sectors combined, there is a scarcity constraint. Everything that is spent by all levels of government, plus everything that is spent by the private sector, must add up to the total income available at any point in time. Hence every government action has an opportunity cost, just as in the market sector.

Competition. Although we typically think of competition as a private market phenomenon, it is also present in collective action. Given the scarcity constraint government also faces, bureaucrats, appointed officials, and elected representatives will always be in competition for available government funds. Furthermore, the individuals within any government agency or institution will act as individuals do in the private sector: They will try to obtain higher wages, better working conditions, and higher job-level classifications. They will compete and act in their own, not society's, interest.

Similarity of Individuals. Contrary to popular belief, there are not two types of individuals, those who work in the private sector and those who work in the public sector; rather, individuals working in similar positions can be considered similar. The difference, as we shall see, is that the individuals in government face a different **incentive structure** than those in the private sector. For example, the costs and benefits of being efficient or inefficient differ when one goes from the private to the public sector.

▶ **Incentive structure**
The system of rewards and punishments individuals face with respect to their own actions.

One approach to predicting government bureaucratic behaviour is to ask what incentives bureaucrats face. Take Canada Post as an example. The bureaucrats running that Crown Corporation are human beings with qualities similar to those possessed by workers in comparable positions at, say, Northern Telecom or Canadian Airlines. Yet the Post Office does not function like either of these companies. The difference can be explained, at least in part, in terms of the incentives provided for managers in the two types of institutions. When the bureaucratic managers and workers at Northern Telecom make incorrect decisions, work slowly, produce shoddy products, and are generally "inefficient," the profitability of the company declines. The owners—millions of shareholders—express their displeasure by selling some of their shares of company stock. The market value, as tracked on the stock exchange, falls. But what about Canada Post? If a manager, a worker, or a bureaucrat in the Post Office gives shoddy service, there is no straightforward mechanism by which the organization's owners—the taxpayers—can express their dissatisfaction. Despite the Post Office's status as a "government corporation," taxpayers as shareholders do not really own shares of stock in the organization that they can sell.

The key, then, to understanding purported inefficiency in the government bureaucracy is not found in an examination of people and personalities but rather in an examination of incentives and institutional arrangements.

Differences Between Market and Collective Decision Making

There are probably more dissimilarities between the market sector and the public sector than there are similarities.

Government Goods at Zero Price. The majority of goods that governments produce are furnished to the ultimate consumers without direct money charge. **Government, or political, goods** can be either private goods or public goods. The fact that they are furnished to the ultimate consumer free of charge does not mean that the cost to society of those goods is zero, however; it only means that the price charged is zero. The full opportunity cost to society is the value of the resources used in the production of goods produced and provided by the government.

> ▶ **Government, or political, goods**
> Goods (and services) provided by the public sector; they can be either private or public goods.

For example, none of us pays directly for each unit of consumption of most highways nor for police protection. Rather, we pay for all these things indirectly through the taxes that support our governments—federal, provincial, and municipal. This special feature of government can be looked at in a different way. There is no longer a one-to-one relationship between the consumption of a government-provided good and the payment for that good. Consumers who pay taxes collectively pay for every political good, but the individual consumer may not be able to see the relationship between the taxes paid and the consumption of the good. Indeed, most taxpayers will find that their tax bill is the same whether or not they consume, or even like, government-provided goods.

Use of Force. All governments are able to engage in the legal use of force in their regulation of economic affairs. For example, governments can exercise the use of expropriation, which means that if you refuse to pay your taxes, your bank account and other assets may be seized by Revenue Canada. In fact, you have no choice in the matter of paying taxes to governments. Collectively, we decide the total size of government through the political process, but individually we cannot determine how much service we pay for just for ourselves during any one year.

> **Try Preview Question 1:**
> What problems will you encounter if you refuse to pay a portion of your income tax because you oppose spending on military defence?

Voting Versus Spending. In the private market sector, a dollar voting system is in effect. This dollar voting system is not equivalent to the voting system in the public sector. There are, at minimum, three differences:

1. In a political system, one person gets one vote, whereas in the market system, the dollars one spends count as votes.
2. The political system is run by **majority rule**, whereas the market system is run by **proportional rule**.
3. The spending of dollars can indicate intensity of want, whereas because of the all-or-nothing nature of political voting, a vote cannot.

> ▶ **Majority rule**
> A collective decision-making system in which group decisions are made on the basis of 50.1 percent of the vote. In other words, whatever more than half of the electorate votes for, the entire electorate has to accept.

> ▶ **Proportional rule**
> A decision-making system in which actions are based on the proportion of the "votes" cast and are in proportion to them. In a market system, if 10 percent of the "dollar votes" are cast for blue cars, 10 percent of the output will be blue cars.

Ultimately, the main distinction between political votes and dollar votes here is that political outcomes may differ from economic outcomes. Remember that economic efficiency is a situation in which, given the prevailing distribution of income, consumers get the economic goods they want. There is no corresponding situation using political voting. Thus we can never assume that a political voting process will lead to the same decisions that a dollar voting process will lead to in the marketplace.

Indeed, consider the dilemma every voter faces. Usually a voter is not asked to decide on a single issue (although this happens); rather, a voter is asked to choose among candidates who present a large number of issues and state a position on each of them. Just consider the average Member of Parliament who has to vote on hundreds of different issues during a five-year term. When you vote for that representative, you are voting for a person who must make hundreds of decisions during the next five years.

> **Try Preview Question 2:**
> What is the essence of the public-choice model?

The Role of Bureaucrats

▶ **Bureaucrats**
Nonelected government officials who are responsible for the day-to-day operation of government and the observance of its regulations and laws.

▶ **Bureaucracy**
An administrative system run by a large staff following rules and procedures set down by government.

Government programs require people to deliver them. This is manifested today in the form of well-established bureaucracies, in which **bureaucrats** (nonelected officials) work. **Bureaucracies** can exert great influence on matters concerning themselves—the amount of funding granted them and the activities in which they engage. In the political marketplace, well-organized bureaucracies can even influence the expression of public demand itself. In many cases, they organize the clientele (interest groups), coach that clientele on what is appropriate, and stick up for the "rights" of the clientele.

Gauging Bureaucratic Performance

It is tempting, but incorrect, to think of bureaucrats as mere "technocrats," executors of orders and channels of information, in this process. They have at least two incentives to make government programs larger and more resistant to attack than we might otherwise expect. First, society has decided that, in general, government should not be run on a profit-making basis. Measures of performance other than bottom-line profits must be devised. In the private market, successful firms typically expand to serve more customers; although this growth is often incidental to the underlying profitability, the two frequently go hand in hand. In parallel, performance in government is often measured by the number of clients served, and rewards are distributed accordingly. As a result, bureaucrats have an incentive to expand the size of their clientele—not because it is more profitable (beneficial) to society but because that is how bureaucrats' rewards are structured.

In general, performance measures that are not based on long-run profitability are less effective at gauging true performance. This makes it potentially easier for the government bureaucrat to appear to perform well, collect rewards for measured performance, and then leave for greener pastures. To avoid this, a much larger proportion of the rewards given bureaucrats are valuable only as long as they continue being bureaucrats—large staffs, expensive offices, generous pensions, and the like. Instead of getting large current salaries (which can be saved for a rainy day), they get rewards that disappear if their jobs disappear. Naturally, this increases the incentives of bureaucrats to make sure that their jobs don't disappear.

The federal government found recently that non-salary rewards were not sufficient to keep its top bureaucrats in the public service. More and more government executives were being lured away to the private sector with its promise of higher salaries. In 1996 alone, at least six deputy ministers and assistant deputy ministers left for private sector jobs. The government responded early in 1998 with salary increases that ranged from 4 to 19 percent, and implemented a bonus plan for performance that would take salaries even higher. The great majority of public servants were not impressed: they have had a single 3 percent raise between 1991 and 1998 and were not expecting great increases in the foreseeable future.

Rational Ignorance

At this point you may well be wondering why this system still goes on. The answer lies in rational ignorance on the part of voters, ignorance that is carefully cultivated by the members of special interest groups.

On most issues, there is little incentive for the individual voter to expend resources to determine how to vote. Moreover, the ordinary course of living provides most of us with enough knowledge to decide whether we should invest in learning more about a given issue. For example, suppose that Canadian voters were asked to decide if the sign marking the entrance to an obscure national park should be enlarged. Most voters would decide that the potential costs and benefits of this decision are negligible: The new sign is unlikely to be the size of Prince Edward Island, and anybody who has even heard of the national park in question probably already has a pretty good idea of its location. Thus most voters would choose to remain rationally ignorant about the exact costs and benefits of enlarging the sign, implying that (1) many will choose not to vote at all and (2) those who do vote will simply flip a coin or cast their ballot based on some other, perhaps ideological, grounds.

Why Be Rationally Ignorant?   For most political decisions, majority rule prevails. Only a coalition of voters representing slightly more than 50 percent of those who vote is needed. Whenever a vote is taken, the result is going to involve costs and benefits. Voters, then, must evaluate their share of the costs and benefits of any budgetary expenditure. Voters, however, are not perfectly informed. That is one of the crucial characteristics of the real world—information is a resource that is costly to obtain. Rational voters will, in fact, decide to remain at some level of ignorance about government programs because the benefits from obtaining more information may not be worth the cost, given each individual voter's extremely limited impact on the outcome of an election. For the same reason, voters will fail to inform themselves about taxes or other revenue sources to pay for proposed expenditures because they know that for any specific expenditure program, the cost to them individually will be small. At this point it might be useful to contrast this situation with what exists in the nonpolitical private market sector of the economy. In the private market sector, the individual chooses a mix of purchases and bears fully the direct and indirect consequences of this selection (ignoring for the moment the problem of externalities).

PAYING FOR THE PUBLIC SECTOR

Jean-Baptiste Colbert, the seventeenth-century French finance minister, said the art of taxation was in "plucking the goose so as to obtain the largest amount of feathers with the least possible amount of hissing." In Canada, governments have designed a variety of methods of plucking the private-sector goose. To analyse any tax system, we must first understand the distinction between marginal tax rates and average tax rates.

Marginal and Average Tax Rates

If somebody says, "I pay 28 percent in taxes," you cannot really tell what that person means unless you know whether the individual is referring to average taxes paid or

▶ **Marginal tax rate**
The change in the tax payment divided by the change in income, or the percentage of additional dollars that must be paid in taxes. The marginal tax rate is applied to the highest tax bracket of taxable income reached.

▶ **Tax bracket**
A specified interval of income to which a specific and unique marginal tax rate is applied.

▶ **Average tax rate**
The total tax payment divided by total income. It is the proportion of total income paid in taxes.

the tax rate on the last dollars earned. The latter concept has to do with the **marginal tax rate**.[2]

The marginal tax rate is expressed as follows:

$$\text{Marginal tax rate} = \frac{\text{change in taxes due}}{\text{change in taxable income}}$$

It is important to understand that the marginal tax rate applies only to the income in the highest **tax bracket** reached, where a tax bracket is defined as a specified level of taxable income to which a specific and unique marginal tax rate is applied.

The **average tax rate** is not the same thing as the marginal tax rate, which is defined as follows:

$$\text{Average tax rate} = \frac{\text{total taxes due}}{\text{total taxable income}}$$

Taxation Systems

No matter how governments raise revenues—from income taxes, sales taxes, or other taxes—all of those taxes can fit into one of three types of taxation systems—proportional, progressive, and regressive, expressing a relationship between the percentage tax, or tax rate, paid and income. To determine whether a tax system is proportional, progressive, or regressive, we simply ask the question, What is the relationship between the average tax rate and the marginal tax rate?

▶ **Proportional taxation**
A tax system in which regardless of an individual's income, the tax bill comprises exactly the same proportion. Also called a flat-rate tax.

Proportional Taxation.   **Proportional taxation** means that regardless of an individual's income, the taxes comprise exactly the same proportion. In terms of marginal versus average tax rates, in a proportional taxation system, the marginal tax rate is always equal to the average tax rate. If every dollar is taxed at 20 percent, then the average tax rate is 20 percent, as is the marginal tax rate.

A proportional tax system is also called a flat-rate tax. Taxpayers at all income levels end up paying the same percentage of their income in taxes. If the proportional tax rate were 20 percent, an individual with an income of $10,000 would pay $2,000 in taxes, while an individual making $100,000 would pay $20,000, the identical 20 percent rate being levied on both.

▶ **Progressive taxation**
A tax system in which as income increases, a higher percentage of the additional income is taxed. The marginal tax rate exceeds the average tax rate as income rises.

Progressive Taxation.   Under **progressive taxation**, as a person's taxable income increases, the percentage of income paid in taxes also increases. In terms of marginal versus average tax rates, in a progressive system, the marginal tax rate is above the average tax rate. If you are taxed 5 percent on the first $10,000 you make, 10 percent on the next $10,000 you make, and 30 percent on the last $10,000 you make, you face a progressive income tax system. Your marginal tax rate is always above your average tax rate.

---

[2] The word *marginal* means "incremental" (or "decremental") here.

INTERNATIONAL EXAMPLE
Marginal Tax Rates Around the World

Table 5.1
Marginal Tax Rates in the Industrialized World, 1994

	Combined Marginal Tax Rate (%) for an Average Production Worker	Marginal Tax Rate (%) for Highest Income Bracket
Australia	35.4	48.4
Canada	49.3	48.1
France	55.3	59.2
Germany	53.4	53.0
Italy	37.0	51.0
Japan	40.8	61.0
New Zealand	33.0	33.0
United Kingdom	35.0	40.0
United States	27.1	44.1

Source: Canadian Tax Foundation

Canadians frequently complain that we pay too much income tax, especially when compared to the United States. While we do pay almost twice what Americans pay in personal income tax, we are not the most highly taxed people in the world.

The Organisation for Economic Co-operation and Development surveyed tax rates in the industrialized world. Table 5.1 shows marginal tax rates for an average production worker, and for workers in the highest income bracket. For a Canadian production worker making about $32,000 per year, the combined marginal tax rate—income taxes plus contributions to the Canada Pension Plan plus Employment Insurance premiums—is about 49.3 percent. Only France and Germany have higher combined rates. Yet, the simple marginal income tax rate for the highest income bracket is 48.1 percent, one of the lowest.

Canada's personal income tax structure is also less progressive than many other countries'. Workers earning only 1.6 times the average production worker's salary fall into the highest income bracket, while in the United States and Japan a worker does not pay the top marginal rate until income is 9.6 times the average production worker's pay.

For critical analysis: Would you expect to see a relationship between the social services provided in a country and the combined marginal tax rate or the simple marginal tax rate? Why?

▶ **Regressive taxation**
A tax system in which as more dollars are earned, the percentage of tax paid on them falls. The marginal tax rate is less than the average tax rate as income rises.

Try Preview Question 3:
In what ways do regressive, proportional, and progressive tax structures differ?

Regressive Taxation. With **regressive taxation**, a smaller percentage of taxable income is taken in taxes as taxable income increases. The marginal rate is below the average rate. As income increases, the marginal tax rate falls, and so does the average tax rate. The Goods and Services Tax (GST) is regressive. Someone earning $10,000 per year pays the same 7 percent sales tax on a tube of toothpaste as someone earning $100,000 per year. But the tube of toothpaste takes up a much larger proportion of the low income earner's budget, so the marginal tax rate for that person is higher. The federal government tries to address this inequity by giving GST rebates to low income earners who apply for them in their income tax returns each year.

Concepts in Brief

- Marginal tax rates are applied to marginal tax brackets, defined as spreads of income over which the tax rate is constant.
- Tax systems can be proportional, progressive, or regressive, depending on whether the marginal tax rate is the same as, greater than, or less than the average tax rate as income rises.

THE MOST IMPORTANT FEDERAL TAXES

The federal government imposes income taxes on both individuals and corporations, and collects sales taxes as well as a variety of other taxes.

The Federal Personal Income Tax

Table 5.2
Federal Marginal Income Tax Rates

These rates became effective in 1992. Taxpayers also pay a surcharge of 3 percent on taxes payable to $12,500 and an additional 5 percent on taxes payable above $12,500.

Marginal Tax Bracket	Marginal Tax Rate
$0–$29,590	17%
$29,590–$59,180	26%
$59,180 and up	29%

Source: Revenue Canada

The most important tax in the Canadian economy is the federal personal income tax, which accounts for about 50 percent of all federal revenues. All Canadian citizens, resident aliens, and most others who earn income in Canada are required to pay federal income tax on all taxable income. The tax rates that are paid depend on the amount of taxable income earned, as can be seen in Table 5.2. Marginal income tax rates at the federal level have varied from as low as 4 percent after the passage of the Income Tax Act in 1917, to as high as 98 percent during World War II. In 1992, the government reduced the top marginal tax rate and cut the number of income tax brackets to three, but broadened the definition of taxable income. The effect of these changes was to make Canada's tax system less progressive.

Advocates of a more progressive income tax system in Canada argue that such a system redistributes income from the rich to the poor, taxes people according to their ability to pay, and taxes people according to the benefits they receive from government. Although there is much controversy over the "redistributional" nature of our progressive tax system, there is no strong evidence that in fact the tax system has ever done much income redistribution in this country. Currently, about 80 percent of all Canadians, rich or poor, pay roughly the same proportion of their income in federal income tax.

The Treatment of Capital Gains

> ▶ **Capital gain**
> The positive difference between the purchase price and the sale price of an asset. If a share of stock is bought for $5 and then sold for $15, the capital gain is $10.

> ▶ **Capital loss**
> The negative difference between the purchase price and the sale price of an asset.

The difference between the buying and selling price of an asset, such as a share of stock or a plot of land, is called a **capital gain** if it is a profit, and a **capital loss** if it is not. Capital gains are taxed at ordinary income marginal tax rates. The taxable part of a capital gain is 75 percent of the net amount of your capital gains minus your capital losses for the year.

Capital gains are not always real. If in one year you pay $100,000 for a house you plan to rent and sell it for 50 percent more 10 years later, your nominal capital gain is $50,000. But what if, during those 10 years, there had been inflation such that average prices had also gone up by 50 percent? Your real capital gain would be zero. But you still have to pay taxes on that $50,000. To counter this problem, many economists have argued that capital gains should be indexed to the rate of inflation.

The Corporate Income Tax

Corporate income taxes account for about 12 percent of all federal taxes collected, and 3.5 percent of all provincial taxes collected. Corporations are generally taxed at a flat rate of 28 percent on the difference between their total revenues (or receipts) and their expenses.

Double Taxation.   Because individual shareholders must pay taxes on the dividends they receive, paid out of after-tax profits by the corporation, corporate profits are taxed twice. If you receive $1,000 in dividends, you have to declare it as income, and you must pay taxes at your marginal tax rate. Before the corporation was able to pay you those dividends, it had to pay taxes on all its profits, including any that it put back into the company or did not distribute in the form of dividends. Eventually the new investment made possible by those **retained earnings**—profits not given out to shareholders—along with borrowed funds will be reflected in the increased value of the stock in that company. When you sell your shares in that company, you will have to pay taxes on the difference between what you paid for them and what you sold them for. In both cases, dividends and retained earnings (corporate profits) are taxed twice.

> ▶ **Retained earnings**
> Earnings that a corporation saves, or retains, for investment in other productive activities; earnings that are not distributed to stockholders.

Who Really Pays the Corporate Income Tax?   Corporations can exist only as long as consumers buy their products, employees make their goods, shareholders (owners) buy their shares, and bondholders buy their bonds. Corporations *per se* do not do anything. We must ask, then, who really pays the tax on corporate income. This is a question of **tax incidence**. (The question of tax incidence applies to all taxes, includ-

> ▶ **Tax incidence**
> The distribution of tax burdens among various groups in society.

ing sales and payroll taxes.) There remains considerable debate about the incidence of corporate taxation. Some economists say that corporations pass their tax burdens on to consumers by charging higher prices. Other economists believe that it is the shareholders who bear most of the tax. Still others believe that employees pay at least part of the tax by receiving lower wages than they would otherwise. Because the debate is not yet settled, we will not hazard a guess here as to what the correct conclusion should be. Suffice to say that you should be cautious when you advocate increasing corporation income taxes. You may be the one who ends up paying the increase, at least in part, if you own shares in a corporation, buy its products, or work for it.

Try Preview Question 4:

Who pays the corporate income tax?

Concepts in Brief

- Because corporations must first pay an income tax on most earnings, the personal income tax shareholders pay on dividends received (or realized capital gains) constitutes double taxation.
- The corporate income tax is paid by one or more of the following groups: shareholder-owners, consumers of corporate-produced products, and employees in corporations.

Unemployment and Pension Taxes

An increasing percentage of federal revenues is accounted for each year by taxes (other than income taxes) levied on payroll. These payroll taxes are for Canada Pension Plan (CPP) benefits and Employment Insurance (EI).

Employment Insurance is a compulsory federal program which provides income assistance in the event of unemployment. EI premiums are paid by employees, and matched by employers. (The employer's contribution is really paid, at least in part, in the form of a reduced wage paid to employees.) Self-employed people must pay both shares. The maximum personal contribution to EI in 1997 was $1,131. EI premiums become part of the government's general revenues; as of 1997, there was a large surplus in the EI account which helped the government balance the budget for the 1998-99 fiscal year.

Thinking Critically About the Media   Employment Insurance

Countless articles have been written about the problem with the Employment Insurance (EI) system in Canada. They all make reference to the employer and employee "contributions" to the EI fund. One gets the impression that EI premiums paid by employees go into a special government account and that employees do not pay for their employers' "contribution" to this account. Both concepts are not merely flawed but grossly misleading. EI premiums are mixed in with the rest of government taxes collected and spent every year. The "contributions" are not contributions at all; they are merely taxes paid to the federal government. The so-called employer contribution, which matches the employee payments, is not in fact paid for by employers but rather by employees because of the lower wages that they are paid. Anybody who quits a job and becomes self-employed finds this out when the time comes to pay one's self-employment taxes (Employment Insurance "contributions"), which effectively double the payments previously being made as an employee.

In 1997, the CPP premium payable on eligible earnings to $32,300 was 3 percent, with employers contributing an equal share on behalf of the employee. CPP premiums do not form part of the government's general revenue, but are managed separately from the government budget. The CPP is a system in which current workers subsidize already retired workers. With the coming retirement of the post-war "baby boomers," the number of retired people will grow much more rapidly than the number of current workers. In anticipation of increased outlays in pension plan benefits, the combined (employer-employee) premium will rise to 9.9 percent of eligible earnings by the year 2003.

The GST

The Goods and Services Tax (GST) is a sales tax which makes up about 14 percent of federal government revenues. Consumers pay a 7 percent tax on virtually all goods and services they purchase in addition to any applicable provincial sales taxes. The GST is a regressive tax since it taxes consumption at the same rate for both the rich and the poor. The federal government tries to mitigate this, however, by giving a rebate of up to $76 four times a year to low income earners. While consumers must pay GST on imports, Canadian exports are exempt. Visitors to Canada may apply for a rebate of the GST they paid on their Canadian purchases when they leave the country.

Some economists argue that in spite of the regressive nature of sales taxes, a tax like the GST is preferable to an income tax. Income taxes tax all income, whether it is spent or saved. Therefore, they argue, saving is discouraged. However, a sales tax taxes only income that is consumed, and so saving is encouraged. The Issues and Applications section at the end of this chapter revisits the pros and cons of this topic.

SPENDING, GOVERNMENT SIZE, AND TAX RECEIPTS

The size of the public sector can be measured in many different ways. One way is to count the number of public employees. Another is to look at total government outlays. Government outlays include all of its expenditures on employees, rent, electricity, and the like. In addition, total government outlays include transfer payments, such as welfare, Employment Insurance benefits, and old age security payments. In Figure 5.2, you see that government outlays prior to World War I did not exceed 8 percent of annual national income. There was a spike during World War I, a significant increase during the Great Depression, and then a huge spike during World War II. Contrary to previous postwar periods, government outlays as a percentage of total national income did not gradually fall, but rather rose fairly regularly until the mid-1970s. Since then, government expenditures have been around 22.5 percent of gross domestic product.

Figure 5.2

Total Government Outlays over Time

Here you see that total government outlays remained small until the 1930s, except during World War I. Since World War II, government outlays have not fallen back to their historical average.

Sources: Statistics Canada, *Canadian Economic Observer,* and M.C. Urquhart and K.A.H. Buckley, *Historical Statistics of Canada.*

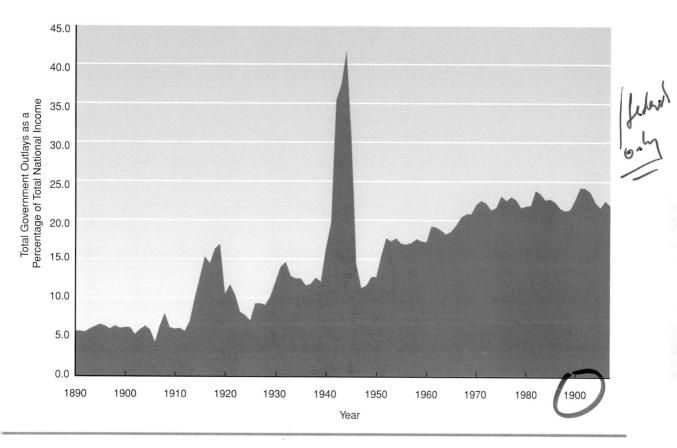

Government Receipts

The main revenue raiser for all levels of government is taxes. We show in the two pie diagrams in Figure 5.3 the percentage of receipts from various taxes obtained by the federal government and by provincial and municipal governments.

The Federal Government.   The largest source of receipts for the federal government is the individual income tax. During the 1997-98 fiscal year, it accounted for 50.3 percent of all federal revenues. After that come Employment Insurance premiums which account for 14.6 percent of total revenues. Next come the GST revenues, corporate income taxes, and a number of other items, such as taxes on imported goods and excise taxes on such things as gasoline and alcoholic beverages.

Provincial and Municipal Governments.   As can be seen in Figure 5.3, there is quite a bit of difference between the origin of receipts for provincial and munici-

Figure 5.3
Sources of Government Tax Receipts

About 65 percent of federal revenues come from income and Employment Insurance taxes, whereas provincial and municipal government revenues are spread more evenly across sources, with less emphasis on taxes based on individual income.

Source: Statistics Canada.

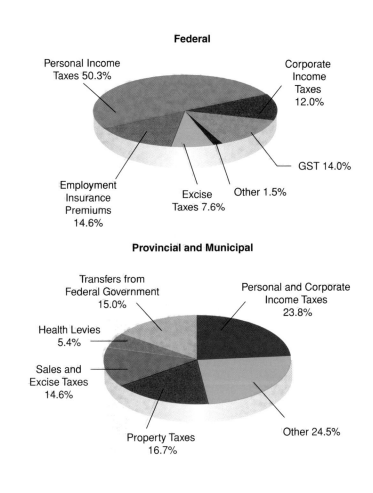

Federal

Personal Income Taxes 50.3%

Corporate Income Taxes 12.0%

GST 14.0%

Other 1.5%

Excise Taxes 7.6%

Employment Insurance Premiums 14.6%

Provincial and Municipal

Transfers from Federal Government 15.0%

Personal and Corporate Income Taxes 23.8%

Health Levies 5.4%

Sales and Excise Taxes 14.6%

Other 24.5%

Property Taxes 16.7%

pal governments and for the federal government. Personal and corporate income taxes account for only 23.8 percent of total provincial and municipal revenues. The next largest source of receipts is from property taxes (used by municipal governments), sales taxes (used mainly by provincial governments), and transfers from the federal government.

Comparing Federal with Provincial and Municipal Spending. A typical federal government budget is given in Figure 5.4. The largest three categories are interest on the debt, elderly benefits, and transfers to the provinces, which together constitute over 60 percent of the total federal budget.

The makeup of provincial and municipal expenditures is quite different. Education and health are the biggest categories, accounting for almost 45 percent of all expenditures.

Figure 5.4
Federal Government Spending Compared to Provincial and Municipal Spending

The federal government's spending habits are quite different from those of the provinces and municipalities. The categories of most importance in the federal budget are interest on the debt, elderly benefits, and transfers to the provinces, which make up over 60 percent. The two most important categories at the provincial and municipal levels are education and health care, which make up almost 45 percent.

Source: Statistics Canada.

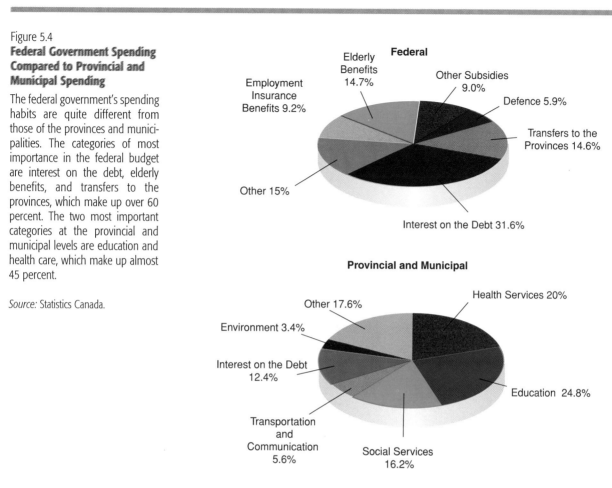

Concepts in Brief

- Total government outlays including transfers have continued to grow since World War II and now account for about 45 percent of yearly total national output.
- Government spending at the federal level is different from that at the provincial and municipal levels. At the federal level, interest on the debt, elderly benefits, and transfers to the provinces account for over 60 percent of the federal budget. At the provincial and municipal levels, education and health comprise almost 45 percent of all expenditures.

Should We Switch to a Flat Tax?

Concepts Applied: Average versus marginal tax rates, opportunity cost, progressive income tax system

Each year, Canadian taxpayers spend numerous hours preparing their taxes or hire accountants to do so for them. Switching to a national sales tax, one alternative to our current system, would lead to the downsizing of Revenue Canada and all of the expenses associated with that organization.

Since the enactment of the federal income tax, Canadians have faced a progressive system. The top marginal tax rate soared to 98 percent in 1943, dropped to 80 percent in 1948, dropped again to 60 percent in 1968, and settled at 47 percent starting in 1971. The government reduced the top marginal tax rate to 34 percent in 1983; today it stands at 29 percent. The idea behind a progressive tax system is that the "rich" should pay more. In actuality, what happens is quite a different story. In Figure 5.5 you see that regardless of what the top tax rate is, the federal government obtains around 48 percent

of its annual income as tax revenues.

Why? Because people respond to incentives. At high marginal tax rates, the following occurs: (1) rich people hire more tax lawyers and accountants to help them figure out loopholes in the tax system to avoid high marginal tax rates; (2) some people change their investments to take advantage of loopholes that allow them to pay lower marginal tax rates; (3) some people drop out of the labour force, particularly secondary income earners, such as lower-paid working women; and (4) more people engage in off-the-books "underground" activities for cash on which no income taxes are paid.

An Alternative: The Flat Tax

For decades, many economists have argued in favour of scrapping our progressive income tax system and replacing it with a so-called flat tax. The idea behind a flat tax is simple. To calculate what you owe, simply subtract the appropriate exemption from your income and multiply the rest by the flat tax rate, say, 20 percent. For example, a family of four might be able to earn as much as $25,000 or $35,000 a year before it paid any income tax. The major benefits of such a system, according to its advocates, would be the following: (1) fewer resources devoted to figuring out one's taxes; (2) fewer tax lawyers and accountants, who could then be engaged in more productive activities; (3) higher saving and investment; and (4) more economic growth. Opponents of a flat tax argue that (1) federal revenues will fall and a federal budget deficit will occur; and (2) the rich will pay few taxes.

Another Alternative: A National Sales Tax

Alternatively, we could apply some form of a value added tax (VAT) in place of the current income tax. VATs are common throughout Europe. A value-added tax is assessed on the value added by a firm at each stage of production. It is a tax on the value of products that firms sell minus the value of the materials that it bought and used to produce the products. Such a tax is collected by all businesses and remitted directly to the federal government. One of the major benefits of a VAT is that it would significantly downsize Revenue Canada and the expenses associated with that government department. A VAT of, say, 15 to 20 percent in lieu of a federal income tax would be quite similar to a consumption tax.

A Consumption Tax

With a consumption tax, taxpayers pay taxes only on what they consume (spend) out of income, not what they earn. One way to determine such consumption in any year is simply to subtract what is

Figure 5.5
**Changing Maximum
Marginal Income Tax Rates
and Revenues Collected**

At the top of the diagram, you can see listed the top marginal tax rates from 1960 to 1995. On the side is the percentage of total annual income collected by the federal government from the income tax system. No matter how high the marginal income tax rate has been, the government has collected about the same percentage of national income in taxes.

Source: W. Irwin Gillespie, *Tax, Borrow & Spend: Financing Federal Spending in Canada 1867-1990.*

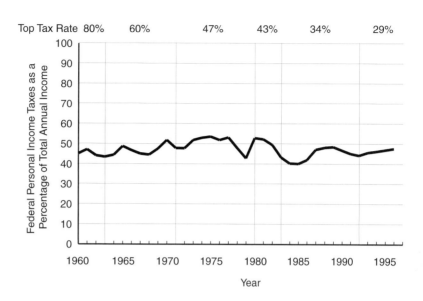

saved from what is earned. The difference is consumption, and that is the base to which a consumption tax would apply. (A consumption tax is actually equivalent to the GST on all goods and services purchased.) In essence, a consumption tax provides an unlimited deduction for saving. As such, it encourages more saving. As you learned in Chapter 2, the less people choose to consume today, the faster the production possibilities curve will shift outward to the right, leading to more economic growth.

What About Fairness?

Every time a new tax system is discussed, the issue of fairness arises. Is it fair, as with a flat federal income tax, that everybody pay the same marginal tax rate, no matter how much each individual earns? Stephen Entin of the Institute for Research on the Economics of Taxation thinks it is: "It is hard to find a definition of 'fairness' more compelling than the idea that every citizen is treated equally." What about a consumption tax, which might be regressive because the poor spend a larger portion of their income than the rich? Is

that a "fair" system? For most economists, these are difficult questions, because they are in the realm of the normative, the value-laden. We can point out that an examination of the evidence shows what reality is. Simply stated, when marginal income tax rates are high, the rich do not, in fact, pay a higher average tax rate than when marginal tax rates are lower. It behooves the rich to find methods to reduce tax liabilities and to expend resources to influence politicians to insert an increasing number of loopholes in the *Tax Act* in order to reduce effective marginal tax rates on those who earn a lot.

For Critical Analysis

1. Do you think employees at Revenue Canada would be for or against the flat-tax system? Explain your choice.

2. Why is a flat-tax system more efficient than a progressive income tax system?

CHAPTER SUMMARY

1. Government can correct external costs through taxation, legislation, and prohibition. It can correct external benefits through financing or production of a good or service, subsidies, and regulation.

2. Government provides a legal system in which the rights of private ownership, the enforcement of contracts, and the legal status of businesses are provided. In other words, government sets the legal rules of the game and enforces them.

3. Public goods, once produced, can be consumed jointly by additional individuals at zero opportunity cost. If users of public goods know that they will be taxed on the basis of their expressed valuation of those public goods, their expressed valuation will be low. They expect to get a free ride.

4. Merit goods (chosen as such, collectively, through the political process) may not be purchased at all or not in sufficient quantities at market clearing prices. Therefore, government subsidizes or provides such merit goods at a subsidized or zero price to specified classes of consumers.

5. When it is collectively decided that something is a demerit good, government taxes, regulates, or prohibits the manufacture, sale, and use of that good.

6. The market sector and the public sector both face scarcity, feature competition, and contain similar individuals. They differ in that many government, or political, goods are provided at zero price, collective action may involve the use of force, and political voting can lead to different results than dollar voting.

7. Bureaucrats often exert great influence on the course of policy because they are in charge of the day-to-day operation of current policy and provide much of the information needed to formulate future policy. Bureaucracies often organize their clientele, coach clients on what is appropriate, and stick up for their rights.

8. Marginal tax rates are those paid on the last dollar of income, whereas average taxes rates are determined by the proportion of income paid in income taxes.

9. With a proportional income tax system, marginal rates are constant. With a regressive system, they go down as income rises, and with a progressive system, they go up as income rises.

10. Government spending at the federal level is different from that at the provincial and municipal levels. Interest on the debt, elderly benefits, and transfers to the provinces account for over 60 percent of the federal budget.

DISCUSSION OF PREVIEW QUESTIONS

1. **What problems will you encounter if you refuse to pay a portion of your income tax because you oppose spending on military defence?**

   You must share in military defence collectively with the rest of the country. Unlike private goods, defence is a public good and must be consumed collectively. You receive benefits from defence whether you choose to or not; the exclusion principle does not work for public goods, such as military defence. The government could make the exclusion principle work better by deporting you to foreign shores if you don't wish to pay for defence. This is typically not done. If you were allowed to forgo taxes allocated to the armed forces, Revenue Canada would be swamped with similar requests. Everyone would have an incentive to claim no benefits from defence (whether true or not) because it must be consumed collectively. So, if you refuse, you may go to jail.

2. **What is the essence of the public-choice model?**

   The essence of the public-choice model is that politicians, bureaucrats, and voters will act so as to maximize their own self-interest (or economic well-being) rather than the community's. In other words, because such people are human, they are subject to the same motivations and drives as the rest of us. They will usually make decisions in terms of what benefits them, not society as a whole. Such an assumption permits economists to apply economic maximization principles to voters, candidates, elected officials, and policymakers.

3. **In what ways do regressive, proportional, and progressive tax structures differ?**

   Under a regressive tax structure, the average tax rate (the percentage of income paid in taxes) falls as income rises. The marginal tax rate is below the average tax rate. Proportional tax structures are those in which the average tax rate remains constant as income rises; the marginal tax rate equals the average tax rate. Under a progressive tax structure, the average tax rate rises as income rises; the marginal tax rate is above the average tax rate. Our federal personal income tax system is an example of a progressive system.

4. **Who pays the corporate income tax?**

   Ultimately, only people can be taxed. As a consequence, corporate taxes are paid by people: corporate owners (in the form of reduced dividends and less stock appreciation for shareholders), consumers of corporate products (in the form of higher prices for goods), and/or employees working for corporations (in the form of lower wages).

PROBLEMS

(Answers to the odd-numbered problems appear at the back of the book.)

5-1. Consider the following system of taxation, which has been labelled *degressive*. The first $5,000 of income is not taxed. After that, all income is assessed at 20 percent (a proportional system). What is the marginal tax rate on $3,000 of taxable income? $10,000? $100,000? What is the average tax rate on $3,000? $10,000? $100,000? What is the maximum average tax rate?

5-2. You are offered two possible bonds to buy as part of your investing program. One is a corporate bond yielding 9 percent. The other is a tax-exempt municipal bond yielding only 6 percent. Assuming that you are certain you will be paid your interest and principal on these two bonds, what marginal tax bracket must you be in to decide in favour of the tax-exempt bond?

5-3. Consider the following tax structure:

Income Bracket	Marginal Tax Rate
$0–$1,500	0%
$1,501–$2,000	14%
$2,001–$3,000	20%

Mr. Smith has an income of $2,500 per annum. Calculate his tax bill for the year. What is his average tax rate? His highest marginal tax rate?

5-4. In 1997, Canada Pension Plan premiums on wages were 3 percent of wages up to $32,300. No further CPP premiums are paid on earnings above this figure. Calculate the average CPP tax rate for annual wages of (a) $4,000, (b) $51,300, (c) $56,000, (d) $100,000. Is the CPP system a progressive, proportional, or regressive tax structure?

5-5. What is meant by the expression "market failure"?

5-6. TV signals have characteristics of public goods, yet TV stations and commercial networks are private businesses. Analyse this situation.

5-7. Assume that you live in a relatively small suburban neighbourhood called Parkwood. The Parkwood Homeowners' Association collects money from homeowners to pay for upkeep of the surrounding stone wall, lighting at the entrances to Parkwood, and mowing the lawn around the perimeter of the area. Each year you are asked to donate $50. No one forces you to do it. There are 100 homeowners in Parkwood.

    a. What percentage of the total yearly revenue of the homeowners' association will you account for?

    b. At what level of participation will the absence of your $50 contribution make a difference?

    c. If you do not contribute your $50, are you really receiving a totally free ride?

5-8. Assume that the only textile firm that exists has created a negative externality by polluting a nearby stream with the wastes associated with production. Assume further that the government can measure the external costs to the community with accuracy and charges the firm for its pollution, based on the social cost of pollution per unit of textile output. Show how such a charge will lead to a higher selling price for textiles and a reduction in the equilibrium quantity of textiles.

5-9. The existence of information and transactions costs has many implications in economics. What are some of these implications in the context of issues discussed in this chapter?

5-10. A favourite political campaign theme in recent years has been to reduce the size, complexity, and bureaucratic nature of the federal government. Nonetheless, the size of the federal government, however measured, continues to increase. Use the theory of public choice to explain why.

5-11. Figures 5.3 and 5.4 give revenues and expenditures for provincial and municipal governments combined. Visit Statistics Canada's Provincial and Territorial General Government Revenue and Expenditure Site at http://www.statcan.ca/english/Pgdb/State/Government/govt08a.htm and locate your province. Calculate what proportion of total revenues and expenditures each category forms. Compare your percentages to Figures 5.3 and 5.4.

    a. Does your government receive relatively more or less of its revenues from any particular source? What characteristics of your provincial economy would account for this?

    b. Does your government spend relatively more or less of its budget in any particular area? What characteristics of your provincial economy would account for this?

INTERACTING WITH THE INTERNET

File Edit View Go Favorites Help

Back   Forward   Stop   Refresh   Home   Search   Favorites   History   Channels   Fullscreen   Mail   Print   Edit

For both detailed and summary information on the 1998 Canadian federal budget, see

    http://www.fin.gc.ca/toce/1998/buddoclist98-e.html

(Future budgets should have a similar name.) At

    http://www.hrdc-drhc.gc.ca/common/income.shtml

you can find material on Old Age Security, the Canada Pension Plan, and Employment Insurance; it is oriented toward both recipients and people interested in how the system works.

    A federal Web site on employment initiatives and employment opportunities for post-secondary students is

    http://canada.gc.ca/programs/pgrind_e.html#opportunities

Economies in Transition

6

If you visit one of the many thousands of hilly fields in Peru, you will likely meet a peasant family. That family probably has been tilling the soil in the same spot for decades. Most of these families eke out a meagre existence. Very few of them could sell the land they have been cultivating for so many years and pursue an alternative line of work even if they wanted to. To understand why in Peru this is so requires a grasp of the changes that are occurring in the world's economies in transition.

Preview Questions

1. Why does the scarcity problem force all societies to answer the questions *what, how,* and *for whom?*

2. What are the "three *P*s" of pure capitalism?

3. Why do we say that *all* economies are mixed economies?

4. How can economies be classified?

Did You Know That... there used to be a country called the Soviet Union, whose chief of state in 1950 took off his shoe at the United Nations and pounded it on the desk while shouting, "We will bury you"? That person was Nikita Khrushchev; he died in 1971. It took quite a few more years for his country to die, but die it did. The Soviet Union is no more. The 74-year experiment in trying to run an economy without using the price, or market, system will go down in history as one of the greatest social and economic failures of all time. But just because the Soviet Union dissolved itself at the end of 1991 does not mean that the entire world economy automatically became like that of Canada. In particular, the 15 republics of the former Soviet Union, the Soviet "satellite" countries of Eastern Europe, and other nations, including China, are what we call *economies in transition.*

At any point in time, every nation has its own **economic system,** which can be defined as the institutional means through which resources are used to satisfy human wants. No matter what institutional means—marketplace or government—a nation chooses to use, three basic economic questions must always be answered.

▶ **Economic system**
The institutional means through which resources are used to satisfy human wants.

THE THREE BASIC ECONOMIC QUESTIONS

In every country, no matter what the form of government or type of economic system, who is running the government, or how poor or rich the country is, three basic economic questions must be answered. They concern the problem of **resource allocation,** which is simply how resources are to be allocated. As such, resource allocation answers the three basic economic questions of *what, how,* and *for whom* goods and services will be produced.

▶ **Resource allocation**
The assignment of resources to specific uses by determining what will be produced, how it will be produced, and for whom it will be produced.

1. *What and how much will be produced?* Literally billions of different things could be produced with society's scarce resources. Some mechanism must exist that causes some things to be produced and others to remain as either inventors' pipe dreams or individuals' unfulfilled desires.

2. *How will it be produced?* There are many ways to produce a desired item. It is possible to use more labour and less capital or vice versa. It is possible to use more unskilled labour and fewer units of skilled labour. Somehow, in some way, a decision must be made as to the particular mix of inputs, the way they should be organized, and how they are brought together at a particular place.

3. *For whom will it be produced?* Once a commodity is produced, who should get it? In a market economy, individuals and businesses purchase commodities with money income. The question then is what mechanism there is to distribute income, which then determines how commodities are distributed throughout the economy.

Try Preview Question 1:
Why does the scarcity problem force all societies to answer the questions *what, how,* and *for whom?*

THE PRICE SYSTEM AND HOW IT ANSWERS THE THREE ECONOMIC QUESTIONS

As explained in Chapter 4, a price (or market) system is an economic system in which (relative) prices are constantly changing to reflect changes in supply and demand for different commodities. In addition, the prices of those commodities are the signals to everyone within the system as to what is relatively scarce and what is relatively abundant. Indeed, it is the *signalling* aspect of the price system that provides the information to buyers and sellers about what should be bought and what should be produced. The price system, which is characteristic of a market economy, is only one possible way to organize society.

What and How Much Will Be Produced?

In a price system, the interaction of demand and supply for each good determines what and how much to produce. Note, however, that if the highest price that consumers are willing to pay is less than the lowest cost at which a good can be produced, output will be zero. That doesn't mean that the price system has failed. Today consumers do not purchase their own private space shuttles. The demand is not high enough in relation to the supply to create a market. But it may be someday.

How Will It Be Produced?

The question of how output will be produced in a price system relates to the efficient use of scarce inputs. Consider the possibility of using only two types of resources, capital and labour. A firm may have the options given in Table 6.1. It can use various combinations of labour and capital to produce the same amount of output. Two hypothetical combinations are given in the table. How, then, is it decided which combination should be used? In the price system, the **least-cost combination** (technique B in our example) will in fact be chosen because it maximizes profits. We assume that the owners of businesses act as if they are maximizing profits. Recall from Chapter 1 that we assume that individuals act *as if* they are rational.

In a price system, competition *forces* firms to use least-cost production techniques. Any firm that fails to employ the least costly technique will find that other

▶ **Least-cost combination**
The level of input use that produces a given level of output at minimum cost.

Table 6.1
Production Costs for 100 Units of Product X

Technique A or B can be used to produce the same output. Obviously, B will be used because its total cost is less than A's. Using production technique B will generate a $2 savings for every 100 units produced.

Inputs	Input Unit Price	A Production Technique A (input units)	Cost	B Production Technique B (input units)	Cost
Labour	$10	5	$50	4	$40
Capital	8	4	32	5	40
Total cost of 100 units			82		80

companies can undercut its price. In other words, other companies that choose the least-cost production technique will be able to offer the product at a lower price and still make a profit. This lower price will persuade consumers to shift their purchases from the higher-priced firm to the lower-priced one. Inefficient businesses will be forced out of operation.

For Whom Will It Be Produced?

This last question that every economic system must answer involves who gets what. In a market system, the choice about what is purchased is made by individuals, but that choice is determined by the ability to pay. Who gets what is determined by the distribution of money income.

Determination of Money Income. In a price system, a consumer's ability to pay for consumer products is based on the size of that consumer's money income. That in turn depends on the quantities, qualities, and types of the various human and non-human resources that the individual owns and supplies to the marketplace. It also depends on the prices, or payments, for those resources. When you are selling your human resources as labour services, your money income is based on the wages you can earn in the labour market. If you own nonhuman resources—physical capital and land, for example—the level of interest and rents that you are paid for your physical capital and land will clearly influence the size of your money income and thus your ability to buy consumer products.

Which Consumers Get What? In a price system, the distribution of finished products to consumers is based on consumers' ability and willingness to pay the market price for the product. If the market price of compact discs is $18, consumers who are able and willing to pay that price will get those CDs. All others won't.

Here we are talking about the *rationing* function of market prices in a price system. Rather than have a central political figure or agency decide which consumers will get which goods, those consumers who are willing and able to pay the market price obtain the goods. That is to say, relative prices ration the available resources, goods, and services at any point in time among those who place the highest value on those items. If scarcity didn't exist, we would not need any system to ration available resources, goods, and services. All of us could have all of everything that we wanted without taking away from what anyone else obtained.

Concepts in Brief

- Any economic system must answer three questions: (1) *What* will be produced? (2) *How* will it be produced? (3) *For whom* will it be produced?
- In a price system, supply and demand determine the prices at which exchanges take place.
- In a price system, firms choose the least-cost combination use of inputs to produce any given output. Competition forces them to do so.
- In a price system, who gets what is determined by consumers' money income and choices about how to use that money income.

TODAY'S INCREASINGLY ALL-CAPITALIST WORLD

what socialism?

Not long ago, textbooks presented a range of economic systems, usually capitalism, socialism, and communism. **Communism** was intended as a system in which the state disappeared and individuals contributed to the economy according to their productivity, receiving income according to their needs. Under **socialism,** the state owned a major share of productive resources except labour. **Capitalism** has been defined as a system under which individuals hold government-protected private property rights to all goods, including those used in production, and their own labour.

Pure Capitalism in Theory

In its purest theoretical form, market capitalism, or pure capitalism, has the following attributes:

1. Private property rights exist and are upheld by the judicial system.
2. Prices are allowed to seek their own level as determined by the forces of supply and demand. In this sense, pure capitalism is a price system.
3. Resources, including human labour, are free to move in and out of industries and geographic locations. The movement of resources follows the lure of profits—higher expected profits create an incentive for more resources to go where those profits might occur.
4. Risk takers are rewarded by higher profits, but those whose risks turn out to be bad business decisions suffer the consequences directly in terms of reduced wealth.
5. Decisions about what and how much should be produced, how it should be produced, and for whom it should be produced are left to the market. In a pure market capitalist system, all decisions are decentralized and made by individuals in a process of *spontaneous coordination* throughout the economy.

One way to remember the attributes of pure capitalism is by thinking of the three Ps: prices, profits, and private property.

The role of government is limited to provision of certain goods, such as defence, police protection, and a legal framework within which property rights and contracts are enforced.

Pure capitalism has also been called a **laissez-faire** system. The French term means "leave [it] alone" or "let [it] be." A pure capitalist system is one in which the government lets the economic actors in the economy make their own decisions without government constraints.

▶ **Communism**
In its purest form, an economic system in which the state has disappeared and individuals contribute to the economy according to their productivity and are given income according to their needs.

▶ **Socialism**
An economic system in which the state owns the major share of productive resources except labour. Socialism also usually involves the redistribution of income.

▶ **Capitalism**
An economic system in which individuals own productive resources; these individuals can use the resources in whatever manner they choose, subject to common protective legal restrictions.

Try Preview Question 2:
What are the "three Ps" of pure capitalism?

▶ **Laissez-faire**
French for "leave [it] alone"; applied to an economic system in which the government minimizes its interference with the economy.

The Importance of Incentives

It is doubtful that "true" communism ever really existed or could survive in a whole economy. However, various forms of socialism, in which the state owned important parts of the economy, have existed. One can argue that the most important distinguishing feature between capitalist countries and everywhere else is the lack of private property rights. Economics predicts that, for example, when an apartment building is owned by no one (that is, owned by the "state"), there is less incentive for anyone to take care of it. This analysis has predicted well with respect to public housing in Canada. Just imagine an entire country for which all housing is public housing. That is what the former Soviet Union was like. (Note that we are not passing judgment on a system that has few private property rights. Rather, we are simply underscoring the predictions that economists can make regarding how individuals treat such property.)

We pointed out in Chapter 4 that, in a world of scarcity, resources must always be rationed. In economic systems where prices were not allowed to be the rationing device, other methods had to be used. In the former Soviet Union, rationing by queuing (standing in line) was one of the most common. Some economists estimated that the average Russian spent as many hours a week waiting in lines as the average Canadian spends watching television.

Today one might say that the collapse of communism has left the world with one system only, the **mixed economy,** in which decisions about how resources are used are made partly by the private sector and partly by the public sector—capitalism with government. Figure 6.1 represents the size of government relative to annual national output. You can see that even among the traditional capitalist countries of the world, there are great variations. These can be regarded as the different faces of capitalism.

▶ **Mixed economy**
An economic system in which decisions about how resources should be used are made partly by the private sector and partly by the government, or the public sector.

Try Preview Question 3:
Why do we say that *all* economies are mixed economies?

Figure 6.1
Percentage of National Yearly Output Accounted for by Government in Various Countries

Even among countries that have embraced capitalism for a long time, government plays an important, but widely different, role. It constitutes over 60 percent of the economy in Sweden, and about 42 percent in Canada.

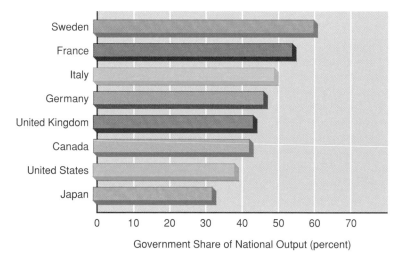

Government Share of National Output (percent)

Try Preview Question 4:
How can economies be classified?

THE DIFFERENT FACES OF CAPITALISM

The world is now left with a single economic system that, thanks to the diversity of human cultures, has a variety of faces. Table 6.2 presents one way to categorize today's economic systems.

Table 6.2
Four Faces of Capitalism

Type of Capitalism	Examples	Characteristics	Problem Areas
Consumer	Canada, United States, New Zealand, Australia, United Kingdom	Borders are relatively open; focus is on profit maximization and laissez-faire.	Low saving and investment rates; income inequality
Producer	Japan, France, Germany	Production is emphasized over consumption; employment is a major policy issue; state controls a relatively large part of the economy.	Consumer dissatisfaction; potential slow future growth rates; inertia within the economy
Family	Indonesia, Malaysia, Thailand, Taiwan	Extended clans dominate business and capital flows.	Lack of modern corporate organizations; lack of money markets
Frontier	Russia, China, Ukraine, Romania, Albania	Many government enterprises pursue for-profit activities; new entrepreneurs emerge every day.	Difficulty of crossing borders; rising criminal activity

Source: Based on, in part, "21st Century Capitalism," *Business Week*, February 23, 1995, p. 19.

Concepts in Brief

- Communism is an economic system under which, in theory, individuals would produce according to their abilities and consume according to their needs. Under socialism, the state owns most major capital goods and attempts to redistribute income.
- Pure capitalism allows for the spontaneous coordination of millions of individuals by allowing the free play of the three *P*s—prices, profits, and property rights. Often, pure capitalism is called a laissez-faire system.
- Incentives matter in any economic system; therefore, in countries that have had few or unenforced property rights, individuals have lacked the incentives to take care of most property that wasn't theirs.
- Most economies today can be viewed as mixed in that they combine private decisions and government controls.

THE TRANSITIONAL PHASE: FRONTIER CAPITALISM

Frontier capitalism describes economies in transition from state ownership and control of most of the factors of production to a system of private property rights in which the price system is used to answer the basic economic questions. Table 6.3 presents theoretical stages in the development of frontier capitalism. Two aspects appear to be the most important: developing the legal system and selling off state-owned businesses.

Table 6.3 **How Frontier Capitalism Develops**	Stage	Characteristics
	I	The central government, as the controller of all economic activities, collapses and starts to disappear. The black market, typically involving government enterprises still owned by the state, expands enormously. Many former state factory managers and other bosses become involved in criminal activities using the state's resources. Government corruption occurs more than before.
	II	Small businesses start to flourish. Families pool funds in order to become entrepreneurs. The rules of commerce are not well understood because there is not yet a well-established commercial law system, nor are property rights well defined or protected by the state.
	III	The economy is growing, but much of its growth is not measured by government statisticians. Small financial markets, such as stock markets, begin to develop. Foreigners cautiously invest in the new stock markets. The government attempts to develop a clear set of commercial laws.
	IV	Foreign corporations are more willing to invest directly in new factories and stores. The state gets serious about selling all businesses that it owns. More resources are devoted to suppressing criminal activity. Commercial law becomes better established and better understood.

Development of the Legal System

In Canada and many other countries, we take a well-established legal system as a given. That does not imply the total absence of a legal system in countries where we are now seeing frontier capitalism. To be sure, the former Soviet Union had a legal system, but virtually none of it had to do with economic transactions, which were carried out by state dictates. Individuals could not own the factors of production, and therefore there were no legal disputes over property rights involving them. Consequently, the legal system in the former Soviet Union and its Eastern European satellites consisted of many volumes of criminal codes—laws against robbery, murder, rape, and theft, as well as so-called economic crimes.

Enter the new world of private property rights and unrestricted exchange of those rights among buyers and sellers. Now what happens when a buyer claims that a seller breached a particular agreement? In Canada, lawyers, courts, and established contract law can be used to settle the dispute. Yet until recently in the frontier economies of the former Soviet Union, there was nothing even vaguely comparable. The rule of law in Canada (and Great Britain—from where much of Canada's law is evolved) has developed over hundreds of years; we cannot expect countries in transition towards full capitalism to create an entire body of law and procedure overnight.

Privatization

The transition towards capitalism requires that the government reduce its role in the economy. This transition involves what has become known as *privatization*. **Privatization** is the transfer of ownership or responsibility for businesses run by the government, so-called *state enterprises*, to individuals and companies in the private sector. Even in capitalist countries, the government has often owned and run various parts of the economy. During and after World War II, it became the norm for many European governments to "nationalize" different industries. This was particularly true in the United Kingdom, where the steel industry was nationalized, for example. In the early 1980s, France nationalized its banking industry. The opposite

▶ **Privatization**

The sale or transfer of state-owned property and businesses to the private sector, in part or in whole. Also refers to contracting out—letting private business take over government-provided services such as garbage collection.

Figure 6.2
The Trend Towards Privatization

Privatization worldwide has been on the upswing since 1985, as shown in part (a). Nationalizations (the opposite of privatizations) reached their peak in about 1970 as is shown in part (b).

Source: OECD and *The Economist,* August 21, 1993, p. 19.

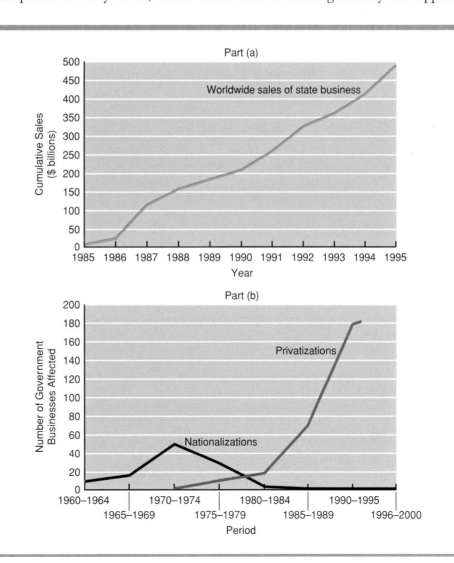

of nationalization is privatization. Late in 1996, Canada privatized air traffic control and sold it to Nav Canada for $1.5 billion.

In the early 1980s, Turkey and Chile were the first capitalist countries to start mass privatization of government-owned businesses. Under Margaret Thatcher, the United Kingdom pioneered the mass privatization of state industry, including the huge road haulage company (NFC), a health care group (Amersham International), telephone services (British Telecom), British Petroleum, and British Aerospace.

A country must employ some method to put government-owned businesses into the hands of the private sector; government-owned businesses are not simply given away to the first party who asks. Imagine if the Canadian government said that it wanted to sell Canada Post. How would it do so? One way is to sell it outright, but there might not be any buyers who would be willing to pay to take over such a giant money-losing corporation. An alternative would involve selling shares of stock to anyone who wanted to buy them at the stated price. This latter technique is indeed the way in which most privatizations have been carried out in established capitalist countries throughout the world over the past 15 or 20 years.

In the former Soviet Union and in Eastern Europe, alternative systems have been devised. For example, citizens, at various times, have been given vouchers granting them the right to purchase a specified number of shares in particular government-owned companies that were being sold off.

The trend in privatization versus nationalization is shown in part (a) of Figure 6.2. The cumulative worldwide sales of state-owned enterprises can be seen in part (b). In Europe, privatization will probably continue into the next century at the rate of over $50 billion a year. Privatization in Latin America will go on for much longer. Finally, privatization in the former Soviet Union and Eastern Europe has in a sense just begun, and may take a long time indeed.

Political Opposition to Privatization

There is often strong political pressure to slow down or even prevent the privatization of state-owned businesses. The political pressure to prevent privatization is derived from simple economics: Managers of state-owned businesses typically have had lifetime job security, better working conditions than they could obtain elsewhere, and little threat of competition. In other words, life for a manager is usually better in a state-owned firm than in that same firm once it has been privatized.

Workers in state-owned firms also believe, often rightly, that their lot in life will not be quite so good if the state-owned firm is sold to the private sector. State-owned firms tend to pay their workers higher wages and give them better fringe benefits, including much better pension plans, than similar firms that are privately owned. For example, an examination of state-owned phone companies in France and Germany shows that they have two to three times as many workers per telephone customer as the private telephone companies in Canada. This comparative overuse of labour in state-owned firms is even more obvious in the republics of the former Soviet Union and in Eastern Europe.

Economists cannot say whether privatization of state-owned firms is good or bad. Rather, economists can simply state that the rigours of a competitive market will generally cause resources to be used more efficiently after privatization occurs. In the process, however, some managers and workers may be made worse off.

Is There a Right Way to Go About the Transition?

Ever since the fall of the Berlin Wall in 1989, economists have debated whether there is a "right" way for former socialist and communist countries to move towards capitalist systems. The once-communist nations have, indeed, embarked on a social experiment in how to move towards a market economy. Basically, they have chosen two methods—a slow one and a fast one. Romania, Russia, and Ukraine have only gradually privatized their economies, whereas the Czech Republic and, to a lesser extent, Poland and Estonia, opted for a "shock treatment."

The rapid move towards a market economy, though not free of problems, has seemed to work better than the go-slow approach. The more slowly the transition occurs, the more the former entrenched bureaucrats in the state-owned businesses have been able to maintain their power over the use of resources. In the meantime, the state-owned businesses continue to use valuable resources inefficiently in these developing countries.

In contrast, a country like the Czech Republic used a voucher system to privatize over 2,000 state-owned enterprises. All citizens were given vouchers—legal rights evidenced on printed certificates—which could be used to purchase shares of stock in state-owned businesses. A stock market quickly developed in which shares of hundreds of companies are now traded every day. After an initial period of transition to a market economy, the Czech Republic has now achieved one of the lowest unemployment rates in Europe.

We will next examine the current situation of two of the largest countries in the world that are in the throes of frontier capitalism. Both are grappling with the problems of the transition from communism to capitalism.

Concepts in Brief

- Today there are four types of capitalism: consumer, producer, family, and frontier. The last begins when a centralized economy starts collapsing and black markets thrive. Eventually small businesses flourish, and then financial markets develop. Finally, foreign investment is attracted, and state-owned businesses are privatized.
- The development of a well-functioning legal system is one of the most difficult problems for an economy in the frontier capitalism stage. Such economies do not have the laws or courts to handle the new system of property right transfers.
- Privatization, or the turning over to the private sector of state-owned businesses, is occurring all over the world in all types of economies. There is much political opposition, however, whenever managers in soon-to-be privatized businesses realize that they may face harder times in a private setting.

RUSSIA AND ITS FORMER SATELLITES, YESTERDAY AND TODAY

Russia was the largest republic in the former Soviet Union. The economic system in place was at times called communism and at other times called command socialism. There is no question that it was a command economy in which there was centralized economic leadership and planning. All economies involve planning, of course; the difference is that in capitalist societies, most of the planning is done by private businesses rather than the government. Leaders in the former Soviet Union believed that its economic planners in Moscow could micromanage an economy that spanned 11 time zones, involved millions of consumers and producers, and affected vast quantities of goods and services.

Imagine trying to run a single business that big! Perhaps more importantly, state ownership in such a large country resulted in unintended consequences throughout the economy. For example, when the government issued production quotas for glass based on the number of panes, the glass produced was almost paper thin and shattered easily. Managers of the glass factories found it took less time to make thin panes of glass which allowed them to produce the required number in the time allotted. In an effort to correct the problem, the government changed its quotas to weight. However, the resulting glass panes were so thick that they were useless. Once again managers found it took less time to meet their quotas if they produced very heavy panes of glass. In short, former Soviet citizens responded rationally to their incentives every time central planners figured out a new way to set production quotas. In the process, untold resources were inefficiently used or completely wasted.

By the time the Soviet Union collapsed in 1991, it consisted of a society in which perhaps one or two percent of the population (the communists, privileged bureaucrats, athletes, and artists) enjoyed a comfortable lifestyle and the rest of the citizens were forced to scrape by. The standard of living of the average citizen prior to the Soviet Union's breakup was at best a quarter, but more realistically one-tenth, of that in Canada. The same was true perhaps to an even greater degree in the former East Germany, Romania, Poland, Hungary, Czechoslovakia (now the Czech Republic and Slovakia), and Albania.

Thinking Critically About the Media   **Taking Russia's Pulse**

When economists and journalists discuss the transition from the centralized Soviet economy to its current market orientation, they lament the tremendous reduction in national output. Official estimates for the period 1989 to 1995, for example, claim that national output dropped by over 50 percent. True though it may be that output dropped during this time, it is not clear what the actual value of that output was to the population. Much of the reduction was in military hardware, such as missiles. How much did the average citizen lose when that output shrank? Also, fewer television sets and radios were produced during this time period—but the ones produced earlier either never worked properly or tended to explode. Steel mills have been shut down in Russia but they had been using technology that was 45 years old. Further, the official Russian state agency that measures the economy, Goskomstat, has none of the sophistication that Statistics Canada has for measuring a nation's output. Even if Goskomstat had better computers and more refined techniques, it would still miss a vast off-the-books economy that won't be counted by government statisticians for years to come. All in all, Russia's 150 million people earn more and live better than what Goskomstat statistics say.

Privatization During Transition

The fact that a former state-owned business in Russia is now privatized does not mean that shareholders control it the way they do in, say, Canada. In Canada, shareholders elect a board of directors, which then chooses upper management. Shareholders can force out directors who have acted improperly, and can also show their disapproval by selling their shares of stock and purchasing shares in another company. It will be some time before the same system of control operates in all recently privatized Russian businesses. Many such businesses are actually controlled by their managers and workers, not by shareholders. One might use the analogy of a divorced couple still sharing the same house and the children.

In some former Soviet satellite countries, one arm of government sells a state-owned firm and another reappears as its owner. This has happened a lot in Poland, for example, where the government's Industrial Development Agency is managing one of the 15 funds that were set up to take over 440 formerly state-owned enterprises.

In the businesses that are being run by worker cooperatives, there is little incentive to fire the least efficient workers or to seek more highly qualified workers. Manager-owners do not often do much better. Manager-owners of recently privatized firms in Russia clearly do not want to surrender control.

The Persistence of Old Ways

The more an economy tends towards pure market capitalism, the less place there is for a government élite that is able to seize economic power and, more importantly, economic privileges. In Russia today, some of the old Communist Party bases of economic power are being redeveloped. Although newspapers and television stations are now privately owned, their owners are increasingly afraid of angering powerful government interests.

Just a few years ago, President Boris Yeltsin created a new political party named "Our House—Russia." The party was and continues to be backed by wealthy banking and business interests. It consists almost entirely of state bureaucrats and provincial governors and administrators, most of whom are former communists. Prior to the downfall of communism, the political élite were able to use special clinics and hospitals. Today the same persons have the same privileges, although the names of the hospitals have changed. Even a new special food store was built for officials with parliamentary identification cards. Under communism, special food stores served to provide Communist Party élite with low-cost, high-quality food without their having to wait in lines. Why such a special food store has cropped up again in Russia's now more capitalistic system remains something of a mystery.

The Inevitable Crime Wave

The shift to a market economy in Russia has brought with it a major increase in crime, particularly organized crime. Currently, virtually every small business pays protection money to some gang. Moscow boasts at least a million unregistered firearms, and the country as a whole has over 30 million of them. According to former *Toronto Star* Moscow reporter Stephen Handelman, "The second Russian revolution of this century is awash in corruption, opportunism, and crime."

One needs to examine the crime statistics more carefully, though, to get a real feeling for what is happening in this nation in transition. Street crime is certainly greater than it used to be under the Soviet régime. But Moscow is still probably safer than many American cities. With respect to "breaking the law," the legal system is in such a state of flux that probably everyone is breaking the law at one time or another. Because the legal system is in its infancy for facilitating private enterprise, business people have had to resort to extralegal methods to collect debts and enforce contracts. Unfortunately, some of these methods involve firearms and violence.

A good analogy for what is happening in Russia today is the violence associated with the illegal production and sale of alcoholic beverages during the United States' experiment with Prohibition (1920–1933) and what is happening in Russia today. The violence associated with the business of illegal booze disappeared with the repeal of Prohibition. It will not disappear so quickly in Russia, but it certainly will eventually fade out as property rights become better established, the legal system increasingly facilitates trade, and the court system gains enough experience to handle legal problems from the business world.

One must also look at what used to exist under the old system. Because everything belonged to "the people," there was little in the way of communications, credit, banking, and computerization. Money was less important than connections and rank in the Communist Party. People who were adept at thriving in such an environment—the Communist Party élite—have had a comparative advantage in the initial stages of transition to a market economy. They maintain their connections with the state bureaucrats who controlled resources. It is not surprising that many of those in power today are the same communists who were in power a decade ago.

All of this is simply a transition. The incidence of certain crimes in Russia has actually fallen, as can be seen in Figure 6.3.

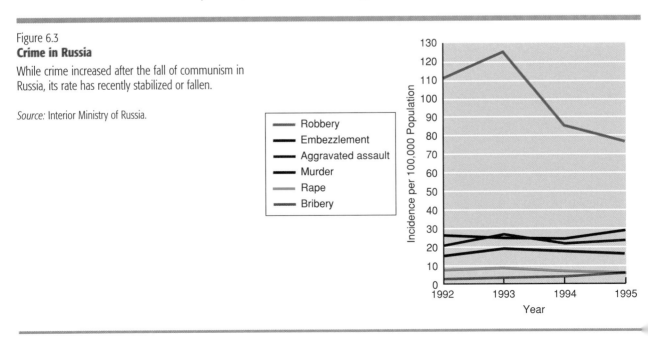

Figure 6.3
Crime in Russia

While crime increased after the fall of communism in Russia, its rate has recently stabilized or fallen.

Source: Interior Ministry of Russia.

INTERNATIONAL EXAMPLE
A Booming Business in Facelifts by Russian Plastic Surgeons

One of the beneficiaries of Russia's economic system in transition is the facelift industry. There is as yet no legal procedure in Russia for imposing liability on physicians for malpractice. Consequently, a patient who desires a facelift or other cosmetic surgery has no consent forms to sign, and the physician has no malpractice (liability) insurance to purchase. People are travelling from outside Russia to take advantage of the resulting relatively inexpensive plastic surgery. According to one of Russia's best-known plastic surgeons, Igor A. Volf, "Surgeons in the West work in a very rigid frame. They are afraid of being sued by their patients—they fear complications. I do the big, bold operations Western doctors are afraid to do." As word of mouth travels, the demand curve for Russian plastic surgeons is shifting outward to the right.

For critical analysis: What are the costs that a Canadian contemplating a facelift in Moscow would have to include in making a rational decision about going there?

Concepts in Brief

- Russia and its former satellite states in Eastern Europe operated under a system of command socialism with much centralized economic planning. The end result was a declining economy in which a small percentage of the population lived extremely well and the rest very poorly.
- Russia and Eastern Europe are privatizing at varying speeds, depending on the level of political opposition.
- Russia has experienced a crime wave during its transition to capitalism. As property rights and the legal system become more efficient, much of the crime associated with illegal economic activities will probably disappear.

THE PEOPLE'S REPUBLIC OF CHINA

The People's Republic of China remains the largest nation on earth and hence the largest with some form of command socialism. However, a decreasing share of the nation's activity is being guided by government. In fact, China started introducing market reforms in various sectors of the economy well before Russia did.

In 1978, the commune system that had been implemented in the 1950s was replaced by what was known as the *household responsibility system*. Each peasant household became responsible for its own plot of land. Whatever was produced in excess of the minimum obligation to the state remained the property of the household. So the incentives for peasant farmers were quite different from those prior to 1978. Peasants were also encouraged to enrich themselves further by engaging in a variety of economic activities. The results were impressive. Between 1979 and 1984, millions of jobs were created in the urban and rural private sector, and farm productivity increased dramatically.

In the 1980s, the highly centralized planning from Beijing, the capital, was relaxed. Decision-making powers were given to state-owned enterprises at the local level. Indeed, China had embarked on a gradual sell-off of state-owned enterprises so that the size of the state-owned sector, which accounted for 70 percent of industrial production in the mid-1980s, dropped to an estimated 40 percent in 1996. The result was an increase in output. The problem with state-owned factories was the **incentive structure.** Managers of those factories never had much incentive to maximize output or minimize cost. Rather, managers of state-owned factories attempted to maximize incomes and benefits for their workers because workers made up a political constituency that was more important than the politicians at the national level.

▶ **Incentive structure**

The motivational rewards and costs that individuals face in any given situation. Each economic system has its own incentive structure. The incentive structure is different under a system of private property than under a system of government-owned property, for example.

Thinking Critically About the Media   **268 Million Chinese Unemployed?**

"China Sees 268 Million Unemployed in 2000." This was the headline a few years ago, reportedly based on statements by mainland Chinese officials in the Labour Ministry. Imagine that—the number of unemployed in China equalling nine times the entire population of men, women, and children in Canada! A frightening prospect, no doubt, but also pure nonsense. Such a large number of unemployed presupposes that there is no way for them to find jobs of any sort. As China shifts towards a market economy, however, many of the unemployed will be able to find jobs in businesses that the current Chinese leadership cannot even conceive of today. That is what happens in a country in transition towards market capitalism. Of course, during the transition, there will be social and human costs associated with higher-than-normal unemployment rates, but that is statistically a temporary blip, not a long-term trend.

Two Decades of Economic Reform

Another major economic reform in China began in 1979, when the central government created a special economic zone in Guangdong province, bordering the nation of Hong Kong. In that special zone, the three Ps of pure capitalism—prices, profits, and private property—have now prevailed for nearly two decades. The result has been economic growth rates that have exceeded those in virtually any other part of the world. Within an area housing less than 1.5 percent of the population, Guangdong province now accounts for about 7 percent of the entire country's industrial output.

Transition Problems in Farming

Even though the Chinese central government was able to increase agricultural production dramatically when it gave peasants the household responsibility system, the agricultural sector has been lagging well behind the industrial sector in recent years. In effect, China has been undergoing an industrial revolution but not an agricultural one. One of the major problems is that peasants do not have legal title to their land. In other words, farmers cannot obtain legal property rights. As a result, the techniques used by agribusiness companies elsewhere in the world cannot be used by most of China's farmers. Peasants, in effect, have their land on loan from the state. The average size of a peasant farm is less than an acre (0.4 hectare) for a family of six. It takes this family about 60 workdays to cultivate this amount of land, whereas a single Canadian farmer can cultivate the same amount of land in about two hours.

Further, there is every incentive for peasant farmers to leave their rural lands and move to the city, where they can earn approximately four times as much income.

A Major Problem: The Rule of Law

As with virtually all countries experiencing frontier capitalism, China faces the perennial issue of how to establish the rule of law. When no specific property rights exist because resources are owned by "the people," the inevitable result is corruption. As with Russia, there is an atmosphere of lawlessness and unpredictability for anyone doing business. Both the government and the army continue to seek bribes and other favours because those two institutions still control many of the resources and influence the way business is conducted in China.

Only very slowly is the institution of a strong legal system being built up in China. The idea of property rights is slow to take hold in a nation where the communist dogma has long denied the concept. A good example is the state-supported bootleg compact disc factories that were first shut down because of international pressure and then reopened a few years ago. That Western singers and musicians are being denied royalties seems not to bother some mainland Chinese government officials.

INTERNATIONAL EXAMPLE
A Tale of Two Countries

Approximately 6 million Chinese, most of whom are directly from or descended from those on mainland China, live in the state of Hong Kong. This colony was leased to the British in the nineteenth century and reverted to Chinese ownership in mid-1997. During its years as a British colony covering a mere 1034 square kilometres (399 square miles), Hong Kong became the world's eighth-largest trading nation, with a higher per capita income than the United Kingdom or France. Total annual output from its 6 million residents exceeded 20 percent of the output of 1.2 billion mainland Chinese. Hong Kong has long been the favourite example of economists who wish to show the efficiency of a system that follows the three *P*s—prices, profits, and private property.

Perhaps more importantly, Hong Kong demonstrates the benefits of a strong legal system. A *Fortune* magazine survey of 500 corporate executives in 32 countries rated Hong Kong above London and New York as the best city for doing business in 1996. Commentators have argued that mainland China does not need Hong Kong's money but rather its rule of law. For decades, these laws have provided businesses with predictable rules governing civil and criminal disputes. Hong Kong has had an independent judicial system, contrary to the one almost completely dominated by the Communist Party on the mainland. Whether the mainland's takeover of Hong Kong results in China's learning from Hong Kong remains to be seen.

For critical analysis: Reread the discussion of comparative versus absolute advantage in Chapter 2. Hong Kong is basically a barren land with no natural resources. What does this say about absolute versus comparative advantage?

The Slow Pace of Privatization

Virtually all state-owned companies in China have provided cradle-to-grave social welfare benefits to their workers. The process of privatization, which started gradually years ago, first requires that these companies slowly eliminate many of these social welfare programs. Such programs are one of the reasons that over 50 percent of state-owned enterprises are losing money every year. You can see from Figure 6.4 which industrial enterprises have the greatest amount of state involvement. It clearly will be many years before the Chinese government is completely (if ever) out of the petroleum and tobacco businesses. But as Figure 6.5 shows, a growing percentage of firms are escaping from state control.

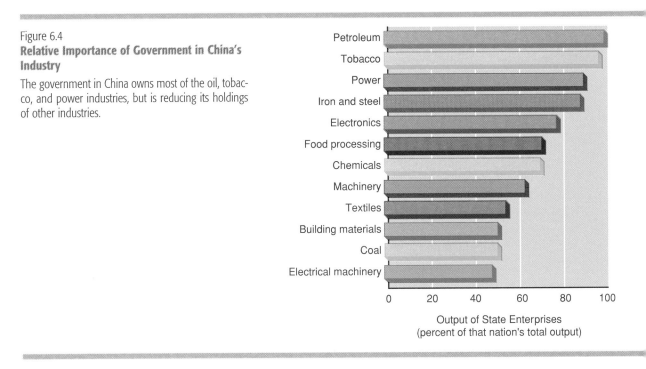

Figure 6.4
Relative Importance of Government in China's Industry

The government in China owns most of the oil, tobacco, and power industries, but is reducing its holdings of other industries.

Figure 6.5
The Changing Face of China's Business Ownership
State ownership of all industries in China has fallen from 78 percent in 1978 to only 41 percent in 1996.

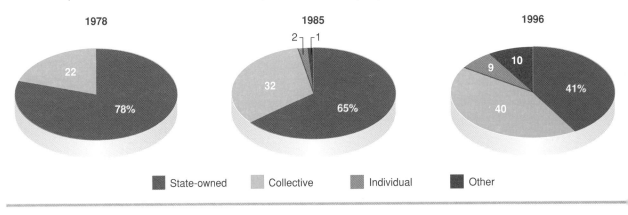

The trend towards privatization in China is inevitably leading to labour dislocations. As state-owned enterprises become privatized, new technology will be introduced that will require fewer labour hours per unit of output. Workers have been, and will continue to be, laid off in recently privatized firms. Laid-off workers will have to seek employment elsewhere, and in the process unemployment rates will rise, at least temporarily.

INTERNATIONAL EXAMPLE
China Eliminates Saturday Work

 In 1995, the Chinese government granted its 450 million urban labourers and students Saturdays off. That adds up to about 1.4 billion extra hours of leisure time every week (labourers and students had been putting in a four-hour Saturday workday). The major beneficiaries of this government edict, besides urban labourers and students, seem to be travel agents. They counted the change in work rules as a windfall.

For critical analysis: What happened to the demand curve for leisure travel after the five-day workweek was instituted?

Concepts in Brief

* China started instituting market reforms in 1979 when it created special economic zones in which the three *P*s of capitalism were allowed to work. Problems remain in agriculture because peasant farmers cannot obtain property rights in land.
* The rule of law as capitalist countries know it is coming slowly to China. Government officials sometimes break contract agreements with foreign investors.
* The process of privatization started years ago but is proceeding slowly. The state still owns most of the businesses in oil, tobacco, power, and iron and steel.

Thinking Critically About the Media   Rich Industrial Nations—Really?

Virtually all news commentators and research organizations continue to classify countries such as Canada, the United States, the United Kingdom, and France as industrial economies. Such an appellation today is a misnomer. In the industrial economies of today, less than one-third of the output is from "industry." Two-thirds of the jobs in so-called industrial economies are from services—doctors, lawyers, computer programmers, and Internet facilitators. Indeed, it might be more appropriate to call the richer countries *knowledge economies* because that is where the primary source of growth will lie—the storage, processing, and distribution of knowledge.

FUTURE ECONOMIC POWER SHIFTS

The fact that there are so many economies in transition today is not just a momentary curiosity. It has implications for the future with respect to which nations will become economic powerhouses. Look at the three parts of Figure 6.6. You see in part (a) that in the mid-1990s, the United States was clearly the world's largest economy. Japan and China were not even half its size. Now look at part (b), which shows

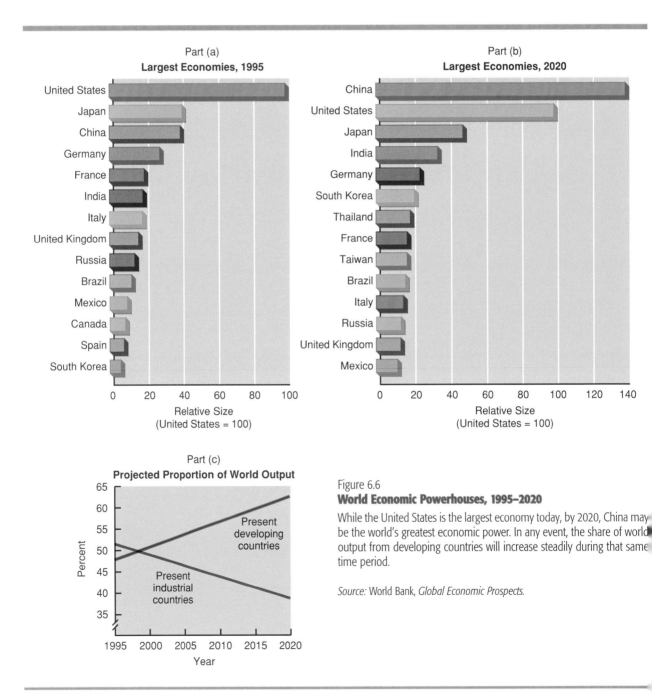

Figure 6.6

World Economic Powerhouses, 1995–2020

While the United States is the largest economy today, by 2020, China may be the world's greatest economic power. In any event, the share of world output from developing countries will increase steadily during that same time period.

Source: World Bank, *Global Economic Prospects.*

the World Bank's prediction of the largest economies in the year 2020. The leading economic powerhouse then is predicted to be China, with the United States a distant second. (These numbers reflect the total size of the economy, not how rich the average citizen is.) Japan will still be among the top three, but India and Indonesia will have expanded dramatically relative to 1995. Indeed, Asia, including India, will be a major economic power in the year 2020. These developments are reflected in part (c) of Figure 6.6, where we show the projected shares of world output of today's industrial countries relative to today's developing countries. Realize, however, that the fact that developing Asian countries will dramatically increase the size of their economies does not mean that westerners will be worse off. Rather, the incomes of most westerners will also increase, but not as rapidly. Given that per-person incomes are generally higher in the West than in Asia, westerners will still remain rich by historical standards. The rest of the world is simply catching up with us.

Issues and Applications

The Peruvian Transition from No Ownership to Clear Title

Concepts Applied: Property rights, incentives, markets, economies in transition

Formal markets do not easily develop where private ownership does not exist. This is the case in Peru, where farmers till family land for generations without a clear title for that land.

By at least one estimate, more than 75 percent of the population of Peru is involved in the "informal society." This term was coined by Peruvian economist Hernando de Soto to emphasize the fact that Peru's official economy is quite small.

Only 20 percent of Peru's land is legally owned. On the remaining 80 percent, which has no true legal ownership, peasant families till the soil as they have done for generations.

Constructing *Pueblos Jovenes*

Cities are actually constructed on the unowned land. They are called *pueblos jovenes*, which means "young cities." Sometimes people who have been living there for a long time or who have tilled the land surrounding them try to register the land in their names. The process can take anywhere from six months to two years, though, and costs thousands of dollars in fees, much more than any peasant family is normally able to pay.

No Ownership, No Market, No Incentive

It is difficult, if not impossible, to create markets when ownership is nonexistent. Informal markets do evolve, and that is what has happened throughout Peru. But without specifically defined property rights, individuals cannot exchange land, for example. Consequently, in Peru, for generations, no large-scale farming has occurred, nor have peasant families experienced much incentive to improve the value of the property on which they farm. It is also not surprising that in the *pueblos jovenes*, construction has been of the flimsiest nature, even by families who have inherited substantial sums of money. If a peasant family doesn't know if it can keep its land, the incentive to invest in it is understandably low.

"Suitcase" Farming

The lack of property rights has created a culture of so-called suitcase farmers in the Upper Huallaga and Rio Apurimac valleys. What the farmers produce, though, is not for normal consumption. It is coca bushes, which provide the raw ingredients for cocaine Peruvian suitcase farmers plant these bushes, cultivate them, quickly sell them to Colombian buyers, and move off the land.

Enter a New System

Since the beginning of the 1990s, Peru's parliament has passed a number of new property laws. Today, for a nominal cost, it is possible to register ownership of property in a month or so. So far, at least 150,000 families have obtained title to their land for $15 to $20 per parcel.

For a family to establish title to land, the local leaders in the "informal" neighbourhoods have to attest that a family has indeed been using the parcel for generations. If no other family contests ownership of that property, it becomes possible for the family to register ownership.

One group objects to providing well-defined property rights to land: the drug dealers who buy coca plants. They are worried that establishing private property rights to land will discourage the suitcase farmers, leading to a smaller supply of the raw ingredient for cocaine. Not surprisingly, the main office of the Peruvian Institute for Liberty and Democracy, a group that is helping peasants register their land, has been bombed several times.

For Critical Analysis

1. What alternatives would suitcase farmers have if they were given clear ownership rights to the land that they farm?

2. Is it possible to have wealth without legal property rights?

CHAPTER SUMMARY

1. The price system answers the resource allocation and distribution questions relating to what and how much will be produced, how it will be produced, and for whom it will be produced. The question of what to produce is answered by the value people place on a good—the highest price they are willing to pay for it. How goods are produced is determined by competition, which inevitably results in least-cost production techniques. Finally, goods and services are distributed to the individuals who are willing and able to pay for them. This answers the question about for whom goods are produced.

2. Pure capitalism can be defined by the three *P*s: prices, profits, and private property.

3. Communism is an economic system in which, theoretically, individuals would produce according to their abilities and consume according to their needs. Under socialism, the state owns most major capital goods and attempts to redistribute income. Most economies today can be viewed as mixed, in that they rely on a combination of private decisions and government controls.

4. Incentives matter in any economic system; consequently, in countries that have had few or unenforced property rights, individuals have lacked the incentives to take care of property

that wasn't theirs.

5. Today there are four types of capitalism: consumer, producer, family, and frontier. The last emerges when a centralized economy starts collapsing and black markets thrive. Eventually, small businesses flourish and financial markets develop. Finally, foreign investment is attracted, and state-owned businesses are privatized.

6. The development of a well-functioning legal system is one of the most difficult problems for an economy in the frontier capitalism stage. Such economies do not have the laws or courts to handle property right protection and transfers.

7. Privatization, or turning over state-owned businesses to the private sector, is occurring all over the world in all types of economies. There is much political opposition, however, whenever managers in soon-to-be-privatized businesses realize that they may face harder times in a private setting.

8. Russia and its former satellite states in Eastern Europe operated under a system of command socialism with much centralized economic planning. The end result was a declining economy in which a small percentage of the population lived extremely well and the rest very poorly.

9. Russia has experienced a crime wave during its transition to capitalism. As property rights and the legal system become more efficient, much of the crime associated with illegal economic activities will probably disappear.

10. China started instituting true market reforms in 1979, when it created special economic zones in which the three *P*s of capitalism—prices, profits, and private property—were allowed to work. Problems remain in agriculture because peasant farmers cannot obtain property rights to land.

11. The process of privatization in China started years ago but is proceeding slowly. The state still owns most of the businesses in oil, tobacco, power, and iron and steel.

12. The United States and Japan will remain economic powerhouses, but China could take the lead over the next 25 years. Other Asian countries, including Indonesia, India, Taiwan, South Korea, and Thailand, will become economically much stronger than they are today. Canada will become relatively less powerful, but will still be wealthy compared to the rest of the world.

DISCUSSION OF PREVIEW QUESTIONS

1. Why does the scarcity problem force all societies to answer the questions *what, how,* and *for whom*?

Scarcity exists for a society because people want more than their resources will allow them to have. Society must decide *what* to produce because of scarcity. But if wants are severely restricted and resources are relatively superabundant, the question of *what* to produce is trivial— society simply produces *everything* that everyone wants. Superabundant resources relative to restricted wants also make the question of *how* to produce trivial. If scarcity doesn't exist, superabundant resources can be combined in *any* manner; waste and efficiency have no meaning without scarcity. Similarly, without scarcity, *for whom* is meaningless; *all* people can consume *all* they want.

2. What are the "three *P*s" of pure capitalism?

They are prices, profits, and property rights. In a pure capitalist economic system, prices are allowed to change when supply or demand changes. Prices are the signals to all about the relative scarcity of different resources. Profits are not constrained. When profits are relatively great in an industry, more resources flow to it. The converse is also true. Finally, property rights exist and are supported by the legal system.

3. Why do we say that *all* economies are mixed economies?

No economy in the real world is purely capitalistic. Resource allocation decisions in all economies are made by some combination of private individuals and governments. Even under an idealized capitalistic economy, important roles are played by the government; it is generally agreed that government is required for some income redistribution, national defence, protection of property rights, and so on.

4. How can economies be classified?

All societies must resolve the three fundamental economic problems: what, how, and for whom? One way to classify economies is according to the manner in which they answer these questions. In particular, we can classify them according to the degree to which *individuals* privately are allowed to make these decisions. Under pure command socialism, practically all economic decisions are made by a central authority; under pure capitalism, practically all economic decisions are made by private individuals pursuing their own economic self-interest.

PROBLEMS

(Answers to the odd-numbered problems appear at the back of the book.)

6-1. Suppose that you are an economic planner and you have been told by your country's political leaders that they want to increase automobile production by 10 percent over last year. What other industries will be affected by this decision?

6-2. Some argue that prices and profits automatically follow from well-established property rights. Explain how this might occur.

6-3. A business has found that it makes the most profits when it produces $172 worth of output of a particular product. It can choose from three possible techniques, A, B, and C, to produce the desired level of output. The table gives the amount of inputs these techniques use along with each input price.
  a. Which technique will the firm choose, and why?
  b. What would the firm's maximum profit be?
  c. If the price of labour increases to $4 per unit, which technique will be chosen, and why? What will happen to profits?

| | Production Technique | | | |
	Input Unit Price	A (units)	B (units)	C (units)
Input				
Land	$10	7	4	1
Labour	2	6	7	18
Capital	15	2	6	3
Entrepreneurship	8	1	3	2

6-4. Answer the questions on the basis of the accompanying graph.

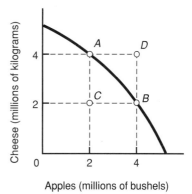

Apples (millions of bushels)

  a. A switch to a decentralized, more market-oriented economy might do what to the production possibilities curve, and why?
  b. What point on the graph represents an economy with unemployment?

6-5. The table gives the production techniques and input prices for 100 units of product X.

| | Production Technique | | | |
	Input Unit Price	A (units)	B (units)	C (units)
Input				
Labour	$10	6	5	4
Capital	8	5	6	7

  a. In a market system, which techniques will be used to produce 100 units of product X?
  b. If the market price of a unit of X is $1, which technique will lead to the greatest profit?
  c. The output of X is still $1, but the price of labour and capital changes so that labour is $8 and capital is $10. Which production technique will be used?
  d. Using the information in (c), what is the potential profit of producing 100 units of X?

6-6. The table gives the production techniques and input prices for one unit of product Y.

| | Input Unit Price | Production Technique | | |
		A (units)	B (units)	C (units)
Input				
Labour	$10	1	3	2
Capital	5	2	2	4
Land	4	3	1	1

a. If the market price of a unit of product Y is $50, which technique generates the greatest potential profit?

b. If input unit prices change so that labour is $10, capital is $10, and land is $10, which technique will be chosen?

c. Assuming that the unit cost of each input is $10 and the price of a unit of Y is $50, which technique generates the greatest profit?

6-7. Visit the World Bank's Selected World Development Indicators website at http://www.worldbank.org/html/iecdd/wdipdf.htm. Open Table 1, Basic Indicators. Notice that the countries are arranged by the size of their economies (GNP per capita) from small to large.

a. Find Canada. What income level group of countries is Canada in?

b. Select one of the low-income economies. Compare its per person GNP with that of Canada. How much larger, in percentage terms, is Canada than your low-income country?

c. Compare the life expectancy at birth in your low-income country with that of a middle-income country and with that of Canada. What conclusions can you draw about health as a country develops? Why do you think this happens?

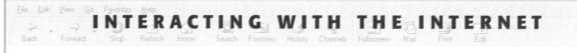

INTERACTING WITH THE INTERNET

Extensive information on Eastern European economic conditions, with an emphasis on financial matters, can be found (for a fee) at

http://www.securities.com/

An excellent source for general information on these and other countries is the CIA's *World Factbook*,

http://www.odci.gov/cia/publications/pubs.html

Information on Canada's relationship with developing countries can be found at the Web site of the Canadian International Development Agency (CIDA) at

http://w3.acdi-cida.gc.ca/

The Organisation for Economic Co-operation and Development (OECD) has extensive information on its Web site about its 29 member countries which include many Eastern European countries as well as the developed western countries. Most of the information is free. You can access the OECD Web site at

http://www.oecd.org/

PART 2

Dimensions of Microeconomics

Consumer Choice

Even if you live in the city, you can surely appreciate the existence of Pacific Rim National Park, the Rocky Mountains, and the great wilderness areas in the north and other parts of the country. And even if you have never seen a whale, you may receive some satisfaction from knowing that whales have not been made extinct. Thus you may feel a certain loss when an environmental disaster, such as a huge oil spill, occurs. Should your feelings of loss be taken into account when government officials attempt to determine the policy response to environmental damage? To answer this question, you need to know how consumers make choices and the values they place on those choices.

Preview Questions

1. What is the law of diminishing marginal utility?

2. How does a consumer maximize total utility?

3. What happens to consumer optimum when price changes?

4. How can the law of diminishing marginal utility account for the law of demand?

Did You Know That... in a typical year, a Canadian family spends about 15 percent of its income on food and about the same on housing? Within individual families, however, these relative percentages may be quite different. Some families devote a much higher percentage of their income to housing than others. What determines how much each family spends on different items in their budget? One explanation is simply tastes—the values that family members place on different items on which they can spend their income. The saying "you can't argue with tastes" suggests that different individuals have different preferences on how to allocate their limited incomes. Although there is no real theory of what determines people's tastes, we can examine some of the behaviour that underlies how consumers react to changes in the prices of the goods and services that they purchase. Recall from Chapter 3 that people generally purchase less at higher prices than at lower prices. This is called the law of demand.

Because the law of demand is important, its derivation is useful as it allows us to arrange the relevant variables, such as price, income, and tastes, in a way that lets us understand the real world better and even perhaps generate predictions about it. One way of deriving the law of demand involves an analysis of the logic of consumer choice in a world of limited resources. In this chapter, therefore, we discuss what is called *utility analysis*.

UTILITY THEORY

When you buy something, you do so because of the satisfaction you expect to receive from having and using that good. For everything that you like to have, the more you have of it, the higher the level of satisfaction you receive. Another term that can be used for satisfaction is **utility,** or want-satisfying power. This property is common to all goods that are desired. The concept of utility is purely subjective, however. There is no way that we can measure the amount of utility that a consumer might be able to obtain from a particular good, for utility does not imply "useful" or "utilitarian" or "practical." For this reason, there can be no accurate scientific assessment of the utility that someone might receive by consuming a frozen dinner or a movie relative to the utility that another person might receive from that same good or service. Nevertheless, we can infer whether a person receives more utility from consuming one good versus another by that person's behaviour. For example, if an individual buys more coffee than tea (when both tea and coffee are priced equally), we are able to say that the individual receives more utility from consuming coffee than from consuming tea.

The utility that individuals receive from consuming a good depends on their tastes and preferences. These tastes and preferences are normally assumed to be given and stable for a particular individual. It is tastes which determine how much utility that individual derives from consuming a good, and this in turn determines how that individual allocates income. People spend a greater proportion of their incomes on goods they like. But we cannot explain why tastes are different among

▶ **Utility**
The want-satisfying power of a good or service.

individuals. For example, we cannot explain why some people like yoghurt but others do not.

We can analyse in terms of utility the way consumers decide what to buy, just as physicists have analysed some of their problems in terms of what they call "force." No physicist has ever seen a unit of force, and no economist has ever seen a unit of utility. In both cases, however, these concepts have proved useful for analysis.

Throughout this chapter, we will be discussing **utility analysis,** which is the analysis of consumer decision making based on utility maximization.

▶ **Utility analysis**
The analysis of consumer decision making based on utility maximization.

Utility and Utils

Economists once believed that utility could be measured. In fact, there is a school of thought based on utility theory called *utilitarianism,* developed by the English philosopher Jeremy Bentham (1748–1832). Bentham held that society should seek the greatest happiness for the greatest number. He sought to apply an arithmetic formula for measuring happiness. He and his followers developed the notion of measurable utility and invented the **util** to measure it. For the moment, we will also assume that we can measure satisfaction using this representative unit. Our assumption will allow us to quantify the way we examine consumer behaviour.[1] Thus the first chocolate bar that you eat might yield you four utils of satisfaction; the first peanut cluster, six utils; and so on. Today, no one really believes that we can actually measure utils, but the ideas forthcoming from such analysis will prove useful in our understanding of the way in which consumers choose among alternatives.

▶ **Util**
A representative unit by which utility is measured.

Total and Marginal Utility

Consider the satisfaction, or utility, that you receive each time that you rent and watch a video on your VCR. To make the example straightforward, let's say that there are hundreds of videos to choose from each year and that each of them is of the same quality. Let's say that you normally rent one video per week. You could, of course, rent two, or three, or four per week. Presumably, each time you rent another video per week, you will get additional satisfaction, or utility. The question, though, that we must ask is, given that you are already renting one per week, will the next one rented that week give you the same amount of additional utility?

That additional, or incremental, utility is called **marginal utility,** where *marginal,* as before, means "incremental" or "additional." (Marginal changes also refer to decreases, in which cases we talk about *decremental* changes.) The concept of marginality is important in economics because we make decisions at the margin. At any particular point, we compare additional (marginal) benefits with additional (marginal) costs.

▶ **Marginal utility**
The change in total utility due to a one-unit change in the quantity of a good or service consumed.

---

[1] What follows is typically called *cardinal utility analysis* by economists. It requires cardinal measurement. Numbers such as 1, 2, and 3 are cardinal numbers. We know that 2 is exactly twice as many as 1 and that 3 is exactly three times as many as 1. You will see in Appendix B at the end of this chapter a type of consumer behaviour analysis that requires only *ordinal* measurement of utility, meaning ranked or ordered. *First, second,* and *third* are ordinal numbers; nothing can be said about their exact size relationships. We can only talk about their importance relative to each other. Temperature, for example, is an ordinal ranking. One hundred degrees Celsius is not twice as warm as 50 degrees Celsius. All we can say is that 100 degrees Celsius is warmer than 50 degrees Celsius.

Applying Marginal Analysis to Utility

The specific example presented in Figure 7.1 will clarify the distinction between total utility and marginal utility. The table in part (a) shows the total utility and the marginal utility of watching videos each week. Marginal utility is the difference between total utility derived from one level of consumption and total utility derived from another level of consumption. A simple formula for marginal utility is this:

$$\text{Marginal utility} = \frac{\text{change in total utility}}{\text{change in number of units consumed}}$$

Part (a)

(1) Number of Videos Watched per Week	(2) Total Utility (utils per week)	(3) Marginal Utility (utils per week)
0	0	
		10 (10 − 0)
1	10	
		6 (16 − 10)
2	16	
		3 (19 − 16)
3	19	
		1 (20 − 19)
4	20	
		0 (20 − 20)
5	20	
		−2 (18 − 20)
6	18	

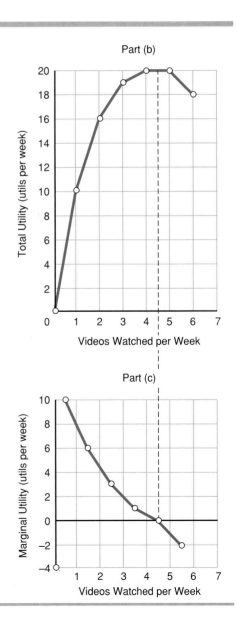

Part (b)

Part (c)

Figure 7.1

Total and Marginal Utility of Watching Videos

If we were able to assign specific values to the utility derived from watching videos each week, we could obtain a marginal utility schedule similar in pattern to the one shown in part (a). In column 1 is the number of videos watched per week; in column 2, the total utility derived from each quantity; and in column 3, the marginal utility derived from each additional quantity, which is defined as the change in total utility due to a change of one unit of watching videos per week. Total utility from part (a) is plotted in part (b). Marginal utility is plotted in part (c), where you see that it reaches zero where total utility hits its maximum at between four and five units.

In our example, when a person has already watched two videos in one week and then watches another, total utility increases from 16 utils to 19. Therefore, the marginal utility (of watching one more video after already having watched two in one week) is equal to three utils.

GRAPHIC ANALYSIS

We can transfer the information in part (a) of Figure 7.1 onto a graph, as we do in parts (b) and (c). Total utility, which is represented in column 2 of part (a), is transferred to part (b).

Total utility continues to rise until four videos are watched per week. This measure of utility remains at 20 utils through the fifth video, and at the sixth video per week it falls to 18 utils; we assume that at some quantity consumed per unit time period, boredom sets in. This is shown in part (b).

Marginal Utility

If you look carefully at parts (b) and (c) of Figure 7.1, the notion of marginal utility becomes very clear. In economics, the term *marginal* always refers to a change in the total. The marginal utility of watching three videos per week instead of two videos per week is the increment in total utility and is equal to three utils per week. All of the points in part (c) are taken from column 3 of the table in part (a). Notice that marginal utility falls throughout the graph. A special point occurs after four videos are watched per week because the total utility curve in part (b) is unchanged after the consumption of the fourth video. That means that the consumer receives no additional (marginal) utility from watching the fifth video. This is shown in part (c) as *zero* marginal utility. After that point, marginal utility becomes negative.

In our example, when marginal utility becomes negative, it means that the consumer is fed up with watching videos and would require some form of compensation to watch any more. When marginal utility is negative, an additional unit consumed actually lowers total utility by becoming a nuisance. Rarely does a consumer face a situation of negative marginal utility. Whenever this point is reached, goods become in effect "bads." A rational consumer will stop consuming at the point at which marginal utility becomes negative, even if the good is free.

Concepts in Brief

- Utility is defined as want-satisfying power; it is a power common to all desired goods and services.
- We arbitrarily measure utility in units called utils.
- It is important to distinguish between total utility and marginal utility. Total utility is the total satisfaction derived from the consumption of a given quantity of a good or service. Marginal utility is the change in total utility due to a one-unit change in the consumption of the good or service.

DIMINISHING MARGINAL UTILITY

▶ **Diminishing marginal utility**

The principle that as more of any good or service is consumed, its extra benefit declines. Otherwise stated, increases in total utility from the consumption of a good or service become smaller and smaller as more is consumed during a given time period.

Notice that in part (c) of Figure 7.1, marginal utility is continuously declining. This property has been named the principle of **diminishing marginal utility.** It is not a concept that can be proved, but economists and others have believed in it for years and it has even been called a law. This supposed law concerns a psychological, or subjective, utility that you receive as you consume more and more of a particular good. Stated formally, the law is as follows:

As an individual consumes more of a particular commodity, the total level of utility, or satisfaction, derived from that consumption usually increases. Eventually, however, the rate at which it increases diminishes as more is consumed.

Take a hungry individual at a dinner table. The first serving is greatly appreciated, and the individual derives a substantial amount of utility from it. The second serving does not have quite as much impact as the first one, and the third serving is likely to be even less satisfying. This individual experiences diminishing marginal utility of food and stops eating. This is true for most people. All-you-can-eat restaurants count on this fact; a second helping of ribs may provide some marginal utility, but the third helping would have only a little or even negative marginal utility. The fall in the marginal utility of other goods is even more dramatic.

Consider for a moment the opposite possibility—increasing marginal utility. Under such a situation, the marginal utility after consuming, say, one hamburger would increase. The second hamburger would be more valuable to you, and the third would be even more valuable yet. If increasing marginal utility existed, each of us would consume only one good or service! Rather than observing that "variety is the spice of life," we would see that monotony in consumption was preferred. We do not observe this, and therefore we have great confidence in the concept of diminishing marginal utility.

Try Preview Question 1:

What is the law of diminishing marginal utility?

EXAMPLE | Newspaper Vending Machines Versus Candy Vending Machines

Have you ever noticed that newspaper vending machines nearly everywhere in Canada allow you to put in the correct change—the cost of one newspaper—lift up the door, and take as many newspapers as you want? Contrast this type of vending machine with candy machines. They are completely locked at all times. You must designate the candy that you wish, normally by using some type of keypad. The candy then drops down to a place where you reach to retrieve it but from which you cannot grab any other candy. The difference between these two types of vending machines is explained by diminishing marginal utility. Newspaper companies dispense newspapers from coin-operated boxes that allow dishonest people to take more copies than they pay for. What would a dishonest person do with more than one copy of a newspaper, however? The marginal utility of a second newspaper is normally zero. The benefit of storing excessive newspapers is usually nil because yesterday's news has no value. But the same analysis does not hold for candy. The marginal utility of a second candy bar is certainly less than the first, but it is normally not zero. Moreover, one can store candy for relatively long periods of time at relatively low cost. Consequently, food vending machine companies have to worry about dishonest users of their machines and must make their machines much more theftproof than newspaper companies do.

For critical analysis: Can you think of a circumstance under which a substantial number of newspaper purchasers might be inclined to take more than one newspaper out of a vending machine?

Thinking Critically About the Media   **It's Priceless!**

Museums around the world are filled with one-of-a-kind art objects. In particular, many museums have items that were crafted by humans thousands of years ago. Occasionally, one of these unique artifacts is stolen. The media are quick to point out that because of the unique nature of the stolen object, it is "priceless." The implication is that the utility humans receive from the stolen object is in fact without limits, or infinite. In a world of scarcity, however, nothing can be truly "priceless." If, rather than being stolen, the art object were put up for sale at auction, it would fetch some price below infinity.

OPTIMIZING CONSUMPTION CHOICES

▶ **Consumer optimum**
A choice of a set of goods and services that maximizes the level of satisfaction for each consumer, subject to limited income.

Every consumer has a limited income. Choices must be made. When a consumer has made all choices about what to buy and in what quantities, and when the total level of satisfaction, or utility, from that set of choices is as great as it can be, we say that the consumer has *optimized*. When the consumer has attained an optimum consumption set of goods and services, we say that individual has reached **consumer optimum.**[2]

Consider a simple two-good example. The consumer has to choose between spending income on the rental of videos at $5 each and on purchasing deluxe hamburgers at $3 each. Let's say that the last dollar spent on hamburgers yields three utils of utility but the last dollar spent on video rentals yields 10 utils. Wouldn't this consumer increase total utility if some dollars were taken away from hamburger consumption and allocated to video rentals? The answer is yes. Given diminishing marginal utility, more dollars spent on video rentals will reduce marginal utility per last dollar spent, whereas fewer dollars spent on hamburger consumption will increase marginal utility per last dollar spent. The optimum—where total utility is maximized—might occur when the satisfaction per last dollar spent on both hamburgers and video rentals per week is equal for the two goods. Thus the amount of goods consumed depends on the prices of the goods, the income of the consumers, and the marginal utility derived from each good.

Table 7.1 (page 170) presents information on utility derived from consuming various quantities of videos and hamburgers. Columns 4 and 8 show the marginal utility per dollar spent on videos and hamburgers, respectively. If the prices of both goods are zero, individuals will consume each as long as their respective marginal

---

[2] Optimization typically refers to individual decision-making processes. When we deal with many individuals interacting in the marketplace, we talk in terms of an equilibrium in the marketplace. Generally speaking, equilibrium is a property of markets rather than of individual decision making.

Table 7-1
Total and Marginal Utility from Consuming Videos and Hamburgers on an Income of $26

(1) Videos per Period	(2) Total Utility of Videos per Period (utils)	(3) Marginal Utility (utils) MU_v	(4) Marginal Utility per Dollar Spent (MU_v/P_v) (price = $5)	(5) Hamburgers per Period	(6) Total Utility of Hamburgers per Period (utils)	(7) Marginal Utility (utils) MU_h	(8) Marginal Utility per Dollar Spent (MU_h/P_h) (price = $3)
0	0.0	—	—	0	0	—	—
1	50.0	50.0	10.0	1	25	25	8.3
2	95.0	45.0	9.0	2	47	22	7.3
3	135.0	40.0	8.0	3	65	18	6.0
4	171.5	36.5	7.3	4	80	15	5.0
5	200.0	28.5	5.7	5	89	9	3.0

utility is positive (at least five units of each and probably much more). It is also true that a consumer with infinite income will continue consuming goods until the marginal utility of each is equal to zero. When the price is zero or the consumer's income is infinite, there is no effective constraint on consumption.

Consumer optimum is attained when the marginal utility of the last dollar spent on each good yields the same utility, and income is completely exhausted. The individual's income is $26. From columns 4 and 8 of Table 7.1, maximum equal marginal utilities occur at the consumption level of four videos and two hamburgers (the marginal utility per dollar spent equals 7.3). Notice that the marginal utility per dollar spent for both goods is also (approximately) equal at the consumption level of three videos and one hamburger, but here total income is not completely exhausted. Likewise, the marginal utility per dollar spent is (approximately) equal at five videos and three hamburgers, but the expenditures necessary for that level of consumption exceed the individual's income.

Table 7.2 shows the steps taken to arrive at consumer optimum. The first video would yield a marginal utility per dollar of 10, while the first hamburger would yield a marginal utility of only 8.3 per dollar. Because it yields the higher marginal utility per dollar, the video is purchased. This leaves $21 of income. The second video yields a higher marginal utility per dollar (9, versus 8.3 for hamburgers), so it is also purchased, leaving an unspent income of $16. At the third purchase, the first hamburger now yields a higher marginal utility per dollar than the next video (8.3 versus 8), so the first hamburger is purchased. This leaves income of $13 to spend. The process continues until all income is exhausted and the marginal utility per dollar spent is equal for both goods.

To restate, consumer optimum requires the following:

Try Preview Question 2:
How does a consumer maximize total utility?

A consumer's money income should be allocated so that the last dollar spent on each good purchased yields the same amount of marginal utility (when all income is spent).

Table 7-2
Steps to Consumer Optimum

In each purchase situation described here, the consumer always purchases the good with the higher marginal utility per dollar spent (MU/P). For example, at the time of the third purchase, the marginal utility per last dollar spent on videos is 8, but it is 8.3 for hamburgers, and $16 of income remains, so the next purchase will be a hamburger. Here $P_v = \$5$ and $P_h = \$3$.

	Choices					
	Videos		Hamburgers			
Purchase	Unit	(MU_v/P_v)	Unit	$(MU_h/(P_h)$	Buying Decision	Remaining Income
1	First	10.0	First	8.3	First video	$26 − $5 = $21
2	Second	9.0	First	8.3	Second video	$21 − $5 = $16
3	Third	8.0	First	8.3	First hamburger	$16 − $3 = $13
4	Third	8.0	Second	7.3	Third video	$13 − $5 = $ 8
5	Fourth	7.3	Second	7.3	Fourth video and	$ 8 − $5 = $ 3
					second hamburger	$ 3 − $3 = $ 0

A Little Math

We can state the rule of consumer optimum in algebraic terms by examining the ratio of marginal utilities and prices of individual products. This is sometimes called the *utility maximization rule*. The rule simply states that a consumer maximizes personal satisfaction when allocating money income in such a way that the last dollars spent on good A, good B, good C, and so on, yield equal amounts of marginal utility. Marginal utility (MU) from good A is indicated by MU of good A. For good B, it is MU of good B. Our algebraic formulation of this rule, therefore, becomes

$$\frac{MU \text{ of good A}}{\text{price of good A}} = \frac{MU \text{ of good B}}{\text{price of good B}} = \ldots = \frac{MU \text{ of good Z}}{\text{price of good Z}}$$

The letters A, B, ..., Z indicate the various goods and services that the consumer might purchase.

We know, then, that the marginal utility of good A divided by the price of good A must equal the marginal utility of any other good divided by its price in order for the consumer to maximize utility. Note, though, that the application of the utility maximization rule is not an explicit or conscious act on the part of consumers. Rather, this is a model of consumer optimum.

HOW A PRICE CHANGE AFFECTS CONSUMER OPTIMUM

Consumption decisions are summarized in the law of demand, which states that the amount purchased is inversely related to price. We can now see why by using the law of diminishing marginal utility.

Purchase decisions are made such that the value of the marginal utility of the last unit purchased and consumed is just equal to the price that had to be paid. No consumer will, when optimizing, buy 10 units of a good per time period when the personal valuation placed on the tenth unit is less than the price of the tenth unit.

If we start out at consumer optimum and then observe a price decrease, we can predict that consumers will respond to the price decrease by consuming more. Why? Because before the price change, the marginal utility of the last unit was about equal to the price paid for the last unit. Now, with a lower price, it is possible to consume more than before and still not have the marginal utility be less than the price, because the price has fallen. If the law of diminishing marginal utility holds, the purchase and consumption of additional units will cause marginal utility to fall. Eventually it will fall to the point at which it is equal to the price of the final good consumed. The limit to this increase in consumption is given by the law of diminishing marginal utility. At some point, the marginal utility of an additional unit will be less than what the person would have to give up (price) for that additional unit, and the person will stop buying.

A hypothetical demand curve for video rentals per week for a typical consumer is presented in Figure 7.2. At a rental price of $5 per video, the marginal utility of the last video rented per week is MU_1. At a rental price of $4 per video per week, the marginal utility is represented by MU_2. Because of the law of diminishing marginal utility—with the consumption of more videos, the marginal utility of the last unit of these additional videos is lower—MU_2 must be less than MU_1. What has happened is that at a lower price, the number of video rentals per week increased from two to three; marginal utility must have fallen. At a higher consumption rate, the marginal utility falls to meet the lower price for video rentals per week.

Try Preview Question 3:

What happens to consumer optimum when price changes?

Figure 7.2
Video Rental Prices and Marginal Utility

The rate of video rentals per week will increase as long as the marginal utility per last video rental per week exceeds the cost of that rental. A reduction in price from $5 to $4 per video rental causes consumers to increase consumption until marginal utility falls from MU_1 to MU_2 (because of the law of diminishing marginal utility).

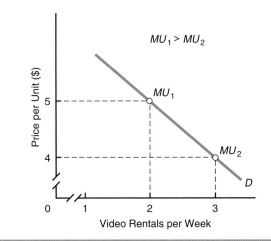

The Substitution Effect

▶ **Substitution effect**
The tendency of people to substitute cheaper commodities for more expensive commodities.

▶ **Principle of substitution**
The principle that consumers and producers shift away from goods and resources that become relatively higher priced in favour of goods and resources that are now relatively lower priced.

▶ **Purchasing power**
The value of money for buying goods and services. If your money income stays the same but the price of one good that you are buying goes up, your effective purchasing power falls and vice versa.

▶ **Real-income effect**
The change in people's purchasing power that occurs when, other things being constant, the price of one good that they purchase changes. When that price goes up, real income, or purchasing power, falls, and when that price goes down, real income increases.

What is happening as the price of video rentals falls is that consumers are substituting the now relatively cheaper video rentals for other goods and services, such as restaurant meals and live concerts. We call this the **substitution effect** of a change in price of a good because it occurs when consumers substitute relatively cheaper goods for relatively more expensive ones.

We assume that people desire a variety of goods and pursue a variety of goals. That means that few, if any, goods are irreplaceable in meeting demand. We are generally able to substitute one product for another to satisfy demand. This is commonly referred to as the **principle of substitution.**

Let's assume now that there are several goods, not exactly the same, and perhaps even very different from one another, but all serving basically the same purpose. If the relative price of one particular good falls, we will most likely substitute in favour of the lower-priced good and against the other similar goods that we might have been purchasing. Conversely, if the price of that good rises relative to the price of the other similar goods, we will substitute in favour of them and not buy as much of the now higher-priced good.

If the price of some item that you purchase goes down while your money income and all other prices stay the same, your ability to purchase goods goes up. That is to say that your effective **purchasing power** is increased, even though your money income has stayed the same. If you purchase 20 litres of gas a week at 60 cents per litre, your total outlay for gas is $12. If the price goes down by 50 percent, to 30 cents a litre, you would have to spend only $6 a week to purchase the same number of litres of gas. If your money income and the prices of other goods remain the same, it would be possible for you to continue purchasing 20 litres of gas a week *and* to purchase more of other goods. You will feel richer and will indeed probably purchase more of a number of goods, including perhaps even more gasoline.

The converse will also be true. When the price of one good you are purchasing goes up, without any other change in prices or income, the purchasing power of your income will drop. You will have to reduce your purchases of either the now higher-priced good or other goods (or a combination).

In general, this **real-income effect** is usually quite small. After all, unless we consider broad categories, such as housing or food, a change in the price of one particular item that we purchase will have a relatively small effect on our total purchasing power. Thus we expect the substitution effect usually to be more important than the real-income effect in causing us to purchase more of goods that have become cheaper and less of goods that have become more expensive.

THE DEMAND CURVE REVISITED

Linking the "law" of diminishing marginal utility and the utility maximization rule gives us a negative relationship between the quantity demanded of a good or service and its price. As the relative price of video rentals goes up, for example, the quantity demanded will fall; and as the relative price of video rentals goes down, the quantity demanded will rise. Figure 7.2 shows this demand curve for video rentals. As the price of video rentals falls, the consumer can maximize total utility only by renting more videos, and vice versa. In other words, the relationship between price and quantity desired is simply a downward-sloping demand curve. Note, though, that this downward-sloping demand curve (the law of demand) is derived under the assumption of constant tastes and incomes. You must remember that we are keeping these important determining variables constant when we simply look at the relationship between price and quantity demanded.

Try Preview Question 4:
How can the law of diminishing marginal utility account for the law of demand?

Marginal Utility, Total Utility, and the Diamond-Water Paradox

Even though water is essential to life and diamonds are not, water is cheap and diamonds are dear. The economist Adam Smith in 1776 called this the "diamond-water paradox." The paradox is easily understood when we make the distinction between total utility and marginal utility. The total utility of water greatly exceeds the total utility derived from diamonds. What determines the price, though, is what happens on the margin. We have relatively few diamonds, so the marginal utility of the last diamond consumed is high. The opposite is true for water. Total utility does not determine what people are willing to pay for a unit of a particular commodity; marginal utility does. Look at the situation graphically in Figure 7.3. We show the demand curve for diamonds, labelled $D_{diamonds}$. The demand curve for water is labelled D_{water}. We plot quantity in terms of kilograms per unit time period on the horizontal axis. On the vertical axis we plot price in dollars per kilogram. We use kilograms as our common unit of measurement for water and for diamonds. We could just as well have used gallons, acre-feet, or litres.

Figure 7.3
The Diamond-Water Paradox

We pick kilograms as a common unit of measurement for both water and diamonds. To demonstrate that the demand and supply of water are immense, we have put a break in the horizontal quantity axis. Although the demand for water is much greater than the demand for diamonds, the marginal valuation of water is given by the marginal value placed on the last unit of water consumed. To find that, we must know the supply of water, which is given as S_1. At that supply, the price of water is P_{water}. But the supply for diamonds is given by S_2. At that supply, the price of diamonds is $P_{diamonds}$. The total valuation that consumers place on water is tremendous relative to the total valuation consumers place on diamonds. What is important for price determination, however, is the marginal valuation, or the marginal utility received.

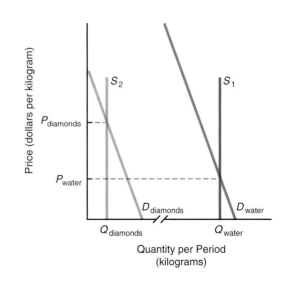

Notice that the demand for water is many, many times the demand for diamonds (even though we really don't show this in the diagram). We draw the supply curve of water as S_1 at a quantity of Q_{water}. The supply curve for diamonds is given as S_2 at quantity $Q_{diamonds}$. At the intersection of the supply curve of water with the demand curve of water, the price per kilogram is P_{water}. The intersection of the supply curve of diamonds with the demand curve of diamonds is at $P_{diamonds}$. Notice that $P_{diamonds}$ exceeds P_{water}. Diamonds sell at a higher price than water.

INTERNATIONAL EXAMPLE
The World of Water in Saudi Arabia

The diamond-water paradox deals with the situation in which water, although necessary for life, may be much cheaper than some luxury item. In Saudi Arabia, as you might expect, the contrary can be true. A litre of water costs five times as much as a litre of gasoline, whereas a pair of custom-made British wool dress pants costs only $25. These relative prices are quite different from what we are used to seeing in Canada. Water costs next to nothing, a litre of gas about 60 cents, and custom-made wool pants at least $200. To understand what has happened in Saudi Arabia, simply substitute gasoline for water and water for diamonds in Figure 7.3.

For critical analysis: List some of the effects on human behaviour that such a high relative price of water would cause.

Concepts in Brief

* The law of diminishing marginal utility tells us that each successive marginal unit of a good consumed adds less extra utility.
* Each consumer with a limited income must make a choice about the basket of commodities to purchase; economic theory assumes that the consumer chooses the basket of commodities that yields optimum consumption. The consumer maximizes total utility by equating the marginal utility of the last dollar spent on one good with the marginal utility per last dollar spent on all other goods. That is the state of consumer optimum.
* To remain in consumer optimum, a price decrease requires an increase in consumption; a price increase requires a decrease in consumption.
* Each change in price has a substitution effect and a real-income effect. When price falls, the consumer substitutes in favour of the relatively cheaper good. When price falls, the consumer's real purchasing power increases, causing the consumer to purchase more of most goods. The opposite would occur when price increases. Assuming that the law of diminishing marginal utility holds, the demand curve must slope downward.

Issues and Applications

Contingent Valuation: Pricing the "Priceless"

Concepts Applied: Utility, total utility, demand curve

It is difficult to estimate the dollar amount an average citizen is willing to pay to keep Banff National Park's air clean. One way economists attempt to derive the demand for pristine wilderness is to use contingent valuation.

Obviously, not everything has a price. That is because not everything is bought and sold in the marketplace. Much of what occurs in the environment is outside the marketplace. A wilderness area so remote that hardly anyone visits it certainly has a value, but what is it? Just because few people visit doesn't mean it has little worth. If the wilderness were privately owned and the owner received virtually no income from occasional visitors, that does not mean that it has virtually no value.

When Disaster Occurs

When the wilderness area with few visitors is harmed by some disaster of human origin, such as an oil spill, what has been lost? If your house is burned down, you can get a pretty accurate idea of what the insurance company will give you by looking at the housing market for an alternative. Such is not the case with an oil-blighted wilderness area in the far reaches of the north.

Nonuse Satisfaction

Even people who never use the wilderness area may place a value on it. They may place a value on the opportunity to preserve the wilderness for their grandchildren and on the mere knowledge that

such a pristine wilderness area exists. The question, then, is, how do we get an accurate valuation of these nonuse values?

Contingent Valuation

Some economists believe that they can obtain an estimate of the demand curve for a wilderness area, for example, that includes nonuse values by conducting opinion polls. In this technique, called *contingent valuation*, people are asked what they are willing to pay for a particular benefit or what they would accept as compensation for its loss. This technique was used in developing multi-billion-dollar damage claims against Exxon after its oil tanker, the *Exxon Valdez*, went aground in Alaska in 1989. In essence, these contingent valuation surveys asked people *not* living in Alaska to place a value on the utility they lost by virtue of the fact that a part of Alaska's pristine beauty was harmed.

Criticisms of Opinion Data

Many economists are critical of opinion surveys conducted to estimate utility. They point out that such estimates of supposed willingness to pay are without strong meaning if individuals don't actually have to make the payments. One opinion survey estimated the average individual's willingness to pay to prevent the extinction of the whooping crane at $200 per year. That comes to almost $3 billion per year for all Canadian adults. Given that there are fewer than 170 whooping cranes in existence, this total represents about $23.6 million per bird *per year*. There are literally thousands of species that might be protected. Even if households' average willingness to pay is only $10 per year per endangered species, summing that amount over all environmental "goods" would exceed the average family's yearly income many times.

The way in which opinion survey questions are phrased also reveals their weaknesses. In one study, the people interviewed said they would be willing to pay $90 a year to preserve clean air in Banff National Park. In a follow-up survey, when they were asked about paying for competing claims of cleaner air in Toronto and in the eastern provinces as well, they were willing to spend only $16 a year to preserve clean air in Banff National Park.

Finally, when people are asked their willingness to accept money in exchange for a harm to a resource rather than their willingness to pay to prevent that identical harm, the dollar values they cite are substantially higher.

For Critical Analysis

1. Why can't opinion polls be used effectively to estimate demand curves?
2. How do individuals normally express their perceived level of satisfaction for a good or a service in the marketplace?

CHAPTER SUMMARY

1. As an individual consumes more of a particular commodity, the total level of utility, or satisfaction, derived from that consumption increases. However, the *rate* at which it increases diminishes as more is consumed. This is known as the law of diminishing marginal utility.

2. An individual reaches consumer optimum when the marginal utility per last dollar spent on each commodity consumed is equal to the marginal utility per dollar spent on every other good.

3. When the price of a particular commodity goes up, to get back into an optimum position, the consumer must reduce consumption of the now relatively more expensive commodity. As this consumer moves back up the marginal utility curve, marginal utility increases. A change in price has both a substitution effect and a real-income effect. As the price goes down, for example, the consumer substitutes in favour of the cheaper good, and also as the price goes down, real purchasing power increases, causing a general increase in consumer purchases of most goods and services.

4. It is possible to derive a downward-sloping demand curve by using the principle of diminishing marginal utility.

DISCUSSION OF PREVIEW QUESTIONS

1. **What is the law of diminishing marginal utility?**
The law of diminishing marginal utility states that as an individual consumes more and more units of a commodity per unit of time, eventually the extra benefit derived from consuming successive units will fall. Thus the fourth hamburger consumed in an eight-hour period yields less satisfaction than the third, and the third less than the second. The law is quite general and holds for almost any commodity.

2. **How does a consumer maximize total utility?**
This question deals with the maximization of utility derived not from the consumption of one commodity but from the consumption of all commodities that the individual wants, subject to an income constraint. The rule is that maximization of total utility requires that the last dollar spent on each commodity consumed by the individual have the same marginal utility. Stated differently, the consumer should purchase goods and services up to the point where the consumer's marginal utilities per dollar (marginal utility divided by price) for all commodities are equated and all income is spent (or saved for future spending). For example, assume that you are about to spend all of your income but discover that the marginal utility per dollar's worth for bread will be 10 utils and the marginal utility per dollar's worth of milk will be 30 utils. This means that the last dollar you are going to spend on bread will increase your total utility by 10, whereas the last dollar you are going to spend on milk will increase your total utility by 30. By spending one dollar more on milk and one dollar less on bread, you raise your total utility by about 20 utils, while your total dollar expenditures remain constant. This reallocation causes the marginal utility per dollar's worth of milk to fall and the marginal utility per dollar's worth of bread to rise. To maximize total utility, you will continue to buy more or less of each commodity until the marginal utilities per dollar's worth of all goods you consume are equated.

3. **What happens to consumer optimum when price changes?**
Assume that you have reached an optimum: The marginal utilities per dollar's worth for all the goods you purchase are equated. Assume that the last dollar spent on each of the commodities you purchase increases your total utility by 20 utils. Now suppose that the price of bread falls

while all other prices remain constant. Because the price of bread has fallen, the last dollar spent on bread now has a higher marginal utility. This is true because at a lower price for bread, a $1 coin can purchase a greater quantity of bread. This means that marginal utility per dollar's worth of bread now *exceeds* 20 utils, whereas the marginal utility per dollar's worth of each of the other goods you purchase still equals 20 utils. In short, you are no longer optimizing; your old pattern of expenditures does not maximize your total utility. You can now increase your total utility by purchasing more bread. Note that a reduction in the price of bread (other things held constant) leads to your purchasing more bread per unit of time.

4. **How can the law of diminishing marginal utility account for the law of demand?**

When a consumer is optimizing, total utility is maximized. An increase in expenditures on any specific commodity will necessarily lead to a reduction in expenditure on another commodity and a reduction in overall total utility. Why? Because of the law of diminishing marginal utility. For example, suppose that you are maximizing your overall total utility and that the marginal utility per dollar's worth of each commodity you purchase is 20 utils. Suppose that you experiment and spend another dollar on bread—and therefore spend one dollar less on milk. Your total utility must fall because you will receive less than 20 utils for the next dollar's worth of bread, and you lose 20 utils by spending a dollar less on milk. Thus, on net balance, you lose utility. We can see intuitively, then, that because you get less and less additional benefit from consuming more and more bread (or any other commodity), the price of bread (or any other commodity) *must fall* before you will voluntarily purchase more of it. That is how diminishing marginal utility helps explain the law of demand.

PROBLEMS

(Answers to the odd-numbered problems appear at the back of the book.)

7-1. Suppose that you are standing in the checkout line of a grocery store. You have five kilograms of oranges and three ears of corn. A kilogram of oranges costs 30 cents; so does an ear of corn. You have $2.40 to spend. You are satisfied that you have reached the highest level of satisfaction, or total utility. A friend comes along and tries to convince you that you have to put some of the corn back and replace it with oranges. From what you know about utility analysis, how would you explain this disagreement?

7-2. To increase marginal utility, the consumer must decrease consumption (other things being constant). This sounds paradoxical. Why is it a correct statement nonetheless?

7-3. Assume that Alice Warfield's marginal utility is 100 utils for the last hamburger she consumed. If the price of hamburgers is $1 apiece, what is Warfield's marginal utility per dollar's worth of hamburger? What is her marginal utility per dollar's worth if the price is 50 cents per hamburger? If the price is $2? How do we calculate marginal utility per dollar's worth of specific commodities?

7-4. A fall in the price of one good leads to more of that good being consumed, other things remaining constant. How might this increase in consumption be broken down?

7-5. Consider the table at the top of page 179. Following the utility maximization rule, how much of each good will be consumed?

Quantity of Good A	Marginal Utility of Good A	Price of Good A	Quantity of Good B	Marginal Utility of Good B	Price of Good B
100	15	$4.51	9	7	$1.69
101	12	4.51	10	5	1.69
102	8	4.51	11	3	1.69
103	6	4.51	12	2	1.69

7-6. If total utility is increasing as more is consumed, what is happening to marginal utility?

7-7. Yesterday you were consuming four eggs and two strips of bacon. Today you are consuming three eggs and three strips of bacon. Your tastes did not change overnight. What might have caused this change? Are you better or worse off?

7-8. The marginal utility of X is five times the marginal utility of Y, but the price of X is only four times the price of Y. How can this disequilibrium be remedied?

7-9. Look at the accompanying table, then answer the questions that follow.

Quantity of X Consumed	Total Utility (utils)
0	0
1	20
2	50
3	70
4	80

a. What is the marginal utility of consuming the first unit of X?
b. What is the marginal utility of consuming the fourth unit of X?
c. When does marginal utility start to diminish?

MORE ADVANCED CONSUMER CHOICE THEORY

It is possible to analyse consumer choice verbally, as we did for the most part in Chapter 7. The theory of diminishing marginal utility can be fairly well accepted on intuitive grounds and by introspection. If we want to be more formal and perhaps more elegant in our theorizing, however, we can translate our discussion into a graphic analysis with what we call indifference curves and the budget constraint. Here we discuss these terms and their relationship and demonstrate consumer equilibrium in geometric form.

ON BEING INDIFFERENT

What does it mean to be indifferent? It usually means that you don't care one way or the other about something—you are equally disposed to either of two alternatives. With this interpretation in mind, we will turn to two choices, video rentals and restaurant meals. In part (a) of Figure B-1, we show several combinations of video rentals and restaurant meals per week that a representative consumer considers equally satisfactory. That is to say, for each combination, A, B, C, and D, this consumer will have exactly the same level of total utility.

The simple numerical example that we have used happens to concern video rentals and restaurant meals per week. This example is used to illustrate general features of indifference curves and related analytical tools that are necessary for deriving the demand curve. Obviously, we could have used any two commodities. Just remember that we are using a *specific* example to illustrate a *general* analysis.

We can plot these combinations graphically in part (b) of Figure B-1, with restaurant meals per week on the horizontal axis and video rentals per week on the vertical axis. These are our consumer's indifference combinations—the consumer finds each

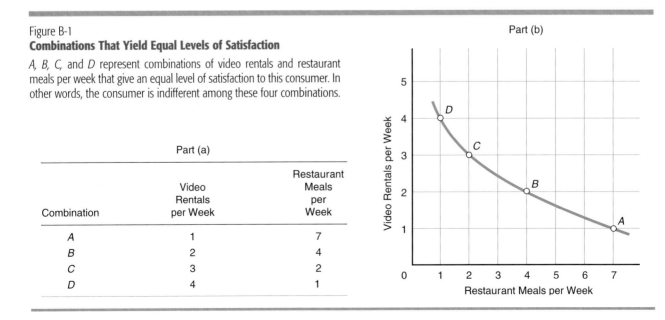

Figure B-1
Combinations That Yield Equal Levels of Satisfaction

A, B, C, and D represent combinations of video rentals and restaurant meals per week that give an equal level of satisfaction to this consumer. In other words, the consumer is indifferent among these four combinations.

Part (a)

Combination	Video Rentals per Week	Restaurant Meals per Week
A	1	7
B	2	4
C	3	2
D	4	1

▶ **Indifference curve**
A curve composed of a set of consumption alternatives, each of which yields the same total amount of satisfaction.

combination as acceptable as the others. When we connect these combinations with a smooth curve, we obtain what is called the consumer's **indifference curve.** Along the indifference curve, every combination of the two goods in question yields the same level of satisfaction. Every point along the indifference curve is equally desirable to the consumer. For example, four video rentals per week and one restaurant meal per week will give our representative consumer exactly the same total satisfaction as two video rentals per week and four restaurant meals per week.

PROPERTIES OF INDIFFERENCE CURVES

Indifference curves have special properties relating to their slope and shape.

Downward Slope

The indifference curve shown in part (b) of Figure B-1 slopes downward; that is, it has a negative slope. Now consider Figure B-2. Here we show two points, *A* and *B*. Point *A* represents four video rentals per week and two restaurant meals per week. Point *B* represents five video rentals per week and six restaurant meals per week. Clearly, *B* is always preferred to *A* because *B* represents more of everything. If *B* is always preferred to *A*, it is impossible for points *A* and *B* to be on the same indifference curve because the definition of the indifference curve is a set of combinations of two goods that are equally preferred.

Curvature

The indifference curve that we have drawn in part (b) of Figure B-1 is special. Notice that it is curved. Why didn't we just draw a straight line, as we have usually done for a demand curve? To find out why we don't posit straight-line indifference curves, con-

Figure B-2
Indifference Curves: Impossibility of an Upward Slope

Point *B* represents a consumption of more video rentals per week and more restaurant meals per week than point *A*. *B* is always preferred to *A*. Therefore, *A* and *B* cannot be on the same indifference curve, which is positively sloped, because an indifference curve shows equally preferred combinations of the two goods.

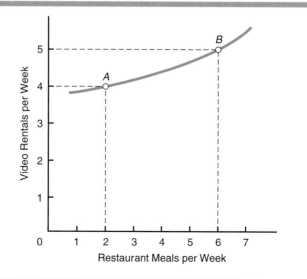

sider the implications. We show such a straight-line indifference curve in Figure B-3. Start at point *A*. The consumer has no restaurant meals and five video rentals per week. Now the consumer wishes to go to point *B*. He or she is willing to give up only one video rental in order to get one restaurant meal. Now let's assume that the consumer is at point *C*, consuming one video rental and four restaurant meals per week. If the consumer wants to go to point *D*, he or she is again willing to give up one video rental in order to get one more restaurant meal per week.

In other words, no matter how many videos the consumer rents, he or she is willing to give up one video rental to get one restaurant meal per week—which does not seem plausible. Doesn't it make sense to hypothesize that the more videos the consumer rents per week, the less he or she will value an *additional* video rental? Presumably, when the consumer has five video rentals and no restaurant meals per week, he or she should be willing to give up more than one video rental in order to get one restaurant meal. Therefore, a straight-line indifference curve as shown in Figure B-3 no longer seems plausible.

In mathematical jargon, an indifference curve is convex with respect to the origin. Let's look at this in part (a) of Figure B-1. Starting with combination *A*, the consumer has one video rental but seven restaurant meals per week. To remain indifferent, the consumer would have to be willing to give up three restaurant meals to obtain one more video rental (as shown in combination *B*). However, to go from combination *C* to combination *D*, notice that the consumer would have to be willing to give up only one restaurant meal for an additional video rental per week. The quantity of the substitute considered acceptable changes as the rate of consumption of the original item changes.

Consequently the indifference curve in part (b) of Figure B-1 will be convex when viewed from the origin.

Figure B-3
Implications of a Straight-Line Indifference Curve

If the indifference curve is a straight line, the consumer will be willing to give up the same number of video rentals (one for one in this simple example) to get one more restaurant meal per week, whether the consumer has no restaurant meals or a lot of restaurant meals per week. For example, the consumer at point *A* has five video rentals and no restaurant meals per week. He or she is willing to give up one video rental in order to get one restaurant meal per week. At point *C*, however, the consumer has only one video rental and four restaurant meals per week. Because of the straight-line indifference curve, this consumer is willing to give up the last video rental in order to get one more restaurant meal per week, even though he or she already has four.

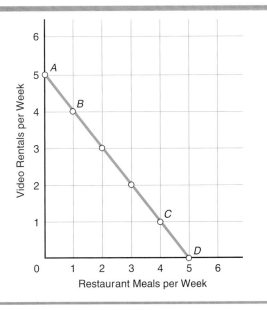

THE MARGINAL RATE OF SUBSTITUTION

Instead of using marginal utility, we can talk in terms of the marginal rate of substitution between restaurant meals and video rentals per week. We can formally define the consumer's marginal rate of substitution as follows:

> The marginal rate of substitution is equal to the change in the quantity of one good that just offsets a one-unit change in the consumption of another good, such that total satisfaction remains constant.

We can see numerically what happens to the marginal rate of substitution in our example if we rearrange part (a) of Figure B-1 into Table B-1. Here we show restaurant meals in the second column and video rentals in the third. Now we ask the question, What change in the consumption of video rentals per week will just compensate for a three-unit change in the consumption of restaurant meals per week and leave the consumer's total utility constant? The movement from *A* to *B* increases video rental consumption by one. Here the marginal rate of substitution is 3:1—a three-unit decrease in restaurant meals requires an increase of one video rental to leave the consumer's total utility unaltered. Thus the consumer values the three restaurant meals as the equivalent of one video rental. We do this for the rest of the table and find that as restaurant meals decrease further, the marginal rate of substitution goes from 3:1 to 1:1. The marginal rate of substitution of restaurant meals for video rentals per week falls as the consumer obtains more video rentals. That is, the consumer values successive units of video rentals less and less in terms of restaurant meals. The first video rental is valued at three restaurant meals; the last (fourth) video rental is valued at only one restaurant meal. The fact that the marginal rate of substitution falls is sometimes called the *law of substitution*.

Table B-1

Calculating the Marginal Rate of Substitution

As we move from combination *A* to combination *B*, we are still on the same indifference curve. To stay on that curve, the number of restaurant meals decreases by three and the number of video rentals increases by one. The marginal rate of substitution is 3:1. A three-unit decrease in restaurant meals requires an increase in one video rental to leave the consumer's total utility unaltered.

(1) Combination	(2) Restaurant Meals per Week	(3) Video Rentals per Week	(4) Marginal Rate of Substitution of Restaurant Meals for Video Rentals
A	7	1	
			3:1
B	4	2	
			2:1
C	2	3	
			1:1
D	1	4	

In geometric language, the slope of the consumer's indifference curve (actually, the negative of the slope) measures the consumer's marginal rate of substitution. Notice that this marginal rate of substitution is purely subjective or psychological.

THE INDIFFERENCE MAP

Let's now consider the possibility of having both more video rentals *and* more restaurant meals per week. When we do this, we can no longer stay on the same indifference curve that we drew in Figure B-1. That indifference curve was drawn for equally satisfying combinations of video rentals and restaurant meals per week. If the individual can now attain more of both, a new indifference curve will have to be drawn, above and to the right of the one shown in part (b) of Figure B-1. Alternatively, if the individual faces the possibility of having less of both video rentals and restaurant meals per week, an indifference curve will have to be drawn below and to the left of the one in part (b) of Figure B-1. We can map out a whole set of indifference curves corresponding to these possibilities.

Figure B-4 shows three possible indifference curves. Indifference curves that are higher than others necessarily imply that for every given quantity of one good, more of the other good can be obtained on a higher indifference curve. Looked at another way, if one goes from curve I_1 to I_2, it is possible to consume the same number of restaurant meals *and* be able to rent more videos per week. This is shown as a movement from point *A* to point *B* in Figure B-4. We could do it the other way. When we move from a lower to a higher indifference curve, it is possible to rent the same number of videos *and* to consume more restaurant meals per week. Thus the higher a consumer is on the indifference map, the greater that consumer's total level of satisfaction.

Figure B-4
A Set of Indifference Curves

An infinite number of indifference curves can be drawn. We show three possible ones. Realize that a higher indifference curve represents the possibility of higher rates of consumption of both goods. Hence a higher indifference curve is preferred to a lower one because more is preferred to less. Look at points *A* and *B*. Point *B* represents more video rentals than point *A*; therefore, bundles on indifference curve I_2 have to be preferred over bundles on I_1 because the number of restaurant meals per week is the same at points *A* and *B*.

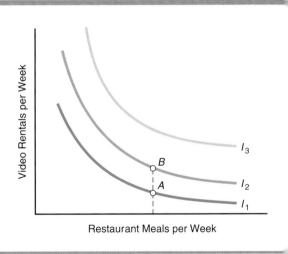

THE BUDGET CONSTRAINT

▶ **Budget constraint**

All of the possible combinations of goods that can be purchased (at fixed prices) with a specific budget.

Our problem here is to find out how to maximize consumer satisfaction. To do so, we must consult not only our *preferences*—given by indifference curves—but also our *market opportunities*—given by our available income and prices, called our **budget constraint.** We might want more of everything, but for any given budget constraint, we have to make choices, or trade-offs, among possible goods. Everyone has a budget constraint; that is, everyone faces a limited consumption potential. How do we show this graphically? We must find the prices of the goods in question and determine the maximum consumption of each allowed by our budget. For example, let's assume that videos rent for $10 apiece and restaurant meals cost $20. Let's also assume that our representative consumer has a total budget of $60 per week. What is the maximum number of videos the consumer can rent? Six. And the maximum number of restaurant meals per week he or she can consume? Three. So now, as shown in Figure B-5, we have two points on our budget line, which is sometimes called the *consumption possibilities curve.* These anchor points of the budget line are obtained by dividing money income by the price of each product. The first point is at *b* on the vertical axis; the second, at *b'* on the horizontal axis. The budget line is linear because prices are given.

Any combination along line *bb'* is possible; in fact, any combination in the coloured area is possible. We will assume, however, that the individual consumer completely uses up the available budget, and we will consider as possible only those points along *bb'*.

Slope of the Budget Constraint

The budget constraint is a line that slopes downward from left to right. The slope of that line has a special meaning. Look carefully at the budget line in Figure B-5. Remember from our discussion of graphs in Appendix A that we measure a negative slope by the ratio of the fall in *Y* over the run in *X*. In this case, *Y* is video rentals per week and *X* is restaurant meals per week. In Figure B-5, the fall in *Y* is −2 video rentals per week (a drop from 4 to 2) for a run in *X* of one restaurant meal per week (an increase from 1 to 2); therefore, the slope of the budget constraint is −2/1, or −2. This slope of the budget constraint represents the rate of exchange between video rentals and restaurant meals; it is the realistic rate of exchange, given their prices.

Figure B-5
The Budget Constraint

The line *bb'* represents this individual's budget constraint. Assuming that video rentals cost $10 each, restaurant meals cost $20 each, and the individual has a budget of $60 per week, a maximum of six video rentals or three restaurant meals can be bought each week. These two extreme points are connected to form the budget constraint. All combinations within the coloured area and on the budget constraint line are feasible.

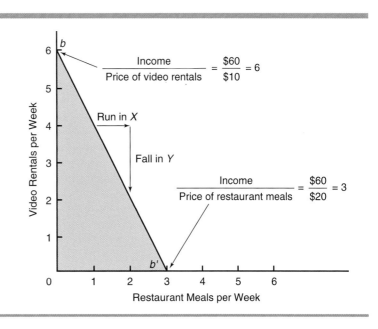

Now we are ready to determine how the consumer achieves the optimum consumption rate.

CONSUMER OPTIMUM REVISITED

Consumers will try to attain the highest level of total utility possible, given their budget constraints. How can this be shown graphically? We draw a set of indifference curves similar to those in Figure B-4, and we bring in reality—the budget constraint bb'. Both are drawn in Figure B-6. Because a higher level of total satisfaction is represented by a higher indifference curve, we know that the consumer will strive to be on the highest indifference curve possible. However, the consumer cannot get to indifference curve I_3 because the budget will be exhausted before any combination of video rentals and restaurant meals represented on indifference curve I_3 is attained. This consumer can maximize total utility, subject to the budget constraint, only by being at point E on indifference curve I_2 because here the consumer's income is just being exhausted. Mathematically, point E is called the tangency point of the curve I_2 to the straight line bb'.

Consumer optimum is achieved when the marginal rate of substitution (which is subjective) is just equal to the feasible, or realistic, rate of exchange between video rentals and restaurant meals. This realistic rate is the ratio of the two prices of the goods involved. It is represented by the absolute value of the slope of the budget constraint. At point E, the point of tangency between indifference curve I_2 and budget constraint bb', the rate at which the consumer wishes to substitute video rentals for restaurant meals (the numerical value of slope of the indifference curve) is just equal to the rate at which the consumer *can* substitute video rentals for restaurant meals (the slope of the budget line).

Figure B-6
Consumer Optimum

A consumer reaches an optimum when he or she ends up on the highest indifference curve possible, given a limited budget. This occurs at the tangency between an indifference curve and the budget constraint. In this diagram, the tangency is at E.

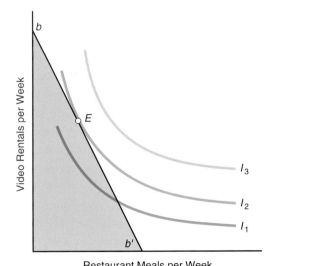

EFFECTS OF CHANGES IN INCOME

A change in income will shift the budget constraint *bb'* in Figure B-6. Consider only increases in income and no changes in price. The budget constraint will shift outward. Each new budget line will be parallel to the original one because we are not allowing a change in the relative prices of video rentals and restaurant meals. We would now like to find out how an individual consumer responds to successive increases in income when relative prices remain constant. We do this in Figure B-7. We start out with an income that is represented by a budget line *bb'*. Consumer optimum is at point *E*, where the consumer attains the highest indifference curve I_1, given the budget constraint *bb'*. Now we let income increase. This is shown by a shift outward in the budget line to *cc'*. The consumer attains a new optimum at point *E'*. That is where a higher indifference curve, I_2, is reached. Again, the consumer's income is increased so that the new budget line is *dd'*. The new optimum now moves to *E"*. This is where indifference curve I_3 is reached. If we connect the three consumer optimum points, *E*, *E'*, and *E"*, we have what is called an income-consumption curve. The **income-consumption curve** shows the optimum consumption points that would occur if income for that consumer were increased continuously, holding the prices of video rentals and restaurant meals constant.

▶ **Income-consumption curve**

The set of optimum consumption points that would occur if income were increased, relative prices remaining constant.

Figure B-7
Income-Consumption Curve

We start off with income sufficient to yield budget constraint *bb'*. The highest attainable indifference curve is I_1, which is just tangent to *bb'* at *E*. Next we increase income. The budget line moves outward to *cc'*, which is parallel to *bb'*. The new highest indifference curve is I_2, which is just tangent to *cc'* at *E'*. We increase income again, which is represented by a shift in the budget line to *dd'*. The new tangency point of the highest indifference curve, I_3, with *dd'*, is at point *E"*. When we connect these three points, we obtain the income-consumption curve.

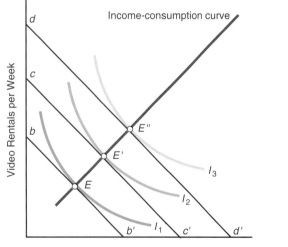

THE PRICE-CONSUMPTION CURVE

In Figure B-8 (page 188), we hold money income and the price of video rentals constant while we lower the price of restaurant meals. As we keep lowering the price of restaurant meals, the quantity of meals that could be purchased if all income were

Figure B-8
Price-Consumption Curve

As we lower the price of restaurant meals, income measured in terms of restaurant meals per week increases. We show this by rotating the budget constraint from *bb'* to *bb''* and finally to *bb'''*. We then find the highest indifference curve that is attainable for each successive budget constraint. For budget constraint *bb'*, the highest indifference curve is I_1, which is tangent to *bb'* at point E. We do this for the next two budget constraints. When we connect the optimum points, E, E', and E'', we derive the price-consumption curve, which shows the combinations of the two commodities that a consumer will purchase when money income and the price of one commodity remain constant while the other commodity's price changes.

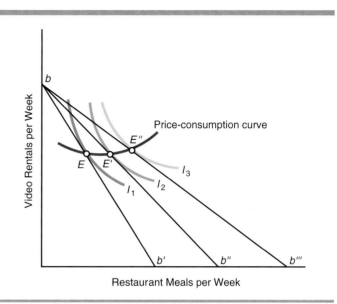

▶ **Price-consumption curve**

The set of consumer optimum combinations that the consumer would choose as the price of one good changes, while money income and the price of the other good remain constant.

spent on restaurant meals increases; thus the extreme points for the budget constraint keep moving outward to the right as the price of restaurant meals falls. In other words, the budget line rotates outward from *bb'* to *bb''* and *bb'''*. Each time the price of restaurant meals falls, a new budget line is formed. There has to be a new optimum point. We find it by locating on each new budget line the highest attainable indifference curve. This is shown at points E, E', and E''. We see that as price decreases for restaurant meals, the consumer purchases more restaurant meals per week. We call the line connecting points E, E', and E'' the **price-consumption curve.** It connects the tangency points of the budget constraints and indifference curves, thus showing the amounts of two goods that a consumer will buy when money income and the price of one commodity are held constant while the price of the remaining good changes.

DERIVING THE DEMAND CURVE

We are now in a position to derive the demand curve using indifference curve analysis. In part (a) of Figure B-9, we show what happens when the price of restaurant meals decreases, holding both the price of video rentals and income constant. If the price of restaurant meals decreases, the budget line rotates from *bb'* to *bb''*. The two optimum points are given by the tangency at the highest indifference curve that just touches those two budget lines. This is at E and E'. But those two points give us two price-quantity pairs. At point E, the price of restaurant meals is $20; the quantity demanded is 2. Thus we have one point that we can transfer to part (b) of Figure B-9. At point E', we have another price-quantity pair. The price has fallen to $10; the quantity demanded has increased to 5. We therefore transfer this other point to part (b). When we connect these two points (and all the others in between), we derive the demand curve for restaurant meals; it slopes downward.

Figure B-9
Deriving the Demand Curve

In part (a), we show the effects of a decrease in the price of restaurant meals from $20 to $10. At $20, the highest indifference curve touches the budget line *bb'* at point *E*. The quantity of restaurant meals consumed is two. We transfer this combination–price, $20; quantity demanded, 2–down to part (b). Next we decrease the price of restaurant meals to $10. This generates a new budget line, or constraint, which is *bb''*. Consumer optimum is now at *E'*. The optimum quantity of restaurant meals demanded at a price of $10 is five. We transfer this point–price, $10; quantity demanded, 5–down to part (b). When we connect these two points, we have a demand curve, *D*, for restaurant meals.

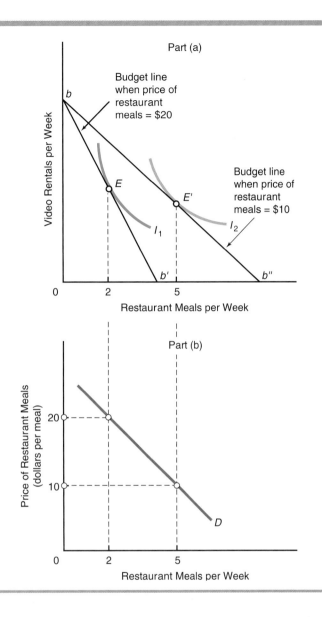

APPENDIX SUMMARY

1. Along an indifference curve, the consumer experiences equal levels of satisfaction. That is to say, along any indifference curve, every combination of the two goods in question yields exactly the same level of satisfaction.

2. Indifference curves usually slope downward and are usually convex to the origin.

3. To measure the marginal rate of substitution, we find out how much of one good has to be given

up in order to allow the consumer to consume one more unit of the other good while still remaining on the same indifference curve. The marginal rate of substitution falls as one moves down an indifference curve.

4. Indifference curves represent preferences. A budget constraint represents opportunities—how much can be purchased with a given level of income. Consumer optimum is obtained when the highest indifference curve is just tangent to the

budget constraint line; at that point, the consumer reaches the highest feasible indifference curve.

5. When income increases, the budget constraint shifts outward to the right, parallel to the previous budget constraint line.

6. As income increases, the consumer optimum moves up to higher and higher indifference

curves. When we connect those points with a line, we derive the income-consumption curve.

7. As the price of one good decreases, the budget line rotates. When we connect the tangency points of the highest indifference curves to these new budget lines, we derive the price-consumption curve.

PROBLEMS

(Answers to the odd-numbered problems appear at the back of the book.)

B-1. Suppose that a consumer prefers A to B and B to C but insists that she also prefers C to A. Explain the logical problem here.

B-2. Suppose that you are indifferent among the following three combinations of food (f) and drink (d): $1f$ and $10d$, $2f$ and $7d$, $3f$ and $2d$. Calculate the marginal rate of substitution in consumption between the two goods. Does the substitution of the third f imply a greater sacrifice of d than the second did?

B-3. Construct a budget line from the following information: nominal income of $100 per week; price of beef, P_b, $2 per pound; price of shelter, P_s, $20 per week; all income is spent on beef and shelter. Suppose that your money income remains constant, the price of beef doubles to $4 per pound, and the price of housing falls to $10 per week. Draw the new budget line. Are you now better off or worse off? What do you need to know before deciding?

B-4. Given the following three combinations of goods, $A = 3x + 4y$, $B = 4x + 6y$, and $C = 5x + 4y$, answer the following questions:
   a. Is any one bundle preferred to the other two?
   b. Could a consumer possibly find B and C to be equally acceptable? How about A and C?

B-5. Calculate the marginal rate of substitution of burritos for yogurt for the following consumer's indifference schedule:

Servings of Yogurt per Week	Burritos per Week
10	1
6	2
3	3
1	4

B-6. Assume that you are consuming only yogurt (Y) and gymnasium exercise (G). Each serving of yogurt costs $4, and each visit to the gym costs $8. Given your food and exercise budget, you consume 15 servings of yogurt and five visits to the gym each week. One day, the price of yogurt falls to $3 per serving and the price of gym visits increases to $10. Now you buy 20 servings of yogurt and four gym visits per week.
   a. Draw the old and new budget constraints, and show the two equilibrium bundles of yogurt servings and visits to the gym.
   b. What is your weekly budget for food and exercise?

B-7. Explain why each of the following statements is or is not consistent with our assumptions about consumer preferences.
   a. I can't decide whether to go abroad this summer or to stay at home.
   b. That is mine. You cannot have it. There is nothing you can do to make me change my mind.
   c. I love hot pretzels with mustard at football games. If I had my way, I would never stop eating them.

Demand and Supply Elasticity

Farming has always been a difficult way to make a living in Canada. A farmer's livelihood is vulnerable to adverse weather conditions, infestations of pests, and wildly fluctuating prices for crops. The pests can be controlled with chemical or organic solutions, but only sometimes will a farmer survive bad weather. When weather destroys crops, or, alternatively, when it helps farmers grow bumper crops, prices can rise or fall dramatically and markedly affect farm incomes. Are farmers able to do anything about fluctuating prices? To answer this question, you need to know more about the price elasticity of demand.

8

Preview Questions

1. How is total revenue related to the price elasticity of demand?

2. What are the determinants of the price elasticity of demand?

3. What is the income elasticity of demand?

4. What is the price elasticity of supply?

Did You Know That... following the pro-baseball strike in the middle of the 1994-1995 baseball season, the Toronto Blue Jays group and season ticket sales fell by about 50 percent? In an effort to attract fans again, beer prices at the SkyDome were reduced by 20 percent. How could reducing beer prices affect baseball game attendance? The answer lies in understanding the relationship between the quantities that people demand at lower prices relative to the quantities of other goods that people demand at the same time. While attendance did not rise to the usual 51,000 capacity, it rose to about 42,000 and the ball club stayed solvent.

It is not only pro-sports clubs that have to know about how individuals respond to prices; it is important that all businesses take into account consumer response to changing prices. If McDonald's lowers its prices by 10 percent, will fast-food consumers respond by buying so many more Big Macs that the company's revenues will rise? At the other end of the spectrum, can Rolls Royce dealers "get away" with a 2 percent increase in prices? In other words, will Rolls Royce purchasers respond so little to the relatively small increase in price that the total revenues received for Rolls Royce sales will not fall and may actually rise? The only way to answer these questions is to know how responsive people in the real world will be to changes in prices. Economists have a special name for price responsiveness—*elasticity,* which is the subject of this chapter.

PRICE ELASTICITY

To begin to understand what elasticity is all about, just keep in mind that it means "responsiveness" or "stretchiness." Here we are concerned with the price elasticity of demand and the price elasticity of supply. We wish to know the extent to which a change in the price of, say, petroleum products will cause the quantity demanded and the quantity supplied to change, other things held constant. Let's restrict our discussion at first to the demand side.

Price Elasticity of Demand

▶ **Price elasticity of demand (E_p)**

The responsiveness of the quantity demanded of a commodity to changes in its price; defined as the percentage change in quantity demanded divided by the percentage change in price.

We will formally define the **price elasticity of demand,** which we will label E_p, as follows:

$$E_p = \frac{\text{percentage change in quantity demanded}}{\text{percentage change in price}}$$

What will price elasticity of demand tell us? It will tell us the relative amount by which the quantity demanded will change in response to a change in the price of a particular good.

Consider an example in which a 10 percent rise in the price of oil leads to a reduction in quantity demanded of only 1 percent. Putting these numbers into the formula, we find that the price elasticity of demand for oil in this case equals the percentage change in quantity demanded divided by the percentage change in price, or

$$E_p = \frac{-1\%}{+10\%} = = .1$$

An elasticity of -.1 means that a 1 percent *increase* in the price would lead to a mere 0.1 percent *decrease* in the quantity demanded. If you were now told, in contrast, that the price elasticity of demand for oil was -1, you would know that a 1 percent increase in the price of oil would lead to a 1 percent decrease in the quantity demanded.

Relative Quantities Only. Notice that in our elasticity formula, we talk about *percentage* changes in quantity demanded divided by *percentage* changes in price. We are therefore not interested in the absolute changes, only in relative amounts. This means that it doesn't matter if we measure price changes in terms of cents, dollars, or hundreds of dollars. It also doesn't matter whether we measure quantity changes in bushels, grams, or litres. The percentage change will be independent of the units chosen.

POLICY EXAMPLE   Increasing Taxes on Cigarettes

Smoking is responsible for a variety of illnesses, including emphysema and lung cancer. In the 1980s, the federal government launched a two-pronged attack on smoking in an effort to reduce the costs to society. Virtually all smoking-related advertising was banned, even the printing of cigarette brandnames on T-shirts. Smoking was prohibited in all public areas and work sites under federal jurisdiction, and on all flights of domestic airlines. Part two involved a steep increase in the price of cigarettes via an increase in the sales tax, both at the federal level and at the provincial level. The price of cigarettes went up by over 30 percent in a three-year period. By the beginning of 1992, a package of cigarettes cost $5.50. This dramatic increase brought about a reduction in quantity demanded. As the price rose, per capita cigarette consumption dropped by 7 percent in 1989, an additional 6.5 percent in 1990, and a further 13 percent in 1991.

Data over a longer period of time confirm the responsiveness of cigarette consumers to price increases. From 1980 to 1993, the inflation-corrected price of cigarettes increased by 60 percent. Over the same time span, the estimated reduction in adult smoking was 43 percent. The approximate price elasticity of demand was therefore 43 percent ÷ 60 percent = 0.72. That means that in the long run, for every 10 percent increase in the relative price of cigarettes, the expected reduction in adult smoking will be about 7 percent.

For critical analysis: Does the rise of cigarette smuggling which followed the tax increases suggest that the price elasticity of demand for cigarettes is not 0.72? If so, would it be larger or smaller?

Always Negative. The law of demand states that quantity demanded is *inversely* related to the relative price. An increase in the price of a good leads to a decrease in the quantity demanded. If a decrease in the relative price of a good should occur, the quantity demanded would increase by a certain percentage. The point is that price elasticity of demand will always be negative. By convention, *we will ignore the minus sign in our discussion from this point on.*

Basically, the greater the *absolute* price elasticity of demand (disregarding sign), the greater the demand responsiveness to relative price changes—a small change in price has a great impact on quantity demanded. The smaller the absolute price elasticity of demand, the smaller the demand responsiveness to relative price changes—a large change in price has little effect on quantity demanded.

Thinking Critically About the Media   **"If They Doubled the Price, We'd Still Drink Coffee"**

Every time there is a frost in Brazil, the price of coffee beans rises, and everyone fears a big rise in the price of coffee. Members of the media interview coffee drinkers and ask how they will respond to the higher prices. Not surprisingly, even when coffee prices soared 150 percent a few years ago, some interviewees said they had to have their cup of coffee no matter what. But if that were true for all coffee drinkers, why don't coffee prices rise as much as bean prices? If what coffee drinkers tell us were really true, their price elasticity of demand would be zero, and the retail price of coffee could skyrocket. But it never does. The truth is, interviewing coffee drinkers (or other consumers) about intentions tells us little. We need to examine the change in total market quantity demanded after an increase in price. The data make it clear: At least some people drink less coffee when the relative price goes up.

Concepts in Brief

- Elasticity is a measure of the price responsiveness of the quantity demanded and quantity supplied.
- The price elasticity of demand is equal to the percentage change in quantity demanded divided by the percentage change in price.
- Price elasticity of demand is calculated in terms of percentage changes in quantity demanded and in price. Thus it is expressed as a unitless, dimensionless number.
- The law of demand states that quantity demanded and price are inversely related. Therefore, the price elasticity of demand is always negative, because an increase in price will lead to a decrease in quantity demanded, and a decrease in price will lead to an increase in quantity demanded. By convention, we ignore the negative sign in discussions of the price elasticity of demand.

Calculating Elasticity

To calculate the price elasticity of demand, we have to compute percentage changes in quantity demanded and in price. To obtain the percentage change in quantity demanded, we divide the change in the quantity demanded by the original quantity demanded:

$$\frac{\text{Change in quantity demanded}}{\text{Original quantity demanded}}$$

To find the percentage change in price, we divide the change in price by the original price:

$$\frac{\text{Change in price}}{\text{Original price}}$$

There is an arithmetic problem, though, when we calculate percentage changes in this manner. The percentage change, say, from 2 to 3—50 percent—is not the same as the percentage change from 3 to 2—$33\frac{1}{3}$ percent. In other words, it makes a difference where you start. One way out of this dilemma is simply to use average values.

To compute the price elasticity of demand, we need to deal with the average change in quantity demanded caused by the average change in price. That means that we take the average of the two prices and the two quantities over the range we are considering and compare the change with these averages. For relatively small changes in price, the formula for computing the price elasticity of demand then becomes

$$E_p = \frac{\text{change in quantity}}{\text{sum of quantities} / 2} \div \frac{\text{change in price}}{\text{sum of prices} / 2}$$

We can rewrite this more simply if we do two things: (1) We can let Q_1 and Q_2 equal the two different quantities demanded before and after the price change and let P_1 and P_2 equal the two different prices. (2) Because we will be dividing a percentage by a percentage, we simply use the ratio, or the decimal form, of the percentages. Therefore,

$$E_p = \frac{\Delta Q}{(Q_1 + Q_2)/2} \div \frac{\Delta P}{(P_1 + P_2)/2}$$

where the Greek letter Δ stands for "change in."

INTERNATIONAL EXAMPLE
The Price Elasticity of Demand for Newspapers

Newspaper owners are always seeking to increase their paper's circulation, not because they want the revenue generated from the sales of the paper, but because the larger the circulation, the more the newspaper can charge for its advertising space. The source of most of a paper's revenues—and profits—is its advertisers.

One newspaper owner, Rupert Murdoch, ran an experiment to see how high he could boost sales of a particular newspaper by lowering its price. For one day, he lowered the price of the British daily paper *Today* from 25 pence to 10 pence. According to London's *Financial Times*, the sales of *Today* almost doubled that day, increasing the circulation from 590,000 to 1.05 million copies. We can estimate the price elasticity of demand for *Today* by using the formula presented earlier (under the assumption, of course, that all other things were held constant):

$$E_p = \frac{\Delta Q}{(Q_1 + Q_2)/2} \div \frac{\Delta P}{(P_1 + P_2)/2}$$

$$= \frac{1,050,000 - 590,000}{(590,000 + 1,050,000)/2} \div \frac{25 \text{ pence} - 10 \text{ pence}}{(10 \text{ pence} + 25 \text{ pence})/2}$$

$$= \frac{460,000}{820,000} \div \frac{15 \text{ pence}}{17.5 \text{ pence}} = 0.65$$

The price elasticity of demand of 0.65 means that a 1 percent decrease in price will lead to a 0.65 percent increase in quantity demanded.

For critical analysis: Would the estimated price elasticity of the *Today* newspaper have been different if we had not used the average-values formula? How?

▶ **Elastic demand**

A demand relationship in which a given percentage change in price will result in a larger percentage change in quantity demanded. Total expenditures and price changes are inversely related in the elastic region of the demand curve.

▶ **Unit elasticity of demand**

A demand relationship in which the quantity demanded changes exactly in proportion to the change in price. Total expenditures are invariant to price changes in the unit-elastic region of the demand curve.

▶ **Inelastic demand**

A demand relationship in which a given percentage change in price will result in a less than proportionate percentage change in the quantity demanded. Total expenditures and price are directly related in the inelastic region of the demand curve.

PRICE ELASTICITY RANGES

We have names for the varying ranges of price elasticities, depending on whether a 1 percent change in price elicits more or less than a 1 percent change in the quantity demanded.

1. *Elastic demand.* We say that a good has an **elastic demand** whenever the price elasticity of demand is greater than 1. A 1 percent change in price causes a change of more than 1 percent in the quantity demanded.
2. *Unit elasticity of demand.* In a situation of **unit elasticity of demand,** a 1 percent change in price causes a response of exactly a 1 percent change in the quantity demanded.
3. *Inelastic demand.* In a situation of **inelastic demand,** a 1 percent change in price causes a response of less than a 1 percent change in the quantity demanded. The most extreme inelastic demand is *perfectly inelastic;* no matter what the price, the quantity demanded remains the same, so the price elasticity of demand is zero.

When we say that a commodity's demand is elastic, we are indicating that consumers are relatively responsive to changes in price. When we say that a commodity's demand is inelastic, we are indicating that its consumers are relatively unresponsive to price changes. When economists say that demand is inelastic, it does not mean that quantity demanded is totally unresponsive to price changes. Remember, the law of demand suggests that there will be some responsiveness in quantity demanded to a price change. The question is how much. That's what elasticity attempts to determine.

Extreme Elasticities

▶ **Perfectly inelastic demand**

A demand that exhibits zero responsiveness to price changes; no matter what the price is, the quantity demanded remains the same.

▶ **Perfectly elastic demand**

A demand that has the characteristic that even the slightest increase in price will lead to zero quantity demanded.

There are two extremes in price elasticities of demand. One extreme represents total unresponsiveness of quantity demanded to price changes, which is referred to as **perfectly inelastic demand,** or zero elasticity. The other represents total responsiveness, which is referred to as infinitely, or **perfectly elastic demand.**

We show perfect inelasticity in part (a) of Figure 8.1. Notice that the quantity demanded per year is 8 million units, no matter what the price. Hence for any percentage price change, the quantity demanded will remain the same, and thus the change in the quantity demanded will be zero. Look back at our formula for computing elasticity. If the change in the quantity demanded is zero, the numerator is also zero, and a nonzero number divided into zero results in an answer of zero too. Hence there is perfect inelasticity. At the opposite extreme is the situation depicted in part (b) of Figure 8.1. Here we show that at a price of 30 cents, an unlimited quantity will be demanded. At a price that is only slightly above 30 cents, no quantity will be demanded. There is complete, or infinite, responsiveness here, and hence we call the demand schedule in part (b) infinitely elastic.

Figure 8.1
Extreme Price Elasticities

In part (a), we show complete price unresponsiveness. The demand curve is vertical at the quantity of 8 million units per year. This means that the price elasticity of demand is zero. In part (b), we show complete price responsiveness. At a price of 30 cents, in this example, consumers will demand an unlimited quantity of the particular good in question. This is a case of infinite price elasticity of demand.

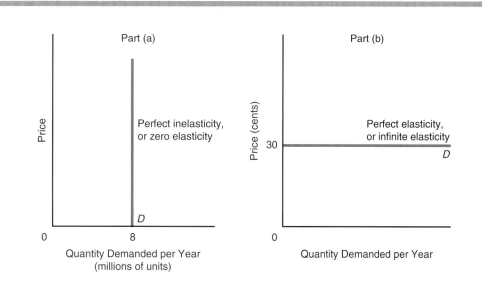

Concepts in Brief

- One extreme elasticity occurs when a demand curve is vertical. It has zero price elasticity of demand; it is completely inelastic.
- Another extreme elasticity occurs when a demand curve is horizontal. It has completely elastic demand; its price elasticity of demand is infinite.

ELASTICITY AND TOTAL REVENUES

Suppose that you are in charge of the pricing decision for a cellular telephone service company. How would you know when it is best to raise or not to raise prices? The answer depends in part on the effect of your pricing decision on total revenues, or the total receipts of your company. (The rest of the equation is, of course, your cost structure, a subject we examine in Chapter 10.) It is commonly thought that the way to increase total receipts is to increase price per unit. But is this always the case? Is it possible that a rise in price per unit could lead to a decrease in total revenues? The answers to these questions depend on the price elasticity of demand.

Let's look at Figure 8.2. In part (a), column 1 shows the price of cellular telephone service in dollars per minute, and column 2 represents billions of minutes per year. In column 3, we multiply column 1 by column 2 to derive total revenue because total revenue is always equal to the number of units (quantity) sold times the price per unit, and in column 4, we calculate values of elasticity. Notice what happens to total revenues throughout the schedule. They rise steadily as the price rises from 10 cents to 50 cents per minute; but when the price rises further to 60 cents per minute, total revenues remain constant at $3 billion. At prices per minute higher than 60 cents, total revenues fall as price increases. Indeed, if prices are above 60 cents per minute, total revenues can be increased only by *cutting* prices, not by raising them.

Labelling Elasticity

The relationship between price and quantity on the demand schedule is given in columns 1 and 2 of part (a) in Figure 8.2. In part (b), the demand curve, *D*, representing that schedule is drawn. In part (c), the total revenue curve representing the data in column 3 is drawn. Notice first the level of these curves at small quantities. The demand curve is at a maximum height, but total revenue is zero, which makes sense according to this demand schedule—at a price of $1.10 and above, no units will be purchased, and therefore total revenue will be zero. As price is lowered, we travel down the demand curve, and total revenues increase until price is 60 cents per minute, remain constant from 60 cents to 50 cents per minute, and then fall at lower unit prices. Corresponding to those three sections, demand is elastic, unit-elastic, and inelastic. Hence we have three relationships among the three types of price elasticity and total revenues.

1. *Elastic demand.* A negative relationship exists between small changes in price and changes in total revenues. That is to say, if price is lowered, total revenues will rise when the firm faces demand that is elastic, and if it raises price, total revenues will fall. Consider another example. If the price of Diet Coke™ were raised by 25 percent and the price of all other soft drinks remained constant, the quantity demanded of Diet Coke™ would probably fall dramatically. The decrease in quantity demanded due to the increase in the price of Diet Coke™ would lead in this example to a reduction in the total revenues of the Coca-Cola Company. Therefore, if demand is elastic, price and total revenues will move in *opposite* directions.

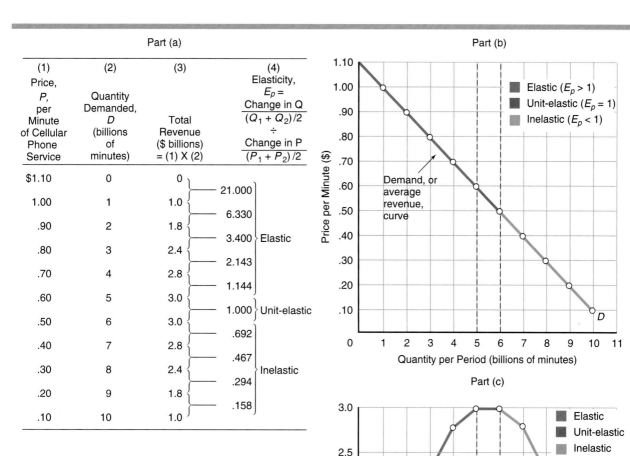

Figure 8.2

The Relationship Between Price Elasticity of Demand and Total Revenues for Cellular Phone Service

In part (a), we show the elastic, unit-elastic, and inelastic sections of the demand schedule according to whether a reduction in price increases total revenues, causes them to remain constant, or causes them to decrease, respectively. In part (b), we show these regions graphically on the demand curve. In part (c), we show them on the total revenue curve.

2. *Unit-elastic demand.* Changes in price do not change total revenues. When the firm is facing demand that is unit-elastic, if it increases price, total revenues will not change; if it decreases price, total revenues will not change either.
3. *Inelastic demand.* A positive relationship exists between changes in price and total revenues. When the firm is facing demand that is inelastic, if it raises price, total revenues will go up; if it lowers price, total revenues will fall. Consider another example. You have just invented a cure for the common cold that has been approved by Health Canada for sale to the public. You are not sure what price you should charge, so you start out with a price of $1 per pill. You sell 20 million pills at that price over a year. The next year, you decide to raise the price by 25 percent, to $1.25. The number of pills you sell drops to 18 million per year. The price increase of 25 percent has led to a 10 percent decrease in quantity demanded. Your total revenues, however, will rise to $22.5 million because of the price increase. We therefore conclude that if demand is inelastic, price and total revenues move in the *same* direction.

The elastic, unit-elastic, and inelastic areas of the demand curve are shown in Figure 8.2. For prices from $1.10 per minute of cellular phone time to 60 cents per minute, as price decreases, total revenues rise from zero to $3 billion. Demand is price-elastic. When price changes from 60 cents to 50 cents, however, total revenues remain constant at $3 billion; demand is unit-elastic. Finally, when price falls from 50 cents to 10 cents, total revenues decrease from $3 billion to $1 billion; demand is inelastic. In parts (b) and (c) of Figure 8.2, we have labelled the sections of the demand curve accordingly, and we have also shown how total revenues first rise, then remain constant, and finally fall.

The relationship between price elasticity of demand and total revenues brings together some important microeconomic concepts. Total revenues, as we have noted, are the product of price per unit times number of units sold. The law of demand states that along a given demand curve, price and quantity changes will move in opposite directions: One increases as the other decreases. Consequently, what happens to the product of price times quantity depends on which of the opposing changes exerts a greater force on total revenues. But this is just what price elasticity of demand is designed to measure—responsiveness of quantity demanded to a change in price. The relationship between price elasticity of demand and total revenues is summarized in Table 8.1.

Try Preview Question 1:
How is total revenue related to the price elasticity of demand?

Table 8.1 **Relationship Between Price Elasticity of Demand and Total Revenues**	Price Elasticity of Demand		Effect of Price Change on Total Revenues (TR)	
			Price Decrease	Price Increase
	Inelastic	$(E_p < 1)$	TR ↓	TR ↑
	Unit-elastic	$(E_p = 1)$	No change in TR	No change in TR
	Elastic	$(E_p > 1)$	TR ↑	TR ↓

INTERNATIONAL EXAMPLE

A Pricing Decision at Disneyland Paris

Several years after it opened with great fanfare, the $4 billion US investment in Disneyland Paris (formerly called EuroDisney) was in trouble. In an attempt to improve profits (actually, to decrease losses), Disney management decided to lower prices starting in the summer of 1995. Entrance fees during peak periods (April 1 to October 1) dropped from 250 francs (about $60) to 195 francs (about $48). Was this 22 percent reduction in ticket prices a good management strategy for Disney officials? That depends in part on what happened to total revenues. As it turned out, park attendance increased by 700,000 visitors. Thus total revenues increased by more than 22 percent, indicating that the demand for Disneyland Paris is elastic in the price range between $48 to $60.

For critical analysis: What other factors may have affected attendance at Disneyland Paris?

Concepts in Brief

- Price elasticity of demand is related to total revenues (and total consumer expenditures).
- When demand is elastic, the change in price elicits a change in total revenues (and total consumer expenditures) in the direction opposite to that of the price change.
- When demand is unit-elastic, a change in price elicits no change in total revenues (or in total consumer expenditures).
- When demand is inelastic, a change in price elicits a change in total revenues (and in consumer expenditures) in the same direction as the price change.

DETERMINANTS OF THE PRICE ELASTICITY OF DEMAND

We have learned how to calculate the price elasticity of demand. We know that, theoretically, it ranges numerically from zero, completely inelastic, to infinity, completely elastic. What we would like to do now is come up with a list of the determinants of the price elasticity of demand. The price elasticity of demand for a particular commodity at any price depends, at a minimum, on the following:

1. The existence, number, and quality of substitutes
2. The percentage of a consumer's total budget devoted to purchases of that commodity
3. The length of time allowed for adjustment to changes in the price of the commodity

Existence of Substitutes

The closer the substitutes for a particular commodity and the more substitutes there are, the greater will be its price elasticity of demand. At the limit, if there is a perfect substitute, the elasticity of demand for the commodity will be infinite. Thus even the slightest increase in the commodity's price will cause an enormous reduction in the quantity demanded: quantity demanded will fall to zero. We are really talking about two goods that the consumer believes are exactly alike and equally desirable, like five-dollar bills whose only difference is serial numbers. When we talk about less extreme examples, we can only speak in terms of the number and the similarity of substitutes that are available. Thus we will find that the more narrowly we define a good, the closer and greater will be the number of substitutes available. For example, the demand for a Diet Coke™ may be highly elastic because consumers can switch to Diet Pepsi™. The demand for diet drinks in general, however, is relatively less elastic because there are fewer substitutes.

Share of Budget

We know that the greater the percentage of a total budget spent on the commodity, the greater the person's price elasticity of demand for that commodity. The demand for pepper is thought to be very inelastic merely because individuals spend so little on it relative to their total budgets. In contrast, the demand for things such as transportation and housing is thought to be far more elastic because they occupy a large part of people's budgets—changes in their prices cannot be ignored so easily without sacrificing a lot of other alternative goods that could be purchased.

Consider a numerical example. A household earns $40,000 a year. It purchases $4 of pepper per year and $4,000 of transportation services. Now consider the spending power of this family when the price of pepper and the price of transportation both go up by 100 percent. If the household buys the same amount of pepper, it will now spend $8. It will thus have to reduce other expenditures by $4. This $4 represents only 0.01 percent of the entire household budget. By contrast, a doubling of transportation costs requires that the family spend $8,000—$4,000 more—on transportation, if it is to purchase the same quantity. That increased expenditure on transportation of $4,000 represents 10 percent of total expenditures that must be switched from other purchases. We would therefore predict that the household will react differently to the doubling of prices for pepper than it will for transportation. It will buy almost the same amount of pepper but will spend significantly less on transportation.

Time for Adjustment

When the price of a commodity changes and that price change persists, more people will learn about it. Further, consumers will be better able to revise their consumption patterns the longer the time period they have to do so. And in fact, the longer the time they do take, the less costly it will be for them to engage in this revision of consumption patterns. Consider a price decrease. The longer the price decrease persists, the greater will be the number of new uses that consumers will discover for the particular commodity, and the greater will be the number of new users of that particular commodity.

It is possible to make a very strong statement about the relationship between the price elasticity of demand and the time allowed for adjustment:

> The longer any price change persists, the greater the elasticity of demand, other things held constant. Elasticity of demand is greater in the long run than in the short run.

Let's take an example. Suppose that the price of electricity goes up 50 percent. How do you adjust in the short run? You can turn the lights off more often, you can stop using the stereo as much as you do, and so on. Otherwise it's very difficult to cut back on your consumption of electricity. In the long run, though, you can devise methods to reduce your consumption. Instead of using electric heaters, the next time you have a house built you will install gas heating. Instead of using an electric stove, the next time you move you will have a gas stove installed. You will purchase fluorescent bulbs because they use less electricity. The more time you have to think about it, the more ways you will find to cut your electricity consumption. We would expect, therefore, that the short-run demand curve for electricity would be relatively inelastic (in the price range around P_e), as demonstrated by D_1 in Figure 8.3. However, the long-run demand curve may exhibit much more elasticity (in the neighbourhood of P_e), as demonstrated by D_3. Indeed, we can think of an entire family of demand curves such as those depicted in that figure. The short-run demand curve is for the period when there is no time for adjustment. As more time is allowed, the demand curve goes first to D_2 and then all the way to D_3. Thus in the neighbourhood of P_e, elasticity differs for each of these curves. It is greater for the less steep curves (but, slope alone does not measure elasticity for the entire curve).

Figure 8.3
Short-Run and Long-Run Price Elasticity of Demand

Consider an equilibrium situation in which the market price is P_e and the quantity demanded is Q_e. Then there is a price increase to P_1. In the short run, as evidenced by the demand curve D_1, we move from equilibrium quantity demanded, Q_e, to Q_1. After more time is allowed for adjustment, the demand curve rotates at original price P_e to D_2. Quantity demanded falls again, now to Q_2. After even more time is allowed for adjustment, the demand curve rotates at price P_e to D_3. At the higher price P_1, in the long run, the quantity demanded falls all the way to Q_3.

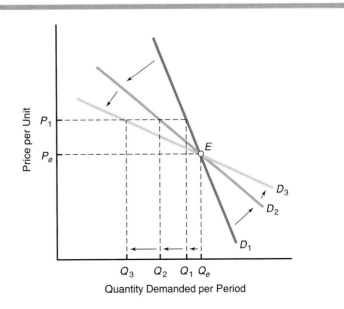

How to Define the Short Run and the Long Run. We've mentioned the short run and the long run. Is the short run one week, two weeks, one month, two months? Is the long run three years, four years, five years? The answer is that there is no single answer. What we mean by the long run is the period of time necessary for consumers to make a full adjustment to a given price change, all other things held constant. In the case of the demand for electricity, the long run will be however long it takes consumers to switch over to cheaper sources of heating, to buy houses that are more energy-efficient, to purchase appliances that are more energy-efficient, and so on. The long-run elasticity of demand for electricity therefore relates to a period of at least several years. The short run—by default—is any period less than the long run.

Try Preview Question 2:

What are the determinants of the price elasticity of demand?

| EXAMPLE | What Do Real-World Price Elasticities of Demand Look Like? |

In Table 8.2, we present demand elasticities for selected goods. None of them is zero, and the largest is 3.8–a far cry from infinity. Remember that even though we are leaving off the negative sign, there is an inverse relationship between price and quantity demanded, and the minus sign is understood. Also remember that these elasticities represent averages over given price ranges. Choosing different price ranges would yield different elasticity estimates for these goods.

Economists have consistently found that estimated price elasticities of demand are greater in the long run than in the short run, as seen in Table 8.2. There you see, for example, in the far-right column that the long-run price elasticity of demand for tires and related items is 1.2, whereas the estimate for the short run is .8. Throughout the table, you see that all estimates of long-run price elasticities of demand exceed their short-run counterparts.

Table 8.2
Demand Elasticity for Selected Goods

Here are estimated demand elasticities for selected goods. All of them are negative, although we omit the minus sign. We have given some estimates of the long-run price elasticities of demand. The long run is associated with the time necessary for consumers to adjust fully to any given price change.

Category	Estimated Elasticity	
	Short Run	Long Run
Lamb	2.65	—
Bread	.15	—
Tires and related items	.8	1.2
Auto repair and related services	1.4	2.4
Radio and television repair	.5	3.8
Legitimate theatre and opera	.2	.31
Motion pictures	.87	3.7
Foreign travel by U.S. residents	.1	1.8
Taxicabs	.6	—
Local public transportation	.6	1.2
Intercity bus	.2	2.2
Electricity	.1	1.8
Jewellery and watches	.4	.6

Sources: P.S. George and G.A. King, *Consumer Demand for Food Commodities in the United States with Projections for 1980* (Berkeley: University of California Press, 1971); Herbert Scarf and J.B. Shoven, *Applied Equilibrium Analysis,* (New York: Cambridge University Press, 1984).

For critical analysis: Explain the intuitive reasoning behind the difference between long-run and short-run price elasticity of demand.

CROSS ELASTICITY OF DEMAND

In Chapter 3, we discussed the effect of a change in the price of one good on the demand for a related good. We defined substitutes and complements in terms of whether a reduction in the price of one caused a decrease or an increase, respectively, in the demand for the other. If the price of compact discs is held constant, the amount of CDs demanded (at any price) will certainly be influenced by the price of a close substitute such as audiocassettes. If the price of stereo speakers is held constant, the amount of stereo speakers demanded (at any price) will certainly be affected by changes in the price of stereo amplifiers.

▶ **Cross elasticity of demand (E_{xy})**

The percentage change in the quantity demanded of one good (holding its price constant) divided by the percentage change in the price of a related good.

What we now need to do is come up with a numerical measure of the price responsiveness of demand to the prices of related goods. This is called the **cross elasticity of demand (E_{xy}),** which is defined as the percentage change in the quantity demand of one good divided by the percentage change in the price of the related good. In equation form, the cross elasticity of demand for good X with respect to good Y is

$$E_{xy} = \frac{\text{percentage change in quantity demanded of good X}}{\text{percentage change in price of good Y}}$$

Alternatively, the cross elasticity of demand for good Y with respect to good X would use the percentage change in the quantity demanded of good Y as the numerator and the percentage change in the price of good X as the denominator.

When two goods are substitutes, the cross elasticity of demand will be positive. For example, when the price of margarine goes up, the demand for butter will rise too as consumers shift away from the now relatively more expensive margarine to butter. A producer of margarine could benefit from a numerical estimate of the cross elasticity of demand between butter and margarine. For example, if the price of butter went up by 10 percent and the margarine producer knew that the cross elasticity of demand was 1, the margarine producer could estimate that the demand for margarine would also go up by 10 percent at any given price. Plans for increasing margarine production could then be made.

When two related goods are complements, the cross elasticity of demand will be negative (and we will not disregard the minus sign). For example, when the price of stereo amplifiers goes up, the demand for stereo speakers will fall. This is because as prices of amplifiers increase, the quantity of amplifiers demanded will naturally decrease. Because amplifiers and stereo speakers are often used together, the demand for speakers is likely to fall. Any manufacturer of stereo speakers must take this into account in making production plans.

If goods are completely unrelated, their cross elasticity of demand will be zero.

POLICY EXAMPLE   Should Public Libraries Be Shut Down?

The public library has been an institution in Canada for years. Most public libraries are paid for out of property taxes. Some policymakers argue that there is no reason to subsidize public libraries anymore. Why? Because individuals are gradually shifting their demand from the use of *physical* public libraries to on-line information services, such as Netscape, and others available over the Internet. As the price of on-line information has fallen, the demand for traditional library services has dropped. Though no one has calculated the exact cross elasticity of demand for traditional library services, the decrease in usage of such libraries shows that it is significant.

For critical analysis: Compare your costs of using a library with those for using on-line information services.

INCOME ELASTICITY OF DEMAND

In Chapter 3, we discussed the determinants of demand. One of those determinants was income. Briefly, we can apply our understanding of elasticity to the relationship between changes in income and changes in demand. We measure the responsiveness of quantity demanded to income changes by the **income elasticity of demand (E_i):**

▶ **Income elasticity of demand (E_i)**

The percentage change in the quantity demanded of any good holding its price constant, divided by the percentage change in income; the responsiveness of demand to changes in income, holding the goods relative price constant.

$$E_i = \frac{\text{percentage change in quantity demanded}}{\text{percentage change in income}}$$

holding relative price constant.

Income elasticity of demand refers to a *horizontal shift* in the demand curve in response to changes in income, whereas price elasticity of demand refers to a movement *along* the curve in response to price changes. Thus income elasticity of demand is calculated at a given price, and price elasticity of demand is calculated at a given income.

A simple example will demonstrate how income elasticity of demand can be computed. Table 8.3 gives the relevant data. The product in question is compact discs. We assume that the price of compact discs remains constant relative to other prices. In period 1, six CDs per month are purchased. Income per month is $400. In period 2, monthly income increases to $600, and the quantity of CDs demanded per month increases to eight. Using the same mid-point formula that we used in computing the price elasticity of demand, we get:

$$E_i = \frac{(8-6)/7}{(600-400)/500} = \frac{2/7}{2/5} = \frac{5}{7} = 0.714$$

Notice that the sign of the income elasticity of demand is positive. That is because as income rises, the quantity of CDs demanded also increases. In Chapter 3, we defined this kind of good as a "normal" good—one that we want more of as our income increases. An "inferior" good is one that we want less of as our income increases. The sign of the income elasticity of demand for an inferior good will therefore be negative, since quantity demanded will decrease as income increases. It is important to retain the negative sign on the income elasticity of demand for an inferior good, since the sign tells us whether the good is in fact normal or inferior.

You have just been introduced to three types of elasticities. Two of them—the price elasticity of demand (E_p), and income elasticity (E_i)—are the two most important factors in influencing the quantity demanded for most goods. Reasonably accurate estimates of these can go a long way towards making accurate forecasts of demand for goods or services.

Try Preview Question 3:
What is the income elasticity of demand?

Table 8.3 **How Income Affects Quantity of CDs Demanded**	Period	Number of CDs Demanded per Month	Income per Month
	1	6	$400
	2	8	600

EXAMPLE   **Frequent Flyer Miles as Income**

For the past 10 years, airlines have been discovering that consumers measure their incomes in more than one way. Most airlines now offer frequent flyer points for air travel, and many are affiliated with other carriers and businesses as well. For example, Air Canada gives frequent flyer points for travel on United Airlines and for renting cars from Budget Rent-a-Car. Travellers can also apply for a Visa card that gives them one frequent flyer mile for every dollar charged. The first of these programs began in 1981. Air Canada started its Aeroplan program in 1984 with 14,000 members; five months later it had 62,000. Now there are over 2 million members. Worldwide there are more than 42 million members of various plans, with over 2 trillion points outstanding.

At the same time, airlines have found the demand for their services increasing. Air Canada alone reported a 16 percent increase in passenger volumes between 1995 and 1996, with much of the increment attributed to "free flights" earned through frequent flyer programs. It appears that air travellers count their frequent flyer miles as part of their incomes, thus they demand more air travel as their incomes increase.

For critical analysis: The federal government has decided that the value of flights paid for with frequent flyer miles earned while travelling on business should be considered part of an individual's income—and thus be liable to income tax. What effect will this have on the income elasticity of demand for air travel?

Concepts in Brief

● Some determinants of price elasticity of demand are (1) the existence, number, and quality of substitutes, (2) the share of the total budget spent on the good in question, and (3) the length of time allowed for adjustment to a change in prices.

● Cross elasticity of demand measures one good's demand responsiveness to another's price changes. For substitutes, it is positive; for complements, it is negative.

● Income elasticity of demand tells you by what percentage demand will change for a particular percentage change in income.

ELASTICITY OF SUPPLY

▶ **Price elasticity of supply (E_s)**

The responsiveness of the quantity supplied of a commodity to a change in its price; the percentage change in quantity supplied divided by the percentage change in price.

The **price elasticity of supply (E_s)** is defined similarly to the price elasticity of demand. Supply elasticities are generally positive; this is because at higher prices, larger quantities will generally be forthcoming from suppliers. The definition of the price elasticity of supply is as follows:

$$E_s = \frac{\text{percentage change in quantity supplied}}{\text{percentage change in price}}$$

Classifying Supply Elasticities

Just as with demand, there are different types of supply elasticities. They are similar in definition to the types of demand elasticities.

   If a 1 percent increase in price elicits a greater than 1 percent increase in the quantity supplied, we say that at the particular price in question on the supply schedule, *supply is elastic.* The most extreme elastic supply is called **perfectly elastic supply**—the slightest reduction in price will cause quantity supplied to fall to zero.

▶ **Perfectly elastic supply**

A supply characterized by a reduction in quantity supplied to zero when there is the slightest decrease in price.

   If, conversely, a 1 percent increase in price elicits a less than 1 percent increase in the quantity supplied, we refer to that as an *inelastic supply.* The most extreme inelastic supply is called **perfectly inelastic supply**—no matter what the price, the quantity supplied remains the same.

▶ **Perfectly inelastic supply**

A supply for which quantity supplied remains constant, no matter what happens to price.

   If the percentage change in the quantity supplied is just equal to the percentage change in the price, we call this *unit-elastic supply.*

   We show in Figure 8.4 two supply schedules, S and S'. You can tell at a glance, without reading the labels, which one is infinitely elastic and which one is perfectly inelastic. As you might expect, most supply schedules exhibit elasticities that are somewhere between zero and infinity.

Figure 8.4
The Extremes in Supply Curves

Here we have drawn two extremes of supply schedules: S is a perfectly elastic supply curve; S' is a perfectly inelastic one. In the former, an unlimited quantity will be supplied at price P_1. In the latter, no matter what the price, the quantity supplied will be Q_1. An example of S' might be the supply curve for fresh fish on the morning the boats come in.

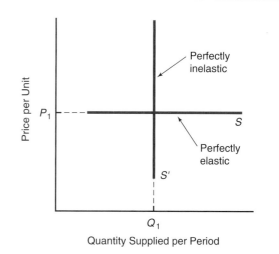

Price Elasticity of Supply and Length of Time for Adjustment

We pointed out earlier that the longer the time period allowed for adjustment, the greater the price elasticity of demand. It turns out that the same proposition applies to supply. The longer the time for adjustment, the more elastic the supply curve. Consider why this is true:

1. The longer the time allowed for adjustment, the more firms are able to figure out ways to increase (or decrease) production in an industry.
2. The longer the time allowed for adjustment, the more resources can flow into (or out of) an industry through expansion (or contraction) of existing firms.

We therefore talk about short-run and long-run price elasticities of supply. The short run is defined as the time period during which full adjustment has not yet taken place. The long run is the time period during which firms have been able to adjust fully to the change in price.

Consider an increase in the price of housing. In the very short run, when there is no time allowed for adjustment, the amount of housing offered for rent or for sale is relatively inelastic. However, as more time is allowed for adjustment, current owners of the housing stock can find ways to increase the amount of housing they will offer for rent from given buildings. The owner of a large house can decide, for example, to have two children move into one room so that a "new" extra bedroom can be rented out. This can also be done by the owner of a large house who decides to move into an apartment and rent each floor of the house to a separate family. Thus the quantity of housing supplied will increase. With more time, landlords will find it profitable to build new rental units.

We can show a whole set of supply curves similar to the ones we generated for demand. As Figure 8.5 shows, when nothing can be done in the short run, the supply curve is vertical, S_1. As more time is allowed for adjustment, the supply curve rotates to S_2 and then to S_3, becoming more elastic as it rotates.

Try Preview Question 4:
What is the price elasticity of supply?

Figure 8.5
Short-Run and Long-Run Price Elasticity of Supply

Consider a situation in which the price is P_e and the quantity supplied is Q_e. In the short run, we hypothesize a vertical supply curve, S_1. With the price increase to P_1, therefore, there will be no change in the short run in quantity supplied; it will remain at Q_e. Given some time for adjustment, the supply curve will rotate to S_2. The new amount supplied will increase to Q_1. The long-run supply curve is shown by S_3. The amount supplied again increases to Q_2.

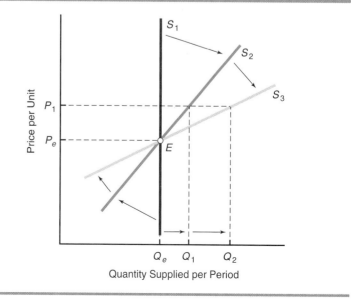

Concepts in Brief

- Price elasticity of supply is calculated by dividing the percentage change in quantity supplied by the percentage change in price.
- Usually, price elasticities of supply are positive—higher prices yield larger quantities supplied.
- Long-run supply curves are more elastic than short-run supply curves because the longer the time allowed, the more resources can flow into or out of an industry when price changes.

Issues and Applications

Productivity Improvements and Farm Incomes

Concepts Applied: Price elasticity of demand, productivity increases, supply shifts

Canadian farmers face more problems than other businesses in maintaining steady incomes. For example, foreign suppliers can affect world supply, which when combined with the inelastic demand for food products results in dramatic fluctuations in farm revenues.

Farmers often have trouble making ends meet in these days of increased global competition and declining government subsidies. This is not new, however. Canadian wheat farmers in the early twentieth century suffered similar problems as domestic and worldwide supplies of wheat fluctuated. Demand for food in general, and for wheat in particular, tends to be inelastic. Unfortunately, early Canadian farmers did not understand the effect an inelastic demand for their product would have on their incomes.

During the first decade of the twentieth century, the fertile agricultural land of the Prairies was being settled, and supply of wheat was rapidly expanding. Production rose from about 55 million bushels in 1900 to more than 230 million bushels in 1911. Because of increasing domestic demand, price fluctuated only slightly.

With the advent of World War I, however, European production of wheat came virtually to a stop. Canadian farmers experienced a great increase in demand for their product, and price rose by 124 percent by the end of the war. Farmers welcomed the increase in their incomes.

However, when the war ended, European farmers began producing again, satisfying the European demand for wheat. The price of wheat in Canada fell almost to pre-war levels. Farmers, concerned about their declining incomes, invested in new technology to improve their crop yields. However, because the demand for wheat was inelastic, the increased supply depressed prices even further, and farm incomes in fact declined.

Figure 8.6 illustrates the Canadian market for wheat during the first three decades of the twentieth century. Prior to World War I, the demand for wheat was $D_{pre-war}$ and Canadian supply was $S_{pre-war}$. When European production ceased, Europe looked to

Figure 8.6

The Market for Wheat in Canada, 1910-1930

Prior to World War I, Canadian farmers satisfied the Canadian demand for wheat, $D_{pre-war}$, with supply, $S_{pre-war}$. When European farmers stopped producing, demand for Canadian wheat increased to $D_{war-time}$. Price rose from P_0 to P_1, increasing farm incomes. After the war, demand returned to its original position, and prices and farm incomes fell. Farmers, trying to bolster their incomes, increased their supply to $S_{post-war}$, depressing price to P_2.

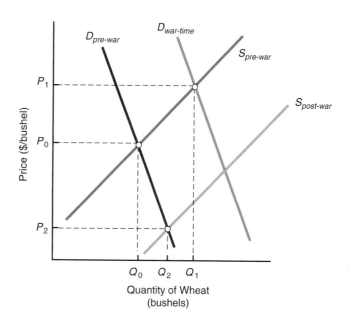

Canada for wheat, increasing demand to $D_{war-time}$. Price rose to P_1 and quantity traded rose to Q_1. Farm incomes increased from P_0Q_0 to P_1Q_1, a radical increase. However, demand returned to about the pre-war level following the war. The return to smaller incomes induced farmers to increase their productivity which had the effect of increasing supply to $S_{post-war}$. You can see the effect on farm incomes as price fell to P_2 and quantity traded increased only to Q_2.

The federal government stepped in and regulated wheat sales in an effort to stabilize incomes. The Canadian Wheat Board still markets all Canadian wheat, although some farmers now feel that they understand the economics of farming well enough to operate independently of the Wheat Board.

For Critical Analysis

1. Instead of increasing productivity, what could early Canadian farmers have done to raise their incomes?

2. If the demand for wheat had been elastic, would the farmers have felt the same need to increase productivity to bolster their incomes?

CHAPTER SUMMARY

1. Price elasticity of demand is a measure of the percentage change in quantity demanded relative to the percentage change in price, given income, the prices of other goods, and time. Because of the law of demand, price elasticity of demand is always negative.

2. We classify demand as *elastic* if a 1 percent change in price leads to a more than 1 percent change in quantity demanded, *unit-elastic* if it leads to exactly a 1 percent change in quantity demanded, and *inelastic* if it leads to less than a 1 percent change in quantity demanded.

3. When facing a perfectly elastic demand, the slightest increase in price leads to zero quantity demanded; when facing a perfectly inelastic demand, no matter what the price, the quantity demanded remains unchanged. Perfect inelasticity means absolutely no price responsiveness.

4. Price elasticity of demand falls as we move down a straight-line demand curve. It goes from infinity to zero. Elasticity and slope are not equivalent; for example, the slope of a straight-line curve is always constant, whereas elasticity changes as we move along a linear curve. A vertical demand curve is perfectly inelastic; a horizontal demand curve is perfectly elastic.

5. Price elasticity of demand depends on (a) the existence, number, and quality of substitutes, (b) the share of total budget accounted for by the commodity, and (c) the length of time allowed for adjustment to changes in price of the commodity.

6. Cross elasticity of demand measures the responsiveness of the demand for one product, either a substitute or a complement, to changes in the price of another product. When the cross elasticity of demand is negative, the two commodities under study are complements; when the cross elasticity of demand is positive, they are substitutes.

7. Income elasticity of demand is given by the percentage change in quantity demanded divided by the percentage change in income, given relative price. When the income elasticity of demand is positive, the good in question is a normal good; when the income elasticity of demand is negative, the good is an inferior good.

8. Price elasticity of supply is given by the percentage change in quantity supplied divided by the percentage change in price. The greater the time allowed for adjustment, the greater the price elasticity of supply.

DISCUSSION OF PREVIEW QUESTIONS

1. How is total revenue related to the price elasticity of demand?

Total revenue is defined as price times quantity demanded; because price changes lead to changes in quantity demanded, total revenue and elasticity are intimately related. If, over the price range in question, demand is inelastic, this means that buyers are relatively unresponsive to price changes. Intuitively, then, we know that if price rises and quantity demanded does not fall by much, total revenue will rise. Conversely, if price falls and quantity demanded rises only slightly, total revenue will fall. If, over the price range in question, demand is elastic, buyers will be quite responsive to price changes. We can tell intuitively that if price rises and quantity demanded falls greatly, total revenue will fall. Similarly, if price falls and quantity demanded rises greatly, total revenue will rise. Finally, if we are in the range of unit elasticity, given percentage changes in price will lead to equal percentage changes in quantity. Thus total revenue remains unaffected in the unit-elasticity range.

2. What are the determinants of the price elasticity of demand?

Three major determinants of price elasticity of demand are (a) the existence, number, and quality of substitutes, (b) the share of the total budget that the commodity represents, and (c) the length of time buyers have to react to price changes. Clearly, the more substitutes and the better they are, the greater will be the price elasticity of demand. Therefore, the price elasticity of demand rises as we consider the commodities "fruit," then "oranges," then "Mandarin oranges"; more and better substitutes exist for a specific brand of oranges than for the fruit group. Also, when a commodity takes up a small percentage of the consumer budget (other things being constant), we expect the price elasticity of demand to be lower, compared with items important to a budget. Presumably, buyers will have a greater incentive to shop around and seek substitutes for high-cost items than for low-cost items. Finally, for a given percentage change in price, quantity responsiveness (and therefore elasticity) will increase with the time period allowed for adjustment. With the passage of time, buyers are better able to find and use substitutes.

3. What is the income elasticity of demand?
Income elasticity of demand refers to the responsiveness of buyers to income changes, given relative price. Technically, income elasticity of demand is defined as the percentage change in quantity demanded divided by the percentage change in income. The resulting measure is referred to as being income-elastic, unit-elastic, or income-inelastic, depending on whether or not it is greater than, equal to, or less than 1.

4. What is the price elasticity of supply?
Price elasticity of supply refers to the responsiveness of sellers to changes in price. Technically, price elasticity of supply is defined as the percentage change in quantity supplied divided by the percentage change in price. The resulting measure can be greater than, equal to, or less than the number 1—referred to as elastic, unit-elastic, and inelastic supply, respectively. The longer the adjustment time, the greater the quantity responsiveness of sellers to given price changes (and hence the greater the price elasticity of supply).

PROBLEMS

(Answers to the odd-numbered problems appear at the back of the book.)

8-1. Use the following hypothetical demand schedule for tea to answer the questions.

Quantity Demanded per Week (kilograms)	Price per Kilogram	Elasticity
1,000	$ 5	
800	10	
600	15	
400	20	
200	25	

a. Using the mid-point formula, determine the elasticity of demand for each price change. (Example: When price changes from $5 to $10, quantity demanded changes from 1,000 to 800 kilograms, so the elasticity of demand, using average values, is $\frac{1}{3}$, or .33.)

b. The data given in the demand schedule would plot as a straight-line demand curve. Why is demand more elastic the higher the price?

8-2. Calculate the price elasticity of demand for the product in the table below using average values for the prices and quantities in your formula. Over the price range in question, is this demand schedule inelastic, unit-elastic, or elastic? Is total revenue greater at the lower price or the higher price?

Price per Unit	Quantity Demanded
$4	22
6	18

8-3. Calculate the income elasticity of demand for the product in the following table, using average values for incomes and quantities.

Quantity of VCRs per Year	Per Capita Annual Group Income
1,000	$15,000
2,000	20,000

a. Is the demand for this product income-elastic or income-inelastic?

b. Would you consider this commodity a luxury or a necessity?

8-4. Can any demand curve possibly be perfectly inelastic ($E_p = 0$) regardless of price? Explain.

8-5. A new mobile home park charges nothing whatsoever for water used by its inhabitants. Consumption is 100,000 litres per month. The decision is then made to charge according to how much each mobile home owner uses, at a rate of $10 per 1,000 litres. Consumption declines to 50,000 litres per month. What is the difficulty here in accurately estimating the price elasticity of the demand for water by these residents?

8-6. Which of the following cross elasticities of demand would you expect to be positive and which to be negative?
  a. Tennis balls and tennis racquets
  b. Tennis balls and golf balls
  c. Dental services and toothpaste
  d. Dental services and candy
  e. Soft drinks and ice cubes
  f. Soft drinks and fruit juices

8-7. Suppose that the price of salt rises from 15 cents to 17 cents a kilogram. The quantity demanded decreases from 525 kilograms to 475 kilograms per month, and the quantity supplied increases from 525 kilograms to 600 kilograms per month. (Use averages in calculating elasticities.)
  a. Calculate the price elasticity of demand (E_p) for salt.
  b. Is the demand for salt price-elastic or price-inelastic?
  c. Calculate the elasticity of supply (E_s) for salt.
  d. Is the supply for salt price-elastic or price-inelastic?

8-8. Suppose that an automobile dealer cuts his car prices by 15 percent. He then finds that his car sales revenues have increased by 10 percent.
  a. What can you say about the price elasticity of demand for cars?
  b. What will happen to the dealer's total revenue?

8-9. For any given relative price, would you think that the demand for canal transportation was more or less elastic in 1840 than in 1890? How about the demand for rail transportation before and after the Model T Ford? The demand for transatlantic cable-laying equipment before and after communications satellites? The demand for slide rules before and after introduction of the pocket-sized calculator? Why?

The Financial Environment of Business

The number of Canadian companies that are run by women is growing faster than any other kind of business. Women-led businesses now comprise one-quarter to one-third of all firms in every province. Employment by these firms is expanding four times faster than the average rate across the country. While the Canadian Top 100 Businesses employed 1.5 million people in 1997, women-led businesses employed 1.7 million. Nevertheless, women often have trouble finding financing for their enterprises. To understand why, you need to know more about the financial environment of business.

Preview Questions

1. What are the main organizational forms that firms take, and what are their advantages and disadvantages?

2. What are the major differences between stocks and bonds?

3. What are corporations' primary sources of financial capital?

4. What gives rise to the problems of adverse selection and moral hazard?

Did You Know That... there are over 2.1 million businesses in Canada? All of these businesses need money to get under way. Therefore they turn to financial markets to raise money. They seek **financial capital.**

You've been introduced to the term *physical capital* as one of the five factors of production. In that context, capital consists of the goods that do not directly satisfy human wants but are used to make other goods. *Financial capital* is the money that is made available to purchase capital goods.

Different types of businesses are able to raise financial capital in different ways. Your first step in understanding the firm's financial environment is therefore to understand the way firms are organized.

▶ **Financial capital**

Money used to purchase capital goods such as buildings and equipment.

THE LEGAL ORGANIZATION OF FIRMS

We all know that firms differ from one another. Some sell frozen yoghurt, others make automobiles; some advertise, some do not; some have annual sales of a few thousand dollars, others have sales in the billions of dollars. The list of differences is probably endless. Yet for all this diversity, the basic organization of *all* firms can be thought of in terms of a few simple structures, the most important of which are the sole proprietorship, the partnership, and the corporation.

Sole Proprietorships

▶ **Sole proprietorship**

A business owned by one individual who makes the business decisions, receives all the profits, and is legally responsible for all the debts of the firm.

The most common form of business organization is the **sole proprietorship**. A sole proprietorship is owned by a single individual who makes the business decisions, receives all the profits, and is legally responsible for all the debts of the firm. Although sole proprietorships are numerous, generally they are rather small businesses, with annual sales typically under $50,000. For this reason, even though there are more than a million sole proprietorships in Canada, they account for only a small percent of all business revenues.

Advantages of Sole Proprietorships. Sole proprietorships offer several advantages as a form of business organization. First, they are *easy to form and to dissolve*. In the simplest case, all one must do to start a business is to start working; to dissolve the firm, one simply stops working. Even a more complicated proposition such as starting a restaurant or a small retail shop, involves only meeting broadly defined health and zoning rules, and the payment of a modest business licence fee to the local government. To go out of business, one simply locks the front door. The second advantage of the sole proprietorship is that *all decision-making power resides with the sole proprietor*. The owner decides what and how much will be offered for sale, what the hours of operation will be, and who will perform what tasks. No partners, shareholders, or board of directors need be consulted. The third advantage is that its *profit is taxed only once*. All profit is treated by law as the net income of the sole proprietor and as such is subject only to personal income taxation.

▶ Unlimited liability
A legal concept whereby the personal assets of the owner of a firm can be seized to pay off the firm's debts.

Disadvantages of Sole Proprietorships. The most important disadvantage of a sole proprietorship is that the sole proprietor faces **unlimited liability** *for the debts of the firm.* This means that the owner is personally responsible for all of the firm's debts. Thus the owner's personal assets—home, car, savings account, coin collection—can be subject to seizure by the firm's creditors. The second disadvantage is that it has *limited ability to raise funds* to expand the business or even simply to help it survive bad times. Because the success of a sole proprietorship depends so heavily on the good judgment and hard work of but one person—the owner—many lenders are reluctant to lend large sums to a sole proprietorship. Thus, much of the financing of sole proprietorships often comes from the personal funds of the owner, which helps explain why sole proprietorships are usually small. The third disadvantage of sole proprietorships is that they normally *end with the death of the sole proprietor.* This, of course, creates added uncertainty for prospective lenders or employees, for a freak accident or sudden illness can turn a prosperous firm into a bittersweet memory.

Partnerships

▶ Partnership
A business owned by two or more co-owners, or partners, who share the responsibilities and the profits of the firm and are individually liable for all of the debts of the partnership.

The second important form of business organization is the **partnership.** Partnerships are far less numerous than sole proprietorships but tend to be significantly larger, with average sales many times greater. A partnership differs from a sole proprietorship chiefly in that there are two or more co-owners, called partners. They share the responsibilities of operating the firm and its profits, and they are *each* legally responsible for *all* of the debts incurred by the firm. In this sense, a partnership may be viewed as a sole proprietorship with more than one owner. The partners may contribute equal or different amounts of financial capital to the firm, may have widely different operating responsibilities, and may share the profits in any way they see fit. Not surprisingly, partnerships share many of the advantages and disadvantages of sole proprietorships.

Advantages of Partnerships. The first advantage of a partnership is that it is *easy to form.* In fact, it is almost as easy as forming a sole proprietorship, except that it requires two or more participants. Second, partnerships, like sole proprietorships, often help *reduce the costs of monitoring job performance.* This is particularly true when interpersonal skills are important for successful performance and in lines of business where, even after the fact, it is difficult to measure performance objectively. Thus, lawyers and accountants often organize themselves as partnerships. In professions such as these, a spectacular success may consist of a greatly reduced jail term or a greatly reduced tax bill for a client. In such circumstances, partners have far more incentive to monitor their own work performance than they would as employees, because the partners share in the profits of the firm. A third advantage of the partnership is that it *permits more effective specialization* in occupations where, for legal or other reasons, the multiple talents required for success are unlikely to be uniform across individuals. Finally, partnerships share with sole proprietorships the advantage that the income of the partnership is treated as personal income and thus is subject only to personal taxation.

Disadvantages of Partnerships. Not surprisingly, partnerships also have their disadvantages. First, the *partners each have unlimited liability.* Thus the personal assets of *each* partner are at risk due to debts incurred on behalf of the partnership by *any* of the partners. One partner's poor business judgment may impose substantial losses on all the other partners, a problem the sole proprietor need not worry about. Second, *decision making is generally more costly* in a partnership than in a sole proprietorship; there are more people involved in making decisions, and they may have differences of opinion that must be resolved before action is possible. Finally, *dissolution of the partnership is generally necessary* when a partner dies or voluntarily withdraws, or when one or more partners wish to remove someone from the partnership. As with sole proprietorships, this creates potential uncertainty for creditors and employees.

Corporations

▶ **Corporation**
A legal entity that may conduct business in its own name just as an individual does; the owners of a corporation, called shareholders, own shares of the firm's profits and enjoy the protection of limited liability.

A **corporation** is a legal entity that may conduct business in its own name just as an individual does. The owners of a corporation are called *shareholders* because they own shares of the profits earned by the firm. By law, shareholders enjoy **limited liability,** which means that if the corporation incurs debts that it cannot pay, creditors have no recourse to the shareholders' personal property. Corporations are far less numerous than sole proprietorships, but because of their large size, they are responsible for over 90 percent of all business revenues in Canada. Many, such as Seagram's, PetroCanada, McCains, and Canadian Tire, are so large that their annual sales are measured in billions of dollars and their names are household words.

▶ **Limited liability**
A legal concept whereby the responsibility, or liability, of the owners of a corporation is limited to the value of the shares in the firm that they own.

Advantages of Corporations. The fact that corporations conduct most of the nation's business suggests that the corporation offers significant advantages as a form of business organization. Perhaps the greatest of these is that the owners of a corporation (the shareholders) enjoy *limited liability.* The liability of shareholders is limited to the value of their shares. The second advantage arises because the law treats a corporation as a legal entity in and of itself; thus the corporation *continues to exist* even if one or more owners cease to be owners. A third advantage of the corporation stems from the first two: Corporations are well positioned for *raising large sums of financial capital.* People are able to buy ownership shares or lend money to the corporation knowing that their liability is limited to the amount of money they invest, and that the corporation's existence does not depend on the life of any one of the firm's owners.

▶ **Dividends**
Portion of a corporation's profits paid to its owners (shareholders).

Disadvantages of Corporations. The chief disadvantage of the corporation is the fact that corporate income is subject to *double taxation.* The profits of the corporation are subject first to corporate taxation. Then, if any of the after-tax profits are distributed to shareholders as **dividends,** such payments are treated as personal income to the shareholders and subject to personal taxation. The combined effect is that owners of corporations pay about twice as much in taxes on corporate income as they do on other forms of income.

A second disadvantage of the corporation is that corporations are potentially subject to problems associated with the *separation of ownership and control.* Specifically, it is common for the owners (shareholders) of corporations to have little, if anything, to do with the actual management of the firm. Instead, these tasks are handled by professional managers who may have little or no ownership interest in the firm. The objective of the shareholders is presumably to maximize the value of their holdings. Unless their sole compensation is in the form of shares of stock in the corporation, however, the objective of the managers may differ from this. For example, managers may choose to have more luxurious offices than are needed for the efficient operation of the firm. If there are costs to the shareholders in preventing such behaviour, the result may be that the market value of the firm is not maximized.

Try Preview Question 1:
What are the main organizational forms that firms take, and what are their advantages and disadvantages?

In principle, such problems could arise with a partnership or a sole proprietorship if the owner or partners hired a manager to take care of day-to-day operations. Nevertheless, the separation of ownership and control is widely regarded as a more important problem for corporations; their attractiveness as a means of raising financial capital from many investors makes them subject to higher costs of agreement among owners with respect to penalties for managers who fail to maximize the value of the firm.

Concepts in Brief

* Sole proprietorships are the most common form of business organization. Each is owned by a single individual who makes all business decisions, receives all the profits, and has unlimited liability for the firm's debts.
* Partnerships are much like sole proprietorships, except that two or more individuals, or partners, share the decisions and the profits of the firm. In addition, each partner has unlimited liability for the debts of the firms.
* Corporations are responsible for the largest share of business revenues. The owners, called shareholders, share in the firm's profits but normally have little responsibility for the firm's day-to-day operations. They enjoy limited liability for the debts of the firm.

METHODS OF CORPORATE FINANCING

When the Dutch East India Company was founded in 1602, it raised financial capital by selling shares of its expected future profits to investors. The investors thus became the owners of the company, and their ownership shares eventually became known as "shares of stock," or simply *stocks*. The company also issued notes of indebtedness, which involved borrowing money in return for interest on the funds, plus eventual repayment of the principal amount borrowed. Today, we call these notes of indebtedness *bonds*. As the company prospered over time, some of its revenues were used to pay lenders the interest and principal owed them; of the profits that remained, some were paid to shareholders in the form of dividends, and some were retained by the company for reinvestment in further enterprises. The methods of financing used by the Dutch East India Company nearly four centuries ago—stocks, bonds, and reinvestment—remain the principal methods of financing for today's corporations.

▶ **Share of stock**
A legal claim to a share of a corporation's future profits; if it is *common* stock, it incorporates certain voting rights regarding major policy decisions of the corporation; if it is *preferred stock,* its owners are accorded preferential treatment in the payment of dividends.

▶ **Bond**
A legal claim against a firm, usually entitling the owner of the bond to receive a fixed annual coupon payment, plus a lump-sum payment at the bond's maturity date. Bonds are issued in return for funds lent to the firm.

Try Preview Question 2:
What are the major differences between stocks and bonds?

A **share of stock** in a corporation is simply a legal claim to a share of the corporation's future profits. If there are 100,000 shares of stock in a company and you own 1,000 of them, you own the right to 1 percent of that company's future profits. If the stock you own is *common stock,* you also have the right to vote on major policy decisions affecting the company, such as the selection of the corporation's board of directors. Your 1,000 shares would entitle you to cast 1 percent of the votes on such issues. If the stock you own is *preferred stock,* you also own a share of the future profits of the corporation, but you do *not* have regular voting rights. You do, however, get something in return for giving up your voting rights: preferential treatment in the payment of dividends. Specifically, the owners of preferred stock generally must receive at least a certain amount of dividends in each period before the owners of common stock can receive *any* dividends.

A **bond** is a legal claim against a firm, entitling the owner of the bond to receive a fixed annual *coupon* payment, plus a lump-sum payment at the maturity date of the bond.[1] Bonds are issued in return for funds lent to the firm; the coupon payments represent interest on the amount borrowed by the firm, and the lump-sum payment at maturity of the bond generally equals the amount originally borrowed by the firm. Bonds are *not* claims to the future profits of the firm; legally, bondholders are to be paid whether the firm prospers or not. To help ensure this, bondholders generally must receive their coupon payments each year, and any principal that is due, before *any* shareholders can receive dividend payments.

You can see a comparison of stocks and bonds in Table 9.1.

Table 9.1	Stocks	Bonds
The Difference Between Stocks and Bonds	1. Stocks represent ownership.	1. Bonds represent debt.
	2. Common stocks do not have a fixed dividend rate.	2. Interest on bonds must always be paid, whether or not any profit is earned.
	3. Stockholders can elect a board of directors, which controls the corporation.	3. Bondholders usually have no voice in or control over management of the corporation.
	4. Stocks do not have a maturity date; the corporation does not usually repay the stockholder.	4. Bonds have a maturity date on which the bondholder is to be repaid the face value of the bond.
	5. All corporations issue or offer to sell stocks. This is the usual definition of a corporation.	5. Corporations need not issue bonds.
	6. Stockholders have a claim against the property and income of a corporation after all creditors' claims have been met.	6. Bondholders have a claim against the property and income of a corporation that must be met before the claims of stockholders.

---

[1] Coupon payments on bonds get their name from the fact that bonds once had coupons attached to them when they were issued. Each year, the owner would clip a coupon off the bond and send it to the issuing firm in return for that year's interest on the bond.

▶ **Reinvestment**
Profits (or depreciation reserves) used to purchase new capital equipment.

Reinvestment takes place when the firm uses some of its profits to purchase new capital equipment rather than paying the money out as dividends to shareholders. Although sales of stock are an important source of financing for new firms, reinvestment and borrowing are the principal means of financing for existing firms. Indeed, reinvestment by established firms is such an important source of financing that it dominates the other two sources of corporate finance, amounting to roughly 75 percent of new financial capital for corporations in recent years. Also, small businesses, which are the source of much current growth, usually cannot rely on the stock market to raise investment funds.

Try Preview Question 3:
What are corporations' primary sources of financial capital?

Primary and Secondary Financial Markets

Both businesses and investors engage in financial transactions in primary and secondary financial markets.

Primary Markets. If you have ever heard of a "new issue," you are familiar with one aspect of a primary securities market. A **primary market** is one in which newly issued securities are bought and sold. A company that is raising money for the first time goes to the primary market, usually to sell its stock. Corporations can also sell newly issued bonds in primary securities markets. Sometimes you may read about large corporations, such as Northern Telecom, issuing new bonds.

▶ **Primary market**
A financial market in which newly issued securities are bought and sold.

▶ **Secondary market**
A financial market in which previously issued securities are bought and sold.

Secondary Markets. A **secondary market** is one in which existing securities are exchanged. When you read about what happened on the stock market today, that is information about a secondary market. Secondary markets are important to primary markets because they make stocks and bonds sold in primary markets more liquid. Most of the activities of stockbrokers involve dealings for investors in secondary market transactions. The stockbroker is an intermediary who brings together buyers and sellers of various stocks and bonds. In return for the broker's services, which include executing market exchanges for buyers and sellers, the broker receives a commission, or brokerage fee.

THE MARKETS FOR STOCKS AND BONDS

Economists often refer to the "market for wheat" or the "market for labour." For stocks and bonds, there really are markets—centralized, physical locations where exchange takes place. The largest stock exchange in Canada is the Toronto Stock Exchange (TSE) which accounts for over 80 percent of the value of shares traded on Canadian stock exchanges. Major stock and bond markets, or exchanges, are located in New York and in other financial capitals of the world, such as London and Tokyo. Although the exact process by which exchanges are conducted in these markets varies slightly from one to another, the process used on the TSE is representative of the principles involved.[2]

---

[2] A number of stocks and bonds are traded in so-called over-the-counter (OTC) markets, which, although not physically centralized, otherwise operate in much the same way as the TSE and so are not treated separately in this text.

More than 1,600 stocks are traded by leading brokerage firms—about 100 of them—that own "seats" on the TSE. These seats, which are actually rights to buy and sell shares of stock on the floor of the TSE, can themselves be exchanged. In recent years, their value has fluctuated between $37,000 and $60,000 each. These prices reflect the fact that stock trades on the TSE are ultimately handled by the firms owning these seats, and the firms earn commissions on each trade. As trading volume rises, as it did during the 1980s, the value of the seats rises.

The Theory of Efficient Markets

At any point in time, there are tens of thousands, even millions of persons looking for any bit of information that will enable them to forecast correctly the future prices of stocks. Responding to any information that seems useful, these people try to buy low and sell high. The result is that all publicly available information that might be used to forecast stock prices gets taken into account by those with access to the information and the knowledge and ability to learn from it, leaving no forecastable profit opportunities. And because so many people are involved in this process, it occurs quite swiftly. Indeed, there is some evidence that *all* information entering the market is fully incorporated into stock prices within less than a minute of its arrival. One view of the stock market is that most public information you will obtain will prove to have little value.

▶ **Random walk theory**
The theory that there are no predictable trends in security prices that can be used to "get rich quick."

The result of this process is that stock prices tend to follow a *random walk*, which is to say that the best forecast of tomorrow's price is today's price. This is called the **random walk theory.** Although large values of the random component of stock price changes are less likely than small values, nothing else about the magnitude or direction of a stock price change can be predicted. Indeed, the random component of stock prices exhibits behaviour much like what would occur if you rolled two dice and subtracted 7 from the resulting score. On average, the dice will show a total of 7, so after you subtract 7, the result will be zero. It is true that rolling a 12 or a 2 (resulting in a net score of +5 or -5) is less likely than rolling an 8 or a 6 (yielding a net score of +1 or -1). Nevertheless, positive and negative net scores are equally likely, and the expected net score is zero.

Inside Information

▶ **Inside information**
Information that is not available to the general public about what is happening in a corporation.

Isn't there any way to "beat the market"? The answer is yes—but normally only if you have **inside information** that is not available to the public. Suppose that your best friend is in charge of new product development at Ballard Power Systems, the leading developer of automobile fuel cells. Your friend tells you that a researcher has just come up with a radical new fuel cell that automobile manufacturers will want to use. No one but your friend and the researcher—and now you—is aware of this. You could indeed make money using this information by purchasing shares of Ballard Power Systems and then selling them (at a higher price) as soon as the new product is publicly announced. There is one problem: Share trading based on inside information such as this is illegal, punishable by substantial fines and even imprisonment. So unless you happen to have a stronger than average desire for a long vacation in a corrections institution, you might be better off investing in Ballard after the new development is publicly announced.

EXAMPLE	How to Read the Financial Press: Stock Prices

Table 9.2, reproduced from the *Globe and Mail*, contains information about the stocks of four companies. Across the top of the financial page are a series of column headings. Under the heading "Stock" we find the name of the company–in the first row, for example, is Molson Breweries, the beer maker. The two columns to the left of the company's name show the highest and lowest prices at which that company's shares traded during the past 52 weeks.

Table 9.2
Reading Stock Quotes

| 52-week | | | | | | | | | | | |
Hi	Lo	Stock	Sym	Div	Hi	Lo	Close	Chg	Vol (100s)	Yield	P/E Ratio
27.75	22.5	Molson	MOL.B	0.72	27.4	27.3	27.4	+0.15	40	2.6	62.3
11.75	9.75	Monrc Dv	MON	0.10	10.10	9.75	9.75	-0.25	655	1.0	16.8
0.65	.115	Moneta Por j	ME		0.18	0.18	0.18		60		
32.00	23.10	Montrusco	MTA	0.84	29.50	29.00	29.00	-0.25	42	2.9	25.4

The summary of stock market information presented on the financial pages of many newspapers reveals the following:

52 weeks Hi/Lo: The highest and lowest prices, in dollars per share, of the stock during the previous 52 weeks

Stock: The name of the company (frequently abbreviated)

Sym: Highly abbreviated name of the company, as it appears on the stock exchange ticker tape

Div: Dividend paid, in dollars per share

Hi: Highest price at which the stock traded that day

Lo: Lowest price at which the stock traded that day

Close: Last price at which the stock traded that day

Chg: Net change in the stock's price from the previous day's closing price

Vol (100s): Number of shares traded during the day, in hundreds of shares

Yield: Yield in percent per year; the dividend divided by the price of the stock

P/E Ratio: Price-earnings ratio; the price of the stock divided by the earnings (profits) per share of the company

Immediately to the right of the company's name you will find the company's *symbol* on the TSE. This symbol (omitted by some newspapers) is simply the unique identifier used by the exchange when it reports information about the stock. For example, the designation MOL.B is used by the exchange as the unique identifier for the firm Molson Breweries.

The dividend column, headed "Div," shows the annual dividend (in dollars and cents) that the company has paid over the preceding year on each share of its stock. In Molson's case, this amounts to 72 cents per share.

The next four columns of information for each firm summarize the behaviour of the firm's share price on the latest trading day. On this particular day, the highest price at which Molson shares traded was $27.40, the lowest price was $27.30, and the last (or closing) price at which it traded was $27.40 per share. The *net change* in the price of Molson's shares was +$0.15, which means that it closed the day at a price of 15 cents per share higher than it *closed* the day before.

The "Yield" column is derived by dividing the dividend by the closing price of the stock. In Molson's case, the yield is 2.6 percent ($0.72 ÷ $27.40). In a sense, the company is paying interest on the stock at a rate of about 2.6 percent. The column heading "P/E" stands for *price-earnings ratio*. To obtain the entries for this column, the firm's total earnings (profits) for the year are divided by the number of the firm's shares in existence to give the earnings per share. When the price of the share is divided by the earnings per share, the result is the price-earnings ratio.

The column to the left of the Yield column shows the total *volume* of the shares of the stock traded that day, measured in hundreds of shares.

For critical analysis: Is there necessarily any relationship between the net change in a stock's price and how many shares have been sold on a particular day?

Concepts in Brief

- Many economists believe that asset markets, especially the stock market, are efficient, meaning that one cannot make a higher than normal rate of return without having inside information (information that the general public does not possess).
- Stock prices normally follow a random walk, meaning that you cannot predict changes in future stock prices based on information about stock price behaviour in the past.

GLOBAL CAPITAL MARKETS

Financial institutions in Canada are tied to the rest of the world via their lending capacities. In addition, integration of all financial markets is increasing. Distinctions among financial institutions and between financial institutions and nonfinancial institutions have blurred. As the legal barriers that have preserved such distinctions are dismantled, multinational corporations offering a wide array of financial services are becoming dominant worldwide.

Globalizing Financial Markets

The globalization of financial markets is not entirely new. Canadian banks developed worldwide branch networks in the 1950s and 1960s for loans, cheque clearing, and foreign exchange (currency) trading.

Foreign exchange—the buying and selling of foreign currencies—became a 24-hour, worldwide market in the 1970s. Instruments tied to government bonds, foreign exchange, stock market indexes, and commodities (grains, metals, oil) are now traded increasingly in financial futures markets in all the world's major centres of commerce.

Most financial firms are coming to the conclusion that to survive as a force in any one of the world's leading financial markets, a firm must have a significant presence in all of them. In 1998, the Royal Bank of Canada announced a merger with the Bank of Montreal, and the Canadian Imperial Bank of Commerce similarly announced a merger with the Toronto-Dominion Bank, with a view to increasing the size of their capital base and their ability to compete in global capital markets. The federal government, however, expressing concern for the banks' possibly diminishing domestic presence, refused to approve the two mergers. It is predicted that by the turn of the twenty-first century, between 30 and 50 financial institutions will be at the centres of world finance—New York, London, Tokyo, and Frankfurt—and they will be competing in all those markets to do business with the world's major corporations and portfolio managers.

Today, major corporate borrowers throughout the world can choose to borrow from a wide variety of lenders, located all over the world. The 24 leading industrialized nations borrowed an estimated $850 billion US on the international capital markets in 1996, according to the Organization for Economic Cooperation and Development (OECD).

Concepts in Brief

- Financial markets throughout the world have become increasingly integrated, leading to a global financial market. Interbank lending and borrowing, foreign exchange trading, and common stock sales now occur virtually 24 hours a day throughout the world.
- Four Canadian banks applied to merge into two in order to better compete in the global financial market. The federal government refused to approve to mergers.

PROBLEMS IN CORPORATE GOVERNANCE

▶ **Separation of ownership and control**
The situation that exists in corporations in which the owners (shareholders) are not the people who control the operation of the corporation (managers). The goals of these two groups are often different.

Many corporations issue stock to raise financial capital that they will use to fund expansion or modernization. The decision to raise capital in this way is ordinarily made not by the owners of the corporation—the holders of its stock—but by the company's managers. This **separation of ownership and control** in corporations leads to incentive problems. Managers may not act in the best interest of shareholders. Further incentive problems arise when corporations borrow money in financial markets. These corporate governance problems have to do with information that is not the same for everyone.

Asymmetric Information:
The Perils of Adverse Selection and Moral Hazard

▶ **Asymmetric information**
Information possessed by one side of a transaction but not the other. The side with more information will be at an advantage.

▶ **Adverse selection**
The circumstance that arises in financial markets when borrowers who are the worst credit risks are the ones most likely to seek loans.

If you invest in a corporation, you give purchasing power to the managers of that corporation. Those managers have much more information about what is happening to the corporation and its future than you do. The inequality of information between the two parties is called **asymmetric information.** If asymmetric information exists before a transaction takes place, we have a circumstance of **adverse selection.** In financial markets, adverse selection occurs because borrowers who are the worst credit risks (and thus likely to yield the most adverse outcomes) are the ones most likely to seek, and perhaps to receive, loans.

Consider two firms seeking to borrow funds by selling bonds. Suppose that one of the firms, the Dynamic Corporation, is pursuing a project with a chance of yielding large profits and a large chance of bankruptcy. The other firm, the Reliable Company, intends to invest in a project that is guaranteed to yield the competitive rate of return, thereby ensuring repayment of its debts. Because Dynamic knows the chance is high that it will go bankrupt and never have to pay its debts, it can offer a high interest rate on the bonds it issues. Unless prospective bond purchasers can distinguish perfectly between the two firms' projects, they will select the high-yielding bonds offered by Dynamic and refuse to buy the low-yielding bonds offered by Reliable. Firms like Reliable will be unable to get funding, yet lenders will lose money on firms like Dynamic. Adverse selection thus makes investors less likely to lend to anyone and more inclined to charge higher interest rates when they do lend.

▶ **Moral hazard**

A problem that occurs because of asymmetric information *after* a transaction occurs. In financial markets, a person to whom money has been lent may indulge in more risky behaviour, thereby increasing the probability of default on the debt.

Moral hazard occurs as a result of asymmetric information *after* a transaction occurs. To continue with our example of the Dynamic Corporation, once the firm has sold the bonds, it must choose among alternative strategies in executing its project. Lenders face the hazard that Dynamic may choose strategies that are contrary to the lenders' well-being and thus "immoral" from their perspective. Because bondholders are entitled to a fixed amount regardless of the firm's profits, Dynamic has an incentive to select strategies offering a small chance of high profits, thereby enabling the owners to keep the largest amount after paying bondholders. Such strategies are also the riskiest—ones that make it more likely that lenders will not be repaid—so the presence of moral hazard makes lenders less likely to lend to anyone and more inclined to charge higher interest rates when they do lend.

Try Preview Question 4:

What gives rise to the problems of adverse selection and moral hazard?

INTERNATIONAL EXAMPLE
Moral Hazard and the International Monetary Fund

The International Monetary Fund (IMF) is a financial agency supported by 181 countries around the world. Its mandate is to stabilize the international monetary system, which often means helping developing countries that are in need of temporary financing. Unfortunately, however, the IMF seems able to respond only *after* a financial crisis, rather than *before*, as witnessed by the Mexican crisis of 1995 when the government had to devalue the peso by 30 percent to avert a full-scale financial collapse.

Canada has advocated an overhaul of the IMF, suggesting that it carry out full-scale surveillance of member countries' financial accounts in order to anticipate potential trouble spots. In this regard, Canada has also advocated increased funding.

The opposition to Canada's position argues that if the IMF were better funded, developing countries would not work as hard to avert financial crises. In a classic case of moral hazard, those countries would know that the IMF was there with more funding to use to bail them out of trouble.

For critical analysis: Would a tightening of funding to the IMF make member countries less vulnerable to financial crisis?

The Principal-Agent Problem

▶ **Principal-agent problem**
The conflict of interest that occurs when agents–managers of firms–pursue their own objectives to the detriment of the goals of the firms' principals, or owners.

A type of moral hazard problem that occurs within firms is called the **principal-agent problem.** The shareholders who own a firm are referred to as *principals,* and the managers who operate the firm are the *agents* of the owners. When the managers do not own all of a firm (as is usually the case), a separation of ownership and control exists, and if the stockholders have less information about the firm's opportunities and risks than the managers do (as is also usually the case), the managers may act in their own self-interests rather than in the interests of the shareholders.

Consider, for example, the choice between two investment projects, one of which involves an enormous amount of work but also promises high profits, while the other requires little effort and promises small returns. Because the managers must do all the work while the shareholders receive all the profits, the managers' incentives are different from those of the shareholders. In this case, the presence of moral hazard will induce the managers to choose the "good life," the easy but low-yielding project—an outcome that fails to maximize the economic value of the firm.

Solving Principal-Agent and Moral Hazard Problems

▶ **Collateral**
An asset pledged to guarantee the repayment of a loan.

▶ **Incentive-compatible contract**
A loan contract under which a significant amount of the borrower's assets are at risk, providing an incentive for the borrower to look after the lender's interests.

The dangers associated with asymmetric information are well known to participants in financial markets, who regularly undertake vigorous steps to minimize its costly consequences. For example, research companies such as Standard & Poor's gather financial data and other information about corporations and sell the information to their subscribers. When even this is insufficient to eliminate the dangers of adverse selection, lenders often require that borrowers post **collateral**—assets that the borrower will forfeit in the event that repayment of a debt is not made. A variant of this strategy, designed to reduce moral hazard problems, is called the **incentive-compatible contract:** Lenders make sure that borrowers have a large amount of their own assets at risk so that the incentives of the borrower are compatible with the interests of the lender. Although measures such as these cannot eliminate the losses caused by asymmetric information, they reduce them below what would otherwise be the case.

EXAMPLE Encouraging Executives to Own a Share of the Company

One way to minimize the principal-agent problem is to induce executives to purchase stock in the companies for which they work. An increasing number of corporations are providing directors and top management with stock options as part of their compensation packages. These include Noranda Inc., Barrick Gold Corp., and the big five chartered banks. Noranda Inc. even provides interest-free loans to help executives exercise their stock options.

Do shareholders benefit from top management's owning "a piece of the rock"? One study indicated that companies in which the chief executives had significant ownership experienced a 4 percent higher annual rate of return over a five-year period than similar companies that did not encourage executives to own stock.

For critical analysis: Is there any way you can use this information to determine in which corporations you should invest?

Concepts in Brief

- When two parties to a transaction have different amounts of information, we call this asymmetric information. Whenever asymmetric information occurs before a transaction takes place, it can result in adverse selection. Adverse selection causes borrowers who are the worst credit risks to be the ones most likely to seek loans.
- When asymmetric information occurs after a transaction, this can cause moral hazard. Lenders often face the hazard that borrowers will choose more risky actions after borrowers have taken out loans.
- The separation of ownership and control in today's large corporations can give rise to the principal-agent problem, whereby the agents (managers) may have interests that differ from those of the principals (shareholders).
- Several methods exist for solving the principal-agent and moral hazard problems. They include requiring lenders to post collateral and devising incentive-compatible contracts in which borrowers have a large amount of their own assets at risk.

Issues and Applications

Small Business Financing

Concepts Applied: Human capital, venture capital, loan repayment schemes

Small business owners often encounter difficulty obtaining financing for expansion projects. The problem is especially acute for female entrepreneurs who typically use more human than physical capital and have little collateral to offer as security for loans.

When businesses apply for loans with commercial banks and finance companies, the financial institutions typically look for three things. They want to see a track record of solid financial management, they want to see annual sales topping $200,000 per year, and they want the business owner to have collateral for the loan. While large companies often do not have a problem meeting these requirements, small companies—especially new entrepreneurial firms—do. Women-led firms are typically small businesses, with less than three employees. With the recent rapid expansion of such firms, few of these female entrepreneurs have a track record of sound management to show the banks. Frequently, too, these new firms are consultancies or small-scale retail outlets, where little physical capital is required, and hence little collateral is available. The capital being used is primarily human capital—the skills of the owners, most of whom are well-educated—but a kind of capital that banks do not take as collateral.

This problem is not unique to women-led firms. Most small firms have trouble finding financing. This problem has become more acute in the last 10 years. Since 1985, the ranks of the self-employed have swelled by 32 percent to a total of 2.1 million Canadians, but the commercial banks and finance companies have been slow to respond to these changing business conditions. Fortunately, others have not.

Alternative Financing

Business Development Bank of Canada. The Business Development Bank of Canada (BDB) is sponsored by the federal government to help new businesses get started. It provides three kinds of financing: patient capital, micro-business capital, and working capital. The patient capital program will lend $250,000 to new high-tech firms lacking the collateral for conventional financing. Repayment takes the form of interest on the debt and royalties on sales. The micro-business program will lend $25,000 to entrepreneurs starting out, on condition that the entrepreneur accepts "coaching" from a retired businessperson working as a counsellor for the BDB. The working capital program provides extra financing of up to $100,000 to established firms who are at the end of their lines of credit. In 1995, the BDB's loans increased by 15.7 percent over the previous year to $827 million. By the end of 1995, 14,399 small businesses had loans with the bank.

Venture Capital. A firm obtains venture capital by accepting funds from an investor in exchange for part ownership of the business. Recently, labour-sponsored venture capital funds have arisen, offering benefits to both investors and to businesses. Investors who lend money to these funds receive 50 percent of their investment back in tax refunds. If the loan is made through a retirement savings plan, they receive a further tax refund. The business gets the financing, and pays dividends to the fund. The success of venture capital funds is demonstrated by their record: In 1995, venture capital funds invested $669 million in 364 businesses. Between 1991 and 1996, firms supported by venture capital funds created 40,573 jobs, spent $789 million on research and development, and made over $6 billion dollars in export sales.

For Critical Analysis

1. Are the Business Development Bank and venture capital funds edging out the commercial banks by financing these small businesses?
2. What kind of safeguards could the BDB and venture capital funds use in funding small entrepreneurial firms to circumvent adverse selection and moral hazard problems?

CHAPTER SUMMARY

1. Sole proprietorships are the most common form of business organization. Each is owned by a single individual who makes all business decisions, receives all the profits, and has unlimited liability for the firm's debts.

2. Partnerships are much like sole proprietorships, except that two or more individuals, or partners, share the decisions and the profits of the firm; each partner has unlimited liability for the debts of the firm.

3. Corporations are responsible for the largest share of business revenues. The owners, called shareholders, share in the firm's profits but normally have little responsibility for the firm's day-to-day operations. Owners of corporations enjoy limited liability for the debts of the firm.

4. When two parties to a transaction have different amounts of information, we call this asymmetric information. Whenever asymmetric information occurs before a transaction takes place, it can result in adverse selection. Adverse selection causes borrowers who are the worst credit risks to be the ones most likely to seek loans.

5. When asymmetric information occurs after a transaction, this can cause moral hazard. Lenders often face the hazard that borrowers will choose more risky actions after borrowers have taken out loans.

6. The separation of ownership and control in today's large corporation has led to the principal-agent problem, whereby the agents (managers) may have interests that differ from those of the principals (shareholders).

7. Several methods exist for solving the principal-agent and moral hazard problems, including requiring lenders to post collateral and devising incentive-compatible contracts in which borrowers have a large amount of their own assets at risk.

DISCUSSION OF PREVIEW QUESTIONS

1. **What are the main organizational forms that firms take, and what are their advantages and disadvantages?**

   The primary organizational forms businesses take are the sole proprietorship, the partnership, and the corporation. The sole proprietorship is owned by a single person, the proprietor, who makes the business decisions, is entitled to all the profits, and is subject to unlimited liability—that is, is personally responsible for all debts incurred by the firm. The partnership differs from the sole proprietorship chiefly in that there are two or more owners, called partners. They share the responsibility for decision making, share the firm's profits, and individually bear unlimited liability for the firm's debts. The net income, or profits, of both sole proprietorships and partnerships is subject only to personal income taxes. Both types of firms legally cease to exist when the proprietor or a partner gives up ownership or dies. The corporation differs from sole proprietorships and partnerships in three important dimensions. Owners of corporations enjoy limited liability; that is, their responsibility for the debts of the corporation is limited to the value of their ownership shares. In addition, the income from corporations is subject to double taxation—corporate taxation when income is earned by the corporation and personal taxation when after-tax profits are paid as dividends to the owners. Finally, corporations do not legally cease to exist due to a change of ownership or the death of an owner.

2. **What are the major differences between stocks and bonds?**

   Stocks represent ownership in a corporation. They are called equity capital. Bonds represent the debt of a corporation. They are part of the debt capital of a corporation. Bond owners normally receive a fixed interest payment on a regular basis, whereas owners of stock are not normally guaranteed any dividends. If a corporation goes out of business, bondholders have first priority on whatever value still exists in the entity. Owners of stock get whatever is left over. Finally, if the corporation is very successful, owners of stock can reap the increases in the market value of their shares of stock. In contrast, the market value of corporate bonds is not so closely tied to the profits of a corporation but is rather influenced by how interest rates are changing in the economy in general

3. **What are corporations' primary sources of financial capital?**

   The main sources of financial capital for corporations are stocks, bonds, and reinvestment of profits. Stocks are ownership shares, promising a share of profits, sold to investors. Common stocks also embody voting rights regarding the major decisions of the firm; preferred stocks typically have no voting rights but enjoy priority status in the payment of dividends. Bonds are notes of indebtedness, issued in return for the loan of money. They typically promise to pay interest in the form of annual coupon payments, plus repayment of the original principal amount upon maturity. Bondholders are generally promised payment before any payment of dividends to shareholders, and for this reason bonds are less risky than stocks. Reinvestment involves the purchase of assets by the firm, using retained profits or depreciation reserves it has set aside for this purpose. No new stocks or bonds are issued in the course of reinvestment, although its value is fully reflected in the price of existing shares of stock..

4. **What gives rise to the problems of adverse selection and moral hazard?**

   The problems of adverse selection and moral hazard arise out of asymmetric information between parties to a transaction. In the case of adverse selection, the asymmetric information exists *before* a transaction takes place. For example, a company may offer high rates of interest on its bonds to attract financing. An investor, lured by the high returns, buys the bonds. If the company knows it will shortly go bankrupt and will never have to pay the interest, there exists a case of adverse selection. The investor has adversely selected the company for investment. Had the information about the possible bankruptcy been available at the time of the transaction—that is, had the information been symmetric—the investor would not have chosen to invest in the company.

If asymmetric information between parties arises *after* a transaction, it is a case of moral hazard. For example, the investor who buys the above company's bonds is entitled to a fixed rate of return. The company now has an incentive to use the funds to maximize its own return and increase its own profits after paying the investor. However, in maximizing its returns, the company may use high-risk means to achieve its end—means that create hazard for the investor. The investor did not know the company would make these risky moves; had the investor known the company's strategies, it might have been able to resell its bonds to someone else to avoid the risk.

PROBLEMS

(Answers to the odd-numbered problems appear at the back of the book.)

9-1. Which kind of firm—a sole proprietorship, a partnership, or a corporation—would need the largest dollar amount of financing? Which would need the lowest dollar amount of financing? Explain your answer.

9-2. Suppose that federal tax policy were changed to exempt the first $10,000 in dividends each year from personal taxation. How would this affect the choice of organizational form for businesses?

9-3. How would the change in corporate tax policy mentioned in Problem 9-2 affect the method of financing that corporations use?

*9-4. Consider a firm that wishes to borrow $10,000 for one year. Suppose that there is a 20 percent chance that this firm will go out of business before the end of the year (repaying none of its debts) and an 80 percent chance that it will survive and repay all of its debts. If potential lenders can earn 10 percent per year by lending to other firms that are certain to repay their debts, what rate of interest will the risky firm have to offer if it is to be able to borrow the $10,000?

9-5. Visit the Web site http://www.tse.com/ investor/quot_set.html. Choose two noncomposite indexes (for example, telephone utilities and food processing) from the index quote search engine.
   a. How many shares have traded on each index in the last 24 hours?
   b. Is one index increasing in value more than the other? How can you tell?
   c. If you could purchase shares in just one of the indexes you selected, which would you choose? Explain your answer.

*This problem is optional; algebra is required.

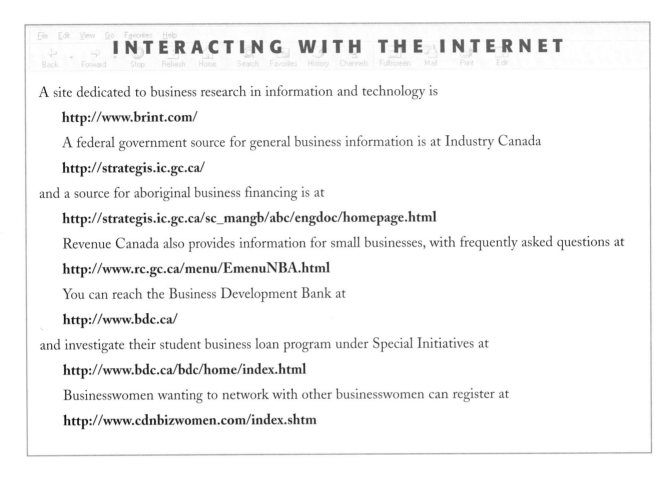

INTERACTING WITH THE INTERNET

A site dedicated to business research in information and technology is

http://www.brint.com/

A federal government source for general business information is at Industry Canada

http://strategis.ic.gc.ca/

and a source for aboriginal business financing is at

http://strategis.ic.gc.ca/sc_mangb/abc/engdoc/homepage.html

Revenue Canada also provides information for small businesses, with frequently asked questions at

http://www.rc.gc.ca/menu/EmenuNBA.html

You can reach the Business Development Bank at

http://www.bdc.ca/

and investigate their student business loan program under Special Initiatives at

http://www.bdc.ca/bdc/home/index.html

Businesswomen wanting to network with other businesswomen can register at

http://www.cdnbizwomen.com/index.shtm

PART 3

Market Structure, Resource Allocation, and Regulation

Chapter 10

The Firm: Cost and Output Determination

Chapter 12

Monopoly

Chapter 14

Regulation and Anticombines Policy

Chapter 11

Perfect Competition

Chapter 13

Monopolistic Behaviour, Oligopoly, and Strategic Behaviour

The Firm: Cost and Output Determination

The technology of communication is changing rapidly. From letters and telegrams, we progressed to telephones and teleprinters, and now we have advanced further to fax machines and e-mail. Even so, telecommunication is about to enter yet another new era—"wireless" communication not only of the spoken word, but also of video and data. What drives businesses to invest in these news types of technology? To understand this issue, you must learn more about how businesses determine costs, profits, and output.

Preview Questions

1. How does the economist's definition of profit differ from the accountant's?

2. What distinguishes the long run from the short run?

3. How does the law of diminishing marginal returns account for an *eventually* increasing marginal cost curve for a firm in the short run?

4. Why is the short-run average total cost curve U-shaped?

Did You Know That... there are more than 25 steps in the process of manufacturing a simple lead pencil? In the production of an automobile, there are literally thousands. At each step, the manufacturer can have the job done by workers or machines or some combination of the two. The manufacturer must also figure out how much to produce each month. Should a new machine be bought that can replace 10 workers? Should more workers be hired, or should the existing workers be paid overtime? If the price of aluminum is rising, should the company try to make do with plastic? What you will learn about in this chapter is how producers can select the best combination of inputs for any given output that is desired.

Before we look at the firm's costs, we need to define a firm.

THE FIRM

▶ **Firm**

A business organization that employs resources to produce goods or services for profit. A firm normally owns and operates at least one plant in order to produce.

We define a business, or **firm**, as follows:

> A firm is an organization that brings together factors of production—labour, land, physical capital, human capital, and entrepreneurial skill—to produce a product or service that it hopes can be sold at a profit.

A typical firm will have an organizational structure consisting of an entrepreneur, managers, and workers. The entrepreneur is the person who takes the risks, mainly of losing personal wealth. In compensation, the entrepreneur will get any profits that are made. Recall from Chapter 2 that entrepreneurs take the initiative in combining land, labour, and capital to produce a good or a service. Entrepreneurs are the ones who innovate in the form of new production and new products. The entrepreneur also decides whom to hire to manage the firm. Some economists maintain that the true quality of an entrepreneur becomes evident through the selection of managers. Managers, in turn, decide who should be hired and fired and how the business generally should be set up. The workers ultimately use the other inputs to produce the products or services that are being sold by the firm. Workers and managers are paid contractual wages. They receive a specified amount of income for a specified time period. Entrepreneurs are not paid contractual wages. They receive no reward specified in advance. The entrepreneurs make profits if there are any, for profits accrue to those who are willing to take risks. Because the entrepreneur gets only what is left over after all expenses are paid, that individual is often referred to as a *residual claimant*. The entrepreneur lays claim to the residual—whatever is left.

Profit and Costs

Most people think of profit as the difference between the amount of revenues a business takes in and the amount it spends for wages, materials, and so on. In a bookkeeping sense, the following formula could be used:

Accounting profits = total revenues − explicit costs

▶ **Explicit costs**
Costs that business managers must take account of because they must be paid; examples are wages, taxes, and rent.

where **explicit costs** are expenses that the business managers must take account of because they must actually be paid out by the firm. This definition of profit is known as **accounting profit.** It is appropriate when used by accountants to determine a firm's taxable income. Economists are more interested in how a firm's managers react not just to changes in explicit costs but also to changes in **implicit costs,** defined as expenses that business managers do not have to pay out of pocket, but which are costs to the firm nonetheless because they represent an opportunity cost. These are noncash costs—they do not involve any direct cash outlay by the firm and must therefore be measured by the alternative cost principle. That is to say, they are measured by what the resources (land, capital) currently used in producing a particular good or service could earn in other uses. Economists therefore use the full opportunity cost of all resources as the figure to subtract from revenues to obtain a definition of profit. Another definition of implicit cost is therefore the opportunity cost of using factors that a producer does not buy or hire but already owns.

▶ **Accounting profit**
Total revenues minus total explicit costs.

▶ **Implicit costs**
Expenses that managers do not have to pay out of pocket and hence do not normally explicitly calculate, such as the opportunity cost of factors of production that are owned; examples are owner-provided capital and owner-provided labour.

Opportunity Cost of Capital

▶ **Normal rate of return**
The amount that must be paid to an investor to induce investment in a business; also known as the opportunity cost of capital.

Firms enter or remain in an industry if they earn, at minimum, a **normal rate of return.** People will not invest their wealth in a business unless they obtain a positive normal (competitive) rate of return—that is, unless their investment pays off. Any business wishing to attract capital must expect to pay at least the same rate of return on that capital as all other businesses (of similar risk) are willing to pay. Put another way, when a firm requires the use of a resource in producing a particular product, it must bid against alternative users of that resource. Thus the firm must offer a price that is at least as much as other users are offering to pay. For example, if individuals can invest their wealth in almost any publishing firm and get a rate of return of 10 percent per year, each firm in the publishing industry must *expect* to pay 10 percent as the normal rate of return to current and future investors. This 10 percent is a *cost to the firm,* the **opportunity cost of capital.** The opportunity cost of capital is the amount of income, or yield, that could have been earned by investing in the next-best alternative. Capital will not stay in firms or industries in which the expected rate of return falls below its opportunity cost, that is, what could be earned elsewhere. If a firm owns some capital equipment, it can either use it or lease it and earn a return. If the firm uses the equipment for production, part of the cost of using that equipment is the forgone revenue that the firm could have earned had it leased out that equipment.

▶ **Opportunity cost of capital**
The normal rate of return, or the available return on the next-best alternative investment. Economists consider this a cost of production, and it is included in our cost examples.

Opportunity Cost of Owner-Provided Labour and Capital

Sole proprietorships often grossly exaggerate their profit rates because they understate the opportunity cost of the labour that the proprietor provides to the business. Here we are referring to the opportunity cost of labour. For example, you may know people who run small grocery stores. These people will sit down at the end of the year and figure out what their "profits" are. They will add up all their sales and subtract what they had to pay to other workers, what they had to pay to their suppliers, what they had to pay in taxes, and so on. The end result they will call "profit." They normally will not, however, have figured into their costs the salary that they could have made if they had worked for somebody else in a similar type of job. By working for themselves, they become residual claimants—they receive what is left after all explicit costs have been accounted for. However, part of the costs should include the salary the owner-operator could have received working for someone else.

Consider a simple example of a skilled auto mechanic working 14 hours a day, six days a week, at a service station owned by that individual. Compare this situation to how much that mechanic could earn working the same 84 hours a week, but for a trucking company. This self-employed auto mechanic might have an opportunity cost of about $20 an hour. For the 84-hour week in the mechanic's own service station, $1,680 is forfeited. Unless the service station shows accounting profits of more than that per week, the mechanic is losing money in an economic sense.

Another way of looking at the opportunity cost of running a business is that opportunity cost consists of all explicit and implicit costs. Accountants only consider explicit costs. Therefore, accounting profit ends up being the residual after only explicit costs are subtracted from total revenues.

This same analysis can apply to owner-provided capital, such as land or buildings. The fact that the owner owns the building or the land where the business operates does not mean that it is "free." Rather, use of the building and land still has an opportunity cost—the value of the next-best alternative use for those assets.

Accounting Profits Versus Economic Profits

▶ **Economic profits**
Total revenues minus total opportunity costs of all inputs used, or the total of all implicit and explicit costs.

The term *profits* in economics means the income that entrepreneurs earn, over and above all costs including their own opportunity cost of time, plus the opportunity cost of the capital they have invested in their business. Profits can be regarded as total revenues minus total costs—which is how accountants think of them—but we must now include *all* costs. Our definition of **economic profits** will be the following:

$$\text{Economic profits} = \text{total revenues} - \text{total opportunity cost of all inputs used}$$

or

$$\text{Economic profits} = \text{total revenues} - (\text{explicit} + \text{implicit costs})$$

Try Preview Question 1:
How does the economist's definition of profit differ from the accountant's?

Remember that implicit costs include a normal rate of return on invested capital. We show this relationship in Figure 10.1.

The Goal of the Firm: Profit Maximization

When we examined the theory of consumer demand, utility (or satisfaction) maximization by the individual provided the basis for the analysis. In the theory of the firm and production, *profit maximization* is the underlying hypothesis of our predictive theory. The goal of the firm is to maximize economic profits, and the firm is expected to try to make the positive difference between total revenues and total costs as large as it can.

Our justification for assuming profit maximization by firms is similar to our belief in utility maximization by individuals. To obtain labour, capital, and other resources required to produce commodities, firms must first obtain financing from investors. In general, investors are indifferent about the details of how a firm uses the money they provide. They are most interested in the earnings on this money, and the risk of obtaining lower returns or losing the money they have invested. Firms that can provide relatively

Figure 10.1
Simplified View of Economic and Accounting Profit

We see on the right column that accounting profit is the difference between total revenues and total explicit accounting costs. Conversely, we see on the left column that economic profit is equal to total revenues minus economic costs. Economic costs equal explicit accounting costs plus all implicit costs, including a normal rate of return on invested capital.

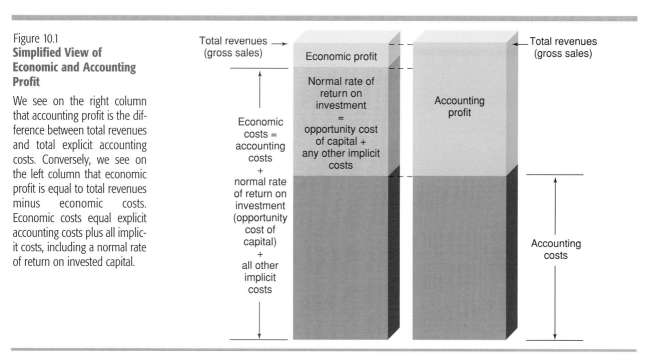

Total revenues (gross sales)

Economic profit

Normal rate of return on investment
=
opportunity cost of capital +
any other implicit costs

Economic costs = accounting costs
+
normal rate of return on investment (opportunity cost of capital)
+
all other implicit costs

Accounting profit

Total revenues (gross sales)

Accounting costs

higher risk-corrected returns will therefore have an advantage in obtaining the financing needed to continue or expand production. Over time we would expect a policy of profit maximization to become the dominant mode of behaviour for firms that survive.

Concepts in Brief

- Accounting profits differ from economic profits. Economic profits are defined as total revenues minus total costs, where costs include the full opportunity cost of all of the factors of production plus all other implicit costs.
- Sole proprietorships often fail to consider the opportunity cost of the labour services provided by the owner.
- The full opportunity cost of capital invested in a business is generally not included as a cost when accounting profits are calculated. Thus accounting profits often overstate economic profits.
- We assume throughout these chapters that the goal of the firm is to maximize economic profits.

SHORT RUN VERSUS LONG RUN

In Chapter 8, we discussed short-run and long-run price elasticities of supply and demand. For consumers, the long run meant the time period during which all adjustments to a change in price could be made, and anything shorter than that was considered the short run. For suppliers, the long run was the time in which all adjustments could be made, and anything shorter than that was the short run.

Now that we are discussing firms only, we will maintain a similar distinction between the short and the long run, but we will be more specific. In the theory of the firm, the **short run** is defined as any time period that is so short that there is at least one input, such as current **plant size,** that the firm cannot alter.[1] In other words, during the short run, a firm makes do with whatever big machines and factory size it already has, no matter how much more it wants to produce because of increased demand for its product. We consider the plant and heavy equipment, the size or amount of which cannot be varied in the short run, as fixed resources. In agriculture and in some other businesses, land may be a fixed resource.

There are, of course, variable resources that the firm can alter when it wants to change its rate of production. These are called *variable inputs* or *variable factors of production.* Typically, the variable inputs of a firm are its labour and its purchases of raw materials. In the short run, in response to changes in demand, the firm can, by definition, vary only its variable inputs.

The **long run** can now be considered the period of time in which *all* inputs can be varied. Specifically, in the long run, the firm can alter its plant size. How long is the long run? That depends on each individual industry. For Wendy's or McDonald's, the long run may be four or five months, because that is the time it takes to add new franchises. For a steel company, the long run may be several years, because that's how long it takes to plan and build a new plant. An electric utility might need over a decade to build a new dam, for example.

Short run and *long run* in our discussion are in fact management planning terms that apply to decisions made by managers. The firm can operate only in the short run in the sense that decisions must be made in the present. The same analysis applies to your own behaviour. You may have many long-run plans about graduate school, vacations, and the like, but you always operate in the short run—you make decisions every day about what you do every day.

THE RELATIONSHIP BETWEEN OUTPUT AND INPUTS

A firm takes numerous inputs, combines them using a technological production process, and ends up with an output. There are, of course, a great many factors of production, or inputs. We classify production inputs in two broad categories (ignoring land)—labour and capital. The relationship between output and these two inputs

---

▶ Short run
The time period when at least one input, such as plant size, cannot be changed.

▶ Plant size
The physical size of the factories that a firm owns and operates to produce its output. Plant size can be defined by floor area, by maximum physical capacity, and by other physical measures.

▶ Long run
The time period in which all factors of production can be varied.

Try Preview Question 2:
What distinguishes the long run from the short run?

---

[1] There can be many short runs but only one long run. For ease of analysis, in this section we simplify the case to one short run and talk about short-run costs.

is as follows:

Output per time period = some function of capital and labour inputs

Mathematically, the production relationship can be written $Q = f(K, L)$, where Q = output per time period, K = capital, and L = labour.

▶ **Production**

Any activity that results in the conversion of resources into products that can be used in consumption.

We have used the word *production* but have not defined it. **Production** is any process by which resources are transformed into goods or services. Production includes not only making things but also transporting them, retailing, repackaging them, and so on. Notice that if we know that production occurs, we do not necessarily know the value of the output. The production relationship tells nothing about the worth or value of the inputs or the output.

INTERNATIONAL EXAMPLE
Europeans Use More Capital

Since 1970, the 15 nations of the European Union (EU) have increased their total annual output of goods and services about as much as Canada. But over this same time period, the EU has dramatically increased the amount of capital relative to the amount of labour it uses in its production processes. Business managers in the EU have substituted capital for labour much more than in Canada because the cost of labour (wages corrected for inflation) has increased by almost 60 percent in the EU but by only 25 percent in Canada.

For critical analysis: How does a firm decide when to buy more machines?

The Production Function: A Numerical Example

▶ **Production function**

The relationship between inputs and output. A production function is a technological, not an economic, relationship.

The relationship between the amount of physical output the firm can produce and the quantity of capital and labour used to produce it is sometimes called a **production function**. The production function specifies the maximum possible output that can be produced with a given amount of inputs. It also specifies the minimum amount of inputs necessary to produce a given level of output. Firms that are inefficient or wasteful in their use of capital and labour will obtain less output than the production function in theory will show. However, no firm can obtain more output than the production function shows. Since the production function is a technological relationship between inputs and output, it follows that an improvement in technology that allows the firm to produce more output with the same amount of inputs (or the same output with fewer inputs) results in a new production function.

Look at part (a) of Figure 10.2. It shows a production function relating total output of pocket calculators in column 2 to the quantity of labour measured in workers in column 1. When there are zero workers, there is zero output. When there are five workers per hour of input (given the capital stock), there is a total output of 62 calculators per hour. (Ignore for the moment the rest of that part.) Part (b) of Figure 10.2 shows this particular production function graphically. Note again that it relates to the short run and that it is for an individual firm.

Figure 10.2
Diminishing Returns, the Production Function, and Marginal Product: A Hypothetical Case of Pocket Calculator Production

Marginal product is the addition to the total product that results when one additional worker is hired. Thus the marginal product of the fourth worker is 13 pocket calculators. With 4 workers, 52 calculators are produced, but with three workers, only 39 are produced; the difference is 13. In part (b), we plot the numbers from columns (1) and (2) of part (a). In part (c), we plot the numbers from columns (1) and (4) of part

(a). When we go from zero workers to one, marginal product is 8. When we go from one worker to two, marginal product increases to 16. After two workers, marginal product declines, but it is still positive. Total product (output) reaches its peak at seven workers, so after seven workers marginal product becomes -5 calculators per hour.

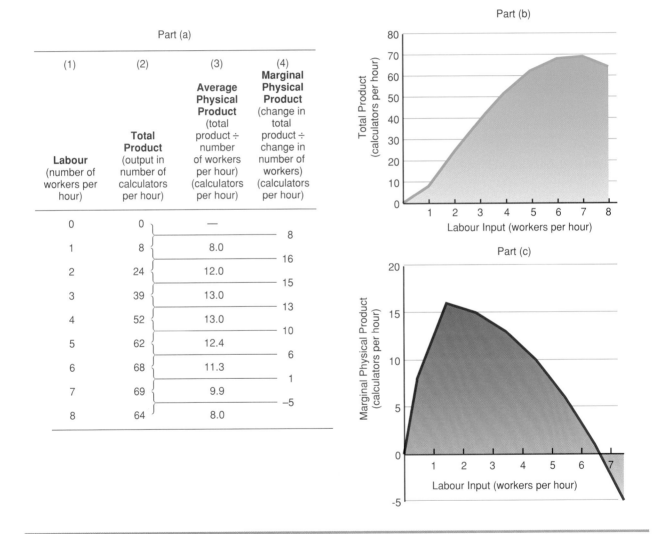

Part (a)

(1)	(2)	(3)	(4)
		Average Physical Product (total product ÷ number of workers per hour) (calculators per hour)	**Marginal Physical Product** (change in total product ÷ change in number of workers) (calculators per hour)
	Total Product		
Labour (number of workers per hour)	(output in number of calculators per hour)		
0	0	—	
			8
1	8	8.0	
			16
2	24	12.0	
			15
3	39	13.0	
			13
4	52	13.0	
			10
5	62	12.4	
			6
6	68	11.3	
			1
7	69	9.9	
			-5
8	64	8.0	

Part (b) shows a total physical product curve, or the maximum amount of physical output that is possible when we add successive equal-sized units of labour while holding all other inputs constant. The graph of the production function in part (b) is not a straight line. In fact, it peaks at seven workers per hour and then starts to go

▶**Law of diminishing (marginal) returns**
The observation that after some point, successive equal-sized increases in a variable factor of production, such as labour, added to fixed factors of production, will result in smaller increases in output.

▶**Average physical product**
Total product divided by the variable input.

▶**Marginal physical product**
The physical output that is due to the addition of one more unit of a variable factor of production; the change in total product occurring when a variable input is increased and all other inputs are held constant; also called *marginal productivity* or *marginal return.*

down. To understand why it starts to go down with an individual firm in the short run, we have to analyse in detail the **law of diminishing (marginal) returns**.

But before that, let's examine the meaning of columns 3 and 4 of part (a) of Figure 10.2—that is, average and marginal physical product.

Average and Marginal Physical Product

The **average physical product** of labour is the total product divided by the number of workers expressed in output per hour. You can see in column 3 of part (a) of Figure 10.2 that the average physical product of labour first rises and then steadily falls after four workers are hired.

Remember that *marginal* means "additional." Hence the **marginal physical product** of labour is the change in total product that occurs when a worker joins an existing production process. (The term *physical* here emphasizes the fact that we are measuring in terms of physical units of production, not in dollar terms.) It is also the *change* in total product that occurs when that worker quits or is laid off an existing production process. The marginal physical product of labour therefore refers to the *change in output caused by a one-unit change in the labour input.* (Marginal physical product is also referred to as *marginal productivity* and *marginal return.*)

DIMINISHING MARGINAL RETURNS

The concept of diminishing marginal returns—also known as diminishing marginal product—applies to many situations. If you put a seat belt across your lap, a certain amount of safety is obtained. If you add another seat belt over your shoulder, some additional safety is obtained, but less than when the first belt was secured. When you add a third seat belt over the other shoulder, the amount of *additional* safety obtained is even smaller.

The same analysis holds for firms in their use of productive inputs. When the returns from hiring more workers are diminishing, it does not necessarily mean that more workers won't be hired. In fact, workers will be hired until the returns, in terms of the *value* of the *extra* output produced, are equal to the additional wages that have to be paid for those workers to produce the extra output. Before we get into that decision-making process, let's demonstrate that diminishing returns can be represented graphically and can be used in our analysis of the firm.

Measuring Diminishing Returns

How do we measure diminishing returns? First, we limit the analysis to only one variable factor of production (or input)—let's say the factor is labour. Every other factor of production, such as machines, must be held constant. Only in this way can we calculate the marginal returns from using more workers and know when we reach the point of diminishing marginal returns.

The marginal productivity of labour may increase rapidly at the very beginning. A firm starts with no workers, only machines. The firm then hires one worker, who finds it difficult to get the work started. But when the firm hires more workers, each is able to specialize, and the marginal productivity of those additional workers may actually be greater than it was with the previous few workers. Beyond some point, however, diminishing returns must set in, not because new workers are less qualified, but because each worker has (on average) fewer machines with which to work (remember, all other inputs are fixed). In fact, eventually the firm will become so crowded that workers will start to get in each other's way. At that point, total production declines and marginal physical product becomes negative.

Using these ideas, we can define the law of diminishing returns as follows:

> As successive equal increases in a variable factor of production are added to fixed factors of production, there will be a point beyond which the extra, or marginal, product that can be attributed to each additional unit of the variable factor of production will decline.

Note that the law of diminishing returns is a statement about the *physical* relationships between inputs and outputs that we have observed in many firms. If the law of diminishing returns were not a fairly accurate statement about the world, what would stop firms from hiring additional workers forever?

An Example of the Law of Diminishing Returns

Look again at Figure 10.2. The numbers in part (a) illustrate the law of diminishing marginal returns and are presented graphically in part (c). Marginal productivity (returns from adding more workers) first increases, then decreases, and finally becomes negative.

When one worker is hired, total output goes from 0 to 8. Thus marginal physical product is 8 calculators per hour. When the second worker is hired, total product goes from 8 to 24 calculators per hour. Marginal physical product therefore increases to 16 calculators per hour. When a third worker is hired, total product again increases, from 24 to 39 calculators per hour. This represents a marginal physical product of only 15 calculators per hour. Therefore, the point of diminishing marginal returns occurs after two workers are hired.

Notice that after seven workers per hour, marginal physical product becomes negative. That means that the hiring of an eighth worker would create a situation that reduces total product. Sometimes this is called the *point of saturation*, indicating that given the amount of fixed inputs, there is no further positive use for more of the variable input. We have entered the region of negative marginal returns.

Concepts in Brief

- The technological relationship between output and input is called the production function. It relates output per time period to the several inputs, such as capital and labour.
- After some rate of output, the firm generally experiences diminishing marginal returns.
- The law of diminishing returns states that if all factors of production are held constant except one, equal increments in that one variable factor will eventually yield decreasing increments in output.

SHORT-RUN COSTS TO THE FIRM

You will see that costs are the extension of the production ideas just presented. Let's consider the costs the firm faces in the short run. To keep our example simple, assume that there are only two factors of production, capital and labour. Our definition of the short run will be the time during which capital is fixed but labour is variable.

In the short run, a firm incurs certain types of costs. We label all costs incurred **total costs**. Then we break total costs down into total fixed costs and total variable costs, which we will explain shortly. Therefore,

Total costs (TC) = total fixed costs (TFC) + total variable costs (TVC)

▶ **Total costs**
The sum of total fixed costs and total variable costs.

Remember that these total costs include both explicit and implicit costs, including the normal rate of return on investment.

After we have looked at the elements of total costs, we will find out how to compute average and marginal costs.

Total Fixed Costs

Let's look at an ongoing business such as Chrysler Canada. The decision makers in that corporate giant can look around and see big machines, thousands of parts, huge buildings, and a multitude of other components of plant and equipment that have already been bought and are in place. Chrysler has to take account of the technological obsolescence of this equipment, no matter how many vehicles it produces. The payments on the loans taken out to buy the equipment will all be exactly the same. The opportunity costs of any land that Chrysler owns will all be exactly the same. These costs are more or less the same for Chrysler no matter how many automobiles it produces.

The opportunity cost (or normal rate of return) of capital must be included along with other costs. Remember that we are dealing in the short run, during which capital is fixed. If investors in Chrysler Canada have already put $100 million into a new factory addition, the opportunity cost of that capital invested is now, in essence, a *fixed cost*. Why? Because in the short run, nothing can be done about that cost; the investment has already been made. This leads us to a very straightforward definition of fixed costs: All costs that do not vary—that is, all costs that do not depend on the rate of production—are called **fixed costs**.

▶ **Fixed costs**
Costs that do not vary with output. Fixed costs include such things as rent on a building. These costs are fixed for a certain period of time; in the long run, they are variable.

Let's now take as an example the fixed costs incurred by our producer of pocket calculators. This firm's total fixed costs will equal the cost of the rent on its equipment and the insurance it has to pay. We see in part (a) of Figure 10.3 (page 246) that total fixed costs per hour are $10. In part (b), these total fixed costs are represented by the horizontal line at $10 per hour. They are invariant to changes in the output of calculators per hour—no matter how many are produced, fixed costs will remain at $10 per hour.

▶ **Variable costs**
Costs that vary with the rate of production. They include wages paid to workers and purchases of materials.

Total Variable Costs

Total **variable costs** are costs whose magnitude varies with the rate of production. One obvious variable cost is wages. The more the firm produces, the more labour it

Figure 10.3

Costs of Production: A Hypothetical Case of Pocket Calculator Production

In part (a), the derivation of columns (5) through (9) are given in parentheses in each column heading. For example, column 7, average variable costs, is derived by dividing column 4, total variable costs, by column 2, total output per hour. Note that marginal cost (MC) in part (c) intersects average variable costs (AVC) at the latter's minimum point. Also, MC intersects average total costs (ATC) at the latter's minimum point.

Part (a)

(1)	(2)	(3)	(4)	(5)	(6)	(7)	(8)	(9)
Labour	Total Output (Q/hour)	Total Fixed Costs (TFC)	Total Variable Costs (TVC) $5 × (1)	Total Costs (TC) (5) = (3) + (4)	Average Fixed Costs (AFC) (3) ÷ (2)	Average Variable Costs (AVC) (4) ÷ (2)	Average Total Costs (ATC) (5) ÷ (2)	Marginal Costs (MC) (9) = change in (5) ÷ change in (2)
0	0	$10	$ 0	$10	—	—	—	
								$0.63
1	8	10	5	15	$1.25	$0.63	$1.88	
								0.31
2	24	10	10	20	0.42	0.42	0.83	
								0.33
3	39	10	15	25	0.26	0.38	0.64	
								0.38
4	52	10	20	30	0.19	0.38	0.58	
								0.50
5	62	10	25	35	0.16	0.40	0.56	
								0.83
6	68	10	30	40	0.15	0.44	0.59	
								5.00
7	69	10	35	45	0.14	0.51	0.65	

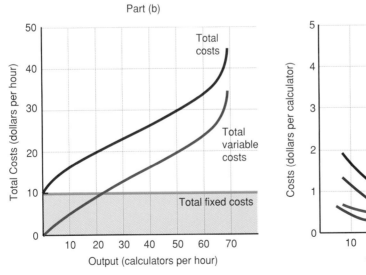

Part (b)

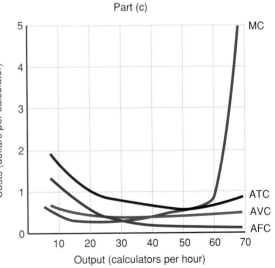

Part (c)

has to hire; therefore, the more wages it has to pay. Another variable cost is parts. In the assembly of calculators, for example, microchips must be bought. The more calculators that are made, the more chips must be bought. Part of the rate of depreciation (the rate of wear and tear) on machines that are used in the assembly process can also be considered a variable cost if depreciation depends partly on how long and how intensively the machines are used. Total variable costs are given in part (a) of Figure 10.3 in column 4. (For simplicity we have assumed here that labour is the only variable factor of production, and that each worker is paid $5 per hour.) These costs are translated into the total variable cost curve in part (b). Notice that the total variable cost curve lies below the total cost curve by the vertical distance of $10. This vertical distance represents, of course, total fixed costs.

Short-Run Average Cost Curves

In part (b) of Figure 10.3 we see total costs, total variable costs, and total fixed costs. Now we want to look at average cost. The average cost concept is one in which we are measuring cost per unit of output. It is a matter of arithmetic to figure the averages of these three cost concepts. We can define them as follows:

$$\text{Average total costs (ATC)} = \frac{\text{total costs (TC)}}{\text{output (}Q\text{)}}$$

$$\text{Average variable costs (AVC)} = \frac{\text{total variable costs (TVC)}}{\text{output (}Q\text{)}}$$

$$\text{Average fixed costs (AFC)} = \frac{\text{total fixed costs}}{\text{output (}Q\text{)}}$$

The arithmetic is done in columns 6, 7, and 8 in part (a) of Figure 10.3. The numerical results are translated into a graphical format in part (c). Because total costs (TC) equal variable costs (TVC) plus fixed costs (TFC), the difference between average total costs (ATC) and average variable costs (AVC) will always be identical to average fixed costs (AFC). That means that average total costs and average variable costs move together as output expands.

Now let's see what we can observe about the three average cost curves in Figure 10.3.

> **Average fixed costs**
> Total fixed costs divided by the number of units produced.

Average Fixed Costs (AFC). **Average fixed costs** continue to fall throughout the output range. In fact, if we were to continue the diagram farther to the right, we would find that average fixed costs would get closer and closer to the horizontal axis. That is because total fixed costs remain constant. As we divide this fixed number by a larger and larger number of units of output, the resulting AFC has to become smaller and smaller. In business, this is called "spreading the overhead."

> **Average variable costs**
> Total variable costs divided by the number of units produced.

Average Variable Costs (AVC). The **average variable cost** curve takes a form that is U-shaped: First it falls; then it starts to rise. It is possible for the AVC curve to take other shapes in the long run.

Average Total Costs (ATC). This curve has a shape similar to that of the AVC curve. However, it falls even more dramatically in the beginning and rises more slowly after it has reached a minimum point. It falls and then rises because **average total costs** are the summation of the AFC curve and the AVC curve. Thus when AFC and AVC are both falling, ATC must fall too. At some point, however, AVC starts to increase while AFC continues to fall. Once the increase in the AVC curve outweighs the decrease in the AFC curve, the ATC curve will start to increase and will develop its familiar U shape.

▶ **Average total costs**

Total costs divided by the number of units produced; sometimes called per-unit total costs.

Marginal Cost

We have stated repeatedly that the basis of decisions is always on the margin—movement in economics is always determined at the margin. This dictum also holds true within the firm. Firms, according to the analysis we use to predict their behaviour, are very interested in their **marginal costs**. Because the term *marginal* means "additional" or "incremental" (or "decremental," too) here, marginal costs refer to costs that result from a one-unit change in the production rate. For example, if the production of 68 calculators per hour costs a firm $40, and the production of 69 calculators costs it $45 per hour, the marginal cost of producing the sixty-ninth calculator is $5.

Marginal costs can be measured by using the formula

▶ **Marginal costs**

The change in total costs due to a one-unit change in production rate.

$$\text{Marginal cost} = \frac{\text{change in total cost}}{\text{change in output}}$$

We show the marginal costs of calculator production per hour in column 9 of part (a) in Figure 10.3, calculated according to the formula just given.

This marginal cost schedule is shown graphically in part (c) of Figure 10.3. Just like average variable costs and average total costs, marginal costs first fall and then rise. The U shape of the marginal cost curve is a result of increasing and then diminishing marginal returns. At lower levels of output, the marginal cost curve declines. The reasoning is that as marginal physical product increases with each addition of output, the marginal cost of this last unit of output must fall. Conversely, when diminishing marginal returns set in, marginal physical product decreases (and eventually becomes negative); it follows that the marginal cost of the last unit must rise. These relationships are clearly reflected in the geometry of parts (b) and (c) of Figure 10.3.

In summary:

As long as marginal physical product rises, marginal cost will fall, and when marginal physical product starts to fall (after reaching the point of diminishing marginal returns), marginal cost will begin to rise.

Try Preview Question 3:

How does the law of diminishing marginal returns account for an *eventually* increasing marginal cost curve for a firm in the short run?

EXAMPLE	The Cost of Driving a Car

Each year the Canadian Automobile Association publishes a study on the annual cost of owning and driving an automobile. The 1996 study found that driving a new 1996 Chevrolet Cavalier 4-door sedan involved the following:

Costs per kilometre
Gasoline and oil: 5.82 cents
Maintenance: 2.23 cents
Tires: 0.95 cents

Annual costs
Insurance: $1164
Licence and registration: $118.81
Financing charges: $864

Based on an average annual driving distance of 24,000 kilometres, total costs amounted to $5,733.17 per year, or $15.71 per day.

However, the average cost of driving a car varied depending on distance driven. At 18,000 kilometres per year, the cost was 40.9 cents per kilometre; at 24,000 kilometres per year, it was 35.9 cents; and at 32,000 kilometres per year, the cost was 32.3 cents per kilometre. (Depreciation was not factored into these numbers.)

For critical analysis: Which costs are total fixed costs, total variable costs, average total costs, and marginal costs?

The Relationship Between Average and Marginal Costs

Let's now look at the relationship between average costs and marginal costs. There is always a definite relationship between averages and marginals. Consider your grade point average. Say your GPA is currently B. If you take an economics course and earn an A, what will happen to your GPA? It must increase. When your grade in a marginal course (the economics course) is higher (above) your GPA, it pulls your average up. If you subsequently take an accounting course and earn a C, your GPA will fall.

There is a similar relationship between average variable costs and marginal costs. When marginal costs are less than average costs, the latter must fall. Conversely, when marginal costs are greater than average costs, the latter must rise. When you think about it, the relationship makes sense. The only way for average variable costs to fall is for the extra cost of the marginal unit produced to be less than the average variable cost of all the preceding units. For example, if the average variable cost for 24 calculators is 42 cents each, the only way for the average variable cost of 25 calculators to be less than that of 24 is for the variable costs attributable to the last calculator—the marginal cost—to be less than the average of the previously produced calculators. In this particular case, if average variable cost falls to 41 cents per calculator, total variable cost for the 25 calculators would be 25 times 41 cents or $10.25. Total variable cost for 24 calculators is 24 times 42 cents or $10.08. The marginal cost is therefore $10.25 minus $10.08, or 17 cents which is less than the average variable cost of 24 calculators—that is, less than 42 cents.

A similar type of computation can be carried out for rising average variable costs. The only way for average variable costs to rise is for the cost of additional units to be more than that for units already produced. But the incremental cost is the marginal cost. In this particular case, the marginal costs have to be higher than the average variable costs.

There is also a relationship between marginal costs and average total costs. Remember that average total cost is equal to total cost divided by the number of units produced. Remember also that marginal cost does not include any fixed costs. Fixed costs are, by definition, fixed and cannot influence marginal costs. Our example can therefore be repeated substituting average total cost for average variable cost.

These rising and falling relationships can be seen in Figure 10.3, where MC intersects AVC and ATC at their respective minimum points.

Minimum Cost Points

At what rate of output of calculators per day does our producer experience the minimum average total costs? Column 8 in part (a) of Figure 10.3 shows that the minimum average total cost is 56 cents, which occurs at an output rate of 62 calculators per hour. We can also find this minimum cost by finding the point in part (c) of Figure 10.3 at which the marginal cost curve intersects the average total cost curve. This should not be surprising. When marginal cost is below average total cost, average total cost falls. When marginal cost is above average total cost, average total cost rises. At the point where average total cost is neither falling nor rising, marginal cost must then be equal to average total cost. When we represent this graphically, the marginal cost curve will intersect the average total cost curve at the latter's minimum.

The same analysis applies to the intersection of the marginal cost curve and the average variable cost curve. When are average variable costs at a minimum? According to part (a) of Figure 10.3, average variable costs are at a minimum of 38 cents at an output rate of 52 calculators per hour. This is where the marginal cost curve intersects the average variable cost curve in part (c) of Figure 10.3.

Concepts in Brief

- Total costs equal total fixed costs plus total variable costs.
- Fixed costs are those that do not vary with the rate of production; variable costs are those that do vary with the rate of production.
- Average total costs equal total costs divided by output (ATC = TC/Q).
- Average variable costs equal total variable costs divided by output (AVC = TVC/Q).
- Average fixed costs equal total fixed costs divided by output (AFC = TFC/Q).
- Marginal cost equals the change in total cost divided by the change in output (MC = ΔTC/ΔQ).
- The marginal cost curve intersects the minimum point of the average total cost curve and the minimum point of the average variable cost curve.

THE RELATIONSHIP BETWEEN DIMINISHING MARGINAL RETURNS AND COST CURVES

There is a unique relationship between output and the shape of the various cost curves we have drawn. Let's consider specifically the relationship between marginal cost and the example of diminishing marginal physical returns in part (a) of Figure 10.4 (page 252). It turns out that if wage rates are constant, the shape of the marginal cost curve in part (d) of Figure 10.4 is both a reflection of and a consequence of the law of diminishing returns. Let's assume that each unit of labour can be purchased at a constant price. Further assume that labour is the only variable input. We see that as more workers are hired, marginal physical product first rises and then falls after the point at which diminishing returns are encountered. Thus the marginal cost of each extra unit of output will first fall as long as marginal physical product is rising, and then it will rise as long as marginal physical product is falling. Recall that marginal cost is defined as

$$MC = \frac{\text{change in total cost}}{\text{change in output}}$$

Because the price of labour is assumed to be constant, the change in total cost is simply the constant price of labour, W (we are increasing labour by only one unit). The change in output is simply the marginal physical product (MPP) of the one-unit increase in labour. Therefore, we see that

$$\text{Marginal cost} = \frac{W}{\text{MPP}}$$

This means that initially, when there are increasing returns, marginal cost falls (we are dividing W by increasingly larger numbers), and later, when diminishing returns set in and marginal physical product is falling, marginal cost must increase (we are dividing W by smaller numbers). As marginal physical product increases, marginal cost decreases, and as marginal physical product decreases, marginal cost must increase. Thus when marginal physical product reaches its maximum, marginal cost necessarily reaches its minimum. To illustrate this, assume that a worker at our pocket calculator factory is paid $5 per hour. When we go from zero labour input to one unit, output increases by eight calculators. Each of those eight calculators has a marginal cost of 63 cents Now the second unit of labour is hired, and it too costs $5 per hour. Output increases by 16. Thus the marginal cost is $5 ÷ 16 = 31 cents. We continue the experiment. We see that the next unit of labour yields only 15 additional calculators, so marginal cost starts to rise to 33 cents. The following unit of labour increases marginal physical product by only 13, so marginal cost becomes $5 ÷ 13 = 38 cents.

All of the foregoing can be restated in relatively straightforward terms:

Firms' short-run cost curves are a reflection of the law of diminishing marginal returns. Given any constant price of the variable input, marginal costs decline as long as the marginal product of the variable resource is rising. At the point at which diminishing marginal returns begin, marginal costs begin to rise as the marginal product of the variable input begins to decline.

Part (a)

(1) Labour	(2) Total Product (number of calculators per hour)	(3) Average Physical Product (calculators per worker per hour) (3) = (2) ÷ (1)	(4) Marginal Physical Product (4) = change in (2) ÷ change in (1)	(5) Average Variable Cost (5) = (W = $5) ÷ (3)	(6) Marginal Cost (6) = (W = $5) ÷ (4)
0	0	—	—	—	—
1	8	8	8	$0.63	$0.63
2	24	12	16	0.42	0.31
3	39	13	15	0.38	0.33
4	52	13	13	0.38	0.38
5	62	12.4	13	0.40	0.50
6	68	11.3	10	0.44	0.83
7	69	9.9	6	0.55	5.00
			1		

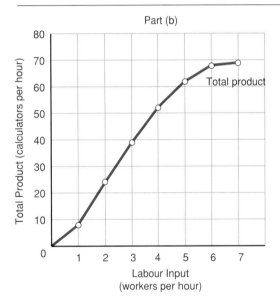

Part (b)

Part (c)

Figure 10.4
The Relationship Between Physical Output and Costs

As the number of workers increases, the total number of calculators produced rises, as shown in parts (a) and (b). In part
(c), marginal product (MP) first rises and then falls. Average
product (AP) follows. The mirror image of part (c) is shown
in part (d), in which MC and AVC first fall and then rise.

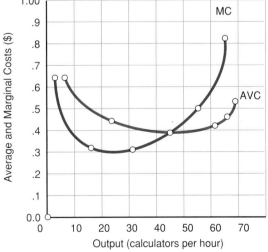

Part (d)

The result is a marginal cost curve that slopes down, hits a minimum, and then slopes up. The average total cost curve and average variable cost curve are of course affected. They will have their familiar U shape in the short run. Again, to see this, recall that

$$\text{AVC} = \frac{\text{total variable costs}}{\text{total output}}$$

As we move from zero labour input to one unit in part (a) of Figure 10.4, output increases from zero to eight calculators. The total variable costs are the price per worker, W ($5), times the number of workers (1). Because the average product of one worker (column 3) is eight, we can write the total product, eight, as the average product, eight, times the number of workers, one. Thus we see that

$$\text{AVC} = \frac{\$5 \times 1}{8 \times 1} = \frac{\$5}{8} = \frac{W}{\text{AP}}$$

From column 3 in part (a) of Figure 10.4, we see that the average product increases, reaches a maximum, and then declines. Because AVC = W / AP, average variable cost decreases as average product increases and increases as average product decreases. AVC reaches its minimum when average product reaches its maximum. Furthermore, because ATC = AVC + AFC, the average total cost curve inherits the relationship between the average variable cost and diminishing returns.

Try Preview Question 4:
Why is the short-run average total cost curve U-shaped?

LONG-RUN COST CURVES

The long run is defined as a time period during which full adjustment can be made to any change in the economic environment. Thus in the long run, *all* factors of production are variable. Long-run curves are sometimes called *planning curves,* and the long run is sometimes called the **planning horizon.** We start out our analysis of long-run cost curves by considering a single firm contemplating the construction of a single plant. The firm has three alternative plant sizes from which to choose on the planning horizon. Each particular plant size generates its own short-run average total cost curve. Now that we are talking about the difference between long-run and short-run cost curves, we will label all short-run curves with an S and long-run curves with an L; short-run average (total) costs will be labelled SAC, and long-run average cost curves will be labelled LAC.

▶ **Planning horizon**
The long run, during which all inputs are variable.

Part (a) of Figure 10.5 (page 254) shows three short-run average cost curves for three successively larger plants. Which is the optimal size to build? That depends on the anticipated normal, sustained (permanent) rate of output per time period. Assume for a moment that the anticipated normal, sustained rate is Q_1. If a plant of size 1 is built, the average costs will be C_1. If a plant of size 2 is built, we see on SAC$_2$ that the average costs will be C_2, which is greater than C_1. Thus if the anticipated rate of output is Q_1, the appropriate plant size is the one from which SAC$_1$ was

Figure 10.5

Preferable Plant Size and the Long-Run Average Cost Curve

If the anticipated permanent rate of output per unit time period is Q_1, the optimal plant to build would be the one corresponding to SAC_1 in part (a) because average costs are lower. However, if the permanent rate of output increases to Q_2, it will be more profitable to have a plant size corresponding to SAC_2. Unit costs fall to C_3.

If we draw all the possible short-run average cost curves that correspond to different plant sizes and then draw the envelope (a curve tangent to each member of a set of curves) to these various curves, SAC_1–SAC_8, we obtain the long-run average cost curve, or the planning curve, as shown in part (b).

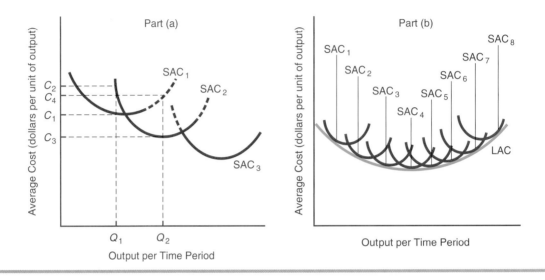

derived.

However, if the anticipated permanent rate of output per time period goes from Q_1 to Q_2 and a plant of size 1 had been decided on, average costs would be C_4. If a plant of size 2 had been decided on, average costs would be C_3, which is clearly less than C_4.

In choosing the appropriate plant size for a single-plant firm during the planning horizon, the firm will pick the size whose short-run average cost curve generates an average cost that is lowest for the expected rate of output.

Long-Run Average Cost Curve

▶ **Long-run average cost curve**

The locus of points representing the minimum unit cost of producing any given rate of output, given current technology and resource prices.

▶ **Planning curve**

The long-run average cost curve.

If we now assume that the entrepreneur faces an infinite number of choices of plant sizes in the long run, we can conceive of an infinite number of SAC curves similar to the three in part (a) of Figure 10.5. We are not able, of course, to draw an infinite number; we have drawn quite a few, however, in part (b) of Figure 10.5. We then draw the "envelope" to all these various short-run average cost curves. The resulting envelope is the **long-run average cost curve.** This long-run average cost curve is sometimes called the **planning curve,** for it represents the various average costs attainable at the planning stage of the firm's decision making. It represents the locus (path) of points giving the least unit cost of producing any given rate of output. Note that the LAC curve is *not* tangent to each individual SAC curve at the latter's minimum points. This is true only at the minimum point of the LAC curve. Then and only then are minimum long-run average costs equal to minimum short-run average costs.

WHY THE LONG-RUN AVERAGE COST CURVE IS U-SHAPED

▶ **Economies of scale**

Decreases in long-run average costs resulting from increases in output.

▶ **Constant returns to scale**

No change in long-run average costs when output increases.

▶ **Diseconomies of scale**

Increases in long-run average costs that occur as output increases.

Notice that the long-run average cost curve, LAC in part (b) of Figure 10.5 is U-shaped, similar to the U shape of the short-run average cost curve developed earlier in this chapter. The reason behind the U shape of the two curves is not the same, however. The short-run average cost curve is U-shaped because of the law of diminishing marginal returns. But the law cannot apply to the long run, because in the long run, all factors of production are variable; there is no point of diminishing marginal returns because there is no fixed factor of production. Why, then, do we see the U shape in the long-run average cost curve? The reason has to do with economies of scale, constant returns to scale, and diseconomies of scale. When the firm is experiencing **economies of scale,** the long-run average cost curve slopes downward—an increase in scale and production leads to a fall in unit costs. When the firm is experiencing **constant returns to scale,** the long-run average cost curve is at its minimum point, such that an increase in scale and production does not change unit costs. When the firm is experiencing **diseconomies of scale,** the long-run average cost curve slopes upward—an increase in scale and production increases unit costs. These three sections of the long-run average cost curves are broken up into parts (a), (b), and (c) in Figure 10.6.

Reasons for Economies of Scale

We shall examine three of the many reasons a firm might be expected to experience economies of scale: specialization, the dimensional factor, and improved productive equipment.

Figure 10.6
Economies of Scale, Constant Returns to Scale, and Diseconomies of Scale Shown with the Long-Run Average Cost Curve

Long-run average cost curves will fall when there are economies of scale, as shown in part (a). They will be constant (flat) when the firm is experiencing constant returns to scale, as shown in part (b). They will rise when the firm is experiencing diseconomies of scale, as shown in part (c).

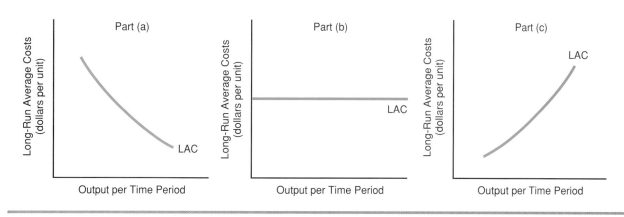

Specialization. As a firm's scale of operation increases, the opportunities for specialization in the use of resource inputs also increase. This is sometimes called *increased division of tasks* or *operations*. Gains from such division of labour or increased specialization are well known. When we consider managerial staffs, we also find that larger enterprises may be able to put together more highly specialized staffs.

Dimensional Factor. Large-scale firms often require proportionately less input per unit of output simply because certain inputs do not have to be physically doubled in order to double the output. Consider the cost of storage of oil. The cost of storage is basically related to the cost of steel that goes into building the storage container; however, the amount of steel required goes up less than in proportion to the volume (storage capacity) of the container (because the volume of a container increases more than proportionately with its surface area).

Improved Productive Equipment. The larger the scale of the enterprise, the more the firm is able to take advantage of larger-volume (output capacity) types of machinery. Small-scale operations may not be able profitably to use large-volume machines that can be more efficient per unit of output. Also, smaller firms often cannot use technologically more advanced machinery because they are unable to spread out the high cost of such sophisticated equipment over a large output.

For any of these reasons, the firm may experience economies of scale, which means that equal percentage increases in output result in a decrease in average cost. Thus output can double, but total costs will less than double; hence average cost falls. Note that the factors listed for causing economies of scale are all *internal* to the firm; they do not depend on what other firms are doing or what is happening in the economy.

EXAMPLE   Goods Versus Ideas

Numerous economic studies have shown that the production of many consumer goods have constant unit costs once production is under way. Otherwise stated, the production of most goods appears to look like part (b) in Figure 10.6. Ideas, in contrast, often have exceedingly high costs for the first "unit" of knowledge. Once that first unit is produced, though, both the marginal and average costs for production of additional units are essentially zero. Numerous costs are involved in producing the ideas for new technology. Once those ideas are produced, they can be disseminated electronically on the Internet to everybody in the world at relatively small additional cost.

For critical analysis: Draw the appropriate long-run average cost curve for ideas.

Why a Firm Might Experience Diseconomies of Scale

One of the basic reasons a firm can expect to run into diseconomies of scale is that there are limits to the efficient functioning of management. Moreover, as more workers are hired, a more than proportionate increase in managers and staff people may be needed, and this could cause increased costs per unit. This is so because larger levels of output imply successively larger *plant* size, which in turn implies successively larger *firm* size. Thus as the level of output increases, more people must be hired, and the firm gets bigger. However, as this happens, the support, supervisory, and administrative staff, and the general paperwork of the firm all increase. As the layers of supervision grow, the costs of information and communication grow more than proportionately; hence the average unit cost will start to increase.

Some observers of corporate giants claim that many of them are experiencing some diseconomies of scale today. Witness the problems that General Motors and IBM had in the early 1990s. Some analysts say that the financial problems that they have experienced are at least partly a function of their size relative to their smaller, more flexible competitors, who can make decisions faster and then take more rapid advantage of changing market conditions. This seems to be particularly true with IBM. It apparently adapted very slowly to the fact that the large mainframe computer business was declining as micro- and mini-computers became more and more powerful.

MINIMUM EFFICIENT SCALE

▶ **Minimum efficient scale (MES)**

The lowest rate of output per unit time at which long-run average costs for a particular firm are at a minimum.

Economists and statisticians have obtained actual data on the relationship between changes in all inputs and changes in average cost. It turns out that for many industries, the long-run average cost curve does not resemble that shown in part (b) of Figure 10.5. Rather, it more closely resembles Figure 10.7. What you observe there is a small portion of declining long-run average costs (economies of scale) and then a wide range of outputs over which the firm experiences relatively constant economies of scale. At the output rate when economies of scale end and constant economies of scale start, the **minimum efficient scale (MES)** for the firm is encountered. It occurs at point *A*. (The point is, of course, approximate. The more smoothly the curve declines into its flat portion, the more approximate will be our estimate of the MES.) The minimum efficient scale will always be the lowest rate of output

Figure 10.7
Minimum Efficient Scale

This long-run average cost curve reaches a minimum point at *A*. After that point, long-run average costs remain horizontal, or constant, and then rise at some later rate of output. Point *A* is called the minimum efficient scale for the firm because that is the point at which it reaches minimum costs. It is the lowest rate of output at which the average long-run costs are minimized.

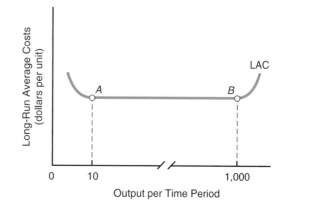

at which long-run average costs are minimized. In any industry with a long-run average cost curve similar to the one in Figure 10.7, larger firms will have no cost-saving advantage over smaller firms as long as the smaller firms have at least obtained the minimum efficient scale at point *A*.

Among its uses, the minimum efficient scale gives us a rough measure of the degree of competition in an industry. If the MES is small relative to industry demand, the degree of competition in that industry is likely to be high because there is room for many efficiently sized plants. Conversely, when the MES is large relative to industry demand, the degree of competition is likely to be small because there is room for a relatively small number of efficiently sized plants or firms. Looked at another way, if it takes a very large scale of plant to obtain minimum long-run average cost, the output of just a few of these very large firms can fully satisfy total market demand. This means that there isn't room for a large number of smaller plants if maximum efficiency is to be obtained in the industry.

Concepts in Brief

- The long run is often called the planning horizon. The long-run average cost curve is the planning curve. It is found by drawing a line tangent to one point on a series of short-run average cost curves, each corresponding to a different plant size.
- The firm can experience economies of scale, diseconomies of scale, and constant returns to scale, all according to whether the long-run average cost curve slopes downward, slopes upward, or is horizontal (flat). Economies of scale refer to what happens to average cost when all factors of production are increased.
- We observe economies of scale for a number of reasons, among which are specialization, improved productive equipment, and the dimensional factor, because large-scale firms require proportionately less input per unit of output. The firm may experience diseconomies of scale primarily because of limits to the efficient functioning of management.
- The minimum efficient scale occurs at the lowest rate of output at which long-run average costs are minimized.

Issues and Applications

Wireless Communications

Concepts Applied: Fixed costs, technological change, minimum efficient scale of production

Wires and telephone poles may be a thing of the past as wireless cable communication takes over. Long-run average costs of both technologies will determine where each will be used.

Part of living in Canada is communicating with others over long distances by mail, by telephone, and more recently by e-mail. We think little of picking up the phone in Newfoundland and calling Saskatchewan or British Columbia. How is it that we can sit comfortably on one side of the country and talk to someone else on the other? Our voices are carried by wire across this vast land of ours. A drive across the Prairies is all we need to convince us that we are connected with each other—for kilometre after kilometre the telephone poles bear the evidence of the cables which physically join us together.

New Technology

There is a new technology on its way, however, that may eventually replace all those telephone poles and kilometres of wire. It is variously referred to as "wireless cable" or "virutal fibre" communications. The two main technologies are local multipoint communications (LMCS) and multichannel multipoint distribution systems (MMDS), both of which broadcast two-way video, voice and data communications, as well as provide Internet access, via airwaves

from fixed point to fixed point. All subscribers will require is a table-top box to translate the digital signals to sight and sound signals.

Why will this new technology replace the old? First, LMCS and MMDS transmit information by sound wave which is much faster than by landline. In addition, this technology can transmit a much greater amount of data at any time. Second, it is much less expensive to construct and maintain wireless technology. While existing telephone companies estimate it will take billions of dollars to update their technology to match the speed of the wireless kind, the wireless companies estimate that they can construct enough transmission towers to serve all of Canada for well under $1 billion. Since all companies wish to maximize profit, the less expensive technology will eventually win out.

Wireless Technology in Action

The earthquake which hit Kobe, Japan, in January of 1995 virtually destroyed Kobe's telecommunications network. Broadband Networks Inc. of Winnipeg went in and established an LMCS network which, by mid-1996, served 250,000 wireless apartments and businesses. The first North American application of digital commercial wireless operation began in Brandon, Manitoba, in October 1996. SkyCable Inc. of Brandon is now servicing many homes and businesses in the area. Due to the small fixed costs of production, these two firms were able to reach their minimum efficient scale of production and make profits by serving relatively small markets.

Complete Replacement?

It is unlikely that LMCS and MMDS will ever completely replace existing landline technology. In some more remote areas, it may be less costly to leave the current infrastructure in place than to build new. Some consumers may also not be comfortable with the notion of their telephone conversations "out there" in the ethernet. Finally, there are still some bugs to be worked out of the new technology. Waving leaves and tree branches have been known to distort, or even to interrupt, transmission. What areas will be served by wireless cable, which areas will not, will likely be decided based on long-run average costs of service.

For Critical Analysis

1. After the transmission towers for LMCS and MMDS have been constructed, where might diminishing marginal returns set in?

2. How long will the long run be for firms in the wireless cable business?

CHAPTER SUMMARY

1. It is important in economics to distinguish between accounting profits and economic profits. Accounting profits are equal to total revenues minus total explicit costs. Economic profits are equal to total revenues minus total opportunity costs of all factors of production.

2. The short run for the firm is defined as the period during which plant size cannot be altered. The long run is the period during which all factors of production can be varied.

3. Fixed costs are costs that cannot be altered in the short run. Fixed costs are associated with assets that the firm owns that cannot be profitably transferred to another use. Variable costs are associated with input costs that vary as the rate of output varies. Wages are a good example of a variable cost.

4. There are definitional relationships between average, total, and marginal costs:

$$\text{ATC} = \frac{\text{TC}}{Q}$$

$$\text{AVC} = \frac{\text{TVC}}{Q}$$

$$\text{AFC} = \frac{\text{TFC}}{Q}$$

$$\text{MC} = \frac{\text{change in TC}}{\text{change in } Q}$$

5. When marginal costs are less than average costs, average costs are falling. When marginal costs are greater than average costs, average costs are rising. The marginal cost curve intersects the average variable cost curve and the average total cost curve at their minimum points.

6. When we hold constant all factors of production except one, an increase in that factor will lead to a change in total physical product. That is how we derive the total physical product curve. The marginal physical product curve is derived from looking at the change in total physical product.

7. After some output rate, firms enter the region of diminishing marginal returns, or diminishing marginal physical product. In other words, after some point, each increment of the variable input will yield a smaller and smaller increment in total output.

8. Given a constant wage rate, the marginal cost curve is the mirror image of the marginal physical product curve. Thus because of the law of diminishing marginal returns, marginal costs will eventually rise.

9. We derive the long-run average cost curve by connecting a smooth line that is just tangent to all of the short-run average cost curves. This long-run average cost curve is sometimes called the planning curve.

10. It is possible for a firm to experience economies of scale, constant returns to scale, or diseconomies of scale, in which case a proportionate increase in *all* inputs will lead, respectively, to decreasing, constant, or increasing average costs. Firms may experience economies of scale because of specialization, the dimensional factor, and the ability to purchase improved productive equipment. Firms may experience diseconomies of scale because of the limitations of efficient management.

11. The long-run average cost curve will be downward-sloping, horizontal, or upward-sloping, depending on whether there are economies of scale, constant returns to scale, or diseconomies of scale.

12. Minimum efficient scale occurs at the lowest rate of output at which long-run average costs are minimized.

DISCUSSION OF PREVIEW QUESTIONS

1. **How does the economist's definition of profit differ from the accountant's?**

The accountant defines total profits as total revenues minus total costs; the economist defines total profits as total revenues minus total opportunity costs of all inputs used. In other words, the economist takes into account implicit as well as explicit costs; the economist's definition stresses that an opportunity cost exists for all inputs used in the production process. Specifically, the economist estimates the opportunity cost for invested capital, the owner's time, inventories on hand, and so on. Because the economist's definition of costs is more inclusive, accounting profits will exceed economic profits; economic profits exist only when all the opportunity costs are taken into account.

2. **What distinguishes the long run from the short run?**

The short run is defined as any time period when there is at least one factor of production that a firm cannot vary; in the long run, *all* factors of production can be varied by the firm. Because each industry is likely to be unique in its ability to vary all inputs, the long run differs from industry to industry. Presumably the long run is a lot shorter (in absolute time periods) for firms in the carpentry or plumbing industry than for firms in the automobile or steel industry. In most economic models, labour is usually assumed to be the variable input in the short run, whereas capital is considered to be fixed in the short run; this assumption is fairly descriptive of the real-world situation.

3. **How does the law of diminishing marginal returns account for an *eventually* increasing marginal cost curve for a firm in the short run?**

Assume that labour is the only variable factor of production. *Eventually,* the law of diminishing returns comes into play (prior to this point, specialization benefits might increase the marginal product of labour), and the marginal product of labour falls. That is, beyond the point of diminishing returns, extra labourers contribute less to total product than immediately preceding labourers do, per unit of time. In effect, this means that if output is to be increased by equal amounts (or equal "batches"), more and more labour time will be required due to its lower marginal product. Later units of output, which are physically identical to earlier units of output, embody more labour time. If wages are constant, later units, which require more worker-hours, have a higher marginal cost. We conclude that beyond the point of diminishing returns, the marginal cost of output rises for the firm in the short run. Prior to the point of diminishing returns, the marginal cost curve falls, due to rising marginal product of labour.

4. **Why is the short-run average total cost curve U-shaped?**

Average total cost (ATC) equals the sum of average fixed costs (AFC) and average variable costs (AVC); that is, ATC = AFC + AVC. The AFC curve continuously falls because it is derived by dividing a constant number (total fixed costs) by larger and larger numbers (output levels). It falls rapidly at first, then slowly. The AVC curve falls during the early output stages because the benefits of specialization cause the marginal physical product of labour to rise and the marginal cost of output to fall; beyond the point of diminishing returns, the marginal physical product of labour falls, eventually forcing marginal cost to rise above AVC, and therefore AVC rises too. As we go from zero output to higher and higher output levels per unit of time, AFC and AVC both initially fall; therefore, ATC falls too. At some point beyond the point of diminishing marginal returns, AVC rises and outweighs the now slowly falling AFC curve; the net result is that somewhere beyond the point of diminishing marginal returns, the ATC curve rises. Because the ATC curve falls at low output levels and rises at higher output levels, we describe it as U-shaped. Of course, it doesn't look exactly like a *U*, but it is close enough.

PROBLEMS

(Answers to the odd-numbered problems appear at the back of the book.)

10-1. "Now that I have paid off my van, it won't cost me anything except for the running expenses, such as gas, oil, and tune-ups, when I use it." What is wrong with this reasoning?

10-2. Examine this table.

Units of Labour (per eight-hour day)	Marginal Product of Labour (per eight-hour day)
1	2
2	4
3	6
.	.
.	.
.	.
12	20
13	10
14	5
15	3
16	2

a. Suppose that this firm wants to increase output over the short run. How much labour time is required to produce the first unit? The second and third? Do the fourth, fifth, and sixth units of output require more or less labour time than the earlier units?

b. Suppose that we have hired 11 labourers and now want to increase the short-run output in batches of 20. To produce the first batch of 20 (beyond the eleventh labourer), how many labour hours are required? What will the next batch of 20 cost, in labour hours? Do additional batches of 20 cost more or less than earlier batches (beyond the eleventh labourer)?

c. What do parts (a) and (b) imply about the relationship between the marginal product of labour and labour time embodied in equal increments of output?

10-3. Refer to the table in Problem 10-2. Assume that wage rates equal $1 per eight-hour day.

a. By hiring the twelfth unit of labour, what was the cost to the firm of this first batch of 20?

b. What was the marginal cost of output in that range? (Hint: If 20 units cost $1, what did *one* unit cost?)

c. What will the next batch of 10 cost the firm?

d. What is the marginal cost of output over that range?

e. What is happening to the marginal cost of output?

f. How are the marginal product of labour and the marginal cost of output related?

10-4. Your school's basketball team had a foul-shooting average of .800 (80 out of 100) before last night's game, during which they shot 5 for 10 at the foul line.

a. What was their marginal performance last night?

b. What happened to the team's foul-shooting average?

c. Suppose that their foul shooting in the next game is 6 for 10. What is happening to their marginal performance?

d. Now what is the team average foul-shooting percentage?

10-5. Define long-run average total cost. In light of the fact that businesses are operated day to day in the short run, of what use is the concept of long-run average total cost to the entrepreneur?

10-6. A recent college graduate turns down a $20,000-per-year job offer in order to open his own business. He borrows $150,000 to purchase equipment. Total sales during his first year are $250,000. Total labour costs for the first year are $160,000, and raw material costs are $50,000. He pays $15,000 interest on the loan per year. Estimate the economic profit of this business for the first year.

10-7. Examine this table.

Output (units)	Average Fixed Cost	Total Cost
0	–	$200
5	$40	300
10	20	380
20	10	420
40	5	520

a. Find the average variable cost at each level of production.
b. What is the marginal cost of increasing output from 10 to 20 units? From 20 to 40 units?
c. Find the average total cost at each level of production.

10-8. You are given the following graph.

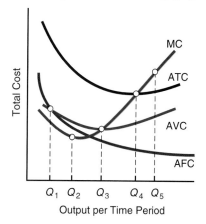

a. At what output level is AVC at a minimum?
b. At what output level is ATC at a minimum?
c. At what output level is MC at a minimum?
d. At what output level do the AVC and MC curves intersect?
e. At what output level do the ATC and MC curves intersect?

10-9. Fill in the missing values for marginal, average, and total product in the following table. Assume that capital and labour are the only two inputs in the production function and that capital is held fixed.

Units of Labour	Total Product	Marginal Product	Average Product
6	120	–	20
7	147		21
8		23	
9			20

Perfect Competition

Preview Questions

1. How much will a perfect competitor produce in the short run?

2. What is the perfectly competitive firm's short-run supply curve?

3. Can a perfectly competitive firm earn economic profits?

4. Why is the perfectly competitive market structure considered economically efficient?

In towns and cities across Canada, local retailers are losing out in the competitive record business. They are falling victim to the aggressive competition of such large-scale discount chains as Future Shop and Virgin Records. Typically, when a record giant like Virgin opens up a new store, local retailers fear for their businesses—and with good reason. They are often unable to meet the low prices offered by the big discounters. Is this type of competition inevitable, and is there anything that local merchants can do to stop it? An understanding of the model of perfect competition will clarify this issue.

Did You Know That... in Canada, there are tens of thousands of copy shops? There are also several thousand desktop publishing companies offering their services. The number of companies wanting to sell CD-ROM development is much smaller but growing. The number of companies offering to write software applications is somewhere inbetween, but that is only in Canada. Today, because of the cheapness and rapidity of modern telecommunications, much of the software code that goes into computer applications programs produced by Canadian companies is written in India and elsewhere. *Competition* is the word that applies to all of these situations. As used in common speech, *competition* simply means "rivalry." In perfectly competitive situations, individual buyers and sellers cannot affect the market price—it is determined by the market forces of demand and supply. In this chapter we examine what has become known as perfect competition.

CHARACTERISTICS OF A PERFECTLY COMPETITIVE MARKET STRUCTURE

▶ **Perfect competition**

A market structure in which the decisions of individual buyers and sellers have no effect on market price.

▶ **Perfectly competitive firm**

A firm which is such a small part of the total industry that it cannot affect the price of the product it sells.

▶ **Price taker**

A competitive firm that must take the price of its product as given because the firm cannot influence its price.

We are interested in studying how a firm acting within a perfectly competitive market structure makes decisions about how much to produce. In a situation of **perfect competition,** each firm is such a small part that it cannot affect the price of the product in question. That means that each **perfectly competitive firm** in the industry is a **price taker**—the firm takes price as a given, something determined *outside* the individual firm.

This definition of a competitive firm is obviously idealized, for in one sense the individual firm *has* to set prices. How can we ever have a situation in which firms regard prices as set by forces outside their control? The answer is that even though every firm sets its own prices, a firm in a perfectly competitive situation will find that it will eventually have no customers at all if it sets its price above the competitive price. The best example is in agriculture. Although the individual farmer can set any price for a bushel of carrots, if that price doesn't coincide with the market price of a bushel of similar-quality carrots, no one will purchase the carrots at a higher price; nor would the farmer be inclined to reduce revenues by selling below the market price.

Let's examine the reasons a firm in a perfectly competitive industry ends up being a price taker.

1. *There must be a large number of buyers and sellers.* When this is the case, no one buyer or one seller has any influence on price.

2. *The product sold by the firms in the industry must be homogeneous.* The product sold by each firm in the industry must be a perfect substitute for the product sold by each other firm. Buyers must be able to choose from a large number of sellers of a product that the buyers believe to be the same.

3. *Any firm can enter or leave the industry without serious impediments.* Firms in a competitive industry cannot be hampered in their ability to get resources or relocate resources. They move labour and capital in pursuit of profit-making opportunities to whatever business venture gives them their highest expected rate of return on their investment.

4. *Both buyers and sellers have equally good information.* Consumers have to be able to find out about lower prices charged by competing firms. Firms have to be able to find out about cost-saving innovations in order to lower production costs and prices, and they have to be able to learn about profitable opportunities in other industries.

INTERNATIONAL EXAMPLE
The Global Coal Market

A good real-world example of perfect competition is the market for coal. Coal is a fossil fuel that started as luxurious vegetation growing in the swamps that covered much of the world about 300 million years ago. Today, coal is found in nearly every region of the world, although the most commercially important deposits are in Asia, Australia, Europe, and North America. The United Kingdom led the world in coal production until about a century ago.

Throughout the world, coal is produced in thousands of different mines. The purchasers of coal, such as steel mills and electric utility generating companies, constantly keep track of the prices of coal output throughout the world. If the price of coal goes up, there are literally thousands of known untapped coal deposits that can be developed. If the price of coal drops, coal mines can be closed. So the market for coal probably conforms as closely as possible to the assumptions underlining the model of perfect competition.

For critical analysis: There are actually several different grades of coal. Does this seriously violate assumption 2 for a perfectly competitive industry?

THE DEMAND CURVE OF THE PERFECT COMPETITOR

When we discussed substitutes in Chapter 8, we pointed out that the more substitutes there were and the more similar they were to the commodity in question, the greater was the price elasticity of demand. Here we assume for the perfectly competitive firm that it is producing a commodity that has perfect substitutes. That means that if the individual firm raises its price one penny, it will lose all of its business. This, then, is how we characterize the demand schedule for a perfectly competitive firm: It is the going market price as determined by the forces of market supply and market demand—that is, where the market demand curve intersects the market supply curve. The single-firm demand curve in a perfectly competitive industry is perfectly elastic at the going market price. Remember that with a perfectly elastic demand curve, any increase in price leads to zero quantity demanded.

We show the market demand and supply curves in part (a) of Figure 11.1. Their intersection occurs at the price of $5. The commodity in question is computer diskettes, and we assume for the purposes of this exposition that all diskettes are perfect substitutes for all others. At the going market price of $5 apiece, a hypothetical individual demand curve for a diskette producer who sells a very, very small part of total industry production is shown in part (b). At the market price, this firm can sell all the output it wants. At the market price of $5 each, which is where the demand curve for the individual producer lies, consumer demand for the diskettes of that one producer is perfectly elastic. This can be seen by noting that if the firm raises its price, consumers, who are assumed to know that this supplier is charging more than other producers, will buy elsewhere, and the producer in question will have no sales at all. Thus the demand curve for that producer is perfectly elastic. We label the individual producer's demand curve *d*, whereas the *market* demand curve is always labelled *D*.

Figure 11.1
The Demand Curve for a Diskette Producer

At $5–where market demand, *D*, and market supply, *S*, intersect–the individual firm faces a perfectly elastic demand curve, *d*. If it raises its price even one penny, it will sell no diskettes at all. Notice the difference in the quantities of diskettes represented on the horizontal axis of parts (a) and (b).

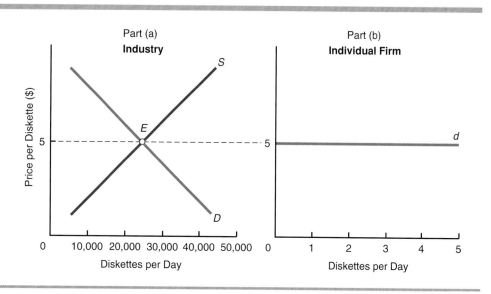

The media are quick to announce price increases in industries that have big firms. In particular, there is a media fascination with oil company behaviour. After all, Imperial Oil, headquartered in Toronto, has annual sales that exceed $160 million and profits that exceed $5 million per year. Chevron, Petro-Canada, Shell, and Irving Oil are smaller, but their profits are still in the millions of dollars a year. The public usually sees nothing wrong with an article stating that "they

decided to raise the price of gasoline." The oil market is worldwide, however. Even within Canada, Imperial Oil accounts for less than 20 percent of total oil sales. The price of oil (net of taxes) is determined by market demand and market supply, not arbitrarily by decision makers in oil companies. They are simply responding to their estimates of the intersection of world demand and supply curves.

HOW MUCH SHOULD THE PERFECT COMPETITOR PRODUCE?

As we have shown, a perfect competitor has to accept the price of the product as a "given." If the firm raises its price, it sells nothing; if it lowers its price, it makes less money per unit sold than it otherwise could. The firm has one decision left: How much should it produce? We will apply our model of the firm to this question to come up with an answer. We'll use the *profit-maximization model,* which assumes that firms attempt to maximize their total profits—the positive difference between total revenues and total costs.

Total Revenues

▶ **Total revenues**
The price per unit times the total quantity sold.

Every firm has to consider its *total revenues,* or TR. **Total revenues** are defined as the quantity sold multiplied by the price. (They are the same as total receipts from the sale of output.) The perfect competitor must take the price as a given.

Look at Figure 11.2. Columns 1 and 2 show total output and sales per day and the total cost of producing that output. Column 3 is the market price, P, of $5 per diskette, which is also equal to average revenue (AR) because

$$AR = \frac{TR}{Q} = \frac{PQ}{Q} = P$$

where Q stands for quantity. If we assume that all units sell for the same price, it becomes apparent that another name for the demand curve is the *average revenue curve* (this is true regardless of the type of market structure under consideration).

Column 4 shows the total revenues, or TR, as equal to the market price, P, times the total output in sales per day, or Q. Thus TR = PQ. We are assuming that the market supply and demand schedules intersect at a price of $5 and that this price holds for all the firm's production. We are also assuming that because our diskette maker is a small part of the market, it can sell all that it produces at that price. Thus part (b) of Figure 11.2 shows the total revenue curve as a straight line. For every unit of sales, total revenue is increased by $5.

Comparing Total Costs with Total Revenues

Total costs are also plotted in part (b). Remember, the firm's costs always include a normal rate of return on investment. So whenever we refer to total costs, we are not talking about accounting costs but about economic costs. When the total cost curve is above the total revenue curve, the firm is experiencing losses. When it is below the total revenue curve, the firm is making profits.

By comparing total costs with total revenues, we can calculate the number of diskettes the individual competitive firm should produce per day. Our analysis rests on the assumption that the firm will attempt to maximize total profits. In part (a) of Figure 11.2, we see that total profits reach a maximum at a production rate of either seven or eight diskettes per day. We can see this graphically in part (b) of the figure. The firm will maximize profits where the total revenue curve exceeds the total cost

Part (a)

(1) Total Output and Sales per Day (Q)	(2) Total Costs (TC)	(3) Market Price (P)	(4) Total Revenues (TR) (4) = (3) × (1)	(5) Total Profit (TR − TC) (5) = (4) − (2)	(6) Average Total Cost (ATC) (6) = (2) ÷ (1)	(7) Average Variable Cost (AVC)	(8) Marginal Cost (MC) (8) = Change in (2) / Change in (1)	(9) Marginal Revenue (MR) (9) = Change in (4) / Change in (1)
0	$10	$5	$ 0	−$10	—	—		
1	15	5	5	− 10	$15.00	$5.00	$5	$5
2	18	5	10	− 8	9.00	4.00	3	5
3	20	5	15	− 5	6.67	3.33	2	5
4	21	5	20	− 1	5.25	2.75	1	5
5	23	5	25	2	4.60	2.60	2	5
6	26	5	30	4	4.33	2.67	3	5
7	30	5	35	5	4.28	2.86	4	5
8	35	5	40	5	4.38	3.12	5	5
9	41	5	45	4	4.56	3.44	6	5
10	48	5	50	2	4.80	3.80	7	5
11	56	5	55	− 1	5.09	4.18	8	5

Figure 11.2
Profit Maximization

Profit maximization occurs where marginal revenue equals marginal cost. Part (a) indicates that this point occurs at a rate of sales of between seven and eight diskettes per day.

In part (b), we find maximum profits where total revenues exceed total costs by the largest amount. This occurs at a rate of production and sales per day of seven or eight diskettes.

In part (c), the marginal cost curve, MC, intersects the marginal revenue curve at a rate of output and sales of somewhere between seven and eight diskettes per day.

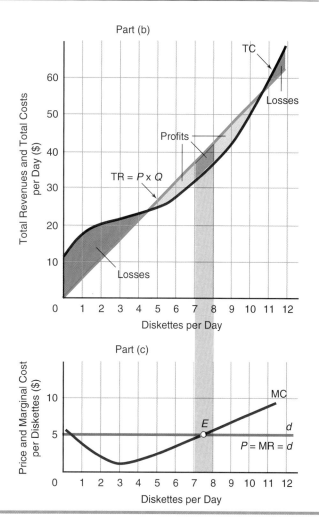

Part (b)

Part (c)

▶ **Profit-maximizing rate of production**

The rate of production that maximizes total profits, or the difference between total revenues and total costs; also, the rate of production at which marginal revenue equals marginal cost.

curve by the greatest amount. That occurs at a rate of output and sales of either seven or eight diskettes per day; this rate is called the **profit-maximizing rate of production.** (If output were continuously divisible or we were dealing with extremely large numbers of diskettes, we would get a unique profit-maximizing output.)

We can also find this profit-maximizing rate of production for the individual competitive firm by looking at marginal revenues and marginal costs.

USING MARGINAL ANALYSIS TO DETERMINE THE PROFIT-MAXIMIZING RATE OF PRODUCTION

It is possible—indeed, preferable —to use marginal analysis to determine the profit-maximizing rate of production. We end up with the same results derived in a different manner, one that focuses more on where decisions are really made—on the margin. Managers examine changes in costs and relate them to changes in revenues. In fact, we almost always compare changes in cost with changes in benefits, where change is occurring at the margin, whether it be with respect to how much more or less to produce, how many more workers to hire or fire, or how much more to study or not study.

▶ **Marginal revenue**

The change in total revenues resulting from a change in output (and sale) of one unit of the product in question.

Marginal revenue represents the change in total revenues attributable to changing production by one unit of the product in question. Hence a more formal definition of marginal revenue is

$$\text{Marginal revenue} = \frac{\text{change in total revenues}}{\text{change in output}}$$

In a perfectly competitive market, the marginal revenue curve is exactly equivalent to the price line or the individual firm's demand curve, because the firm can sell all of its output (production) at the market price. Thus in Figure 11.1, the demand curve, d, for the individual producer is at a price of $5—the price line is coincident with the demand curve. But so is the marginal revenue curve, for marginal revenue in this case also equals $5.

The marginal revenue curve for our competitive diskette producer is shown as a line at $5 in part (c) of Figure 11.2. Notice again that the marginal revenue curve is equal to the price line, which is equal to the individual firm's demand, or average revenue, curve, d.

When Are Profits Maximized?

Now we add the marginal cost curve, MC, taken from column 8 in part (a) of Figure 11.2. As shown in part (c) of that figure, the marginal cost curve first falls and then starts to rise because of the law of diminishing returns, eventually intersecting the marginal revenue curve and then rising above it. Notice that the numbers for both the marginal cost schedule, column 8 in part (a), and the marginal revenue schedule, column 9 in part (a), are printed *between* the rows on which the quantities appear. This indicates that we are looking at a *change* between one rate of output and the next.

In part (c), the marginal cost curve intersects the marginal revenue curve somewhere between seven and eight diskettes per day. The firm has an incentive to produce and sell until the amount of the additional revenue received from selling one more diskette just equals the additional costs incurred for producing and selling that diskette. This is how the firm maximizes profit. Whenever marginal cost is less than marginal revenue, the firm will always make more profit by increasing production.

Now consider the possibility of producing at an output rate of 10 diskettes per day. The marginal cost curve at that output rate is higher than the marginal revenue (or d) curve. The firm would be spending more to produce that additional output than it would be receiving in revenues; it would be foolish to continue producing at this rate.

But how much should it produce? It should produce at point E, where the marginal cost curve intersects the marginal revenue curve from below.[1] The firm should continue production until the cost of increasing output by one more unit is just equal to the revenues obtainable from that extra unit. This is a fundamental rule in economics:

> Profit maximization normally occurs at the rate of output at which marginal revenue equals marginal cost.

For a perfectly competitive firm, this is at the intersection of the demand schedule, d, and the marginal cost curve, MC. When MR exceeds MC, each additional unit of output adds more to total revenues than to total costs, causing losses to decrease or profits to increase. When MC is greater than MR, each unit produced adds more to total cost than to total revenues, causing profits to decrease or losses to increase. Therefore, profit maximization occurs when MC equals MR. In our particular example, our profit-maximizing, perfectly competitive diskette producer will produce at a rate of either seven or eight diskettes a day. (If we were dealing with a very large rate of output, we would come up with an exact profit-maximizing rate.)

Try Preview Question 1:

How much will a perfect competitor produce in the short run?

Concepts in Brief

- Four fundamental characteristics of the market in perfect competition are (1) a large number of buyers and sellers, (2) a homogeneous product, (3) unrestrained exit from and entry into the industry by other firms, and (4) good information in the hands of both buyers and sellers.
- A perfectly competitive firm is a price taker. It has no control over price and consequently has to take price as a given, but it can sell all that it wants at the going market price.
- The demand curve for a perfect competitor is a line at the going market price. The demand curve is also the perfect competitor's marginal revenue curve because marginal revenue is defined as the change in total revenue due to a one-unit change in output.
- Profit is maximized at the rate of output where the positive difference between total revenues and total costs is the greatest. This is the same level of output at which marginal revenue equals marginal cost. The perfectly competitive firm produces at an output rate at which marginal cost equals the price per unit of output, because MR = P.

---

[1] The marginal cost curve, MC, also cuts the marginal revenue curve, d, from above at an output rate of less than 1 in this example. This intersection should be ignored because it is irrelevant to the firm's decisions.

SHORT-RUN PROFITS

To find what our competitive individual diskette producer is making in terms of profits in the short run, we have to add the average total cost curve to part (c) of Figure 11.2. We take the information from column 6 in part (a) and add it to part (c) to get Figure 11.3. Again the profit-maximizing rate of output is between seven and eight diskettes per day. If we have production and sales of seven diskettes per day, total revenues will be $35 a day. Total costs will be $30 a day, leaving a profit of $5 a day. If the rate of output in sales is eight diskettes per day, total revenues will be $40 and total costs will be $35, again leaving a profit of $5 a day. In Figure 11.3, the lower boundary of the rectangle labelled "Profits" is determined by the intersection of the profit-maximizing quantity line represented by vertical dashes and the average total cost curve. Why? Because the ATC curve gives us the cost per unit, whereas the price ($5), represented by d, gives us the revenue per unit, or average revenue. The difference is profit per unit. So the height of the rectangular box representing profits equals profit per unit, the length equals the amount of units produced, and when we multiply these two quantities, we get total profits. Note, as pointed out earlier, that we are talking about *economic profits* because a normal rate of return on investment is included in the average total cost curve, ATC.

It is certainly possible, also, for the competitive firm to make short-run losses. We give an example in Figure 11.4, where we show the firm's demand curve shifting from d_1 to d_2. The going market price has fallen from $5 to $3 per diskette because of changes in market supply or demand conditions (or both). The firm will

Figure 11.3
Measuring Total Profits

Profits are represented by the shaded area. The height of the profit rectangle is given by the difference between average total costs and price ($5), where price is also equal to average revenue. This is found by the vertical difference between the ATC curve and the price, or average revenue, line d, at the profit-maximizing rate of output of between seven and eight diskettes per day.

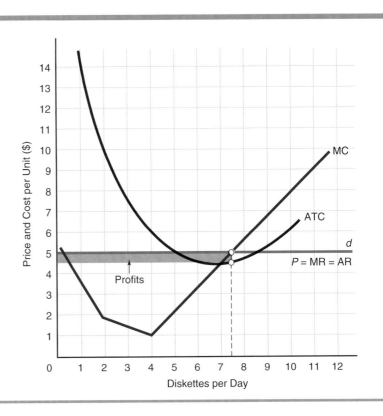

Figure 11.4
Minimization of Short-Run Losses

In cases in which average total costs exceed the average revenue, or price (and price is greater than or equal to average variable cost), profit maximization is equivalent to loss minimization. This again occurs where marginal cost equals marginal revenue. Losses are shown in the shaded area.

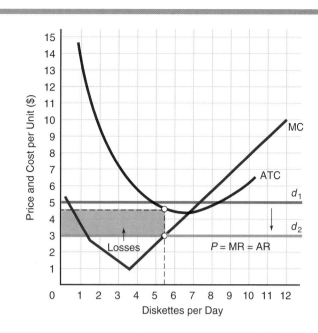

always do the best it can by producing where marginal revenue equals marginal cost. We see in Figure 11.4 that the marginal revenue (d_2) curve is intersected (from below) by the marginal cost curve at an output rate of about $5\frac{1}{2}$ diskettes per day. The firm is clearly not making profits because average total costs at that output rate are greater than the price of $3 per diskette. The losses are shown in the shaded area. By producing where marginal revenue equals marginal cost, however, the firm is minimizing its losses; that is, losses would be greater at any other output.

THE SHORT-RUN SHUTDOWN PRICE

In Figure 11.4, the firm is sustaining economic losses. Will it go out of business? In the long run it will, but surprisingly, in the short run the firm will not go out of business, for as long as the loss from staying in business is less than the loss from shutting down, the firm will continue to produce. A firm *goes out of business* when the owners sell its assets to someone else. A firm temporarily *shuts down* when it stops producing, but it still is in business.

Now how can we tell when the firm is sustaining economic losses in the short run and it is still worthwhile not to shut down? The firm must compare the cost of producing (while incurring losses) with the cost of closing down. The cost of staying in production in the short run is given by the total *variable* cost. Looking at the problem on a per-unit basis, as long as average variable cost (AVC) is covered by average revenues (price), the firm is better off continuing to produce. If average variable costs are exceeded even a little bit by the price of the product, staying in production produces some revenues in excess of variable costs that can be applied towards covering fixed costs.

A simple example will demonstrate this situation. The price of a product is $8, and average total costs equal $9 at an output of 100. In this example, average total costs are broken up into average variable costs of $7 and average fixed costs of $2. Total revenues, then, equal $8 × 100, or $800, and total costs equal $9 × 100, or $900. Total losses therefore equal $100. However, this does not mean that the firm will shut down. After all, if it does shut down, it still has fixed costs to pay. And in this case, because average fixed costs equal $2 at an output of 100, the fixed costs are $200. Thus the firm has losses of $100 if it continues to produce, but it has losses of $200 (the fixed costs) if it shuts down. The logic is fairly straightforward:

> As long as the price per unit sold exceeds the average *variable* cost per unit produced, the firm will be covering at least part of the opportunity cost of the investment in the business—that is, part of its fixed costs.

Calculating the Short-Run Break-Even Price

▶ **Short-run break-even price**

The price at which a firm's total revenues equal its total costs. At the break-even price, the firm is just making a normal rate of return on its capital investment. (It is covering its explicit and implicit costs.)

Look at demand curve d_1 in Figure 11.5. It just touches the minimum point of the average total cost curve, which, as you will remember, is exactly where the marginal cost curve intersects the average total cost curve. At that price, which is about $4.30, the firm will be making exactly zero short-run economic profits. That price is called the **short-run break-even price,** and point E_1 therefore occurs at the short-run break-even price for a competitive firm. It is the point at which marginal revenue, marginal cost, and average total cost are all equal (that is, at which $P = MC$ and $P = ATC$). The break-even price is the one that yields zero short-run economic profits or losses.

Figure 11.5
Short-Run Shutdown and Break-Even Prices

We can find the short-run break-even price and the short-run shutdown price by comparing price with average total costs and average variable costs. If the demand curve is d_1, profit maximization occurs at output E_1, where MC equals marginal revenue (the d curve). Because the ATC curve includes all relevant opportunity costs, point E_1 is the break-even point, and zero economic profits are being made. The firm is earning a normal rate of return. If the demand curve falls to d_2, profit maximization (loss minimization) occurs at the intersection of MC and MR (the d_2 curve), or E_2. Below this price, it does not pay for the firm to continue in operation because its average variable costs are not covered by the price of the product.

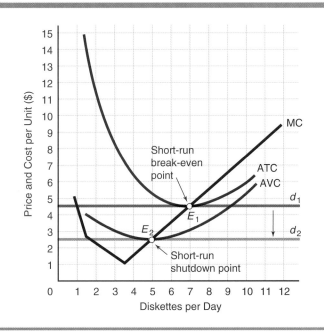

Calculating the Short-Run Shutdown Price

To calculate the firm's shutdown price, we must introduce the average variable cost (AVC) to our graph. In Figure 11.5, we have plotted the AVC values from column 7 in part (a) of Figure 11.2. For the moment, consider two possible demand curves, d_1 and d_2, which are also the firm's respective marginal revenue curves. Therefore, if demand is d_1, the firm will produce at E_1, where that curve intersects the marginal cost curve. If demand falls to d_2, the firm will produce at E_2. The special feature of the hypothetical demand curve, d_2, is that it just touches the average variable cost curve at the latter's minimum point, which is also where the marginal cost curve intersects it. This price is the **short-run shutdown price.** Why? Below this price, the firm would be paying out more in variable costs than it is receiving in revenues from the sale of its product. Each unit it sold would add to its losses. Clearly, the way to avoid incurring these additional losses, if price falls below the shutdown point, is in fact to shut down operations.

The intersection of the price line, the marginal cost curve, and the average variable cost curve is labelled E_2. The resulting short-run shutdown price is valid only for the short run because, of course, in the long run the firm will not stay in business at a yield less than a normal rate of return and hence at least zero economic profits.

▶ **Short-run shutdown price**

The price that just covers average variable costs. It occurs just below the intersection of the marginal cost curve and the average variable cost curve.

THE MEANING OF ZERO ECONOMIC PROFITS

The fact that we labelled point E_1 in Figure 11.5 the break-even point may have disturbed you. At point E_1, price is just equal to average total cost. If this is the case, why would a firm continue to produce if it were making no profits whatsoever? If we again make the distinction between accounting profits and economic profits, then at that price the firm has zero economic profits but positive accounting profits. Recall that accounting profits are total revenues minus total explicit costs. What is ignored in such accounting is the reward offered to investors—the opportunity cost of capital—plus all other implicit costs.

In economic analysis, the average total cost curve includes the full opportunity cost of capital. Indeed, the average total cost curve includes the opportunity cost of *all* factors of production used in the production process. At the short-run break-even price, economic profits are, by definition, zero. Accounting profits at that price are not, however, equal to zero; they are positive. Consider an example. A clock manufacturer sells clocks at some price. The owners of the firm have supplied all the funds in the business. They have borrowed no money from anyone else, and they explicitly pay the full opportunity cost to all factors of production, including any managerial labour that they themselves contribute to the business. Their salaries show up as a cost in the books and are equal to what they could have earned in the next-best alternative occupation. At the end of the year, the owners find that after they subtract all explicit costs from total revenues, they have earned $100,000. Let's say that their investment was $1 million. Thus the rate of return on that investment is 10 percent per year. We will assume that this turns out to be equal to the rate of return that, on average, all other clock manufacturers make in the industry.

This $100,000, or 10 percent rate of return, is actually, then, a competitive, or normal, rate of return on invested capital in that industry or in other industries with similar risks. If the owners had made only $50,000, or 5 percent on their investment, they would have been able to make higher profits by leaving the industry. The 10 percent rate of return is the opportunity cost of capital. Accountants show it as a profit; economists call it a cost. We include that cost in the average total cost curve, similar to the one shown in Figure 11.5. At the short-run break-even price, average total cost, including this opportunity cost of capital, will just equal that price. The firm will be making zero economic profits but a 10 percent *accounting* rate of return.

Now we are ready to derive the firm's supply curve.

THE PERFECT COMPETITOR'S SHORT-RUN SUPPLY CURVE

What does the supply curve for the individual firm look like? Actually, we have been looking at it all along. We know that when the price of diskettes is $5, the firm will supply seven or eight of them per day. If the price falls to $3, the firm will supply five or six diskettes per day. And if the price falls below $3, the firm will shut down in the short run. Hence in Figure 11.6, the firm's supply curve is the marginal cost curve above the short-run shutdown point. This is shown as the solid part of the marginal cost curve. *The definition, then, of the individual firm's supply curve in a competitive industry is its marginal cost curve equal to and above the point of intersection with the average variable cost curve.*

Try Preview Question 2:

What is the perfectly competitive firm's short-run supply curve?

The Short-Run Industry Supply Curve

In Chapter 3, we indicated that the market supply curve was the summation of individual supply curves. At the beginning of this chapter, we drew a market supply curve in Figure 11.1. Now we want to derive more precisely a market, or industry, supply curve to reflect individual producer behaviour in that industry. First we must ask, What is an industry? It is merely a collection of firms producing a particular

Figure 11.6
The Individual Firm's Short-Run Supply Curve

The individual firm's supply curve is the portion of its marginal cost curve above the minimum point on the average variable cost curve.

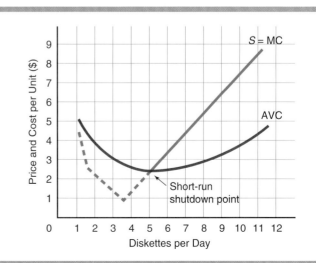

product. Therefore, we have a way to figure out the total supply curve of any industry: We add the quantities that each firm will supply at every possible price. In other words, we sum the individual supply curves of all the competitive firms *horizontally*. The individual supply curves, as we just saw, are simply the marginal cost curves of each firm.

Consider doing this for a hypothetical world in which there are only two diskette producers in the industry, firm A and firm B. These two firms' marginal cost curves are given in parts (a) and (b) of Figure 11.7. The marginal cost curves for the two separate firms are presented as MC_A in part (a) and MC_B in part (b). Those two marginal cost curves are drawn only for prices above the minimum average variable cost for each firm. Hence we are not including any of the marginal cost curves below minimum average variable cost. In part (a), for firm A, at $4, the quantity supplied would be 7. At $6, the quantity supplied would be 9. In part (b), we see the two different quantities that would be supplied by firm B corresponding to those two prices. Now for the $4 price we add horizontally the quantities 7 and 10. This gives us one point, *F*, for our short-run **industry supply curve,** *S*. We obtain the other point, *G*, by doing the same horizontal adding of quantities at $6. When we connect points *F* and *G*, we obtain industry supply curve *S*, which is also marked SMC, indicating that it is the horizontal summation of the marginal cost curves (above the respective minimum average variable cost of each firm).[2] Because the law of diminishing returns makes marginal cost curves rise, the short-run supply curve of a perfectly competitive industry must be upward-sloping.

▶ **Industry supply curve**
The locus of points showing the minimum prices at which given quantities will be forthcoming; also called the market supply curve.

Figure 11.7
Deriving the Industry Supply Curve
Marginal cost curves above minimum average variable cost are presented in parts (a) and (b) for firms A and B. We horizontally sum the two quantities supplied, 7 and 10, at $4. This gives us point *F* in part (c). We do the same thing for the quantities at $6. This gives us point *G*. When we connect those points, we have the industry supply curve, *S*, which is the horizontal summation of the firms' marginal cost curves above their respective minimum average costs.

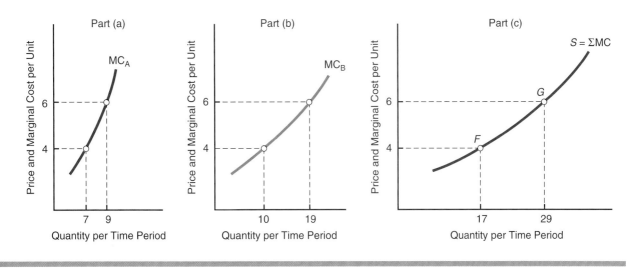

---

[2] The capital Greek sigma, Σ, is the symbol for summation.

Factors That Influence the Industry Supply Curve

As you have just seen, the industry supply curve is the horizontal summation of all of the individual firms' marginal cost curves above their respective minimum average variable cost points. This means that anything that affects the marginal cost curves of the firm will influence the industry supply curve. Therefore, the individual factors that will influence the supply schedule in a competitive industry can be summarized as the factors that cause the variable costs of production to change. These are factors that affect the individual marginal cost curves, such as changes in the individual firm's productivity, in factor costs (wages paid to labour, prices of raw materials, etc.), in taxes, and in anything else that would influence the individual firm's marginal cost curve.

All of these are *ceteris paribus* conditions of supply. Because they affect the position of the marginal cost curve for the individual firm, they affect the position of the industry supply curve. A change in any of these will shift the market supply curve.

Concepts in Brief

- Short-run average profits or average losses are determined by comparing average total costs with price (average revenue) at the profit-maximizing rate of output. In the short run, the perfectly competitive firm can make economic profits or economic losses.
- The competitive firm's short-run break-even output occurs at the minimum point on its average total cost curve, which is where the marginal cost curve intersects the average total cost curve.
- The competitive firm's short-run shutdown output is at the minimum point on its average variable cost curve, which is also where the marginal cost curve intersects the average variable cost curve. Shutdown will occur if price falls below average variable cost.
- The firm will continue production at a price that exceeds average variable costs even though the full opportunity cost of capital is not being met; at least some revenues are going towards paying fixed costs.
- At the short-run break-even price, the firm is making zero economic profits, which means that it is just making a normal rate of return in that industry.
- The firm's short-run supply curve is the portion of its marginal cost curve equal to or above minimum average variable costs. The industry short-run supply curve is a horizontal summation of the individual firms' marginal cost curves above their respective minimum average variable costs.

COMPETITIVE PRICE DETERMINATION

How is the market, or "going," price established in a competitive market? This price is established by the interaction of all the suppliers (firms) and all the demanders. The market demand schedule, *D*, in part (a) of Figure 11.8 represents the demand

Figure 11.8
Industry Demand and Supply Curves and the Individual Firm Demand Curve

The industry demand curve is represented by *D* in part (a). The short-run industry supply curve is *S* and equal to ΣMC. The intersection of the demand and supply curves at *E* determines the equilibrium or market clearing price at P_e. The individual firm demand curve in part (b) is set at the market clearing price determined in part (a). If the producer has a marginal cost curve MC, this producer's individual profit-maximizing output level is at q_e. For AC_1, economic profits are zero; for AC_2, profits are negative; and for AC_3, profits are positive.

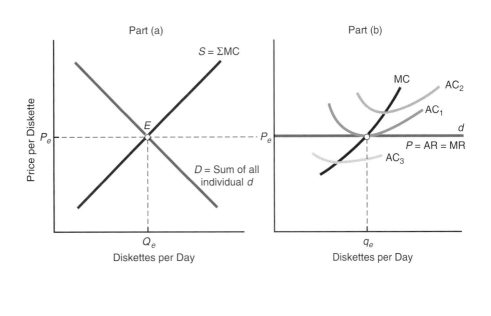

schedule for the entire industry, and the supply schedule, *S*, represents the supply schedule for the entire industry. Price P_e is established by the forces of supply and demand at the intersection of *D* and the short-run industry supply curve, *S*. Even though each individual firm has no control or effect on the price of its product in a competitive industry, the interaction of *all* the producers and buyers determines the price at which the product will be sold. We say that the price P_e and the quantity Q_e in part (a) of Figure 11.8 constitute the competitive solution to the pricing-quantity problem in that particular industry. It is the equilibrium where quantity demanded equals quantity supplied, and both suppliers and demanders are maximizing. The resulting individual firm demand curve, *d*, is shown in part (b) of Figure 11.8 at the price P_e.

In a purely competitive industry, the individual producer takes price as a given and chooses the output level that maximizes profits. (This is also the equilibrium level of output from the producer's standpoint.) We see in part (b) of Figure 11.8 that this is at q_e. If the producer's average costs are given by AC_1, q_e is also the short-run break-even output (see Figure 11.5); if its average costs are given by AC_2, at q_e, AC exceeds price (average revenue), and the firm is incurring losses. Alternatively, if average costs are given by AC_3, the firm will be making economic profits at q_e. In the former case, we would expect, over time, that people will cease production (exit the industry), causing supply to shift inward, whereas in the latter case, we would expect people to enter the industry to take advantage of the economic profits, thereby causing supply to shift outward. We now turn to these long-run considerations.

Try Preview Question 3:
Can a perfectly competitive frim earn economic profits?

THE LONG-RUN INDUSTRY SITUATION: EXIT AND ENTRY

In the long run in a competitive situation, firms will be making zero economic profits. In the long run, we surmise that firms in perfect competition will tend to have average total cost curves that just touch the price (marginal revenue) curve, or individual demand curve *d*. How does this occur? It is through an adjustment process that depends on economic profits and losses.

Exit and Entry of Firms

Look again at Figures 11.3 and 11.4. The existence of either profits or losses is a signal to owners of factors of production both within and outside the industry. If the industry is characterized by firms showing economic profits as represented in Figure 11.3, this will signal owners of resources elsewhere in the economy that they, too, should enter this industry. If, by contrast, there are firms in the industry like the ones suffering economic losses represented in Figure 11.4, this signals resource owners outside the industry to stay out. It also signals resource owners within the industry not to reinvest and if possible to leave the industry. It is in this sense that we say that profits direct resources to their highest-valued use. In the long run, resources will flow into industries in which profitability is highest and will flow out of industries in which profitability is lowest.

The price system therefore allocates productive resources according to the relative expected rates of return on alternative investments. Entry restrictions will thereby hinder economic efficiency, and thus welfare, by not allowing resources to flow to their highest-valued use. Similarly, exit restrictions (such as plant closing laws) will act to trap resources (temporarily) in sectors in which their value is below that in alternative uses. Such laws will also inhibit the ability of firms to respond to changes in the domestic and international marketplace; yet to judge their desirability, we must weigh these factors against the costs to employees and local economies from such sudden economic disruptions.

Not every industry presents an immediate source of opportunity for every firm. In a brief period of time, it may be impossible for a firm that produces frying pans to switch to the production of computers, even if there are very large profits to be made. Over the long run, however, we would expect to see such a change, whether or not the frying pan producers want to change over to another product. In a market economy, investors supply firms in the more profitable industry with more investment funds, which they take from firms in less profitable industries. (Also, profits give existing firms internal investment funds for expansion.) Consequently, resources needed in the production of more profitable goods, such as labour, will be bid away from lower-valued opportunities. Investors and other suppliers of resources respond to market **signals** about their highest-valued opportunities.

Market adjustment to changes in demand will occur regardless of the wishes of the managers of firms in less profitable markets. They can either attempt to adjust their product line to respond to the new demands, be replaced by managers who are more responsive to new conditions, or see their firms go bankrupt as they find them-

▶ **Signals**
Compact ways of conveying to economic decision makers information needed to make decisions. A true signal not only conveys information but also provides the incentive to react appropriately. Economic profits and economic losses are such signals.

selves unable to replace worn-out plant and equipment.

In addition, when we say that in a competitive long-run equilibrium situation firms will be making zero economic profits, we must realize that at a particular point in time it would be pure coincidence for a firm to be making *exactly* zero economic profits. Real-world information is not as precise as the curves we use to simplify our analysis. Things change all the time in a dynamic world, and firms, even in a very competitive situation, may for many reasons not be making exactly zero economic profits. We say that there is a *tendency* towards that equilibrium position, but firms are adjusting all the time to changes in their cost curves and in their individual demand curves.

EXAMPLE   Whittling Away at Apple's Profit Margins

Successful new products yield higher than competitive profits. That, of course, is the incentive that induces firms to introduce new products. Competition, over time, is supposed to cut back gradually on those above-normal profits. This pattern of events occurred with Apple Computer Company. Apple introduced the first truly user-friendly graphics interface computer in the mid-1980s. It offered the first, and for several years the only, mouse-driven machine and programming that used simple icons and pull-down menus to guide users. It chose not to license its operating software technology to anyone else. Consequently, it was able to keep high profit margins, above 50 percent, for the first five years of its sales of Macintosh computers. Then the competing system—IBM and IBM-compatibles supported by the Microsoft disk operating system (MS-DOS)—started to get easier to use. Moreover, competition within the IBM-compatible PC market, involving literally hundreds of entrants, kept driving the price of PCs down. Microsoft's introduction of the Windows graphics interface made PCs work more like Macs and further eroded Apple's market position. In the face of declining market share, Apple started reducing its prices and hence its profit margins. By the time the most user-friendly PC operating system, Windows 95, appeared, Apple had lowered its profit margin to less than 25 percent.

For critical analysis: Why did Apple lose market share in the personal computer industry?

Long-Run Industry Supply Curves

In part (a) of Figure 11.8, we drew the summation of all of the portions of the individual firms' marginal cost curve above each firm's respective minimum average variable costs as the upward-sloping supply curve of the entire industry. We should be aware, however, that a relatively steep upward-sloping supply curve may be appropriate only in the short run. After all, one of the prerequisites of a competitive industry is free entry.

Remember that our definition of the long run is a period of time in which adjustments can be made. The **long-run industry supply curve** is a supply curve showing the relationship between quantities supplied by the entire industry at dif-

▶ Long-run industry supply curve

A market supply curve showing the relationship between price and quantities forthcoming after firms have been allowed the time to enter into or exit from an industry, depending on whether there have been positive or negative economic profits.

ferent prices after firms have been allowed either to enter or to leave the industry, depending on whether there have been positive or negative economic profits. Also, the long-run industry supply curve is drawn under the assumption that entry and exit have been completed.

The long-run industry supply curve can take one of three shapes, depending on whether input costs stay constant, increase, or decrease as the number of firms in the industry changes. In Chapter 9, we assumed that input prices remained constant to the firm regardless of the firm's rate of output. When we look at the entire industry, when all firms are expanding and new firms are entering, they may simultaneously bid up input prices.

Constant-Cost Industries. In principle, there are small enough industries that use such a small percentage of the total supply of inputs necessary for their production that firms can enter the industry without bidding up input prices. In such a situation, we are dealing with a **constant-cost industry.** Its long-run industry supply curve is therefore horizontal and is represented by S_L in part (a) of Figure 11.9.

We can work through the case in which constant costs prevail. We start out in part (a) with demand curve D_1 and supply curve S_1. The equilibrium price is P_1. Market demand shifts rightward to D_2. In the short run, the equilibrium price rises to P_2. This generates positive economic profits for existing firms in the industry. Such economic profits induce resources to flow into the industry. The existing firms expand and/or new firms enter. The short-run supply curve shifts outward to S_2. The new intersection with the new demand curve is at E_3. The new equilibrium price is again P_1. The long-run supply curve is obtained by connecting the intersections of the corresponding pairs of demand and supply curves, E_1 and E_3. Labelled S_L, it is

▶ **Constant-cost industry**
An industry whose total output can be increased without an increase in long-run per-unit costs; an industry whose long-run supply curve is horizontal.

Figure 11.9
Constant-Cost, Increasing-Cost, and Decreasing-Cost Industries
In part (a), we show a situation in which the demand curve shifts from D_1 to D_2. Price increases from P_1 to P_2; however, in time the short-run supply curve shifts outward because positive profits are being earned, and the equilibrium shifts from E_2 to E_3. The market clearing price is again P_1. If we connect points such as E_1 and E_3, we come up with the long-run supply curve S_L. This is a constant-cost industry. In part (b),

costs are increasing for the industry, and therefore the long-run supply curve slopes upward and long-run prices rise from P_1 to P_2. In part (c), costs are decreasing for the industry as it expands, and therefore the long-run supply curve slopes downward such that long-run prices decline from P_1 to P_2.

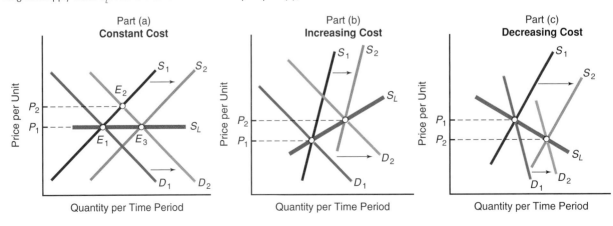

horizontal; its slope is zero. In a constant-cost industry, long-run supply is perfectly elastic. Any shift in demand is eventually met by an equal shift in supply so that the long-run price is constant at P_1.

Retail trade is often given as an example of such an industry because output can be expanded or contracted without affecting input prices. Banking is another example.

Increasing-Cost Industries. In an **increasing-cost industry,** expansion by existing firms and the addition of new firms cause the price of inputs specialized within that industry to be bid up. As costs of production rise, the ATC curve and the firms' MC curve shift upward, causing short-run supply curves (each firm's marginal cost curve) to shift upward. The result is a long-run industry supply curve that slopes upward, as represented by S_L in part (b) of Figure 11.9. Examples are residential construction and coal mining—both use specialized inputs that cannot be obtained in ever-increasing quantities without causing their prices to rise.

Decreasing-Cost Industries. An expansion in the number of firms in an industry can lead to a reduction in input costs and a downward shift in the ATC and MC curves. When this occurs, the long-run industry supply curve will slope downward. An example is given in part (c) of Figure 11.9. This is a **decreasing-cost industry.**

▶ **Increasing-cost industry**
An industry in which an increase in industry output is accompanied by an increase in long-run per-unit costs, such that the long-run industry supply curve slopes upward.

▶ **Decreasing-cost industry**
An industry in which an increase in output leads to a reduction in long-run per-unit costs, such that the long-run industry supply curve slopes downward.

LONG-RUN EQUILIBRIUM

In the long run, the firm can change the scale of its plant, adjusting its plant size in such a way that it has no further incentive to change. It will do so until profits are maximized. Figure 11.10 shows the long-run equilibrium of the perfectly competitive firm. Given a price of P and a marginal cost curve, MC, the firm produces at output Q_e. Because profits must be zero in the long run, the firm's short-run average costs (SAC) must equal P at Q_e, which occurs at minimum SAC. In addition, because we are in long-run equilibrium, any economies of scale must be exhausted so that we are on the minimum point of the long-run average cost curve (LAC). In other words, the long-run equilibrium position is where "everything is equal," which

Figure 11.10
Long-Run Firm Competitive Equilibrium

In the long run, the firm operates where price, marginal revenue, marginal cost, short-run minimum average cost, and long-run minimum average cost are all equal. This occurs at point E.

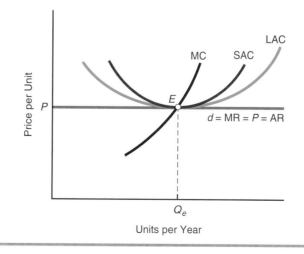

is at point E in Figure 11.10. There, *price* equals *marginal revenue* equals *marginal cost* equals *average cost* (minimum, short-run, and long-run).

Perfect Competition and Minimum Average Total Cost

Look again at Figure 11.10. In long-run equilibrium, the perfectly competitive firm finds itself producing at output rate Q_e. At that rate of output, the price is just equal to the minimum long-run average cost as well as the minimum short-run average cost. In this sense, perfect competition results in the production of goods and services using the least costly combination of resources. This is an important attribute of a perfectly competitive long-run equilibrium, particularly when we wish to compare the market structure of perfect competition with other market structures that are less than perfectly competitive. We will examine these other market structures in later chapters.

COMPETITIVE PRICING: MARGINAL COST PRICING

In a perfectly competitive industry, each firm produces where its marginal cost curve intersects its marginal revenue (d) curve from below. Thus perfectly competitive firms always sell their goods at a price that just equals marginal cost. This represents an optimal pricing situation because the price that consumers pay reflects the opportunity cost to society of producing the good. Recall that marginal cost is the amount that a firm must spend to purchase the additional resources needed to expand output by one unit. Given competitive markets, the amount paid for a resource will be the same in all of its alternative uses. Thus MC reflects relative resource input use; that is, if the MC of good 1 is twice the MC of good 2, one more unit of good 1 requires twice the resource input of one more unit of good 2. Because under perfect competition, price equals marginal cost, the consumer, in determining allocation of income on purchases on the basis of relative prices, is actually allocating income on the basis of relative resource input use.

Marginal Cost Pricing

▶ **Marginal cost pricing**
A system of pricing in which the price charged is equal to the opportunity cost to society of producing one more unit of the good or service in question. The opportunity cost is the marginal cost to society.

The competitive firm produces up to the point at which the market price just equals the marginal cost. Herein lies the element of the optimal nature of a competitive solution. It is called **marginal cost pricing.** The competitive firm sells its product at a price that just equals the cost to society—the opportunity cost—for that is what the marginal cost curve represents. (But note that it is the self-interest of firm owners that causes price to equal marginal social cost.) In other words, the marginal benefit to consumers, given by the price that they are willing to pay for the last unit of the good purchased, just equals the marginal cost to society of producing the last unit. (If the marginal benefit exceeds the marginal cost (P>MC), too little is being produced in that people value additional units more than the cost to society of producing them; if P<MC, the opposite is true.)

When an individual pays a price equal to the marginal cost of production, the cost to the user of that product is equal to the sacrifice or cost to society of producing that quantity of that good as opposed to more of some other good. (We are assuming that all marginal social costs are accounted for.) The competitive solution, then, is called *efficient*, in the economic sense of the word. Economic efficiency means that it is impossible to increase the output of any good without lowering the *value* of the total output produced in the economy. No juggling of resources, such as labour and capital, will result in an output that is higher in total value than the value of all of the goods and services already being produced. In an efficient situation, it is impossible to make one person better off without making someone else worse off. All resources are used in the most advantageous way possible, and society therefore enjoys an efficient allocation of productive resources. All goods and services are sold at their opportunity cost, and marginal cost pricing prevails throughout.

Try Preview Question 4:
Why is the perfectly competitive market structure considered economically efficient?

Market Failure

Although perfect competition does offer many desirable results, situations arise when perfectly competitive markets cannot efficiently allocate resources. Either too many or too few resources are used in the production of a good or service. These situations are instances of **market failure.** Externalities and public goods are examples. For reasons discussed in later chapters, perfectly competitive markets cannot efficiently allocate resources in these situations, and alternative allocation mechanisms are called for. Finally, the rate of innovation by perfectly competitive firms may be socially suboptimal, and the distribution of income may differ from what our normative judgment indicates. In all cases, alternative market structures, or government intervention, *may* improve the economic outcome.

▶ **Market failure**
A situation in which an unrestrained market operation leads to either too few or too many resources going to a specific economic activity.

| **POLICY EXAMPLE** | Can the Government Cure Market Failure Due to Asymmetric Information, or Are Lemons Here to Stay? |

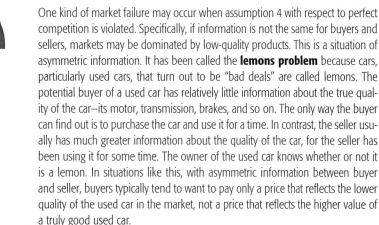

▶ **Lemons problem**
The situation in which consumers, who do not know details about the quality of a product, are willing to pay no more than the price of a low-quality product, even if a higher-quality product at a higher price exists.

One kind of market failure may occur when assumption 4 with respect to perfect competition is violated. Specifically, if information is not the same for buyers and sellers, markets may be dominated by low-quality products. This is a situation of asymmetric information. It has been called the **lemons problem** because cars, particularly used cars, that turn out to be "bad deals" are called lemons. The potential buyer of a used car has relatively little information about the true quality of the car—its motor, transmission, brakes, and so on. The only way the buyer can find out is to purchase the car and use it for a time. In contrast, the seller usually has much greater information about the quality of the car, for the seller has been using it for some time. The owner of the used car knows whether or not it is a lemon. In situations like this, with asymmetric information between buyer and seller, buyers typically tend to want to pay only a price that reflects the lower quality of the used car in the market, not a price that reflects the higher value of a truly good used car.

From the car seller's point of view, given that the price of used cars will tend to reflect average qualities, all of the owners of known lemons will want to put their cars up for sale. The owners of high-quality used cars will be more reluctant to do so. The logical result of this adverse selection is a disproportionate number of lemons on the used car market and consequently relatively fewer sales than would exist if information were symmetric.

So lemons will be overpriced and great-running used cars will be underpriced. Is there room for government policy to improve this market? Because the government has no better information than used-car buyers, it cannot provide any improved information. What most provincial governments have done, though, is require used-car vendors to take back their vehicles and refund the sale price if the buyer demands it within some specified period of time (often 30 days) following the sale.

For critical analysis: If used-car dealers depend on repeat customers, is the lemons problem reduced or eliminated?

Concepts in Brief

- The competitive price is determined by the intersection of the market demand curve and the market supply curve; the market supply curve is equal to the horizontal summation of the portions of the individual marginal cost curves above their respective minimum average variable costs.
- In the long run, competitive firms make zero economic profits because of entry and exit of firms into and out of the industry whenever there are industrywide economic profits or economic losses.
- A constant-cost industry will have a horizontal long-run supply curve. An increasing-cost industry will have an upward-sloping long-run supply curve. A decreasing-cost industry will have a downward-sloping long-run supply curve.
- In the long run, a competitive firm produces where price, marginal revenue, marginal cost, short-run minimum average cost, and long-run minimum average cost are all equal.
- Competitive pricing is essentially marginal cost pricing, and therefore the competitive solution is called efficient because marginal cost represents the social opportunity cost of producing one more unit of the good; when consumers face a price equal to the full opportunity cost of the product they are buying, their purchasing decisions will lead to an efficient use of available resources.

Issues and Applications

Future Shop Versus the Traditional Record Retailers

Concepts Applied: Competition, marginal cost pricing, entry, and exit

Traditional record retailers faced stiff competition when retail giants like Future Shop entered the record market. They drove prices down below minimum ATC for smaller retailers, forcing the smaller companies to exit the market.

Sam Sniderman ("Sam the Record Man") opened his first record store in Toronto in 1937. Until recently, he enjoyed remarkable success, capturing a large part of the Canadian record market and opening over 100 more stores in the process. However, Sam is gradually losing his market share to large-chain discounters like Future Shop, which are selling CDs at lower prices than Sam can afford. While consumers benefit from the discounters, independent retailers are hurt.

The Benefits of Diversified Inventory

One reason Future Shop can undercut the traditional record retailers is that it started as an electronics outlet. In 1994, it entered the record business in British Columbia, and gained a part of the market by offering CDs at marginal cost $2 to $5 less than the same titles were selling in Toronto and Ottawa. Future Shop was able to afford this pricing because of the profits it earned on its electronics sales. (The "record business" is still referred to as such even though it is now dominated by CDs.)

Other Record Retailers Fight Back

Because of Future Shop's cutthroat pricing, other retailers were forced to reduce their prices too. The result was that some smaller stores and chains like A&A Records went bankrupt, while other record retailers have entered the industry ready to compete. Virgin Records, a British chain, and Tower Records, a US chain, both opened their first Canadian "megastores" in 1996. Why do Virgin and Tower think they can compete in this market while A&A could not? They use centralized purchasing for all their outlets and order tremendous quantities. They therefore enjoy a lower per-unit cost than the smaller outlets.

The Benefits to Consumers

Competition for the record market has driven CD prices lower in Canada than almost anywhere in the world, and to almost one-half of prices in Britain, Australia, and Asia. For example, a new Céline Dion CD selling for $16.99 in Vancouver sold at the same time for $31.62 in London, England. And it is not only Canadian CDs that sell cheaply. A new release from the British band, Oasis, sold for $14.99 in Vancouver and $27 on its own turf.

Competition theoretically leads to maximum value of output for a given set of inputs over a specified period of time. That does not mean that in the process some individuals and businesses will not be hurt. The experience in the Canadian record industry highlights the fact that there may always be losers when entrepreneurs attempt to force prices down to their marginal cost.

For Critical Analysis

1. With the entry of large firms like Future Shop into the retail record industry, does the market remain one of perfect competition? Why or why not?

2. Do you think the record selling industry would be a decreasing, constant, or increasing cost industry? Why?

CHAPTER SUMMARY

1. We define a competitive situation as one in which individual firms cannot affect the price of the product they produce. This is usually when the firm is very small relative to the entire industry. A firm in a perfectly competitive situation is called a price taker; it must take price as a given.

2. The firm's total revenues will equal the price of the product times the quantity sold. Because the competitive firm can sell all it wants at the same price (the "going" price), total revenues equal the going price times the quantity the firm decides to sell.

3. The firm maximizes profits when marginal cost equals marginal revenue. The marginal revenue to the firm is represented by its own perfectly elastic demand curve. This is because marginal revenue is defined as the change in total revenues due to a change in output and sales by one unit. But the competitive firm can sell all it wants at the same price; therefore, its marginal revenue will equal the price, which will equal its average revenue.

4. A perfectly competitive firm ends up in the long run making zero economic profits. However, it still makes a normal, or competitive, rate of return because that is the opportunity cost of

capital. The competitive rate of return on investment is included in the costs as we have defined them for the firm.

5. The firm will always produce along its marginal cost curve unless the price falls below average variable costs; this would be the shutdown price. It occurs at the intersection of the average variable cost curve and the marginal cost curve. Below that price, it is not profitable to stay in production because variable costs will not be completely covered by revenues.

6. The supply curve of the firm is exactly equal to its marginal cost curve above the shutdown price. The supply curve of the industry is equal to the horizontal summation of all the supply curves of the individual firms. This is a short-run industry supply curve, and it slopes upward.

7. The long-run supply curve will be upward-sloping, horizontal, or downward-sloping, depending on whether the industry is facing increasing, constant, or decreasing costs. The industry may have an upward-sloping long-run supply curve if it faces diseconomies of scale or increasing costs. The industry may have a downward-sloping long-run supply curve if it faces economies of scale or decreasing costs.

DISCUSSION OF PREVIEW QUESTIONS

1. How much will a perfect competitor produce in the short run?

A perfect competitor will produce at the profit-maximizing rate of output; it will maximize the positive difference between total revenues and total costs. Another way of viewing this process is through analysing marginal revenue (MR) and marginal cost (MC). The firm can maximize total profits by producing all outputs for which MR exceeds MC. Thus if MR>MC, the firm will produce the unit in question; if MR<MC, the firm will not produce the unit in question. If MC>MR, the extra cost of produc-

ing that unit is greater than the extra revenue that the firm can earn by selling it; producing a unit for which MC>MR leads to a reduction in total profits or an increase in total losses. In short, the perfect competitor will produce up to the output rate at which MR = MC; by doing so, it will have produced all units for which MR>MC, and it will be maximizing total profits.

2. What is the perfectly competitive firm's short-run supply curve?

A supply curve indicates the various quantities

per unit of time that will be offered, voluntarily, at different prices, other things being constant. Under perfect competition, price (P) equals marginal revenue (MR), and because the profit-maximizing output occurs where P = MC, it follows that any price above MC will induce more output until MC is driven up to equal that price. Thus the marginal cost curve is the firm's short-run supply schedule. We qualify this to note that because the firm has a shutdown point at the minimum average variable cost point, the technical short-run supply curve is the firm's marginal cost curve *above* the minimum average variable cost point.

3. **Can a perfectly competitive firm earn economic profits?**

In the short run, yes; in the long run, no. Though it is possible for a perfectly competitive firm to earn profits in the short run, our assumption of free (unfettered but not costless) entry forces us to conclude that any positive economic (abnormal) profits will be bid away. This will happen because excess profits induce entry into the industry, which amounts to an increase in industry supply. Given demand, an increase in supply will cause market price to fall, thereby shifting the individual firm's demand curve downward.

This process continues until economic profits equal zero; free entry allows new entrants to compete away economic profits.

4. **Why is the perfectly competitive market structure considered economically efficient?**

The perfectly competitive market structure is considered economically efficient for two reasons: In the long run, economic profits are zero, and price equals marginal cost. We discuss each in turn. Profits are a signal; if economic profits are positive, the signal is that society wants *more* of this good; if economic profits are negative, this means that society wants *less* of this good; when economic profits are zero, just the "right" quantity of resources is being allocated to the production of a good. Also, the marginal cost of a good represents the social opportunity cost of producing one more unit of that good; the price of a good represents society's marginal valuation of that commodity. When price equals marginal cost, the value to society of the last unit produced (its price) is just offset by what society had to give up in order to get it (its marginal cost). Because under perfect competition, long-run economic profits equal zero and price equals marginal cost, an efficient allocation of resources exists.

PROBLEMS

(Answers to the odd-numbered problems appear at the back of the book.)

11-1. In the accompanying table, we list cost figures for a hypothetical firm. We assume that the firm is selling in a perfectly competitive market. Fill in all the blanks.

Output (units)	Fixed Cost	Average Fixed Cost (AFC)	Variable Cost	Average Variable Cost (AVC)	Total Cost	Average Total Cost (ATC)	Marginal Cost (MC)
1	$100	$_____	$40	$_____	$_____	$_____	$_____
2	100	_____	70	_____	_____	_____	_____
3	100	_____	120	_____	_____	_____	_____
4	100	_____	180	_____	_____	_____	_____
5	100	_____	250	_____	_____	_____	_____
6	100	_____	330	_____	_____	_____	_____

a. How low would the market price of its output have to go before the firm would shut down in the short run?

b. What is the price of its output at which the firm would just break even in the short run? (This is the same price below which the firm would go out of business in the long run.) What output would the firm produce at that price?

c. If the price of its output were $76, what rate of output would the firm produce, and how much profit would it earn?

11-2. Consider the accompanying graph. Then answer the questions.

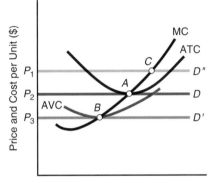

a. Which demand curve indicates that the firm is earning normal profits?

b. Which demand curve indicates that the firm is earning abnormal profits?

c. Which demand curve indicates that the firm is indifferent between shutting down and producing?

d. Which curve is the firm's supply curve?

e. Below which price will the firm shut down?

11-3. In a perfectly competitive market, what is the difference between the demand the industry faces and the demand an individual firm faces?

11-4. Why might a firm continue to produce in the short run, even though the going price is less than its average total cost?

11-5. A firm in a perfectly competitive industry has total revenue of $200,000 per year when producing 2,000 units of output per year.

a. Find the firm's average revenue.

b. Find the firm's marginal revenue.

c. Assuming that the firm is maximizing profits, what is the firm's marginal cost?

d. If the firm is at long-run equilibrium, what are its short-run average costs?

11-6. The accompanying graph is for firm J. Study it; then answer the questions.

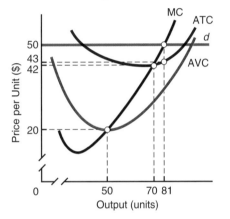

a. How many units will firm J sell in order to maximize profits?

b. What is firm J's total profit from selling the amount of output in part (a)?

c. At what price will firm J shut down in the short run?

d. If the cost curves shown represent production at the optimal long-run plant size, at what price will firm J shut down in the long run?

11-7. You have a friend who earns $25,000 a year working for a collection agency. In a savings account she has $200,000 that she inherited. She is earning 6 percent per year on that money. She quits her job and buys a car wash with the $200,000. At the end of one year, she shows you her tax return. It indicates that the car wash had a pretax profit of $40,000. "What do you think about that?" she remarks. What is your answer?

Monopoly

Your genes make up your inherited physical characteristics. Genes are found in strands of genetic material called chromosomes. Each gene carries a "code" that is the chemical equation which translates hereditary information into proteins. Scientists are identifying new genes on a regular basis now. The discovery of new gene data has led, and will continue to lead, to the development of drugs necessary for the prevention, treatment, and cure of many life-threatening diseases. Much of the information relating to these new genetic data is owned by one drug company, SmithKline Beecham. Does this company therefore have market power? To answer this question, you need to study the theory and reality of monopoly.

Preview Questions

1. For the monopolist, marginal revenue is less than selling price. Why?

2. What is the profit-maximizing rate of output for the monopolist?

3. What are some common misconceptions about monopolists?

4. What is the cost to society of monopoly?

Did You Know That... the Central Selling Organization (CSO), a marketing group based in London, England, sells about 80 percent of the world's rough-cut diamonds each year, collecting handling fees of about 12 percent? The CSO is owned by South Africa's De Beers, the world's largest diamond mining company, controlled by Harry Oppenheimer. In any given year, the CSO sells between US$5 and US$6 billion in diamonds, making around US$500 million a year in profits. It spends relatively little each year on advertising—"A diamond is forever." For all intents and purposes, there is one seller of rough-cut diamonds in the world, and you can be certain that this principal seller attempts to extract the maximum amount of profit possible under the circumstances.

Single sellers of goods and services exist all around you. The company that sells food in your school cafeteria has most probably been granted the exclusive right to do so by your college or university. The ski resort that offers you food at the top of the mountain does not allow anyone else to open a restaurant next to it. When you run a business that is the only one of its type in a particular location, you can usually charge a higher price per constant-quality unit than when there is intense competition. In this chapter you will read more about situations in which competition is restricted. We call these situations *monopoly*.

DEFINITION OF A MONOPOLIST

The word *monopoly* probably brings to mind notions of a business that gouges the consumer, sells faulty products, and gets unconscionably rich. But if we are to succeed in analysing and predicting the behaviour of noncompetitive firms, we will have to be more objective in our definition. Although most monopolies in Canada are relatively large, our definition will be equally applicable to small businesses: A **monopolist** is the *single supplier* of a good or service for which there is no close substitute.

> ▶ **Monopolist**
>
> A single supplier that comprises its entire industry for a good or service for which there is no close substitute.

In a monopoly market structure, the firm (the monopolist) and the industry are one and the same. Occasionally there may be a problem in identifying an industry and therefore determining if a monopoly exists. For example, should we think of aluminum and steel as separate industries, or should we define the industry in terms of basic metals? Our answer depends on the extent to which aluminum and steel can be substituted in the production of a wide range of products.

As we shall see in this chapter, a seller prefers to have a monopoly than to face competitors. In general, we think of monopoly prices as being higher than prices under perfect competition and of monopoly profits as being higher than profits under perfect competition (which are, in the long run, merely equivalent to a normal rate of return). How does a firm obtain a monopoly in an industry? Basically, there must be *barriers to entry* that enable firms to receive monopoly profits in the long run. Barriers to entry are restrictions on who can start a business or who can stay in a business.

BARRIERS TO ENTRY

For any amount of monopoly power to continue to exist in the long run, the market must be closed to entry in some way. Either legal means or certain aspects of the industry's technical or cost structure may prevent entry. We will discuss several of the barriers to entry that have allowed firms to reap monopoly profits in the long run (even if they are not pure monopolists in the technical sense).

Ownership of Resources Without Close Substitutes

Preventing a newcomer from entering an industry is often difficult. Indeed, some economists contend that no monopoly acting without government support has been able to prevent entry into the industry unless that monopoly has had the control of some essential natural resource. Consider the possibility of one firm's owning the entire supply of a raw material input that is essential to the production of a particular commodity. The exclusive ownership of such a vital resource serves as a barrier to entry until an alternative source of the raw material input is found, or an alternative technology not requiring the raw material in question is developed. A good example of control over a vital input is the Aluminum Company of America, a firm that prior to World War II controlled the world's bauxite, the essential raw material in the production of aluminum. Such a situation is rare, though, and is usually temporary.

Problems in Raising Adequate Capital

Certain industries require a large initial capital investment. The firms already in the industry can, according to some economists, obtain monopoly profits in the long run because no competitors can raise the large amount of capital needed to enter the industry. This is called the "imperfect" capital market argument employed to explain long-run, relatively high rates of return in certain industries. These industries are generally ones in which large fixed costs must be incurred merely to start production. Their fixed costs are generally for expensive machines necessary to the production process.

EXAMPLE   "Intel Inside"

Many observers of today's high-stakes high-technology world argue that the world's largest manufacturer of microprocessors, Intel, is a monopoly. They point out that to compete effectively with Intel, a potential adversary would have to invest billions of dollars. Intel provides the critical microprocessor chip that goes into the majority of the world's personal computers. Each new generation of microprocessor quickly becomes the industry standard for all IBM-compatible personal computers. Apple computers for years used a Motorola-made chip. In an attempt to fight back against Intel, Apple, Motorola, and IBM formed an alliance that did develop the Power PC microprocessor. So far, though, it has not made serious inroads into Intel's market. A few companies have attempted to clone Intel's chips, but they have not been very successful for both legal and technical reasons.

For critical analysis: Intel spends billions of dollars developing each new generation of microprocessor. Would it spend more or less if it had a smaller share of the microprocessor market?

Economies of Scale

Sometimes it is not profitable for more than one firm to exist in an industry. This is so if, in order to realize lower unit costs, one firm would have to produce such a large quantity that there would be insufficient demand to warrant a second producer of the same product. Such a situation may arise because of a phenomenon we discussed in Chapter 10, economies of scale. When economies of scale exist, total costs increase less than proportionately to the increase in output. That is, proportional increases in output yield proportionately smaller increases in total costs, and per-unit costs drop. The advantage in economies of scale lies in the fact that larger firms (with larger output) have lower costs that enable them to charge lower prices, and that drives smaller firms out of business.

▶ **Natural monopoly**

A monopoly that arises from the peculiar production characteristics in an industry. It usually arises when there are large economies of scale relative to the industry's demand such that one firm can produce at a lower average cost than can be achieved by multiple firms.

When economies of scale occur over a wide range of outputs, a **natural monopoly** may develop. The natural monopoly is the firm that first takes advantage of persistent declining long-run average costs as scale increases. The natural monopolist is able to underprice its competitors and eventually force all of them out of the market.

In Figure 12.1, we have drawn a downward-sloping long-run average cost curve (LAC). Recall that when average costs are falling, marginal costs are less than average costs. We can apply the same analysis in the long run. When the long-run average cost curve (LAC) is falling, the long-run marginal cost curve (LMC) will be below the LAC.

In our example, long-run average costs are falling over such a large range of production rates that we would expect only one firm to survive in such an industry. That firm would be the natural monopolist. It would be the first one to take advantage of the decreasing average costs; that is, it would construct the large-scale facilities first. As its average costs fell, it would lower prices and get an increasingly larger share of the market. Once that firm had driven all other firms out of the industry, it would set its price to maximize profits.

Figure 12.1

The Cost Curves That Might Lead to a Natural Monopoly: The Case of Electricity

Whenever long-run average costs are falling, so, too, will be long-run marginal costs. Also, long-run marginal costs (LMC) will always be below long-run average costs (LAC). A natural monopoly might arise in such a situation. The first firm to establish the low unit cost capacity would be able to take advantage of the lower average total cost curve. This firm would drive out all rivals by charging a lower price than the others could sustain at their higher average costs.

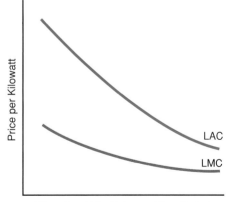

Legal or Governmental Restrictions

Both the federal and provincial governments can also erect barriers to entry. These include public franchises, licences, patents, tariffs, and specific regulations that tend to limit entry.

Public Franchises and Licences. In many industries, it is illegal to enter without a government licence. For example, you could not open a medical practice in Canada without first obtaining a licence from the Canadian College of Physicians and Surgeons. Standards are closely monitored by the government to protect the health and safety of consumers. By restricting entry to the profession, doctors' earnings remain relatively high.

A public franchise is necessary to enter markets such as the provision of cable television service. The Canadian Radio-television and Telecommunications Commisson (CRTC) must approve all applications for entry, and in many cases grants local, or geographical, monopolies to cable TV providers. Because these franchises are restricted, long-run monopoly profits might be earned by firms like Rogers Cablesystems which are already in the industry.

POLICY EXAMPLE   Should Canada Post Remain a Monopoly—or Does It Matter?

Canada Post has been granted a monopoly on first-class mail by the government. Until fairly recently it had a *de facto* monopoly on parcel delivery as well. Any monopoly power that Canada Post had with respect to parcel delivery, however, has been whittled away by the more efficient and cheaper United Parcel Service. For urgent delivery, Federal Express, Purolator, and other courier companies have further eroded Canada Post's monopoly. In the 1990s, technology has perhaps rendered the most fatal blow to Canada Post's position. The fax machine is usually cheaper and certainly faster than mailing a letter domestically or internationally. Now that fax modems are routinely installed in all new personal computers, faxing may become ubiquitous. So, too, may the use of electronic mail. With over 40 million users of the Internet active today, e-mail offers an almost free substitute for mailing a letter.

For critical analysis: In what ways might Canada Post slow down the erosion of its monopoly position?

Patents. A patent is issued to an inventor to provide protection from having the invention copied or stolen for a period of 20 years. Suppose that engineers working for Northern Telecom discover a way to build fibre optic cable that requires half the amount of inputs of regular cable, and transmits data twice as fast. If Nortel is successful in obtaining a patent on this discovery, it can (in principle) prevent others from copying it. The patent holder has a monopoly. However, it is the patent holder's responsibility to defend the patent. That means that Northern Telecom—like other patent owners—must expend resources to prevent others from imitating its invention. If in fact the costs of enforcing a particular patent are greater than the benefits, the patent may not bestow any monopoly profits on its owner. The policing costs would be just too high.

INTERNATIONAL EXAMPLE
Patents as Intellectual Property

A patent may bestow on its owner a monopoly for a given time period. So, too, may copyrights. Trademarks don't actually bestow monopoly power, but they do in certain cases have extreme value. Coca-Cola can exploit its trademark by licensing it for clothes and other items. So, too, can the Hard Rock Cafe. Both of those companies have done so. Copyrights, trademarks, patents, and the like are all part of what is known as intellectual property. Songs, music, computer programs, and designs are all intellectual property. Indeed, some economists believe that the world value of intellectual property now exceeds the value of physical property such as real estate, buildings, and equipment. Not surprisingly, in the corporate world, when a business buys another business, the lawyers for the purchasing company have to be seriously concerned with the acquired company's intellectual property portfolio. What intellectual property rights in terms of patents, trademarks, and copyrights does the soon-to-be-acquired company actually own?

For critical analysis: Why doesn't the ownership of a well-known trademark bestow true monopoly power on its owner?

▶ **Tariffs**
Taxes on imported goods.

Tariffs. Tariffs are special taxes that are imposed on certain imported goods. They have the effect of making imports relatively more expensive than their domestic counterparts so that consumers switch to the relatively cheaper domestically made products. If the tariffs are high enough, imports become overpriced, and domestic producers gain monopoly advantage as the sole suppliers. Many countries have tried this protectionist strategy by using high tariffs to shut out foreign competitors.

Regulations. During much of the twentieth century, government regulation of the Canadian economy has increased, especially along the dimensions of safety and quality. For example, pharmaceutical quality-control regulations enforced by Health and Welfare Canada may require that each pharmaceutical company install computerized testing machines that require elaborate monitoring and maintenance. Presumably, this large fixed cost can be spread over a greater number of units of output by larger firms than by smaller firms, thereby putting the smaller firms at a competitive disadvantage. It will also deter entry to the extent that the scale of operation of a potential entrant must be sufficiently large to cover the average fixed costs of the required equipment. We examine regulation in more detail in Chapter 14.

Concepts in Brief

* A monopolist is defined as a single seller of a product or a good for which there is no good close substitute.
* To maintain a monopoly, there must be barriers to entry. Barriers to entry include ownership of resources without close substitutes; large capital requirements in order to enter the industry; economies of scale; legally required licences and public franchises; patents; tariffs; and safety and quality regulations.

THE DEMAND CURVE A MONOPOLIST FACES

A *pure monopolist* is the sole supplier of *one* product, good, or service. A pure monopolist faces a demand curve that is the demand curve for the entire market for that good.

> The monopolist faces the industry demand curve because the monopolist is the entire industry.

Because the monopolist faces the industry demand curve, which is by definition downward-sloping, its decision-making process with respect to how much to produce is not the same as for a perfect competitor. When a monopolist changes output, it does not automatically receive the same price per unit that it did before the change.

Profits to Be Made from Increasing Production

How do firms benefit from changing production rates? What happens to price in each case? Let's first review the situation among perfect competitors.

Marginal Revenue for the Perfect Competitor. Recall that a competitive firm has a perfectly elastic demand curve. That is because the competitive firm is such a small part of the market that it cannot influence the price of its product. It is a *price taker.* If the forces of supply and demand establish that the price per constant-quality pair of shoes is $50, the individual firm can sell all the pairs of shoes it wants to produce at $50 per pair. The average revenue is $50, the price is $50, and the marginal revenue is also $50.

Let us again define marginal revenue:

> Marginal revenue equals the change in total revenue due to a one-unit change in the quantity produced and sold.

In the case of a competitive industry, each time a single firm changes production by one unit, total revenue changes by the going price, and price is always the same. Marginal revenue never changes; it always equals price, or average revenue. Average revenue was defined as total revenue divided by quantity demanded, or

$$\text{Average revenue} = \frac{\text{TR}}{Q} = \frac{PQ}{Q} = P$$

Marginal Revenue for the Monopolist. What about a monopoly firm? Because a monopoly is the entire industry, the monopoly firm's demand curve is the market demand curve. The market demand curve slopes downward, just like the other demand curves that we have seen. Therefore, to sell more of a particular product, given the industry demand curve, the monopoly firm must lower the price. Thus the monopoly firm moves *down* the demand curve. If all buyers are to be charged the same price, the monopoly must lower the price on all units sold in order to sell more. It cannot just lower the price on the *last* unit sold in any given time period in order to sell a larger quantity.

Put yourself in the shoes of a monopoly ferryboat owner. You have a government-bestowed franchise, and no one can compete with you. Your ferryboat goes between two islands. If you are charging $1 per crossing, a certain quantity of your services will be demanded. Let's say that you are ferrying 100 people a day each way at that price. If you decide that you would like to ferry more individuals, you must lower your price to all individuals—you must move *down* the existing demand curve for ferrying services. To calculate the marginal revenue of your change in price, you must first calculate the total revenues you received at $1 per passenger per crossing and then calculate the total revenues you would receive at, say, 90 cents per passenger per crossing.

It is sometimes useful to compare monopoly markets with perfectly competitive markets. The only way the monopolist can increase sales is by getting consumers to spend more of their incomes on the monopolist's product and less on all other products combined. Thus the monopolist is constrained by the entire market demand curve for its product. We see this in Figure 12.2, which compares the demand curves of the perfect competitor and the monopolist.

Here we see the fundamental difference between the monopolist and the competitor. The competitor doesn't have to worry about lowering price to sell more. In a purely competitive situation, the competitive firm accounts for such a small part of the market that it can sell its entire output, whatever that may be, at the same price. The monopolist cannot. The more the monopolist wants to sell, the lower the price it has to charge on the last unit (and on *all* units put on the market for sale). Obviously, the extra revenues the monopolist receives from selling one more unit are going to be smaller than the extra revenues received from selling the next-to-last unit. The monopolist has to lower the price on the last unit to sell it because it is facing a downward-sloping demand curve and the only way to move down the demand curve is to lower the price on all units.

Figure 12.2
Demand Curves for the Perfect Competitor and the Monopolist

The perfect competitor in part (a) faces a perfectly elastic demand curve, d. The monopolist in part (b) faces the entire industry demand curve, which slopes downward.

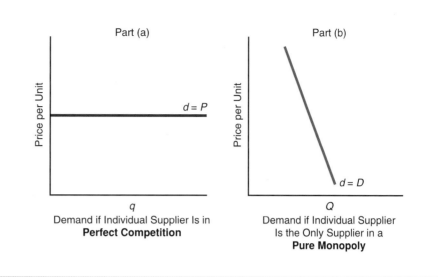

Part (a)

$d = P$

Price per Unit

q

Demand if Individual Supplier Is in
Perfect Competition

Part (b)

$d = D$

Price per Unit

Q

Demand if Individual Supplier Is the Only Supplier in a
Pure Monopoly

The Monopolist's Marginal Revenue: Less than Price

An essential point is that for the monopolist, marginal revenue is always less than price. To understand why, look at Figure 12.3, which shows a unit increase in sales

Figure 12.3
Marginal Revenue: Always Less than Price

The price received for the last unit sold is equal to P_2. The revenues received from selling this last unit are equal to P_2 times one unit, or the area of the vertical column. However, if a single price is being charged for all units, total revenues do not go up by the amount of the area represented by that column. The price had to be reduced on all the previous Q units that were being sold at price P_1. Thus we must subtract area B–the rectangle between P_1 and P_2 from the origin to Q–from area A in order to derive marginal revenue. Marginal revenue is therefore always less than price.

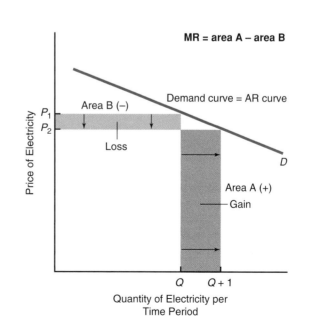

MR = area A − area B

Demand curve = AR curve

P_1
P_2

Area B (−)

Loss

Price of Electricity

D

Area A (+)

Gain

Q $Q + 1$

Quantity of Electricity per
Time Period

due to a reduction in the price of a commodity from P_1 to P_2. After all, the only way that sales can increase, given a downward-sloping demand curve, is for the price to fall. Price P_2 is the price received for the last unit. Thus price P_2 times the last unit sold represents what is received from the last unit sold. That is equal to the vertical column (area A). Area A is one unit wide by P_2 high.

But price times the last unit sold is *not* the addition to *total* revenues received from selling that last unit. Why? Because price had to be reduced on all previous units sold (Q) in order to sell the larger quantity $Q + 1$. The reduction in price is represented by the vertical distance from P_1 to P_2 on the vertical axis. We must therefore subtract area B from area A to come up with the *change* in total revenues due to a one-unit increase in sales. Clearly, the change in total revenues—that is, marginal revenue—must be less than price because marginal revenue is always the difference between areas A and B in Figure 12.3. For example, if the initial price is $8 and quantity demanded is 3, to increase quantity to 4 units, it is necessary to decrease price to $7, not just for the fourth unit, but on all three previous units as well. Thus at a price of $7, marginal revenue is $7 - $3 = $4 because there is a $1 per unit price reduction on three previous units. Hence marginal revenue, $4, is less than price, $7.

Try Preview Question 1:
For the monopolist, marginal revenue is less than selling price. Why?

ELASTICITY AND MONOPOLY

The monopolist faces a downward-sloping demand curve (its average revenue curve). That means that it cannot charge just *any* price with no changes in quantity (a common misconception) because, depending on the price charged, a different quantity will be demanded.

Earlier we defined a monopolist as the single seller of a well-defined good or service with no *close* substitute. This does not mean, however, that the demand curve for a monopoly is vertical or exhibits zero price elasticity of demand. (Indeed, as we shall see, the profit-maximizing monopolist will never operate in a price range in which demand is inelastic.) After all, consumers have limited incomes and alternative wants. The downward slope of a monopolist's demand curve occurs because individuals compare the marginal satisfaction they will receive to the cost of the commodity to be purchased. Take the example of telephone service. Even if miraculously there were absolutely no substitute whatsoever for telephone service, the market demand curve would still slope downward. At lower prices, people will add more phones and separate lines for different family members.

Furthermore, the demand curve for telephone service slopes downward because there are at least several *imperfect* substitutes, such as letters, telegrams, in-person conversations, and CB and VHF-FM radios. Thus even though we defined a monopolist as a single seller of a commodity with no *close* substitute, we can talk about the range of *imperfect* substitutes. The more such imperfect substitutes there are, the more elastic will be the monopolist's demand curve, all other things held constant.

Concepts in Brief

* The monopolist estimates its marginal revenue curve, where marginal revenue is defined as the change in total revenues due to a one-unit change in quantity sold.
* For the perfect competitor, price equals marginal revenue equals average revenue. For the monopolist, price is always greater than marginal revenue. For the monopolist, marginal revenue is always less than price because price must be reduced on all units to sell more.
* The price elasticity of demand for the monopolist depends on the number and similarity of substitutes. The more numerous and more similar the substitutes, the greater the price elasticity of demand of the monopolist's demand curve.

COSTS AND MONOPOLY PROFIT MAXIMIZATION

To find out the rate of output at which the perfect competitor would maximize profits, we had to add cost data. We will do the same thing now for the monopolist. We assume that profit maximization is the goal of the pure monopolist, just as for the perfect competitor. The perfect competitor, however, has only to decide on the profit-maximizing rate of output because price was given. The competitor is a price taker. For the pure monopolist, we must seek a profit-maximizing *price-output combination* because the monopolist is a **price searcher.** We can determine this profit-maximizing price-output combination with either of two equivalent approaches—by looking at total revenues and total costs or by looking at marginal revenues and marginal costs. We shall examine both approaches.

▶ **Price searcher**

A firm that must determine the price-output combination that maximizes profit because it faces a downward-sloping demand curve.

The Total Revenues–Total Costs Approach

We show hypothetical demand (rate of output and price per unit), revenues, costs, and other data in part (a) of Figure 12.4. In column 3, we see total revenues for our hypothetical monopolist, and in column 4, we see total costs. We can transfer these two columns to part (b). The difference between the total revenue and total cost diagram in part (b) and the one we showed for a perfect competitor in Chapter 11 is that the total revenue line is no longer straight. Rather, it curves. For any given demand curve, in order to sell more, the monopolist must lower the price. Thus, the basic difference between a monopolist and a perfect competitor has to do with the demand curve for the two types of firms. Monopoly market power is derived from facing a downward-sloping demand curve.

Figure 12.4
Monopoly Costs, Revenues, and Profits

In part (a), we give hypothetical demand (rate of output and price per unit), revenues, costs, and other relevant data. As shown in part (b), the monopolist maximizes profits where the positive difference between TR and TC is greatest. This is at an output rate of 8 or 9. Put another way, profit maximization occurs where marginal revenue equals marginal cost, as shown in part (c). This is at the unique output rate of 9 units. (The MC curve must cut the MR curve from below.)

Part (a)

(1) Output (units)	(2) Price per Unit	(3) Total Revenues (TR) (3) = (2) x (1)	(4) Total Costs (TC)	(5) Total Profit (5) = (3) – (4)	(6) Marginal Cost (MC)	(7) Marginal Revenue (MR)
0	$8.00	$ .00	$10.00	–$10.00		
					$4.00	$7.75
1	7.75	7.75	14.00	– 6.20		
					3.50	7.25
2	7.50	15.00	17.50	– 2.30		
					3.25	6.75
3	7.25	21.75	20.75	1..00		
					3.05	6.25
4	7.00	28.00	23.80	4.20		
					2.90	5.75
5	6.75	33.75	26.70	7.05		
					2.80	5.25
6	6.50	39.00	29.50	9.50		
					2.75	4.75
7	6.25	43.75	32.25	11.50		
					3.15	4.25
8	6.00	48.00	35.10	12.60		
					3.75	3.75
9	5.75	51.75	38.30	12.60		
					4.15	3.25
10	5.50	55.00	42.30	11.70		
					5.25	2.75
11	5.25	57.75	48.55	9.20		
					9.95	2.25
12	5.00	60.00	58.50	1.50		
					13.50	1.75
13	4.75	61.75	72.00	– 10.25		
					17.00	1.25
14	4.50	63.00	89.00	– 26.00		
					21.00	0.75
15	4.25	63.75	110.00	– 46.25		

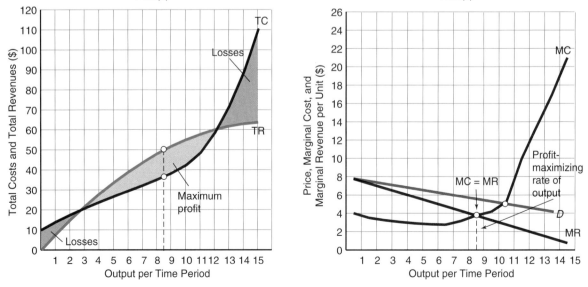

Profit maximization involves maximizing the positive difference between total revenues and total costs. This occurs at an output rate of 8 or 9 units.

The Marginal Revenue–Marginal Cost Approach

Profit maximization will also occur where marginal revenue equals marginal cost. This is as true for a monopolist as it is for a perfect competitor (but the monopolist will charge a higher price). When we transfer marginal cost and marginal revenue information from columns 6 and 7 in part (a) of Figure 12.4 to part (c), we see that marginal revenue equals marginal cost at an output rate of 9 units. Remember that a marginal cost of $3.75 refers to the extra cost of producing the 9th unit of output; a marginal revenue of $3.75 refers to the extra revenue earned by selling the 9th unit of output. Therefore, the monopolist will not stop at producing and selling 8 units of output, but will continue until marginal cost equals marginal revenue. Profit maximization occurs at the same output as in part (b).

Why Produce Where Marginal Revenue Equals Marginal Cost? If the monopolist goes past the point where marginal revenue equals marginal cost, marginal cost will exceed marginal revenue. That is, the incremental cost of producing any more units will exceed the incremental revenue. It just wouldn't be worthwhile, as was true also in perfect competition. But if the monopolist produces less than that, it is also not making maximum profits. Look at an output rate of 7 units in Figure 12.4. Here the monopolist's marginal revenue is $4.75, but marginal cost is only $2.75. Marginal revenue exceeds marginal cost on the last unit sold; the profit for the 7th unit of output is equal to $2.00, or the difference between marginal revenue and marginal cost. The monopolist would be foolish to stop at 7 units of output because if output is expanded, marginal revenue will still exceed marginal cost, and therefore total profits will rise. In fact, the profit-maximizing monopolist will continue to expand output and sales until marginal revenue equals marginal cost, which is at 9 units of output. The monopolist won't produce at an output rate of 11 because here, as we see, marginal cost is $5.25 and marginal revenue is $2.75. The difference of $2.50 represents the *reduction* in total profits from producing that additional unit. Total profits will rise as the monopolist reduces its rate of output back toward 9 units of output.

Try Preview Question 2:
What is the profit-maximizing rate of output for the monopolist?

Thinking Critically About the Media   Price Increases Everywhere

Almost daily, stories appear in the media about price increases. They are usually presented as specific decisions by specific companies: "Ford announced a 3.2 percent increase in car prices" or "Stelco announced a 2.4 percent increase in its price of steel." One gets the impression that virtually all businesses in Canada raise prices whenever they want. Nothing could be further from the truth. Business pricing decisions depend on changes in cost and in demand. Just because individual firms have to have a price list does not mean that those prices are arbitrary. Even a monopolist faces a demand curve that is not perfectly inelastic.

What Price to Charge for Output?

How does the monopolist set prices? We know the quantity is set at the point at which marginal revenue equals marginal cost. The monopolist then finds out how much can be charged—how much the market will bear—for that particular quantity. We know that the demand curve is defined as showing the *maximum* price for which a given quantity can be sold. That means that our monopolist knows that to sell 9 units, it can charge only $5.75 because that is the price at which that specific quantity is demanded. This price is found by drawing a vertical line from the quantity to the market demand curve. Where that line hits the market demand curve, the price is determined. We find that price by drawing a horizontal line from the demand curve over to the price axis; that gives us the profit-maximizing price of $5.75.

The basic procedure for finding the profit-maximizing short-run price-quantity combination for the monopolist is first to determine the profit-maximizing rate of output, by either the total revenue–total cost method or the marginal revenue–marginal cost method, and then to determine by use of the demand curve, *D*, the maximum price that can be charged to sell that output.

Don't get the impression that just because we are able to draw an exact demand curve in Figure 12.4, real-world monopolists have such perfect information. The process of price searching by a less than perfect competitor is just that—a process. A monopolist can only estimate the actual demand curve and therefore can only make an educated guess when it sets its profit-maximizing price. This is not a problem for the perfect competitor because price is given already by the intersection of market demand and market supply. The monopolist, in contrast, reaches the profit-maximizing output-price combination by trial and error.

CALCULATING MONOPOLY PROFIT

We have talked about the monopolist's profit, but we have yet to indicate how much profit the monopolist makes. We have actually shown total profits in column 5 of part (a) in Figure 12.4. We can also find total profits by adding an average total cost curve to part (c) of that figure. We do that in Figure 12.5. When we add the average total cost curve, we find that the profit that a monopolist makes is equal to the shaded area [or total revenues (P × Q) minus total costs (ATC × Q)]. Given the demand curve and a uniform pricing system (i.e., all units sold at the same price), there is no way for a monopolist to make greater profits than those shown by the shaded area. The monopolist is maximizing profits where marginal cost equals marginal revenue. If the monopolist produces less than that, it will be forfeiting some profits. If the monopolist produces more than that, it will be forfeiting some profits.

The same is true of a perfect competitor. The competitor produces where marginal revenues equal marginal costs because it produces at the point where the marginal cost curve intersects the perfectly elastic firm demand curve. The perfectly elastic firm demand curve represents the marginal revenue curve for the pure competitor, for the same average revenues are obtained on all the units sold. Perfect

Figure 12.5
Monopoly Profit

We find monopoly profit by subtracting total costs from total revenues at an output rate of 9, labelled Q_m, which is the profit-maximizing rate of output for the monopolist. The profit-maximizing price is therefore $5.75 and is labelled P_m. Monopoly profit is given by the shaded area, which is equal to total revenues (P × Q) minus total costs (ATC × Q). This diagram is similar to part (c) of Figure 12.4, with the short-run average total cost curve (ATC) added.

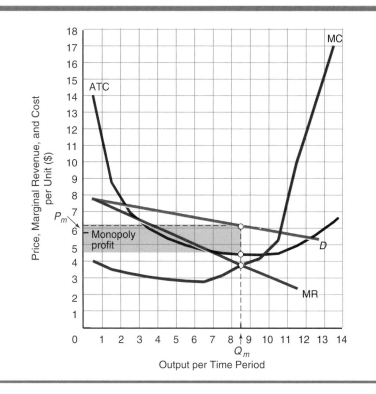

competitors maximize profits at MR = MC, as do pure monopolists. But the perfect competitor makes no true economic profits in the long run; rather, all it makes is a normal, competitive rate of return.

In Chapter 11, we talked about companies experiencing short-run economic profits because they had, for example, invented something new. Competition, though, gradually eroded those higher than normal profits. The fact that a firm experiences higher than normal profits today does not mean that it has a monopoly forever. Try as companies may, keeping competitors away is never easy.

No Guarantee of Profits

The term *monopoly* conjures up the notion of a greedy firm ripping off the public and making exorbitant profits. However, the mere existence of a monopoly does not guarantee high profits. Numerous monopolies have gone bankrupt. Figure 12.6 shows the monopolist's demand curve as D and the resultant marginal revenue curve as MR. It does not matter at what rate of output this particular monopolist operates; total costs cannot be covered. Look at the position of the average total cost curve. It lies everywhere above D (the average revenue curve). Thus there is no price-output combination that will allow the monopolist even to cover costs, much less earn profits. This monopolist will, in the short run, suffer economic losses as shown by the shaded area. The graph in Figure 12.6 depicts a situation for millions of typical monopolies that exist; they are called inventions. The owner of a patented invention

Figure 12.6
Monopolies: Not Always Profitable

Some monopolists face the situation shown here. The average total cost curve, ATC, is everywhere above the average revenue, or demand, curve, D. In the short run, the monopolist will produce where MC = MR at point E. Output Q_m will be sold at price P_m, but cost per unit is C_1. Losses are the shaded rectangle. Eventually, the monopolist will go out of business.

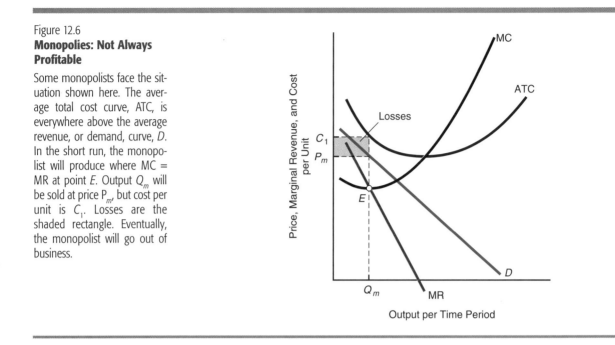

Try Preview Question 3:

What are some common misconceptions about monopolists?

or discovery has a pure legal monopoly, but the demand and cost curves may be such that production is not profitable. Every year at inventors' conventions, one can see many inventions that have never been put into production because they were deemed "uneconomic" by potential producers and users.

Concepts in Brief

- The basic difference between a monopolist and a perfect competitor is that a monopolist faces a downward-sloping demand curve, and therefore marginal revenue is less than price.
- The monopolist must choose the profit-maximizing price-output combination—the output at which marginal revenue equals marginal cost and the highest price possible as given by the demand curve for that particular output rate.
- Monopoly short-run profits are found by looking at average total costs compared to price per unit. This difference multiplied by quantity sold at that price determines monopoly profit.
- A monopolist does not necessarily earn a profit. If the average total cost curve lies entirely above the demand curve for a monopoly, production will not be profitable.

ON MAKING HIGHER PROFITS: PRICE DISCRIMINATION

In a perfectly competitive market, each buyer is charged the same price for every unit of the particular commodity (corrected for differential transportation charges). Because the product is homogeneous and we also assume full knowledge on the part of the buyers, a difference in price cannot exist. Any seller of the product who tried to charge a price higher than the going market price would find that no one would purchase it from that seller.

In this chapter we have assumed until now that the monopolist charged all consumers the same price for all units. A monopolist, however, may be able to charge different people different prices or different prices for successive units sought by a given buyer. When there is no cost difference, either one or a combination of these strategies is called **price discrimination.** A firm will engage in price discrimination whenever feasible to increase profits. A price-discriminating firm is able to charge some customers more than other customers.

Returning to Figure 12.4, you will note that our hypothetical monopolist earned $12.60 profit on the sale of 9 units of output. How would a firm that could price discriminate act differently?

A price-discriminating monopolist would, in the extreme, charge a different price for each unit of output according to the demand for his product. Thus it would sell the first unit for $7.75, the second for $7.50, the third for $7.25 and so on, until the price it could charge for the next unit of output just equalled the marginal cost of producing it. In our example, therefore, the price discriminator would sell 11 units of output, with the eleventh unit selling for $5.25, just equal to its marginal cost.

▶ **Price discrimination**

Selling a given product at more than one price, with the price difference being unrelated to differences in cost.

Figure 12.7
Additional Profits from Price Discriminating

The single-price monopoly will sell Q_s units of output for the price of P_s and will earn revenues equal to the shaded area P_sQ_s. The perfect price-discriminating monopolist will continue to sell output until MC is equal to demand, that is until Q_d units of output are sold. The perfect price discriminator will earn revenues equal to the shaded area plus the striped area. Hence, for any cost structure, the price discriminator will earn higher profits than the single-price monopoly.

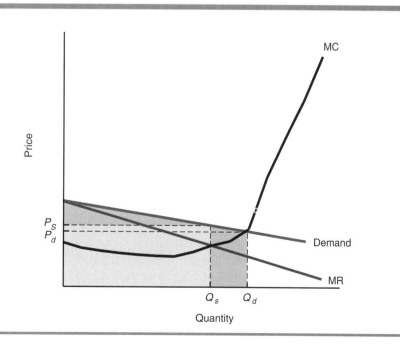

How much extra profit would it make? Total revenue would be $71.50—the sum of each of the prices charged for the eleven units sold ($7.75 + $7.50 + $7.25 + $7.00 + $6.75 + $6.50 + $6.25 + $6.00 + $5.75 + $5.50 + $5.25). Total cost would be unchanged at $48.55, and the resulting profit would be $22.95. Figure 12.7 reproduces Figure 12.4 and highlights the extra revenues which accrue to the price-discriminating monopolist.

It is interesting to note that a monopolist which can price discriminate will usually produce a greater amount of output than a single-price monopoly. In fact, if the monopolist can perfectly price discriminate as in the above example, it will produce where price equals marginal cost—the perfectly competitive output.

Most monopolies, however, cannot charge a separate price for each unit of output. Instead they sell blocks of output for different prices. For example, most electric utilities charge businesses less for electricity than they charge households. Airlines charge less for economy seats than for business-class seats.

We can also say that a uniform price does not necessarily indicate an absence of price discrimination. Charging all customers the same price when production costs vary by customer is actually a case of price discrimination.

Necessary Conditions for Price Discrimination

Four conditions are necessary for price discrimination to exist:

1. *The firm must face a downward-sloping demand curve.* In order to charge different consumers different prices, the firm must have some control over price setting.
2. *The firm must be able to separate markets at a reasonable cost.* The monopoly must be able to determine which consumers are willing to pay high prices and which are not in a relatively simple manner. If the cost of segregating the market is high, it will offset the extra profit gained from price discrimination.
3. *The buyers in the various markets must have different price elasticities of demand.* Buyers who are willing to pay high prices typically have fewer substitutes to choose from; hence their demand is relatively price inelastic. Consumers with more elastic demands usually are less willing to pay high prices for goods and services.
4. *The firm must be able to prevent resale of the product or service.* If the purchaser of the monopoly's product can resell it to a higher-price buyer, then the low-price purchaser, and not the firm, captures the profit that accrues from price discrimination.

For example, charging students a lower price than nonstudents for a movie can be done relatively easily. The cost of checking student IDs is apparently not significant. Also, it is fairly easy to make sure that students do not resell their tickets to nonstudents.

It must be made clear at the outset that charging different prices to different people or for different units that reflect differences in the cost of service to those particular people does not amount to price discrimination. This is **price differentiation:** differences in price that reflect differences in marginal cost.

▶ **Price differentiation**
Establishing different prices for similar products to reflect differences in marginal cost in providing those commodities to different groups of buyers.

INTERNATIONAL EXAMPLE
Fuji Film Price Discrimination

For years, Kodak argued that the Japanese film company, Fuji, was "dumping" its film in North America. In effect, Kodak was arguing that Fuji was price-discriminating. Because, according to Kodak, Fuji had effectively blocked Kodak from successfully competing in Japan, Fuji faced a less elastic demand for film in Japan than it did in North America, where Kodak dominated the market. Part (a) of Figure 12.8 shows the relatively inelastic demand curve, D_J, that Fuji faces domestically. In Canada and the United States, Fuji faces a relatively elastic demand curve, D_{NA}. For the sake of simplicity, marginal cost is assumed to be constant for Fuji. At profit maximization, marginal revenue must equal marginal cost. Here we have a common marginal cost, MC. There are two sets of marginal revenue curves, however—MR_J and MR_{NA}. For profit maximization, $MR_J = MR_{NA}$ = MC. (In essence, it is as if the Fuji film sold in Japan and in North America were two different goods having exactly the same marginal cost to produce.) The market for Fuji film in Japan is given in part (a) of Figure 12.8. MC = MR at Q_J, sold at price P_J. Buyers of Fuji film in Canada and the United States have a more elastic demand because of competition from Kodak. They ended up paying only P_{NA} for quantity Q_{NA}. P_{NA} is lower than P_J. (Since this analysis was completed, Kodak has been successful in having the courts force Fuji to raise its prices in North America.)

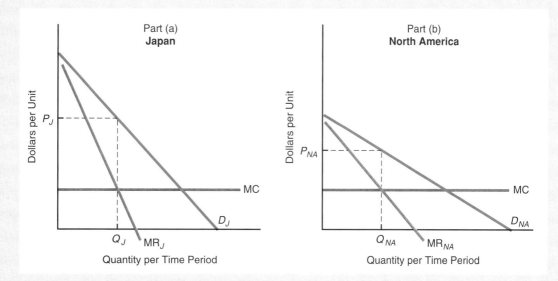

Figure 12.8   **Price Discrimination in Film by Fuji**
The Japanese film industry is protected from foreign competition and therefore faces a relatively inelastic demand curve, D_J, in part (a). In North America, as shown in part (b), the industry faces competition such that its demand curve, D_{NA}, is more elastic. (For simplicity, the marginal cost curve is assumed to be horizontal.) Profit maximization occurs in each market where MC = MR. In Japan, that is at Q_J, at which point film can be sold at a price of P_J. In North America, profit maximization occurs at Q_{NA}, at which point film can be sold at a price of P_{NA}. Prices charged in Japan for the same film are higher than prices charged in North America.

For critical analysis: Assuming that price discrimination was being undertaken by Fuji, who was benefiting?

THE SOCIAL COST OF MONOPOLIES

Let's run a little experiment. We will start with a purely competitive industry that has numerous firms, each unable to affect the price of its product. The supply curve of the industry is equal to the horizontal sum of the marginal cost curves of the individual producers above their respective minimum average variable costs. In part (a) of Figure 12.9, we show the market demand curve and the market supply curve in a perfectly competitive situation. The competitive price in equilibrium is equal to P_e, and the equilibrium quantity at that price is equal to Q_e. Each individual competitor faces a demand curve (not shown) that is coincident with the price line P_e. No individual supplier faces the market demand curve, D.

Figure 12.9
The Effects of Monopolizing an Industry

In part (a), we show a competitive situation in which equilibrium is established at the intersection of D and S at point E. The equilibrium price would be P_e, and the equilibrium quantity would be Q_e. Each individual competitive producer faces a demand curve that is a horizontal line at the market clearing price, P_e. What happens if the industry is suddenly monopolized? We assume that the costs stay the same; the only thing that changes is that the monopolist now faces the entire downward-sloping demand curve. In part (b), we draw the marginal revenue curve. Marginal cost is S because that is the horizontal summation of all the individual marginal cost curves. The monopolist therefore produces at Q_m and charges price P_m. P_m in part (b) is higher than P_e in part (a), and Q_m is less than Q_e. We see, then, that a monopolist charges a higher price and produces less than an industry in a competitive situation.

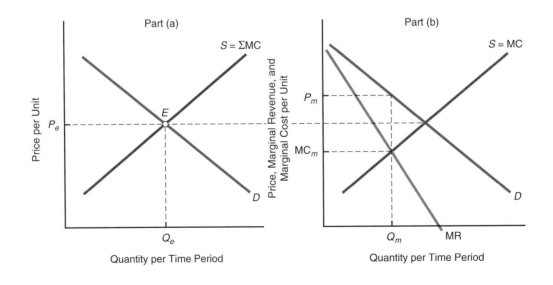

Now let's assume that a monopolist comes in and buys up every single competitor in the industry. In so doing, we'll assume that the monopolist does not affect any of the marginal cost curves or demand. We can therefore redraw D and S in part (b) of Figure 12.9, exactly the same as in part (a).

How does this monopolist decide how much to charge and how much to produce? If the monopolist is profit maximizing, it is going to look at the marginal revenue curve and produce at the output where marginal revenue equals marginal cost. But what is the marginal cost curve in part (b) of Figure 12.9? It is merely S because we said that S was equal to the horizontal summation of the portions of the individual marginal cost curves above each firm's respective minimum average variable cost. The monopolist therefore produces quantity Q_m and sells it at price P_m. Notice that Q_m is less than Q_e and that P_m is greater than P_e. A monopolist therefore produces a smaller quantity and sells it at a higher price. This is the reason usually given when economists criticize monopolists. Monopolists raise the price and restrict production, compared to a competitive situation. For a monopolist's product, consumers are forced to pay a price that exceeds the marginal cost of production. Resources are misallocated in such a situation—too few resources are being used in the monopolist's industry, and too many are used elsewhere.

Notice from Figure 12.9 that by setting MR = MC, the monopolist produces at a rate of output where P > MC (compare P_m to MC). The marginal cost of a commodity (MC) represents what society had to give up in order to obtain the last unit produced. Price, by contrast, represents what buyers are willing to pay to acquire that last unit. Thus the price of a good represents society's valuation of the last unit produced. The monopoly outcome of P > MC means that the value to society of the last unit produced is greater than its cost (MC); hence not enough of the good is being produced. As we have pointed out before, these differences between monopoly and competition arise not because of differences in costs, but rather because of differences in the demand curves the individual firms face. The monopolist has monopoly power because it faces a downward-sloping demand curve. The individual perfect competitor faces a perfectly elastic demand curve.

Before we leave the topic of the cost to society of monopolies, we must repeat that our analysis is based on an heroic assumption. That assumption is that the monopolization of the perfectly competitive industry does not change the cost structure. If monopolization results in higher marginal cost, the cost to society is even greater. Conversely, if monopolization results in cost savings, the cost, if any, to society is less than we infer from our analysis. Indeed, we could have presented a hypothetical example in which monopolization led to such a dramatic reduction in average cost that society actually benefited. Such a situation is a possibility in industries in which economies of scale exist for a very great range of outputs.

Try Preview Question 4:

What is the cost to society of monopoly?

Concepts in Brief

- Four conditions are necessary for price discrimination: (1) The firm must face a downward-sloping demand curve, (2) the firm must be able to distinguish markets, (3) buyers in different markets must have different price elasticities of demand, and (4) resale of the product or service must be preventable.
- A monopolist can make higher profits if it can price discriminate. Price discrimination requires that two or more identifiable classes of buyers exist whose price elasticities of demand for the product or service are different and that these two classes of buyers can be distinguished at little cost.
- Price differentiation should not be confused with price discrimination. The former occurs when differences in price reflect differences in marginal cost.
- Monopoly results in a lower quantity being sold because the price is higher than it would be in an ideal perfectly competitive industry in which the cost curves were essentially the same as the monopolist's.

Issues and Applications

The Right to Develop Drugs Based on Genetic Data

Concepts Applied: Market power, price searcher, monopoly

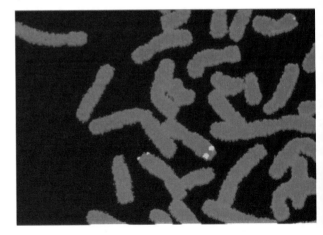

The pharmaceutical company SmithKline Beecham, through a research pact with Human Genome Sciences, Inc., claims to have isolated almost 50,000 human genes. Roche Holding of Switzerland and Glaxo Holdings of the United Kingdom have formed similar alliances, but none has been as successful as SmithKline. The question for each company is whether it should use its successful gene discoveries in developing its own drugs, or sell or license the genetic sequences to other drug companies.

The pharmaceutical company SmithKline Beecham has a monopoly over much of the information about the genes in human chromosomes. SmithKline recoups its huge investment in gene research by licensing the information to other companies.

The Controversy

Because the area in question relates to health care, there is controversy. Does not SmithKline owe to humanity the valuable information it has? A few years ago, academic researchers called on SmithKline to make public its information on the molecular arrangement of a gene. The molecular sequence is the "biological blueprint" of a gene. Knowledge of it allows a company to make a drug that will enhance or block the gene's functioning in order to treat a disease. Researchers have already learned the molecular sequence for the gene that causes breast cancer, the gene that causes obesity, and the gene that causes type II (non-insulin-dependent) diabetes.

Monopoly Returns Needed

According to George Poste, SmithKline's research director, his company is not about to publish the initial information on the molecular arrangement of a gene. "The more people who get access to sequence data, the greater the number of competitors we have." After all, SmithKline paid US$125 million for its association with Human Genome, Inc. SmithKline wants to make at least a normal rate of return on that investment.

The New Market in Genes

SmithKline decided to sell the rights to genes rather than exploit the new information itself in the form of new drugs. The firm decided that even large pharmaceutical companies can handle only a small percentage of the genetic data that are available. SmithKline believes that it can earn higher profits by obtaining licensing royalties on the new drugs based on its genetic discoveries than by developing them itself. Presumably, it charges higher than its marginal cost at all times. After all, it is in a classic monopoly position. It owns the rights to the genetic data. If it were to charge marginal cost, that would be effectively zero. That is the nature of many discoveries today. There are huge initial costs for the first unit but zero marginal costs for each additional unit. SmithKline could pass on genetic data over the Internet essentially free, if it chose to do so.

For Critical Analysis

1. Is it "bad" for the economy that SmithKline is not charging a price equal to marginal cost for its genetic data discoveries?

2. Does SmithKline have a pure monopoly with respect to genetic data?

CHAPTER SUMMARY

1. We formally define a monopolist as the single supplier of a product or service with no close substitute. A monopolist faces the entire industry demand curve because the monopolist *is* the industry. Pure monopolists are rare.

2. A monopolist can usually remain a monopolist only if other firms are prevented from entering the industry and sharing in the monopoly profits. One barrier to entry is government restrictions. Patents are another.

3. A monopoly could arise because of firm economies of scale, which are defined as a situation in which an increase in output leads to a more than proportionate decrease in average

total costs. If this were the case, average total costs would be falling as production increased. The first company to produce a great deal and take advantage of firm economies of scale could conceivably lower price and drive everyone else out of the industry. This would be a natural monopolist.

4. Health and quality regulations can be a barrier to entry because the increased fixed costs put smaller firms at a competitive disadvantage.

5. The marginal revenue that a monopolist receives is defined in the same way as the marginal revenue that a competitor receives. Nevertheless, because the monopolist faces the industry

demand curve, it must lower price to increase sales, not only on the last unit sold, but also on all the preceding units. The monopolist's marginal revenue is therefore equal to the price received on the last unit sold minus the reduction in price on all the previous units times the number of previous units sold.

6. The profit-maximizing price that the monopolist charges is the maximum price that it can get away with while still selling everything produced up to the point where marginal revenue equals marginal cost. We find this price by extending a vertical line from the intersection of the marginal revenue curve and the marginal cost curve up to the demand curve and then over to the vertical axis, which measures price.

7. Total profits are total revenues minus total costs. Total revenues are equal to the price of the product (the profit-maximizing price) times the quantity produced (the quantity found at the intersection of the marginal revenue and marginal cost curves). Total costs are equal to the quantity produced times average total costs. The difference between these total costs and total revenues is profits.

8. It can be shown that a competitive industry, if monopolized, will end up charging a higher price for its product but supplying a lower quantity of it. That is why monopolies are considered "bad" in an economic analysis. The monopolist will restrict production and increase price.

9. If a monopolist can effectively separate demanders into groups according to their demand elasticities, it can become a price-discriminating monopolist. (Resale between groups that were charged different prices must be prevented.) Price discrimination should not be confused with price differentiation, which occurs when differences in price reflect differences in marginal cost.

10. Four conditions are necessary for price discrimination to exist: (1) The firm must face a downward-sloping demand curve, (2) the firm must be able to distinguish markets, (3) buyers in different markets must have different price elasticities of demand, and (4) the firm must be able to prevent resale of the product.

11. Monopoly involves costs to society because the higher price leads to a reduction in output and consumption of the monopolized good.

DISCUSSION OF PREVIEW QUESTIONS

1. **For the monopolist, marginal revenue is less than selling price. Why?**

   In the perfectly competitive model, the firm's selling price equals its marginal revenue (MR) because the firm can sell all it wants to sell at the going market price. This is not the case for the monopolist, which, as the sole supplier, faces the (downward-sloping) demand curve for the product. Thus the monopolist can sell more only by lowering price on all units sold per time period, assuming that it can't discriminate on price. Thus the monopolist's marginal revenue will equal price (which it gains from selling one more unit) *minus* the revenue that it loses from selling previously produced units at a lower price.

2. **What is the profit-maximizing rate of output for the monopolist?**

   A monopolist will produce up to the point where marginal cost (MC) equals marginal revenue (MR). For example, if the output rate for the monopolist at which MR = MC is 80,000 units per week and MR is falling while MC is rising, any output beyond 80,000 units will have MC > MR; to produce units beyond 80,000 units will lower total profits. To produce at a rate less than

80,000 units per week would mean that not all the outputs at which MR > MC will be produced; hence total profits would not be maximized. Total profits are maximized at the output rate where MR = MC because all outputs for which MR > MC will be produced.

3. **What are some common misconceptions about monopolists?**

Many people think that a monopolist charges the highest price possible. This is untrue; the monopolist tries to maximize *total profits*, not price. The monopolist produces where MR = MC and *then* charges the highest price consistent with that output rate. Note that a monopolist can't charge any price *and* sell any amount; it must choose a price and have the amount that it can sell be determined by the demand curve, or it must choose an output rate (where MR = MC) and have selling price determined where that quantity intersects the demand curve. Another common misconception is that a monopolist must earn economic profits. This is not the case. To take an extreme example, if the monopolist's average cost curve lies above the demand curve, the monopolist will be suffering economic losses.

4. **What is the cost to society of monopoly?**

Because barriers to entry exist under monopoly, a monopolist could theoretically earn economic profits in the long run. Because profits are a signal that society wants more resources in that area, a misallocation of resources could exist; not enough resources flow to production of the monopolized commodity. Also, because the monopolist's selling price (P) exceeds its marginal revenue (MR) and the profit-maximizing output rate is where MR = MC (marginal cost), P > MR = MC, or simply P > MC (unlike under the perfectly competitive market structure, where P = MC). The marginal cost of the commodity reflects what society had to give up in order to get the last unit produced, and price is what buyers have to pay in order to get it. Because P > MC under monopoly, buyers must pay *more* to get this commodity than they must give up in order to get it; hence not enough of this commodity is produced. In short, under monopoly, price is higher and output is less than under perfect competition.

PROBLEMS

(Answers to the odd-numbered problems appear at the back of the book.)

12-1. Use the graph to answer the questions.

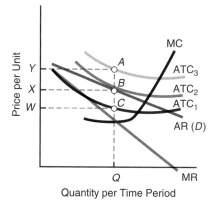

Quantity per Time Period

a. Suppose that a monopolist faces ATC_1. Define the rectangle that shows the monopolist's total costs at output rate Q. Also define the rectangle showing total revenue. Is the monopolist showing an economic loss, break-even (normal profit), or an economic profit? What is the significance of the MC = MR output?

b. Suppose that the monopolist faces ATC_2. Define the rectangle that shows the monopolist's total costs at output rate Q. Also define the rectangle showing total revenue. Is the monopolist showing an economic loss, break-even (normal profit), or an economic profit?

What is the significance of the MC = MR output?

c. Suppose that the monopolist faces ATC_3. Define the rectangle that shows the monopolist's total costs at output rate Q. Also define the rectangle showing total revenue. Is the monopolist showing an economic loss, break-even (normal profit), or an economic profit? What is the significance of the MC = MR output?

12-2. Suppose that a monopolist faces the following demand schedule. Compute marginal revenue.

Price	Quantity Demanded	Marginal Revenue
$1,000	1	$ _____
920	2	$ _____
840	3	$ _____
760	4	$ _____
680	5	$ _____
600	6	$ _____
520	7	$ _____
440	8	$ _____
350	9	$ _____
260	10	$ _____

12-3. State the necessary conditions for price discrimination. Then discuss how they might apply to the medical services of a doctor.

12-4. In the text, we indicated that a monopolist will produce at the rate of output at which MR = MC and will then charge the highest price consistent with that output level. What conditions would exist if the monopolist charged a lower price? A higher price?

12-5. Summarize the relationship between price elasticity of demand and marginal revenue.

12-6. Explain why a monopolist will never set a price (and produce the corresponding output) at which the demand is price-inelastic.

12-7. Examine the revenue and cost figures for a monopoly firm in the following table.
a. Fill in the empty columns.
b. At what rate(s) of output would the firm operate at a loss?
c. At what rate(s) of output would the firm break even?
d. At what rate(s) of output would the firm be maximizing its profits, and what would those profits be?

Price	Quantity Demanded	Total Revenue	Marginal Revenue	Total Cost	Marginal Cost	Profit or Loss
$20	0	$ _____	$ _____	$ 4	$ _____	$ _____
16	1	_____	_____	10	_____	_____
12	2	_____	_____	14	_____	_____
10	3	_____	_____	20	_____	_____
7	4	_____	_____	28	_____	_____
4	5	_____	_____	40	_____	_____
0	6	_____	_____	54	_____	_____

12-8. Answer the questions based on the accompanying graph for a monopolist.

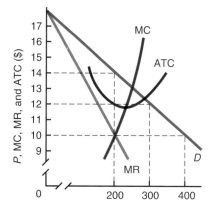

a. If this firm is a profit maximizer, how much output will it produce?

b. At what price will the firm sell its output?

c. How much profit or loss will this firm realize?

d. ATC is at its minimum at what cost per unit?

12-9. Examine this information for a monopoly product.

Price	Quantity
$10.00	1,000
8.00	2,000
6.00	3,000
4.00	4,000
2.00	5,000
0.50	6,000

a. Calculate total revenue.

b. Calculate marginal revenue.

c. What is the maximum output that the producer of this product would ever produce?

d. Why would this firm never produce more than the output amount in part (c)?

12-10. Suppose that a single-price monopolist and a comparable perfectly competitive industry experience a cost increase that causes average and marginal cost curves to shift upward by 10 percent. Will the resulting increase in market price be greater or less for the monopolist than for the perfectly competitive industry?

13

Monopolistic Competition, Oligopoly, and Strategic Behaviour

For most of this century, two firms have dominated the Canadian market for beer—John Labatt Ltd. and Molson Brewing Co. Ltd. Industry observers estimate that 45 to 50 percent of Canadians drink a Labatt's Blue at least once a year. Molson's Canadian brand itself likely holds an 11 percent market share. Beginning in 1984, however, small breweries, called "microbreweries," began opening up, challenging the "big two" with high quality "craft" beers. Labatt and Molson appear to have decided not to fight the entry of these competitors. To understand this strategic behaviour, you need to learn more about markets that are not perfectly competitive, but at the same time are not pure monopolies.

Preview Questions

1. What are the characteristics of the monopolistically competitive market structure?

2. How does the monopolistic competitor determine the equilibrium price-output combination?

3. How does the monopolistically competitive market structure differ from that of perfect competition?

4. What are the characteristics of the oligopolistic market structure?

Did You Know That... the so-called father of the modern department store, John Wanamaker, once said, "Half the money I spend on advertising is wasted. The trouble is, I don't know which half"? Obviously, Canadian businesses do not know either, for they continue to advertise more each year. Total annual advertising expenditures in Canada amount to billions of dollars. The number of ads popping up on the Internet's World Wide Web shows that Canadian businesses will leave no stone unturned in their quest to let people know about their existence, what they have to sell, how they sell it, where it can be bought, and at what price.

Advertising did not show up in our analysis of perfect competition. Nonetheless, it plays a large role in industries that cannot be described as perfectly competitive but cannot be described as pure monopolies either. A combination of consumers' preferences for variety, and competition among producers has led to similar but differentiated products in the marketplace. This situation has been described as monopolistic competition, the subject of the first part of this chapter. In the second part of the chapter, we look at how firms that are neither perfect competitors nor pure monopolists make strategic decisions. Such decisions do not exist for pure monopolists, who do not have to worry about actual competitors. And clearly, perfect competitors cannot make any strategic decisions, for they must take the market price as given. We call firms that have the ability to make strategic decisions oligopolies, which we will define more formally later in this chapter.

MONOPOLISTIC COMPETITION

In the 1920s and 1930s, economists became increasingly aware that there were many industries for which both the perfectly competitive model and the pure monopoly model did not apply and did not seem to yield very accurate predictions. Theoretical and empirical research was instituted to develop some sort of middle ground. Two separately developed models of **monopolistic competition** resulted. American economist Edward Chamberlin published *The Theory of Monopolistic Competition* in 1933. The same year, Britain's Joan Robinson published *The Economics of Imperfect Competition*. In this chapter we will outline the theory as presented by Chamberlin. Chamberlin defined monopolistic competition as a market structure in which there is a relatively large number of producers offering similar but differentiated products.

> **Monopolistic competition**
> A market situation in which a large number of firms produce similar but not identical products. Entry into the industry is relatively easy.

Monopolistic competition therefore has the following features:

1. Significant numbers of sellers in a highly competitive market
2. Differentiated products
3. Sales promotion and advertising
4. Easy entry of new firms in the long run

Even a cursory look at the Canadian economy leads to the conclusion that monopolistic competition is the dominant form of market structure in Canada. Indeed, that is true of all developed economies.

Number of Firms

In a perfectly competitive situation, there is an extremely large number of firms; in pure monopoly, there is only one. In monopolistic competition, there is a large number of firms, but not as many as in perfect competition. This fact has several important implications for a monopolistically competitive industry.

1. *Small share of market.* With so many firms, each firm has a relatively small share of the total market. Thus it has only a very small amount of control over the market clearing price.
2. *Lack of collusion.* With so many firms, it is very difficult for all of them to get together to collude—to cooperate in setting a pure monopoly price (and output). Price rigging in a monopolistically competitive industry is virtually impossible. Also, barriers to entry are minor, and the flow of new firms into the industry makes collusive agreements less likely. The large number of firms makes the monitoring and detection of cheating very costly and extremely difficult. This difficulty is compounded by differentiated products and high rates of innovation; collusive agreements are easier for a homogeneous product than for heterogeneous ones.
3. *Independence.* Because there are so many firms, each one acts independently of the others. No firm attempts to take into account the reaction of all of its rival firms—that would be impossible with so many rivals. Rivals' reactions to output and price changes are largely ignored.

Product Differentiation

▶ **Product differentiation**
The distinguishing of products by brand name, colour, and other minor attributes. Product differentiation occurs in other than perfectly competitive markets in which products are, in theory, homogeneous, such as wheat or corn.

Perhaps the most important feature of the monopolistically competitive market is **product differentiation**. We can say that each individual manufacturer of a product has an absolute monopoly over its own product, which is slightly differentiated from other similar products. This means that the firm has some control over the price it charges. Unlike the perfectly competitive firm, it faces a downward-sloping demand curve.

Consider the abundance of brand names for toothpaste, soap, gasoline, vitamins, shampoo, and most other consumer goods, as well as for a great many services. We are not obliged to buy just one type of television set, just one type of jeans, or just one type of footwear. There are usually a number of similar but differentiated products from which to choose. One reason is that the greater a firm's success at product differentiation, the greater the firm's pricing options.

Each separate differentiated product has numerous similar substitutes. This clearly has an impact on the price elasticity of demand for the individual firm. Recall that one determinant of price elasticity of demand is the availability of substitutes. The greater the number of substitutes available, other things being equal, the greater the price elasticity of demand. If the consumer has a vast array of alternatives that are just about as good as the product under study, a relatively small increase in the price of that product will lead many consumers to switch to one of the many close substitutes. Thus the ability of a firm to raise the price above the price of close substitutes is very small. The result of this is that even though the demand curve slopes downward, it does so only slightly. In other words, it is relatively elastic (over that price range) compared to a monopolist's demand curve. In the extreme case, with perfect competition, the substitutes are perfect because we are dealing with only one particular undifferentiated product. In that case, the individual firm has a perfectly elastic demand curve.

Ease of Entry

For any current monopolistic competitor, potential competition is always lurking in the background. The easier—that is, the less costly—entry is, the more a current monopolistic competitor must worry about losing business.

A good example of a monopolistically competitive industry is the computer software industry. Many small firms provide different programs for many applications. The fixed capital costs required to enter this industry are small; all you need are skilled programmers. In addition, there are few legal restrictions. The firms in this industry also engage in extensive advertising in over 150 computer publications.

Sales Promotion and Advertising

Monopolistic competition differs from perfect competition in that no individual firm in a perfectly competitive market will advertise. A perfectly competitive firm, by definition, can sell all that it wants to sell at the going market price anyway. Why, then, would it spend even one cent on advertising? Furthermore, by definition, the perfect competitor is selling a product that is identical to the product that all other firms in the industry are selling. Any advertisement that induces consumers to buy more of that product will, in effect, be helping all the competitors, too. A perfect competitor therefore cannot be expected to incur any advertising costs (except for all firms in an industry collectively agreeing to advertise to urge the public to buy more pork or drink more milk).

But because the monopolistic competitor has at least some monopoly power, advertising may result in increased profits. Advertising is used to increase demand and to differentiate one's product. How much advertising should be undertaken? It should be carried to the point at which the additional revenue from one more dollar of advertising just equals that one dollar of marginal cost.

Advertising as Signalling Behaviour.   Recall from Chapter 11 that signals are compact gestures or actions that convey information. For example, high profits in an industry are signals that resources should flow to that industry. Individual companies can explicitly engage in signalling behaviour. They do so by establishing brand names or trademarks, and then promoting them heavily. This is a signal to prospective consumers that this is a company that plans to stay in business. Before the modern age of advertising, banks faced a problem of signalling their soundness. They chose to do this by constructing large, imposing, granite and marble buildings.

Stone communicated permanence. The effect was to give the bank's customers confidence that they were not doing business with a fly-by-night operation.

When IBM extensively advertises its brand name, it incurs substantial costs. The only way it can recoup those costs is by selling lots of computers over a long period of time. Thus heavy advertising of its brand name is a signal to personal computer buyers that IBM is interested in each customer's repeat business.

But what about advertising that does not seem to convey any information, not even about price? What good is an advertisement for, say, Toyota, that simply states, "Oh what a feeling—Toyota"?

Try Preview Question 1:

What are the characteristics of the monopolistically competitive market structure?

EXAMPLE   Can Advertising Lead to Efficiency?

Advertising budgets by major retailers may just seem like an added expense, not a step on the road to economic efficiency. According to research by economists Kyle Bagwell and Garey Ramey, just the opposite is true. When retailers advertise heavily, they increase the number of shoppers that come to their store. Such increased traffic allows retailers to offer a wider selection of goods, to invest in cost-reduction technology (such as computerized inventory and satellite communications), and to exploit manufacturers' quantity discounts. Such cost reductions can help explain the success of Zellers, Canadian Tire, and Home Depot. Consequently, Bagwell and Ramey conclude that advertising can help promote efficiency even if it provides no "hard" information. Advertising signals to consumers where they can find big-company, low-priced, high-variety stores.

For critical analysis: Which is true: "We are bigger because we are better" or "We are better because we are bigger"?

Concepts in Brief

- Monopolistic competition is a market structure that lies between pure monopoly and perfect competition.
- A monopolistically competitive market structure has (1) a large number of sellers, (2) differentiated products, (3) advertising, and (4) easy entry of firms in the long run.
- Because of the large number of firms, each has a small share of the market, making collusion difficult; the firms are independent.

PRICE AND OUTPUT FOR THE MONOPOLISTIC COMPETITOR

Now that we are aware of the assumptions underlying the monopolistic competition model, we can analyse the price and output behaviour of each firm in a monopolistically competitive industry. We assume in the analysis that follows that the desired product type and quality have been chosen. We further assume that the budget and the type of promotional activity have already been chosen and do not change.

The Individual Firm's Demand and Cost Curves

Because the individual firm is not a perfect competitor, its demand curve slopes downward, as is shown in all three parts of Figure 13.1. Hence it faces a marginal revenue curve that is also downward-sloping and below the demand curve. To find the profit-maximizing rate of output and the profit-maximizing price, we go to the

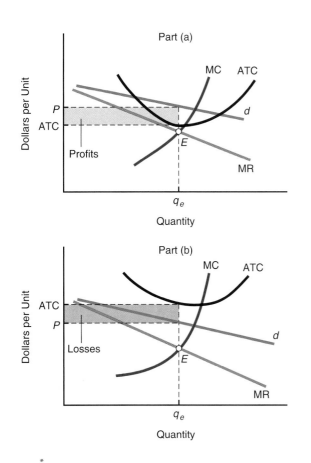

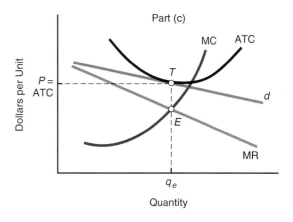

Figure 13.1

Short-Run and Long-Run Equilibrium with Monopolistic Competition

In part (a), the typical monopolistic competitor is shown making economic profits. If that were the situation, there would be entry into the industry, forcing the demand curve for the individual monopolistic competitor leftward. Eventually, firms would find themselves in the situation depicted in part (c), where zero economic profits are being made. In part (b), the typical firm is in a monopolistically competitive industry making economic losses. If that were the case, firms would leave the industry. Each remaining firm's demand curve would shift outward to the right. Eventually, the typical firm would find itself in the situation depicted in part (c).

output where the marginal cost curve intersects the marginal revenue curve from below. That gives us the profit-maximizing output rate. Then we draw a vertical line up to the demand curve. That gives us the price that can be charged to sell exactly that quantity produced. This is what we have done in Figure 13.1. In each part, a marginal cost curve intersects the marginal revenue curve at E. The profit-maximizing rate of output is q_e, and the profit-maximizing price is P.

Short-Run Equilibrium

In the short run, it is possible for a monopolistic competitor to make economic profits—profits over and above the normal rate of return or beyond what is necessary to keep that firm in that industry. We show such a situation in part (a) of Figure 13.1. The average total cost curve is drawn in below the demand curve, d, at the profit-maximizing rate of output, q_e. Economic profits are shown by the shaded rectangle in that part.

Losses in the short run are clearly also possible. They are presented in part (b) of Figure 13.1. Here the average total cost curve lies everywhere above the individual firm's demand curve, d. The losses are marked as the shaded rectangle.

Just as with any market structure or any firm, in the short run it is possible to observe either economic profits or economic losses. (In the long run such is not the case with monopolistic competition, however.) In either case, the price does not equal marginal cost but rather is above it. Therefore, there is some misallocation of resources, a topic that we will discuss later in this chapter.

The Long Run: Zero Economic Profits

The long run is where the similarity between perfect competition and monopolistic competition becomes more obvious. In the long run, because so many firms produce substitutes for the product in question, any economic profits will disappear with competition. They will be reduced to zero—either through the entry of new firms that see a chance to make a higher rate of return than elsewhere, or by changes in the product quality and advertising outlays of existing firms in the industry. (Profitable products will be imitated by other firms.) As for economic losses in the short run, they will disappear in the long run because the firms that suffer them will leave the industry. They will go into another business where the expected rate of return is at least normal. Parts (a) and (b) of Figure 13.1 therefore represent only short-run situations for a monopolistically competitive firm. In the long run, the average total cost curve will just touch the individual firm's demand curve d at the particular price that is profit-maximizing for that particular firm. This is shown in part (c) of Figure 13.1.

A word of warning: This is an idealized, long-run equilibrium situation for each firm in the industry. It does not mean that even in the long run we will observe every single firm in a monopolistically competitive industry making exactly zero economic profits or just a normal rate of return. We live in a dynamic world. All we are saying is that if this model is correct, the rate of return will tend towards normal—economic profits will tend towards zero.

Try Preview Question 2:

How does the monopolistic competitor determine the equilibrium price-output combination?

COMPARING PERFECT COMPETITION WITH MONOPOLISTIC COMPETITION

If both the monopolistic competitor and the perfect competitor make zero economic profits in the long run, how are they different? The answer lies in the fact that the demand curve for the individual perfect competitor is perfectly elastic. Such is not the case for the individual monopolistic competitor; its demand curve is less than perfectly elastic. This firm has some control over price. Price elasticity of demand is not infinite.

We see the two situations in Figure 13.2. Both parts show average total costs just touching the respective demand curves at the particular price at which the firm is selling the product. Notice, however, that the perfect competitor's average total costs are at a minimum. This is not the case with the monopolistic competitor. The equilibrium rate of output is to the left of the minimum point on the average total cost curve where price is greater than marginal cost. The monopolistic competitor cannot expand output to the point of minimum cost without lowering price, and then marginal cost would exceed marginal revenue. A monopolistic competitor at profit

---

Figure 13.2
Comparison of the Perfect Competitor with the Monopolistic Competitor

In part (a), the perfectly competitive firm has zero economic profits in the long run. The price is set equal to marginal cost, and the price is P_1. The firm's demand curve is just tangent to the minimum point on its average total cost curve, which means that the firm is operating at an optimum rate of production. With the monopolistically competitive firm

in part (b), there are also zero economic profits in the long run. The price is greater than marginal cost; the monopolistically competitive firm does not find itself at the minimum point on its average total cost curve. It is operating at a rate of output to the left of the minimum point on the ATC curve.

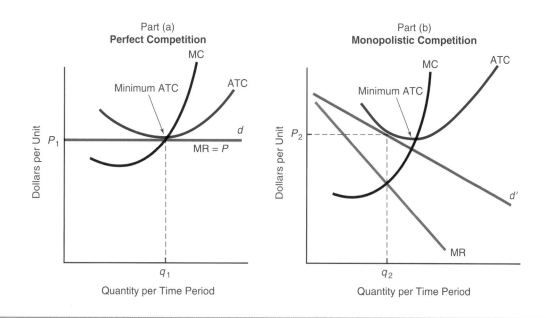

maximization charges a price that exceeds marginal cost. In this respect it is similar to the monopolist.

It has consequently been argued that monopolistic competition involves waste because minimum average total costs are not achieved and price exceeds marginal cost. There are too many firms, each with excess capacity, producing too little output. According to critics of monopolistic competition, society's resources are being wasted.

Chamberlin had an answer to this criticism. He contended that the difference between the average cost of production for a monopolistically competitive firm in an open market and the minimum average total cost represented what he called the cost of producing "differentness." Chamberlin did not consider this difference in cost between perfect competition and monopolistic competition a waste. In fact, he argued that it is rational for consumers to have a taste for differentiation; consumers willingly accept the resultant increased production costs in return for choice and variety of output.

Try Preview Question 3:
How does the monopolistically competitive market structure differ from that of perfect competition?

Concepts in Brief

- In the short run, it is possible for monopolistically competitive firms to make economic profits or economic losses.
- In the long run, monopolistically competitive firms will make zero economic profits—that is, they will make a normal rate of return.
- Because the monopolistic competitor faces a downward-sloping demand curve, it does not produce at the minimum point on its average total cost curve. Hence we say that a monopolistic competitor has higher average total costs per unit than a perfect competitor would have.
- Chamberlin argued that the difference between the average cost of production for a monopolistically competitive firm and the minimum average total cost at which a competitive firm would produce is the cost of producing "differentness."

OLIGOPOLY

There is another important market structure that we have yet to discuss. It involves a situation in which a few large firms dominate an entire industry. They are not competitive in the sense that we have used the term; they are not even monopolistically competitive. And because there are several of them, a pure monopoly does not exist. We call such a situation an **oligopoly**, which consists of a small number of interdependent sellers. Each firm in the industry knows that other firms will react to its changes in prices, quantities, and qualities. An oligopoly market structure can exist for either a homogeneous or a differentiated product.

▶ **Oligopoly**
A market situation in which there are very few sellers. Each seller knows that the other sellers will react to its changes in prices and quantities.

Characteristics of Oligopoly

Oligopoly is characterized by the small number of interdependent firms that constitute the entire market.

Small Number of Firms. How many is "a small number of firms"? More than two but less than 100? The question is not easy to answer. Basically, though, oligopoly exists when a handful of firms dominate the industry enough to set prices. The top few firms in the industry account for an overwhelming percentage of total industry output.

Oligopolies usually involve three to five big companies dominating the industry. The Canadian banking industry is dominated by five large firms: the Royal Bank, the Toronto-Dominion Bank, the Canadian Imperial Bank of Commerce, the Bank of Montreal, and the Bank of Nova Scotia. From World War II until the 1970s, the automobile industry was dominated by three large firms: General Motors, Chrysler, and Ford.

Interdependence. All markets and all firms are, in a sense, interdependent. But only when a few large firms dominate an industry does the question arise of **strategic dependence** of one on the others' actions. The firms must recognize that they are interdependent. Any action on the part of one firm with respect to output, price, quality, or product differentiation will cause a reaction on the part of other firms. A model of such mutual interdependence is difficult to build, but examples are not hard to find in the real world. Oligopolists in the supermarket industry, for example, are constantly reacting to each other.

▶ **Strategic dependence**
A situation in which one firm's actions with respect to price, quality, advertising, and related changes may be strategically countered by the reactions of one or more other firms in the industry. Such dependence can exist only when there are a limited number of major firms in an industry.

Recall that in the model of perfect competition, each firm ignores the reactions of other firms because each is able to sell all that it wants at the going market price. At the other extreme, the pure monopolist does not have to worry about the reaction of current rivals because there are none. In an oligopolistic market structure, the managers of firms are like generals in a war: They must attempt to predict the reaction of rival firms. It is a strategic game.

| **Thinking Critically About the Media** | **The "Big Three"** |

Media references to the automobile industry often make mention of the "Big Three," referring to Ford, General Motors, and Chrysler. Historically, the "Big Three" have accounted for about 90 percent of the value of total domestic sales of motor vehicles. Thus it would seem that the automobile market is a classic case of an oligopoly. Thirty years ago that was true; today it is not. The "Big Three" can no longer concern themselves merely with one another's reactions; they now have to worry about Toyota, Nissan, BMW, and a dozen other foreign competitors. Imports now account for almost 30 percent of total new car sales in Canada. The "Big Three" would love to be pure oligopolists in the Canadian market again, but increasing world trade has made that impossible.

Why Oligopoly Occurs

Why are some industries dominated by a few large firms? What causes an industry that might otherwise be competitive to tend towards oligopoly? We can provide some partial answers here.

Economies of Scale. Perhaps the strongest reason that has been offered for the existence of oligopoly is economies of scale. Recall that economies of scale are defined as a situation in which a doubling of output results in less than a doubling of total costs. When economies of scale exist, the firm's average total cost curve will slope downward as the firm produces more and more output. Average total cost can be reduced by continuing to expand the scale of operation. Smaller firms in such a situation will have a tendency to be inefficient. Their average total costs will be greater than those incurred by a large firm. Little by little, they will go out of business or be absorbed into the larger firm.

Barriers to Entry. It is possible that certain barriers to entry have prevented more competition in oligopolistic industries. They include legal barriers, such as patents, and control and ownership over critical supplies. Indeed, we can find periods in the past when firms maintained market power because they were able not only to erect a barrier to entry but also to keep it in place year after year. In principle, the chemical, electronics, and aluminum industries have been at one time or another either monopolistic or oligopolistic because of the ownership of patents and the control of strategic inputs by specific firms.

Oligopoly by Merger. Another reason that oligopolistic market structures may sometimes develop is that firms merge. A merger is the joining of two or more firms under single ownership or control. The merged firm naturally becomes larger, enjoys greater economies of scale as output increases, and may ultimately have a greater ability to control the market price for its product.

There are three types of mergers: horizontal, vertical, and conglomerate. A **horizontal merger** involves firms selling a similar product. If two shoe manufacturing firms merge, that is a horizontal merger. If a group of firms, all producing steel, merge into one, that is also a horizontal merger. A **vertical merger** occurs when one firm merges with either a firm from which it purchases an input or a firm to which it sells its output. Vertical mergers occur, for example, when a coal-using electrical utility purchases a coal-mining firm, or when a shoe manufacturer purchases retail shoe outlets. A **conglomerate merger** happens when two firms in unrelated industries merge. If an automobile manufacturer purchases a chain of restaurants, the result is a conglomerate merger. (Obviously, vertical and conglomerate mergers cannot create an oligopoly as we have defined it.)

We have been talking about oligopoly in a theoretical manner until now. It is time to look at the actual picture of oligopolies in Canada.

Measuring Industry Concentration

As we have stated, oligopoly is a situation in which a few interdependent firms control a large part of total output in an industry. This has been called industry concentration. Before we show the concentration statistics in Canada, let's determine how industry concentration can be measured.

▶ **Horizontal merger**
The joining of firms that are producing or selling a similar product.

▶ **Vertical merger**
The joining of a firm with another to which it sells an output or from which it buys an input.

▶ **Conglomerate merger**
The joining of two firms from unrelated industries.

Table 13.1
Computing the Four-Firm Concentration Ratio

Firm	Annual Sales ($ millions)	
1	150 ⎫	
2	100 ⎬ = 400	Total number of firms in industry = 25
3	80 ⎪	
4	70 ⎭	
5 through 25	50	
Total	450	

Four-firm concentration ratio $= \dfrac{400}{450} = 88.9\%$

▶ **Concentration ratio**
The percentage of all sales contributed by the leading four or leading eight firms in an industry; sometimes called the *industry concentration ratio.*

Concentration Ratio. The most popular way to compute industry concentration is to determine the percentage of total sales or production accounted for by the top four or top eight firms in an industry. This gives the four- or eight-firm **concentration ratio**. An example of an industry with 25 firms is given in Table 13.1. We can see in that table that the four largest firms account for almost 90 percent of total output in the hypothetical industry. That is an example of an oligopoly.

Table 13.2
Four-Firm Domestic Concentration Ratios for Selected Canadian Industries

Industry	Percentage of Value of Total Domestic Shipments Accounted for by the Top Four Firms
Tobacco products	99
Beer	93
Petroleum and coal products	75
Storage	72
Non-alcoholic beverages	69
Transportation equipment	68
Communications	65
Primary metals	63
Metal mining	59

Source: Statistics Canada.

Canadian Concentration Ratios. Table 13.2 shows the four-firm domestic concentration ratios for various industries. Is there any way that we can show or determine which industries to classify as oligopolistic? There is no definite answer. If we arbitrarily picked a four-firm concentration ratio of 70 percent, we could indicate that tobacco products, beer, petroleum and coal products, and storage were oligopolistic. But we would always be dealing with an arbitrary definition.

The concept of an industry is necessarily arbitrary. As a consequence, concentration ratios rise as we narrow the definition of an industry and fall as we broaden it. Thus we must be certain that we are satisfied with the measurement of the industry under study before we jump to conclusions about whether the industry is too concentrated as evidenced by a high measured concentration ratio.

Cartels

▶ **Cartel**

An association of producers in an industry that agree to set common prices and output quotas to prevent competition.

Manufacturers and sellers have often attempted to form an organization that acts as one and tries to capture 100 percent of the market. This is called a **cartel**, and it is frequently international in scope. Cartels are an attempt by their members to earn higher than competitive profits. They set common prices and output quotas for their members. The key to the success of a cartel is keeping one member from competing against other members by expanding production and thereby lowering price. The formation of cartels is illegal in Canada. One of the most successful international cartels ever is the Organization of Petroleum Exporting Countries (OPEC), an association of the world's largest oil-producing countries, including Saudi Arabia, which at times has accounted for a significant percentage of the world's crude oil output. OPEC effectively organized a significant cutback on the production of crude oil in the wake of the so-called Yom Kippur War in the Middle East in 1973. Within one year, the spot price of crude oil jumped from US$2.12 to US$7.61 per barrel on the world market. By the early 1980s, the price had risen to over US$30.

Most cartels do not have as much success.

INTERNATIONAL EXAMPLE
"We're Just Trying to Keep the Market Stable"

The stated goal of most international cartels is keeping markets "stable." In reality, cartel members are seeking higher prices (and profits) for their product. But to achieve their aims, the producing countries have to be willing to withhold some of their production from the world market. In this way, the world price of a commodity does not fall if world production increases.

Nowhere are international cartels as prevalent as in the market for commodities. For coffee there is the Association of Coffee Producing Countries. Cocoa has the International Cocoa Organization. There is even an ostrich cartel called the Little Karoo Agricultural Cooperative.

The federal government has at times sanctioned the equivalent of a cartel. A meeting in 1994 in Ottawa, involving executives from a dozen global aluminum producers and government officials representing Canada, the United States, the European Union, and three other nations, ultimately resulted in an agreement by all those attending to reduce aluminum production. All such reductions were voluntary, except by Russia. In exchange for cutting primary aluminum production by 500,000 tonnes over a two-year period, Russia received the promise of financial support from the West in updating and improving its aluminum smelters. Government officials nevertheless claim that "the markets are still open."

For critical analysis: The price of gasoline today (corrected for inflation) is about 50 percent of what it was in 1984. What does that tell you about the long-run effectiveness of global cartels?

Oligopoly, Efficiency, and Resource Allocation

Although oligopoly is not the dominant form of market structure in Canada, oligopolistic industries do exist. To the extent that oligopolies have market power, they lead to resource misallocations, just as monopolies do. Oligopolies charge prices that exceed marginal cost. But what about oligopolies that occur because of economies of scale? One could argue that consumers end up paying lower prices than if the industry were composed of numerous smaller firms.

All in all, there is no definite evidence of serious resource misallocation in Canada because of oligopolies. Canadian firms face a lot of competition from the rest of the world, hence they are able to exercise little real market power.

Concepts in Brief

* An oligopoly is a market situation in which there are a small number of interdependent sellers.
* Oligopoly may result from (1) economies of scale, (2) barriers to entry, and (3) mergers.
* Horizontal mergers involve the joining of firms selling a similar product.
* Vertical mergers involve the merging of one firm either with the supplier of an input or the purchaser of its output.
* Industry concentration can be measured by the percentage of total sales accounted for by the top four or top eight firms.
* Cartels collude to restrict output and raise price in order to earn higher profits for their members.

STRATEGIC BEHAVIOUR AND GAME THEORY

▶ **Best response function**
The manner in which one oligopolist reacts to a change in price, output, or quality made by another oligopolist in the industry.

▶ **Game theory**
A way of describing the various possible outcomes in any situation involving two or more interacting individuals when those individuals are aware of the interactive nature of their situation and plan accordingly. The plans made by these individuals are known as *game strategies*.

At this point, we should be able to show oligopoly price and output determination in the way we showed it for perfect competition, pure monopoly, and monopolistic competition, but we cannot. Whenever there are relatively few firms competing in an industry, each can and does react to the price, quantity, quality, and product innovations that the others undertake. In other words, each oligopolist has a **best response function**. Oligopolistic competitors are interdependent. Consequently, the decision makers in such firms must employ strategies. And we must be able to model their strategic behaviour if we wish to predict how prices and outputs are determined in oligopolistic market structures. In general, we can think of the reactions of other firms to one firm's actions as part of a game that is played by all firms in the industry. Not surprisingly, economists have developed **game theory** models to describe firms' rational interactions. Game theory is the analytical framework in which two or more individuals, companies, or nations compete for certain payoffs that depend on the strategy that the others employ. Poker is such a game situation because it involves a strategy of bluffing.

Some Basic Notions About Game Theory

▶ **Cooperative game**

A game in which the players explicity collude to make themselves better off. As applied to firms, it involves companies colluding in order to make higher than competitive rates of return.

▶ **Noncooperative game**

A game in which the players neither negotiate nor collude in any way. As applied to firms in an industry, this is the common situation in which there are relatively few firms and each has some ability to change price.

▶ **Zero-sum game**

A game in which the any gains within the group are exactly offset by equal losses by the end of the game.

▶ **Negative-sum game**

A game in which players as a group lose at the end of the game.

▶ **Positive-sum game**

A game in which players as a group are better off at the end of the game.

▶ **Strategy**

Any rule that is used to make a choice, such as "Always pick heads"; any potential choice that can be made by players in a game.

▶ **Dominant strategies**

Strategies that always yield the highest benefit. Regardless of what other players do, a dominant strategy will yield the most benefit for the player using it.

Games can be either cooperative or noncooperative. If firms get together to collude or form a cartel, that is considered a **cooperative game**. Whenever it is too costly for firms to negotiate such collusive agreements and to enforce them, they are in a **noncooperative game** situation. Most strategic behaviour in the marketplace would be described as a noncooperative game.

Games can be classified by whether the payoffs are negative, zero, or positive. A **zero-sum game** is one in which one player's losses are offset by another player's gains; at any time, sum totals are zero. If two retailers have an absolutely fixed total number of customers, the customers that one retailer wins over are exactly equal to the customers that the other retailer loses. A **negative-sum game** is one in which players as a group lose at the end of the game (although one perhaps by more than the other, and it's possible for one or more players to win). A **positive-sum game** is one in which players as a group end up better off. Some economists describe all voluntary exchanges as positive-sum games. After an exchange, both the buyer and the seller are better off than they were prior to the exchange.

Strategies in Noncooperative Games.   Players, such as decision makers in oligopolistic firms, have to devise a **strategy**, which is defined as a rule used to make a choice. The goal of the decision maker is of course to devise a strategy that is more successful than alternative strategies. Whenever a firm's decision makers can come up with certain strategies that are generally successful no matter what actions competitors take, these are called **dominant strategies**. The dominant strategy always yields the unique best action for the decision maker no matter what action the other "players" undertake. Relatively few business decision makers over a long period of time have successfully devised dominant strategies. We know this by observation: Few firms in oligopolistic industries have maintained relatively high profits consistently over time.

EXAMPLE   The Prisoners' Dilemma

One real-world example of simple game theory involves what happens when two people, both involved in a bank robbery, are later caught. What should they do when questioned by police? The result has been called the prisoners' dilemma. The two suspects, Sam and Carol, are interrogated separately and confronted with alternative potential periods of imprisonment. The interrogator indirectly indicates to Sam and Carol the following:

1. If both confess to the bank robbery, they will both go to jail for five years.
2. If neither confesses, they will each be given a sentence of two years on a lesser charge.
3. If one prisoner confesses, that prisoner goes free and the other one, who did not confess, will serve 10 years on bank robbery charges.

▶ **Payoff matrix**

A matrix of outcomes, or consequences, of the strategies available to the players in a game.

You can see the prisoners' alternatives in the **payoff matrix** in Figure 13.3. The two options for each prisoner are "confess" and "don't confess." There are four possibilities:

1. Both confess.
2. Neither confesses.
3. Sam confesses but Carol doesn't.
4. Carol confesses but Sam doesn't.

Figure 13.3
The Prisoners' Dilemma Payoff Matrix

Regardless of what the other prisoner does, each person is better off if he or she confesses. So confessing is the dominant strategy and each ends up behind bars for five years.

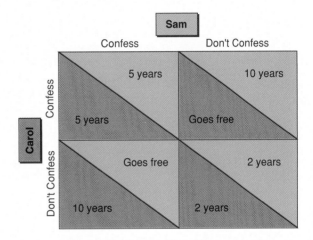

In Figure 13.3, all of Sam's possible outcomes are shown on the upper half of each rectangle, and all of Carol's possible outcomes are shown on the lower half.

By looking at the payoff matrix, you can see that if Carol confesses, Sam's best strategy is to confess also—he'll get only 5 years instead of 10. Conversely, if Sam confesses, Carol's best strategy is also to confess—she'll get 5 years instead of 10. Now let's say that Sam is being interrogated and Carol doesn't confess. Sam's best strategy is still to confess, because then he goes free instead of serving two years. Conversely, if Carol is being interrogated, her best strategy is still to confess even if Sam hasn't. She'll go free instead of serving 10 years. To confess is a dominant strategy for Sam. To confess is also a dominant strategy for Carol. The situation is exactly symmetrical. So this is the **prisoners' dilemma**. The prisoners know that both prisoners will be better off if neither confesses. Yet it is in each individual prisoner's interest to confess, even though the collective outcome of each prisoner's pursuing his or her own interest is inferior for both.

▶ **Prisoners' dilemma**

A famous strategic game in which two prisoners have a choice between confessing and not confessing to a crime. If neither confesses, they serve a minimum sentence. If both confess, they serve a maximum sentence. If one confesses and the other doesn't, the one who confesses goes free. The dominant strategy is always to confess.

For critical analysis: Can you apply the prisoners' dilemma to the firms in a two-firm industry that agree to split the market? (Hint: Think about the payoff to cheating on the market-splitting agreement.)

Applying Game Theory to Pricing Strategies

We can apply game strategy to two firms—oligopolists—that have to decide on their pricing strategy. Each can choose either a high or a low price. Their payoff matrix is shown in Figure 13.4. If they each choose high prices, they can each make $6 million, but if they each choose low prices, they will only make $4 million each. If one sets a high price and the other a low one, the low-priced firm will make $8 million, but the high-priced firm will only make $2 million. As in the prisoners' dilemma, in the absence of collusion, they will end up choosing low prices.

Figure 13.4
Game Theory and Pricing Strategies

This payoff matrix shows that if both oligopolists choose a high price, each makes $6 million. If they both choose a low price, each makes $4 million. If one chooses a low price and the other doesn't, the low-priced firm will make $8 million. Unless they collude, however, they will end up at the low-priced solution.

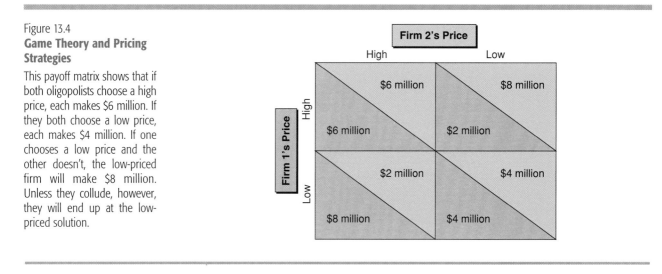

Opportunistic Behaviour

In the prisoners' dilemma, it was clear that cooperative behaviour—both parties standing firm without admitting to anything—leads to the best outcome for both players. But each prisoner (player) stands to gain by cheating. Such action is called **opportunistic behaviour**. Our daily economic activities involve the equivalent of the prisoners' dilemma all the time. We could engage in opportunistic behaviour. You could write a cheque for a purchase knowing that it is going to bounce because you have just closed that bank account. When you agree to perform a specific task for pay, you could perform your work in a substandard way. When you go to buy an item, the seller might be able to cheat you by selling you a defective item.

▶ **Opportunistic behaviour**
Actions that ignore the possible long-run benefits of cooperation and focus solely on short-run gains.

In short, if all of us—sellers and buyers—engaged in opportunistic behaviour all of the time, we would always end up in the bottom right-hand box of the prisoners' dilemma payoff matrix in Figure 13.3. We would constantly be acting in a world of non-cooperative behaviour. That is not the world in which most of us live, however. Why not? Because most of us engage in repeat transactions. Manufacturers would like us to keep purchasing their products. Sellers would like us to keep coming back to their stores. As a seller of labour services, each of us would like to keep our jobs, get promotions, or be hired away by another firm at a higher wage rate. We engage in a **tit-for-tat strategic behaviour**. In tit-for-tat strategy, manufacturers and sellers continue to guarantee their merchandise, in spite of cheating by a small percentage of consumers.

▶ **Tit-for-tat strategic behaviour**
In game theory, cooperation that continues so long as the other players continue to cooperate.

INTERNATIONAL EXAMPLE
Collapsing Oil Prices

Sometimes, the tit-for-tat strategy is costly to market participants. Recall that the Organization of Petroleum Exporting Countries (OPEC) is a global cartel whose members control much of the world's output of crude oil. Under the terms of the tit-for-tat strategy, each OPEC member continues to cooperate as long as the other members do likewise. If anyone cheats on the cartel, the appropriate tit-for-tat response is to cut the price of crude oil and keep cutting prices until the original cheater reverts to the higher price previously agreed on by the cartel members. Saudi Arabia, the largest oil-producing member of OPEC, appears to have followed this strategy. It has effectively said to other members of OPEC, "If you stick to your agreed-on production limits, so shall we; but if you expand production beyond those limits, so shall we." Sometimes Saudi Arabia has difficulty knowing whether an OPEC member has cheated. When Iraq and Iran were at war in the 1980s, both depended on oil production to finance their defence expenditures. Saudi Arabia thought they were both cheating on the OPEC agreements by expanding production. They claimed otherwise, but Saudi Arabia responded tit-for-tat by hiking production. Prices collapsed: In just one year (1985 to 1986), crude oil prices plunged from US$24.10 to US$12.50 per barrel.

For critical analysis: Why would you expect a major crude oil producer, such as Saudi Arabia, to take the lead in enforcing a tit-for-tat strategy?

PRICE RIGIDITY AND THE KINKED DEMAND CURVE

Let's hypothesize that the decision makers in an oligopolistic firm assume that rivals will react in the following way: They will match all price decreases (in order not to be undersold) but not price increases (because they want to capture more business). There is no collusion. The implications of this best response function are rigid prices and a kinked demand curve.

Nature of the Kinked Demand Curve

In Figure 13.5 (page 336), we draw a kinked demand curve, which assumes that oligopolists match price decreases but not price increases. We start off at a given price of P_0 and assume that the quantity demanded at the price for this individual oligopolist is q_0. The starting price of P_0 is usually the stable market price. If the oligopolist assumes that rivals will not react, it faces demand curve d_1d_1 with marginal revenue curve MR_1. Conversely, if it assumes that rivals will react, it faces demand curve d_2d_2 with marginal revenue curve MR_2. More than likely, the oligopoly firm will

Figure 13.5
The Kinked Demand Curve

If the oligopolist firm assumes that rivals will not match price changes, it faces demand curve d_1d_1 and marginal revenue curve MR_1. If it assumes that rivals will match price changes, it faces demand curve d_2d_2 and marginal revenue curve MR_2. If the oligopolist believes that rivals will not react to price increases but will react to price decreases, at prices above P_0 it faces demand curve d_1d_1 and at prices below P_0 it faces the other demand curve, d_2d_2. The overall demand curve will therefore have a kink, as is seen in part (b) at price P_0. The marginal revenue curve will have a vertical break, as shown by the dashed line in part (b).

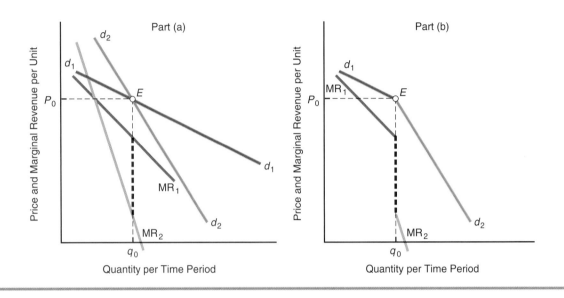

assume that if it lowers price, rivals will react by matching that reduction to avoid losing their respective shares of the market. The oligopolist that initially lowers its price will not greatly increase its quantity demanded. So when it lowers its price, it believes that it will face demand curve d_2d_2. But if it increases price above P_0, rivals will probably not follow suit. Thus a higher price than P_0 will cause quantity demanded to decrease rapidly. The demand schedule to the left of and above point E will be relatively elastic, as represented by d_1d_1. At prices above P_0, the relevant demand curve is d_1d_1, whereas below price P_0, the relevant demand curve will be d_2d_2. Consequently, at point E there will be a kink in the resulting demand curve. This is shown in part (b) of Figure 13.5, where the demand curve is labelled d_1d_2. The resulting marginal revenue curve is labelled MR_1MR_2. It has a discontinuous portion, or gap, represented by the boldfaced dashed vertical lines in both parts.

Price Rigidity

The kinked demand curve analysis may help explain why price changes might be infrequent in an oligopolistic industry without collusion. Each oligopolist can see only harm in a price change: If price is increased, the oligopolist will lose many of its customers to rivals who do not raise their prices. That is to say, the oligopolist moves up from point E along demand curve d_1 in part (b) of Figure 13.5. However, if an oligopolist lowers its price, given that rivals will lower their prices too, its sales will not increase very much. Moving down from point E in part (b) of Figure 13.5, we see that the demand curve is relatively inelastic. If the elasticity is less than 1, total revenues will fall rather than rise with the lowering of price. Given that the production of a larger output will increase total costs, the oligopolist's profits will fall. The lowering of price by the oligopolist might start a price war in which its rival firms will charge an even lower price.

The theoretical reason for price inflexibility under the kinked demand curve model has to do with the discontinuous portion of the marginal revenue curve shown in part (b) of Figure 13.5, which we reproduce in Figure 13.6. Assume that marginal cost is represented by MC. The profit-maximizing rate of output is q_0, which can be sold at a price of P_0. Now assume that the marginal cost curve rises to MC'. What will happen to the profit-maximizing rate of output? Nothing. Both quantity and price will remain the same for this oligopolist.

Remember that the profit-maximizing rate of output is where marginal revenue equals marginal cost. The shift in the marginal cost curve to MC' does not change the profit-maximizing rate of output in Figure 13.6 because MC' still cuts the marginal revenue curve in the latter's discontinuous portion. Thus the equality between marginal revenue and marginal cost still holds at output rate q_0 even when the marginal cost curve shifts upward. What will happen when marginal costs fall to MC"? Nothing. This oligopolist will continue to produce at a rate of output q_0 and charge a price of P_0. Whenever the marginal cost curve cuts the discontinuous portion of the marginal revenue curve, fluctuations (within limits) in marginal cost will not affect output or price because the profit-maximizing condition MR = MC will hold. The result is that even when firms in an oligopolistic industry such as this experience increases or decreases in costs, their prices do not change as long as MC cuts MR in the discontinuous portion. Hence prices are seen to be rigid in oligopolistic industries if oligopolists react the way we assume they do in this model.

Figure 13.6

Changes in Cost May Not Alter the Profit-Maximizing Price and Output

As long as the marginal cost curve intersects the marginal revenue curve in the latter's discontinuous portion, the profit-maximizing price P_0 (and output q_0) will remain unchanged even with changes in MC. (However, the firm's rate of profit will change.)

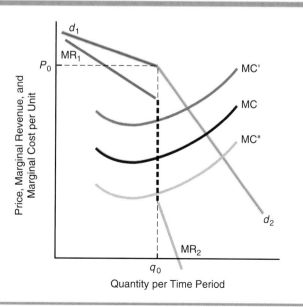

Criticisms of the Kinked Demand Curve

One of the criticisms directed against the kinked demand curve is that we have no idea how the existing price, P_0, came to be. If every oligopolistic firm faced a kinked demand curve, it would not pay for it to change prices. The problem is that the kinked demand curve does not show us how demand and supply originally determine the going price of an oligopolist's product.

As far as the evidence goes, it is not encouraging. Oligopoly prices do not appear to be as rigid, particularly in the upward direction, as the kinked demand curve theory implies. During the 1970s and early 1980s, when prices in the economy were rising overall, oligopolistic producers increased their prices frequently. Evidence of price changes during the Great Depression showed that oligopolies changed prices much more frequently than monopolies.

Try Preview Question 4:
What are the characteristics of the oligopolistic market structure?

EXAMPLE	Do Pet Products Have Nine Lives?

A. J. Heinz's Pet Products Company knows all about the kinked demand curve. It makes 9-Lives cat food. To meet increased competition (at lower prices) from Nestlé, Quaker, and Purina, Heinz dropped the wholesale price of a case of 9-Lives more than 22 percent. Finally, Heinz had "had enough." It decided to buck the trend by raising prices. The result? A disaster, because none of Heinz's four major competitors increased their prices. Heinz's market share dropped from 23 percent to 15 percent almost overnight.

For critical analysis: What does Heinz's experience with 9-Lives suggest about the price elasticity of demand for its product?

Concepts in Brief

- Each oligopolist has a best response function because oligopolistic competitors are interdependent. They must therefore engage in strategic behaviour. One way to model this behaviour is to use game theory.
- Games can be either cooperative or non-cooperative. A cartel is cooperative. When a cartel breaks down and its members start cheating, the industry becomes a non-cooperative game.
- In a zero-sum game, one player's losses are exactly offset by another player's gains. In a negative-sum game, all players collectively lose, perhaps one more than the others. In a positive-sum game, the players as a group end up better off.
- Decision makers in oligopolistic firms must devise a strategy. A dominant strategy is one that is generally successful no matter what actions competitors take.
- The kinked demand curve oligopoly model predicts that major shifts in marginal cost will cause any change in industry price.

STRATEGIC BEHAVIOUR WITH IMPLICIT COLLUSION: A MODEL OF PRICE LEADERSHIP

What if oligopolists do not actually collude to raise prices and share markets but do so implicitly? There are no formal cartel arrangements and no formal meetings. Nonetheless, there is tacit collusion. One example of this is the model of **price leadership**.

▶ **Price leadership**
A practice in many oligopolistic industries in which the largest firm publishes its price list ahead of its competitors, who then match those announced prices. Also called *parallel pricing*.

In this model, the basic assumption is that the dominant firm, usually the biggest, sets the price and allows other firms to sell all they can at that price. The dominant firm then sells the rest. The dominant firm always makes the first move in a price leadership model. By definition, price leadership requires that one firm be the leader. Because of laws against collusion, firms in an industry cannot communicate this directly. That is why it is often natural for the largest firm to become the price leader. In the automobile industry during the period of General Motors' dominance (until the 1980s), that company was traditionally the price leader. At various times in the breakfast food industry, Kellogg was the price leader. In the banking industry, the Bank of Montreal has been the price leader in announcing changes in its prime rate, the interest rate charged on loans offered to the best credit risks. Typically, five or six hours after the Bank of Montreal would increase or decrease its prime rate, the other major banks would announce the same change in their prime rate.

Price Wars

▶ **Price war**
A pricing campaign designed to drive competing firms out of a market by repeatedly cutting prices.

Price leadership may not always work. If the price leader ends up much better off than the firms that follow, the followers may in fact not set prices according to those set by the dominant firm. The result may be a **price war**. The dominant firm lowers its prices a little bit, but the other firms lower theirs even more. Price wars have occurred in many industries. Supermarkets within a given locale often engage in price wars, especially during holiday periods. One may offer turkeys at so much per kilogram on Wednesday; competing stores cut their price on Thursday, so the first store cuts its price even more on Friday. We see price wars occur frequently at gas stations. They usually last for only a few days, however.

> ### EXAMPLE   Air Wars
>
>
> From the beginning of air travel in Canada, Air Canada and Canadian Airlines International have dominated the market for domestic flights. Their dominance was challenged in 1996, however, when Greyhound Airlines entered the market. Initially, Canadian Airlines tried to block the entry of this firm through appeals to the federal government, but ultimately it was unsuccessful.
>
> Why did Canadian Airlines try to keep Greyhound out of the market? Because it feared that the new airline would offer cheaper fares to travellers. Canadian was right; what ensued over the summer of 1996 was a price war. Air fares plum-

metted by 50 to 60 percent as Greyhound offered no-frills service–no frequent flyer plan, no inflight meals, no business-class seats.

Canadian Airlines and Air Canada fought back with some low fares, but their weapon of choice was "quality" service. The two major airlines offered more flights to more destinations, and both forged alliances with other airlines–Air Canada with Lufthansa and Canadian Airlines with British Airways–so that Canadian travellers could travel to any European location and earn frequent flyer points the whole way. In addition, both airlines upgraded their VIP lounges in Vancouver and Toronto airports; they now offer private rooms with showers, fax machines, laptop connections, and Internet access.

In early 1998, Greyhound Airlines went bankrupt. Nevertheless, it has had an effect on air fares. Air Canada's 1996 profit was down 60 percent, and Canadian Airlines was forced to ask for concessions from its employees to keep from going bankrupt. The real victors in this price war were the consumers.

For critical analysis: Why do you think Air Canada and Canadian Airlines fought back by offering more costly "quality service" instead of lower fares?

DETERRING ENTRY INTO AN INDUSTRY

Some economists believe that all decision making by existing firms in a stable industry involves some type of game playing. An important part of game playing does not have to do with how existing competitors might react to a decision by others. Rather, it has to do with how potential competitors might react. Strategic decision making requires that existing firms in an industry come up with strategies to deter entrance into that industry. One important way is, of course, to get a municipal, provincial, or federal government to restrict entry. Another way is to adopt certain pricing and investment strategies that may deter entry.

Increasing Entry Costs

▶ **Entry deterrence strategy**

Any strategy undertaken by firms in an industry, either individually or together, with the intent or effect of raising the cost of entry into the industry by a new firm.

One **entry deterrence strategy** is to raise the cost of entry by a new firm. The threat of a price war is one technique. To sustain a long price war, existing firms might invest in excess capacity so that they can expand output if necessary. When existing firms invest in excess capacity, they are signalling potential competitors that they will engage in a price war.

Another way that existing domestic firms can raise the entry cost of foreign firms is by getting the federal government to pass stringent environmental or health and safety standards. These typically raise costs more for foreign producers, often in developing countries, than for domestic producers.

Limit-Pricing Strategies

If existing firms make it clear to potential competitors that the existing firms will not change their output rate after entry, this is a signal. It tells potential firms that the existing firm will simply lower its market price (moving down the firm demand curve) until it sells the same quantity as before the new entry came into the industry. The existing firms limit their price to be above competitive prices, but if there is a new entrant, the new limit price will be below the one at which the new firm can make a profit. This is called the **limit-pricing model**.

▶ **Limit-pricing model**
A model that hypothesizes that a group of colluding sellers will set the highest common price that they believe they can charge without new firms seeking to enter that industry in search of relatively high profits.

Raising Customers' Switching Costs

If an existing firm can make it more costly for customers to switch from its product or service to a competitor's, the existing firm can deter entry. There are a host of ways in which existing firms can raise customers' switching costs. Makers of computer equipment have in the past produced operating systems and software that would not run on competitors' computers. Any customer wanting to change from one computer system to another faced a high switching cost.

EXAMPLE	High Switching Costs in the Credit World

One way banks keep their customers is by raising the cost of switching to a different bank. Two years ago, the Canadian Imperial Bank of Commerce (CIBC) offered a $650 rebate if customers renewed their mortgages rather than switching to another bank. Additionally, their names were entered in a draw for $5,000. Even though interest rates continued to fall, few customers at the CIBC moved their accounts. After all, to refinance a mortgage at another bank meant that the customer would lose out on the rebate.

Another example of high switching costs in the credit world involves the General Motors credit card, which offers a 5 percent rebate towards a new GM car (to a maximum of $3,500). If you have used this card for several years and have not yet accumulated $3,500 towards the purchase of a new General Motors vehicle, there is little chance you will switch to the Ford rebate card.

For critical analysis: What other credit card systems are in effect that raise switching costs across credit cards?

Concepts in Brief

* One type of strategic behaviour involving implicit collusion is price leadership. The dominant firm is assumed to set the price and then allows other firms to sell all that they want to sell at that price. Whatever is left over is sold by the dominant firm. The dominant firm always makes the first move in a price leadership model. If the nondominant firms decide to compete, they may start a price war.

* One strategic decision may be to attempt to raise the cost of entry of new firms into an industry. The threat of a price war is one technique. Another is to lobby the federal government to pass stringent environmental or health and safety standards in an attempt to keep out foreign competition.

• If existing firms limit prices to a level above competitive prices before entry but are willing to reduce it, this is called a limit-pricing model.
• Another way to raise the cost to new firms is to make it more costly for customers to switch from one product or service to a competitor's.

COMPARING MARKET STRUCTURES

Now that we have looked at perfect competition, pure monopoly, monopolistic competition, and oligopoly, we are in a position to compare the attributes of these four different market structures. We do this in summary form in Table 13.3, in which we compare the number of sellers, their ability to set price, and whether product differentiation exists, and we give some examples of each of the four market structures.

Table 13-3
Comparing Market Structures

Market Structure	Number of Sellers	Unrestricted Entry and Exit	Ability to Set Price	Long-Run Economic Profits Possible	Product Differentiation	Nonprice Competition	Examples
Perfect competition	Numerous	Yes	None	No	None	None	Agriculture, coal
Monopolistic competition	Many	Yes	Some	Not for most firms	Considerable	Yes	Toothpaste, toilet paper, soap, retail trade
Oligopoly	Few	Partial	Some	Yes	Frequent	Yes	Cigarettes, steel, banks
Pure monopoly	One	No (for entry)	Considerable	Yes	None (product is unique)	Yes	Electric company, provincial telephone company

Issues and Applications

Game Theory: Opening Up the Brewing Industry

Concepts Applied: Game theory, strategic behaviour, entry deterrence

Craft beers with exotic names like Dragon's Breath Pale Ale and Warthog Lager are slowly gaining a share of the beer market. Labatt and Molson beer companies have found it too expensive to fight their entry.

anadians drink about 5.6 billion bottles of beer each year. The Labatt and Molson companies produce the lion's share of this beer–about 93 percent of it. Over the last 15 years, however, their market share has been eroded by competition from "microbreweries."

There are now about 40 microbreweries in Canada producing craft beers with exotic names like Satan Red, Dragon's Breath Pale Ale, and Warthog Lager. As Canadians have aged, they have begun to drink less and discriminate more, turning from the old standards–Labatt's Blue and Molson Canadian–to the high-quality craft beers. To date the microbreweries have captured about a 4 percent market share country-wide. In British Columbia, they have captured at least a 10 percent share of the beer market. Industry analysts suggest that a 1 percent share of the beer market is worth about $16 million in profits. So why have Molson and Labatt not fought the entry of microbreweries to the industry? We can use game theory to help us answer this question.

Constructing the Game

The two players in this game are: (1) Molson and Labatt, which currently dominate the market for beer; and (2) a representative microbrewery which wants to enter the market. Molson and Labatt can fight entry or acquiesce. Fighting entry would cost each firm $1 million. The microbrewery's strategies are to enter the industry–which requires a $1 million fixed cost investment–or to stay out. If the firm successfully enters the market, it will capture a 1 percent market share worth $16 million. If it encounters a fight from the major breweries, however, it will lose the $1 million earmarked for set-up costs.

The Payoffs

Figure 13.7 shows the payoff matrix for this game. If Molson and Labatt fight entry but are unsuccessful, they spend $2 million on the fight and lose $16 million in profits to the successful microbrewery. If they fight and win, they spend $2 million fighting, but retain the market share. If Molson and Labatt acquiesce, they lose a 1 percent market share to the microbrewery, for a payoff of negative $16 million. If they acquiesce and the microbrewery stays out, they spend nothing and lose nothing.

If the microbrewery chooses to enter the market and the major breweries fight, the firm spends $1 million on fighting off the two companies. If the microbrewery enters but Molson and Labatt acquiesce, the microbrewery earns a $16 million profit less the $1 million set-up costs. If the microbrewery stays out, there are no profits and no costs involved.

The Solution

Molson and Labatt know that if the microbrewery wants to enter the market, fighting will cost them $18 million, while acquiescing

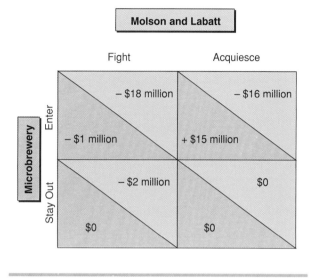

Figure 13.7
Payoff Matrix

will cost $16 million in lost profits. If the microbrewery decides to stay out of the market, then fighting will cost them $2 million, while acquiescing will cost nothing. In either case, the two breweries choose to acquiesce.

The microbrewery knows that if Labatt and Molson want to fight entry, it is better off staying out of the market and not losing its $1 million. If, however, they want to acquiesce, the microbrewery is better off entering. Since Molson and Labatt's dominant strategy is to acquiesce, the microbrewery enters the market.

No Symmetrical Solution

This game is not symmetrical since the microbrewery has no dominant strategy. If the major brewers decided to fight, the microbrewery would not enter the market. Nevertheless, Molson and Labatt choose not to fight since fighting is an expensive undertaking. By behaving strategically, Molson and Labatt face increasing competition from small, high-quality brands.

For Critical Analysis

1. Is this game a positive-sum, zero-sum, or negative-sum game? How do you know?

2. What strategies, besides fighting, could Labatt and Molson use to deter entry by the microbreweries?

CHAPTER SUMMARY

1. Numerous market situations lie between the extremes of pure competition and pure monopoly. Monopolistic competition and oligopoly are two of these situations.

2. Monopolistic competition is a theory developed by economist Edward Chamberlin in 1933. It refers to a market composed of specific product groups in which the different companies involved have slight monopoly powers because each has a product slightly different from the others. Examples of product groups might include the toothpaste and soap industries. The monopolistic competitor ends up with zero economic profits because there is free entry into the industry. However, according to Chamberlin, the monopolistic competitor does not produce where price equals marginal costs and therefore does not produce at the minimum point on the average total cost curve.

3. Advertising occurs in industries in which the firms are not pure price takers. The basic goal of advertisers is to increase demand for their product.

4. In the short run, it is possible for a monopolistic competitor to make economic profits or economic losses. In the long run, monopolistic competitors make zero economic profits (that is, they make just the normal rate of return).

5. When we compare monopolistic competition with perfect competition, we find that the monopolistic competitor does not produce where average total costs are at a minimum, whereas the perfect competitor does.

6. Oligopoly is a market situation in which there are just a few firms. Each firm knows that its rivals will react to a change in price. Oligopolies are usually defined as industries in which the four-firm concentration ratio is relatively high.

7. Oligopolies are characterized by relatively high barriers to entry, interdependence, product differentiation, and growth through merger.

8. Each oligopolist has a best response function because oligopolistic competitors are interdependent and must therefore engage in strategic behaviour. One way to model this behaviour is to use game theory.

9. Games can be either cooperative or non-cooperative. A cartel is cooperative. When a cartel breaks down and its members start cheating, the industry becomes a non-cooperative game. In a zero-sum game, one player's losses are exactly offset by another player's gains. In a negative-sum game, players as a group lose, perhaps one more than the others. In a positive-sum game, players as a group end up better off.

10. The kinked demand curve oligopoly model indicates that prices will be relatively rigid unless demand or cost conditions change substantially.

11. Price leadership is strategic behaviour that involves implicit collusion. The dominant firm is assumed to set the price and then allows other firms to sell all that they want to sell at that price. Whatever is left over is sold by the dominant firm. The dominant firm always makes the first move. If the nondominant firms decide to compete, they may start a price war.

12. One strategic decision may be to attempt to raise the cost of entry of new firms into an industry. The threat of a price war is one technique. Another is to lobby the federal government to pass stringent environmental or health and safety standards in an attempt to keep out foreign competition. A third is to make it more costly for customers to switch from one product or service to a competitor's.

DISCUSSION OF PREVIEW QUESTIONS

1. **What are the characteristics of the monopolistically competitive market structure?**

   The monopolistically competitive market structure lies between the extremes of monopoly and perfect competition, but closer to the latter. Under monopolistic competition, there are a large number of sellers, each with a small market share, acting independently of one another, producing a differentiated product. This product differentiation is advertised; advertising emphasizes product differences or, on occasion, "creates" differences.

2. **How does the monopolistic competitor determine the equilibrium price-output combination?**

   The monopolistic competitor has some control over price; it faces a downward-sloping demand curve. The monopolistic competitor must lower price in order to increase sales; the marginal revenue curve for the monopolistic competitor is therefore downward-sloping. In equilibrium, the profit-maximizing rate of output will therefore be where the upward-sloping (increasing) marginal cost curve intersects the downward-sloping (decreasing) marginal revenue curve. The output rate being thus established, price is set at the corresponding market clearing level. Any other output rate would lead to a reduction in total profits.

3. **How does the monopolistically competitive market structure differ from that of perfect competition?**

   Like the perfect competitor, the monopolistic competitor acts independently of its competitors and is able to earn economic profits only in the short run; competition from entrants eliminates long-run economic profits under both market structures. Yet an important difference exists in the two models: The perfect competitor faces a perfectly elastic demand curve, whereas the monopolistic competitor faces a downward-sloping demand curve. Because economic profits must equal zero in the long run, the demand (average revenue) curve must be tangent to the average total cost (ATC) curve in both models. Under perfect competition, a perfectly elastic demand curve can only be tangent to a U-shaped ATC curve at the latter's minimum point (where its slope is zero). Under monopolistic competition, the demand curve must be tangent to the firm's ATC somewhere to the left of the ATC's minimum point. Thus under perfect competition, long-run equilibrium will be at minimum ATC, whereas under monopolistic competition, long-run equilibrium will be at a higher ATC—and at a lower output rate.

4. **What are the characteristics of the oligopolistic market structure?**

   Like the monopolistically competitive market structure, oligopoly lies between the extremes of perfect competition and monopoly. However, oligopoly is closer to being unique; under oligopoly, a small number of firms dominate the market, and the firms cannot act independently. An oligopolist must take into account the reactions of its rivals when it sets policy; this interdependence makes the oligopoly model unique. It also makes the price-output decision a complex one for the oligopolists—and hence for economists who analyse this market structure. It is believed that oligopolies emerge because great economies of scale, in conjunction with a limited market demand, allow the few largest to drive out competitors. Also, oligopolies may arise because of barriers to entry and mergers.

PROBLEMS

(Answers to the odd-numbered problems appear at the back of the book.)

13-1. Suppose that you own a monopolistically competitive firm that sells automobile tune-ups at a price of $25 each. You are currently selling 100 per week. As the owner-operator, you initiate an ad campaign on a local AM radio station. You promise to smooth out any ill-running car at a price of $25. The result is that you end up tuning 140 cars per week. What is the "marginal revenue" of this ad campaign? What additional information do you need to determine whether your profits have risen?

13-2. The graph depicts long-run equilibrium for a monopolistic competitor.

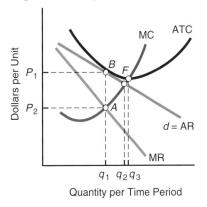

Quantity per Time Period

a. Which output rate represents equilibrium?
b. Which price represents equilibrium?
c. Which labelled point indicates that economic profits are zero?
d. Which labelled point indicates minimum ATC?
e. Is ATC at the equilibrium output rate above or at minimum ATC?
f. Is the equilibrium price greater than, less than, or equal to the marginal cost of producing at the equilibrium output rate?

13-3. The following table indicates some information for industry A.

Firm	Annual Sales ($ millions)
1	200
2	150
3	100
4	75
5 through 30	300

a. What is the four-firm concentration ratio for this industry (with just 30 firms)?
b. Assume that industry A is the steel industry. What would happen to the concentration index if we redefined industry A as the cold rolled-steel industry? As the metals industry?

13-4. Explain how, in the long run, any economic profits will be eliminated in a monopolistically competitive industry.

13-5. Explain why an oligopolist's demand curve might be kinked.

13-6. The table at the top of the next page gives some cost and demand data for an oligopolistic industry. There are five firms. Assume that each one faces the same long-run total cost curve and that each firm knows that any change in price will be matched by all other firms in the industry.
a. Fill in the blanks.
b. What will the profit-maximizing rate of output be for each firm?
c. What price will be charged for this output?
d. What will the profits be for each of the five firms?

Price	Quantity Demanded	Total Revenue	Marginal Revenue	Quantity Demanded ÷ Number of Firms	Total Revenue ÷ Number of Firms	Marginal Revenue ÷ Number of Firms	Individual Firm Quantity Supplied	Long-Run Total Costs	Long-Run Marginal Costs
$20	5	$ _____	$ _____	_____	_____		1	$20	$ _____
18	10	_____	_____	_____	_____	_____	2	30	_____
16	15	_____	_____	_____	_____	_____	3	36	_____
14	20	_____	_____	_____	_____	_____	4	44	_____
12	25	_____	_____	_____	_____	_____	5	60	_____

13-7. Suppose that you run a movie theatre. At your price of $5 per person, you sell 5,000 tickets per week. Without changing your price, you initiate a $1,000-per-week advertising campaign. Assuming that all your nonadvertising costs are totally unrelated to the number of weekly viewers you have, how much additional revenue must you generate to justify continuation of the ad campaign? How many more customers would this require?

13-8. Study the accompanying graph for a firm in an oligopolistic industry.

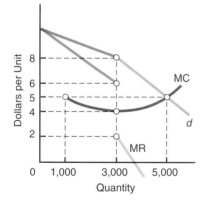

a. How much will this oligopolistic firm produce?

b. At what price will the firm sell this output?

c. How much can marginal cost vary without causing a change in price?

13-9. There are only two firms in an industry. They collude to share the market equally. They jointly set a monopoly price and split the quantity demanded at that price. Here are their options.

a. They continue to collude (no cheating) and make $10 million each in profits.

b. One firm cheats on the agreement, but the other firm doesn't. The firm that cheats makes $12 million a year in profit, whereas the firm that doesn't cheat makes $7 million in profit.

c. They both cheat and each one makes $6 million a year in profit.

Construct a payoff matrix for these two firms. How does this situation relate to the prisoners' dilemma?

14

Regulation and Competition Policy

Preview Questions

1. What is a natural monopoly, and how does one arise?

2. If natural monopolies are required to price at marginal cost, what problem emerges?

3. What are some means of regulating a natural monopoly?

4. Why have economists been re-evaluating the government's role as an economic regulator?

About 7.2 million Canadians read daily newspapers. Of those 7.2 million readers, 41.4 percent read papers owned or controlled by one man—Conrad Black. From his start in 1985, Mr. Black, through his company Hollinger Inc., steadily built his holdings so that today he is the third largest newspaper publisher in the world, and the single largest newspaper publisher in Canada. Some view Mr. Black as a hard-working creative businessman. Others fear that he will use his newspapers to push his right-wing political agenda and unduly influence public opinion; they want the government to prohibit the growing concentration of ownership in the print media. To understand this issue, you need to know more about regulation and competition policy.

Did You Know That... each year thousands of pages of new or modified federal regulations are published? These regulations, found in the *Canada Gazette,* cover virtually every aspect of the way business can be conducted, products can be built, and services can be offered. In addition, every province and municipality publishes regulations relating to worker safety, restaurant cleanliness, and the number of lights needed in each room in a day-care centre. There is no question about it, Canadian business activities are highly regulated. Consequently, how regulators should act to increase economic efficiency and how they actually act are important topics for understanding our economy today. In addition to regulation, the government has one additional weapon to use in its attempts to prevent restraints of trade. It is called anticombines law, and it is the subject of the later part of this chapter.

Let's look first at how government might best regulate a single firm that has obtained a monopoly because of constantly falling long-run average costs, a situation known as a natural monopoly.

NATURAL MONOPOLIES REVISITED

You will recall from our discussion of natural monopolies in Chapter 12 that whenever a single firm has the ability to produce all of the industry's output at a lower per-unit cost than other firms attempting to produce less than total industry output, a natural monopoly arises. Natural gas and electric utilities are examples. Long-run average costs for those firms typically fall as output increases. In a natural monopoly, economies of large-scale production dominate, leading to a single-firm industry.

The Pricing and Output Decision of the Natural Monopolist

We show data for a hypothetical natural monopoly in part (a) of Figure 14.1 (page 350). Demand data is in columns 1 and 2, with marginal revenue in column 3. Total cost is in column 4. Notice that marginal cost in column 5 is constant over the range of demand provided. This might be typical of a hydroelectric utility—once the necessary dams are constructed, electricity can be produced at a relatively constant cost. Average total cost is in column 6.

Columns 1, 2, 3, 5, and 6 are graphed in part (b). The intersection of MR and MC is at $4. The monopolist will therefore produce 5,000 units and charge a price of $8 per unit.

What do we know about a monopolist's solution to the price-quantity question? When compared to a competitive situation, we know that consumers end up paying more for the product, and consequently they purchase less of it than they would purchase under competition. The monopoly solution is economically inefficient from society's point of view; the price charged for the product is higher than the opportunity cost to society, and consequently there is a misallocation of resources. That is, the price does not equal the true marginal cost of producing the good because the true marginal cost is at the intersection *A*, not at $8.

Try Preview Question 1:
What is a natural monopoly, and how does one arise?

Figure 14.1
Profit Maximization and Regulation Through Marginal Cost Pricing

The profit-maximizing monopolist here would produce at the point in part (b) where marginal costs equal marginal revenue, which means production of 5,000 units of output. The price charged would be $8. If a regulatory commission attempted to regulate natural monopolies so that price equalled long-run marginal cost, the commission would make the monopolist set production at the point where the marginal cost curve intersects the demand curve. This is shown in part (c). The quantity produced would be 9,000 units, and the price would be $4. However, average costs at 9,000 units are equal to $5.56. Losses would ensue, equal to the shaded area. It would be self-defeating for a regulatory commission to force a natural monopoly to produce at an output rate at which MC = P without subsidizing some of its costs because losses would eventually drive the natural monopolist out of business.

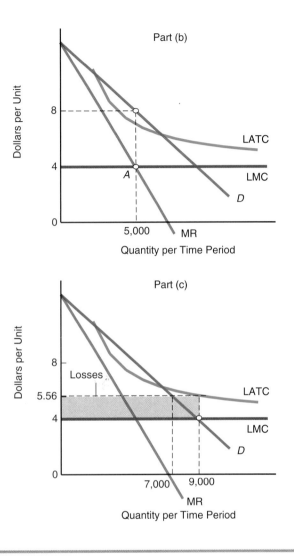

Part (a)

(1)	(2)	(3)	(4)	(5)	(6)
			Long-Run	Long-Run	Long-Run
Output (units)	Price per Unit	Marginal Revenue (MR)	Total Cost (TC)	Marginal Cost (MC)	Average Cost (ATC)
0	$13.00		$14,000		—
		12.00		$4.00	
1,000	12.00		18,000		$18.00
		10.00		4.00	
2,000	11.00		22,000		11.00
		8.00		4.00	
3,000	10.00		26,000		8.67
		6.00		4.00	
4,000	9.00		30,000		7.50
		4.00		4.00	
5,000	8.00		34,000		6.80
		2.00		4.00	
6,000	7.00		38,000		6.33
		0		4.00	
7,000	6.00		42,000		6.00
		−2.00		4.00	
8,000	5.00		46,000		5.75
		−4.00		4.00	
9,000	4.00		50,000		5.56
		−6.00		4.00	
10,000	3.00		54,000		5.40
		−8.00		4.00	
11,000	2.00		58,000		5.27
		−10.00		4.00	
12,000	1.00		62,000		5.17

Regulating the Natural Monopolist

Assume that the government wants the natural monopolist to produce at an output at which price equals marginal cost, so that the value of the satisfaction that individuals receive from the marginal unit purchased is just equal to the marginal cost to society. Where is that solution in part (b) of Figure 14.1? It is at the intersection of the marginal cost curve and the demand curve, where price equals $4. If a regulatory commission forces the natural monopolist to engage in marginal cost pricing, and hence to produce 9,000 units to sell for $4 each, how large will the monopolist's profits be? Profits, of course, are the *positive* difference between total revenues and total costs. Total revenues equal price times output, and total costs equal average costs times output. At 9,000 units, average cost is equal to $5.56, higher than the price that the regulatory commission forces our natural monopolist to charge. Profits turn out to be losses and are equal to the shaded area in part (c) of Figure 14.1. Thus regulation that forces a natural monopolist to produce and price as if it were in a competitive situation would also force that monopolist into negative profits, or losses. Obviously, the monopolist would rather go out of business than be subject to such regulation.

As a practical matter, then, regulators can't force a natural monopolist to engage in marginal cost pricing. Consequently, regulation of natural monopolies has often taken the form of allowing the regulated natural monopolist to set price where LAC intersects *D*, at 7,000 units of output, in part (c) of Figure 14.1. This is called *average cost pricing*. Average cost includes what the regulators deem a "fair" rate of return on investment.

While average cost pricing is not socially optimal—at 7,000 units of output, price is still $2 above marginal cost—it does result in more output being produced at a lower cost to consumers. Regulators must beware, however, of problems associated with average cost pricing. Unless there are safeguards in place to ensure that the monopoly is cost efficient, the firm has no incentive to keep average costs low. It is easier for the firm to condone inefficiencies in the form of very generous fringe benefits and large expense accounts for executives, all of which inflate average costs. In the extreme, the monopoly could allow its average costs, and hence its regulated price, to rise to the profit-maximizing level of $8.

Try Preview Question 2:
If natural monopolies are required to price at marginal cost, what problem emerges?

INTERNATIONAL EXAMPLE

European Post Offices: Natural Monopolies and How to Evade Them

Both in Canada and in the European Union (EU), the postal service has been a legal monopoly. Governments have argued that their post offices are natural monopolies because of economies of scale. In Europe, governments set the postal price where MR = MC, as in part (b) of Figure 14.1, rather than where MC = *D*, as in part (c).

Enter third-party mail handlers as a way to erode such monopoly power. In the Netherlands, the government-owned telecommunications company Koninklijke PTT Nederland formed an international mail joint venture with KLM Royal Dutch Airlines called Interpost. Interpost's foreign mail rates, especially to North America and Asia, are sometimes as low as 25 percent of what a German or French person would have to pay. Third-party mail handlers are now picking up bulk mail in countries surrounding the Netherlands, trucking it in, and then letting Interpost send it out.

A similar activity is occurring as a way to avoid state-owned telephone companies in the EU. People in Europe can now call computers in Canada and the United States, then hang up, and the computer calls back. An open line is established, thereby allowing the European to call North American numbers (and elsewhere) as if the caller were here. The savings sometimes exceeds 70 percent.

For critical analysis: If postal services are natural monopolies, why do we need laws preventing private firms from competing with them?

Concepts in Brief

* A natural monopoly arises when one firm can produce all of an industry's output at a lower per-unit cost than other firms.
* The first firm to take advantage of the declining long-run average cost curve can undercut the prices of all other sellers, forcing them out of business, thereby obtaining a natural monopoly.
* A natural monopolist allowed to maximize profit will set quantity where marginal revenue equals long-run marginal cost. Price is determined from the demand curve at that quantity.
* A natural monopolist that is forced to set price equal to long-run marginal cost will sustain losses.

REGULATION

The federal government began regulating social and economic activity early in our history, but the amount of government regulation has increased in the twentieth century. There are three types of government regulation:

1. Regulation of natural monopolies
2. Regulation of inherently competitive industries
3. Regulation for public welfare across all industries, or so-called "social regulation"

For example, various provincial commissions regulate the rates and quality of service of electric power companies, which are considered natural monopolies. Dairy farming and interprovincial trucking are inherently competitive industries but have nonetheless been subject to government regulation. And federal and provincial governments impose occupational, health, and safety rules on a wide variety of employers.

Objectives of Economic Regulation

▶ **Cost-of-service regulation**
Regulation based on allowing prices to reflect only the actual cost of production and no monopoly profits.

▶ **Rate-of-return regulation**
Regulation that seeks to keep the rate of return in the industry at a competitive level by not allowing excessive prices to be charged.

Economic regulation is typically intended to control the prices that regulated enterprises are allowed to charge. Various public utility commissions across the country regulate the rates (prices) of electrical utility companies and telephone operating companies. This has usually been called rate regulation. The goal of rate regulation has, in principle, been the prevention of both monopoly profits and predatory competition.

Two traditional methods of rate regulation have involved cost-of-service regulation and rate-of-return regulation. A regulatory commission using **cost-of-service regulation** allows the regulated companies to charge only prices that reflect the actual average cost of providing the services to the customer. In a somewhat similar vein, regulatory commissions using the **rate-of-return regulation** method allow regulated companies to set prices that ensure a normal, or competitive, rate of return on the investment in the business. We implied these two types of regulation when dis cussing part (b) of Figure 14.1. If the long-run average cost curve in that figure includes a competitive rate of return on investment, regulating the price at $5.56, where LAC = D, is an example of rate-of-return regulation.

A major problem with regulating monopolies concerns the quality of the service or product involved. Consider the many facets of telephone service: getting a dial tone, hearing other voices clearly, getting the operator to answer quickly, having out-of-order telephone lines repaired rapidly, putting through a long-distance call quickly and efficiently—the list goes on and on. But regulation of a telephone company usually dealt with the prices charged for telephone service. Of course, regulators were concerned with the quality of service, but how could that be measured? Indeed, it cannot be measured very easily. Therefore, it is extremely difficult for any type of regulation to be successful in regulating the *price per constant-quality unit*. Certainly, it is possible to regulate the price per unit, but we don't really know that the quality remains unchanged when the price is not allowed to rise "enough." Thus if regulation doesn't allow prices to rise, quality of service may be lowered, thereby raising the price per constant-quality unit.

Try Preview Question 3:
What are some means of regulating a natural monopoly?

POLICY EXAMPLE   Can the CRTC Effectively Regulate Cable TV?

The Canadian Radio-television and Telecommunications Commission (CRTC) is a federal agency established to ensure that Canadian-made programs have a chance to be broadcast in Canada. The CRTC accomplishes this through its power to grant and renew broadcasting licences. The current standard is that Canadian broadcasters must include in their programming 60 percent Canadian content measured over a day, with at least 50 percent Canadian content in the evening hours. The CBC faces even greater content quotas.

Is the CRTC really ensuring that Canadians view Canadian-made programming? Not really. The spread of satellite dishes and pay-TV, for example, make TV stations like WSBK in Boston and WGN in Chicago and KTLA in Los Angeles as accessible as Canadian stations. And the CRTC has no regulatory powers over those American broadcasters.

For critical analysis: Is there any way the CRTC could ensure that the American channels carry Canadian content?

Social Regulation

As mentioned, social regulation reflects concern for public welfare across all industries. In other words, regulation is focused on the impact of production on the environment and society, the working conditions under which goods and services are produced, and sometimes the physical attributes of goods. The aim is a better quality of life for all through a less polluted environment, better working conditions, and safer and better products. For example, Health Canada attempts to protect against impure and unsafe foods, drugs, cosmetics, and other potentially hazardous prod-

Table 14.1   **Some Federal Regulatory Agencies**

Agency	Jurisdiction	Date Formed	Major Regulatory Functions
Canadian Dairy Commission	Product Markets	1967	Sets support prices for milk used in making dairy products for the domestic market.
Canadian Radio-television and Telecommunications Commission	Product Markets	1976	Regulates broadcasting to balance interests of consumers, the creative community, and distribution industries.
Canada Labour Relations Board	Labour Markets	1948	Enforces the *Canada Labour Code* where workers are direct employees of the federal government, or the employers fall within the authority of Parliament.
Bank of Canada	Financial Markets	1934	Regulates credit and currency and ensures the soundness of Canadian financial institutions.
Atomic Energy Control Board	Energy and Environment	1946	Enforces health, safety, security and environmental standards for the use of nuclear energy, and licenses users of radioactive material.
Canadian Food Inspection Agency	Health and Safety	1997	Sets and enforces standards for food quality and food delivery systems.
Transport Canada	Health and Safety	1936	Establishes and enforces regulations necessary for safety in civil aviation, marine transport, and rail transport.

ucts; the Atomic Energy Control Board (AECB) controls the use and disposal of all radioactive materials to ensure the health, safety, and security of the public and the preservation of the environment; the Workers' Compensation Board attempts to protect workers against work-related injuries and illnesses; and the Canadian Human Rights Commission seeks to ensure fair access for all to jobs.

Table 14.1 lists some major federal regulatory agencies and their areas of concern. Although most people agree with the idea behind such social regulation, many disagree on whether we have too much regulation—whether it costs us more than the benefits we receive. Some contend that the costs that firms incur in abiding by regulations run into billions of dollars per year. The result is higher production costs, which are then passed on to consumers. Also, the resources invested in complying with regulatory measures could be invested in other uses. Furthermore, extensive regulation may have an anti-competitive effect because it may represent a relatively greater burden for smaller firms than for larger ones.

But the *potential* benefits of more social regulation are many. For example, the water we drink in some cities is known to be contaminated with cancer-causing chemicals; air pollution from emissions, and toxic wastes from production processes cause many illnesses. Some contaminated areas have been cleaned up, but many other problem areas remain.

The benefits of social regulation may not be easy to measure and may accrue to society for a long time. Furthermore, it is difficult to put a dollar value on safer working conditions and a cleaner environment. In any case, the debate goes on. However, it should be pointed out that the controversy is generally not about whether we should have social regulation, but about when and how it is being done and whether we take *all* of the costs and benefits into account. For example, is regulation best carried out by federal, provincial, or local authorities? Is a specific regulation economically justified through a complete cost-benefit analysis?

Creative Response and Feedback Effects: Results of Regulation

▶ **Creative response**
Behaviour on the part of a firm that allows it to comply with the letter of the law but violate the spirit, significantly lessening the law's effect.

Regulated firms commonly try to avoid the effects of regulation whenever they can. In other words, the firms engage in **creative response,** which is a response that conforms to the letter of the law but undermines its spirit. Take federal laws requiring male-female pay-equity: The wages of women must be on a par with those paid to males who are performing the same tasks. Employers that pay the same wages to both males and females are clearly not in violation of the law. However, wages are only one component of total employee compensation. Another component is fringe benefits, such as on-the-job training. Because on-the-job training is difficult to observe from outside the firm, employers could offer less on-the-job training to women and still not be in technical violation of pay-equity laws. This unobservable difference would mean that males were able to acquire skills that could raise their future income even though current wages among males and females were equal, in compliance with the law.

Individuals have a type of creative response that has been labelled a *feedback effect*. Regulation may alter individuals' behaviour after the regulation has been put into effect. If regulation requires fluoridated water, then parents know that their children's teeth have significant protection against tooth decay. Consequently, the feedback effect on parents' behaviour is that they may be less concerned about how many sweets their children eat.

EXAMPLE   The Effectiveness of Auto Safety Regulation

A good example of the feedback effect has to do with automotive safety regulation. Since the 1960s, the federal government has required automobile manufacturers to make cars increasingly safer. Some of the earlier requirements involved nonprotruding door handles, collapsible steering columns, and shatterproof glass. More recent requirements involve daytime running lights, better seat belts, and airbags. The desired result was fewer injuries and deaths for drivers involved in accidents. According to economist Sam Peltzman, however, due to the feedback effect, drivers have gradually started driving more recklessly. Automobiles with more safety features have been involved in a disproportionate number of accidents.

For critical analysis: The feedback effect has also been called the law of unintended consequences. Why?

EXPLAINING REGULATORS' BEHAVIOUR

Regulation has usually been defended by contending that government regulatory agencies are needed to correct market imperfections. We are dealing with a non-market situation because regulators are paid by the government and their decisions are not determined or constrained by the market. A number of theories have been put forward to describe the behaviour of regulators. These theories can help us understand how regulation has often harmed consumers through higher prices and less choice, and benefited producers through higher profits and fewer competitive forces. Two of the best-known theories of regulatory behaviour are the *capture hypothesis* and the *share-the-gains, share-the-pains theory*.

The Capture Hypothesis

▶ **Capture hypothesis**
A theory of regulatory behaviour that predicts that the regulators will eventually be captured by the special interests of the industry being regulated.

It has been observed that with the passage of time, regulators often end up adopting the views of the regulated. According to the **capture hypothesis,**[1] no matter what the reason for a regulatory agency's having been set up, it will eventually be captured by the special interests of the industry that is being regulated. Consider the reasons.

Who knows best about the industry that is being regulated? The people already in the industry. Who, then, will be asked to regulate the industry? Again, people who have been in the industry. And people who used to be in the industry have allegiances and friendships with others in the industry.

Also consider that whenever regulatory hearings are held, the affected consumer groups will have much less information about the industry than the people already in the industry, the producers. Additionally, the cost to any one consumer to show up at a regulatory hearing to express concern about a change in the rate structure will certainly exceed any perceived benefit that consumer could obtain from going to the rate-making hearing.

Because they have little incentive to do so, consumers and taxpayers will not be well organized, nor will they be greatly concerned with regulatory actions. But the special interests of the industry are going to be well organized and well defined. Political entrepreneurs within the regulatory agency see little payoff in supporting the views of consumers and taxpayers anyway. After all, few consumers understand the benefits deriving from regulatory agency actions. Moreover, how much could a consumer directly benefit someone who works in an agency? Regulators have the most incentive to support the position of a well-organized special-interest group within the industry that is being regulated.

▶ **Share-the-gains, share-the-pains theory**
A theory of regulatory behaviour in which the regulators must take account of the demands of three groups: legislators, who established and who oversee the regulatory agency; members of the regulated industry; and consumers of the regulated industry's products or services.

"Share the Gains, Share the Pains"

A somewhat different view of regulators' behaviour is given in the **share-the-gains, share-the-pains theory.**[2] This theory looks at the specific aims of the regulators. It

---

[1] See George Stigler, *The Citizen and the State: Essays on Regulation* (Chicago: University of Chicago Press, 1975).

[2] See Sam Peltzman, "Towards a More General Theory of Regulation," *Journal of Law and Economics*, 19 (1976), pp. 211–240.

argues that a regulator simply wants to continue in the job. To do so, the regulator must obtain the approval of both the legislators who established and oversee the regulatory agency, and the industry that is being regulated. A third group that must be taken into account is, of course, the customers of the industry.

Under the capture hypothesis, only the special interests of the industry being regulated had to be taken into account by the regulators. The share-the-gains, share-the-pains model contends that such a position is too risky because customers who are really hurt by improper regulation will complain to legislators, who might fire the regulators. Thus each regulator has to attach some weight to these three separate groups. What happens if there is an abrupt increase in fuel costs for electrical utilities? The capture theory would predict that regulators would relatively quickly allow for a rate increase in order to maintain the profits of the industry. The share-the-gains, share-the-pains theory, however, would predict that there will be an adjustment in rates, but not as quickly or as completely as the capture theory would predict. The regulatory agency is not completely captured by the industry; it has to take account of legislators and consumers.

THE COSTS OF REGULATION

There is no truly accurate way to measure the costs of regulation. However, in recent years, that cost has been growing, and more and more complex regulations are passed into law. In 1994, for example, it took 1,000 more pages to print the federal government's 818 new regulations than it did to print the 844 new regulations passed in 1974. But actual direct costs to taxpayers are only a small part of the overall cost of regulation. Pharmaceutical-manufacturing safety standards raise the price of drugs. Automobile safety standards raise the price of cars. Environmental controls on manufacturing raise the price of manufactured goods. All of these increased prices add to the cost of regulation. Studies suggest that the cost of administering federal regulations is about $50 billion per year. When you add the cost of enforcing regulations at the municipal and provincial levels, the total rises to $86 billion, or about 12 percent of each year's GDP! Not surprisingly, the increasing cost of regulation on occasion has brought about cries for **deregulation**, the removal of old regulations.

▶ **Deregulation**
The elimination or phasing out of regulations on economic activity.

Short-Run Versus Long-Run Effects of Deregulation

The short-run effects and the long-run effects of deregulation are quite different. In the short run, a regulated industry that becomes deregulated may experience numerous temporary adjustments. One is the inevitable shakeout of higher-cost producers with the accompanying removal of excess monopoly profits. Another is the sometimes dramatic displacement of workers who have laboured long and hard in the formerly regulated industry. The level of service for some consumers may fall; for example, after the deregulation of the Canadian National Railway (CNR), service to many small communities was eliminated as the CNR offloaded over 2,000 kilometres of track. The power of unions in the formerly regulated industry may decrease. And bankruptcies may cause disruptions, particularly in the local economy where the headquarters of the formerly regulated firm are located.

Those who support deregulation, or at least less regulation, contend that there are long-run, permanent benefits. These include lower prices that are closer to marginal cost. Furthermore, fewer monopoly profits are made in the deregulated industry. Such proponents argue that deregulation has positive *net* benefits.

Thinking Critically About the Media | **Deregulation of Airlines and Safety**

Every time there is a major commercial airline crash that involves death and injury, the media have a field day. Some journalists have even argued that such airline crashes are due to deregulation of the airline industry. Though it may be true that there are more airline fatalities today than prior to deregulation in the 1970s and 1980s, air-line safety has increased significantly. Lower airline prices, coupled with increasing population, have caused airline traffic to increase dramatically. Even if a larger number of accidents seem to be occurring, the number of *fatal accidents per 100,000 departures* has decreased almost 75 percent since 1978.

Deregulation and Contestable Markets

A major argument in favour of deregulation is that when government-imposed barriers to entry are removed, competition will cause firms to enter markets that previously had only a few firms with market power due to those entry barriers. Potential competitors will become actual competitors, and prices will fall towards a competitive level. Recently, this argument has been bolstered by a relatively new model of efficient firm behaviour that predicts competitive prices in spite of a lack of a large number of firms. This model is called the **theory of contestable markets.** Under the theory of contestable markets, most of the outcomes predicted by the theory of perfect competition will occur in certain industries with relatively few firms. Specifically, where the theory of contestable markets is applicable, the few firms may still produce the output at which price equals marginal cost in both the short run and the long run. These firms will receive zero economic profits in the long run.

▶ **Theory of contestable markets**

A hypothesis concerning pricing behaviour that holds that even though there are only a few firms in an industry, they are forced to price their products more or less competitively because of the ease of entry by outsiders. The key aspect of a contestable market is relatively costless entry into and exit from the industry.

Unconstrained and Relatively Costless Entry and Exit. For a market to be perfectly contestable, firms must be able to enter and leave the industry easily. Freedom of entry and exit implies an absence of nonprice constraints and of serious fixed costs associated with a potential competitor's decision to enter a contestable market. Such an absence of important fixed costs results if the firm need buy no specific durable inputs in order to enter, if it uses up all such inputs it does purchase, or if all of its specific durable inputs are saleable upon exit without any losses beyond those normally incurred from depreciation. The important issue is whether potential entrants can easily get their investment out at any time in the future.

The mathematical model of perfect contestability is complex, but the underlying logic is straightforward. As long as conditions for free entry prevail, any excess profits, or any inefficiencies on the part of incumbent firms, will serve as an inducement for potential entrants. By entering, new firms can temporarily profit at no risk to themselves from the less than competitive situation in the industry. Once competitive conditions are again restored, these firms will leave the industry just as quickly.

Benefits of Contestable Markets. Contestable markets have several desirable characteristics. One has to do with profits. Profits that exceed the opportunity cost of capital will not exist in the long run because of freedom of entry, just as in a perfectly competitive industry. The elimination of "excess" profits can occur even with only a couple of firms in an industry. The threat of entry will cause them to expand output to eliminate excess profit.

Also, firms that have cost curves that are higher than those of the most efficient firms will find that they cannot compete. These firms will be replaced by entrants whose cost curves are consistent with the most efficient technology. In other words, in contestable markets, there will be no cost inefficiencies in the long run.

Rethinking Regulation Using Cost-Benefit Analysis

Try Preview Question 4:
Why have economists been re-evaluating the government's role as an economic regulator?

Rather than considering deregulation as the only solution to "too much" regulation, some economists argue that regulation should simply be put to a cost-benefit test. Specifically, the cost of existing and proposed regulations should be compared to the benefits. Unless it can be demonstrated that regulations generate net positive benefits (benefits greater than costs), such regulations should not be in effect.

EXAMPLE   Cutting Through the "Red Tape"

Since 1975, governments at every level in Canada have collectively implemented approximately 100,000 regulations dealing with everything from land use and environmental protection to building codes and packaging. In many cases, provincial regulations overlap federal regulations, leaving businesses with mounds of "red tape" to cut through each year. Governments in Canada have recognized the need to simplify regulatory procedures, and many of them are working on it now.

The federal government has adopted a cost-benefit approach to reviews of current regulations. Every federal regulatory agency must use a software-based business impact test to measure the effect on the private sector of proposed changes to their regulations. This is no small task—the Treasury Board estimates that between 1993 and 1998, over 800 regulatory revisions took place.

The provinces, too, are looking to streamline their regulations. Alberta has introduced "sunset" schedules which trigger reviews of the effectiveness of regulations every three years. Saskatchewan has committed to review all its regulations for necessity and efficiency, and to reduce overall regulation by 25 percent within the next 10 years. Other governments are developing cost-saving targets: New Brunswick reduced its regulatory costs by 25 percent in 1996 alone!

While these governments recognize the importance of regulating certain industries to provide safety and security for consumers, they are trying to do so without unduly penalizing the business community. In this way they hope to achieve, as one Treasury Board booklet put it, "smarter" regulatory management.

For critical analysis: What costs are attached to reviewing and revising regulations?

Concepts in Brief

- It is difficult to regulate the price per constant-quality unit because it is difficult to measure all dimensions of quality.
- The capture hypothesis holds that regulatory agencies will eventually be captured by special interests of the industry. This is because consumers are a diffuse group who individually are not affected greatly by regulation, whereas industry groups are well focused and know that large amounts of potential profits are at stake and depend on the outcome of regulatory proceedings.
- In the share-the-gains, share-the-pains theory of regulation, regulators must take account of the interests of three groups: the industry, legislators, and consumers.
- The short-run effects of deregulation often include bankruptcy and disrupted service. The long-run results in deregulated industries should include better service, more variety, and lower costs. One argument in favour of deregulation involves the theory of contestable markets—if entry and exit are relatively costless, the number of firms in an industry is irrelevant in terms of determining whether consumers pay competitive prices.

COMPETITION POLICY

It is the express aim of our government to foster efficiency and competition in the economy. To this end, numerous attempts have been made to legislate against business practices that seemingly destroy the competitive nature of the system. This is the general idea behind anticombines legislation: If the courts can prevent collusion among sellers of a product, monopoly prices will not result; there will be no restriction of output if the members of an industry are not allowed to join together in restraint of trade. Remember that the competitive solution to the price-quantity problem is one in which the price of the item produced is equal to its marginal social opportunity cost. Also, no *economic* profits are made in the long run.

The History of Anticombines Legislation

Anticombines legislation has a long history in Canada. *An Act for the Protection and Suppression of Combinations in Restraint of Trade* was passed by the federal government in 1889, and amended in 1892 to become Section 502 of the Criminal Code. This new law made it a criminal offence to act to unduly restrict competition in the marketplace. Over the next 100 years, the Act was amended many more times.

The *Anticombines Act* of 1910

The *Anticombines Act* of 1910 expanded and clarified the powers bestowed under the 1889 Act. It set out procedures for initiating and investigating complaints of restrictive trade practice. On petition from any six persons, a judge could now order investigation of an alleged crime.

In 1915, the government established a board whose duties included regulating prices and preventing persons or firms from hoarding necessities in order to drive up price and increase profits. The courts, however, declared in 1922 that this board was unconstitutional under the terms of the *British North America Act*. Accordingly, in 1923, the government again amended the *Anticombines Act* to allow for a constitutional investigative body.

Evolution of Anticombines Law

Over the first half of the twentieth century, the interpretation of anticombines law evolved to apply to three main offences: price fixing that unduly restricted competition; mergers or monopolies acting contrary to the public interest; and unfair trade practices. Convictions under the anticombines legislation were difficult to obtain, however, because of the Criminal Code requirement of proof beyond a reasonable doubt.

Thus in 1960, the government passed an amendment to the *Combines Investigation Act* making offences under the Act civil, rather than criminal, matters. By applying the less restrictive burden of proof required in civil cases, the Restrictive Trade Practices Commission won many more convictions of offending companies.

The federal government added to the scope and power of the *Combines Investigation Act* in 1976. The Act was extended to cover service industries which had hitherto been exempt, and sections were added dealing with misleading advertising. The Restrictive Trade Practices Commission was given power to protect consumers by keeping suppliers from refusing to supply without good reason, from restricting the way in which a good is sold, and from requiring tied sales.

The *Competition Act* of 1986

In June of 1986, the government repealed the *Combines Investigation Act* and replaced it with the *Competition Act* and the *Competition Tribunal Act*. The purpose of this new legislation is "to maintain and encourage competition in Canada in order to promote the efficiency and adaptability of the Canadian economy." The new Competition Tribunal which replaced the old Restrictive Trade Practices Commission is a quasi-judicial body with fairly wide-ranging powers to issue orders and to fine offenders. The maximum fine for price-fixing, for example, is $10 million!

The *Competition Act* classifies anti-competitive behaviour as "abuse of dominant position" by monopolies or combines, and mergers which "prevent or substantially lessen competition." General restrictive trade practices such as pyramid selling schemes, as well as tied sales and misleading advertising are also considered anti-competitive. Canada's anticombines legislation now applies to all economic activities except collective bargaining, amateur sports, securities underwriting, and government-regulated industries.

POLICY EXAMPLE   Breaking the Tight Grip of Interac

The issue of "abuse of dominant position" came to the fore in late 1995 when George Addy, Director of the Competition Bureau, ruled that the Interac organization had acted to restrain trade by preventing retailers and other financial institutions from gaining direct access to the system.

The "charter members" of Interac—Bank of Montreal, Royal Bank of Canada, Canadian Imperial Bank of Commerce, Bank of Nova Scotia, Toronto-Dominion Bank, National Bank of Canada, Canada Trustco, and the network of credit unions and *caisses populaires*—had long resisted widening their network for security reasons, forcing retailers and others to use a charter member as an intermediary.

The group challenging the status quo was a mixed bag of non-banks, including investment houses Midland Walwyn, Richardson Greenshields of Canada, Mackenzie Financial Corp., and Trimark Investment Management Inc., as well as the Canadian Life and Health Insurance Association, and the Retail Council of Canada. All wanted to issue their own Interac cards to their customers and set up their own networks of cash machines. With changes taking place in the banking industry, non-banks increasingly are offering deposit services to the public. However, without direct access to Interac, the non-banks must pay whatever service charge the intermediary stipulates, and swallow increases in service charges or risk losing customers. The challengers argued that this reduced their ability to compete in the financial market.

Following Mr. Addy's decision, the charter members agreed to open the Interac network to non-banks. This change should allow for more competition for the consumer's discretionary income.

For critical analysis: With the widening of access to Interac, what do you predict will happen to service charges for using ATMs which belong to a competitor's system?

Concepts in Brief

- The first anticombines law was *An Act for the Protection and Suppression of Combinations in Restraint of Trade*, passed in 1889, which made it illegal to unduly restrict competition in the marketplace.
- The *Anticombines Act* of 1910 set out procedures for reporting and investigating alleged anti-competitive behaviour.
- In 1960, anti-competitive behaviour was made a civil offence instead of a criminal offence. Because of the less restrictive burden of proof, many more convictions were won.
- The *Competition Act* of 1986 was aimed at maintaining and encouraging an efficient and competitive Canadian economy.

Issues and Applications

Competition Policy for Non-economic Concerns?

Concepts Applied: Anticombines policies, corporate concentration

The National Post, a Hollinger Inc. publication, made its debut on October 27, 1998. Hollinger's extensive ownership of Canadian newspapers does not restrict competition for advertising space in the print media.

In mid-1996, Conrad Black, publisher of almost 650 newspapers worldwide, approached the Bureau of Competition Policy for approval of his plan to acquire 50.7 percent of Southam Inc., publisher of 32 Canadian daily papers. The Bureau gave its consent, making Mr. Black and his company, Hollinger Inc., the largest newspaper publisher in Canada. Table 14.2 shows the distribution of Hollinger's holdings across the country. In all, it owns 59 of 105 daily newspapers, including all of those in Saskatchewan, Prince Edward Island, and Newfoundland.

The Controversy

Hollinger's purchase of Southam brought forth howls of outrage from the Council of Canadians. The Council, a 60,000-member, non-profit national lobby group, feared that freedom of the press and editorial diversity would be seriously threatened by this growing concentration of ownership. The Council filed an appeal of the Bureau's decision, but had missed the deadline for submitting appeals. It then sued the federal government, arguing that the Canadian Constitution guarantees freedom of expression for news-

Table 14.2
Distribution of Daily Newspapers Controlled by Hollinger Inc.

Province	Number of Daily Papers Owned or Controlled by Hollinger Inc.
British Columbia	12
Alberta	3
Saskatchewan	5
Manitoba	0
Ontario	25
Quebec	4
New Brunswick	0
Nova Scotia	3
Prince Edward Island	2
Newfoundland	2

paper readers, and asking the federal government to step in to regulate the newspaper business. The federal court ruled that the lawsuit did not have grounds to proceed.

The Decision

The Bureau of Competition Policy defended its decision by declaring that Hollinger Inc. was not unduly restricting competition with its purchase of Southam Inc. The Bureau looked strictly at the competitive aspects of the newspaper business, and particularly at the effect of the purchase on advertising space. Since the purchase of Southam Inc. meant only a change of ownership, and not a change in the number of newspapers, the availability of advertising space was not affected. Thus, the Bureau approved the purchase. Later, the Bureau noted that its mandate did not include passing judgment on editorial diversity.

The Response

Mr. Black, for his part, brushed off his critics. Since in addition to the print media there are 60 or more television channels and hundreds of radio stations across Canada, he explained that he could not possibly control editorial diversity. Mr. Black then expressed an interest in going national. He purchased the *Financial Post* and incorporated it in his new national newspaper, the *National Post*, which debuted on October 27, 1998.

For Critical Analysis

1. Is there an argument for growing concentration of print ownership due to economies of scale?

2. How would a regulatory agency measure whether there is a threat to editorial diversity or freedom of expression?

CHAPTER SUMMARY

1. Regulation may be applied to a natural monopoly, which arises when, for example, the average total cost curve falls over a very large range of production rates. In such a situation, only one firm can survive. It will be the firm that can expand production and sales faster than the others to take advantage of the falling average total costs. If regulation seeks to force the natural monopolist to produce at the point where the marginal cost curve (supply curve in the competitive case) intersects the demand curve, the natural monopolist will incur losses, because when average total costs are falling, marginal costs are below average total costs. The regulators face a dilemma.

2. There are several ways of regulating monopolies, the most common ones being a cost-of-service basis or a rate-of-return basis. Under cost-of-service regulation, the regulated monopolies are allowed to charge prices that reflect only reasonable costs. Under rate-of-return regulation, the regulated monopolies are allowed to set rates so as to make a competitive rate of return for the equity shareholders. Supposedly, no monopoly profits can therefore be earned.

3. The capture hypothesis predicts that because of the diffuse interests of consumers as compared to the well-focused interests of industry members, regulators will eventually be captured by those whom they regulate.

4. The share-the-gains, share-the-pains theory predicts that regulators must take account not only of the desires of members of the industry but also of the wishes of legislators and consumers.

5. The short-run effects of deregulation can include bankruptcy and disrupted service. The long-run results in deregulated industries should include better service, more variety, and lower costs.

6. One argument in favour of deregulation involves the theory of contestable markets—if entry and exit are relatively costless, the number of firms in an industry is irrelevant in terms of determining whether consumers pay competitive prices.

7. Some economists argue that all actual and proposed regulation be subject to strict cost-benefit analysis.

8. Anticombines legislation is designed to encourage competition and efficiency in the Canadian economy. The *Competition Act* and the *Competition Tribunal Act* form the major anticombines policy today.

DISCUSSION OF PREVIEW QUESTIONS

1. **What is a natural monopoly, and how does one arise?**

   A natural monopoly is a situation in which the long-run average cost curve falls persistently as output expands. Thus the natural monopolist is a firm that by expanding is able to charge a price lower than its competitors can, thereby eliminating them. A natural monopolist arises due to tremendous economies of scale; expanding output causes ATC to fall.

2. **If natural monopolies are required to price at marginal cost, what problem emerges?**

   We have noted in earlier chapters that efficiency requires that people pay the marginal cost for a good or a service. If regulators grant a firm monopoly privileges (recognizing it as a natural monopoly and regulating it to keep it in line) but force it to price at its marginal cost of production, a problem emerges. Because long-run ATC is persistently falling, it follows that long-run marginal cost must be below long-run ATC. Forcing a firm to charge a price equal to marginal cost implies that average revenue = price = marginal cost < average total cost (AR = P = MC < ATC). It follows that AR < ATC, and therefore the regulated natural monopolist would experience *negative* economic profits. In that case, it would shut down unless subsidized. In short, forcing a regulated natural monopolist to price at marginal cost may be socially beneficial, but such a policy requires that the natural monopolist be subsidized to cover the resulting economic losses to the firm.

3. What are some means of regulating a natural monopoly?

Two important means of regulating a natural monopoly are cost-of-service and rate-of-return. Cost-of-service regulation aims at requiring a natural monopolist to price at levels that would result from a more competitive situation. In effect, the natural monopolist is required to charge the average cost of providing

the service in question, thereby ensuring zero economic profits. The rate-of-return form of regulation in effect allows a natural monopolist to price at rates that permit it an *overall* "normal" rate of return, because the natural monopolist will remain in operation only if it earns at least a normal return on invested capital.

4. Why have economists been re-evaluating the government's role as an economic regulator?

Presumably, regulation is an attempt to prevent monopoly abuses and to simulate a competitive market structure where one would not otherwise exist. Yet much academic research indicates that this is not the case; regulated industries apparently behave more like monopolies than the overall manufacturing sector does. Some analysts have claimed that the regulated firms sooner or later "capture" the regulatory agencies; before long, regulated industries have the protection and sanction of the regulatory bodies! Hence many economists favour deregulation.

PROBLEMS

(Answers to the odd-numbered problems appear at the back of the book.)

14-1. The accompanying graph depicts a situation for a monopolist.

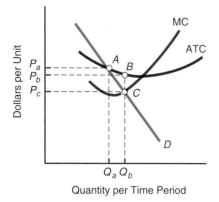

a. If this monopolist were required to price at marginal cost, what would the quan-

tity and price be?

b. What rectangle would indicate total economic losses if this monopolist were required to price at marginal cost?

14-2. "The elimination of all tariffs would dissipate more monopoly power than any other single government action." What do tariffs (taxes on imported goods only) have to do with monopoly power?

14-3. Assume that you are in charge of enforcing the *Workers' Compensation Act*. If you are not constrained to consider the costs of new regulations that increase worker health and safety, what *will* constrain your behaviour, if anything? If you now must consider the costs of your new rules, how might you go about your job?

14-4. Why is the right of free entry insufficient to prevent sustained economic profits within a natural monopoly?

14-5. Suppose that you own the only natural hot springs in your province. Why would we *not* expect to see the provincial government regulating the price you charge?

14-6. "Philosophically, I am vehemently opposed to government interference in the marketplace. As the owner of a neighbourhood pub, however, I can tell you that deregulation will be bad for the citizenry. You would not want a neighbourhood pub on every corner, would you?" Why would you predict that a neighbourhood pub owner would defend regulation of the liquor industry in this way?

14-7. Visit the Canadian Business Service Centre's Web site at www.cbsc.org/fedbis/search.html. Search for "Competition Act" using the search box on the left side of the screen. Choose one of the Competition Act topics that come up, and answer the following questions.

a. What is the offence described under the Competition Act?
b. Why is it an offence?
c. Is the offence civil or criminal in nature?
d. What is the range of penalties available to the Competition Tribunal to apply to violators?
e. Can you find a decision at the Competition Tribunal's Web site listed below which involves the offence you have found?

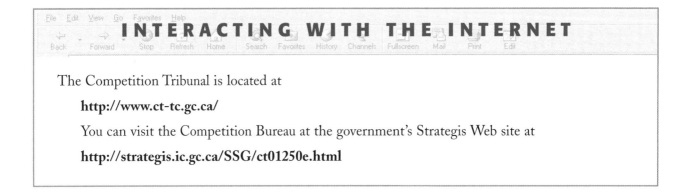

INTERACTING WITH THE INTERNET

The Competition Tribunal is located at

http://www.ct-tc.gc.ca/

You can visit the Competition Bureau at the government's Strategis Web site at

http://strategis.ic.gc.ca/SSG/ct01250e.html

PART 4

Productive Factors, Poverty, the Environment, and Development

Chapter 15

Labour Demand and Supply

Chapter 17

Rent, Interest, and Profits

Chapter 19

Environmental Economics

Chapter 21

Cybernomics

Chapter 16

Unions and Labour Market Monopoly Power

Chapter 18

Income and Poverty

Chapter 20

Development: Economic Growth Around the World

Labour Demand and Supply

Except for a relatively small First Nations population, North America has been peopled by immigrants for hundreds of years. Many Canadians are proud of their foreign origins, be they Asian, European, African, Latin American, or Middle Eastern. Immigration today, nonetheless, has become a major policy issue. In particular, some politicians and labour unions argue that current immigration is hurting the Canadian economy and is thus pushing down the wages of nonimmigrant Canadian workers. Before you can analyse this issue, you need to know about the basic model of labour demand and supply.

Preview Questions

1. When hiring labour, what general rule will be followed by employers who wish to maximize profits?

2. What is the profit-maximizing rate of employment for a perfectly competitive firm?

3. How is an industry wage rate determined?

4. What is the profit-maximizing rate of employment for an imperfectly competitive firm?

Did You Know That... in 1996, the Chairman of the Bank of Montreal, Matthew Barratt, was paid a total of $3,880,000 in salary and benefits? In contrast, if you are a typical college or university student, the most you can hope to make during the first year after graduating is between $25,000 and $40,000, or approximately one one-hundredth of Barratt's annual income. Leaving aside whether he is worth it, to understand why firms pay different workers different wages requires an understanding of the demand for and supply of labour.

A firm's demand for inputs can be studied in much the same manner as we studied the demand for output in different market situations. Again, various market situations will be examined. Our analysis will always end with the same commonsense conclusion: A firm will hire employees up to the point beyond which it isn't profitable to hire any more. It will hire employees to the point at which the marginal benefit of hiring a worker will just equal the marginal cost. Basically, in every profit-maximizing situation, it is most profitable to carry out an activity up to the point at which the marginal benefit equals the marginal cost. Remembering that guideline will help you in analysing decision making at the firm level. We will start our analysis under the assumption that the market for input factors is perfectly competitive. We will further assume that the output market is perfectly competitive. This provides a benchmark against which to compare other situations in which labour markets or product markets are not perfectly competitive.

COMPETITION IN THE PRODUCT MARKET

Let's take as our example a compact disc (CD) manufacturing firm that is in competition with many companies selling the same kind of product. Assume that the labourers hired by our CD maker do not need any special skills. This firm sells its product in a perfectly competitive market. A CD manufacturer also buys labour (its variable input) in a perfectly competitive market. A firm that hires labour under perfectly competitive conditions hires only a tiny proportion of all the workers who are potentially available. By "potentially available" we mean all the workers in a given geographic area who possess the skills demanded by our perfect competitor. In such a market, it is always possible for the individual firm to pick up extra workers without having to offer a higher wage. Thus, the supply of labour to the firm is perfectly elastic—that is, represented by a horizontal line at the going wage rate established by the forces of supply and demand in the entire labour market. The firm is a price taker in the labour market.

MARGINAL PHYSICAL PRODUCT

Look at part (a) of Figure 15.1. In column 1, we show the number of workers per week that the firm can hire. In column 2, we show total physical product (TPP) per

Figure 15.1
Marginal Revenue Product

In part (a), column 4 shows marginal revenue product (MRP), which is the amount of additional revenue the firm receives for the sale of that additional output. Marginal revenue product is simply the amount of money the additional worker brings in—the combination of that worker's contribution to production and the revenue that that production will bring to the firm. For this perfectly competitive firm, marginal revenue is equal to the price of the product, or $6 per unit. At a weekly wage of $498, the profit-maximizing employer will pay for only 12 workers because then the marginal revenue product is just equal to the wage rate or weekly salary.

Part (a)

(1) Labour Input (workers per week)	(2) Total Physical Product (TPP) CDs per Week	(3) Marginal Physical Product (MPP) CDs per Week	(4) Marginal Revenue (MR = P = $6 net) x MPP = Marginal Revenue Product (MRP) ($ per additional worker)	(5) Wage Rate ($ per week) = Marginal Factor Cost (MFC) = Change in Total Costs Change in Labour
6	882			
		118	708	498
7	1,000			
		111	666	498
8	1,111			
		104	624	498
9	1,215			
		97	582	498
10	1,312			
		90	540	498
11	1,402			
		83	498	498
12	1,485			
		76	456	498
13	1,561			

In part (b), we find the number of workers the firm will want to hire by observing the wage rate that is established by the forces of supply and demand in the entire labour market. We show that this employer is hiring labour in a perfectly competitive labour market and therefore faces a perfectly elastic supply curve represented by s at $498 per week. As in all other situations, we basically have a supply and demand model; in this example, the demand curve is represented by MRP, and the supply curve is s. Equilibrium occurs at their intersection.

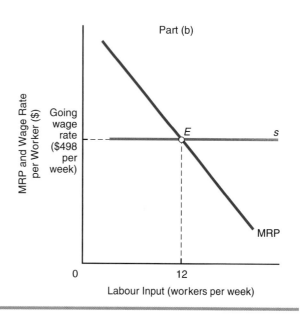

week, the total *physical* production that different quantities of the labour input (in combination with a fixed amount of other inputs) will generate in a week's time. In column 3, we show the additional output gained when a CD maker adds workers to its existing manufacturing facility. This column, the **marginal physical product (MPP) of labour,** represents the extra (additional) output attributed to employing additional units of the variable input factor. If this firm adds a seventh worker, the MPP is 118. The law of diminishing marginal returns predicts that additional units of a variable factor will, after some point, cause the MPP to decline, other things being held constant.

▶ **Marginal physical product (MPP) of labour**
The change in output resulting from the addition of one more worker. The MPP of the worker equals the change in total output accounted for by hiring the worker, holding all other factors of production constant.

Why the Decline in MPP?

We are assuming all other nonlabour factors of production are held constant. So if our CD maker wants to add one more worker to its production line, it has to crowd all the existing workers a little closer together because it does not increase its capital stock (the production equipment). Therefore, as we add more workers, each one has a smaller and smaller fraction of the available capital stock with which to work. If one worker uses one machine, adding another worker usually won't double the output because the machine can run only so fast and for so many hours per day. In other words, MPP declines because of the law of diminishing marginal returns.

Marginal Revenue Product

We now need to translate into a dollar value the physical product that results from hiring an additional worker. This is done by multiplying the marginal physical product by the marginal revenue of the firm. Because our CD firm is selling its product in a perfectly competitive market, marginal revenue is equal to the price of the product. If the seventh worker's MPP is 118 and the marginal revenue is $6 per CD, the **marginal revenue product (MRP)** is $708 (118 × $6). The MRP is shown in column 4 of part (a) of Figure 15.1. *The marginal revenue product represents the worker's contribution to the firm's total revenues.*

▶ **Marginal revenue product (MRP)**
The marginal physical product (MPP) times marginal revenue. The MRP gives the additional revenue obtained from a one-unit change in labour input.

When a firm operates in a competitive product market, the marginal physical product times the product price is also sometimes referred to as the *value of marginal product (VMP).* Because price and marginal revenue are the same for a perfectly competitive firm, the VMP is also the MRP.

In column 5 of part (a) of Figure 15.1, we show the wage rate, or *marginal factor cost,* of each worker. The marginal cost of workers is the extra cost incurred in employing that factor of production. We call that cost the **marginal factor cost (MFC).** Otherwise stated,

▶ **Marginal factor cost (MFC)**
The cost of using an additional unit of an input. For example, if a firm can hire all the workers it wants at the going wage rate, the marginal factor cost of labour is the wage rate.

$$\text{Marginal factor cost} \equiv \frac{\text{change in total cost}}{\text{change in amount of resource used}}$$

Because each worker is paid the same competitively determined wage of $498 per week, the MFC is the same for all workers. And because the firm is buying labour in a perfectly competitive labour market, the wage rate of $498 per week really represents the firm's supply curve of labour. That curve is perfectly elastic because the firm can purchase all labour at the same wage rate, considering that it is a minuscule part of the entire labour-purchasing market. (Recall the definition of perfect competition.) We show this perfectly elastic supply curve as *s* in part (b) of Figure 15.1.

General Rule for Hiring

Virtually every optimizing rule in economics involves comparing marginal benefits with marginal cost. The general rule, therefore, for the hiring decision of a firm is this:

> The firm hires workers up to the point at which the additional cost associated with hiring the last worker is equal to the additional revenue generated by that worker.

In a perfectly competitive situation, this is the point at which the wage rate just equals the marginal revenue product. If the firm hired more workers, the additional wages would not be covered by additional increases in total revenue. If the firm hired fewer workers, it would be forfeiting the contributions that those workers could make to total profits.

Therefore, referring to columns 4 and 5 in part (a) of Figure 15.1, we see that this firm would certainly employ the seventh worker, because the MRP is $708 while the MFC is only $498. The firm would continue to employ workers up to the point at which MFC = MRP because as workers are added, they contribute more to revenue than to cost.

Try Preview Question 1:

When hiring labour, what general rule will be followed by employers who wish to maximize profits?

The MRP Curve: Demand for Labour

We can also use part (b) of Figure 15.1 to find how many workers our firm should hire. First, we draw a straight line across from the going wage rate, which is determined by demand and supply in the labour market. The straight line is labelled *s* to indicate that it is the supply curve of labour for the *individual* firm purchasing labour in a perfectly competitive labour market. That firm can purchase all the labour it wants of equal quality at $498 per worker. This perfectly elastic supply curve, *s*, intersects the marginal revenue product curve at 12 workers per week. At the intersection, *E*, the wage rate is equal to the marginal revenue product. Equilibrium for the firm is obtained when the firm's demand curve for labour, which turns out to be its MRP curve, intersects the firm's supply curve for labour, shown as *s*. The firm in our example would not hire the thirteenth worker, who will add only $456 to revenue but $498 to cost. If the price of labour should fall to, say, $456 per worker, it would become profitable for the firm to hire an additional worker; there is an increase in the quantity of labour demanded as the wage decreases.

Try Preview Question 2:

What is the profit-maximizing rate of employment for a perfectly competitive firm?

DERIVED DEMAND

We have identified an individual firm's demand for labour curve as its MRP curve. Under conditions of perfect competition in both product and labour markets, MRP is determined by multiplying MPP times the product's price. This suggests that the demand for labour is a **derived demand.** That is to say that our CD firm does not want to purchase the services of labour just for the services themselves. Factors of production are rented or purchased not because they give any intrinsic satisfaction to the firms' owners but because they can be used to manufacture output that is expected to be sold for profit.

▶ **Derived demand**

Input factor demand derived from demand for the final product being produced.

We know that an increase in the market demand for a given product raises the product's price (all other things held constant), which in turn increases the marginal revenue product, or demand for the resource. Figure 15.2 illustrates the effective role played by changes in product demand in a perfectly competitive product market. The MRP curve shifts whenever there is a change in the price of the final product that the workers are making. If, for example, the market price of CDs goes down, the MRP curve will shift downward to the left from MRP_0 to MRP_1. We know that $MRP = MPP \times MR$. If marginal revenue (here the output price) falls, so, too, does the demand for labour; at the same going wage rate, the firm will hire fewer workers. This is because at various levels of labour use, the marginal revenue product of labour falls so that at the initial equilibrium, the price of labour (here the MFC) becomes greater than MRP. Thus the firm would reduce the number of workers hired. Conversely, if the marginal revenue (output price) rises, the demand for labour will also rise, and the firm will want to hire more workers at each and every possible wage rate.

We just pointed out that $MRP = MPP \times MR$. Clearly, then, a change in marginal productivity, or in the marginal physical product of labour, will shift the MRP curve. If the marginal productivity of labour decreases, the MRP curve, or demand

---

Figure 15.2

Demand for Labour, a Derived Demand

The demand for labour is derived from the demand for the final product being produced. Therefore, the marginal revenue product curve will shift whenever the price of the product changes. If we start with the marginal revenue product curve MRP at the going wage rate of $498 per week, 12 workers will be hired. If the price of CDs goes down, the marginal product curve will shift to MRP_1, and the number of workers hired will fall to 10. If the price of CDs goes up, the marginal revenue product curve will shift to MRP_2, and the number of workers hired will increase to 15.

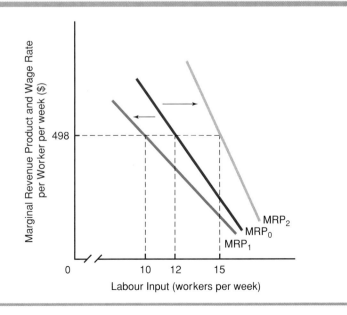

curve, for labour will shift inward to the left. Again, this is because at every quantity of labour used, the MRP will be lower. A lower quantity of labour will be demanded at every possible wage rate.

THE MARKET DEMAND FOR LABOUR

The downward-sloping portion of each individual firm's marginal revenue product curve is also its demand curve for the one variable factor of production—in our example, labour. When we go to the entire market for a particular type of labour in a particular industry, we find that quantity of labour demanded will vary as the wage rate changes. Given that the market demand curve for labour is made up of the individual firm demand curve for labour, we can safely assume that the market demand curve for labour will look like D in part (b) of Figure 15.3: It will slope downward. That market demand curve for labour in the CD industry shows the quantities of labour demanded by all of the firms in the industry at various wage rates.

It is important to note that the market demand curve for labour is not a simple horizontal summation of the labour demand curves of all individual firms. Remember that the demand for labour is a derived demand. Even if we hold labour productivity constant, the demand for labour still depends on both the wage rate and the price of the final output. Assume that we start at a wage rate of $20 per hour and employment level 10 in part (a) of Figure 15.3. If we sum all such employment levels—point a in part (a)—across firms, we get a market quantity demanded of

Figure 15.3
Derivation of the Market Demand Curve for Labour
The market demand curve for labour is not simply the horizontal summation of each individual firm's demand curve for labour. If wage rates fall from $20 to $10, all firms will increase employment and therefore output, causing the price of the product to fall. This causes the marginal revenue product curve of each firm to shift inward, as from d_0 to d_1 in part (a). The resulting market demand curve, D, in part (b) is therefore less elastic than it would be if output price remained constant.

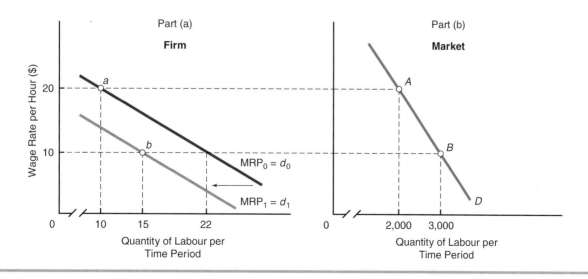

Try Preview Question 3:

How is an industry wage rate determined?

2,000—point *A* in part (b)—at the wage rate of $20. A decrease in the wage rate to $10 per hour induces individual firms' employment level to increase toward a quantity demanded of 22. As all firms simultaneously increase employment, however, there is a shift in the product supply curve such that output increases. Hence the price of the product must fall. The fall in the output price in turn causes a downward shift of each firm's MRP curve (d_0) to MRP_1 (d_1) in part (a). Thus each firm's employment of labour increases to 15 rather than to 22 at the wage rate of $10 per hour. A summation of all such employment levels gives us 3,000—point *B*—in part (b).

DETERMINANTS OF DEMAND ELASTICITY FOR INPUTS

Just as we were able to discuss the price elasticity of demand for different commodities in Chapter 8, we can discuss the price elasticity of demand for inputs. The price elasticity of demand for labour is defined in a manner similar to the price elasticity of demand for goods: the percentage change in quantity demanded divided by the percentage change in the price of labour. When the numerical value of this ratio is less than 1, it is inelastic; when it is 1, unit-elastic; and when it is greater than 1, elastic.

There are four principal determinants of the price elasticity of demand for an input. The price elasticity of demand for a variable input will be greater:

1. The greater the price elasticity of demand for the final product
2. The easier it is for a particular variable input to be substituted for by other inputs
3. The larger the proportion of total costs accounted for by a particular variable input
4. The longer the time period being considered

Consider some examples. An individual radish farmer faces an extremely elastic demand for radishes, given the existence of many competing radish growers. If the farmer's labourers tried to obtain a significant wage increase, the farmer couldn't pass on the resultant higher costs to radish buyers. So any wage increase to the individual radish farmer would lead to a large reduction in the quantity of labour demanded.

Clearly, the easier it is for a producer to switch to using another factor of production, the more responsive that producer will be to an increase in an input's price. If plastic and aluminum can easily be substituted in the production of, say, car bumpers, then a price rise in aluminum will cause car makers to reduce greatly their quantity of aluminum demanded.

When a particular input's costs account for a very large share of total costs, any increase in that input's price will affect total costs relatively more. If labour costs are 80 percent of total costs, a company will cut back on employment more aggressively than if labour costs were only 8 percent of total costs, for any given wage increase.

Finally, over longer periods, firms have more time to figure out ways to economize on the use of inputs whose prices have gone up. Furthermore, over time, technological change will allow for easier substitution in favour of relatively cheaper inputs and against inputs whose prices went up. At first, a pay raise obtained by a strong telephone company union may not result in many layoffs, but over time, the telephone company will use new technology to replace many of the now more expensive workers.

Concepts in Brief

- The change in total output due to a one-unit change in one variable input, holding all other inputs constant, is called the marginal physical product (MPP). When we multiply marginal physical product times marginal revenue, we obtain the marginal revenue product (MRP).
- A firm will hire workers up to the point at which the additional cost of hiring one more worker is equal to the additional revenues generated. For the individual firm, therefore, its MRP of labour curve is also its demand for labour curve.
- The demand for labour is a derived demand, derived from the demand for final output. Therefore, if the price of final output changes, this will cause a shift in the MRP curve (which is also the firm's demand for labour curve).
- Input price elasticity of demand depends on final product elasticity, the ease of other input substitution, the relative importance of the input's cost in total costs, and the time allowed for adjustment.

WAGE DETERMINATION

Having developed the demand curve for labour (and all other variable inputs) in a particular industry, let's turn to the labour supply curve. By adding supply to the analysis, we can come up with the equilibrium wage rate that workers earn in an industry. We can think in terms of a supply curve for labour that slopes upward in a particular industry. At higher wage rates, more workers will want to enter that particular industry. The individual firm, however, does not face the entire *market* supply curve. Rather, in a perfectly competitive case, the individual firm is such a small part of the market that it can hire all the workers that it wants at the going wage rate. We say, therefore, that the industry faces an upward-sloping supply curve but that the individual *firm* faces a perfectly elastic supply curve for labour.

The demand curve for labour in the CD industry is D in Figure 15.4 (page 378), and the supply curve of labour is S. The equilibrium wage rate of $498 a week is established at the intersection of the two curves. The quantity of workers both supplied and demanded at that rate is Q_1. If for some reason the wage rate fell to $400 a week, in our hypothetical example, there would be an excess number of workers demanded at that wage rate. Conversely, if the wage rate rose to $600 a week, there would be an excess quantity of workers supplied at that wage rate.

Figure 15.4
The Equilibrium Wage Rate and the CD Industry
The industry demand curve for labour is *D*. We put in a hypothetical upward-sloping labour supply curve for the CD industry, *S*. The intersection is at point *E*, giving an equilibrium wage rate of $498 per week and an equilibrium quantity of labour demanded of Q_1. At a price above $498 per week, there will be an excess quantity of workers supplied. At a price below $498 per week, there will be an excess quantity of workers demanded.

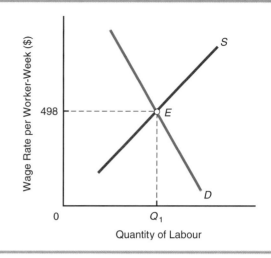

We have just found the equilibrium wage rate for the entire CD industry. The individual firm must take that equilibrium wage rate as given in the competitive model used here because the individual firm is a very small part of the total demand for labour. Thus each firm purchasing labour in a perfectly competitive market can purchase all of the input it wants at the going market price.

POLICY EXAMPLE **Should the Minimum Wage Be Raised to Help Young People?**

The equilibrium wage rate model shown in Figure 15.4 does not apply when the government sets a minimum wage rate below which employers are not allowed to pay workers and workers are not allowed to offer their services. Recall from Chapter 4 that in general, a minimum wage (if set above equilibrium) creates an excess quantity of labour supplied (a surplus) at that legal minimum. Thus young people probably would not be helped by an increase in minimum wages. Look at Figure 15.5. There you see the unemployment rate for young people ages 15 to 19. As minimum wages across the country rose during the 1990s, so did the rate of unemployment for young people. It started falling again only around 1993. Why? In part because what is important is the real, inflation-corrected minimum wage rate. In real terms, the minimum wage fell until about 1989. Then it rose until 1993 and started falling again, exactly coincident with the reduction in the unemployment rate for young people. So to answer the policy question, raising the minimum wage probably would not help young people as a group, although it might help some young people who retain their jobs at the higher wage rate.

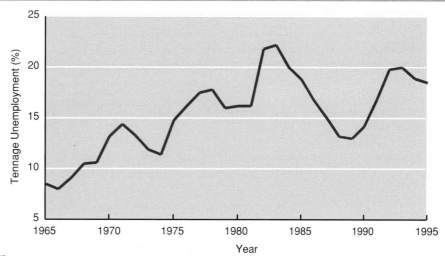

Figure 15.5
Teenage Unemployment and the Real Minimum Wage
Although the minimum wage has risen over the past 30 years, the real minimum wage has fallen since 1993, leading to a decrease in the rate of youth unemployment since then.

Source: M.C. Urquhart and K.A.H. Buckley, *Historical Statistics of Canada*; Statistics Canada, *Canadian Economic Observer Historical Supplement*; and Statistics Canada, *Canadian Economic Observer.*

For critical analysis: Why are young people most affected by changes in the minimum wage? (Hint: Which workers have the lowest MRP?)

ALTERNATIVE THEORIES OF WAGE DETERMINATION: EFFICIENCY WAGES AND INSIDERS VERSUS OUTSIDERS

The relatively straightforward analysis of the supply and demand of labour just presented may not fully explain the equilibrium level of wages under certain circumstances. There are two important alternative theories of wage determination that may apply to at least some parts of the economy. We analyse those two theories now.

Efficiency Wages

Let's say that in the CD industry, employers can hire as many workers as they want at the equilibrium weekly wage rate of $498. Associated with that weekly wage rate is a specified amount of employment in each firm. Within each firm, though, there is turnover. Some workers quit to go on to other jobs. Turnover costs are significant. Workers have to be trained. What if a firm, even though it could hire workers at $498 a week, offered employment at $600 a week? Several things might occur. First, current employees would have less desire to look elsewhere to find better jobs. There would be less turnover. Second, those workers who applied for openings might be of higher quality, being attracted by the higher wage rate. Third, workers on the job

▶ **Efficiency wages**

Wages set above competitive levels to increase labour productivity and profits by enhancing the efficiency of the firm through lower turnover, ease of attracting higher-quality workers, and better efforts by workers.

might actually become more productive because they do not want to lose their jobs. They know that alternative competitive wages are $498 a week.

The higher-than-competitive wage rates offered by such a firm have been designated **efficiency wages.** The underlying assumption is that firms operate more efficiently if they pay their workers a higher wage rate.

Insiders and Outsiders

A related view of the labour market involves the notion of insiders within a firm. The insiders are those current employees who have the "inside track" and can maintain their positions because the firm would have to incur costs to replace them. These employee insiders are therefore able to exercise some control over the terms under which new employees (outsiders) are hired by the firm. They keep other potential workers out by not allowing them to offer themselves for work at a lower real wage rate than that being earned by the insiders. As pointed out earlier, the costs of hiring and firing workers are significant. Indeed, the cost of firing one worker may sometimes be relatively high: termination wages, retraining payments, and litigation if the worker believes termination was unjustified. All such costs might contribute to the development of insider-dominated labour markets. They contain significant barriers to entry by outsiders.

▶ **Insider-outsider theory**

A theory of labour markets in which workers who are already employed have an influence on wage bargaining in such a way that outsiders who are willing to work for lower real wages cannot get a job.

So the **insider-outsider theory** predicts that wages may remain higher than the standard supply and demand model would predict even though outsiders are willing to work at lower real wages.

EXAMPLE   Competing for the Boss's Job

Although efficiency wage theory and the insider-outsider theory may explain wages that are somewhat above a competitive level, they have a harder time explaining really big differences in wages within a firm's management structure. CEOs tend to make many times more than vice-presidents do. Senior vice-presidents often make double what a regular vice-president makes. According to one theory, corporations create these big salary differentials, *not* in an attempt to reward the recipients, but rather to create a structure of powerful incentives to get people in the organization to work harder. Pay is based on *relative* performance, relative to one's peers within the management organization. The pay of a vice-president is not what motivates that vice-president; it is the pay of the CEO, to whose job the vice-president aspires. Economists Edward Lazer and Sherwin Rosen call this concept *tournament theory*. They argue that vice-presidents and others under them are involved in a series of tournaments. The winner of each tournament moves up to the next higher level. All aspire to the highest level, that of the CEO.

For critical analysis: If luck plays an unusually large role in a vice-president's rise to the top, will the pay differential between vice-presidents and the CEO have to be relatively large or small compared to a situation in which luck is not important?

SHIFTS IN THE MARKET DEMAND FOR AND SUPPLY OF LABOUR

Just as we discussed shifts in the supply curve and the demand curve for various products in Chapter 3, we can discuss the effects of shifts in supply and demand in labour markets.

Reasons for Labour Demand Curve Shifts

Many factors can cause the demand curve for labour to shift. We have already discussed a number of them. Clearly, because the demand for labour or any other variable input is a derived demand, the labour demand curve will shift if there is a shift in the demand for the final product. There are two other important determinants of the position of the demand curve for labour: changes in labour's productivity and changes in the price of related factors of production (substitutes and complements).

Changes in Demand for Final Product.　The demand for labour or any other variable input is derived from the demand for the final product. The marginal revenue product is equal to marginal physical product times marginal revenue. Therefore, any change in the price of the final product will change MRP. This happened when we derived the market demand for labour. The general rule of thumb is as follows:

> A change in the demand for the final product that labour (or any other variable input) is producing will shift the market demand curve for labour in the same direction.

Changes in Labour Productivity.　The second part of the MRP equation is MPP, which relates to labour productivity. We can surmise, then, that, other things being equal,

> A change in labour productivity will shift the market labour demand curve in the same direction.

Labour productivity can increase because labour has more capital or land to work with, because of technological improvements, or because labour's quality has improved. Such considerations explain why the real standard of living of workers in Canada is higher than in most countries. Canadian workers generally work with a larger capital stock, have more natural resources, are in better physical condition, and are better trained than workers in many countries. Hence the demand for labour in Canada is, other things held constant, greater. Conversely, labour is relatively scarcer in Canada than it is in many other countries. One result of relatively greater demand and relatively smaller supply is a relatively higher wage rate.

EXAMPLE   Does It Pay to Study?

One way to increase labour productivity is to increase skill level. One way to do that, of course, is to go to college. Is there a big payoff? According to a recent study of identical twins carried out by economists Orley Ashenfelter and Alan Krueger, the answer is a resounding yes. They studied the earning patterns of more than 250 identical twins. In this manner, they were able to hold constant heredity, early home life, and so on. They focused on differences in the number of years of schooling. They discovered that each additional year of schooling increased wages almost 16 percent. Four years of post-secondary education yielded a 67 percent increase in monthly wages compared to none at all.

Some economists believe that a university degree is part of **labour market signalling.** Employers do not have much information about the future productivity of job applicants. Typically, the only way to find out is to observe someone working. Employers attempt to reduce the number of bad choices that they might make by using a job applicant's amount of higher education as a signal. According to the labour market signalling theory, even if higher education does not change productivity, it acts as an effective signal of greater individual abilities.

▶ **Labour market signalling**
The process by which a potential worker's acquisition of credentials, such as a degree, is used by the employer to predict future productivity.

For critical analysis: Why does studying identical twins' earnings hold constant many of the factors that can determine differences in wages?

Change in the Price of Related Factors.   Labour is not the only resource used. Some resources are substitutes and some are complements. If we hold output constant, we have the following general rule:

A change in the price of a substitute input will cause the demand for labour to change in the same direction. This is typically called the *substitution effect.*

Note, however, that if the cost of production falls sufficiently, the firm will find it more profitable to produce and sell a larger output. If this so-called *output effect* is great enough, it will override the substitution effect just mentioned, and the firm will end up employing not only more of the relatively cheaper variable input, but also more labour. This is exactly what happened for many years in the Canadian automobile industry. Car makers used more machinery (capital), but employment continued to increase in spite of rising wage rates. The reason: Markets were expanding and the marginal physical productivity of labour was rising faster than its wage rate.

With respect to complements, we are referring to inputs that must be used jointly. Assume now that capital and labour are complementary. In general, we predict the following:

A change in the price of a complementary input will cause the demand for labour to change in the opposite direction.

If the cost of machines goes up but they must be used with labour, fewer machines will be purchased and therefore fewer workers will be used.

Determinants of the Supply of Labour

There are a number of reasons labour supply curves will shift in a particular industry. For example, if wage rates for factory workers in the CD industry remain constant while wages for factory workers in the computer industry go up dramatically, the supply curve of factory workers in the CD industry will shift inward to the left as these workers move to the computer industry.

Changes in working conditions in an industry can also affect its labour supply curve. If employers in the CD industry discover a new production technique that makes working conditions much more pleasant, the supply curve of labour to the CD industry will shift outward to the right.

Job flexibility also determines the position of the labour supply curve. For example, in an industry in which workers are allowed more flexibility, such as the ability to work at home via computer, the workers are likely to work more hours. That is to say, their supply curve will shift outward to the right. Some industries in which firms offer *job sharing*, particularly to people raising families, have found that the supply curve of labour has shifted outward to the right.

Concepts in Brief

- The individual competitive firm faces a perfectly elastic supply curve—it can buy all the labour it wants at the going market wage rate. The industry supply curve of labour slopes upward.
- By plotting an industrywide supply curve for labour and an industrywide demand curve for labour on the same coordinate system, we obtain the equilibrium wage rate in this industry.
- Efficiency wage theory predicts that wages paid above market wages may lead to high productivity because of lower turnover rates and better work effort by existing workers.
- The labour demand curve can shift because (1) the demand for the final product shifts, (2) labour productivity changes, or (3) the price of a related (substitute or complementary) factor of production changes.

MONOPOLY IN THE PRODUCT MARKET

So far we've considered only a perfectly competitive situation, both in selling the final product and in buying factors of production. We will continue our assumption that the firm purchases its factors of production in a perfectly competitive factor market. Now, however, we will assume that the firm sells its product in an *imperfectly* competitive output market. In other words, we are considering the output market structures of monopoly, oligopoly, and monopolistic competition. In all such cases, the firm, be it a monopolist, an oligopolist, or a monopolistic competitor, faces a downward-sloping demand curve for its product. Throughout the rest of this chapter, we will simply refer to a monopoly output situation for ease of analysis. The analysis holds for all industry structures that are less than perfectly competitive. In any event, the fact that our firm now faces a downward-sloping demand curve for its product means that if it wants to sell more of its product (at a uniform price), it has to lower the price, *not just on the last unit, but on all preceding units*. The *marginal revenue* received from selling an additional unit is continuously falling (and is less than price) as the firm attempts to sell more and more. This is certainly different from our earlier discussions in this chapter in which the firm could sell all it wanted at a constant price. Why? Because the firm we discussed until now was a perfect competitor.

Constructing the Monopolist's Input Demand Curve

In reconstructing our demand schedule for an input, we must account for the facts that (1) the marginal *physical* product falls because of the law of diminishing returns as more workers are added, and (2) the price (and marginal revenue) received for the product sold also falls as more is produced and sold. That is, for the monopolist, we have to account for both the diminishing marginal physical product and the diminishing marginal revenue. Marginal revenue is always less than price for the monopolist. The marginal revenue curve is always below the downward-sloping demand curve.

Marginal revenue for the perfect competitor is equal to the price of the product because all units can be sold at the going market price. In our CD example, we assumed that the perfect competitor could sell all it wanted at $6 per compact disc. A one-unit change in sales always led to a $6 change in total revenues. Hence marginal revenue was always equal to $6 for that perfect competitor.

The monopolist, however, cannot simply calculate marginal revenue by looking at the price of the product. To sell the additional output from an additional unit of input, the monopolist has to cut prices on all previous units of output. As output is increasing, then, marginal revenue is falling. The underlying concept is, of course, the same for both the perfect competitor and the monopolist. We are asking exactly the same question in both cases: When an additional worker is hired, what is the benefit? In either case, the benefit is obviously the change in total revenues due to the one-unit change in the variable input, labour. In our discussion of the perfect competitor, we were able simply to look at the marginal physical product and multiply it by the *constant* per-unit price of the product because the price of the product never changed (for the perfect competitor, $P = \text{MR}$).

A single monopolist ends up hiring fewer workers than all of the competitive firms added together. To see this, we must calculate the marginal revenue product for the monopolist. To make it simple, we will look at it as simply the change in total revenues due to a one-unit change in the labour input for a monopolist. This is what we do in part (a) of Figure 15.6, which shows the change in total revenues. Column 6, headed "Marginal Revenue Product," gives the monopolistic firm a quantitative notion of how profitable additional workers and additional production actually are. The marginal revenue product curve for this monopolist has been plotted in part (b) of the figure. To emphasize the steeper slope of the monopolist's MRP curve, MRP_m, the MRP curve for the perfect competitor in Figure 15.1, labelled MRP_c, has been plotted on the same graph.

Part (a)

(1)	(2)	(3)	(4)	(5)	(6)
Labour Input (workers per week)	Total Physical Product (TPP) CDs per week	Marginal Physical Product (MPP) CDs per week	Price of Product (P)	Total Revenue (TR) = (2) × (4)	Marginal Revenue Product (MRP$_m$) = Change in (5) / Change in (1)
7	1,000		$8.00	$ 8,000.00	
		111			$665.80
8	1,111		7.80	8,665.80	
		104			568.20
9	1,215		7.60	9,234.00	
		97			474.80
10	1,312		7.40	9,708.80	
		90			385.60
11	1,402		7.20	10,094.40	
		83			300.60
12	1,485		7.00	10,395.00	
		76			219.80
13	1,561		6.80	10,614.80	

Figure 15.6

A Monopolist's Marginal Revenue Product

The monopolist hires just enough workers to make marginal revenue product equal to the going wage rate. If the going wage rate is $498 per week, as shown by the labour supply curve, s, the monopolist would want to hire between 9 and 10 workers per week. That is the profit-maximizing amount of labour. The MRP curve for the perfect competitor from Figure 15.1 is also plotted (MRP$_c$). The monopolist's MRP curve will always be less elastic than it would be if marginal revenue were constant.

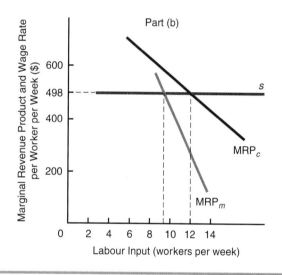

Why does MRP$_m$ represent the monopolist's input demand curve? As always, our profit-maximizing monopolist will continue to hire labour as long as additional profits result. Profits are made as long as the additional cost of more workers is outweighed by the additional revenues made from selling the output of those workers. When the wage rate equals these additional revenues, the monopolist stops hiring. That is, it stops hiring when the wage rate is equal to the marginal revenue product because additional workers would add more to cost than to revenue.

Why the Monopolist Hires Fewer Workers

Because we have used the same numbers as in Figure 15.1, we can see that the monopolist hires fewer worker-weeks than the perfect competitor. That is to say, if we could magically change the CD industry in our example from one in which there is perfect competition in the output market to one in which there is monopoly in the output market, the amount of employment would fall. Why? Because the monopolist must take account of the declining product price that must be charged in order to sell a larger number of CDs. Remember that every firm hires up to the point at which marginal benefit equals marginal cost. The marginal benefit to the monopolist of hiring an additional worker is not simply the additional output times the price of the product. Rather, the monopolist faces a reduction in the price charged on all units sold in order to be able to sell more. So the monopolist ends up hiring fewer workers than all of the perfect competitors taken together, assuming that all other factors remain the same for the two hypothetical examples. But this should not come as a surprise. In considering product markets, by implication we saw that a monopolized CD industry would produce less output than a competitive one. Therefore, the monopolized CD industry would want fewer workers.

Try Preview Question 4:

What is the profit-maximizing rate of employment for an imperfectly competitive firm?

OTHER FACTORS OF PRODUCTION

The analysis in this chapter has been given in terms of the demand for the variable input labour. The same analysis holds for any other variable factor input. We could have talked about the demand for fertilizer, or the demand for the services of tractors by a farmer instead of the demand for labour and reached the same conclusions. The entrepreneur will hire or buy any variable input up to the point at which its price equals the marginal revenue product.

A further question remains: How much of each variable factor should the firm use when all the variable factors are combined to produce the product? We can answer this question by looking at either the profit-maximizing side of the question or the cost-minimizing side.[1]

---

[1] Many economic problems involving maximization of profit or other economic variables have duals, or precise restatements, in terms of *minimization* rather than maximization. The problem "How do we maximize our output, given fixed resources?" for example, is the dual of the problem "How do we minimize our cost, given fixed output?" Noneconomists sometimes confuse their discussions of economic issues by mistakenly believing that a problem and its dual are two problems rather than one. Asking, for example, "How can we maximize our profits while minimizing our costs?" makes about as much sense as asking, "How can we cross the street while getting to the other side?"

Thinking Critically About the Media | **Capital Substitution Threatens Jobs**

Every time there is an improvement in capital productivity, the media figure out ways to discuss the resultant loss of employment because of capital substitution. In the absence of restrictions in the labour market, though, capital substitution simply means that in a particular firm or industry, relatively more capital is used and relatively less labour. There are two additional factors to consider: (1) What about the workers used to make the additional capital? Won't there be increases in employment in the capital-producing industries? (2) The economy is not just machines versus workers. Even though the proportion of workers employed in manufacturing in Canada has dropped since the mid-1970s, the number of jobs has actually increased by over 150,000. Moreover, jobs in service industries, such as software programming, have greatly increased. The Canadian economy has added over 4 million jobs since 1976 despite machines having replaced many workers.

Profit Maximization Revisited

If a firm wants to maximize profits, how much of each factor should be hired (or bought)? As we just saw, the firm will never hire a factor of production unless the marginal benefit from hiring that factor is at least equal to the marginal cost. What is the marginal benefit? As we have pointed out, the marginal benefit is the change in total revenues due to a one-unit change in use of the variable input. What is the marginal cost? In the case of a firm buying in a competitive market, it is the price of the variable factor—the wage rate if we are referring to labour.

The profit-maximizing combination of resources for the firm will be where, in a perfectly competitive situation,

MRP of labour = price of labour (wage rate)

MRP of land   = price of land (rental rate per unit)

MRP of capital = price of capital (cost per unit of service)

Alternatively, we can express this profit-maximizing rule as

$$\frac{\text{MRP of labour}}{\text{price of labour}} = \frac{\text{MRP of land}}{\text{price of land}} = \frac{\text{MRP of capital}}{\text{price of capital}}$$

The marginal revenue product of each of a firm's resources must be exactly equal to its price. If the MRP of labour was $20 and its price was only $15, the firm would be underemploying labour.

Cost Minimization

From the cost minimization point of view, how can the firm minimize its total costs for a given output? Assume that you are an entrepreneur attempting to minimize costs. Consider a hypothetical situation in which if you spend $1 more on labour, you would get 20 more units of output, but if you spend $1 more on machines, you would get only 10 more units of output. What would you want to do in such a situation? Most likely you would wish to hire more workers or sell off some of your machines, for you are not getting as much output per last dollar spent on machines as you are per last dollar spent on labour. You would want to employ factors of production so that the marginal products per last dollar spent on each are equal. Thus the least-cost, or cost minimization, rule will be as follows:

> To minimize total costs for a particular rate of production, the firm will hire factors of production up to the point at which the marginal physical product per last dollar spent on each factor of production is equalized.

That is,

$$\frac{\text{MPP of labour}}{\begin{array}{c}\text{price of labour}\\\text{(wage rate)}\end{array}} = \frac{\text{MPP of capital}}{\begin{array}{c}\text{price of capital}\\\text{(cost per unit of service)}\end{array}} = \frac{\text{MPP of land}}{\begin{array}{c}\text{price of land}\\\text{(rental rate per unit)}\end{array}}$$

All we are saying here is that the profit-maximizing firm will always use *all* resources in such combinations that cost will be minimized for any given output rate. This is commonly called the *least-cost combination of resources*. There is an exact relationship between the profit-maximizing combination of resources and the least-cost combination of resources. In other words, either rule can be used to yield the same cost-minimizing rate of use of each variable resource.[2]

EXAMPLE	Cost Minimization and the Substitution of Software for Labour

The computer revolution, while it is increasing employment in one sector of the economy, may at the same time be decreasing the use of labour in other sectors. In particular, accounting software (capital) is replacing certified general accountants (labour) at an increasing rate. Accounting software has become more plentiful, less costly, easier to use, and more sophisticated in the past several years. Nonetheless, the number of CGAs has risen virtually every year since 1970. A prediction would be that the relative salaries of CGAs should therefore fall in the future (all other things held constant).

The same analysis holds for lawyers. Legal software has proliferated, grown more sophisticated, dropped in price, and become easier to use. Consequently, paralegals are now able to do many of the jobs that lawyers used to do. Not surprisingly, the paralegal profession is expanding rapidly, while the growth in the number of lawyers is starting to slow down.

For critical analysis: Can you apply the same analysis to doctors?

Concepts in Brief

- When a firm sells its output in a monopoly market, marginal revenue is less than price.
- Just as the MRP is the perfectly competitive firm's input demand curve, the MRP is also the monopolist's demand curve.
- For a less than perfectly competitive firm, the profit-maximizing combination of factors will occur where each factor is used up to the point where its MRP is equal to its unit price.
- To minimize total costs for a given output, the profit-maximizing firm will hire each factor of production up to the point where the marginal physical product per last dollar spent on each factor is equal to the marginal physical product per last dollar spent on each of the other factors of production.

---

[2] This can be proved as follows: Profit maximization requires that the price of every input must equal that input's marginal revenue product (the general case). Let i be the input. Then $P_i = \text{MRP}_i$. But MRP_i is equal to marginal revenue times marginal physical product of the input. Therefore, $P_i = \text{MR} \times \text{MPP}_i$. If we divide both sides by MPP_i, we get $P_i/\text{MPP}_i = \text{MR}$. If we take the reciprocal, we obtain $\text{MPP}_i/P_i = 1/\text{MR}$. That is another way of stating our cost minimization rule.

Issues and Applications

Are Immigrants Pushing Down Canadian Wages?

Concepts Applied: Demand for and supply of labour, shifts in the supply curve of labour, real wages, productivity

New Canadians swear an oath of allegiance to the Queen at a citizenship ceremony in Toronto. Economists have found that the traditional view that immigrants push down real wages and take advantage of social programs is not borne out by the evidence.

Immigration has been on the upsurge since the 1930s, as you can see in part (a) of Figure 15.7. But the number of immigrants as a percentage of the population is still less than it was 80 years ago, as can be seen in part (b) of the figure. Thus any notion that immigration is posing an increased threat to Canadian culture certainly does not stand up to the facts.

A Worldwide Phenomenon

Immigration into Canada is just a small part of a worldwide phenomenon of human migration. Today, at least 100 million people live outside the country in which they were born. Most of this migration is not to the richer industrialized countries. Consequently, by 2000, fully 17 of the world's biggest cities will be in the developing world with Mexico City, Mexico (26 million), and São Paulo, Brazil (22 million), in first and second place. New York City will rank fifth.

Just because human migration occurs everywhere does not mean that it is "good" or "bad" for the Canadian economy.

Costs and Benefits of Immigration

One of the basic criticisms of immigrants is that they use the social welfare system more than in proportion to their numbers. This and other issues are currently being investigated by the four federally-funded Centres for Excellence for the Study of Immigration and Integration.

Existing data show, however, that the percentage of immigrant households receiving social assistance is less than Canadian

Figure 15.7
Immigrants in Canada
Since the 1870s, the rate of immigrant arrivals peaked in the years 1900–1910 and is on the rise again today, as is seen in part (a). Nonetheless, the percentage of the Canadian population that is foreign-born is still lower than it was from the 1910s to the 1940s, as is seen in part (b).

Sources: M.C. Urquhart and K.A.H. Buckley, *Historical Statistics of Canada*, and Statistics Canada, Census 1981 and 1991.

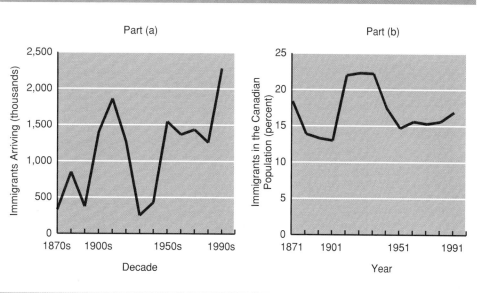

households, 12.5 percent compared to 13.8 percent. After all, immigrants usually arrive when they are young and healthy. Consequently, they generally need fewer welfare services than Canadian-born families. More important, because they are young, they do not require much medical care, nor do they receive Old Age Security payments, two significant government expenditures. Moreover, several studies have found that immigrant families contribute more to government coffers, by way of taxes, than they take out in social services.

Employment and Wages

Another major question with respect to immigration is whether immigrants will force down wages and create unemployment. According to numerous studies, there is virtually no statistically significant change in unemployment rates when immigration increases.

The data on wage rates are inconclusive. While immigrants definitely increase the supply curve of labour, they mainly affect specific parts of the labour market, and then for only a short time.

On an empirical basis, given that Canada has been peopled by immigrants since the 17th century, and that real wage rates have been rising more or less steadily, immigration cannot have reduced real wage rates. What has happened is that all labour has become increasingly productive in spite of large increases in the labour force due to both Canadian births and net immigration.

For Critical Analysis

1. While immigrants increase the supply of labour, they also increase the demand for goods and services. What impact will this increase in demand for goods and services have on the *wage rate*?

2. Canada's population growth rate without immigration is approximately 1.2 children per couple. In the absence of immigration, what effect will this replacement rate have on the labour market and the quantity of output produced?

CHAPTER SUMMARY

1. In a competitive situation in which the firm is a very small part of the entire product and labour market, the firm will want to hire workers up to the point at which the marginal revenue product just equals the going wage rate.

2. The marginal revenue product curve for the individual competitive firm is the input demand curve. The competitive firm hires up to the point at which the wage rate equals the MRP.

3. The summation of all the MRP curves does not equal the market demand curve for labour. The market demand curve for labour is less elastic than the sum of the MRP curves because as more workers are hired, output is increased and the price of the product must fall, lowering the MRP.

4. The demand for labour is derived from the demand for the product produced.

5. The elasticity of demand for an input is a function of several determinants, including the elasticity of demand for the final product. Moreover, the price elasticity of demand for a variable input will usually be larger in the long run than it is in the short run because there is time for adjustment.

6. The firm buying labour in a perfectly competitive labour market faces a perfectly elastic supply curve at the going wage rate because the firm can hire all it wants at that wage rate. The industry supply curve of labour slopes upward.

7. Efficiency wage theory predicts that wages paid above market wages may lead to high productivity because of lower turnover rates and better work effort by existing workers.

8. The demand curve for labour will shift if (a) the demand for final product shifts, (b) labour productivity changes, or (c) the price of a substitute or a complementary factor of production changes.

9. The MRP curve is also the monopolist's input demand curve. Because marginal revenue is less than the price of the product for a monopolist, the monopolist's input demand curve is steeper.

10. A firm minimizes total costs by equating the ratio of marginal physical product of labour divided by the price of labour with the ratio of marginal physical product of machines to the price of capital with all other such ratios for all the different factors of production. This is the mirror of profit maximization.

DISCUSSION OF PREVIEW QUESTIONS

1. When hiring labour, what general rule will be followed by employers who wish to maximize profits?

Employers who wish to maximize total profits will hire labour (or any other factor of production) up to the point at which the marginal cost (MC) of doing so equals the marginal benefit, MB. In that way, they will have used up all instances in which the marginal benefit of hiring labour exceeds the marginal cost of hiring labour. If MB > MC, they will hire more labour; if MB < MC, they will hire less; when MB = MC, they will be maximizing total profits.

2. What is the profit-maximizing rate of employment for a perfectly competitive firm?

The perfectly competitive firm will accept prevailing wage rates; it can hire as much labour as it wishes at the going rate. It follows that the MFC of hiring labour to the perfectly competitive firm is a constant that is equal to the prevailing wage rate; MFC = W, where W is the market wage rate. The MB of hiring labour is the value of the marginal product of an additional unit of labour. The perfectly competitive firm will maximize total profits by hiring labour up to the point at which it drives the MRP down to equal the constant wage rate: MRP = W. This is also how the firm minimizes costs for a given output.

3. How is an industry wage rate determined?

Wage rates are a price; they are the price of labour. As such, wage rates are determined like all prices, by the forces of supply and demand. The market, or industry, wage rate will be determined by the point of intersection of the industry supply of labour curve and the industry demand for labour curve. At the point of intersection, the quantity of labour supplied equals the quantity of labour demanded, and equilibrium exists; both buyers and sellers are able to realize their intentions.

4. What is the profit-maximizing rate of employment for an imperfectly competitive firm?

For an imperfectly competitive firm, P > MR. Thus in the short run the marginal benefit of hiring additional units of labour falls for two reasons: (a) The law of diminishing returns causes marginal physical product to diminish, and (b) to increase sales, price must fall—on previously produced units as well as the new one. Thus the MB of hiring labour equals the *marginal revenue* times the marginal physical product of labour: MB = MRP = MR × MPP.

By assumption, the imperfectly competitive firm is a competitor in the input markets, so in hiring labour it (like the perfect competitor) faces a constant marginal factor cost equal to the going wage rate; MFC = W for the imperfectly competitive firm too. What about the profit-maximizing rate of employment for the imperfectly competitive firm? It hires up to the point at which it drives down the marginal revenue product of labour (MRP = MR × MPP) until it equals the going wage rate; MRP = W is the equilibrium condition in this model.

PROBLEMS

(Answers to the odd-numbered problems appear at the back of the book.)

15-1. Assume that the product in the table is sold by a perfectly competitive firm for $2 per unit.
   a. Use the information in the table to derive a demand schedule for labour.
   b. What is the most that this firm would be willing to pay each worker if five workers were hired?
   c. If the going salary for this quality labour is $200 per week, how many workers will be hired?

Quantity of Labour	Total Physical Product per Week	MPP	MRP
1	250	_____	_____
2	450	_____	_____
3	600	_____	_____
4	700	_____	_____
5	750	_____	_____
6	750		

15-2. The table presents some production function data for a firm in which the only variable input is capital; the labour input is fixed. First fill in the other columns. What quantity of capital will the firm use if the price of capital is $90 per machine-week? If the price of capital is $300 per machine-week, what quantity of capital will the firm use? Explain.

15-3. The accompanying graph indicates labour supply and demand in the construction industry.

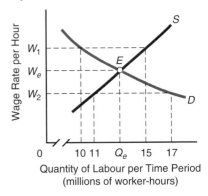

a. When wage rates are W_1 per hour, how many worker-hours do workers intend to offer per unit?
b. How much do businesses intend to buy at this wage rate?
c. Which group can realize its intentions, and which can't?
d. What forces will be set in motion at wage rate W_1, given a free market for labour?

15-4. Using the graph in Problem 15-3, answer the following questions.

Quantity of Capital (machine-weeks)	Total Physical Product per Week	Marginal Physical Product of Capital per Week	Marginal Revenue (product price) per Unit	Marginal Revenue Product per Week
0	0	_____	$10	$ _____
1	25	_____	10	_____
2	45	_____	10	_____
3	60	_____	10	_____
4	70	_____	10	_____
5	75	_____		

a. At wage rate W_2, how many worker-hours do workers intend to offer?
b. At W_2, how many worker-hours do businesses intend to purchase?
c. Which group can realize its intentions, and which can't?
d. What forces will be set in motion at W_2 if a free market for labour exists in this industry?
e. What will the equilibrium wage rate be?

15-5. The price elasticity of demand for the final output product directly affects the elasticity of demand for the input factor. Why?

15-6. Suppose that you are seeking to maximize output for a given outlay. If the marginal physical product of input x is 10 and that of input y is 20, and the prices of the two inputs are $3 and $7, respectively, how should you alter your input mix in order to increase output and profit?

15-7. Suppose that you are a monopolist and labour is the only variable input you employ. You are currently producing 150 units of output and selling them for $20 apiece. You are considering the possibility of hiring an additional full-time employee. You estimate that daily output would increase to 160 units if you hired this additional person and that you would be able to sell all of those units at a price of $19 each. What is the MRP of labour (per worker-day)? Assuming that you take the price of labour as a given, what is the maximum daily wage that would make it in your interest to hire this additional employee?

15-8. When there is only one variable input, how does a monopoly seller's demand for that input differ from that of a perfectly competitive seller?

15-9. Assume that you have graduated from university. You decide to look for a job rather than go for further schooling. Indicate how the following criteria might affect the salary that you will receive and the type of job you may end up taking after you graduate.
a. You want to stay near your family, so you do not consider moving out of your immediate geographic area to find a job.
b. You look only for jobs that allow you to apply the knowledge and skills you have learned in your college major.
c. You now live in the city but decide that you will only work in a rural area.

16

Unions and Labour Market Monopoly Power

Preview Questions

1. **What are the major types of unions?**

2. **What do unions seek to maximize?**

3. **Do unions help workers?**

4. **What is a monopsonist, and how does one determine its profit-maximizing employment rate?**

The average major-league baseball player today earns about $1.8 million a year. The average professional football player earns about $1 million a year. The average professional basketball player earns about $3 million a year. At the same time, professional sports team owners continue to buy and sell professional franchises for tens and hundreds of millions of dollars.

For many years, players' salaries grew relatively slowly. Only since 1989 have they increased significantly. To understand the market for professional sports league players, you have to acquire an understanding of various restrictions in the labour market.

Did You Know That... in 1976, more than 1.5 million Canadian workers were involved in strikes? In the past few years, however, fewer than 100,000 have participated. More than 12 times the number of workdays were lost to strikes in the 1950s than are lost today. The labour landscape has been changing in Canada. Some workers are able to earn more than they would in a competitive labour market because they have obtained a type of monopoly power. These are members of effective **labour unions,** workers' organizations that seek to secure economic improvements for their members.

In forming unions, a certain monopoly element enters into the supply of labour equation. That is because we can no longer talk about a perfectly competitive labour supply situation when active and effective unions bargain as a single entity with management. The entire supply of a particular group of workers is controlled by a single source. Later in the chapter, we will examine the opposite—a single employer who is the sole user of a particular group of workers.

▶ **Labour unions**
Worker organizations that seek to secure economic improvements for their members; they also seek to improve safety, health, and other benefits (such as job security) for their members.

THE CANADIAN LABOUR MOVEMENT

The Canadian labour movement started with local **craft unions**. These were groups of workers in individual trades such as shoemaking, printing, and baking. Initially, workers struggled for the right to band together to bargain as a unit. Until 1872, that right did not exist.

▶ **Craft unions**
Labour unions composed of workers who engage in a particular trade or skill, such as shoemaking, printing, or baking.

Between 1875 and 1907, the US-based Knights of Labor, an organized group of both skilled and unskilled workers, demanded a nine-hour workday, equal pay for men and women, and the replacement of free enterprise with the socialist system. In 1883, the Trades and Labour Congress (TLC) formed as a meeting ground for crafts unions and the Knights of Labor. Several years later, during the last decade of the 19th century, a rapid expansion of American branch plants took place in Canada. Paralleling this growth was international unionism; by 1911, there were 135,000 Canadian members of the American Federation of Labour (AFL).

During World War I, overall union membership grew rapidly, but fell off amidst the prosperity of the 1920s. In response to declining membership, the All-Canadian Congress of Labour (ACCL) was formed to rival the TLC, and divorce Canadian unionism from the United States. In contrast to the TLC, the ACCL was composed of **industrial unions**—unions whose membership came from an entire industry such as steel or automobile manufacturing.

▶ **Industrial unions**
Labour unions that consist of workers from a particular industry, such as automobile manufacturing or steel manufacturing.

Then came the Great Depression. It was a time of both economic and labour turmoil. The American Congress of Industrial Organizations (CIO), a committee of the AFL, joined the TLC but was subsequently expelled from both the AFL and the TLC due to conflicting ideologies with respect to partnerships with business. The CIO then joined the ACCL, which dropped the "A" for "All" and became simply the Canadian Congress of Labour (CCL).

▶ **Collective bargaining**
Bargaining between the management of a company, or a group of companies, and the management of a union, or a group of unions, for the purpose of setting a mutually agreeable contract on wages, fringe benefits, and working conditions for all employees in all the unions involved.

World War II was another time of significant union activity, and in 1944 the federal government enfranchised the public sector with the *Trade Union Act*. In 1946, a Supreme Court decision gave unions the legal right to organize, to engage in **collective bargaining**, and to strike. The "Rand formula" also guaranteed the solvency of unions by ensuring a union check-off—a law stipulating that employees in a union shop must pay dues whether or not they choose to join the union.

In 1956, the TLC and the CCL merged to form the Canadian Labour Congress (CLC) which today has over two million members organized into almost 9,000 locals across the country. Other labour congresses, such as the Canadian Federation of Labour (CFL), the Confederation of National Trade Unions (CNTU) in Quebec, and the AFL-CIO in Canada boast a further 630,000 members. In 1992, total union membership in Canada consisted 3.86 million workers.

INTERNATIONAL EXAMPLE
European Merchant Guilds, the Original Craft Unions

The origin of today's craft unions is found in a type of association that flourished in continental Europe and England during the Middle Ages. Around the eleventh century, merchants started travelling from market to market in a caravan to protect themselves from bandits. The members of the caravan elected a leader whose rules they pledged to obey. The name of such a caravan was Gilde in the Germanic countries of Europe. When the members of the caravan returned home, they frequently stayed in close association. They soon found it beneficial to seek exclusive rights to a particular trade from a feudal lord or, later, from the city government itself. Soon merchant guilds obtained a monopoly over an industry and its related commerce in a city. It supervised the crafts and the wholesale and retail selling of commodities manufactured in that city. Nonmember merchants were not allowed to sell goods at retail and were subject to many restrictions from which members of the guild were exempt.

For critical analysis: Analyse the medieval guild in terms of the insider-outsider theory presented in Chapter 15.

The Current Status of Labour Unions

If you look at Figure 16.1, you can see that union membership grew quite rapidly from the 1940s to the late 1950s. Since 1967, union membership has been fairly stable, and is currently hovering around 34 percent of the civilian labour force. If you remove labour unions in the public sector—federal, provincial, and municipal government workers—private sector union membership in Canada is about 23 percent of the civilian labour force.

The stability of union membership masks substantial changes that have taken place within the labour movement. Since the mid-1960s there has been a large shift

Figure 16.1
Union Membership

Numerically, union membership in Canada has increased dramatically since 1921. After a rapid increase in the percentage of workers in unions from the 1920s to the late 1950s, that percentage has remained relatively static at about 34 percent.

Sources: M.C. Urquhart and K.A.H. Buckley, *Historical Statistics of Canada*, and Statistics Canada, *CALURA, 1992*.

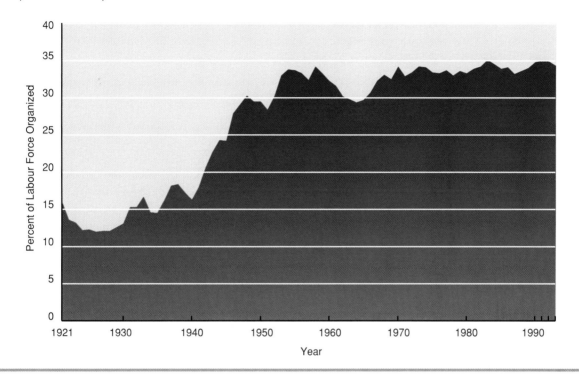

in union membership away from manufacturing and into the services sector, reflecting how Canada's economy has changed. In 1966, 39.2 percent of union members worked in manufacturing; by 1992 that proportion had dropped to 16 percent. At the same time the percentage of union members working in the service sector rose from 9 percent to 37.2 percent.

Try Preview Question 1:

What are the major types of unions?

INTERNATIONAL EXAMPLE
Europe's Management-Labour Councils

Unionization rates are much higher in the European Union (EU) than in Canada, averaging 48 percent. Perhaps more important, most EU countries have institutionalized the concept of management-labour councils. In Germany, legislation dating back to the early 1950s created such councils, requiring that management and labour reach decisions jointly and unanimously. German management-labour councils use up a significant amount of management time. At H. C. Asmussen, a small German distilling company with 300 workers, there are five work councils, some of which meet weekly.

> A directive from the EU has forced 1,500 of the European Union's largest companies to set up Europe-wide worker-management consultative committees. In Canada, no such legislation exists, although there is a management desire to create more "quality circles" (to improve quality and to reduce costs) that involve workers and management. Many unions view these quality circles as a threat and are active in their opposition to them.

For critical analysis: Why do you think unions might be against quality circles involving management and workers?

Concepts in Brief

- The Trades and Labour Congress (TLC), composed primarily of craft unions, was formed in 1883. Membership increased until after World War I.
- The Canadian Congress of Labour (CCL), formerly the All-Canadian Congress of Labour, was formed in 1927 by industrial unions.
- In 1946, the Rand formula gave unions in the right to strike, to bargain collectively, and to collect dues both from members and nonmembers.
- The TLC and the CCL merged in 1956 to form the Canadian Labour Congress (CLC).

UNIONS AND COLLECTIVE BARGAINING CONTRACTS

Unions can be regarded as setters of minimum wages. Through collective bargaining, unions establish minimum wages below which no workers can offer their services. Each year, collective bargaining contracts covering wages as well as working conditions and fringe benefits for about 2 million workers are negotiated. Union negotiators act as agents for all members of the bargaining unit. They bargain with management about the provisions of a labour contract. Once union representatives believe that they have an acceptable collective contract, they will submit it to a vote of the union members. If approved by the members, the contract sets wage rates, maximum workdays, working conditions, fringe benefits, and other matters, usually for the next two or three years. Typically, collective bargaining contracts between management and the union apply also to nonunion members who are employed by the firm or the industry.

Strike: The Ultimate Bargaining Tool

Whenever union-management negotiations break down, union negotiators may turn to their ultimate bargaining tool—the threat, or the reality, of a strike. The first recorded strike in Canadian history occurred in 1671 when shipyard workers in

Quebec conducted a slowdown to secure better wages and working conditions. Strikes make headlines, but in only 4 percent of all labour-management disputes does a strike occur before the contract is signed. In the other 96 percent of cases, contracts are signed without much public fanfare.

The purpose of a strike is to impose costs on stubborn management to force its acceptance of the union's proposed contract terms. Strikes disrupt production and interfere with a company's or an industry's ability to sell goods and services. The strike works both ways, though. Workers draw no wages while on strike (they may be partly compensated out of union strike funds) and are not eligible to claim Employment Insurance benefits.

The impact of a strike is closely related to the ability of striking unions to prevent nonstriking (and perhaps nonunion) employees from continuing to work for the targeted company or industry. Therefore, steps are usually taken to prevent others from working for the employer. **Strikebreakers** can effectively destroy whatever bargaining power rests behind a strike. Numerous methods—including violence on the picket lines—have been used to deter strikebreakers.

▶ **Strikebreakers**
Temporary or permanent workers hired by a company to replace union members who are on strike.

| EXAMPLE | Strikes in Professional Sports |

Professional baseball players have gone on strike twice in the past two decades. In 1994, virtually the entire season was lost. At the start of the following season, team owners hired replacement players at much lower salaries. The results were not quite what fans were used to seeing—and therein lies the rub. Compare this situation with one in which a shoemaking factory suffers a strike. Strikebreakers (substitute "players") can learn the strikers' jobs relatively quickly; the skills involved are not too difficult. But in professional sports, it is hard, if not impossible, to duplicate the skills of the best players. Therefore, professional league players are not so easily replaced. Moreover, current professional sports management cannot figure out ways to automate sports as, say, the telephone industry has done in order to weaken the power of unions in that industry. In general, the more highly trained (either physically or academically) the employee, the more successful a strike will be.

For critical analysis: Why do you typically find unions in occupations that require specialized training?

Thinking Critically About the Media   A $25 Million Contract—or Is It?

Even though the days of professional sports player exploitation are over, the salaries of professional players reported by the media are often grossly exaggerated. Typically, a $25 million contract for a "superstar" is usually for a number of years, say, five. That means that the annual salary is $5 million a year. But it is even less than that. Income received in the future is not as valuable as income received today. Nobody would pay $25 million today in order to be repaid $5 million per year for five years. In other words, the team offering the $25 million contract to be paid out over five years can put much less than $25 million into an interest-bearing savings account and still be able to pay the promised $5 million a year.

UNION GOALS

We have already pointed out that one of the goals of unions is to set minimum wages. In many situations, any wage rate set higher than a competitive market clearing wage rate will reduce total employment in that market. This can be seen in Figure 16.2. We have a competitive market for labour. The market demand curve is D, and the market supply curve is S. The market clearing wage rate will be W_e; the equilibrium quantity of labour will be Q_e. If the union establishes by collective bargaining a minimum wage rate that exceeds W_e, an excess quantity of labour will be supplied (assuming no change in the labour demand schedule). If the minimum wage established by union collective bargaining is W_U, the quantity supplied would be Q_S; the quantity demanded would be Q_D. The difference is the excess quantity supplied, or surplus. Hence the following point becomes clear:

> One of the major roles of a union that establishes a wage rate above the market clearing wage rate is to ration available jobs among the excess number of workers who wish to work in unionized industries.

Note also that the surplus of labour is equivalent to a shortage of jobs at wage rates above equilibrium.

Figure 16.2
Unions Must Ration Jobs

If the union succeeds in obtaining wage rate W_U, the quantity of labour demanded will be Q_D, but the quantity of labour supplied will be Q_S. The union must ration a limited number of jobs to a greater number of workers; the surplus of labour is equivalent to a shortage of jobs at that wage rate.

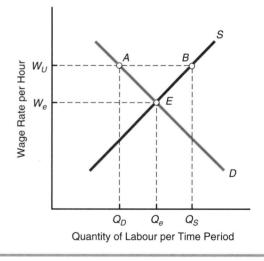

The union may use a system of seniority, a lengthening of the apprenticeship period to discourage potential members from joining, and other such rationing methods. This has the effect of shifting the supply of labour curve to the left in order to support the higher wage, W_U.

There is a trade-off here that any union's leadership must face: Higher wages inevitably mean a reduction in total employment, as more persons are seeking a smaller number of positions. (Moreover, at higher wages, more workers will seek to enter the industry, thereby adding to the surplus that occurs because of the union contract.) Facing higher wages, management may replace part of the workforce with machinery.

Union Strategies

If we view unions as monopoly sellers of a service, we can identify three different wage and employment strategies that they use: ensuring employment for all members of the union, maximizing aggregate income for all workers, and maximizing wage rates for some workers.

Employing All Members in the Union.   Assume that the union has Q_1 workers. If it faces a labour demand curve such as D in Figure 16.3, the only way it can "sell" all of those workers' services is to accept a wage rate of W_1. This is similar to any other demand curve. The demand curve tells the maximum price that can be charged to sell any particular quantity of a good or service. Here the service happens to be labour.

Maximizing Member Income.   If the union is interested in maximizing the gross income of its members, it will normally want a smaller membership than Q_1—namely, Q_2 workers, all employed and paid a wage rate of W_2. The aggregate income to all members of the union is represented by the wages of only the ones who work. Total income earned by union members is maximized where the price elasticity of demand is numerically equal to 1. That occurs where marginal revenue equals zero. In Figure 16.3, marginal revenue equals zero at a quantity of labour Q_2. So we know that if the union obtains a wage rate equal to W_2, and therefore Q_2 workers are demanded, the total income to the union membership will be maximized. In other words, $Q_2 \times W_2$ (the shaded area) will be greater than any other combination of wage rates and quantities of union workers demanded. It is, for example, greater than $Q_1 \times W_1$. Note that in this situation, if the union started out with Q_1 members, there would be $Q_1 - Q_2$ members out of *union* work at the wage rate W_2. (Those out of union work either remain unemployed or go to other industries, which has a depressing effect on wages in nonunion industries due to the increase in supply of nonunion workers there.)

Figure 16.3
What Do Unions Maximize?

Assume that the union wants to employ all its Q_1 members. It will attempt to get wage rate W_1. If the union wants to maximize total wage receipts (income), it will do so at wage rate W_2, where the elasticity of the demand for labour is equal to 1. (The shaded area represents the maximum total income that the union would earn at W_2.) If the union wants to maximize the wage rate for a given number of workers, say, Q_3, it will set the wage rate at W_3.

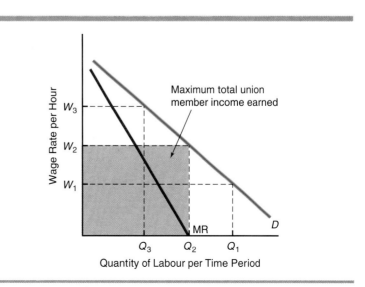

Maximizing Wage Rates for Certain Workers.   Assume that the union wants to maximize the wage rates for some of its workers—perhaps those with the most seniority. If it wanted to keep a quantity of Q_3 workers employed, it would seek to obtain a wage rate of W_3. This would require deciding which workers should be unemployed and which should work, as well as for how long each week or each year they should be employed.

Limiting Entry Over Time

One way to raise wage rates without specifically setting wages is for unions to limit the size of their membership to the extent of their employed workforce when the union was first organized. No workers are put out of work at the time the union is formed. Over time, as the demand for labour in the industry increases, there is no net increase in union membership, so larger wage increases are obtained than would otherwise be the case. We see this in Figure 16.4. Union members freeze entry into their union, thereby obtaining a wage rate of $16 per hour instead of allowing a wage rate of $15 per hour with no restriction on labour supply.

Altering the Demand for Union Labour

Another way in which unions can increase wages is to shift the demand curve for labour outward to the right. This approach compares favourably with the supply restriction approach because it increases both wage rates and employment level. The demand for union labour can be increased by increasing worker productivity, increasing the demand for union-made goods, and decreasing the demand for non-union-made goods.

Figure 16.4
Restricting Supply Over Time

When the union was formed, it didn't affect wage rates or employment, which remained at $14 and Q_1 (the equilibrium wage rate and quantity). However, as demand increased—that is, as the demand schedule shifted outward to D_2 from D_1—the union restricted membership to its original level of Q_1. The new supply curve is S_1S_2, which intersects D_2 at E_2, or at a wage rate of $16. Without the union, equilibrium would be at E_3 with a wage rate of $15 and employment of Q_2.

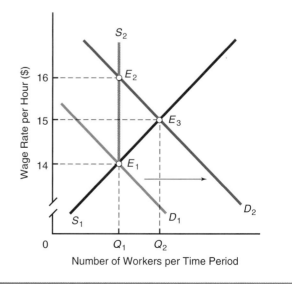

Increasing Worker Productivity.   Supporters of unions have argued that unions provide a good system of industrial jurisprudence. The presence of unions may induce workers to feel that they are working in fair and just circumstances. If so, they work harder, increasing labour productivity. Productivity is also increased when unions resolve differences and reduce conflicts between workers and management, thereby providing a smoother administrative environment.

Increasing Demand for Union-Made Goods.   Because the demand for labour is a derived demand, a rise in the demand for products produced by union labour will increase the demand for union labour itself. One way in which unions attempt to increase the demand for union labour–produced products is by advertising "Look for the union label."

Decreasing the Demand for Non-Union-Made Goods.   When the demand for goods that are competing with (or are substitutes for) union-made goods is reduced, consumers shift to union-made goods, increasing the demand. A good example is when various unions campaign against imports. The result is greater demand for goods "made in Canada," which in turn presumably increases the demand for Canadian union (and nonunion) labour.

Try Preview Question 2:
What do unions seek to maximize?

HAVE UNIONS RAISED WAGES?

We have seen that unions are able to raise the wages of their members if they are successful at limiting the supply of labour in a particular industry. They are also able to raise wages above what wages would otherwise be to the extent that they can shift the demand for union labour outward to the right. This can be done using the methods we have just discussed, including collective bargaining agreements that require specified workers for any given job—for example, by requiring a pilot, a copilot, and an engineer in the cockpit of a jet airplane even if an engineer is not really needed on short flights.

Economists have done extensive research to determine the actual increase in union wages relative to nonunion wages. They have found that in certain industries, such as construction, and in certain occupations, such as commercial airline pilot, the union wage differential can be 50 percent or more. That is to say, unions have been able in some industries and occupations to raise wage rates 50 percent or more above what they would be in the absence of unions.

In addition, the union wage differential appears to increase during recessions. This is because unions often, through collective bargaining, have longer-term contracts than nonunion workers so that they do not have to renegotiate wage rates, even when overall demand in the economy falls.

On average, unions appear to be able to raise the wage rates of their members relative to nonunion members by 10 to 20 percent. Note, though, that when unions increase wages beyond what productivity increases would permit, some union members will be laid off. A redistribution of income from low- to high-seniority union workers is not equivalent to higher wages for *all* union members.

CAN UNIONS INCREASE PRODUCTIVITY?

▶ **Featherbedding**
Any practice that forces employers to use more labour than they would otherwise, or to use existing labour in an inefficient manner.

A traditional view of union behaviour is that unions decrease productivity by artificially shifting the demand curve for union labour outward through excessive staffing and make-work requirements. For example, some economists have traditionally felt that unions tend to bargain for excessive use of workers, as when requiring an engineer on all flights. This is referred to as **featherbedding.** Many painters' unions, for example, resisted the use of paint sprayers and required that their members use only brushes. They even specified the maximum width of the brush. Moreover, whenever a union strikes, productivity drops, and this reduction in productivity in one sector of the economy can spill over into other sectors.

This view of unions has recently been countered by one that unions can actually increase productivity. The new labour economists argue that unions act as a collective voice for their members. In the absence of a collective voice, any dissatisfied worker either simply remains at a job and works in a disgruntled manner, or quits. But unions, as a collective voice, can listen to worker grievances on an individual basis and then apply pressure on the employer to change working conditions and other things. The individual worker does not run the risk of being singled out by the employer and harassed. Also, the individual worker doesn't have to spend time trying to convince the employer that some change in the working arrangement should be made. Given that unions provide this collective voice, worker turnover in unionized industries should be less, and this should contribute to productivity. Indeed, there is strong evidence that worker turnover is reduced when unions are present. Of course, this evidence may also be consistent with the fact that wage rates are so attractive to union members that they will not quit unless working conditions become truly intolerable.

THE BENEFITS OF LABOUR UNIONS

It should by now be clear that there are two opposing views about unions. One portrays them as monopolies whose main effect is to raise the wage rate of high-seniority members at the expense of low-seniority members. The other contends that they can increase labour productivity through a variety of means. Economists Richard B. Freeman and James L. Medoff argue that the truth is somewhere in between. They came up with the following conclusions:

1. Unionism probably raises social efficiency, thereby contradicting the traditional monopoly interpretation of what unions do. Even though unionism reduces employment in the unionized sector, it does permit labour to develop and implement workplace practices that are more valuable to workers. In some settings, unionism is associated with increased productivity.
2. Unions appear to reduce wage inequality.
3. Unions seem to reduce profits.
4. Internally, unions provide a political voice for all workers, and unions have been effective in promoting general social legislation.
5. Unions tend to increase the stability of the workforce by providing services, such as arbitration proceedings and grievance procedures.

Try Preview Question 3:
Do unions help workers?

Freeman and Medoff take a positive view of unionism. But critics of the two economists point out they may have overlooked the fact that many of the benefits that unions provide do not require that unions engage in restrictive labour practices, such as refusing to allow nonmembers to work in any particular company. Unions could still do positive things for workers without restricting the labour market.

Concepts in Brief

- When unions raise wage rates above market clearing prices, they face the problem of rationing a restricted number of jobs to a more than willing supply of workers.
- Unions may pursue any one of three goals: (1) to employ all members in the union, (2) to maximize total income of the union's workers, or (3) to maximize wages for certain, usually high-seniority, workers.
- Unions can increase the wage rate of members by engaging in practices that shift the union labour supply curve inward or shift the demand curve for union labour outward (or both).
- Some economists believe that unions can increase productivity by acting as a collective voice for their members, thereby freeing members from the task of convincing their employers that some change in working arrangements should be made. Unions may reduce employee turnover, thus improving productivity.

MONOPSONY: A BUYER'S MONOPOLY

Let's assume that a firm is a perfect competitor in the product market. The firm cannot alter the price of the product it sells, and it faces a perfectly elastic demand curve for its product. We also assume that the firm is the only buyer of a particular input. Although this situation may not occur often, it is useful to consider. Let's think in terms of a factory town, like those dominated by textile mills or in the mining industry. One company not only hires the workers but also owns the businesses in the community, owns the apartments that workers live in, and hires the clerks, waiters, and all other personnel. This buyer of labour is called a **monopsonist,** the single buyer.

▶ **Monopsonist**
A single buyer of a factor of production.

What does an upward-sloping supply curve mean to a monopsonist in terms of the costs of hiring extra workers? It means that if the monopsonist wants to hire more workers, it has to offer higher wages. Our monopsonist firm cannot hire all the labour it wants at the going wage rate. If it wants to hire more workers, it has to raise wage rates, including the wage of all its current workers (assuming a non-wage-discriminating monopsonist). It therefore has to take account of these increased costs when deciding how many more workers to hire.

INTERNATIONAL EXAMPLE
Monopsony in College Sports

How many times have you read stories about American colleges and universities violating National Collegiate Athletic Association (NCAA) rules? If you keep up with the sports press, these stories about alleged violations occur every year. About 600 four-year colleges and universities in the United States belong to the NCAA, which controls more than 20 sports. In effect, the NCAA operates an intercollegiate cartel that is dominated by universities which operate big-time athletic programs. It operates as a cartel with monopsony (and monopoly) power in four ways:

1. It regulates the number of student athletes that universities can recruit.
2. It often fixes the prices that the university charges for tickets to important intercollegiate sporting events.
3. It sets the prices (wages) and the conditions under which the universities can recruit these student athletes.
4. It enforces its regulations and rules with sanctions and penalties.

The NCAA rules and regulations expressly prohibit bidding for college athletes in an overt manner. Rather, the NCAA requires that all athletes be paid the same for tuition, fees, room, board, and books. Moreover, the NCAA limits the number of athletic scholarships that can be given by a particular university. These rules are ostensibly to prevent the richest universities from "hiring" the best student athletes.

Not surprisingly, from the very beginning of the NCAA, individual universities and colleges have attempted to cheat on the rules in order to attract better athletes. The original agreement among the colleges was to pay no wages. Almost immediately after this agreement was put into effect, colleges switched to offering athletic scholarships, jobs, free room and board, travel expenses, and other enticements. It was not unusual for athletes to be paid $10 an hour to rake leaves when the going wage rate for such work was only $5 an hour. Finally, the NCAA had to agree to permit wages up to a certain amount per year.

If all American universities had to offer exactly the same money wages and fringe benefits, the academically less distinguished colleges in urban areas (with a large potential number of ticket-buying fans) would have the most inducement to violate the NCAA agreements (to compensate for the lower market value of their degrees). They would figure out all sorts of techniques to get the best student athletes. Indeed, such schools have in fact cheated more than other universities and colleges, and their violations have been detected and punished with a relatively greater frequency than those of other colleges and universities.

For critical analysis: American college and university administrators argue that the NCAA rules are necessary to "keep business out of higher education." How can one argue that college athletics is related to academics?

Marginal Factor Cost

The monopsonist faces an upward-sloping supply curve of the input in question because as the only buyer, it faces the entire market supply curve. Each time the monopsonist buyer of labour, for example, wishes to hire more workers, it must raise wage rates. Thus the marginal cost of another unit of labour is rising. In fact, the marginal cost of increasing its workforce will always be greater than the wage rate. This is because in the situation in which the monopsonist pays the same wage rate to everyone in order to obtain another unit of labour, the higher wage rate has to be offered not only to the last worker but also to all its other workers. We call the additional cost to the monopsonist of hiring one more worker the marginal factor cost (MFC).

The marginal factor cost for the last worker is therefore that individual's wages plus the increase in the wages of all other existing workers. As we pointed out in Chapter 15, marginal factor cost is equal to the change in total variable cost due to a one-unit change in the one variable factor of production—in this case, labour. In Chapter 15, marginal factor cost was simply the competitive wage rate because the employer could hire all workers at the same wage rate.

Derivation of a Marginal Factor Cost Curve

Part (a) of Figure 16.5 (page 408) shows the quantity of labour purchased, the wage rate per hour, the total cost of the quantity of labour purchased per hour, and the marginal factor cost per hour for the additional labour bought.

We translate the columns from part (a) to the graph in part (b) of the figure. We show the supply curve as *S*, which is taken from columns 1 and 2. (Note that this is the same as the *average* factor cost curve; hence you can view Figure 16.5 as showing the relationship between average factor cost and marginal factor cost.) The marginal factor cost curve (MFC) is taken from columns 1 and 4. The MFC curve must be above the supply curve whenever the supply curve is upward-sloping. If the supply curve is upward-sloping, the firm must pay a higher wage rate in order to attract a larger amount of labour. This higher wage rate must be paid to all workers; thus the increase in total costs due to an increase in the labour input will exceed the wage rate. Note that in a perfectly competitive input market, the supply curve is perfectly elastic and the marginal factor cost curve is identical to the supply curve.

Employment and Wages Under Monopsony

To determine the number of workers that a monopsonist desires to hire, we compare the marginal benefit to the marginal cost of each hiring decision. The marginal cost is the marginal factor cost curve, and the marginal benefit is the marginal revenue product curve. In Figure 16.6 we assume competition in the output market and monopsony in the input market. A monopsonist finds its profit-maximizing quantity of labour demanded at *E*, where the marginal revenue product is just equal to the marginal factor cost.

Figure 16.5

Derivation of a Marginal Factor Cost Curve

The supply curve, S, in part (b) is taken from columns 1 and 2 of part (a). The marginal factor cost curve (MFC) is taken from columns 1 and 4. It is the increase in the total wage bill resulting from a one-unit increase in labour input.

Part (a)

(1) Quantity of Labour Supplied to Management	(2) Required Hourly Wage Rate	(3) Total Wage Bill (3) = (1) x (2)	(4) Marginal Factor Cost (MFC) = $\frac{\text{Change in (3)}}{\text{Change in (1)}}$
0	—	—	
			$1.00
1	$1.00	$1.00	
			3.00
2	2.00	4.00	
			3.20
3	2.40	7.20	
			4.00
4	2.80	11.20	
			6.80
5	3.60	18.00	
			7.20
6	4.20	25.20	

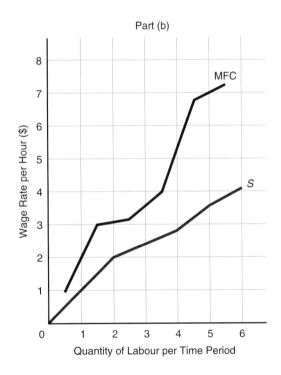

Part (b)

Figure 16.6

Marginal Factor Cost Curve for a Monopsonist

The monopsonist firm looks at a marginal cost curve, MFC, that slopes upward and is above its labour supply curve, S. The marginal benefit of hiring additional workers is given by the firm's MRP curve. The intersection of MFC with MRP, at point E, determines the number of workers hired. The firm hires Q_m workers but has to pay them only W_m in order to attract them. Compare this with the competitive solution, in which the wage rate would have to be W_e and the quantity of labour would be Q_e.

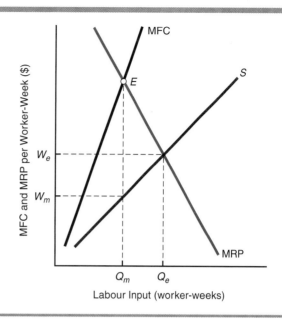

How much is the firm going to pay these workers? In a nonmonopsonistic situation it would face a given wage rate in the labour market, but because it is a monopsonist, it faces the entire supply curve, S.

A monopsonist faces an *upward-sloping* supply curve for labour. Firms do not usually face the market supply curve; most firms can hire all the workers they want at the going wage rate and thus usually face a perfectly elastic supply curve for each factor of production. The market supply curve, however, slopes upward.

The monopsonist therefore sets the wage rate so that it will get exactly the quantity, Q_m, supplied to it by its "captive" labour force. We find that wage rate is W_m. There is no reason to pay the workers any more than W_m because at that wage rate, the firm can get exactly the quantity it wants. The actual quantity used is established at the intersection of the marginal factor cost curve and the marginal revenue product curve for labour—that is, at the point at which the marginal revenue from expanding employment just equals the marginal cost of doing so.

Notice that the profit-maximizing wage rate paid to workers (W_m) is lower than the marginal revenue product. That is to say that workers are paid a wage that is less than their contribution to the monopsonist's revenues. This is sometimes referred to as **monopsonistic exploitation** of labour. The monopsonist is able to do this because each individual worker has little power in bargaining for a higher wage. The organization of workers into a union, though, creates a monopoly supplier of labour, which gives the union some power to bargain for higher wages.

What happens when a monopsonist meets a union? This is the situation called **bilateral monopoly,** defined as a market structure in which a single buyer faces a single seller. An example is a provincial Ministry of Education facing a single teachers' union in the labour market. Another example is a professional players' union facing an organized group of team owners. Such bilateral monopoly situations have indeed occurred in professional baseball and hockey. To analyse bilateral monopoly, we would have to look at the interaction of both sides, buyer and seller. The price outcome turns out to be indeterminate.

▶ **Monopsonistic exploitation**

Exploitation due to monopsony power. It leads to a price for the variable input that is less than its marginal revenue product. Monopsonistic exploitation is the difference between marginal revenue product and the wage rate.

▶ **Bilateral monopoly**

A market structure consisting of a monopolist and a monopsonist.

Try Preview Question 4:

What is a monopsonist, and how does one determine its profit-maximizing employment rate?

We have studied the pricing of labour in various situations, including perfect competition in both the output and input markets and monopoly in both the output and input markets. Figure 16.7 shows four possible situations graphically.

Figure 16.7
Summary of Pricing and Employment Under Various Market Conditions

In part (a), the firm operates in perfect competition in both input and output markets. It purchases labour up to the point where the going rate W_e is equal to MRP$_c$. It hires quantity Q_e of labour. In part (b), the firm is a perfect competitor in the input market but has a monopoly in the output market. It purchases labour up to the point where W_e is equal to MRP$_m$. It hires a smaller quantity of labour, Q_m, than in part (a). In part (c), the firm is a monopsonist in the input market and a perfect competitor in the output market. It hires labour up to the point where MFC = MRP$_c$. It will hire quantity Q_1 and pay wage rate W_c. Part (d) shows bilateral monopoly. The wage outcome is indeterminate.

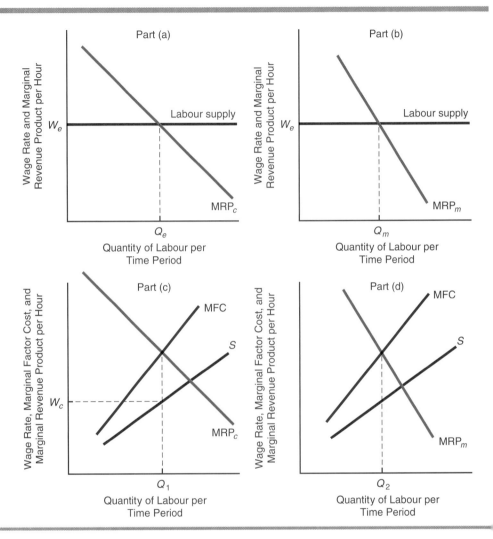

Concepts in Brief

- A monopsonist is a single buyer. The monopsonist faces an upward-sloping supply curve of labour.
- Because the monopsonist faces an upward-sloping supply curve of labour, the marginal factor cost of increasing the labour input by one unit is greater than the wage rate. Thus the marginal factor cost curve always lies above the supply curve.
- A monopsonist will hire workers up to the point at which marginal factor cost equals marginal revenue product. Then the monopsonist will find what minimal wage is necessary to attract that number of workers. This is taken from the supply curve.

Issues and Applications

Pro Sports Means Big Bucks

Concepts Applied: Monopoly, monopsony, bilateral monopoly, collusion, marginal revenue product, marginal factor cost

Blue Jays pitcher Roger Clemens has benefited from membership in the baseball players' union. High players' salaries and team profits are made possible in part by subsidies provided by taxpayers.

A year does not go by without a headline in the sports news that involves multimillion-dollar figures—either a new contract for a professional player that breaks all records, or a team franchise that was just sold for $140 million. For many years, though, the big dollar figures were all on the side of the team owners; professional players faced classic monopsony power by the owners.

The Era of Monopsony Power

Through a variety of restrictions, professional team owners in baseball, basketball, and hockey acted in concert as single buyers of the labour services of players. The result was salaries below players' marginal revenue product. Economists Lawrence Kahn and Peter Sherer estimated that a popular NBA star, such as Wilt Chamberlain, could have earned about $3 million per year (in 1996 dollars) in the early 1970s had he been able to sell his services to the highest bidder. Instead he was paid about $1.7 million (in 1996 dollars). A similar study done by Gerald Scully found that star hitters in baseball were paid almost $3 million per year less than their marginal revenue product in the late 1960s.

Figure 16.8
The Effect of Monopsony Power on Baseball Players' Salaries and the Incomes of Team Owners

The salaries of professional baseball players remained almost flat from 1985 through 1988, the four years during which team owners successfully colluded, as shown in part (a). In part (b), you see that team owners experienced rising net incomes during that same period.

Source: National League.

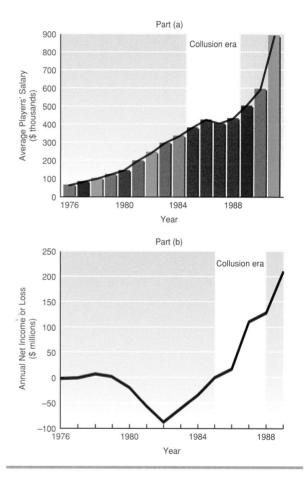

Look at Figure 16.8. In part (a), you see what happened to baseball players' income during a four-year period of strong collusion by baseball team owners. In part (b), you see what happened to profits during the same period.

The Era of Bilateral Monopoly

Through the formation of stronger and stronger players' unions, professional sports have become more of a bilateral monopoly situation. The wage rate is now higher than under pure monopsony, but it is theoretically indeterminate because it depends on the respective bargaining power of the two opposing sides. Strikes in professional baseball and hockey resulted when bargaining did not yield satisfactory results for both sides.

Taxpayers' Dollars Too

One little-known fact concerning both high salaries for professional sports players and large profits for owners of professional teams is that both phenomena are in part the result of taxpayer subsidies. Taxpayers do not give money directly to baseball, hockey, and basketball players, or to team owners. Rather, taxpayers give them money indirectly by subsidizing new stadiums and arenas. Just consider that in 1950, not a single stadium for baseball's National League was owned by the public; today, more than 80 percent of the league's stadiums are publicly owned. For the American League, the comparable numbers are 12 percent in 1950 and

almost 90 percent today. For basketball, the number went from 46 to 76 percent and for hockey, from 0 to 52 percent.

All in all, just since 1992, about $1.5 billion of Canadian and American taxpayers' money has been spent on professional sports stadiums and arenas, with another $2 billion under construction today and plans for yet another $5 billion by 2000.

In essence, taxpayers, whether they are fans or not, are subsidizing professional sports.

For Critical Analysis

1. What is the difference between a monopoly, a monopsony, and a bilateral monopoly?

2. What arguments are there to justify subsidizing professional sports?

CHAPTER SUMMARY

1. The Canadian labour movement started with local craft unions but was very small until the twentieth century. Important organizations in the history of labour in Canada are the Knights of Labor, the Trades and Labour Congress, the Canadian Congress of Labour and the Canadian Labour Congress.

2. In 1946, unions won the right to bargain collectively, to strike, and to collect dues from both members and nonmembers working in organized establishments. This right flowed from a Supreme Court decision referred to as the Rand formula.

3. Unions raise union wage rates relative to nonunion wages. The union wage differential increases during recessions because of the longer-term nature of union collective bargaining contracts.

4. Because unions act as a collective voice for indi-

vidual employees, they may increase productivity by reducing the time that employees spend trying to alter unproductive working arrangements. Unions may also increase productivity by reducing turnover.

5. Monopsony is a situation in which there is only one buyer of a particular input. The single buyer faces an upward-sloping supply curve and must therefore pay higher wage rates to attract additional workers. The single buyer faces a marginal factor cost curve that is upward-sloping and above the supply curve. The buyer hires workers up to the point at which the marginal revenue product equals the marginal factor cost. Then the labour buyer will find out how low a wage rate can be paid to get that many workers.

6. When a single buyer faces a single seller, a situation of bilateral monopsony exists.

DISCUSSION OF PREVIEW QUESTIONS

1. **What are the major types of unions?**

The earliest, and one of the most important forms today, is the craft union, which is an organization of skilled labourers. Another major type

is the industrial union, in which all or most labourers in an industry, such as the steelworkers or mineworkers, unite.

2. What do unions seek to maximize?

Unions do not have unlimited power; in Canada, the rules that have evolved declare that unions can set wage rates *or* the number of labourers who will be employed, but not both. Consequently, a trade-off exists for union leaders: If they maximize wages, some members will become unemployed; if they maximize employment, wages will be relatively low. Union leaders often decide to maximize wages for a given number of workers—presumably the higher-seniority workers. Each union reaches its own decision as to how to resolve the trade-off.

3. Do unions help workers?

If unions are to be considered effective, they must increase real wage rates *above* productivity increases; after all, market forces will increase real wage rates at the rate of productivity change. Yet if real wage rates are increased more rapidly than the rate of productivity increases, unions will cause reduced employment; hence some labourers will be helped (those who retain their jobs at above-productivity wage levels), and some will be hurt (those who lose their jobs). The evidence is that unions are neither a necessary nor a sufficient condition for high real wages. Moreover, labour's overall share of national income has not changed significantly since the 1930s, although *union* labour's share has probably increased relative to nonunion labour's share.

4. What is a monopsonist, and how does one determine its profit-maximizing employment rate?

A monopsonist is a single buyer. A monopsonist hires labour up to the point at which the marginal benefit of doing so equals the marginal cost of doing so. The marginal benefit of hiring labour is labour's marginal revenue product: MB = MRP of labour. The marginal cost of hiring labour must reflect the fact that the monopsonist faces the industry labour supply schedule; hence the monopsonist must increase wage rates in order to hire more labour. Of course, it must increase wage rates for all the labour that it hires, not just the marginal labourer. Thus the MC of hiring labour for a monopsonist (the marginal factor cost, MFC) will be greater than the wage rate. Since the profit-maximizing employment rate is generally where MB = MC, the monopsonist will hire labour up to the point where MRP = MFC. It then pays the lowest wage rate required to attract that quantity of labour. This wage rate will be below the MRP of labour.

PROBLEMS

(Answers to the odd-numbered problems appear at the back of the book.)

16-1. The accompanying graph indicates a monopsonistic firm that is also a perfect competitor in the product market.
  a. What does MRP stand for?
  b. Which is the supply of labour curve?
  c. How many labourers will this firm voluntarily hire?
  d. Given the profit-maximizing employment rate, what is the lowest wage rate that this firm can offer to get this quantity of labour?

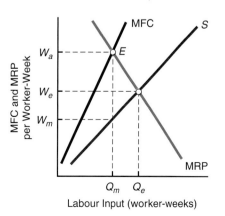

16-2. Does a perfectly competitive firm have to worry about the impact of its own demand for labour on the going wage rate?

16-3. Give examples of perfectly competitive sellers having monopsony power in the input market.

16-4. Suppose that you operate a firm that sells its output in a perfectly competitive market. However, you are the only employer in your island economy. You are currently employing 10 full-time employees at a wage rate of $50 per person per day, and you are producing 100 units of output per day. Labour is your only variable input. The market price of your output is $8 per unit. You estimate that daily output would rise to 108 units per day if you increased your workforce to 11 people. To attract the eleventh worker, you would have to pay a wage rate of $52 to all employees. Should you expand your workforce?

16-5. Imagine yourself managing a plant that is a monopsony buyer of its sole input and is also the monopoly seller of its output. You are currently employing 30 people, producing 20 units of output per day, and selling them for $100 apiece. Your current wage rate is $60 per day. You estimate that you would have to raise your wage scale for all workers to $61 per day in order to attract one more person to your firm. The 31 employees would be able to produce 21 units of output per day, which you would be able to sell at $99.50 apiece. Should you hire the thirty-first employee?

16-6. If a union, in its collective bargaining, sets a wage rate that maximizes total union members' income, will all union members be employed? Explain your answer.

16-7. Why will a union never want to bargain collectively for a wage rate that would exist with perfect competition in the labour market?

16-8. The marginal factor cost curve faced by a firm buying an input in a perfectly competitive market is identical to its supply curve for that input. Why is this not true for a monopsonist? Explain your answer.

16-9. Visit the Canadian Labour Congress Web site at: http://www.clc-ctc.com/. Under "Policy" find the report "The Union Advantage." Table 2 contains comparative data on union and non-union wages.
   a. Who gains more from unionization, men or women?
   b. What occupations gain most from unionization?
   c. What occupations gain least from unionization?

INTERACTING WITH THE INTERNET

The Canadian Labour Congress (CLC) has a substantial amount of material on the organization and issues important to it at

http://www.clc-ctc.ca/

The Trade Union Advisory Committee to the OECD can be found at

http://www.tuac.org/index.html

This site provides a wide range of information on the union movement's global priorities for economic well-being.

Rent, Interest, and Profits

Do you know what the odds are of winning the lottery ? They are the same as the odds of a poker player drawing four royal flushes in a row, all in spades, and then getting up from the card table and meeting four total strangers who were all born on exactly the same day. Nonetheless, "lottomania" continues in most of North America. However, sometimes the announced awards constitute a form of false advertising. To understand why, you have to know how to value money that you receive in the future. You will learn about this in the process of studying rent, interest, and profits in this chapter.

Preview Questions

1. What is rent?
2. What is interest?
3. What is the economic function of interest rates?
4. What is the economic function of profits?

Did You Know That... in Canada, one of the most industrialized countries in the world today, compensation for labour services makes up over 70 percent of national income every year? But what about the other 30 percent? It consists of compensation to the owners of the other factors of production that you read about in Part 1: land, capital, and entrepreneurship. Somebody owns the real estate downtown for which the monthly commercial rents are higher for one square metre than you might pay to rent a whole apartment. Land, obviously, is a factor of production, and it has a market clearing price. Businesses also have to use capital. Compensation for that capital is interest, and it, too, has a market clearing level. Finally, some of you may have entrepreneurial ability that you offer to the marketplace. Your compensation is called profit. In this chapter you will also learn about the sources and functions of profit.

RENT

▶ **Economic rent**

A payment for the use of any resource over and above its opportunity cost.

When you hear the term *rent,* you normally think it means the payment made to property owners for the use of land or apartments. But, the term *rent* has a different meaning in economics. **Economic rent** is payment to the owner of a resource in excess of its opportunity cost—the payment that would be necessary to call forth production of that amount of the resource. Economists originally used the term *rent* to designate payment for the use of land. What was thought to be important about land was that its supply is completely inelastic. Hence the supply curve for land is a vertical line; no matter what the prevailing market price for land, the quantity supplied will remain the same.

Determining Land Rent

The concept of economic rent is associated with the British economist David Ricardo (1772–1823). He looked at two plots of land on which grain was growing, one of which happened to be more fertile than the other. The owners of these two plots sold the grain that came from their land, but the one who owned the more fertile land grew more grain and therefore made more profits. According to Ricardo, the owner of the fertile land was receiving economic rents that were due not to the landowner's hard work or ingenuity but rather to an accident of nature. Ricardo asked his readers to imagine another scenario, that of walking up a road that starts out flat with no rocks and then becomes steeper and rockier. The value of the land falls as one walks up the hill. If a different person owns the top of the hill than the bottom, the highland owner will receive very little in payment from, say, a farmer who wants to cultivate land for wheat production.

Here is how Ricardo analysed economic rent for land. He first simplified his model by assuming that all land is equally productive. Then Ricardo assumed that the quantity of land in a country is *fixed.* Graphically, then, in terms of supply and demand, we draw the supply curve of land vertically (zero price elasticity). In Figure 17.1, the supply curve of land is represented by S. If the demand curve is D_1, it inter-

Figure 17.1

Economic Rent

If indeed the supply curve of land were completely price-inelastic in the long run, it would be depicted by S. At the quantity in existence, Q_1, any and all revenues are economic rent. If demand is D_1, the price will be P_1; if demand is D_2, price will rise to P_2. Economic rent would be $P_1 \times Q_1$ and $P_2 \times Q_1$, respectively.

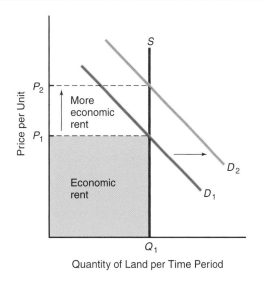

sects the supply curve, S, at price P_1. The entire amount of revenues obtained, $P_1 \times Q_1$, is labelled "Economic rent." If the demand for land increased to D_2, the equilibrium price would rise to P_2. Additions to economic rent are labelled "More economic rent." Notice that the quantity of land remains insensitive to the change in price. Another way of stating this is that the supply curve is perfectly inelastic.

ECONOMIC RENT TO LABOUR

Land and natural resources are not the only factors of production to which the analysis of economic rent can be applied. In fact, the analysis is probably more often applicable to labour. Here is a list of people who provide different labour services, some of whom probably receive large amounts of economic rent:

> Professional sports superstars
> Rock stars
> Movie stars
> World-class models
> Successful inventors and innovators
> World-famous opera stars

Just apply the definition of economic rent to the phenomenal earnings that these people make. They would undoubtedly work for much, much less than they earn. Therefore, much of their earnings constitutes economic rent (but not all, as we shall see). Economic rent occurs because specific resources cannot be replicated exactly. No one can duplicate today's most highly paid entertainment figures, and therefore they receive economic rent.

Economic Rent and the Allocation of Resources

If an extremely highly paid movie star would make the same number of movies at half that individual's current annual earnings, does that mean that 50 percent of the star's income is unnecessary? To answer the question, consider first why the superstar gets such a high income. The answer can be found in Figure 17.1. Substitute *entertainment activities of the superstars* for the word *land.* The high "price" received by the superstar is due to the demand for that person's services. If Michael J. Fox announces that he will work for a measly $1 million a movie and do two movies a year, how is he going to know which production company values his services the most highly? Fox and other movie stars let the market decide where their resources should be used. In this sense, we can say the following:

> Economic rent allocates resources to their highest-valued use.

In other words, economic rent directs resources to the people who can most efficiently use them.

A common counterexample involves rock stars who claim that their tickets are overpriced. Consequently, they agree to perform, say, five concerts with all tickets being sold at the same price, $15. Assume that a star performs these concerts in halls with 20,000 seats. A total of 100,000 individuals per year will be able to see this particular performer. This is represented by point *A* in Figure 17.2. By assumption, this performer is still receiving some economic rent because we are assuming that the supply curve of concerts is vertical at 100,000 seats per year. At a price per ticket of $15, however, the annual quantity of seats demanded will be 150,000, represented by point *B.* The difference between points *A* and *B* is the excess quantity of tickets demanded at the below-market-clearing price of $15 a seat. The *additional* economic rent that could be earned by this performer by charging the clearing price of $25 per seat in this graph would serve as the rationing device that would make the quantity demanded equal to the quantity supplied.

Figure 17.2
The Allocative Function of Rent

If the performer agrees to give five concerts a year "at any price" and there are 20,000 seats in each concert hall, the supply curve of concerts, *S,* is vertical at 100,000 seats per year. The demand curve is given by *D.* The performer wants a price of only $15 to be charged. At that price, the quantity of seats demanded per year is 150,000. The excess quantity demanded is equal to the horizontal distance between points *A* and *B,* or 50,000 seats per year.

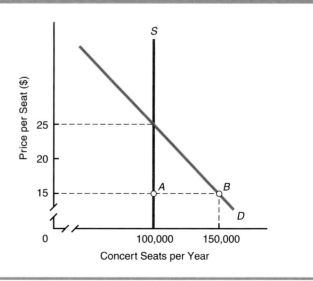

In such situations, which are fairly common, part of the economic rent that could have been earned is dissipated—it is captured, for example, by radio station owners in the form of promotional gains when they are allowed to give away a certain number of tickets on the air (even if they have to pay $15 per ticket) because the tickets are worth $25. Ticket holders who resell tickets at higher prices ("scalpers") also capture part of the rent. Conceivably, at 100,000 seats per year, this performer could charge the market clearing price of $25 per ticket and give away to charity the portion of the economic rent ($10 per ticket) that would be dissipated.

Try Preview Question 1:
What is rent?

INTERNATIONAL EXAMPLE
Economic Rent and the Superstar Income Earners

Table 17.1
Superstar Earnings

Name	Occupation	Earnings (annual US$)
Steven Spielberg	Director/producer, founding partner of DreamWorks studio	$283,000,000
Oprah Winfrey	Television talk show host	104,000,000
Michael Crichton	Author	65,000,000
Tom Cruise	Actor	65,000,000
The Rolling Stones	Rock band	62,000,000
Spice Girls	Rock band	40,000,000
John Grisham	Author	36,000,000
Céline Dion	Pop singer	34,000,000
Kiss	Rock band	21,000,000
Michael Jackson	Pop singer	20,000,000

Source: Forbes, 1997.

Everybody knows that big-time entertainers make big bucks. Just consider Table 17.1, which lists some of the top income-earning entertainers in North America today as estimated by *Forbes* magazine. The difficult question here is how much of those millions of dollars can be called economic rent. Whereas relatively new superstar entertainers would certainly work for much less than they earn, the same may not necessarily be true for superstar entertainers who have been doing the same thing year in and year out for several decades. In other words, given their already extremely high accumulated wealth and their presumably more jaded outlook about their work, perhaps they would work very little if they were not paid tens of millions of dollars a year.

For critical analysis: Even if some superstar entertainers would work for less, what forces cause them to make so much income anyway?

Taxing Away Economic Rent

Some people have argued in favour of imposing high taxes on economic rent. For example, drug companies that have developed *successful* patented drugs make large amounts of economic rent during the life of the patent. That is to say, the marginal cost of production is much less than the price charged. If the government taxed this economic rent completely, those successful drugs already on the market would in fact stay on the market. But there would be long-run consequences. Drug companies would invest fewer resources in discovering new successful drugs. So economic rent is typically a *short-run* phenomenon. In the long run, it constitutes a source of reward for risk taking in society. This is true not only in the drug business but also in entertainment and professional sports.

Concepts in Brief

- Economic rent is defined as payment for a factor of production that is completely inelastic in supply. It is payment for a resource over and above what is necessary to keep that resource in existence at its current level in the long run.
- Economic rent serves an allocative function by guiding available supply to the most efficient use.

INTEREST

The term **interest** is used to mean two different things: (1) the price paid by debtors to creditors for the use of loanable funds and (2) the market return earned by (nonfinancial) capital as a factor of production. Owners of capital, whether directly or indirectly, obtain interest income. Often, businesses go to credit markets to obtain so-called money capital in order to invest in physical capital from which they hope to make a satisfactory return. In other words, in our complicated society, the production of capital goods often occurs because of the existence of credit markets in which borrowing and lending take place. For the moment, we will look only at the credit market.

Interest and Credit

When you obtain credit, you actually obtain money in order to have command over resources today. We can say, then, that interest is the payment for current rather than future command over resources. Thus interest is the payment for obtaining credit. If you borrow $100 from me, you have command over $100 worth of goods and services today. I no longer have that command. You promise to pay me back $100 plus interest at some future date. The interest that you pay is usually expressed as a percentage of the total loan calculated on an annual basis. If at the end of one year you pay me back $110, the annual interest is $10 ÷ $100, or 10 percent. When you go out into the marketplace to obtain credit, you will find that the interest rate charged differs greatly. A loan to buy a house (a mortgage) may cost you 5 to 8 percent annual interest. An instalment loan to buy an automobile may cost you 9 to 14 percent annual interest. The federal government, when it wishes to obtain credit (issues Treasury bills), may have to pay only 3 to 5 percent annual interest. Variations in the rate of annual interest that must be paid for credit depend on the following factors.

1. *Length of loan.* In some (but not all) cases, the longer the loan will be outstanding, other things being equal, the greater will be the interest rate charged.
2. *Risk.* The greater the risk of nonrepayment of the loan, other things being equal, the greater the interest rate charged. Risk is assessed on the basis of the creditworthiness of the borrower, and whether the borrower provides collateral for the loan. Collateral consists of any asset that will automatically become the property of the lender should the borrower fail to comply with the loan agreement.
3. *Handling charges.* It takes resources to set up a loan. Papers have to be filled out and filed, credit references have to be checked, collateral has to be examined, and so on. The larger the amount of the loan, the smaller the handling (or administrative) charges as a percentage of the total loan. Therefore, we would predict that, other things being equal, the larger the loan, the lower the interest rate.

Try Preview Question 2:
What is interest?

What Determines Interest Rates?

The overall level of interest rates can be described as the price paid for loanable funds. As with all commodities, price is determined by the interaction of supply and demand. Let's first look at the supply of loanable funds and then at the demand for them.

The Supply of Loanable Funds.   The supply of loanable funds (credit available) depends on individuals' willingness to save.[1] When you save, you exchange rights to current consumption for rights to future consumption. The more current consumption you give up, the more valuable is a marginal unit of present consumption in comparison with future consumption.

Recall from our discussion of diminishing marginal utility that the more of something you have, the less you value an additional unit. Conversely, the less of something you have, the more you value an additional unit. Thus when you give up current consumption of a good—that is, have less of it—you value an additional unit more. The more you save today, the more utility you attach to your last unit of today's consumption. So to be induced to save more—to consume less—you have to be offered a bigger and bigger reward to match the marginal utility of current consumption you will give up by saving. Because of this, if society wants to induce people to save more, it must offer a higher rate of interest. Hence we expect that the supply curve of loanable funds will slope upward. At higher rates of interest, savers will be willing to offer more current consumption to borrowers, other things being constant.[2] When the income of individuals increases or when there is a change in individual preferences towards more saving, the supply curve of loanable funds will shift outward to the right, and vice versa.

---

[1] Actually, the supply of loanable funds also depends on business and government saving and on the behaviour of the monetary authorities and the banking system. For simplicity of discussion, we ignore these components here.
[2] A complete discussion would include the income effect: At higher interest rates, households receive a higher yield on savings, permitting them to save less to achieve any given target.

The Demand for Loanable Funds. There are three major sources of the demand for loanable funds:

1. Households that want loanable funds for the purchase of services and non-durable goods, as well as consumer durables such as automobiles and homes
2. Businesses that want loanable funds to make investments
3. Governments that want loanable funds, usually to cover deficits—the excess of government spending over tax revenues

We will ignore the government's demand for loanable funds and consider only consumers and businesses.

Loans are taken out both by consumers and by businesses. It is useful to separate the motives underlying the demand for loans by these two groups of individuals. We will therefore treat consumption loans and investment loans separately. In the discussion that follows, we assume that there is no inflation—that is, there is no persistent increase in the overall level of prices.

Consumer Demand for Loanable Funds. In general, consumers demand loanable funds because they tend to prefer earlier consumption to later consumption. That is to say, people subjectively value goods obtained immediately more than the same goods of the same quality obtained later on. Consider that sometimes an individual household's present income falls below the average income level expected over a lifetime. Individuals may go to the credit market to borrow whenever they perceive a temporary dip in their current income—assuming that they expect their income to go back to normal later on. By borrowing, they can spread out purchases more evenly during their lifetimes. In so doing, they're able to increase their lifetime total utility.

Consumers' demand for loanable funds will be inversely related to the cost of borrowing—the rate of interest. Why? For the same reason that all demand curves slope downward: A higher rate of interest means a higher cost of borrowing, and a higher cost of borrowing must be weighed against alternative uses of limited income. At higher costs of borrowing, consumers will forgo current consumption.

POLICY EXAMPLE Should Rent-to-Own Stores Be Regulated?

A growing number of consumers are implicitly borrowing money by dealing with rent-to-own stores that offer them goods such as television sets and refrigerators for low weekly payments. At the end of a very long period, they end up owning the item. For example, a consumer can rent a television for $18 a week and at the end of 91 weeks will own it. Some investigators claim that because the TV is worth only $190 when it's new, consumers are paying over 300 percent annual interest. The Consumers Association of Canada has found many cases where the sale/rental of a refrigerator or sofa yields two or three times what the store paid for it. In 1996, provincial Consumer Ministers vowed to pass legislation forcing rent-to-own stores to describe in their contracts the credit cost in terms of an annual percentage rate. Because the number of rent-to-own stores across Canada has increased from very few in the 1980s to over 150 today, empirically we know that a consumer demand exists for their services. Typically, the people who use them do not qualify for normal consumer credit. That is why they end up paying such implicitly high interest rates.

For critical analysis: What do you think will happen to the growth in rent-to-own stores if the cost-of-credit legislation is passed?

Business Demand for Loanable Funds.   Businesses demand loanable funds to make investments that they believe will increase productivity or profit. Whenever a business believes that by making an investment, it can increase revenues (net of other costs) by more than the cost of capital, it will make the investment. Businesses compare the interest rate they must pay in the loanable funds market with the interest rate they think they can earn by investing. This comparison helps them decide whether to invest.

In any event, we hypothesize that the demand curve for loanable funds by firms for investment purposes will be negatively sloped. At higher interest rates, fewer investment projects will make economic sense to businesses because the cost of capital (loanable funds) will exceed the net revenues derivable from the capital investment. Conversely, at lower rates of interest, more investment projects will be undertaken because the cost of capital will be less than the expected rate of return on the capital investment.

The Equilibrium Rate of Interest

When we add together the demand for loanable funds by households and businesses (and government in more complex models), we obtain a demand curve for loanable funds, as given in Figure 17.3. The supply curve is S. The equilibrium rate of interest is i_e.

Figure 17.3
The Supply of and Demand for Loanable Funds

We draw D as the demand curve for all loanable funds by households and businesses (and governments). It slopes downward. S is the supply curve of credit, or loanable funds. It slopes upward. The intersection of S and D gives the equilibrium rate of interest at i_e.

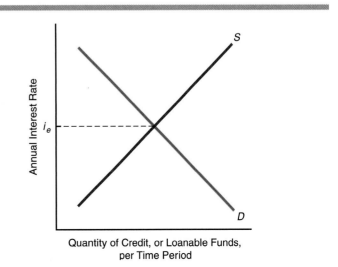

Quantity of Credit, or Loanable Funds,
per Time Period

INTERNATIONAL EXAMPLE
One Consequence of Privatizing Italian Banks: Loan Sharking

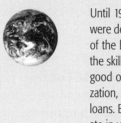

Until 1994, almost all Italian banks were government-owned, and loans usually were decided on political grounds. When the Italian government got out of some of the banking business, though, the newly privatized bank loan officers lacked the skills and experience necessary to judge whether a potential borrower was a good or a bad credit risk. Consequently, during this interim period after privatization, many small businesspersons in Italy were turned away when they sought loans. Bank loan officers steered them to "loan sharks." Many such lenders operate in violation of Italian law and end up charging borrowers 300 to 500 percent per year, well above the posted "equilibrium" interest rate at the nation's biggest banks.

For critical analysis: Who typically ends up agreeing to the high interest rates charged by loan sharks?

Real Versus Nominal Interest Rates

▶ **Nominal rate of interest**
The market rate of interest expressed in today's dollars.

We have been assuming that there is no inflation. In a world of inflation—a persistent rise in an average of all prices—the **nominal rate of interest** will be higher than it would be in a world with no inflation. Basically, nominal, or market, rates of interest rise to take account of the anticipated rate of inflation. If, for example, there is no inflation and none is expected, the nominal rate of interest might be 5 percent for home mortgages. If the rate of inflation goes to 10 percent a year and stays there, everybody will anticipate that inflation rate. The nominal rate of interest will rise to about 15 percent to take account of the anticipated rate of inflation. If the interest rate did not rise to 15 percent, the interest earned at 5 percent would be worth less in the future because inflation would have eroded its purchasing power. We can therefore say that the nominal, or market, rate of interest is approximately equal to the real rate of interest plus the anticipated rate of inflation, or

$$i_n = i_r + \text{anticipated rate of inflation}$$

▶ **Real rate of interest**
The nominal rate of interest minus the anticipated rate of inflation.

where i_n equals the nominal rate of interest and i_r equals the real rate of interest. In short, you can expect to see high nominal rates of interest in periods of high or rising inflation rates. The **real rate of interest** may not necessarily be high, though. We must first correct the nominal rate of interest for the anticipated rate of inflation before determining whether the real interest rate is in fact higher than normal.

The Allocative Role of Interest

In Chapters 3 and 4 we talked about the price system and the role that prices play in the allocation of resources. Interest is a price that allocates loanable funds (credit) to consumers and to businesses. Within the business sector, interest allocates loanable funds to different firms and therefore to different investment projects. Investment, or capital, projects with rates of return higher than the market rate of interest in the credit market will be undertaken, given an unrestricted market for loanable funds. For example, if the expected rate of return on the purchase of a new factory in some industry is 15 percent and loanable funds can be acquired for 11 percent, the investment project may proceed. If, however, that same project had an expected rate of return of only 9 percent, it would not be undertaken. In sum, the interest rate allocates loanable funds to industries whose investments yield the highest returns—where resources will be the most productive.

It is important to realize that the interest rate performs the function of allocating money capital (loanable funds) and that this ultimately allocates real physical capital to various firms for investment projects.

Try Preview Question 3:
What is the economic function of interest rates?

Thinking Critically About the Media   Those Astronomical Interest Rates

The media have a field day when they analyse economic statistics in particular developing countries. You may have read about double- and triple-digit interest rates in such countries as Brazil, Argentina, and Russia. The problem with such stories is that they ignore the difference between nominal and real interest rates. Almost always, astronomically high interest rates are due to people's expectations of very high rates of inflation. Consequently, even with double- and triple-digit nominal interest rates in certain countries, *real* interest rates may be quite low.

Interest Rates and Present Value

Businesses make investments in which they often incur large costs today but don't make any profits until some time in the future. Somehow they have to be able to compare their investment cost today with a stream of future profits. How can they relate present cost to future benefits?

Interest rates are used to link the present with the future. After all, if you have to pay $110 at the end of the year when you borrow $100, that 10 percent interest rate gives you a measure of the premium on the earlier availability of goods and services. If you want to have things today, you have to pay the 10 percent interest rate in order to have current purchasing power.

The question could be put this way: What is the present value (the value today) of $110 that you could receive one year from now? That depends on the market rate of interest, or the rate of interest that you could earn in some appropriate financial institution, such as in a savings account. To make the arithmetic simple, let's assume that the rate of interest is 10 percent. Now you can figure out the **present value** of $110 to be received one year from now. You figure it out by asking the question, How much money must I put aside today at the market interest rate of 10 percent to receive $110 one year from now? Mathematically, we represent this equation as:

▶ **Present value**
The value of a future amount expressed in today's dollars; the most that someone would pay today to receive a certain sum at some point in the future.

$$(1 + 0.1)PV_1 = \$110$$

where PV_1 is the sum that you must set aside now.

Let's solve this simple equation to obtain PV_1:

$$PV_1 = \frac{\$110}{1.1} = \$100$$

That is to say, $100 will accumulate to $110 at the end of one year with a market rate of interest of 10 percent. Thus the present value of $110 one year from now, using a rate of interest of 10 percent, is $100. The formula for present value of any sums to be received one year from now thus becomes

$$PV_1 = \frac{FV_1}{1+i}$$

where

PV_1 = present value of a sum one year hence
FV_1 = future sum of money paid or received one year hence
i = market rate of interest

Present Values for More Distant Periods.   The present-value formula for figuring out today's worth of dollars to be received at a future date can now easily be seen. How much would have to be put in the same savings account today to have $110 two years from now if the account pays a rate of 10 percent per year compounded annually?

After one year, the sum that would have to be set aside, which we will call PV_2, would have grown to $PV_2 \times 1.1$. This amount during the second year would increase to $PV_2 \times 1.1 \times 1.1$, or $PV_2 \times (1.1)^2$. To find the PV_2 that would grow to $110 over two years, let

$$PV_2 \times (1.1)^2 = \$110$$

and solve for PV_2:

$$PV_2 = \frac{\$110}{(1.1)^2} = \$90.91$$

Thus the present value of $110 to be paid or received two years hence, discounted at an interest rate of 10 percent per year compounded annually, is equal to $90.91. In other words, $90.91 put into a savings account yielding 10 percent per year compounded interest would accumulate to $110 in two years.

▶ **Discounting**
The method by which the present value of a future sum or a future stream of sums is obtained.

The General Formula for Discounting.   The general formula for **discounting** becomes

$$PV_t = \frac{FV_t}{(1+i)^t}$$

where t refers to the number of periods in the future the money is to be paid or received.

▶ **Rate of discount**
The rate of interest used to discount future sums back to present value.

Table 17.2 gives the present value of $1 to be received in future years at various interest rates. The interest rate used to derive the present value is called the **rate of discount.**

Table 17.2
Present Value of a Future Dollar

This table shows how much a dollar received at the end of a certain number of years in the future is worth today. For example, at 5 percent a year, a dollar to be received 20 years in the future is worth 37.7 cents; if received in 50 years, it isn't even worth a dime today. To find out how much $10,000 would be worth a certain number of years from now, just multiply the figures in the table by 10,000. For example, $10,000 received at the end of 10 years discounted at a 5 percent rate of interest would have a present value of $6,140.

	Compounded Annual Interest Rate				
Year	3%	5%	8%	10%	20%
1	0.971	0.952	0.926	0.909	0.833
2	0.943	0.907	0.857	0.826	0.694
3	0.915	0.864	0.794	0.751	0.578
4	0.889	0.823	0.735	0.683	0.482
5	0.863	0.784	0.681	0.620	0.402
6	0.838	0.746	0.630	0.564	0.335
7	0.813	0.711	0.583	0.513	0.279
8	0.789	0.677	0.540	0.466	0.233
9	0.766	0.645	0.500	0.424	0.194
10	0.744	0.614	0.463	0.385	0.162
15	0.642	0.481	0.315	0.239	0.0649
20	0.554	0.377	0.215	0.148	0.0261
25	0.478	0.295	0.146	0.0923	0.0105
30	0.412	0.231	0.0994	0.0573	0.00421
40	0.307	0.142	0.0460	0.0221	0.000680
50	0.228	0.087	0.0213	0.00852	0.000109

INTERNATIONAL EXAMPLE
Viager, or Betting on an Early Death (Someone Else's)

In France, it is possible to make a legal bet on when someone is going to die. It is done through a real estate transaction called *viager,* the right for someone to receive periodic payments until that person's death. Apartments and houses are sold via the system of *viager* in the following manner: Typically, a senior citizen agrees to transfer ownership of the apartment or house upon death. In exchange for the future right to own the real estate, the purchaser agrees to pay a specified amount every month until the occupant-owner's death. In essence, then, the future owner is looking at the present value of a stream of payments coupled with the current occupant-owner's life expectancy. Under a fair *viager* contract, the present value of the purchase price is approximately equal to the market price of the real estate. If the occupant-owner dies earlier than anticipated, though, the purchaser pays less. The converse is almost always true also.

For critical analysis: How does present value enter in to the market for the purchase of life insurance policies from terminally ill people? How does this relate to a *viager* contract?

Concepts in Brief

* Interest is the price paid for the use of capital. It is also the cost of obtaining credit. In the credit market, the rate of interest paid depends on the length of the loan, the risk, and the handling charges, among other things.
* The interest rate is determined by the intersection of the supply curve of credit, or loanable funds, and the demand curve for credit, or loanable funds. The major sources for the demand for loanable funds are households, businesses, and governments.
* Nominal, or market, interest rates include a factor to take account of the anticipated rate of inflation. Therefore, during periods of high anticipated inflation, nominal interest rates will be relatively high.
* Payments received or costs incurred in the future are worth less than those received or incurred today. The present value of any future sum is lower the farther it occurs in the future and the greater the discount rate used.

PROFITS

In Chapter 2, we identified entrepreneurship as a factor of production. Profit is the reward that this factor earns. You may recall that entrepreneurship involves engaging in the risk of starting new businesses. In a sense, then, nothing can be produced without an input of entrepreneurial skills.

Until now, we have been able to talk about the demand for and supply of labour, land, and capital. We can't talk as easily about the demand for and supply of entrepreneurship. For one thing, we have no way to quantify entrepreneurship. What measure should we use? We do know that entrepreneurship exists. We cannot, however, easily present a supply and demand analysis to show the market clearing price per unit of entrepreneurship. We must use a different approach, focusing on the reward for entrepreneurship—profit. First we will determine what profit is *not*. Then we will examine the sources of true, or economic, profit. Finally, we will look at the functions of profits in a market system.

Distinguishing Between Economic Profit and Business, or Accounting, Profit

▶ **Economic profit**
The difference between total revenues and the opportunity cost of all factors of production.

▶ **Accounting profit**
Total revenues minus total explicit costs.

In our discussion of rent, we had to make a distinction between the common notions of rent and the economist's concept of economic rent. We must do the same thing when we refer to profit. We always have to distinguish between **economic profit** and **accounting profit.** The accountant calculates profit for a business as the difference between total explicit revenues and total explicit costs. Consider an extreme example. You are given a large farm as part of your inheritance. All of the land, fertilizer, seed, machinery, and tools have been fully paid for by your deceased relative. You take over the farm and work on it diligently with half a dozen workers. At the end of the year, you sell the output for $1 million. Your accountant then subtracts your actual ("explicit") expenses, mainly the wages you paid.

The difference is called profit, but it is not economic profit. Why? Because no accounting was taken of the *implicit* costs of using the land, seed, tools, and machinery. The only explicit cost considered was the workers' wages. But as long as the land could be rented out, the seed could be sold, and the tools and machinery could be leased, there was an opportunity cost to using them. To derive the economic profit that you might have earned last year from the farm, you must subtract from total revenues the full opportunity cost of all factors of production used (which will include both implicit and explicit costs).

In summary, then, accounting profit is used mainly to define taxable income and, as such, may include some returns to both the owner's labour and capital. Economic profit, by contrast, represents a return over and above the opportunity cost of all resources (including a normal return on the owner's entrepreneurial abilities).

When viewed in this light, it is possible for economic profit to be negative, even if accounting profit is positive. Turning to our farming example again, what if the opportunity cost of using all of the resources turned out to be $1.1 million? The economic profit would have been −$100,000. You would have suffered economic losses.

In sum, the businessperson's accounting definition and the economist's economic definition of profit usually do not coincide. Economic profit is a residual. It is whatever remains after all economic, or opportunity, costs have been taken into account.

Explanations of Economic Profit

There are many alternative explanations of profit. Let us examine a few of them: restrictions on entry, innovation, and reward for bearing uninsurable risks.

Restrictions on Entry. We pointed out in Chapter 12 that monopoly profits—a special form of economic profits—are possible when there are barriers to entry, and that economists often call these profits monopoly rents. Entry restrictions exist in many industries, including taxicabs, cable television franchises, and prescription drugs and eyeglasses. Basically, monopoly profits are built into the value of the business that owns the particular right to have the monopoly.

Innovation. A number of economists have maintained that economic profits are created by innovation, which is defined as the creation of a new organizational strategy, a new marketing strategy, or a new product. This source of economic profit was popularized by economics professor Joseph Schumpeter (1883–1950). The innovator creates new economic profit opportunities through innovation. The successful innovator obtains a temporary monopoly position, garnering temporary economic profits. When other firms catch up, those temporary economic profits disappear.

Reward for Bearing Uninsurable Risks There are risks in life, including those involved in any business venture. Many of these risks can be insured, however. You can insure against the risk of losing your house to fire, flood, hurricane, or earthquake. You can do the same if you own a business. You can insure against the risk of theft also. Insurance companies are willing to sell you such insurance because they can predict relatively accurately what percentage of a class of insured assets will suffer losses each year. They charge each insured person or business enough to pay for those fully anticipated losses and to make a normal rate of return.

But there are risks that cannot be insured. If you and a group of your friends get together and pool your resources to start a new business, no amount of statistical calculations can accurately predict whether your business will still be running a year from now or 10 years from now. Consequently, when you start your business you can't buy insurance against losing money, bad management, miscalculations about the size of the market, aggressive competition by big corporations, and the like. Entrepreneurs therefore incur uninsurable risks. According to a theory of profits advanced by economist Frank H. Knight (1885–1973), this is the origin of economic profit.

The Function of Economic Profit

In a market economy, the expectation of profits induces firms to discover new products, new production techniques, and new marketing techniques—literally all the new ways to make higher profits. Profits in this sense spur innovation and investment.

Profits also cause resources to move from lower-valued to higher-valued uses. Prices and sales are dictated by the consumer. If the demand curve is close to the origin, there will be few sales and few profits, if any. The lack of profits therefore means that there is insufficient demand to cover the opportunity cost of production. In the quest for higher profits, businesses will take resources out of areas in which either accounting losses or lower than normal rates of return are being made and put them into areas in which there is an expectation of higher profits. The profit reward is an inducement for an industry to expand when demand and supply conditions warrant it. Conversely, the existence of economic losses indicates that resources in the particular industry are not valued as highly as they might be elsewhere. These resources therefore move out of that industry, or at least no further resources are invested in it. Therefore, resources follow the businessperson's quest for higher profits. Profits allocate resources, just as wages and interest do.

Try Preview Question 4:

What is the economic function of profits?

Concepts in Brief

- Profit is the reward for entrepreneurial talent, a factor of production.
- It is necessary to distinguish between accounting profit and economic profit. Accounting profit is measured by the difference between total revenues and all explicit costs. Economic profit is measured by the difference between total revenues and the total of all opportunity costs of all factors of production.
- Theories of why profits exist include restriction on entry, innovation, and payment to entrepreneurs for taking uninsurable risks.
- The function of profits in a market economy is to allocate scarce resources. Resources will flow to wherever profits are highest.

Issues and Applications

A Million-Dollar Jackpot Doesn't Make a Millionaire

Concepts Applied: Present value

North Americans spend about US$50 billion on lottery tickets every year. Lotteries that are paid in instalments end up paying out, in current dollars, substantially less than the announced value of the winning ticket.

Every year, millions of North Americans play the lottery. We purchase collectively about US$50 billion worth of tickets in this legalized form of gambling. Sometimes the winners are not happy, though.

Suing the Lottery

When one resident of the United States won the lottery, he thought he was an instant millionaire. He discovered, though, that instead of giving him a cheque for $1 million, the lottery foundation was going to pay him $50,000 a year for 20 years for a grand total of $1 million. He went to court charging fraud and deception. In the advertisement for the lottery, it never mentioned the 20-year payment system. The court went along with the lottery foundation in arguing that if the complainant did not like what he won, he could return his ticket and be repaid the dollar that he spent on it.

Present Value Is What Counts

In reality, the millions of dollars of jackpots that are paid in instalments are not really the millions they claim to be. Let's see why. A person wins a $15 million lottery jackpot. Rather than handing that person a cheque for $15 million, the lottery foundation typically pays the winnings in instalments of, say, $750,000 a year over 20 years. Is $750,000 each year for 20 years worth $15 million today? It is true that the $750,000 per year for 20 years does add up to $15 million. But if the lottery gave that person $15 million all at once, it could be invested at the market rate of interest today and it would be worth considerably more 20 years from now.

Thus in actuality, 20 annual payments of $750,000 are worth much less than $15 million. At an interest rate of 10 percent, they are worth only $6,385,500. You can use Table 17.2 to calculate the present value of each $750,000 payment at the end of each year in the future. We can also view this by looking at the value of each of the $750,000 payments. The last instalment of $750,000 in the twentieth year is worth a mere $111,750 today, discounted at 10 percent. If we used a higher discount rate, it would be worth even less in present value.

Now you can see why some lotteries prefer to pay out winnings in instalments rather than in a lump sum.

For Critical Analysis

1. Canadian lotteries pay out in lump sums. Does it cost the lottery foundation more to do this?
2. If the chances of winning a lottery are so low, as pointed out in the first page of this chapter, why do thousands of Canadians continue to buy tickets every week?

CHAPTER SUMMARY

1. Resources that have a fixed supply are paid what is called economic rent. We therefore define economic rent as the payment over and above what is necessary to keep a resource of constant quality and quantity in supply at its current level.

2. Resource owners (including labour owners) of factors with inelastic supply earn economic rent because competition among potential users of those resources bids up the price offered.

3. Interest can be defined as the payment for command over resources today rather than in the future. Interest is typically seen as the payment for credit, but it can also be considered the payment for the use of capital. Interest charged depends on length of loan, risk, and handling charges.

4. The equilibrium rate of interest is determined by the intersection of the demand for credit, or loanable funds, and the supply of credit, or loanable funds.

5. The nominal rate of interest includes a factor that takes account of the anticipated rate of inflation. In periods of high anticipated inflation, nominal, or market, interest rates will be high. Real interest rates may not actually be higher, however, because they are defined as the nominal rate of interest minus the anticipated rate of inflation.

6. The present value of any sum in the future is less than that same sum today. Present value decreases as the sum is paid or obtained further and further in the future and as the rate of discount increases.

7. Frank Knight believed that profit was a payment to entrepreneurs for undertaking risks that are uninsurable. Other reasons why profit exists include restrictions on entry and reward for innovation.

DISCUSSION OF PREVIEW QUESTIONS

1. What is rent?

Rent is payment for the use of land. Economists have long played with the notion that land is completely inelastic in supply, although this is a debatable issue and depends on various definitions. Modern economists now refer to a payment to any factor of production that is in excess of its opportunity cost as economic rent. For example, athletes and entertainers presumably earn economic rent: Beyond some "normal" income, the opportunity cost to superstars of performing is zero; hence "abnormal" income is not necessary to induce them to perform. Note that we usually discuss positively sloped supply schedules indicating that higher relative prices are necessary to induce increased quantity supplied. This is not the case with economic rent.

2. What is interest?

On the most obvious level, interest is a payment for the use of money. On another level, interest can be considered payment for obtaining credit; by borrowing, people (consumers or businesses) obtain command over resources now rather than in the future. Those who wish to make purchases now instead of later are allowed to do so even if they do not currently earn purchasing power. They do so by borrowing, and interest is the price they must pay for the privilege of making expenditures now instead of later.

3. What is the economic function of interest rates?

Interest rates are the price of credit, and like all prices, interest rates play an allocative role. That is, interest is a rationing device. We have said that interest is the price of credit; this credit is allocated to the households and businesses that are willing to pay the highest price (interest rate). Such is the rationing function of credit. On a more fundamental level, we can see that something other than scarce loanable funds is allocated. After all, businesses don't borrow money simply for the privilege of paying interest! The key to understanding what *physical* resources are being allocated is to follow the money: On what do businesses spend this borrowed money? The answer is for the most part, capital goods. Thus the interest rate plays the crucial role of allocating scarce capital goods; the firms that are willing to pay the highest interest rates will be the ones that will be able to purchase the most scarce capital goods. Firms putting capital to the most profitable uses will be able to pay the highest interest rates (and be

most acceptable to lenders) and will therefore receive disproportionately greater quantities of new capital. Interest rates help bring about this capital rationing scheme in a market economy.

4. **What is the economic function of profits?**

Profit is the return on entrepreneurial talent or the price paid to risk takers. Profits also play a rationing role in society. Profits (in conjunction with interest rates) perform the all-important function of deciding which industries (and which firms within an industry) expand and which are forced to contract. Profitable firms can reinvest profits (and offer to pay higher interest rates), while unprofitable firms are forced to contract or go bankrupt. In short, businesses' quests for profits assure that scarce resources flow from less profitable to more profitable uses; profits help society decide which firms are to expand and which are to contract.

PROBLEMS

(Answers to the odd-numbered problems appear at the back of the book.)

17-1. "All revenues obtained by the Italian government from Renaissance art museums are economic rent." Is this statement true or false, and why?

17-2. Some people argue that the extraordinary earnings of entertainment and sports superstars are not economic rent at all but merely the cost of ensuring that a steady stream of would-be stars and starlets continues to flow into the sports and entertainment fields. How would the argument go?

17-3. "If employers paid marginal revenue product (MRP) to each of their inputs, there would be no profits left over." Is this statement true or false, and why?

17-4. The accompanying graph shows the supply of and demand for land. The vertical axis is the price per year received by landowners for permitting the land to be used by farmers.

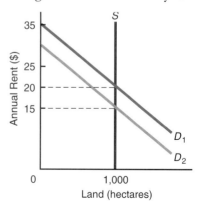

a. Assume that the demand curve for land is D_1. How much economic rent is received by landowners?

b. Now assume that the demand curve for land falls to D_2. How much economic rent is received now?

17-5. The graph shows the demand for and supply of loanable funds.

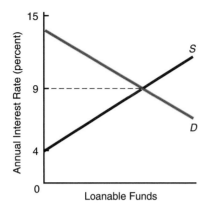

a. What is the equilibrium interest rate?
b. If the supply of loanable funds decreases, what will happen to the equilibrium interest rate?
c. If anticipated inflation is 4 percent for the year, what is the real equilibrium interest rate?

17-6. Make a list of risks that you might face in your life that you believe are insurable. Now make a list of risks that you believe are uninsurable. What is the general distinction between these lists?

17-7. Why do you think that the interest rate you have to pay on an automobile loan is greater than what you have to pay for a loan on a house? Why is the interest rate charged for a loan to purchase a used car usually more than for a loan to purchase a new car?

17-8. At the beginning of the 1980s, virtually all interest rates were much higher than they are in the 1990s. What do you think the major difference is between these two periods that might have caused interest rates to fall so dramatically?

17-9. Assume that everybody has perfect information about all events in the future. What would you expect to happen to economic profits in such a world?

Income and Poverty

By some measures, Canada is one of the richest nations on earth, not only in terms of total annual national income, but also in terms of average annual income per person. Despite such riches, almost 1.4 million Canadian children under the age of 18 live in poverty. Over 40 percent of people who use food banks are children. In fact, Canada ranks second among the industrialized countries, behind only the United States, for the highest rate of child poverty. Can "something" be done to eradicate child poverty? To answer this question, you need to know more about the distribution of income and the facts about poverty in this country.

Preview Questions

1. **What is a Lorenz curve, and what does it measure?**

2. **What has been happening to the distribution of income in Canada?**

3. **What is the difference between income and wealth?**

4. **Why do people earn different incomes?**

Did You Know That... over 300,000 Canadians earn more than $100,000 per year? That constitutes 1 percent of the Canadian population. When you go further up the income ladder, there are only about 2,400 who earn more than $1 million per year, or about 0.008 percent. At the same time, over 5 million Canadians live in poverty. Why is the **distribution of income** the way it is? Economists have devised various theories to explain this distribution. We present some of these theories in this chapter. We also present some of the more obvious institutional reasons why income is not distributed equally in Canada.

▶ **Distribution of income**

The way income is allocated among the population.

INCOME

Income provides each of us with the means of consuming and saving. Income can be derived from a payment for labour services, or a payment for ownership of one of the other factors of production besides labour—land, physical capital, human capital, and entrepreneurship. In addition, individuals obtain spendable income from gifts and government transfers. (Some individuals also obtain income by stealing, but we will not treat this matter here.) Right now, let us examine how money income is distributed across classes of income earners within Canada.

Measuring Income Distribution: The Lorenz Curve

▶ **Lorenz curve**

A geometric representation of the distribution of income. A Lorenz curve that is perfectly straight represents complete income equality. The more bowed a Lorenz curve, the more unequally income is distributed.

We can represent the distribution of money income graphically with what is known as the **Lorenz curve,** named after American-born statistician, Max Otto Lorenz, who proposed it in 1905. The Lorenz curve shows what portion of total money income is accounted for by different proportions of the country's households. Look at Figure 18.1. On the horizontal axis, we measure the *cumulative* percentage of households, lowest-income households first. Starting at the left corner, there are zero households; at the right corner, we have 100 percent of households; and in the middle, we have 50 percent of households. The vertical axis represents the cumulative percentage of money income. The 45-degree line represents complete equality: 50 percent of the households obtain 50 percent of total income, 60 percent of the households obtain 60 percent of total income, and so on. Of course, in no real-world situation is there such complete equality of income; no actual Lorenz curve would be a straight line. Rather, it would be some curved line, like the one labelled "Actual money income distribution" in Figure 18.1. For example, the bottom 50 percent of households in Canada receive about 26 percent of total money income. In Figure 18.2, we show the actual money income distribution Lorenz curve for 1994.

Criticisms of the Lorenz Curve. In recent years, economists have placed less and less emphasis on the shape of the Lorenz curve as an indication of the degree of income inequality in a country. There are five basic reasons the Lorenz curve has been criticized:

Figure 18.1
The Lorenz Curve

The horizontal axis measures the cumulative percentage of house-holds from 0 to 100 percent. The vertical axis measures the cumulative percentage of money income from 0 to 100. A straight line at a 45-degree angle cuts the box in half and represents a line of complete income equality, along which 25 percent of the families get 25 percent of the money income, 50 percent get 50 percent, and so on. The Lorenz curve, showing actual money income distribution, is not a straight line but rather a curved line as shown. The difference between complete money income equality and the Lorenz curve is the inequality gap.

Figure 18.2
Lorenz Curve of Income Distribution, 1994

Notice that there is substantial income inequality in before-tax money distribution.

Source: Statistics Canada.

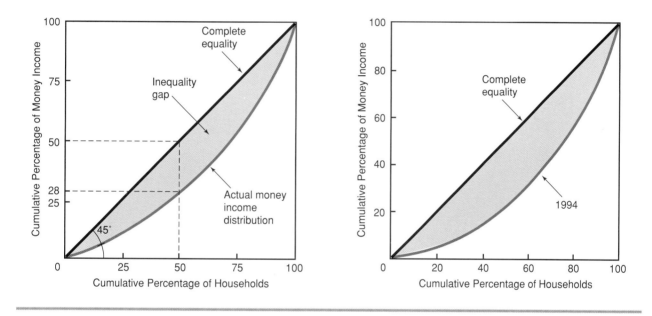

▶ **Income in kind**

Income received in the form of goods and services, such as health care; to be contrasted with money income, which is simply income in dollars, or general pur-chasing power, that can be used to buy *any* goods and services.

1. The Lorenz curve is typically presented in terms of the distribution of *money* income only. It does not include **income in kind,** such as health care, public school education, and goods or services produced and consumed in the home or on the farm.

2. The Lorenz curve does not account for differences in the size of households or the number of wage earners they contain.

3. It does not account for age differences. Even if all families in Canada had exact-ly the same *lifetime* incomes, chances are that young families would have lower incomes, middle-aged families would have relatively high incomes, and retired families would have low incomes. Because the Lorenz curve is drawn at a moment in time, it could never tell us anything about the inequality of *lifetime* income.

4. The Lorenz curve ordinarily reflects money income *before* taxes.

5. It does not measure unreported income from the underground economy, a sub-stantial source of income for some individuals.

Try Preview Question 1:

What is a Lorenz curve, and what does it measure?

Income Distribution in Canada

We could talk about the percentage of income earners within specific income classes—those earning between $20,001 and $30,000 per year, those earning between $30,001 and $40,000 per year, and so on. The problem with this type of analysis is that we live in a growing economy. Income, with some exceptions, is going up all the time. If we wish to make comparisons of the relative share of total income going to different income classes, we cannot look at specific amounts of money income. Instead, we talk about a distribution of income over five groups. Then we can talk about how much the bottom fifth (or quintile) makes compared with the top fifth, and so on. In Table 18.1, we see the percentage share of income for households before direct taxes. The table groups households according to whether they are in the lowest 20 percent of the income distribution, the second lowest 20 percent, and so on. We see that in 1994, the lowest 20 percent had a combined money income of 4.7 percent of the total money income of the entire population. This is a little more than the lowest 20 percent had 25 years ago. Accordingly, the conclusion has been drawn that there have been only slight changes in the distribution of money income. Indeed, considering that the definition of money income used by Statistics Canada includes only wage and salary income, income from self-employment, interest and dividends, and such government transfer payments as Old Age Security and Employment Insurance, we have to agree that the distribution of money income has not changed. *Money* income, however, understates *total* income for individuals who receive in-kind transfers from the government in the form of medical care, government-provided schooling and so on. In particular, since World War II, the share of total income—money income plus in-kind benefits—going to the bottom 20 percent of households has probably more than doubled.

Try Preview Question 2:
What has been happening to the distribution of income in Canada?

Table 18.1
Percentage Share of Money Income for Households Before Direct Taxes

Income Group	1994	1984	1974
Lowest fifth	4.7	4.5	4.0
Second fifth	10.2	10.3	10.9
Third fifth	16.7	17.1	17.7
Fourth fifth	24.8	25.0	24.9
Highest fifth	43.6	43.0	42.5

Source: Statistics Canada.
Note: Figures may not sum to 100 percent due to rounding.

INTERNATIONAL EXAMPLE
Relative Income Inequality Throughout the Richest Countries

According to the World Bank, Canada ranks fifth in income inequality among all the major industrialized countries. Look at Figure 18.3. There you see the ratio of income of the richest 20 percent of households to the poorest 20 percent of households. Should something be done about such income inequality?

Figure 18.3
Relative Income Inequality in the World

According to the World Bank, Canada has the fifth greatest income inequality of all the developed countries.

Source: World Bank.

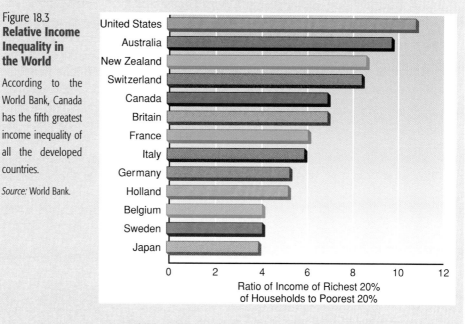

Ratio of Income of Richest 20% of Households to Poorest 20%

Public attitudes towards the government's role in reducing income inequality differ dramatically from country to country. Whereas fewer than 30 percent of Americans believe that government should reduce income differentials, between 60 and 80 percent of Canadians, Britons, Germans, Italians, and Austrians believe it is the government's job.

For critical analysis: Does it matter whether the same families stay in the lowest fifth of income earners over time? In other words, do we need to know anything about mobility across income groups?

Thinking Critically About the Media   Increasing Income Inequality and Working Spouses

The media have been having a field day pointing out that Canada has the fifth greatest income inequality in the industrialized world. Underlying the statistics, though, is a little-known fact: Income inequality is measured with respect to *households*. No distinction is made between one- and two-earner households. If two $80,000-a-year lawyers marry, their household income is now $160,000, and they have moved into a higher income group. Not surprisingly, most single tax returns show smaller earnings than would joint returns of married couples. In 1972, some 22 percent of working-age married couples had two earners; today that figure is 61 percent. Consequently, part of the reported increase in income inequality in Canada is simply due to an increase in the number of working spouses.

The Distribution of Wealth

We have been referring to the distribution of income in Canada. We must realize that income—a flow—can be viewed as a return on wealth (both human and nonhuman)—a stock. A discussion of the distribution of income in Canada is not the same thing as a discussion of the distribution of wealth. A complete concept of wealth would include tangible objects, such as buildings, machinery, land, cars, and houses—nonhuman wealth—as well as people who have skills, knowledge, initiative, talents, and so on—human wealth. The total of human and nonhuman wealth in Canada makes up our country's capital stock. (Note that the terms *wealth* and *capital* are often used only with reference to nonhuman wealth.) The capital stock consists of anything that can generate utility to individuals in the future. A fresh ripe tomato is not part of our capital stock. It has to be eaten before it turns rotten, and once it has been eaten, it can no longer generate satisfaction.

Figure 18.4 shows that the richest 10 percent of Canadian households hold about one-half of all wealth. The problem with those data is that they do not include many important assets. The first of these is workers' claims on private pension plans, contributions to which totalled $19.7 billion in 1995 alone. In addition, $23 billion was contributed to registered retirement savings plans that year. And public pension wealth is also left out. Contributions to the Canada Pension Plan (CPP) and the Quebec Pension Plan (QPP) totalled another $12.8 billion in 1995. Most of this additional wealth is "owned" by the middle class.

Try Preview Question 3:
What is the difference between income and wealth?

Figure 18.4
Measured Total Wealth Distribution

The top 10 percent of households have 50 percent of all measured wealth.

Source: "Death of the Middle Class," *Vancouver Sun*, November 1992.

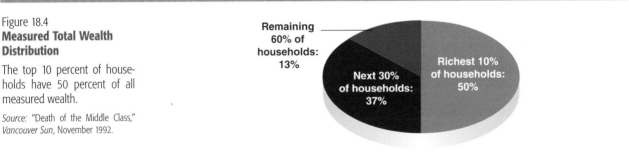

Remaining 60% of households: 13%

Next 30% of households: 37%

Richest 10% of households: 50%

EXAMPLE   Are We Running to Stay in Place?

There are a lot of statistics around which can show that the typical working person in Canada has not experienced an increase in standard of living for the last 20 years. If we correct take-home wages for inflation, that is an accurate statement. Indeed, Statistics Canada has frequently shown that real wages have actually fallen since 1980. There are at least two problems with such statements, though. The first concerns total compensation. Compensation of workers does not consist solely of wages. Whereas in 1971, nonsalary benefits (Workers' Compensation, Employment Insurance, pension payments, and so on) amounted to 8.5 percent of wages, they now come to around 30 percent. Second, even if after-tax real wages have not increased, the typical Canadian household is at least 20 percent better off than in 1971. Why? Because more households have a second breadwinner. Furthermore, fewer babies are being born, so expenses per household are lower.

One other piece of data is telling: Virtually every measure of consumption per capita is growing, year in and year out. Consequently, the majority of Canadians continue to experience increases in their standard of living as measured by their actual purchases of goods and services.

For critical analysis: Why might an individual be most concerned about total compensation?

Concepts in Brief

- The Lorenz curve graphically represents the distribution of income. If it is a straight line, there is complete equality of income. The more it is bowed, the more inequality of income exists.
- The distribution of wealth is not the same as the distribution of income. Wealth includes assets such as houses, stocks, and bonds. Although the apparent distribution of wealth seems to be more concentrated at the top, the data used are not very accurate, and most summary statistics fail to take account of workers' claims on private and public pensions, which are substantial.

DETERMINANTS OF INCOME DIFFERENCES

We know that there are income differences—that is not in dispute. A more important question is why these differences in income occur, for if we know why they do, perhaps we can change public policy, particularly with respect to helping people in the lowest income classes climb the income ladder. What is more, if we know the reasons for income differences, we can ascertain whether any of these determinants have changed over time. We will look at four income difference determinants: age, marginal productivity, inheritance, and discrimination.

Age

▶ **Age-earnings cycle**
The regular earnings profile of an individual throughout that person's lifetime. The age-earnings cycle usually starts with a low income, builds gradually to a peak at around age 50, and then gradually curves down until it approaches zero at retirement.

Age turns out to be a determinant of income because with age comes, usually, more education, more training, and more experience. It is not surprising that within every class of income earners, there seem to be regular cycles of earning behaviour. Most individuals earn more when they are middle-aged than when they are younger or older. We call this the **age-earnings cycle.**

The Age-Earnings Cycle. Every occupation has its own age-earnings cycle, and every individual will probably experience some variation from the average.

Figure 18.5
Typical Age-Earnings Profile

Within every class of income earners there is usually a typical age-earnings profile. Earnings are lowest when starting work at age 18, reach their peak at around age 50, and then taper off until retirement around age 65, when they become zero for most people. The rise in earnings up to age 50 is usually due to increased experience, longer working hours, and better training and schooling. (We abstract from economy-wide productivity changes that would shift the entire curve upward.)

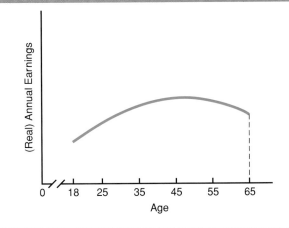

Nonetheless, we can characterize the typical age-earnings cycle graphically in Figure 18.5. Here we see that at age 18, income is relatively low. Income gradually rises until it peaks at about age 50. Then it falls until retirement, when it becomes zero (that is, currently earned income becomes zero, although retirement payments may then commence). The reason for such a regular cycle in earnings is fairly straightforward. When individuals start working at a young age, they typically have no work-related experience. Their ability to produce is less than that of more seasoned workers—that is, their productivity is lower. As they become older, they obtain more training and accumulate more experience. Their productivity rises, and they are therefore paid more. They also generally start to work longer hours. As the age of 50 approaches, the productivity of individual workers usually peaks. So, too, do the number of hours per week that are worked. After this peak in the age-earnings cycle, the detrimental effects of aging—decreases in stamina, strength, reaction time, and the like—usually outweigh any increases in training or experience. Also, hours worked usually start to fall for older people. Finally, as a person reaches retirement, both productivity and hours worked diminish rather drastically.

Note that general increases in overall productivity for the entire workforce will result in an upward shift in the typical age-earnings profile given in Figure 18.5. Thus even at the end of the age-earnings cycle, when just about to retire, the worker would not receive a really low wage compared with the starting wage 45 years earlier. The wage would be higher due to factors that contribute to rising real wages for everyone, regardless of the stage in the age-earnings cycle.

Now we have some idea why specific individuals earn different incomes at different times in their lives, but we have yet to explain why different people are paid different amounts of money for their labour. One way to explain this is to recall the marginal productivity theory developed in Chapter 15.

Marginal Productivity

When trying to determine how many workers a firm would hire, we had to construct a marginal revenue product curve. We found that as more workers were hired, the marginal revenue product fell due to diminishing marginal returns. If the forces of demand and supply established a certain wage rate, workers would be hired until their marginal physical product times marginal revenue was equal to the going wage rate. Then the hiring would stop. This analysis suggests what workers can expect to be paid in the labour market: They can each expect to be paid their marginal revenue product (assuming that there are low-cost information flows and that the labour and product markets are competitive).

In a competitive situation, with mobility of labour resources (at least on the margin), workers who are being paid less than their marginal revenue product will be bid away to better employment opportunities. Either they will seek better employment themselves, or other employers will offer them a slightly higher wage rate. This process will continue until each worker is being paid that individual's marginal revenue product.

You may balk at the suggestion that people are paid their marginal revenue product because you may personally know individuals whose MRP is more or less than what they are being paid. Such a situation may, in fact, exist because we do not live in a world of perfect information or in a world with perfectly competitive input and output markets. Employers cannot always seek out the most productive employees available. It takes resources to research the past records of potential employees, their training, their education, and their abilities. Nonetheless, competition creates a tendency towards equality of wages and MRP.

Determinants of Marginal Productivity.   If we accept marginal revenue product theory, we have a way of finding out how people can earn higher incomes. If they can increase the value of their marginal physical product, they can expect to be paid more. Some of the determinants of marginal physical product are talent, education, experience, and training. Most of these are means by which marginal physical product can be increased. Let's examine them in greater detail.

Talent.   This factor is the easiest to explain but difficult to acquire if you don't have it. Innate abilities and attributes can be very strong, if not overwhelming, determinants of a person's potential productivity. Strength, coordination, and mental alertness are facets of nonacquired human capital and thus have some bearing on the ability to earn income. Someone who is extremely tall has a better chance of being a basketball player than someone who is short. A person born with a superior talent for abstract thinking has a better chance of making a relatively higher income as a mathematician or a physicist than someone who is not born with that talent.

Experience. Additional experience at particular tasks is another way of increasing productivity. Experience can be linked to the well-known *learning curve* that applies when the same task is done over and over. The worker repeating a task becomes more efficient: The worker can do the same task in less time or in the same amount of time but better. Take an example of a person going to work on an automobile assembly line. At first the individual is able to fasten only three bolts every two minutes. Then the worker becomes more adept and can fasten four bolts in the same time plus insert a rubber guard on the bumper. After a few more weeks, another task can be added. Experience allows this individual to improve productivity. The more effectively people learn to do something, the quicker they can do it and the more efficient they are. Hence we would expect experience to lead to higher productivity.

And we would expect people with more experience to be paid more than those with less experience. More experience, however, does not guarantee a higher wage rate. The *demand* for a person's services must also exist. Spending a long time to become a first-rate archer in modern society would probably add very little to a person's income. Experience has value only if the output is demanded by society.

Training. Training is similar to experience but is more formal. Much of a person's increased productivity is due to on-the-job training. Many companies have training programs for new workers. On-the-job training is perhaps responsible for as much of an increase in productivity as is formal education beyond high school.

EXAMPLE   Economists, Aging, and Productivity

Do the actions of professional economists fit the model that predicts a decrease in productivity after some peak at around age 50? Yes, according to economist Daniel Hamermesh. One measure of productivity of economics professors is the number of articles they publish in professional journals. The over-50 economists constitute 30 percent of the profession, but they contribute a mere 6 percent of the articles published in leading economics journals. Of economists between ages 36 and 50, 56 percent submit articles on a regular basis, while only 14 percent of economists over 50 do so.

For critical analysis: Why should we predict that an economist closer to retirement will submit fewer professional journal articles than a younger economist? (Hint: Normally, professors who have tenure can't be fired.)

Investment in Human Capital.   Investment in human capital is just like investment in any other thing. If you invest in yourself by going to college or university, rather than going to work after high school and earning more current income, you will presumably be rewarded in the future with a higher income or a more interesting job (or both). This is exactly the motivation that underlies the decision of many students to obtain a formal higher education. Undoubtedly there would be students going to school even if the rate of return on formal education were zero or negative. But we do expect that the higher the rate of return on investing in ourselves, the more such investment there will be. Statistics Canada data demonstrate conclusively that, on average, high school graduates make more than elementary school graduates, and that university graduates make more than high school graduates. The estimated annual income of a full-time worker with four years of university in the mid-1990s was about $50,000. That person's high school counterpart was estimated to earn only $30,000, which gives a "university premium" of about 67 percent. Generally, the rate of return on investment in human capital is on a par with the rate of return on investment in other areas.

To figure out the rate of return on an investment in a university education, we first have to figure out the marginal costs of going to school. The main cost is not what you have to pay for books, fees, and tuition but rather the income you forgo.

The main cost of education is the income forgone—the opportunity cost of not working. In addition, the direct expenses of going to university must be paid. Not all students forgo all income during their university years. Many work part time. Taking account of those who work part time and those who are supported by grants and other scholarships, the average rate of return on going to university is somewhere between 8 and 12 percent. This is not a bad rate. Of course, this type of computation does leave out all the consumption benefits you get from going to university. Also omitted from the calculations is the change in personality after going to university. You undoubtedly come out a different person. Most people who go through university feel that they have improved themselves both culturally and intellectually in addition to having increased their potential marginal revenue product so that they can make more income. How do we measure the benefit from expanding our horizons and our desire to experience different things in life? This is not easy to measure, and such non-money benefits from investing in human capital are not included in normal calculations.

Inheritance

It is not unusual to inherit cash, jewellery, stocks, bonds, homes, or other real estate. Yet only about 8 percent of income inequality in Canada can be traced to differences in wealth that was inherited. If for some reason the government confiscated all property that had been inherited, there would be very little measured change in the distribution of income in Canada.

Discrimination

Economic discrimination occurs whenever workers with the same marginal revenue product receive unequal pay due to some noneconomic factor such as their race, sex, or age. Alternatively, it occurs when there is unequal access to labour markets. It is possible—and indeed quite obvious—that discrimination affects the distribution of income. Certain groups in our society are not paid wages at rates comparable to those received by other groups, even when we correct for productivity and education. Differences in income remain between whites and nonwhites and between men and women. For example, the median wage for an aboriginal man is about 80 percent that of white men. The median wage rate of women is about 73 percent that of men. What we need to do is discover why differences in income between groups exist and then determine if factors other than discrimination in the labour market can explain them. Then the unexplained part of income differences can rightfully be considered the result of discrimination.

The Doctrine of Comparable Worth. Discrimination can occur because of barriers to entry in higher-paying occupations, and because of discrimination in the acquisition of human capital. Consider the distribution of highest-paying and lowest-paying occupations. The lowest-paying jobs are dominated by females, both white and nonwhite. For example, the proportion of women in secretarial, clerical, janitorial, and food service jobs ranges from 60 percent (food and beverage service) to 80 percent (clerical). Proponents of the **comparable-worth doctrine** feel that

▶ Comparable-worth doctrine

The belief that women should receive the same wages as men if the levels of skill and responsibility in their jobs are equivalent.

female secretaries, janitors, and food service workers should be making salaries comparable to those of male truck drivers or construction workers, assuming that the levels of skill and responsibility in these jobs are comparable. These advocates also believe that a comparable-worth policy would benefit the economy overall. They contend that adjusting the wages of workers in female-dominated jobs upward would create a move towards more efficient and less discriminatory labour markets.

Try Preview Question 4:
Why do people earn different incomes?

THEORIES OF DESIRED INCOME DISTRIBUTION

We have talked about the factors affecting the distribution of income, but we have not yet mentioned the normative issue of how income *ought* to be distributed. This, of course, requires a value judgment. We are talking about the problem of economic justice. We can never completely resolve this problem because there are always going to be conflicting values. It is impossible to give all people what each thinks is just. Nonetheless, two particular normative standards for the distribution of income have been popular with economists. These are income distribution based on productivity and income distribution based on equality.

Productivity

The *productivity standard* for the distribution of income can be stated simply as "To each according to what he or she produces." This is also called the *contributive standard* because it is based on the principle of rewarding according to the contribution to society's total output. It is also sometimes referred to as the *merit standard* and is one of the oldest concepts of justice. People are rewarded according to merit, and merit is judged by one's ability to produce what is considered useful by society.

However, just as any standard is a value judgment, so is the productivity standard. It is rooted in the capitalist ethic and has been attacked vigorously by some economists and philosophers, including Karl Marx, who felt that people should be rewarded according to need and not according to productivity.

We measure a person's productive contribution in a capitalist system by the market value of that person's output. We have already referred to this as the marginal revenue product theory of wage determination.

Do not immediately jump to the conclusion that in a world of income distribution determined by productivity, society will necessarily allow the aged, the infirm, and the physically or mentally challenged to die of starvation because they are unproductive. In Canada today, the productivity standard is mixed with a standard based on people's "needs" so that the aged, the physically and mentally challenged, the involuntarily unemployed, the very young, and other unproductive (in the market sense of the word) members of the economy are provided for through private and public transfers.

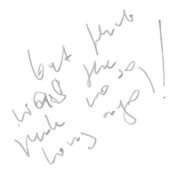

Equality

The *egalitarian principle* of income distribution is simply "To each exactly the same." Everyone would have exactly the same amount of income. This criterion of income distribution has been debated as far back as biblical times. This system of income distribution has been considered equitable, meaning that presumably everybody is dealt with fairly and equally. There are problems, however, with an income distribution that is completely equal.

Some jobs are more unpleasant or more dangerous than others. Should the people undertaking these jobs be paid exactly the same as everyone else? Indeed, under an equal distribution of income, what incentive would there be for individuals to take risky, hazardous, or unpleasant jobs at all? What about overtime? Who would be willing to work overtime without additional pay? There is another problem: If everyone earned the same income, what incentive would there be for individuals to invest in their own human capital—a costly and time-consuming process?

Just consider the incentive structure within a corporation. Recall from Chapter 15 that much of the pay differential between, say, the CEO and all of the vice-presidents is meant to create competition among the vice-presidents for the CEO's job.

The result is higher productivity. If all incomes were the same, much of this competition would disappear, and productivity would fall.

There is some evidence that differences in income lead to higher rates of economic growth. Future generations are therefore made better off. Elimination of income differences may reduce the rate of economic growth and cause future generations to be poorer than they otherwise might have been.

Concepts in Brief

* Most people follow an age-earnings cycle in which they earn relatively small incomes when they first start working, increase their incomes until about age 50, and then slowly experience a decrease in their real incomes as they approach retirement.

* If we accept the marginal revenue product theory of wages, workers can expect to be paid their marginal revenue product. However, full adjustment is never obtained, so some workers may be paid more or less than their MRP.

* Marginal physical productivity depends on talent, education, experience, and training.

* Going to school and receiving on-the-job training can be considered an investment in human capital. The main cost of education is the opportunity cost of not working.

* Proponents of the comparable-worth doctrine contend that disparate jobs can be compared by examining efforts, skill, and educational training and that wages should therefore be paid on the basis of this comparable worth.

* Two normative standards for income distribution are income distribution based on productivity and income distribution based on equality.

POVERTY AND ATTEMPTS TO ELIMINATE IT

Throughout the history of the world, mass poverty has been accepted as inevitable. However, this country and others, particularly in the Western world, have sustained enough economic growth in the past several hundred years so that *mass* poverty can no longer be said to be a problem for these fortunate countries. As a matter of fact, the residual of poverty in Canada strikes us as bizarre, an anomaly. How can there still be so much poverty in a country of such abundance? Having talked about the determinants of the distribution of income, we now have at least some ideas of why some people are destined to remain low-income earners throughout their lives.

There are methods of transferring income from the relatively well-to-do to the relatively poor, and as a country we have been using them for a long time. Today, we have a vast array of income support programs set up for the purpose of redistributing income. However, we know that these programs have not been entirely successful. Are there alternatives to our current income support system? Is there a better method of helping the poor? Before we answer these questions, let's look at the concept of poverty in more detail and at the characteristics of the poor.

We see in Figure 18.6 that the proportion of individuals classified as poor rose from 1980 to 1985 during the recession of the early 1980s. The percentage of poor then fell between 1985 and 1989, only to rise again during the recession of the early 1990s.

Figure 18.6

The Proportion of People Who Are Poor in Canada

The proportion of Canadians classified as poor rose in the early 1980s. It then fell between 1985 and 1989, then it rose again during the early 1990s.

Source: Canadian Council on Social Development.

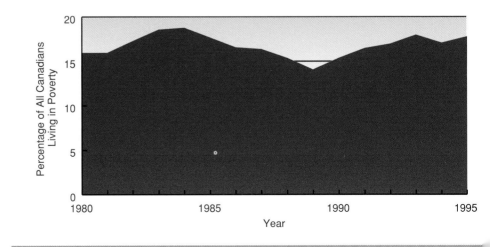

INTERNATIONAL EXAMPLE
Poverty Worldwide and How to Cure It: Suggestions from the UN Summit

For seven days in 1995, delegations from 140 countries gathered in Copenhagen, Denmark, for the United Nations' World Summit for Social Development. According to the UN, 1.3 billion people live in poverty throughout the world. The attendees agreed to a document that commits them to the goal of "eradicating poverty in the world." Nobel Prize–winning economist James Tobin offered one solution: Tax speculative international currency transactions to raise $50 billion a year for the United Nations to support development programs. The delegates also argued for a "20-20 compact." Donor nations should agree to direct 20 percent of their foreign aid to alleviate poverty in less developed countries, and recipient countries should direct 20 percent of their national budgets to the same programs.

For critical analysis: If economist Tobin's idea were put into practice, who would collect the tax, given that the United Nations does not have the power to do so?

Defining Poverty

There is no official poverty line announced each year in Canada. However, Statistics Canada releases income thresholds which it calls low-income cutoffs (LICOs), below which families and individuals are said to be living in "straightened circumstances." The LICO is widely used by both government and nongovernment agencies as a poverty line.

Statistics Canada first defined the LICO in 1959 as 70 percent of the average family income. It reasoned that the average family required one-half of its income to pay for necessities—food, shelter, and clothing. Thus any family which needed 20 percent more than the average for necessities would have insufficient income left for transportation, health care, recreation, and so on. (The choice of 20 percent was arbitrary.) Over time, the LICO has changed as incomes have grown, from 70 percent of average family income in 1959 to 62 percent in 1962, 58.5 percent in 1980, 56.2 percent in 1986, and is currently set at 54.7 percent of the average family income.

The LICO has also been expanded to apply to both families and single persons living in urban and rural areas. In 1995, the LICO for an individual living in a large city was $15,189, and for an urban family of seven it was $40,029. For rural areas, the LICO for a single person was $10,769 and $27,252 for a large family.

Transfer Payments as Income

The LICO is based on pretax income, including wages, net income from self-employment, government transfer payments such as Employment Insurance and Canada Pension Plan benefits, scholarships and alimony payments. Excluded from

Figure 18.7
Relative Poverty: Comparing Household Incomes

This graph shows, on the vertical axis, the ratio of the top 20 percent of income-earning households, after taxes and transfers, to the bottom 20 percent. The decline in the ratio implies that the income gap between the rich and the poor in Canada has been decreasing.

Source: Statistics Canada.

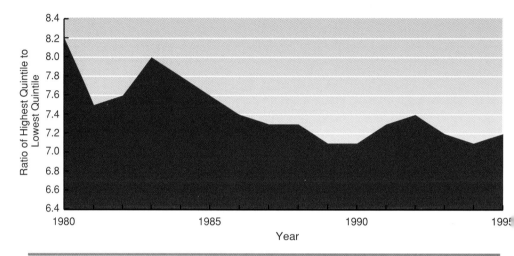

the income calculation are winnings from gambling, inheritances, and income in kind such as food produced on the farm for domestic use. If we correct the LICO for government transfers, the percentage of the population that is below the poverty line drops dramatically. Some economists argue that the way the LICO is calculated makes no sense in a country that redistributed over $60 billion in cash and noncash transfers in 1996.

Furthermore, some of the people living below the poverty line partake in the informal, or underground, sectors of the economy without reporting their income from these sources. And some of the poor obtain benefits from owning their own home. Look at Figure 18.7 to see what has happened to the relative position of this nation's poor. The graph shows the ratio of the top fifth of the country's households to the bottom fifth of the country's households. Since 1984, the gap between the richest and the poorest families has been gradually closing. There are two reasons for this. The poor have been collecting more transfer payments and the rich have been paying a larger share of income taxes.

ATTACKS ON POVERTY: MAJOR FEDERAL INCOME SUPPORT PROGRAMS

There are a variety of federal income support programs designed to help the poor. We examine a few of them here.

Old Age Security

The current Old Age Security Plan came into force in 1952. It provides for income supplements for seniors aged 65 and over, and has three components: old age security (OAS), guaranteed income supplement (GIS) and spouse's allowance (SPA).

The amount of the OAS component payment is dependent on the recipient's length of residence in Canada, with longer residence earning a higher payment. This payment comes out of the federal government's general revenue; it is indexed to the Consumer Price Index (CPI) and is raised four times each year. In 1996, over four million seniors were receiving cheques averaging $400 per month. If the recipient's total income exceeds $53,215, however, 15 cents of each OAS dollar is clawed back through income tax.

The GIS is paid to OAS recipients who have little or no additional income. This supplement is not taxable and its size is dependent on the marital status of the recipient. While the single rate exceeds the married rate, the combined married rate exceeds the single rate. The SPA is paid to the spouse of an OAS and GIS recipient when those pension payments constitute the only income for the family. This benefit is dependent on the spouse passing an income test.

Canada Pension Plan

The Canada Pension Plan (CPP) and its counterpart Quebec Pension Plan (QPP) enroll virtually all employed and self-employed workers between the ages of 18 and 70 years. Both employees and employers must contribute a percentage of the employee's earnings to the plan, which provides insurance against retirement, disability, and death. (A self-employed person must contribute both shares.) No part of the pension payments comes from general government revenues; the CPP is a "pay-as-you-go" plan funded entirely by premiums and investment earnings.

The CPP came into force in 1966; it is fully indexed to the CPI and is adjusted each January. With the increase in the Canadian population, the contributory rates have risen; in 1986, employees and employers paid a combined 3.6 percent of eligible earnings into the plan; by 1997 they paid 5.85 percent. Beginning in 1998, in anticipation of the retirement of our "baby boomers" and the estimated 75 percent increase in the over-65 population, the premium rates will increase significantly to the year 2003, when they will be capped at 9.9 percent. By that time, it is estimated that the CPP fund will grow to $100 billion, sufficient to pay out the necessary pensions.

Benefit payments from the CPP redistribute income to some degree. However, benefit payments are not based on recipient need. Participants' contributions give them the right to benefits even if they would be financially secure without them. Thus the CPP is not an insurance program because people are not guaranteed that the benefits they receive will be in line with the contributions they have made. It is not a personal savings account either. The benefits are legislated by the government. In the future, the government may not be as sympathetic towards older people as it is today. It could (and probably will have to) legislate for lower real levels of benefits instead of higher ones.

Employment Insurance

Employment Insurance (EI) is designed to provide income for the unemployed while they are looking for work. Like the CPP, it is funded by compulsory employee and employer contributions. Unlike the CPP, however, the premiums and benefit payments are part of the federal government's general revenues and expenditures. During 1997, there was a substantial surplus in the EI account which helped the government achieve the budget surplus that year.

The EI program replaced the Unemployment Insurance (UI) plan in 1996. While UI was designed to provide income support to contributors who became unemployed, EI is designed to help the unemployed find work as well. Re-employment benefits, such as retraining funds, act as incentives for the unemployed to find jobs in other fields. Automated job market information and federally funded job search services assist recipients in their quest for work. The federal government has estimated that by the year 2001, this drive to find work for the unemployed will result in up to 100,000 new job opportunities.

No Apparent Reduction in Poverty Rates

In spite of the numerous programs in existence and the hundreds of millions of dollars transferred to the poor, the poverty rate in Canada has shown no long-run tendency to decline. It reached its low of around 14 percent in 1981, peaked at over 18 percent in 1993, and since then has been hovering at just below 18 percent. Is there a way that we can reform welfare to improve the situation? We attempt to shed some light on this question in the Issues and Applications section at the end of this chapter.

Concepts in Brief

- If poverty is defined in absolute terms, economic growth eventually decreases the number of officially defined poor. If poverty is defined relatively, however, we will never eliminate it.
- Major attacks on poverty have been income support programs such as Old Age Security, Canada Pension Plan, and Employment Insurance.
- Although the relative lot of the poor measured by household income seems to have worsened, the after-tax gap between the richest 20 percent and the poorest 20 percent of households has been narrowing.

Issues and Applications

Eradicating Child Poverty

Concepts Applied: Incentives, marginal tax rate

Food banks provide essential nourishment for millions of children who live in poverty. In spite of a federal government resolution to eradicate child poverty by the year 2000, poverty rates are still on the climb.

Figure 18.8
Child Poverty Rate

Since 1989, the child poverty rate in Canada has climbed from 15.3 percent to 21 percent in 1995.

Source: Canadian Council on Social Development.

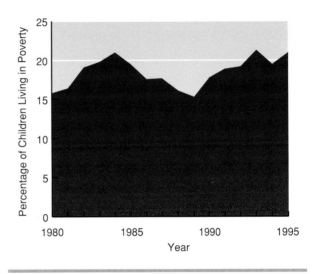

In 1989, the House of Commons passed a resolution to "seek to achieve the goal of eliminating poverty among Canadian children by the year 2000." However, child poverty rates have only climbed since then, as Figure 18.8 shows. One of the reasons for continuing child poverty is that many of the programs designed to help low income families apply only to those families on welfare. The working poor—those with low-paying jobs—don't qualify and so remain below the poverty line.

Work Versus Welfare

In most provinces, families receiving social assistance also receive other benefits for their children. These include free health and dental care and optometric services. Thus finding employment brings with it a penalty: not only does the family lose its welfare payments, it also loses the subsidized services. In 1993, the federal Working Income Supplement was created to address this problem by providing a maximum payment of $1,000 per family to the working poor. Nevertheless, the working poor still lag behind families on social assistance in combined federal and provincial child benefits.

An Integrated Plan

The federal and provincial governments have been working on an integrated child benefit plan to assist all poor families, whether working or receiving social assistance. For its part, the federal government will provide a child tax credit thereby raising a family's after-tax income. To create an incentive for families on welfare to find employment, the provinces will cut welfare payments by a part of the additional disposable income. The working poor, however, will be able to keep the all of the increase. A further condition of this proposal is that the provincial governments redirect the savings on welfare payments to other programs to aid poor children: school lunch programs and health and dental services, for example.

Several of the provinces have already reformed their welfare systems to dovetail with the proposed federal plan, and to create incentives for families on social assistance to find employment. In British Columbia, for example, the BC Family Bonus program provides benefits to both working and non-working families. A maximum bonus of $103 per month per child is paid to families with annual incomes of $18,000 or less. The bonus decreases as family income rises, finally disappearing at an annual income of $41,175 for a family with three children. Thus the bonus acts to soften the effect of increasing marginal tax rates as the family works towards self-sufficiency. A recent study found that in BC the poverty gap for the working poor in general had been reduced by 19 percent, and by 26 percent for single parents. (The poverty gap is that amount of income required to lift families below the poverty line out of poverty.)

Support Payments or Job Creation?

Critics of improved social assistance plans argue that the money put into supporting the poor would be better spent improving economic conditions, which would in turn lead to more jobs for the unemployed. They also suggest that falling welfare cheques act as a better incentive than child tax benefits to induce welfare families

to look for work. And once the families are working, child poverty would be reduced.

For Critical Analysis

1. Do you think that the new integrated child benefit plan will end child poverty in Canada? Why or why not?

2. If the critics of improved social assistance plans succeeded in having money put into supporting the poor allocated instead to improving economic conditions, would this end child poverty?

CHAPTER SUMMARY

1. We can represent the distribution of income graphically with a Lorenz curve. The extent to which the line is bowed from a straight line shows how unequal the distribution of income is.

2. The distribution of pretax money income in Canada has remained fairly steady for the last 25 years. The lowest fifth of income earners still receive only about 5 percent of total pretax money income, while the top fifth of income earners receive over 40 percent.

3. The distribution of wealth is not the same as the distribution of income. Wealth includes assets such as houses, stocks, and bonds. Though the apparent distribution of wealth seems to be more concentrated at the top, the data used are not very accurate, nor do most summary statistics take account of workers' claims on private and public pensions.

4. Most individuals face a particular age-earnings cycle. Earnings are lowest when starting out to work at age 18 to 24. They gradually rise and peak at about age 50, then fall until retirement age. They go up usually because of increased

experience, increased training, and longer working hours.

5. The marginal productivity theory of the distribution of income indicates that workers can expect to be paid their marginal revenue product. The marginal physical product is determined largely by talent, education, experience, and training.

6. Discrimination is usually defined as a situation in which a certain group is paid a lower wage than other groups for the same work.

7. One way to invest in your own human capital is to go to university or college. The investment usually pays off; the rate of return is somewhere between 8 and 12 percent.

8. A definition of poverty made in relative terms means that there will always be poor in our society because the distribution of income will never be exactly equal.

9. The major federal income support programs are Old Age Security (OAS), Canada Pension Plan (CPP) and Employment Insurance (EI).

DISCUSSION OF PREVIEW QUESTIONS

1. What is a Lorenz curve, and what does it measure?

A Lorenz curve indicates the portion of total money income accounted for by given proportions of a country's households. It is a measure of income inequality that can be found by plotting the cumulative percentage of money income on the y axis and the percentage of households on the x axis. Two major problems with using the Lorenz curve to measure income equality are that it typically does not take into account income in kind, such as health care and public school education, and that it does not account for differences in household size (and effort) or age. Adjustments for these would undoubtedly reduce the degree of measured income inequality in Canada.

2. What has been happening to the distribution of income in Canada?

Over the past 50 years, the distribution of *money* income has not changed significantly, but the distribution of *total* income—which includes in-kind government transfers—has changed a great deal. Since the 1960s, *total* income inequality has been reduced significantly. The fact that more (total) income equality has been achieved in Canada in recent years is of tremendous importance, yet few people seem to be aware of this fact.

3. What is the difference between income and wealth?

Income is a *flow* concept and as such is measured per unit of time; we usually state that a person's income is X dollars *per year*. Wealth is a *stock* concept; as such, it is measured at a given point in time. We usually say that a person's wealth is $200,000 or $1 million. If people save out of a given income, it is possible for their wealth to be rising while their income is constant. Technically, a person's wealth may be defined as the value of that individual's assets (human and nonhuman) minus liabilities (wealth being equivalent to net worth) at some point in time.

4. Why do people earn different incomes?

The major theory to account for income differentials in market economies is the marginal productivity theory. This theory says that labourers (as well as other resources) tend to be paid the value of their marginal revenue product. Labourers who are paid less than their MRP will go to other employers who will gladly pay them more (it will be profitable for them to do so); labourers who are being paid more than their MRP may well lose their jobs (at least in the private sector). Thus productivity differences due to age, talent (intelligence, aptitudes, coordination), experience, and training can account for income differences. Of course, imperfect markets can potentially lead to income differences, at a given productivity, due to exploitation and discrimination. Income differences can also be accounted for by differences in nonhuman wealth—individuals can earn income on their property holdings.

PROBLEMS

(Answers to the odd-numbered problems appear at the back of the book.)

18-1. It is often observed that women, on average, earn less than men in Canada. What are some possible reasons for these differences?

18-2. The accompanying graph shows Lorenz curves for two countries.

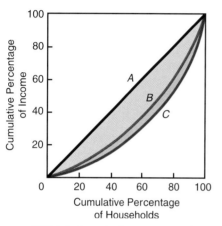

a. Which line indicates complete equality of income?

b. Which line indicates the most income inequality?

c. One country's "income inequality" is described by line *B*. Suppose that this country's income is to be adjusted for age and other variables such that income on the *y* axis reflects *lifetime* income instead of income in a given year. Would the new, adjusted Lorenz curve move inward towards *A* or outward towards *C*?

18-3. What are two common normative standards of income distribution?

18-4. What does it mean when we say that some income support recipients face a 120 percent marginal tax rate if they choose to go to work?

18-5. How might a program that truly made every household's income equal affect economy efficiency?

18-6. Visit the National Anti-Poverty Organization at http://www.napo.onap.ca/napohome.htm and take the poverty quiz.

INTERACTING WITH THE INTERNET

File Edit View Go Favorites Help

Back Forward Stop Refresh Home Search Favorites History Channels Fullscreen Mail Print Edit

An excellent source for all sorts of statistics on Canada is Statistics Canada's Web site at

http://www.statcan.ca/english/Pgdb/

For information from the 1996 Census, visit

http://www.statcan.ca/english/census96/list.htm

Statistics Canada's holdings are quite extensive, so it may take a bit of effort to find what you want.

For official overviews of federal income support programs, visit Human Resources Development Canada at

http://www.hrdc-drhc.gc.ca/common/home.shtml

There you can also find a number of links to various agencies such as the Electronic Labour Exchange and the HRDC National Job Bank, and information about its other programs.

The Canadian Council for Social Development has many statistics on poverty and poverty rates in Canada. You can find the Council's statistics page at

http://www.ccsd.ca/facts.html.

Enivronmental Economics

Most of us eat some fish and other seafood on a regular basis. Across Canada and throughout the world, fish stocks in the wild are dwindling. According to the Food and Agricultural Organization of the United Nations, 70 percent of the world's fisheries are near collapse or already completely depleted. Cod has virtually disappeared from Newfoundland's coastal waters. There are perilously few coho salmon off British Columbia. Why did this problem occur, and is there a technological solution to it today? To answer these questions, you need to know more about environmental economics.

Preview Questions

1. What is a negative externality?

2. What is the optimal quantity of pollution?

3. How can poorly defined property rights create negative externalities?

4. If property rights are poorly defined, *must* negative externalities arise?

CHAPTER OUTLINE

Did You Know That... plants pollute? That's right, plants generate toxins as nature's attempt at protecting them from being eaten. Many of these toxins are known carcinogens. There are, for example, more known carcinogens in that cup of coffee you drink than in all of the pesticide residue on food that you consume in one year. Brussels sprouts, broccoli, mushrooms, potatoes, parsnips, and pears all contain natural carcinogens. When you think of pollution, nonetheless, you are probably thinking of smelly, foul, ugly air emanating from smokestacks across the country, oil spills fouling pristine waters and killing wildlife, and other natural resources being ruined. Today, the Canadian public, in general, appears to be willing to pay more to keep the environment "in good shape." But what does that mean?

As you might expect, after having read the previous chapters in this textbook, the economic way of thinking about the environment has a lot to do with costs. But of course your view of how to clean up the environment has a lot to do with costs also. Are you willing to give up driving your car in order to have a cleaner environment? Or would you pay $2 for a litre of gas to help clean up the environment? In a phrase, how much of your current standard of living are you willing to give up to help the environment? The economic way of looking at ecological issues is often viewed as anti-environmental. But this is not so. Economists want to help citizens and policymakers opt for informed policies that have the maximum possible *net* benefits (benefits minus costs). As you will see, every decision in favour of "the environment" involves a trade-off.

PRIVATE VERSUS SOCIAL COSTS

Human actions often give rise to unwanted side effects—the destruction of our environment is one. Human actions generate pollutants that go into the air and the water. The question that is often asked is, "Why can individuals and businesses continue to create pollution without necessarily paying directly for the negative consequences?"

Until now, we've been dealing with situations in which the costs of an individual's actions are borne directly by the individual. When a business has to pay wages to workers, it knows exactly what its labour costs are. When it has to buy materials or build a plant, it knows quite well what these will cost. An individual who has to pay for car repairs or a theatre ticket knows exactly what the cost will be. These costs are what we term *private costs*. **Private costs** are borne solely by the individuals who incur them. They are *internal* in the sense that the firm or household must explicitly take account of them.

What about a situation in which a business dumps the waste products from its production process into a nearby river, or in which an individual litters a public park or beach? Obviously, a cost is involved in these actions. When the firm pollutes the water, people downstream suffer the consequences. They may not want to swim in or drink the polluted water. They may also be unable to catch as many fish as before because of the pollution. In the case of littering, the people who come along after

▶ **Private costs**

Costs borne solely by the individuals who incur them. Also called *internal costs.*

our litterer has cluttered the park or the beach are the ones who bear the costs. The cost of these actions is borne by people other than those who commit the actions. The creator of the cost is not the sole bearer. The costs are not internalized by the individual or firm; they are external. When we add *external* costs to *internal*, or private, costs, we get **social costs.** Pollution problems—indeed, all problems pertaining to the environment—may be viewed as situations in which social costs exceed private costs. Because some economic participants don't pay the full social costs of their actions but rather only the smaller private costs, their actions are socially "unacceptable." In such situations in which there is a divergence between social and private costs, we therefore see "too much" steel production, automobile driving, and beach littering, to pick only a few of the many possible examples.

> ▶ **Social costs**
> The full costs borne by society whenever a resource use occurs. Social costs can be measured by adding private, or internal, costs to external costs.

The Costs of Polluted Air

Why is the air in cities so polluted from automobile exhaust fumes? When automobile drivers step into their cars, they bear only the private costs of driving. That is, they must pay for the gas, maintenance, depreciation, and insurance on their automobiles. However, they cause an additional cost, that of air pollution, which they are not forced to take account of when they make the decision to drive. Air pollution is a cost because it causes harm to individuals—burning eyes, respiratory ailments, and dirtier clothes, cars, and buildings. The air pollution created by automobile exhaust is a cost that individual operators of automobiles do not yet bear directly. The social cost of driving includes all the private costs plus at least the cost of air pollution, which society bears. Decisions made only on the basis of private costs lead to too much automobile driving or, alternatively, to too little money spent on the reduction of automobile pollution for a given amount of driving. Clean air is a scarce resource used by automobile drivers free of charge. They will use more of it than they would if they had to pay the full social costs.

EXTERNALITIES

> ▶ **Externality**
> A situation in which a private cost diverges from a social cost; a situation in which the costs of an action are not fully borne by the two parties engaged in exchange or by an individual engaging in a scarce-resource-using activity. (Also applies to benefits.)

When a private cost differs from a social cost, we say that there is an **externality** because individual decision makers are not paying (internalizing) all the costs. Some of these costs remain external to the decision-making process. Remember that the full cost of using a scarce resource is borne one way or another by all who live in the society. That is, society must pay the full opportunity cost of any activity that uses scarce resources. The individual decision maker is the firm or the customer, and external costs and benefits will not enter into that individual's or firm's decision-making processes.

We might want to view the problem as it is presented in Figure 19.1 (page 460). Here we have the market demand curve, D, for the product X and the supply curve, S_1, for product X. The supply curve, S_1, includes only internal, or private, costs. The intersection of the demand and supply curves as drawn will be at price P_1 and quantity Q_1 (at E_1). However, we will assume that the production of good X involves externalities that the private firms did not take into account. Those externalities could be air pollution, water pollution, scenery destruction, or anything of that nature.

Figure 19.1
Reckoning with Full Social Costs

The supply curve, S_1, is equal to the horizontal summation (Σ) of the individual marginal cost curves above the respective minimum average variable costs of all the firms producing good X. These individual marginal cost curves include only internal, or private, costs. If the external costs were included and added to the private costs, we would have social costs. The supply curve would shift upward to S_2. In the uncorrected situation, the equilibrium price would be P_1 and the equilibrium quantity would be Q_1. In the corrected situation, the equilibrium price would rise to P_2 and the equilibrium quantity would fall to Q_2.

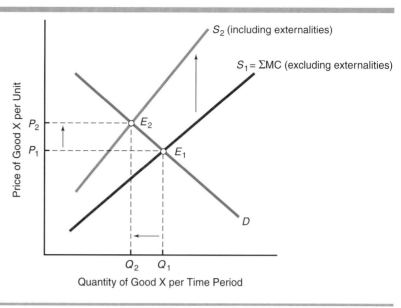

We know that the social costs of producing product X exceed the private costs. We show this by drawing curve S_2. It is above the original supply curve S_1 because it includes the full social costs of producing the product. If firms could be made to bear these costs, the price would be P_2 and the quantity Q_2 (at E_2). The inclusion of external costs in the decision-making process leads to a higher-priced product and a decline in quantity produced. Thus we see that when social costs are not being fully borne by the creators of those costs, the quantity produced is "excessive," because the price is too low.

Try Preview Question 1:
What is a negative externality?

CORRECTING FOR EXTERNALITIES

We can see here an easy method for reducing pollution and environmental degradation. Somehow the signals in the economy must be changed so that decision makers will take into account *all* the costs of their actions. In the case of automobile pollution, we might want to devise some method by which motorists are taxed according to the amount of pollution they cause. In the case of a firm, we might want to devise a system whereby businesses are taxed according to the amount of pollution they create. In this manner, they would have an incentive to install pollution abatement equipment.

The Polluters' Choice

Facing an additional cost of polluting, firms will be induced (1) to install pollution abatement equipment or otherwise change production techniques so as to reduce the amount of pollution, (2) to reduce pollution-causing activity, or (3) simply to pay the price to pollute. The relative costs and benefits of each option for each polluter will determine which one or combination will be chosen. Allowing the choice is the efficient way to decide who pollutes and who doesn't. In principle, each polluter faces the full social cost of its actions and makes a production decision accordingly.

Is a Uniform Tax Appropriate?

It may not be appropriate to levy a *uniform* tax according to physical quantities of pollution. After all, we're talking about social costs. Such costs are not necessarily the same everywhere in Canada for the same action.

Essentially, we must establish the amount of the *economic damages* rather than the amount of the physical pollution. A polluting electrical plant in Toronto will cause much more damage than the same plant in Carstairs, Alberta. There are already innumerable demands on the air in Toronto, so the pollution from smokestacks will not be cleansed away naturally. Millions of people will breathe the polluted air and thereby incur the costs of sore throats, sickness, emphysema, and even early death. Buildings will become dirtier faster because of the pollution, as will cars and clothes. A given quantity of pollution will cause more harm in concentrated urban environments than it will in less dense rural environments. If we were to establish some form of taxation to align private costs with social costs and to force people to internalize externalities, we would somehow have to come up with a measure of *economic* costs instead of *physical* quantities. But the tax, in any event, would fall on the private sector and modify private-sector economic agents' behaviour. Therefore, because the economic cost for the same physical quantity of pollution would be different in different locations according to population density, the natural formation of mountains and rivers, and so forth, so-called optimal taxes on pollution would vary from location to location. (Nonetheless, a uniform tax might make sense when administrative costs, particularly the cost of ascertaining the actual economic costs, are relatively high.)

INTERNATIONAL EXAMPLE
The Black Sea Becomes the Dead Sea:
The Results of Externalities

The Black Sea is one of the dirtiest bodies of water in the world because for nearly 30 years it has been the dumping ground for half of Europe—the repository of phosphorus, inorganic nitrogen, DDT, and mercury, all generated by the 165 million people living around it. Only five out of 26 species of fish that lived in the sea in the 1960s remain. Because of pollution, the approximately 16,500 square kilometres of oyster and blue mussel fields now yield one-tenth of their previous output. Cholera outbreaks have occurred routinely because raw sewage enters the Black Sea virtually everywhere. Prior to the breakup of the Soviet Union, there was virtually no concern for environmental degradation of the Black Sea. Currently, Russia, Georgia, Ukraine, Bulgaria, Romania, and Turkey have agreed to control maritime pollution. Because the cleanup will cost billions, it will not occur very rapidly in these developing countries.

For critical analysis: If the Black Sea were surrounded by just one country, could its degradation be more easily controlled? Why or why not?

Concepts in Brief

- Private costs are costs that are borne directly by consumers and producers when they engage in any resource-using activity.
- Social costs are private costs plus any other costs that are external to the decision maker. For example, the social costs of driving include all the private costs plus any pollution and congestion caused.
- When private costs differ from social costs, externalities exist because individual decision makers are not internalizing all the costs that society is bearing.
- When social costs exceed private costs, we say that there are negative externalities.

Thinking Critically About the Media   **The World's Ecology Is Being Destroyed—or Is It?**

Most media reports about the ecology are negative. There are some encouraging signs nonetheless. As a result of special breeding programs, for example, the whooping crane population has increased from 21 in 1941, to around 160 today. Beaver populations have rebounded from virtual extinction in the nineteenth century. Smog has dissipated in many Canadian cities. And there has been almost no degradation of pristine rivers by *new* water pollution sources in Canada in recent years.

POLLUTION

The term *pollution* is used quite loosely and can refer to a variety of by-products of any activity. Industrial pollution involves mainly air and water, but can also include noise and such concepts as aesthetic pollution, as when a landscape is altered in a negative way. For the most part, we will be analysing the most common forms, air and water pollution.

When asked how much pollution there should be in the economy, many people will respond, "None." But if we ask those same people how much starvation or deprivation of consumer products should exist in the economy, many will again say, "None." Growing and distributing food or producing consumer products creates pollution, however. In effect, therefore, there is no correct answer to how much pollution should be in an economy because when we ask how much pollution there *should* be, we are entering the realm of normative economics. We are asking people to express values. There is no way to disprove somebody's value system scientifically. One way we can approach a discussion of the "correct" amount of pollution would be to set up the same type of marginal analysis we used in our discussion of a firm's employment and output decisions. That is to say, we should pursue measures to reduce pollution only up to the point at which the marginal benefit from further reduction equals the marginal cost of further reduction.

Look at Figure 19.2. On the horizontal axis, we show the degree of cleanliness of the air. A vertical line is drawn at 100 percent cleanliness—the air cannot become any cleaner. Consider the benefits of obtaining a greater degree of air cleanliness.

Figure 19.2

The Optimal Quantity of Air Pollution

As we attempt to get a greater degree of air cleanliness, the marginal cost rises until even the slightest attempt at increasing air cleanliness leads to a very high marginal cost, as can be seen at the upper right of the graph. Conversely, the marginal benefit curve slopes downward: The more pure air we have, the less we value an additional unit of pure air. Marginal cost and marginal benefit intersect at point E. The optimal degree of air cleanliness is something less than 100 percent at Q_0. The price that we should pay for the last unit of air cleanup is no greater than P_0, for that is where marginal cost equals marginal benefit.

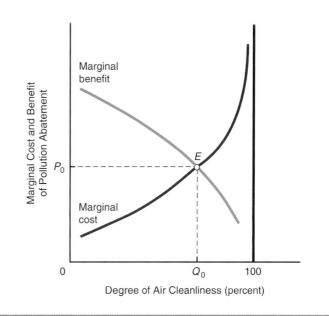

These benefits are represented by the marginal benefit curve, which slopes downward because of the law of diminishing marginal utility. When the air is very dirty, the marginal benefit from air that is a little cleaner appears to be relatively high, as shown on the vertical axis. As the air becomes cleaner and cleaner, however, the marginal benefit of a little bit more air cleanliness falls.

Consider the marginal cost of pollution abatement—that is, the marginal cost of obtaining cleaner air. In the 1960s, automobiles had no pollution abatement devices. Eliminating only 20 percent of the pollutants emitted by internal-combustion engines entailed a relatively small cost per unit of pollution removed. The cost of eliminating the next 20 percent rose, though. Finally, as we now get to the upper limits of removal of pollutants from the emissions of internal-combustion engines, we find that the elimination of one more percentage point of the amount of pollutants becomes astronomically expensive. To go from 97 percent cleanliness to 98 percent cleanliness involves a marginal cost that is many times greater than going from 10 percent cleanliness to 11 percent cleanliness.

It is realistic, therefore, to draw the marginal cost of pollution abatement as an upward-sloping curve, as shown in Figure 19.2. (The marginal cost curve slopes up because of the law of diminishing returns.)

▶ **Optimal quantity of pollution**

The level of pollution for which the marginal benefit of one additional unit of clean air just equals the marginal cost of that additional unit of clean air.

The Optimal Quantity of Pollution

The **optimal quantity of pollution** is defined as the level of pollution at which the marginal benefit equals the marginal cost of obtaining clean air. This occurs at the intersection of the marginal benefit curve and the marginal cost curve in Figure 19.2, at point E, which is analytically exactly the same as for every other economic activity. If we increased pollution control by one more unit greater than Q_0, the marginal cost of that small increase in the degree of air cleanliness would be greater than the marginal benefit to society.

As is usually the case in economic analysis, the optimal quantity of just about anything occurs when marginal cost equals marginal benefit. That is, the optimal quantity of pollution occurs at the point at which the marginal cost of reducing (or abating) pollution is just equal to the marginal benefit of doing so. The marginal cost of pollution abatement rises as more and more abatement is achieved (as the environment becomes cleaner and cleaner, the *extra* cost of cleansing rises). The state of technology is such that early units of pollution abatement are easily achieved (at low cost), but attaining higher and higher levels of environmental quality becomes progressively more difficult (as the extra cost rises to prohibitive levels). At the same time, the marginal benefits of a cleaner and cleaner environment fall; the marginal benefit of pollution abatement declines as the concept of a cleaner and cleaner environment moves from human life-support requirements to recreation to beauty to a perfectly pure environment. The point at which the increasing marginal cost of pollution abatement equals the decreasing marginal benefit of pollution abatement defines the (theoretical) optimal quantity of pollution.

Recognizing that the optimal quantity of pollution is not zero becomes easier when we realize that it takes scarce resources to reduce pollution. It follows that a trade-off exists between producing a cleaner environment and producing other goods and services. In that sense, nature's ability to cleanse itself is a resource that can be analysed like any other resource, and a cleaner environment must take its place with other societal wants.

Try Preview Question2:
What is the optimal quantity of pollution?

Concepts in Brief

- The marginal cost of cleaning up the environment rises as we get closer to 100 percent cleanliness. Indeed, it rises at an increasing rate.
- The marginal benefit of environmental cleanliness falls as we have more of it.
- The optimal quantity of pollution is the quantity at which the marginal cost of cleanup equals the marginal benefit of cleanup.
- Pollution abatement is a trade-off. We trade off goods and services for cleaner air and water, and vice versa.

▶ **Private property rights**
Exclusive rights of ownership that allow the use, transfer, and exchange of property.

▶ **Common property**
Property that is owned by everyone and therefore by no one. Air and water are examples of common property resources.

COMMON PROPERTY

In most cases, you do not have **private property rights**—exclusive ownership rights—to the air surrounding you, nor does anyone else. Air is a **common property**—nonexclusive—resource. Therein lies the crux of the problem. When no one owns a particular resource, no one has any incentive (conscience aside) to consider misuse of that resource. If one person decides not to pollute the air, there normally will be no significant effect on the total level of pollution. If one person decides not to pollute the ocean, there will still be approximately the same amount of ocean pollution—provided, of course, that the individual was previously responsible for only a small part of the total amount of ocean pollution.

Basically, pollution occurs where we have poorly defined private property rights, as in air and common bodies of water. We do not, for example, have a visual pollution problem in people's attics. That is their own property, which they choose to keep as clean as they want, given their preferences for cleanliness as weighed against the costs of keeping the attic neat and tidy.

Where private property rights exist, individuals have legal recourse to any damages sustained through the misuse of their property. When private property rights are well defined, the use of property—that is, the use of resources—will generally involve contracting between the owners of those resources. If you own land, you might contract with another person who wants to use your land for raising cows. The contract would most likely be written in the form of a lease agreement.

Try Preview Question 3:
How can poorly defined property rights create negative externalities?

INTERNATIONAL POLICY EXAMPLE
Should Ivory Imports Be Banned Worldwide?

Not many years ago, an important government official in Kenya burned 2,500 elephant tusks worth an estimated US$4 million. He wanted to dramatize the plight of the African elephant, which poachers had been killing in order to sell their ivory. This "white gold" is worth about US$100 per pound on the international market. At the beginning of the 1990s, the Convention on International Trade and Endangered Species prohibited all trade in ivory. Zimbabwe refuses to accept the import ban. Rather, it passed ownership of much of its elephant population to different tribes. The tribes charge relatively high prices to trophy hunters. Because they retain the benefits from taking care of the elephants and preventing poaching, the elephant population in Zimbabwe is growing rapidly. Elsewhere in Africa, poaching is on the upsurge because the ban on the ivory trade has caused an increase in its price. The problem of elephant extinction is due mainly to the common property nature of elephants in Africa.

For critical analysis: Alligators in the southeast United States can be raised on special farms. The Alligator Farmers Association has argued that "if people want to protect the alligator, the best thing they can do is buy an alligator handbag." Analyse this statement.

Voluntary Agreements and Transactions Costs

Is it possible for externalities to be internalized via voluntary agreement? Take a simple example. You live in a house with a nice view of a lake. The family living below you plants a tree. The tree grows so tall that it eventually starts to cut off your view. In most cities, no one has property rights to views; therefore, you cannot usually go to court to obtain relief. You do have the option of contracting with your neighbour, however.

Voluntary Agreements: Contracting.   You have the option of paying your neighbours (contracting) to cut back the tree. You could start out with an offer of a small amount and keep going up until your neighbours agree or until you reach your limit. Your limit will equal the value you place on having an unobstructed view of the lake. Your neighbours will be willing if the payment is at least equal to the reduction in their intrinsic property value due to a stunted tree. Your offering the payment makes your neighbours aware of the social cost of their actions. The social cost here is equal to the care of the tree plus the cost suffered by you from an impeded view of the lake.

In essence, then, your offer of money income to your neighbours indicates to them that there is an opportunity cost to their actions. If they don't comply, they forfeit the money that you are offering them. The point here is that *opportunity cost always exists, whoever has property rights.* Therefore, we would expect under some circumstances that voluntary contracting will occur to internalize externalities.[1] The question is, When will voluntary agreements occur?

Transaction Costs.   One major condition for the outcome just outlined above is that the **transaction costs**—all costs associated with making and enforcing agreements—must be low relative to the expected benefits of reaching an agreement. (We already looked at this topic briefly in Chapter 4.) If we expand our example to a much larger one such as air pollution, the transaction costs of numerous homeowners trying to reach agreements with the individuals and companies that create the pollution are relatively high. Consequently, we don't expect voluntary contracting to be an effective way to internalize the externality of air pollution.

▶ **Transaction costs**

All costs associated with making, reaching, and enforcing agreements.

Changing Property Rights

In considering the problem of property rights, we can approach it by assuming that initially in a society, many property rights and many resources are not defined. But this situation does not cause a problem so long as no one cares to use the resources for which there are no property rights, or so long as enough of these resources are available that people can have as much as they want at a zero price. Only when and if a use is found for a resource, or the supply of a resource is inadequate at a zero price does a problem develop. The problem requires that something be done about deciding property rights. If not, the resource will be wasted and possibly even destroyed. Property rights can be assigned to individuals who will then assert control; or they may be assigned to government, which can maintain and preserve the resource, charge for its use, or implement some other rationing device. What we have seen with common property such as air and water is that governments have indeed attempted to take over the control of those resources so that they cannot be wasted or destroyed.

---

[1]This analysis is known as the *Coase theorem,* named after its originator, Ronald Coase, who demonstrated that negative or positive externalities do not necessarily require government intervention in situations in which property rights are defined and enforceable and transaction costs are relatively low.

Another way of viewing the pollution problem is to argue that property rights are "sacred" and that there are property rights in every resource that exists. We can then say that each individual does not have the right to act on anything that is not that person's property. Hence no individual has the right to pollute because that amounts to using property that the individual does not specifically own.

Clearly, we must fill the gap between private costs and true social costs in situations in which we have to make up somehow for the fact that property rights are not well defined or assigned. There are three ways to fill this gap: taxation, subsidization, and regulation. Government is involved in all three. Unfortunately, government does not have perfect information and may not pick the appropriate tax, subsidy, or type of regulation. We also have to consider cases in which taxes are hard to enforce or subsidies are difficult to give out to "worthy" recipients. In such cases, outright prohibition of the polluting activity may be the optimal solution to a particular pollution problem. For example, if it is difficult to monitor the level of a particular type of pollution that even in small quantities can cause severe environmental damage, outright prohibition of such pollution may be the only alternative.

Try Preview Question 4:
If property rights are poorly defined, *must* negative externalities arise?

INTERNATIONAL POLICY EXAMPLE
Privatizing the Right to Pollute

In late 1997, negotiators from 159 countries met in Kyoto, Japan, to work out an agreement to limit the emission of greenhouse gases, those gases produced from burning fossil fuels. In recent years, scientists have become convinced that the increase in greenhouse gases is leading to changes in weather patterns around the world—the devastating 1997 flood in southern Manitoba is an example.

Following days of tough negotiations, the countries present finally reached an agreement. Overall, the 38 most developed countries will cut emissions by 5.2 percent. Canada, which accounts for 2 percent of world production of greenhouse gases, will cut its emissions by 6 percent by the year 2012. The European Union will cut its emissions by 8 percent, the United States by 7 percent, and Japan by 6 percent. Interestingly, Australia can increase its emissions by 8 percent, and Iceland by 10 percent!

In spite of the apparent progress made at Kyoto, environmentalists are disappointed. For one thing, the Kyoto agreement creates private property rights in pollution. Each country will be given the right to produce an agreed level of greenhouse gases. Countries able to reduce emissions below the agreed level will be able to sell their unused property rights to countries that fail to meet their targets. The sale of "pollution permits" thus represents the monetization of a social cost, and raises the cost of polluting in the offending countries.

In addition, the Kyoto agreement provides for pollution credits for developed countries that give financial assistance for emission reduction in Third World countries. Environmentalists fear that rich countries like the United States will be able to continue to pollute by purchasing the right to do so.

For critical analysis: How much do you think the rich countries of the world would be prepared to pay for excess pollution rights?

Are There Alternatives to Pollution-Causing Resource Use?

Some people cannot understand why, if pollution is bad, we still use pollution-causing resources such as coal and oil to generate any electricity at all. Why don't we forgo the use of such polluting resources and opt for one that apparently is pollution free, such as solar energy? Contrary to some people's beliefs, there is no nationwide or worldwide conspiracy to prevent us from shifting to solar power. The plain fact is that the cost of generating solar power in most circumstances is much higher than generating that same power through conventional means. We do not yet have the technology that allows us all the luxury of driving solar-powered cars—though such cars do exist. Moreover, with current technology, the solar parts necessary to generate the electricity for the average town would cover massive sections of the countryside, and the manufacturing of those solar parts would itself generate pollution.

WILD SPECIES, COMMON PROPERTY, AND TRADE-OFFS

One of the most distressing common property problems concerns endangered species, usually in the wild. No one is too concerned about the quantity of dogs, cats, cattle, sheep, and horses. The reason is that virtually all of those species are private property. Peregrine falcons, swift foxes, piping plovers, and the like are typically common property. No one has a vested interest in making sure that they perpetuate in good health.

The federal government has passed the *Canadian Endangered Species Protection Act* in an attempt to prevent certain species from dying out, although the Act has yet to be proclaimed. As well, most provincial governments have similar legislation to protect dwindling stocks of wildlife. In the mid-1990s in British Columbia, for example, logging was cut back in two forestry districts when only 30 pairs of nesting spotted owls could be located. Up to 100 jobs in forestry were lost, and the process of generating a plan to save the spotted owl cost taxpayers $1,000,000, or about $17,000 per bird. The issues are not straightforward. Today, the earth has only 0.02 percent of all of the species that have ever lived. Every year, 1,000 to 3,000 new species are discovered and classified. Estimates of how many species are actually dying out vary from a high of 50,000 a year to a low of one every four years.

Concepts in Brief

- A common property resource is one that no one owns—or, otherwise stated, that everyone owns.
- Common property exists when property rights are indefinite or nonexistent.
- When no property rights exist, pollution occurs because no one individual or firm has a sufficient economic incentive to care for the common property in question, be it air, water, or scenery.
- Private costs will not equal social costs when common property is at issue unless only a few individuals are involved and they are able to contract among themselves.

RECYCLING

▶ **Recycling**

The reuse of raw materials derived from manufactured products.

As part of the overall ecology movement, there has been a major push to save scarce resources via recycling. **Recycling** involves reusing paper products, plastics, glass, and metals rather than putting them into solid waste dumps. Many cities have instituted curb-side pick-up recycling programs.

The benefits of recycling are straightforward. Fewer *natural* resources are used. But some economists argue that recycling does not necessarily save *total* resources. For example, recycling paper products may not necessarily save trees, according to A. Clark Wiseman, an economist for Resources for the Future. He argues that an increase in paper recycling will eventually lead to a reduction in the demand for virgin paper and thus for trees. Because most trees are planted specifically to produce paper, a reduction in the demand for trees will mean that certain land now used to grow trees will be put to other uses. The end result may be smaller rather than larger forests, a result that is probably not desired in the long run.

Recycling's Invisible Costs

The recycling of paper can also pollute. Used paper has ink on it that has to be removed during the recycling process. According to the National Wildlife Federation, the product of 98 tonnes of deinked (bleached) fibre generates approximately 39 tonnes of sludge. This sludge has to be disposed of, usually in a landfill. A lot of recycled paper companies, however, are beginning to produce unbleached paper. In general, recycling does create waste that has to be disposed of.

There is also an issue involved in the use of resources. Recycling requires human effort. The labour resources involved in recycling are often many times more costly than the potential savings in scarce resources not used. That means that net resource use, counting all resources, may sometimes be greater with recycling than without it.

Landfills

One of the arguments in favour of recycling is to avoid a solid waste "crisis." Some people believe that we are running out of solid waste dump sites in Canada. This is perhaps true in and near major cities, and indeed the most populated areas of the country might ultimately benefit from recycling programs. In the rest of the country, however, the data do not seem to indicate that we are running out of solid waste landfill sites.

Throughout urban Canada, the disposal price per tonne of city garbage is rising rapidly. Prices vary, of course, for the 20 million tonnes of garbage generated each year. In Toronto, disposal fees are now upwards of $150 per tonne, compared to $10.40 per tonne in 1981. However, disposal prices in rural Canada are actually falling, implying that there is no shortage of space for landfills.

Currently, municipalities burn about 16 percent of their solid waste and recycle a few percentage points more. The amount of solid waste dumped in landfills estimated for 1996 is 13 million tonnes. By 2000, it is expected to drop to 10 million tonnes even as total garbage output rises above 22 million tonnes. In all likelihood, partly because of increased recycling efforts, the amount of solid waste disposal will continue to drop as municipalities restrict the number of landfill sites in response to pressure from community groups who believe that landfills are unsafe.

INTERNATIONAL POLICY EXAMPLE
Can Citizens Recycle Too Much? The Case of Germany

Recycling is popular throughout the European Union, but the Germans have raised it to an art form. Germany has a law requiring that manufacturers or retailers take back their packaging or ensure that 80 percent of it is collected rather than thrown away. What is collected must be recycled or reused. The law covers about 40 percent of the country's garbage. The problem is that German consumers responded more enthusiastically than anticipated: So much plastic packaging has been collected that German recyclers do not have the capacity to use it all. Consequently, Germany has been exporting its recyclable waste to neighbouring Belgium, France, and the Netherlands. France threatened to curb its imports of German recyclable garbage. Belgium even argued in front of the European Parliament that Germany was engaging in unfair competition. In the meantime, the company in charge of recycling Germany's waste, Duales System Deutschland, is losing hundreds of millions of dollars a year. Considering that it costs $2,000 a tonne to recycle plastic, and that the price of petroleum (the main ingredient in plastic) is relatively low, the future of recycling in Germany does not look bright.

For critical analysis: How is it possible to recycle "too much"?

Thinking Critically About the Media   We Are Running Out of Everything!

It is going to be a world with no more oil, natural gas, copper, or zinc. At least that is the impression one gets these days from the media. In reality, as economists have discovered, the real (inflation-corrected) prices for most nonrenewable resources have fallen over the past 125 years. Real energy prices have dropped an average of 1.6 percent per year; major mineral prices have dropped 1.3 to 2.9 percent a year; even the price of land has dropped 0.8 percent per year. Unless supply and demand analysis is no longer valid, those numbers indicate that the supply of nonrenewable resources is increasing faster than the demand.

Should We Save Scarce Resources?

Periodically, the call for recycling focuses on the necessity of saving scarce resources because "we are running out." There is little evidence to back up this claim because virtually every natural resource has fallen in price (corrected for inflation) over the past several decades. In 1980, economist Julian Simon made a $1,000 bet with well-known environmentalist Paul Erlich. Simon bet $200 per resource that any five natural resources that Erlich picked would decline in price (corrected for inflation) by the end of the 1980s. Simon won. (When Simon asked Erlich to renew the bet for $20,000 for the 1990s, Erlich declined.) During the 1980s, the price of virtually every natural resource fell (corrected for inflation), and so did the price of every agricultural commodity. The same was true for every forest product. Though few people remember the dire predictions of the 1970s, many noneconomists throughout the world argued at that time that the world's oil reserves were vanishing. If this were true, the pretax, inflation-corrected price of gasoline would not be the same today as it was in the late 1940s (which it is).

In spite of predictions in the early 1980s by World Watch Institute president Lester Brown, real food prices did not rise. Indeed, the real price of food fell by more than 30 percent for the major agricultural commodities during the 1980s. A casual knowledge of supply and demand tells you that since demand for food did not decrease, supply must have increased faster than demand.

Concepts in Brief

- Recycling involves reusing paper, glass, and other materials rather than putting them into solid waste dumps. Recycling does have a cost both in the resources used for recycling and in the pollution created during recycling, such as the sludge from deinking paper for reuse.
- Landfills are an alternative to recycling. Expansion of these solid waste disposal sites is outpacing demand increases.
- Resources may not be getting scarcer. The inflation-corrected price of most resources has been falling for decades.

Issues and Applications

Technology to the Rescue of Dwindling Fish Stocks

Concepts Applied: Marginal cost, marginal benefit, common property, social cost, private cost, opportunity cost

Overfishing has caused the worldwide stock of fish to be severely limited, and in some cases, totally depleted. Attempts to remedy this problem have come in the form of government imposition of limited-access schemes in which catch limits are set.

Overfishing is a common property problem. An individual who fishes for a living will fish until the marginal benefit equals the marginal cost. That individual considers only actual private costs when computing marginal cost. These include the opportunity cost of investing in equipment, depreciation, and supplies, as well as the individual's opportunity cost of time. What the private fisher does not take into account is the potential cost to society if common property fishing grounds are overfished. The result has been called the "tragedy of the commons." The tragedy occurs because of the overuse of the common property resource. In the case of fish, there is strong evidence that the tragedy of the commons has occurred. Some solutions have already been tried.

Limited-Access Schemes

Some governments, such as New Zealand, have instituted limited-access schemes in which officials set annual catch limits. The right to a percentage of that catch is privately owned and can be traded. Once instituted in New Zealand, according to economist Michael De Alessi, fishers began to practise conservation and limit their harvest. Similar systems have been instituted in Alaska for the Pacific whiting.

Technology and Private Ownership

The tragedy of the commons with respect to fishing involves common property ownership of most migratory species. The territorial waters of Canada extend over millions of square kilometres of ocean. Thus it has never seemed possible for anybody to "own" migratory schools of fish. Today, this is now possible due to branding technologies, including sonar. Scientists have used the Integrated Underseas Surveillance System to track a single blue whale for over 40 days without the use of radio beacons. Because constant monitoring is now technologically feasible, at least with whales, it is possible to enforce private property rights in that species if we so choose.

Satellite technologies allow for the tagging and monitoring of certain species of sea life. Branding fish is another possibility. Fish packers might then compensate fish "ranchers" according to how much of each branded fish was packed. According to economist De Alessi, it is now possible for autonomous underwater vehicles actually to "corral" schools of certain types of fish like herds of sheep. This might be feasible for very expensive fish such as giant bluefin tuna, which routinely fetch up to thousands of dollars each in Tokyo.

Using sonar and satellites, it is also possible to create a "virtual fence." Satellites can provide information on ship location and ship activity even to the extent of knowing when a ship has lowered a net. Boats that are fishing illegally could be identified.

For Critical Analysis

1. In the Canadian west a century ago, land expanses were great and fencing material was relatively expensive. How did ranchers solve the problem of intermingling livestock herds?

2. What are some currently available ways to solve the fish stock depletion problem without using sophisticated new technologies?

CHAPTER SUMMARY

1. In some situations, there are social costs that do not equal private costs—that is, there are costs to society that exceed the cost to the individual. These costs may include air and water pollution, for which private individuals do not have to pay. Society, however, does bear the costs of these externalities. Few individuals or firms voluntarily consider social costs.

2. One way to analyse the problem of pollution is to look at it as an externality. Individual decision makers do not take account of the negative externalities they impose on the rest of society. In such a situation, they produce "too much" pollution and "too many" polluting goods.

3. It might be possible to ameliorate the situation by imposing a tax on polluters. The tax, however, should be dependent on the extent of the economic damages created rather than on the physical quantity of pollution. This tax will therefore be different for the same level of physical pollution in different parts of the country because the economic damage differs, depending on location, population density, and other factors.

4. The optimal quantity of pollution is the quantity at which the marginal cost of cleanup equals the marginal benefit of cleanup. Pollution abate-ment is a trade-off. We trade off goods and services for cleaner air and water, and vice versa.

5. Another way of looking at the externality problem is to realize that it involves the lack of definite property rights. No one owns common property resources such as air and water, and therefore no one takes account of the long-run pernicious effects of excessive pollution.

6. There are alternatives to pollution-causing resource use—for example, solar energy. We do not use solar energy because it is too expensive relative to conventional alternatives, and because the creation of solar parts would generate pollution.

7. Recycling involves reusing paper, glass, and other materials rather than putting them into solid waste dumps. Recycling does have a cost both in the resources used for recycling and in the pollution created during recycling. Landfills are an alternative to recycling. In rural Canada, these solid waste disposal sites are being expanded faster than the demand for them.

8. Resources may not be getting scarcer. The inflation-corrected price of most resources has been falling for decades.

DISCUSSION OF PREVIEW QUESTIONS

1. What is a negative externality?

A negative externality exists if the social costs exceed the private costs of some activity; if parties not involved in that activity are adversely affected, negative externalities are said to exist. Pollution is an example of a negative externality; for example, transactions between automobile producers and users impose costs in the form of pollution on people who neither produce nor consume the autos.

2. What is the optimal quantity of pollution?

The optimal quantity of pollution cannot be zero because at 100 percent cleanliness, the marginal cost of pollution abatement would greatly exceed the marginal benefit. We would have too much pollution abatement; we would be using resources in a socially suboptimal manner. That means that the resources being used in pollution abatement would have a higher value elsewhere in society.

We live in a world of scarce resources. If the value we receive from spending one more dollar on cleaning up the environment is less than the value we would receive by spending that dollar on something else—such as cancer research—we are not allocating our resources efficiently if we still choose to spend that dollar on pollution abatement.

3. How can poorly defined property rights create negative externalities?

Nature's ability to cleanse itself can be considered a scarce resource, and as such, it behooves society to use this resource efficiently. However, if everyone owns natural resources, in effect *no one* owns them. Consequently, people will use natural resources, for good or for ill, as though they were free. Of course, excessive use of natural resources eventually impairs nature's ability to cleanse itself; enter the concept of pollution (an accumulation of unwanted matter). Now the marginal cost to *private* polluters is still zero (or nearly zero), whereas the cost to society of using this (now scarce) resource is positive. In short, third parties are adversely affected when pollution results from the production and consumption of goods that lead to waste, which creates pollution.

4. If property rights are poorly defined, *must* negative externalities arise?

No. If contracting costs are small and enforcement is relatively easy, voluntary contracts will arise and the full opportunity costs of actions will be accounted for. That is, when transaction costs are small, private and social costs will converge, as the parties affected contract with the parties creating the additional costs, and externalities will disappear. What is interesting is that regardless of how property rights are assigned, resources will be allocated in the same way. Of course, the specific assignment of property rights does affect the distribution of wealth, even though resource allocation is independent of the specific property right assignment; what is important for efficient resource allocation is that *someone* have property rights. It should be noted that, unfortunately, the main externalities, such as air and water pollution, are very complex, contracting costs are very high, and enforcement is difficult. As a consequence, free market solutions are not likely to emerge—indeed, they have not.

PROBLEMS

(Answers to the odd-numbered problems appear at the back of the book.)

19-1. Construct a typical supply and demand graph. Show the initial equilibrium price and quantity. Assume that the good causes negative externalities to third parties (persons not involved in the transactions). Revise the graph to compensate for that fact. How does the revised situation compare with the original?

19-2. Construct a second supply and demand graph for any product. Show the equilibrium price and quantity. Assuming that the good generates external benefits, modify the diagram to allow for them. Show the new equilibrium price and quantity. How does the revised situation compare with the original?

19-3. Suppose that polluters are to be charged by government agencies for the privilege of polluting.
  a. How should the price be set?
  b. Which firms will treat waste, and which will pay to pollute?
  c. Is it possible that some firms will be forced to close down because they now have to pay to pollute? Why might this result be good?
  d. If producers are charged to pollute, they will pass this cost on to buyers in the form of higher prices. Why might this be good?

19-4. Why has the free market not developed contractual arrangements to eliminate excess air pollution in major Canadian cities?

19-5. What is the problem with common property resources?

19-6. The accompanying graph shows external costs arising from the production of good Y.

a. Which curve includes only the private costs of producing good Y?
b. Which supply curve includes the external costs of producing good Y?
c. How much of good Y is produced and at what price?
d. Who bears the cost of producing the amount of good Y in part (c)?
e. If external costs are included, how much of good Y should be produced, and at what price should it be sold?

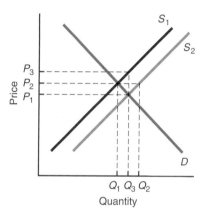

19-7. The table shows the costs and benefits of removing air pollution.

Annual Units of Pollution	Annual Total Air Pollution Damage	Annual Total Costs of Air Pollution Reduction
0	$ 0	$410
1	30	260
2	70	160
3	150	80
4	270	20
5	430	0

a. Find the marginal benefits of pollution reduction.
b. Find the marginal costs of pollution reduction.
c. Assume that society is currently allow-

ing 5 units of air pollution per year. If pollution is reduced to 3 units, what is the net gain or loss to society?
d. Suppose that all air pollution is eliminated. What would be the net gain or loss to society?
e. If air pollution were regulated efficiently, how many units of air pollution would be allowed each year?

19-8. Examine this marginal cost and marginal benefit schedule for air cleanliness.

Quantity (%)	Marginal Benefit	Marginal Cost
0	$50,000	$ 5,000
20	45,000	10,000
40	35,000	15,000
60	25,000	25,000
80	10,000	40,000
100	0	∞

a. Graph the marginal benefit and marginal cost curves.
b. What is the optimal degree of air cleanliness?
c. How much will the optimal amount of air cleanliness cost?
d. What is the optimal amount of air pollution?
e. Would we want a level of zero pollution? Why or why not?

19-9. Explain why it is possible to have too little pollution. What might government do to cause private individuals and businesses to generate too little pollution?

19-10. Visit the International Development Research Centre's "Resource Clock" at http://www.idrc.ca.

a. Which direction is the population clock moving? the productive land clock?
b. What do you think will happen to the price of productive land as the world population increases? Why?

INTERACTING WITH THE INTERNET

Environment Canada is located at

http://www.ec.gc.ca/envhome.html

It has general information and material on its programs, initiatives, rules, regulations, and legislation. It also has "Environmental Action," which describes the role individuals can play in environmental issues.

You can measure your ecological footprint—how many resources you are using relative to other Canadians and to other people around the world—at

http://www.wwfcanada.org/cgi-bin/database-cgi/ecofoot.pl

You can find out how to reduce the size of your footprint at

http://www.wwfcanada.org/footprints/tips.htm

An organization that takes an economist's view towards environmental issues is Resources for the Future at

http://www.rff.org/

Development: Economic Growth Around the World

Many Canadians do not yet use a home-banking program on their computer in order to make transactions with their local bank. But if you live in Brazil, one of the world's developing countries, you can use a system developed by *União de Bancos Brasileiros.* How is it possible that such a technological advancement can take place more rapidly in a less developed country than in one of the most developed countries in the world? The answer lies in understanding what causes economic development and why there may be a bright future for the world's developing economies.

Did You Know That... a 1967 best-selling business book called *The American Challenge* predicted that by 1985, the world's economies would be owned and run by a dozen huge American multinationals, producing over 90 percent of the world's manufactured goods? Of course, nothing could be further from the truth today. American companies remain important in the world economy, but they do not dominate. Since that prediction was made, Germany, Japan, South Korea, Hong Kong, Singapore, and Taiwan grew to become economic powerhouses. Today, there are indeed many "rich" countries, including, of course, Canada. But this country was not always rich. In fact, it was quite poor 200 years ago. If you go back far enough, every country was poor and undeveloped. Why do some countries develop faster than others? In other words, what causes economic development? Although there are no easy answers to this important question, economists now have enough data to know what conditions favour economic growth in the developing world.

PUTTING WORLD POVERTY IN PERSPECTIVE

It is difficult to comprehend the reality of poverty in the world today. At least one-half, if not two-thirds, of the world's population lives at subsistence level, with just enough to eat for survival. The official poverty level in Canada exceeds the average income in at least half the world. That is not to say that we should ignore problems at home with the poor and homeless simply because they are living better than many people elsewhere in the world. Rather, it is necessary for Canadians to keep their perspective on what are considered problems for this country relative to what are considered problems elsewhere.

WHAT IS DEVELOPMENT ECONOMICS?

How did developed countries travel the path from extreme poverty to relative riches? That is the essential issue of development economics. It is the study of why some countries develop and others do not. Further, it is the study of changes in policies that might help developing countries get richer. It is not good enough simply to say that people in diverse countries are different and therefore that is why some countries are rich while some are poor. Economists do not deny that different cultures create different work ethics, but they are unwilling to accept such a pat and fatalistic answer.

Look at any world map. About four-fifths of the countries you will see on that map are considered relatively poor. The goal of students of development economics is to help the more than four billion people with low living standards today join the billion or so who have relatively high living standards.

INDUSTRIALLY ADVANCED ECONOMIES

▶ **Industrially advanced countries (IACs)**
Canada, Japan, the United States, and the countries of Western Europe, all of which have market economies based on a large skilled labour force and a large technically advanced stock of capital goods.

Any system of defining poor countries and rich countries, developing countries and developed countries, is, of course, arbitrary. Nonetheless, it is instructive to examine some figures on the difference between **industrially advanced countries (IACs)** and so-called developing countries. There are 19 IACs. (Excluded from this classification are countries whose economies are based on a single resource, such as oil, but whose industrial development in other fields is minimal.) The latest data available on the IACs (1995) show an estimated per capita income of $16,341, an annual growth rate of about 2.2 percent, and a population growth of about 0.6 percent. At the other end of the scale, the more than 100 developing countries have a per capita income of $980, an annual growth rate of almost 3 percent, and a population growth rate of 2 percent per year, more than three times that of the IACs.

To be sure, we must be careful about accepting such data at face value. There is a tremendous disparity in incomes among the developing countries, and the data are notoriously inaccurate. Nonetheless, it is certain that a tremendous gap exists between average incomes in the IACs and in the developing countries.

Thinking Critically About the Media   **The Gap Between the Rich and the Poor**

Contrary to what we are often told by the media, government statisticians, and politicians, the rich countries are not leaving the poor countries in the dust. The International Monetary Fund revised its estimates of relative size of economies a few years ago and came up with this startling conclusion: The share of world output produced by the rich industrial economies is only 54 percent rather than the 75 percent formerly reported. Because the majority of countries in the developing world are growing faster than those in the developed world, the world's rich countries will dominate the world economy less and less in the future.

Newly Industrialized Economies

Not all developing countries are stuck in abject poverty. The developing countries vary greatly in their ability to experience economic growth, but one group of recently industrialized economies achieved annual growth rates two and three times that of Canada. These newly industrialized economies are the so-called Four Tigers—Singapore, Hong Kong, Taiwan, and South Korea—all on the Pacific Rim. From 1960 to 1995, per capita income in these economies grew sixfold. One of the reasons the newly industrialized countries have grown so rapidly is that a huge increase

Try Preview Question 1:

What is a developing country?

in world trade and in international communications has allowed technology to be disseminated much more quickly today than in the past. Indeed, these countries have advanced so quickly that three of the four now have a higher per capita income than Spain, the United Kingdom, and Italy. Yet during the same 35-year period, a number of sub-Saharan African countries experienced a *fall* in real per capita income.

Concepts in Brief

- Any definition of developing countries or industrially advanced countries (IACs) is arbitrary. Nonetheless, we have identified 19 IACs and over 100 developing countries.
- The IACs have per capita incomes that are roughly 17 times the per capita incomes in the developing countries. Population in developing countries is growing more than three times as fast as in the IACs.
- Four newly industrialized countries on the Pacific Rim—Singapore, Taiwan, South Korea, and Hong Kong—have increased their real per capita incomes sixfold since 1960.

ECONOMIC DEVELOPMENT: INDUSTRY VERSUS AGRICULTURE

One of the most widely discussed theories of development concerns the need for balanced growth, with industry and agriculture given equal importance. One characteristic of many developed countries is their high degree of industrialization, although there are clearly exceptions—Hong Kong, for example. In general, countries with relatively high standards of living are more industrialized than countries with low standards of living. The policy prescription then seems obvious: Less developed countries in which a large percentage of the total resources are devoted to agricultural pursuits should attempt to obtain more balanced growth by industrializing.

Although the theory is fairly acceptable at first glance, it leads to some absurd results. We find in many developing countries with steel factories and automobile plants that the people are actually worse off because of this attempted industrialization. Most developing countries currently cannot profitably produce steel or automobiles because they lack the necessary domestic human and physical capital. They can engage in such industrial activities only with heavy government subsidization of the industry itself. Import restrictions abound, preventing the purchase of foreign, mostly cheaper substitutes for the industrial products that the country itself produces. Also, in general, the existence of subsidies leads to a misallocation of resources and a lower economic welfare for the country as a whole.

INTERNATIONAL EXAMPLE
Industrialized Poverty

Amazingly, some of the poorest countries in the world today have some of the highest rates of industrialization. Industry's share of gross output is greater in sub-Saharan Africa than in Denmark, is greater in Zimbabwe, Botswana, and Trinidad and Tobago than in Japan, and is greater in Argentina than in every country in the European Union!

Agriculture represents a relatively low share of gross output in some of the world's poorest countries. For example, agriculture represents a greater share of national output in Denmark than it does in Trinidad and Tobago. The same is true in Spain relative to Botswana, and in Portugal relative to Gabon. It is clear that industrialization does not necessarily lead to high standards of living.

For critical analysis: If industry represents a large share of gross output in extremely poor countries, what does this tell you about the rate of return on investment in industry in those countries?

The Stages of Development: Agriculture to Industry to Services

If we analyse the development of modern rich countries, we find that they went through three stages. First is the agricultural stage, when most of the population is involved in agriculture. Then comes the manufacturing stage, when much of the population becomes involved in the industrialized sector of the economy. And finally there is a shift towards services. That is exactly what happened in Canada: The so-called tertiary, or service, sector of the economy continues to grow, whereas the manufacturing sector (and its share of employment) is declining in relative importance.

However, it is important to understand the need for early specialization in a country's comparative advantage. We have repeatedly referred to the doctrine of comparative advantage, and it is even more appropriate for the developing countries of the world. If trading is allowed among countries, a country is normally best off if it produces what it has a comparative advantage at producing and imports the rest. This means that many developing countries should continue to specialize in agricultural production or in labour-intensive manufactured goods.

Try Preview Question 2:

Must developing countries develop by industrializing?

How Subsidized Agriculture Affects Developing Countries

Modern Western countries have continually subsidized their own agricultural sectors to allow them to compete more easily with the developing countries in this area. If we lived in a world of no subsidization, we would probably see less food being produced in the highly developed Western world (except for Canada, the United States, and Australia) and much more being produced in the developing countries of the rest of the world. They would trade food for manufactured goods. It would seem, then, that one of the most detrimental aspects of our economic policy for the developing countries has been the continued subsidization of the Canadian farmer. Canada, of course, is not alone; virtually the entire European Union does exactly the same thing.

Even with this situation, however, a policy of using higher taxes on imported goods or domestic manufacturing subsidies in order to increase industrialization in the developing countries may do more harm than good. Industrialization is generally beneficial only if it comes about naturally, when the market conditions are such that the countries' entrepreneurs freely decide to build factories instead of increasing farm output because it is profitable to do so.

Concepts in Brief

- A balanced-growth theory predicts that industry and agriculture must grow together in order for a country to experience growth.
- For many developing countries, balanced growth requires subsidization of manufacturing firms.
- Historically, there are three stages of economic development: the agricultural stage, the manufacturing stage, and the service-sector stage, when a large part of the workforce is employed in providing services.

NATURAL RESOURCES AND ECONOMIC DEVELOPMENT

One theory of development states that for a country to develop, it must have a large natural resource base. The theory continues to assert that much of the world is running out of natural resources, thereby limiting economic growth and development. We must point out that only the narrowest definition of a natural resource could lead to such an opinion. In broader terms, a natural resource is something scarce occurring in nature that we can use for our own purposes. Natural resources therefore include knowledge of the use of something. The natural resources that we could define several hundred years ago did not, for example, include hydroelectric power—no one knew that such a natural resource existed or, indeed, how to make it exist.

In any event, it is difficult to find a strong correlation between the natural resources of a country and its stage of development. Japan has virtually no crude oil and must import most of the natural resources that it uses as inputs for its industrial production. Brazil has huge amounts of natural resources, including fertile soil and abundant minerals, yet Brazil has a much lower per capita income than Japan. Only when we include the human element of natural resources can we say that natural resources determine economic development.

Natural resources by themselves are not particularly useful for economic development. They must be transformed into something usable for either investment or consumption. This leads us to another aspect of development, the trade-off between investment and consumption. The normal way this subject is analysed is by dealing with investment simply as capital accumulation.

CAPITAL ACCUMULATION

It is often asserted that a necessary prerequisite for economic development is a large capital stock—machines and other durable goods that can be used to aid in the production of consumption goods and more capital goods in the future. It is true that industrially advanced countries indeed have larger capital stocks per capita than developing countries. It is also true that the larger the capital stock for any given population, the higher the possible rate of economic growth (assuming that the population makes good use of the capital goods). This is basically one of the foundations for many of the foreign aid programs in which Canada and other countries have engaged. We and other countries have attempted to give developing countries capital so that they, too, might grow. However, the amount of capital that we have actually given to other countries is quite small: a hydroelectric dam here, a factory there.

Thinking Critically About the Media   **The Dark Side of the PC Revolution**

According to more than a handful of articles, the "PC revolution" will increase the gap between the rich and the poor. According to one "expert," technology can only be afforded by the rich, and furthermore, computers displace "hordes of workers." Nothing could be further from the truth. The country that has the most computers in place per capita is the United States, and its unemployment rate has not varied much in the past two decades. Moreover, even if computers are essential to the success of a business, their prices are dropping every month. And what is to prevent several businesses in less developed countries from sharing a PC if the price is too high?

Domestic Capital Formation

How does a developing country accumulate capital? The answer is that it must save, and invest those accumulated savings profitably. Saving, of course, means not consuming. Resources must be released from consumer goods production in order to be used for investment.

Saving and the Poor.   It is often stated that people in developing countries cannot save because they are barely subsisting. This is not actually true. Many anthropological studies—of villages in India, for example—have revealed that saving is in fact going on, but it takes forms that we don't recognize in our money economy; for example, saving may involve storing dried onions that can later be traded for other goods. Some researchers speculate that much saving in developing countries takes the form of rearing children who then feel a moral obligation to support their parents during the latter's retirement. In any event, saving does take place even in the most poverty-stricken areas. In general, there is no pronounced relationship between the *percentage* of income saved and the level of income (over the long run).

Basically, then, saving is a method by which individuals can realize an optimal consumption stream throughout their expected lifetimes. The word *optimal* here does not mean adequate or necessary or decent; it means most desirable from the *individual's* point of view (given that individual's resources).

Evidence of Saving in Developing Countries.   Savings in developing countries do not necessarily flow into what we might consider productive capital formation projects. We do see the results of literally centuries of saving in the form of religious monuments such as cathedrals, and in government buildings. Indeed, one major problem in developing countries is that much of the saving that occurs does not get channelled into productive capital formation. This is also true of much of the foreign aid that has been sent to developing countries. These countries could productively use more factories and a better infrastructure—roads and communications—rather than more government buildings and fancy stadiums built exclusively for merrymaking and sports.

Try Preview Question 3:

Can developing countries create their own capital stock?

Property Rights and Economic Development

If you were in a country in which bank accounts and businesses were periodically expropriated by the government, how willing would you be to leave your money in a savings account or to invest in a business? Certainly, you would be less willing than if such things never occurred. Periodic expropriation of private property rarely occurs in developed countries. It *has* occurred in numerous developing countries, however. For example, private property was once nationalized in Chile and still is in Cuba. In some cases, former owners are compensated, but rarely for the full value of the property taken over by the state.

Empirically, we have seen that, other things being equal, the more certain private property rights are, the more private capital accumulation there will be. People are more willing to invest their savings in endeavours that will increase their wealth in future years. They have property rights in their wealth that are sanctioned and enforced by the government. In fact, some economic historians have attempted to show that it was the development of well-defined private property rights that allowed Western Europe to increase its growth rate after many centuries of stagnation. The degree of certainty with which one can reap the gains from investing also determines the extent to which businesspeople in *other* countries will invest capital in developing countries. The threat of nationalization in some countries may scare away foreign investment that would allow these countries to become more developed.

In a sentence, economic development depends more on individuals who are able to perceive opportunities and then take advantage of those opportunities than it does on capital or natural resources.[1] Risks will not be taken, though, if the risk takers cannot expect a reward. The political institutions must be such that risk takers are rewarded. That requires well-established property rights, lack of the threat of expropriation of profits, and no fear of government nationalization of businesses.

Try Preview Question 4:

Does a lack of protected property rights hinder a developing country's development?

---

[1] The member countries of OPEC might be considered exceptions to this generalization.

Concepts in Brief

- Some policymakers believe that a large capital stock is a prerequisite for economic growth and development. They therefore suggest that developing countries need more capital.
- The human element, however, is vital; the labour force must be capable of using any capital that the developing country acquires. This requires training and education.
- Saving is a prerequisite for capital formation.
- Saving goes on even in poor developing countries, although not necessarily in the same form as in rich developed countries.
- Saving and individual capital accumulation will be greater the more certain individuals are about the safety of their wealth.

THE IMPORTANCE OF AN OPEN ECONOMY

The data are conclusive: Open economies experience faster economic development than economies closed to international trade. That is to say, the less government protects the domestic economy by imposing trade barriers, the faster that economy will experience economic development. According to a study by economists Nouriel Roubini and Xavier Sala-i-Martin, when a country goes from being relatively open to relatively closed via government-enacted trade barriers, it will have a 2.5 percentage point decrease in its growth rate.

Open economies accomplish several things. For one, individuals and businesses end up specializing in those endeavours in which they have a comparative advantage. International trade encourages individuals and businesses to discover ways to specialize so that they can become more productive and earn higher incomes. Increased productivity and the subsequent increase in the rate of economic development are the results. Open economies also allow the importation of already developed technology. For instance, no developing country today needs to spend years to figure out how to make computers or how to use them; that has already been done elsewhere.

The True Cost of Protectionism

A statistical study of the cost of trade barriers might give the impression that taxes on imported goods simply raise their price to domestic consumers. But there is another cost that is normally hidden. Statisticians call it a *Type II error*—the cost of omission. It is the cost of what would have been had there not been tariff barriers. The best example of a Type II error is the cost of overregulating the pharmaceutical industry. If it causes fewer lifesaving drugs to be introduced, it is a Type II error. When trade is restricted in a developing country, that country's people are deprived of a potential larger range of new goods and production processes. Such new foreign products could spur local support businesses, which in turn would cause other businesses to be created. Developing countries that have restricted the entry of computer products have clearly slowed down the development of their own software industry. Trade barriers sometimes guarantee that new goods and services never appear in protected countries. According to economist Paul Romer, because of protectionism, many developing countries do not simply cut back on their consumption of the entire range of goods available to rich countries; rather, they use a smaller quantity of a much smaller range of goods. He calculates that the cumulative forgone benefits from new economic activity blocked by an across-the-board 10 percent tariff in a developing country might be as high as 20 percent of annual national income.

THE IMPORTANCE OF AN EDUCATED POPULATION

Both theoretically and empirically, we know that a more educated workforce aids economic development because it allows individuals to build on the ideas of others. According to economists David Gould and Roy Ruffin, increasing the rate of enrolment in secondary schools by only two percentage points, from 8 to 10 percent, raises the average rate of economic growth by half a percent per year. Thus we must conclude that developing countries can advance more rapidly if they invest more heavily in secondary education. Or stated in the negative, economic development cannot be sustained if a country allows a sizable portion of its population to avoid education. After all, education allows young people who grew up poor to acquire skills that enable them to avoid poverty as adults.

Some of the fastest-growing countries in the world, including the Four Tigers, virtually eliminated illiteracy very early on.

INTERNATIONAL POLICY EXAMPLE
Should School Tuition Vouchers Be Used in Developing Countries?

Nobel Prize–winning economist Gary Becker has argued in favour of a school voucher system in developing countries. According to his scheme, low-income parents would receive the vouchers, which could then be used at any approved school in their country. The participating schools would also have to provide meals for their students. According to Becker, such vouchers would stimulate competition among private and public schools in developing countries. There is a problem for very poor families, however. They want their children to work to provide income. Becker suggests that such families be given a bonus that offsets the income loss while their children are going to school.

For critical analysis: Do parents in developed countries have to be compensated for sending their children to school? Explain.

LETTING COMPANIES DISAPPEAR: CREATIVE DESTRUCTION

Economist Joseph Schumpeter (1883–1950) championed the concept of *creative destruction*. He pointed out that new technologies and successful new businesses end up destroying old jobs, old companies, and old industries. Change is painful and costly, but it is necessary for economic advancement. Nowhere is this more important than in developing countries, where the principle is often ignored.

Developing countries have had a history of supporting current companies and industries by preventing new technologies and new companies from entering the marketplace. The process of creative destruction has not been allowed to work its magic.

One key element in providing the most favourable condition for economic development is allowing businesses to fail. A corollary to this principle is that governments should not consistently use their taxpayers' money to subsidize or even own businesses. It does little good (and normally a lot of harm) for governments in developing countries to own banks, phone companies, electric companies, car companies, or airlines. There are few historical examples of state-owned companies doing other than one thing—draining the public coffers.

Do not get the impression that government-owned and -operated businesses are run by individuals who are somehow less competent than those in the private sector. Rather, the incentive structure for managers in private businesses is different from that for managers in state-owned businesses.

THE RELATIONSHIP BETWEEN POPULATION GROWTH AND ECONOMIC DEVELOPMENT

World population is growing at the rate of 2.8 people each and every second. That turns out to be 242,000 a day, or 88.3 million a year. Today, there are about 5.8 billion people on earth. By the year 2030, according to the United Nations, there will be 8.5 billion. Look at Figure 20.1 (page 488) to see which countries are growing the most.

Now look at Figure 20.2 (page 488). There you see that virtually all of the growth in population comes from developing countries. Some countries, such as Germany, are expected to lose population over the next several decades.

The Conventional Wisdom

Ever since the Reverend Thomas Robert Malthus wrote his essay *The Principle of Population* in 1798, excessive population growth has been a concern. Modern-day Malthusians are able to generate just as much enthusiasm for the concept that population growth is bad. We are told that rapid population growth threatens economic development and the quality of life. This message was made loud and clear by numerous participants in the United Nations' International Conference on Population and Development held in Cairo, Egypt, in the fall of 1994.

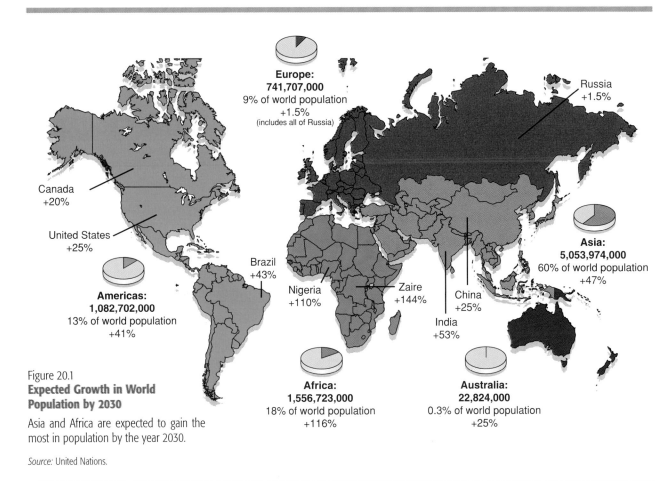

Figure 20.1
Expected Growth in World Population by 2030

Asia and Africa are expected to gain the most in population by the year 2030.

Source: United Nations.

Figure 20.2
Population Growth by 2050

Population will increase dramatically in the developing countries. The industrially advanced countries will grow very little in population over the next half century.

Source: United States Population Reference Bureau.

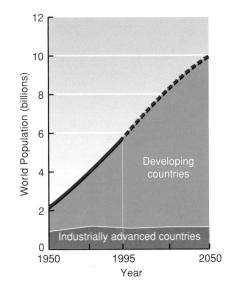

Figure 20.3
Population and Food Supplies

Malthus has been proved wrong: Population has not out-stripped the world's food sup-ply. In fact, for at least the past half century, calories consumed per person have been increas-ing at a rate even faster than the increase in population.

Source: United States Department of Agriculture.

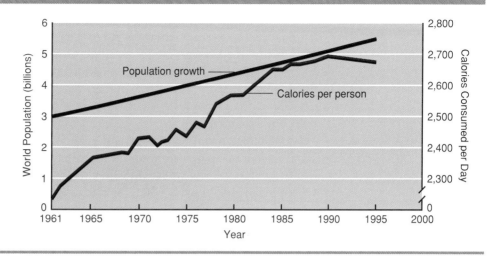

What the Data Show. First of all, according to economist Nicholas Eberstadt, Malthus's prediction that population would outstrip food supplies has never held true for the entire world. Figure 20.3 shows how population has grown over the past 35 years. At the same time, the food supply, measured by calories per person, has also increased somewhat steadily.

Also, the price of food, corrected for inflation, has been falling steadily for over a century. That means that the supply of food is expanding faster than the demand caused by increased population.

Population Density and Economic Development. There is no consistent rela-tionship between population density and economic development. Japan, for example, has a higher per capita income than many Western European countries, yet it has more peo-ple per square kilometre than India, one of the poorest countries. Hong Kong is the most densely populated country. Fifty years ago it was one of the poorest, but today its per capi-ta income exceeds that in France and the United Kingdom. (Hong Kong has almost no natural resources either—it has to import even its drinking water.) As a general proposi-tion, some of the richest countries in the world today are the most densely populated—South Korea, Taiwan, Belgium, the Netherlands, England, Germany, and Japan.

The Relationship Between Population Growth Rates and Economic Development. Again there seems to be little relationship between economic devel-opment and rapid population growth. Consider Malaysia, which grew from a sparsely populated country of villages in the 1890s to a country of cities in the 1930s. During this period, its population increased from 1.5 million to 6 million, but its standard of living also increased, by about 140 percent. Historically, the largest increases in Western living standards took place during the period when the Western population was growing faster than it is in today's developing countries. Also, in spite of relatively high population growth rates, per capita incomes in many, if not most, developing countries are much higher today than they were four decades ago. Much of the population growth in devel-oping countries has occurred because both adults and children live longer than they used to, not necessarily because families are having more children. There are just fewer deaths caused by malnutrition and contagious diseases than there used to be.

The Relationship Between Average Family Income and Size

One thing that economists know for sure is that over the past century, as countries became richer, the average family size fell. Otherwise stated, the more economic development occurs, the slower the population growth rate. Predictions of birthrates in developing countries have often turned out to be overstated if those countries experience rapid economic growth. This was the case in Hong Kong, Mexico, Taiwan, and Colombia.

Recent research on population and economic development has revealed that social and economic modernization has been accompanied by what might be called a fertility revolution—the spread of deliberate family size limitation within marriage and a decline in childbearing. Modernization reduces infant mortality, which in turn reduces the incentive for couples to have many children to make sure that enough will survive to satisfy each couple's demand. Also, modernization lowers the demand for children for a variety of reasons, not least being that couples in more developed countries do not need to rely on their children to take care of them in old age.

Population and Productivity

Specialization turns out to be a function of the size of the market, which is, of course, a function of population. Thus a growing population can help improve the quality of life because it allows individuals to devote their talents to what they are best suited to do—whatever their comparative advantage is. Individuals don't "exhaust" the earth's resources. People create wealth through imagination and innovation. It was not all that long ago that oil was considered useless. So was sand; today, it is used to make silicone and glass from which computer chips and fibre optics are manufactured.

Three hundred years ago, there were one-tenth the number of humans who now live. Yet the world is incredibly more wealthy than it was three centuries ago. Today, there are six times as many Canadians as there were 100 years ago. Yet today we live longer and are about seven times richer per capita.

FOREIGN AID

Many countries, including Canada, extend assistance to developing countries. A number of reasons are given to justify this assistance, which can be in the form of grants, low-interest loans, food, or technical expertise. Although the humanitarian argument in support of foreign aid is often given, security and economics also enter into the discussion. During the Cold War, many Western nations gave foreign aid to developing countries in order to support noncommunist régimes or to prevent communist takeovers. Canada also extends foreign aid to help develop foreign markets for the output of Canadian firms. This is particularly true when foreign aid is tied to the purchase of Canadian products. Tied foreign aid requires that the recipient spend all or part of the sum extended as foreign aid on Canadian-produced goods.

The Results of Foreign Aid

Since the end of World War II, the developed world has transferred about $2.4 trillion (in today's dollars) to developing countries. The results have been mixed. According to one study by economist Peter Bauer, there is little correlation between the level of foreign aid received and changes in living standards. He also found that foreign aid did not necessarily reduce infant mortality rates. His conclusion was that foreign aid simply raised the standard of living of the recipient countries' richest people.

Consider Tanzania. Between 1970 and 1988, this African country received $8.6 billion in aid, four times that country's 1988 gross domestic product. This is the equivalent of someone giving Canada around $3 trillion. During the same period, Sudan was given $9.6 billion, an amount equal to one year's output. Zaire, Togo, Zambia, Mozambique, and Niger each received around $6 billion during the same period. What happened to these billions of dollars? In all of these countries, gross output actually fell. Critics of foreign aid point out that much of the money went into new government centres, showy airports, and grand conference halls. Some of it also went into government officials' Swiss bank accounts. According to economist George Ayittey, Zaire ex-president Mobutu Sese Seko was worth $10 billion at his death, and Zambia's Kenneth Kaunda is currently worth $6 billion.

INTERNATIONAL EXAMPLE
The World Bank and the Development of Poor Countries (or Lack Thereof)

The International Bank for Reconstruction and Development, known as the World Bank, was established in 1944. To date it has lent over $300 billion, mostly to poor countries. However, its accomplishments have recently been questioned. For example, since 1951, India has received $55 billion—more foreign aid than any other country on earth—yet over 40 percent of India's population still lives in poverty. In sub-Saharan Africa, massive amounts of money have gone into development planning, yet that region has a lower per capita income than it did before it received aid.

Another criticism of the World Bank is that its lending policies during the 1970s encouraged large-scale, capital-intensive technology, which helped governments in less developed countries to plunder their natural resources. These large-scale projects displaced millions of poor and tribal peoples. In India, World Bank development projects uprooted over 20 million people. Throughout the world, dam projects have altered natural ecologies. Indeed, a mid-1990's internal review of the bank's lending portfolio found that almost 40 percent of recently evaluated projects did not adhere to established environmental and social policies.

The major problem with the World Bank's lending activities is that they help government bureaucracies flourish with funds that could be used to help individuals in the host countries.

For critical analysis: How does lending to governments in less developed countries hinder market reforms?

Concepts in Brief

- The openness of an economy can determine its rate, or lack thereof, of economic development. Open economies allow, among other things, the importation of technology from the rest of the world.
- The more educated the workforce, the greater the chance of successful economic development, so enrolment in secondary schools is a key determinant of economic growth.
- While many believe population growth hinders economic development, there is little historic relationship between either population density or growth rates and economic growth rates.
- Critics of foreign aid point out that foreign aid will not increase the rate of economic growth unless a well-functioning capital base and infrastructure are in place.

Issues and Applications

Can PCs Bridge the Gap Between Less Advanced and More Advanced Economics?

Concepts Applied: International trade, technology, open economies

The PC revolution allows less advanced economies to benefit from new technology at a low investment cost and at a faster rate than in already developed countries.

The PC revolution is showing up in the world's developing countries, sometimes at a faster pace than in Canada. In its wake is a quickly narrowing competitive gap between the more advanced and the less advanced economies. There are several reasons the PC may be at the heart of improved economies in developing countries.

Low-Price Accessibility

Even in the developed countries, the PC revolution would never have happened without dramatic improvements in microprocessors, memory chips, and software, all occurring while prices continue to drop. Computer technology is now economically viable for most businesses except in the extremely poor countries, according to Eduardo Talero, information technology specialist at the World Bank.

"Necessity: The Mother of Invention"

Another reason PC technology has taken off in some countries is simply that it was needed. The advanced home-banking system in Brazil referred to at the beginning of this chapter did depend on cheap technology and software. Also, high inflation rates in Brazil have meant that people who did not deposit their earnings immediately would see the real value of their wealth drop through inflation. Home banking allows for instantaneous transfers of earnings. Necessity is the mother of invention.

The Benefit of Being a Latecomer

Perhaps just as important for developing countries, the fact that they are latecomers has helped them tremendously. Developing countries by definition have had low levels of technology in their business infrastructure. Consequently, they have not invested large amounts in old systems, such as IBM mainframe computers. When the PC revolution came along, they were able to take advantage of it without waiting for their old equipment to wear out. Economic theory predicts that late starters—developing countries—can benefit from new technology at a much faster rate than the already developed countries. And that is what has been happening.

Bringing Down the Trade Barriers

The developing countries that have reduced their trade barriers fastest have seen technology circulate the most freely and have experienced the greatest benefits. Many Latin American countries are leading the way by allowing unfettered imports of computer equipment and software. The PC market in Latin America is growing at a rate of almost 25 percent a year. Sales in Eastern Europe are growing at 15 percent a year. Software sales are growing even faster.

For Critical Analysis

1. Why do latecomers adopt technology faster than already established economies?

2. Why is an open economy necessary for technological innovation to spread rapidly?

CHAPTER SUMMARY

1. The 19 industrially advanced countries (IACs)— Canada, the United States, Japan, and the countries of Western Europe—have market economies based on a large skilled labour force and a large technically advanced stock of capital goods.

2. One of the major characteristics of developing countries is a high rate of population growth. However, high population growth does not necessarily prevent or retard economic development.

3. Some authorities contend that balanced development of industry and agriculture is necessary for growth in the developing countries. There are, however, exceptions to this rule; Hong Kong is one.

4. Industrialization in many developing countries has involved subsidization of manufacturing. Such subsidization leads to a misallocation of resources and to a lower per capita standard of living for the population even though the country may become more highly industrialized.

5. Capital accumulation is an important determinant of economic development. However, massive transfers of capital to developing countries do not guarantee economic development. Appropriately trained personnel must be available to use the capital given to these countries.

6. Domestic capital formation requires saving—nonconsumption of current income. Even the poorest countries' citizens do some saving. In fact, there is no pronounced relationship between percentage of income saved and level of income.

7. Saving in the developing countries may take on different forms than in more developed countries. For example, having children is a form of saving if those children feel an obligation to support their parents during retirement.

8. The more certain private property rights are, the more private capital accumulation there will be, other things being equal.

DISCUSSION OF PREVIEW QUESTIONS

1. What is a developing country?

Developing countries are arbitrarily defined as those with very low per capita incomes. Relative to developed countries, people in developing countries have lower incomes, life expectancies, literacy rates, and daily caloric intake, and higher infant mortality rates.

2. Must developing countries develop by industrializing?

Proponents of the balanced-growth theory point out that the industrially advanced countries (IACs) are highly industrialized and the developing countries are mostly agrarian. They feel that balanced growth requires that the developing countries expand the manufacturing sector; labourers and other resources should be reallocated to promote industrialization. It is often suggested that the developing countries restrict imports of nonagricultural goods to help industrialization. It is alleged that these countries must industrialize even if their comparative advantage lies in the production of agricultural goods because they can't compete with the subsidized agricultural sectors of the IACs. Yet it is easy to oversell the pro-industrialization balanced-growth approach. Numerous examples of gross inefficiency can be cited when the developing countries attempted to develop steel and automobile industries. Moreover, when the developing countries restrict the imports of manufactured goods, they lower living standards and promote inefficiency. It would seem that the time to develop the industrial sector would be when it is profitable for businesses to do so.

3. Can developing countries create their own capital stock?

It is often asserted that a large capital stock is necessary for economic development, the developing countries are too poor to save sufficient amounts to develop domestic capital formation, and the IACs should therefore give capital to the developing countries. Experts disagree about the validity of each contention. The question under discussion here deals with the second proposition. A good deal of evidence exists to support the notion that the developing countries do save—although in forms that are not easily observed or cannot be readily converted into capital. Even people with extremely low incomes are forced by economic circumstances to provide for future consumption; they often store dried or cured food. On a nationwide scale, much evidence of capital formation exists: cathedrals, pyramids, great walls, fortresses, government buildings, and so on. Of course, the problem is to get savings into forms that can be used to produce goods or services.

4. Does a lack of protected property rights hinder a developing country's development?

Yes. When individuals fear that their property rights will not be protected, they invest in ways that reflect this risk. Thus people in politically and economically unstable countries prefer to accumulate diamonds, gold, silver, and currency in foreign banks rather than invest in factories, equipment, and savings in domestic bank accounts. Similarly, a country that expropriates property or nationalizes industry discourages investment by foreign businesses. Many developing countries could be aided to a great extent by attracting foreign investment—but foreign investors will require property rights guarantees.

PROBLEMS

(Answers to the odd-numbered problems appear at the back of the book.)

20-1. List five developing countries and five industrially advanced countries.

20-2. What problems are associated with advancements in medicine and health that are made available to developing countries?

20-3. Outline a typical pattern of economic development.

20-4. Suppose that you are shown the following data for two countries, known only as country X and country Z:

Country	GDP	Population
X	$ 81 billion	9 million
Z	$135 billion	90 million

a. From this information, which country would you expect to be classified as a developing country? Why?

b. Now suppose that you were also given the following data:

Country	Life Expectancy at Birth (years)	Infant Mortality per 1,000 Live Births	Literacy (%)
X	70	15	60
Z	58	50	70

Are these figures consistent with your answer to part (a)?

c. Should we expect the developing country identified in part (a) to have a much greater population density than the other country?

20-5. Would unrestricted labour immigration end up helping or hurting developing countries? Explain.

20-6. Many countries in Africa have extremely large potential stocks of natural resources. Nonetheless, those natural resources often remain unexploited. Give reasons why this situation continues to exist.

20-7. Sketch a scenario in which population growth causes an increase in income per capita.

20-8. Visit the Organisation for Economic Cooperation and Development (OECD) development indicators Web site at http://www.oecd.org/dac/Indicators/htm/list.htm.

a. What indicators of general development does the OECD use?

b. Now open the general development indicators table. List four of the poorest countries according to per capita GDP. (For example, countries with per capita GDP less than US$500.) What is the life expectancy in these countries?

c. List four of the richer countries according to per capita GDP. (Countries with per capita GDP greater than US$10,000.) What is the life expectancy in these countries?

d. What conclusions can you draw about life expectancy and economic wealth as represented by per capita GDP? Which set of countries would you expect to experience more rapid economic development? Why?

INTERACTING WITH THE INTERNET

Summary macroeconomic data on most countries of the world, including developing ones, can be found in the Penn World Tables at

http://www.nber.org/pwt56.html

If the release number of the data changes, it might be necessary to search from

http://www.nber.org

The World Bank maintains two sites with valuable information on economic development. Perhaps the more important is "Social Indicators of Development," which covers a wide variety of health, demographic, and economic information. It is found at

http://www.ciesin.org/IC/wbank/sid-home.html

Brief reports on countries that borrow from the World Bank are contained in "Trends in Developing Economies," which is located at

http://www.ciesin.org/IC/wbank/tde-home.html

Cybernomics

In the days before inexpensive cassette recorders, record companies did not have to worry about piracy. It was simply too expensive for bootleggers to copy records. Then the cassette recorder became so cheap that pirated versions of popular records were common. Many people made copies for friends, not for profit. Next, with the advent of relatively cheap compact disc reproduction, bootlegged CDs started to show up worldwide. Go to any flea market in many parts of the world, and you can find CDs of live performances by well-known recording artists. These are not copies of existing CDs but unauthorized performance reproductions, for which the artists get paid nothing. Now the digital world has added a new twist—massive copyright violations over the Internet—and with the possibility of perfect quality. How will artists and recording companies cope with the possible onslaught of massive bootlegging? Before you tackle this issue, you need to know a little more about the impact of the Internet on our economic system.

Preview Questions

1. How does technological change affect the demand for labour?

2. What is the main reason the Internet may lead to increased efficiency?

3. If different tax jurisdictions each take their "piece" of an Internet transaction, what might be the long-run result?

4. Why does the software business seem to belie the traditional law of diminishing marginal returns?

CHAPTER OUTLINE

- A World of Continuous Change
- The Age of Information
- Efficiency, Transaction Costs, and E-Commerce
- The Increasing Importance of Brands
- Taxes and the Internet
- The Micro Theory of Business Behaviour with the Internet Added

▶ **Protocol**

The data formatting system that permits computers to access each other and communicate.

▶ **Cybernomics**

The application of economic analysis to human and technological activities related to the use of the Internet in all of its forms.

Did You Know That... the Internet has its origins in a 1966 United States government program designed to provide a communications network for defence-related research that could survive a nuclear calamity? The program, called the Advanced Research Projects Agency Network, soon became the favourite form of communication for researchers and academics in non-defence-related fields. Then the US National Science Foundation established a distributed network, which greatly increased the traffic. The current system is based on a common addressing system and communications **protocol** that was created in 1983. The world has never been the same.

In this chapter, you will explore the new world of **cybernomics**. You will find out about the growing world of electronic commerce, banking, and finance. In addition, you will find out about the changes it is bringing in the theory of the firm, monopoly, and labour markets.

A WORLD OF CONTINUOUS CHANGE

As with all technological changes, there are losers and winners. The cyberspace revolution is creating many winners and, of course, some losers. That is not new. Decades ago, when elevator control systems were automated, elevator operators lost their jobs. When optical character recognition systems were perfected, bank employees who manually sorted cheques were laid off. As word processing systems have become easier to use, the need for typing specialists has diminished. Technological change will almost always reduce the demand for traditional labour services, but at the same time it will increase the demand for new types of labour services. The fear of technological change has been around for centuries, as you can see in the following example.

INTERNATIONAL EXAMPLE

Luddites Unite Against Automated Textile Machinery

In the vicinity of Nottingham, England, towards the end of 1811, an organized band of craftsmen started riots with the aim of destroying the textile machines that were replacing them. The members of the band were called Luddites, after an imaginary leader known as King Ludd. Bands of Luddites were generally masked and operated at night. They were often supported by the local townspeople—but certainly not by threatened employers. One employer, a man named Horsfall, ordered his supporters to open fire on a band of them in 1812. The Luddite movement eventually lost steam by 1817, when prosperity again reigned in England.

For critical analysis: What are some other technological changes that have created job losses?

Try Preview Question 1:

How does technological change affect the demand for labour?

THE AGE OF INFORMATION

Let there be no mistake, the information age is here. What is one of the most important industries in Canada? The answer is information technology, or IT. Sales of the Canadian computing and telecommunications industry have almost doubled during the 1990s, to $70 billion a year. In 1996, the IT sector of the economy accounted for 7.2 percent of GDP. Employment in the IT sector now accounts for around 420,000 workers and is growing. The average IT worker earns wages that are about 60 to 70 percent greater than the average wage in the private sector. This growing sector of the economy consists of high-tech companies that are generating new work practices and new challenges in public policy.

Household and Business Use of the Internet

Figure 21.1 shows the rise in the percentage of households that have a link to the Internet. At the beginning of the 1990s, the number was virtually zero; at the end of 1995, approximately 10 percent of Canadians had Internet access. By the end of 1997, that ratio had increased to about 25 percent—approximately 7 to 8 million Canadians regularly accessing the Internet. Internet users are, on average, highly educated, earn high incomes and spend more than the average Canadian. No wonder businesses are eager to reach out to Internet users!

For the moment, the greatest use of the Internet is electronic mail, or e-mail. Canadian businesses alone send about a billion e-mail messages a year, and that figure is likely to increase. The number of Internet hosts has increased from a few thousand in 1988 to about 20 million today. Worldwide, about 200 million global citizens are connected to the Net. Some estimates for the year 2030 put that number well over a billion.

Figure 21.1
The Internet Invades Canada

Perhaps no other innovation has caught on so quickly in Canada. Not only are more people connecting to the Internet, but they are also using it more. Data for the year 2005 has been estimated for the retailing industry.

Source: Industry Canada, *Canadian Internet Retailing Report.*

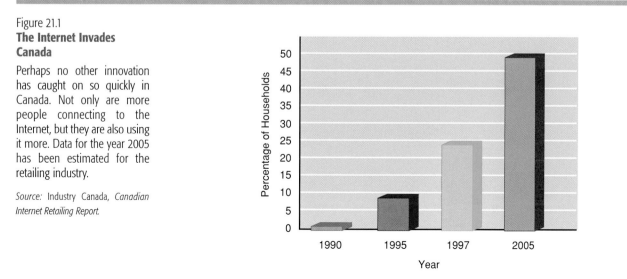

EFFICIENCY, TRANSACTION COSTS, AND E-COMMERCE

In Chapter 4, you learned that individuals turn to markets because markets reduce the costs of exchange, which are called transaction costs. Remember that these are defined as the costs associated with finding out exactly what is being transacted, as well as the cost of enforcing contracts. Entrepreneurs since the beginning of time have attempted to make markets more efficient by figuring out ways to reduce transaction costs.

A big part of transaction costs is the cost of obtaining information. Buyers need information about sellers—their existence, the goods and services they offer, and the prices of those goods and services. A stroll through one's local mall may be a pastime for some, but it is a costly activity for all—time usually does not have a zero opportunity cost. The advent of mail-order shopping reduced transaction costs for many. It also introduced additional competition for retailers located in remote cities. After all, one no longer had to rely solely on the local camera store once camera ads from stores in Toronto and elsewhere started appearing in nationally available print publications.

The Web as a Reducer of Transaction Costs

Enter the Internet and the World Wide Web. The existence of information about numerous goods and services, such as automobiles and cameras, via the Web simply means that transaction costs are being further reduced. This should make the market work more efficiently, and should lead to less variation in price per constant-quality unit for any good offered for sale.

Business-to-Business E-Commerce

▶ **e-commerce**
The use of the Internet in any manner that allows buyers and sellers to find each other. It can involve business selling directly to other businesses or business selling to retail customers. Both goods and services are involved in e-commerce.

The first place that **e-commerce** has been extensively used is for the sale of goods between businesses. A good example is Cisco Systems, Inc., a major producer of Internet computer routers. It estimates that over 40 percent of its orders are already handled through the Internet—to the tune of about US$5 billion a year. The benefits to Cisco of taking orders on-line are many: faster service for its customers, quicker production cycles, and savings on labour and printing charges. Cisco believes that it has reduced overall costs by more than $500 million a year by relying so heavily on e-commerce.

As might be expected, the first companies to take full advantage of the ease of ordering through the Internet have been those involved in information technology, particularly computers and computer parts. If current trends continue, the government estimates that e-commerce in Canada should account for $50 billion to $150 billion of sales by the year 2000.

"E-'Tailing"

While the growth rate in e-commerce at the retail level has been impressive, the total dollar volume is still a mere drop in the bucket compared to retail sales through normal retail outlets. An increasing proportion of Internet users are willing to purchase via the Net, but they do not do so on a regular basis. One issue that concerns retail customers is security. They worry that it is too easy for their credit card number to be stolen off the Net by individuals who wish to use it for fraudulent purposes. The real problem area, though, involves Internet merchants, particularly those selling software for immediate download, for these people have been the victims of cybercrimes much more than consumers who have had their credit cards "lifted" out of cyberspace.

Cybershopping Crooks.   The ease of selling software over the Internet also makes it easy for cybershoppers to defraud Internet sellers of software provided on-line. Occasionally, CyberSource, the owner of the on-line retail source Software.Net, experiences more fraudulent sales than legitimate ones. Cybercrooks use someone else's credit card number to order the software. CyberSource downloads the software almost instantaneously. By the time the seller discovers the fraud, the buyer has a copy of the software and can resell it.

On-line software sellers have struck back. They have developed a computer model that looks at 150 factors to calculate the risk of fraud for any particular purchase. Any on-line company can pay about $1.00 to have a pending credit card request run through the model. There is also an ever more complete name-fraud database that can be used as a reference point.

Better Encryption.   Encryption systems—software systems that prevent anyone else from obtaining information provided on-line—are getting better all the time. Both Netscape's Navigator and Microsoft's Internet Explorer browsers have built-in encryption systems. On-line retailers are developing even better ones. Given the demand for a system that is totally secure, we can predict that concerns over losing a credit card number in cyberspace will virtually disappear over time. In any event, even current encryption systems are much more secure than a telephone conversation with a mail-order company operator to whom you give your credit card number in order to have goods shipped to you.

Using Intelligent Shopping Agents

▶ **Intelligent shopping agents**

Computer programs that an individual or business user of the Internet can instruct to carry out a specific task such as looking for the lowest-priced car of a particular make and model. The agent then searches the Internet (usually just the World Wide Web) and may even purchase the product when the best price has been found.

Intelligent shopping agents are software programs that search the Web to find a specific item that you specify. Using these agents saves the time you might have to spend searching all potential sites through your browser. Suppose that you wanted to order a pair of pants. An intelligent shopping agent would ask you for essential descriptions and then go searching on the Web.

A new software program called XML—for "extensible markup language"—will assist intelligent shopping agents. Preparing a Web home page in XML makes the Web site smart enough to tell other machines what is inside in great detail. In essence, XML puts "tags" on Web pages that describe bits of information. Each group of on-line businesses—travel, financial services, and so on—will have its own set of agreed-on tags. This will allow searching intelligent shopping agents to "flip through" all of the Web sources for a particular item more easily.

Suppose that you are considering the purchase of some airline tickets in the middle of a fare price war. You are not sure how low the ticket prices are going to go.

In the near future, you will be able to tell your intelligent shopping agent to keep looking for a lower fare as the airlines change prices on a daily basis. When the agent finds the best price, it can automatically order the tickets on your behalf.

The development of XML along with better intelligent shopping agents is crucial for the most efficient utilization of the Web. Currently, there are over 450,000 commercial sites selling products on-line, and the number is sure to increase rapidly. In the meantime, certain search engines, such as Excite, offer services to compare listed prices from various cyberstores for a desired product.

The Trend Away from Mass Merchandising

Electronic retailing may reverse the trend towards mass merchandising that we have seen over the past 50 years. This reversal has already taken place in the computer industry. Computer mail-order pioneer Dell does not even start the production of a computer until the customer selects all the features—size of hard drive, amount of memory, processor speed, modem speed, and so on. Over 10 percent of Dell's orders are now through the Internet. Dell asks the customer each feature it wants and gives a menu. Apple is doing the same thing on a full selection of its latest computers. Levi Strauss and Company has a customized jeans site on the Internet—a type of on-line fitting room. A similar plan has been put forth by Custom Foot, a large shoe retailer.

CYBERSPACE EXAMPLE
Buying a Car on the Net

They said it could never be done—selling cars in cyberspace. After all, the thinking went, before purchasing such an expensive item, consumers would want to "kick the tires." For most consumers, that is still true. But a growing number now use the Internet to search for the best price on exactly the car they want. And many more have discovered that the most painless way to start looking for a car is on the Net. You can go to the Auto-net-Guide™ site at www.autonet.ca where you can take a look at all your options in order to narrow your choices.

Once you know what you want, you can start shopping for the actual car via the numerous Web sites for dealers throughout the country. Some dealers are making more than 10 percent of their total sales via the Web. You can also use an on-line car-buying service that processes orders and forwards them to dealers. America's Big Three—Chrysler, General Motors, and Ford—now have their own on-line selling sites.

For critical analysis: Car dealers argue that on-line auto shopping will destroy customer bonds. Why should this matter?

The Advent of the Internet Shopping Mall

Perhaps the wave of the future in Internet retail shopping is the equivalent of today's shopping mall. The biggest player in on-line shopping malls is netMarket.com. Sales for 1997 were US$1.2 billion, and the company anticipates that its sales will more than double every year into the foreseeable future. The netMarket site sells everything from books and videos to cars, travel, CDs, and kitchen appliances. Within the next several years, netMarket will sell about 95 percent of the goods purchased by a typical household. The on-line firm netMarket is like a club warehouse, for it charges about a $75 annual fee. In effect, though, netMarket is not a mall. Rather, it's a megastore that uses the best specialized retailers' efficiencies and discounts. Unlike the typical megastore, such as Wal-Mart or a club warehouse, such as PriceCostco, on-line megastores carry no inventory. They simply pass the orders on electronically to distributors or manufacturers, who then ship the goods from their own warehouses directly to the buyers.

Reduction in the Demand for Retail Space

If more shopping will be done over the Internet in the future, less shopping will be done in traditional retail outlets. Even in those retail outlets that exist, customization may be the order of the day because of new digital scanning and manufacturing systems. Some Levi's stores in the US already allow customers to be scanned electronically to order perfectly fitting jeans. There are also a few stores where customers' feet are scanned electronically for custom-made shoes. If more consumers opt for such custom-made items, retail stores will carry much smaller inventories, keeping on hand only samples or computerized images.

Try Preview Question 2:
What is the main reason the Internet may lead to increased efficiency?

The result will be a reduced demand for commercial retail space. Moreover, there will be a reduced demand for trucking to haul inventory, for electricity to light and heat retail space, and for the paper that is used for all the ordering.

Concepts in Brief

- Extensive use of the Web will lead to greater efficiency through a reduction in transaction costs.
- Most e-commerce is between businesses today.
- Retail business will expand as better encryption methods are used for protecting credit card numbers.
- Internet retailing requires no inventory costs for "malls" that simply send orders to other companies for fulfilment.
- If more Internet retailing occurs, the demand for traditional retail space will decrease over time.

THE INCREASING IMPORTANCE OF BRANDS

Brands have value because they indicate to potential purchasers of a brand-name item that a strong and successful company stands behind it. Successful companies typically have well-recognized brands—think of Seagram's, Microsoft, Levi's, Mercedes-Benz, Sony, Nike. In the world of e-commerce, cybershoppers will increasingly look for branded items to satisfy their purchase desires. Why? Because there will be no salesperson extolling the virtues of a perhaps lower-priced but less well known item.

Brands Created on the Net

That does not rule out new brands establishing themselves on the Net. A case in point is Amazon.com. The most successful virtual bookseller, Amazon.com didn't even exist before it went on-line. Nonetheless, it has established its brand name as a reputable place to purchase books. Amazon offers incentives to other Web site owners to link with it. If you link your Web site to Amazon, you get a 3 to 8 percent commission on each book purchase made by anyone who follows that link and buys that book from Amazon. Because Amazon orders only books that customers have agreed to buy, the return rate is less than one-quarter of 1 percent, versus 30 to 40 percent for the industry overall.

Reputation on the Web is crucial for success. The CEO of Amazon.com makes it clear: "This is the Web. If people feel mistreated by us, they don't tell five people—they tell 5,000."

CYBERSPACE EXAMPLE
Selling CDs On-Line

While Amazon.com is busily selling books on-line, the music industry has had a slower start. According to Juniper Communications, on-line music purchases represent less than half a percent of the US industry's $20 billion total sales. Some small companies are nonetheless doing well. Internet Underground Music Archive at www.iuma.com started in business by selling CDs of bands that were not yet under contract. Today, it carries over 1,000 bands, gets a quarter of a million "hits" (visitors to its site) a day, and is selling CDs at the rate of $1.5 million a day. The on-line CD purchaser gets to listen to a sample song before purchase, and also typically spends less than at a regular retail CD store. Many minor artists are starting their own Web sites to publicize their works and sell them, too.

The real future in on-line CD sales will begin when Web surfers can quickiy and easily download entire albums in digital quality onto blank CDs.

For critical analysis: Who will be affected most by the on-line downloading of digital-quality CDs?

Marketing and Advertising on the Net

If you are marketing a product and you have 20 potential purchasers, you can use the phone to call them. If you want to reach 20 million potential purchasers, you take out a TV ad during the Olympics. What do you do if you want to reach 10,000 people? Typically, you engage in direct-mail advertising, at a cost of 50 cents to $1 per person targeted. But now you've got the Internet. In principle, the Net makes it easier to reach more finely-targeted audiences and to communicate with them. Consider an example. You are using the search engine InfoSeek, and you enter the keywords "airline tickets." When you do so, a banner ad for Dell's pentium computers will appear on top of the resulting list of potential Web sites.

The key difference between a similar-looking ad on a TV screen and one on your computer is important—you can click on the one on your computer for an instant response. For TV advertising (and space ads in newspapers and magazines, too), there is no way of really knowing how many people's behaviour is truly changed. With Internet advertising, all you have to do is count the number of "click-throughs." If Dell finds out that its Pentium computer ad on InfoSeek has only a 1 percent click-through rate, it will rethink that particular type of advertising.

The future of Internet advertising is impressive. America Online (AOL) already has more "viewers" than any single cable television network and more "readers" than most popular magazines. As Internet service providers, browsers, home pages, and the like attract larger and larger audiences, the potential for more extensive advertising is dramatic. Currently, Internet advertising revenues represent only a few percent of the annual $55 billion spent on television advertising. But that proportion will change.

TAXES AND THE INTERNET

Canada has some 8,000 tax jurisdictions. In addition to the 10 provinces and 2 territories, there are thousands of municipalities as well as other taxing districts. Not surprisingly, many of these tax jurisdictions are looking covetously at e-commerce. But there is a big potential problem: taxation confusion.

A single Internet transaction does not just go from one entity to another. The nature of the Internet is such that servers may be located virtually anywhere in the world, and the transaction from one end point to the other may be routed through half a dozen servers in numerous tax jurisdictions. Virtually every tax jurisdiction in Canada has different fees and regulations. If all jurisdictions started imposing their tax structures on every Internet transaction, the result would be total confusion. This chaos would discourage firms from getting involved in electronic commerce and would slow the growth of the use of the Internet.

In October 1998, representatives of 29 member countries of the Organisation for Economic Co-operation and Development (OECD) met in Ottawa to discuss taxation of e-commerce. They agreed that any taxation should be simple, fair, efficient, effective, certain, and flexible. They also agreed that consumption (sales) taxes should be levied where the consumption takes place, but the supply of digitized products should not be taxed as a supply of material goods.

However, in the absence of uniformity of taxation of Net transactions, the mar-

Try Preview Question 3:

If different tax jurisdictions each take their "piece" of an Internet transaction, what might be the long-run result?

ket will still punish governments that attempt to apply relatively high taxes on cyber-transactions. If Toronto, for example, decided to subject on-line service providers to a 10 percent telecommunications tax, the companies would immediately move elsewhere.

CYBERSPACE EXAMPLE
Avoiding Taxes by Selling Offshore

 If you are willing to break the law, you can set up an Internet business in a Caribbean tax haven, such as Anguilla. All you have to do is send your name, phone number, e-mail address, and a proposed Web address for your business to www.offshore.com.ai. You will have a Web site set up, and an Anguillan lawyer will register your corporation. You can open a corporate bank account with the Anguillan branch of Barclays Bank or the local National Bank of Anguilla. You can transfer the $2,200 fee using DigiCash, Inc.'s e-cash—which is untraceable. Anguilla does not impose any taxes on your venture. It does not cooperate with Revenue Canada, either. You can get a corporate credit card and spend your money anywhere you want. Remember, though, that as a citizen or legal resident of Canada, you owe federal income taxes on your worldwide income.

For critical analysis: What types of businesses might individuals seeking to avoid taxes most likely set up on an offshore Web site?

Concepts in Brief

- Brands can be established on the Web itself.
- The Internet allows for a better way of reaching more finely tuned groups of potential customers. It is cheaper, and perhaps even more effective, than traditional direct-mail marketing methods.
- Because any Internet transaction may pass through numerous jurisdictions, confusion may reign for e-commerce unless a uniform taxing policy is adopted.

THE MICRO THEORY OF BUSINESS BEHAVIOUR WITH THE INTERNET ADDED

The theory we discuss in this textbook of the way firms make decisions was developed well before the Internet became even a pipe dream. How has the advent of the Internet changed the theory of the firm? To understand the answers to this question we look at several areas, including pricing and cost of entry.

Pricing

In a competitive market, the perfect competitor has no control over price—the perfect competitor is a *price taker*. The market price simply equals the price at which the market demand curve intersects the market supply curve. A firm with any market power, however, is a *price setter*. The profit-maximizing price occurs at the quantity at which marginal revenue equals marginal cost, with the price being read off the market demand curve.

Marginal Cost for Software.   Consider the issue of marginal cost. Once a software program is developed, the marginal cost of providing one more unit to the world via Internet transmission is very close to zero. Moreover, this marginal cost is probably constant over all of the potential demanders throughout the entire world (at least with respect to the cost incurred by the offering firm). What, then, is the correct pricing decision for a software company that can provide millions of users with its product at a virtually zero marginal cost? You will find the answer in Figure 21.2.

Such a pricing strategy cannot, however, provide revenues to compensate for the initial development costs of the program. So some software providers have come up with different ways to obtain revenues, even while "selling" their programs at a zero price. Microsoft Corporation has offered its Internet Explorer at no charge for years now. It obtains revenues from the advertising that it sells on the Explorer pages. Netscape went one step further at the beginning of 1998 and opened up its entire Navigator program free to the world. Anybody can modify Navigator now to suit a particular environment. The share of Netscape's total revenues from its Navigator browser program had already fallen to 13 percent when it made this policy change. The other 87 percent was obtained from the development of corporate intranets and the like.

Figure 21.2
Pricing When Marginal Cost Equals Zero

For a monopolist, MR = MC at quantity Q_m. The monopoly price would be P_m. For a perfect competitor, MR = MC = 0, so price would be P_{PC} (= 0) and quantity would be Q_{PC}.

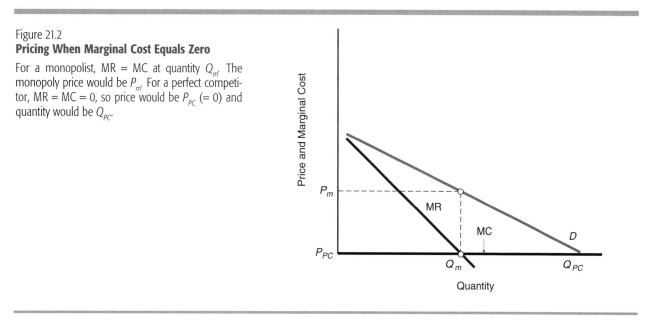

Many software firms have offered their programs free of charge simply to "capture" the names of users to whom it might later sell upgraded versions. This is true, for example, of the free e-mail program Eudora. Some accounting software has also been given away free. The best-known example among game players is Doom. The first few levels of the game are given away free on the Net. Once "hooked" though, players pay extra to get to more difficult levels. Several million copies have now been sold.

No Traditional Law of Diminishing Returns. Recall from Chapter 10 the law of diminishing marginal returns. Also remember that a firm's short-run cost curves are a reflection of the law of diminishing marginal returns. When diminishing marginal returns begin, marginal cost begins to rise.

Software production, now that the Internet exists, does not appear to follow this traditional rule. Once a program has been written, any number of copies can be sent out via the Internet at very little cost, and the cost does not increase with the number of copies. Software companies can cheaply capture a significant market share by giving away a program and then selling follow-up products (upgrades, add-ons, manuals) at higher prices.

Try Preview Question 4:
Why does the software business seem to belie the traditional law of diminishing marginal returns?

Cost of Entry

One thing the Internet has certainly done is reduce the cost of entry, at least for companies willing to sell goods via the Internet. Amazon.com has no inventory, only an Internet site, programmers, and a small staff. Numerous CD retailers on the Internet carry no inventories. The megamalls on the Internet carry no inventories. Entry and operating costs cover simply development of the software retailing programs, paying for the server, and other relatively modest outlays.

CYBERSPACE EXAMPLE
Your Business on the Net for $40,000

If you have an existing retail business, you can set up on the Net for an initial investment of about $40,000. The offer to do so was announced by Pandesic at the beginning of 1998. For the $40,000 fee, a small to mid-sized company can obtain everything it needs to put its business on the Net—and do so in less than six weeks. This includes computer hardware (a server) plus software programs to handle finance, shipping, and inventory. In addition, however, once the retailer is on the Net and up and running, Pandesic takes a fee of 1 to 6 percent of monthly sales. In return, Pandesic provides all of the installation, training, upgrades, and maintenance of the system. This approach was taken by Thin Blue Line, Inc., a small Canadian mountain-bike maker that stormed the US market via its Web site.

For critical analysis: To make a profit, what else must a company do besides get on the Net?

The Global Connection

One thing is certain: Because anybody can set up an e-commerce site from anywhere in the world, the Internet is easing entry into any retailing or wholesaling business. Moreover, foreigners can operate Internet sites just as Canadian citizens can. Thus, worldwide competition is a given on the Internet. Software that can be downloaded from anywhere is a clear example.

Concepts in Brief

- Pricing decisions for software products that can be downloaded from the Internet are difficult. The marginal cost becomes zero, but a product given away doesn't yield revenues to pay for its development.
- Some firms have succeeded by giving away their programs but charging for upgrades and updated versions.
- The Internet is leading to lower costs of entry, especially in retailing.

Issues and Applications

Cyberpiracy

Concepts Applied: Copyright, intellectual property, monopoly, law of demand, marginal cost

Industry (IFPI) estimates that one-fifth of all sales of recorded music are of pirated copies. For CDs, that group estimates that one in three sales is pirated.

This young man is proud of his bootlegged CDs. If unauthorized copies of CDs can be downloaded easily from the Internet, how will this affect the sales of legally produced copies?

The first legal copyright protection was a statute passed in Britain in 1709. Canada's *Copyright Act* was first passed in 1924. Modernization of this Act has been almost continual since the mid-1980s as new methods of illicit copying have proliferated.

However, no law, whether in Canada or elsewhere, has been very effective against the bootlegging of *intellectual property*—any creation whose source is a person's intellect, as opposed to physical property. The International Federation of the Phonographic

First Things First: The Law of Demand

There is a problem with the IFPI estimates, however. When estimating what legitimate CD sales would be in the absence of pirating, the IFPI assumes that pirated copies displace legitimate copies one for one, even though the pirated copies have much lower prices than legitimate copies. This assumption is a clear violation of the law of demand. In fact, there will be a larger quantity demanded at a lower price. Thus the lower-priced pirated copies of recorded music induce purchasers to buy more of them. If pirated copies did not exist, we could not predict that legal sales of CDs would simply replace them one for one. But pirated copies do exist, inflating potential sales estimates.

This same analysis can apply to pirated copies of software. The Business Software Alliance estimates that at least half the global market for software is pirated products. That does not mean, though, that if no pirating occurred, the sales of software would double. Remember the law of demand.

Altruists on the Internet

There has been a major change in pirating with the advent of the Internet. When you purchase a bootlegged CD, the group that produced the pirated version did so to make a profit. In contrast, many Internet devotees offer downloadable copies of software and recorded music at no charge. In other words, organized profit-seeking gangs are not always involved here. Such anarchy on the Internet may have serious long-term repercussions. People invest in producing high-quality intellectual property, be it software programs or recorded music, because they expect to be paid. The more free, unauthorized copies of such intellectual properties that people distribute on the Internet, the lower the payoff to investing in the development of such property. Without ways to reduce the bootlegging of intellectual property (for one can never prevent it completely), there will certainly be a decrease in the growth of investment of people's time, effort, and creative energy in the development of software, recorded music, and other intellectual property.

How to Survive Internet Copying

It used to be that a copy of a record was of lower quality than the original. A copy of a CD on cassette has a poorer sound quality than the CD. But the same cannot be said of digital copying on the Internet. Zeros and ones copy just as well through cyberspace as they do in a sophisticated studio setup.

There are ways, though, for intellectual property owners to improve their chances of retaining direct sales of their products. They can provide more "goodies" along with legally sold CDs in the standard plastic jewel box—the words to the songs, better liner notes, perhaps contests and drawings, and so on. Software providers have already learned that by offering more useful instructional packages with legally purchased programs, they are able to encourage potential buyers to shy away from bootlegged copies.

Finally, a technological breakthrough will help recording companies track down bootleggers. It is a type of "watermarking" system embedded in the digital information stored on a compact disc. It allows investigators to determine whether a CD was obtained legally or illegally.

Perhaps the extreme concern over the fate of recording artists in the digital Internet world is much ado about nothing. After all, when the *Grateful Dead* were touring, they allowed anybody to "bootleg" their live sessions. In the process, they created a cult of fans who could identify a particular concert in a particular city on a given date simply upon hearing the opening bars of a "bootlegged" CD or tape. The result was increased interest in purchasing other *Grateful Dead* recordings and paraphernalia.

For Critical Analysis

1. If CDs can be bootlegged, does the company that produced them retain its monopoly?

2. Most people have at least once copied a computer program or a CD. Is this always bad for the copyright owner of such material?

CHAPTER SUMMARY

1. The twenty-first century is dawning on the age of information. The use of the Internet by businesses has mushroomed, and billions of e-mail messages are sent each year.

2. The rising use of the Internet allows for a reduction in transaction costs. Relatively inexpensive programs for searching for the lowest price on the Web will lead to less variation in the price per constant-quality unit for any given item.

3. The greatest volume of transactions on the Web is between businesses. Retailing on the Web is taking longer to establish itself, in part because of fears that credit card numbers can be stolen in cyberspace. Better encryption programs will ultimately resolve this problem.

4. Increased acceptance of Web shopping will lead

to a reduction in the demand for retail space.

5. Pricing is a problem for software sold on the Web because once the software is produced, it can be distributed at very little cost to literally millions of potential users.

6. Because the Internet has made it easier and cheaper to go into retailing, the cost of entry has fallen. Also, foreign competition now exists that was too expensive to consider before.

DISCUSSION OF PREVIEW QUESTIONS

1. How does technological change affect the demand for labour?

Though technological change undoubtedly reduces the demand for more traditional labour services, that is never the end of the story. Individuals who provide such services are thrown out of work, but at the same time (or perhaps after a time lag), new types of labour services are demanded. Who could have imagined 20 years ago the types of labour services now demanded for Web design, Web marketing, and the like?

2. What is the main reason the Internet may lead to increased efficiency?

The Internet can be viewed as a giant ongoing process that reduces transaction costs. The more quickly buyers can locate sellers, the more efficient our economy becomes. The more competition occurs, even from other parts of the world, the more efficient our economy becomes.

3. If different tax jurisdictions each take their "piece" of an Internet transaction, what might be the long-run result?

To enter the e-commerce world, businesses have to know what they are in for. If they can never tell when, for example, a city government may try to tax an Internet transaction, they may be reluctant to move forward. Because Internet transactions go through many servers in many jurisdictions, too many taxes on a single transaction will hamper the growth of e-commerce.

4. Why does the software business seem to belie the traditional law of diminishing marginal returns?

Generally, after the production of an ever-increasing number of an item, its marginal cost starts to rise, due to diminishing marginal returns. For software production, an increasing number of copies can be distributed on the Internet without any significant rising marginal cost.

PROBLEMS

(The answer to Problem 21-1 appears at the back of the book.)

21-1. Imagine that you are selling a new word processing program that you have decided to give away free of charge on the Internet.

How can you make a profit?

21-2. Assume that you hired a great Web designer to make you a terrific-looking home page for your new business. Does this necessarily mean that you can stay in business?

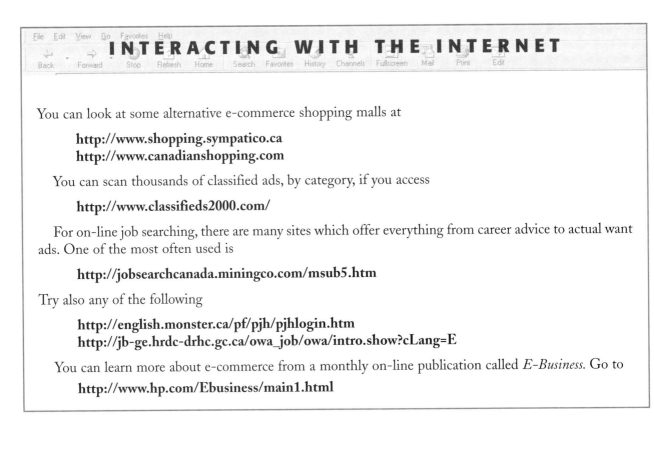

INTERACTING WITH THE INTERNET

You can look at some alternative e-commerce shopping malls at

> **http://www.shopping.sympatico.ca**
> **http://www.canadianshopping.com**

You can scan thousands of classified ads, by category, if you access

> **http://www.classifieds2000.com/**

For on-line job searching, there are many sites which offer everything from career advice to actual want ads. One of the most often used is

> **http://jobsearchcanada.miningco.com/msub5.htm**

Try also any of the following

> **http://english.monster.ca/pf/pjh/pjhlogin.htm**
> **http://jb-ge.hrdc-drhc.gc.ca/owa_job/owa/intro.show?cLang=E**

You can learn more about e-commerce from a monthly on-line publication called *E-Business*. Go to

> **http://www.hp.com/Ebusiness/main1.html**

ANSWERS TO ODD-NUMBERED PROBLEMS

Chapter 1
The Nature of Economics

1-1. A large number of possible factors might affect the probability of death, including age, occupation, diet, and current health. Thus one model would show that the older someone is, the greater is the probability of dying within the next five years; another would show that the riskier the occupation, other things being equal, the greater the probability of dying within five years; and so forth.

1-3. a. We should observe younger drivers to be more frequently involved in traffic accidents than older persons.
   b. Slower monetary expansion should be associated with less inflation.
   c. Professional basketball players receiving smaller salaries should be observed to have done less well in their high school studies.
   d. Employees being promoted rapidly should have lower rates of absenteeism than those being promoted more slowly.

1-5. The decreasing relative attractiveness of mail communication has no doubt decreased students' demand for writing skills. Whether the influence has been a significant one is a subject for empirical research. As for the direction of causation, it may well be running both ways. Cheaper non-written forms of communication may decrease the demand for writing skills. Lower levels of writing skills probably further increase the demand for audio and video communications media.

1-7. a. Normative, involving a value judgment about what should be
   b. Positive, for it is a statement of what has actually occurred
   c. Positive, for it is a statement of what actually is
   d. Normative, involving a value judgment about what should be

Chapter 2
Scarcity and the World of Trade-Offs

2-1. The law of increasing relative cost does seem to hold because of the principle that some resources may be more suited to one productive use than to another. In moving from cheese to apples, the economy will first transfer those resources most easily sacrificed by the cheese sector, holding on to the very specialized (to cheese) factors until the last. Thus different factor intensities will lead to increasing relative costs.

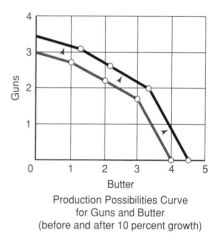

Production Possibilities Curve
for Guns and Butter
(before and after 10 percent growth)

2-3. a. Neither, because each can produce the same total number of jackets per time period (2 jackets per hour)
   b. Neither, because each has the same cost of producing ties ($\frac{2}{3}$ jacket per tie)
   c. No, because with equal costs of production, there are no gains from specialization
   d. Output will be the same as if they did not specialize (16 jackets per day and 24 ties per day)

2-5. a. Only the extra expense of lunch in a restaurant, above what lunch at home would have cost, is part of the cost of going to the game.
   b. This is part of the cost of going to the game because you would not have incurred it if you had watched the game on TV at home.
   c. This is part of the cost of going to the game because you would not have incurred it if you had watched the game on TV at home.

2-7. For most people, air is probably not an economic good because most of us would not pay simply to have a larger volume of the air we are currently breathing. But for almost everyone, clean air is an economic good because most of us would be willing to give something up to have cleaner air.

Appendix A
Reading and Working with Graphs

A-1.

y	x
12	4
9	3
6	2
3	1
0	0
−3	−1
−6	−2
−9	−3
−12	−4

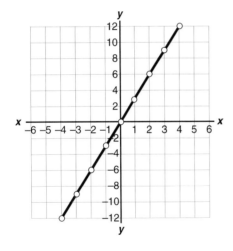

Chapter 3
Demand and Supply

3-1. The equilibrium price is $30. The quantity supplied and demanded is about 1,050 thousand skateboards per year.

3-3. a. The demand curve for vitamin C will shift outward to the right because the product has taken on a desirable new quality. (Change in tastes and preferences)

   b. The demand curve for teachers will shift inward to the left because the substitute good, the interactive educational CD-

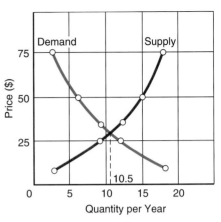

   ROM, is now a lower-cost alternative. (Change in the price of a substitute)

   c. The demand curve for beer will shift outward to the right because the price of a complementary good—pretzels—has decreased. Is it any wonder that pub owners often give pretzels away? (Change in the price of a complement)

3-5. As the graph indicates, demand doesn't change, supply decreases, the equilibrium price of oranges rises, and the equilibrium quantity falls.

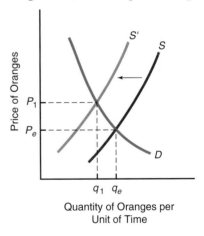

3-7. The speaker has learned well the definition of a surplus but has overlooked one point. The "surpluses" that result from the above-equilibrium minimum prices don't go begging; the excess quantities supplied are in effect purchased by government agencies. In that sense, they are not surpluses at all. When one includes the quantity that is demanded by the government agencies, along with the quantities being bought by private purchasers at the support price, the quantity demanded will equal the quantity supplied, and there will be an equilibrium of sorts.

3-9.   As the graph illustrates, rain consumers are not willing to pay a positive price to have nature's bounty increased. Thus the equilibrium quantity is 200 centimetres per year (the amount supplied freely by nature), and the equilibrium price is zero (the amount that consumers will pay for an additional unit, given that nature is already producing 200 centimetres per year).

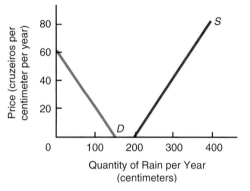

Chapter 4
Extensions of Demand and Supply Analysis

4-1.   a.   The demand curve will shift to the right (increase).

   b.   The supply curve will shift to the right (increase).

   c.   Because the price floor, or minimum price, is below the equilibrium price of 50 cents, there will be no effect on price or quantity.

   d.   Because the price floor is now greater than the equilibrium price, there will be a surplus at the new price of 75 cents.

   e.   Assuming that grapefruits are a substitute for oranges, the demand curve for oranges will shift to the right (increase).

   f.   Assuming that oranges are a normal good, the demand curve will shift to the left (decrease).

4-3.   The "equilibrium" price is $40 per calculator, and the equilibrium quantity is zero calculators per year. This is so because at a price of $40, the quantity demanded—zero—is equal to the quantity supplied—also zero. None will be pro-

duced or bought because the highest price that any consumer is willing to pay for even a single calculator ($30) is below the lowest price at which any producer is willing to produce even one calculator ($50).

4-5.   The equilibrium price is $4 per crate, and the equilibrium quantity is 5 million crates per year. At $2 per crate, the quantity demanded is 9 million crates per year and the quantity supplied is 1 million. This is called a shortage, or excess quantity demanded. The excess quantity demanded is 8 million crates per year. At $5 per crate, the quantity demanded is 2 million crates per year and the quantity supplied is 8 million crates. This is called a surplus, or excess quantity supplied. The excess quantity supplied is 6 million crates per year.

4-7.   As shown in the graph, if the equilibrium price of apples is 10 cents, a price floor of 15 cents will result in a surplus equal to $Q_s - Q_d$. A price floor of 5 cents per apple will have no effect, however, because it is below the equilibrium price and thus does not prevent suppliers and demanders from doing what they want to do—produce and consume Q_e apples at 10 cents each.

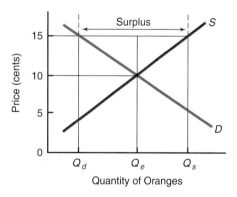

Chapter 5
The Public Sector

5-1.   The marginal tax rate on the first $3,000 of taxable income is 0 percent because no taxes are imposed until $5,000 is earned. The marginal rate on $10,000 is 20 percent, as it is on

$100,000 and all other amounts above the $5,000 level, because for each additional dollar earned after $5,000, 20 cents will be taxed away. The average tax rate, which is the tax amount divided by the pretax income, is 0 for $3,000, 10 percent for $10,000, and 19 percent for $100,000. The average tax rate will approach a maximum of 20 percent as income increases. It cannot reach exactly 20 percent because of the untaxed $5,000 at the beginning. Such is the nature of a degressive tax system.

5-3. Mr. Smith pays nothing on his first $1,500 of income, 14 percent ($70) on the $500 of earnings between $1,500 and $2,000, and 20 percent ($100) on the $500 that he earns above $2,000. Thus Mr. Smith has a total tax bill of $170 on an income of $2,500; his average tax rate is 6.8 percent, and his marginal tax rate is 20 percent.

5-5. Market failure means that the unrestrained operation of a market leads to either too few or too many resources being used in that activity.

5-7. a. If you give and everyone else does also, you account for 1 percent. If you are the only one who gives, you account for 100 percent. If you give nothing, you account for 0 percent, regardless of what others give.

b. In principle, your contribution matters whatever the level of participation. But as a practical matter, if participation is near 100 percent, the absence of your contribution may have little effect.

c. There is no free ride. If you do not make your contribution, total contributions will be lower, and the quality of the services provided will be lower.

5-9. The existence of these costs implies the notion of rational ignorance, so that individuals choose not to be informed about certain issues because the cost of being informed is high relative to any benefit forthcoming from the state of the issue. This also contributes to the growth of special-interest groups because individuals have no strong economic incentive to act against them.

Chapter 6
Economies in Transition

6-1. On the supply side, all of the industries responsible for automobile inputs would have to be considered. This would include steel (and coke and coal), glass, tires (and rubber), plastics, railroads (and thus steel again), aluminum (and electricity), and manufacturers of stereos, hubcaps, and air conditioners, to name a few. On the demand side, you would have to take into account industries involving complements (such as oil, gasoline, concrete, and asphalt) and substitutes (including bicycles, motorcycles, buses, and walking shoes). Moreover, resource allocation decisions regarding labour and the other inputs, complements, and substitutes for these goods must also be made.

6-3. a. Profit equals total revenue minus total cost. Because revenue is fixed (at $172), if the firm wishes to maximize profit, this is equivalent to minimizing costs. To find total costs, simply multiply the price of each input by the amount of the input that must be used for each technique.

Costs of A = ($10)(7) + ($2)(6) + ($15)(2) + ($8)(1) = $120

Costs of B = ($10)(4) + ($2)(7) + ($15)(6) + ($8)(3) = $168

Costs of C = ($10)(1) + ($2)(18) + ($15)(3) + ($8)(2) = $107

Because C has the lowest costs, it yields the highest profits, and thus it will be used.

b. Profit equals $172 - $107 = $65.

c. Each technique's costs rise by the increase in the price of labour multiplied by the amount of labour used by that technique. Because technique A uses the least amount of labour, its costs rise the least, and it thus becomes the lowest-cost technique at $132. (The new cost of B is $182, and the new cost of C is $143.) Hence technique A will be used, resulting in profits of $172 - $132 = $40.

6-5. a. In the market system, the techniques that yield the highest (positive) profits will be used.

b. Profit equals total revenue minus total cost. Because revenue from 100 units is fixed (at $100), if the firm wishes to maximize profit, this is equivalent to minimizing costs. To find total costs, simply multiply the price of each input by the amount of the input that must be used for each technique.

Costs of A = ($10)(6) + ($8)(5) = $100
Costs of B = ($10)(5) + ($8)(6) = $98
Costs of C = ($10)(4) + ($8)(7) = $96

Because technique C has the lowest costs, it also yields the highest profits ($100 - $96 = $4).

c. Following the same methods yields these costs: A = $98, B = $100, and C = $102. Technique A will be used because it is the most profitable.

d. The profits from using technique A to produce 100 units of X are $100 - $98 = $2.

Chapter 7
Consumer Choice

7-1. For you, the marginal utility of the fifth kilogram of oranges is equal to the marginal utility of the third ear of corn. Apparently, your sister's tastes differ from yours—for her, the marginal utilities are not equal. For her, corn's marginal utility is too low, while that of oranges is too high—that's why she wants you to get rid of some of the corn (raising its marginal utility). She would have you do this until marginal utilities, for her, were equal. If you follow her suggestions, you will end up with a market basket that maximizes her utility subject to the constraint of your income. Is it any wonder that shopping from someone else's list is a frustrating task?

7-3. Her marginal utility is 100 at $1. It is 200 at 50 cents, and 50 at $2. To calculate marginal utility per dollar, divide marginal utility by price per unit.

7-5. Optimum satisfaction is reached when marginal utilities per dollar of both goods are equal. This occurs at 102 units of A and 11 units of B. (Marginal utility per dollar is 1.77.)

7-7. Either your income or the relative price of eggs and bacon must have changed. Without more information, you can't make any judgments about whether you are better or worse off.

7-9. a. 20
      b. 10
      c. With consumption of the third unit of X

Appendix B
More Advanced Consumer Choice Theory

B-1. The problem here is that such preferences are inconsistent (*intransitive* is the word that economists use). If this consumer's tastes really are this way, then when confronted with a choice among A, B, and C, she will be horribly confused because A is preferred to B, which is preferred to C, which is preferred to A, which is preferred to B, which is preferred to C, and so on forever. Economists generally assume that preferences are consistent (or *transitive*): If A is preferred to B and B is preferred to C, then A is preferred to C. Regardless of what people may say about their preferences, the assumption of transitivity seems to do quite well in predicting what people actually do.

B-3. With an income of $100 and the original prices, you could have consumed *either* 50 kilograms of beef *or* 5 units of shelter or any linear combination shown by the budget line labelled "Original" on the graph below. With the same income but the new prices, you can now consume 25 kilograms of beef or 10 units of shelter or any linear

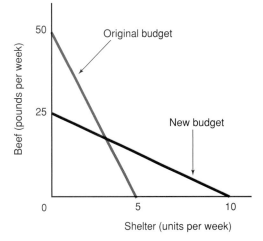

combination shown by the line labelled "New budget." Without information about your preferences, there is no way to tell whether you are better off or worse off. Draw a few indifference curves on the diagram. You will find that if you are a "shelter lover" (your indifference curves are relatively steep), the decline in the relative price of shelter will tend to make you better off. Conversely, if you are a beef lover (your indifference curves are relatively flat), the rise in the relative price of beef will make you worse off.

B-5. The first burrito is substituted at a rate of 10 servings of yoghurt per burrito; the second burrito is substituted at a rate of 4:1; the third at a rate of 3:1; and the fourth at a rate of 2:1.

B-7. a. This person is simply indifferent between going or staying, an attitude that is perfectly consistent with our assumptions about consumer preferences.

b. This statement denies the law of substitution and so is inconsistent with our assumptions about preferences.

c. If we interpret "if I had my way" to mean "if I had an unlimited budget," this statement simply says that there is nonsatiation for these goods for this consumer—which is perfectly consistent with our assumptions about preferences.

Chapter 8
Demand and Supply Elasticity

8-1. a.

Quantity Demanded per Week (kilograms)	Price per Kilogram	Elasticity
1,000	$ 5	
		$\frac{1}{3}$, or .33
800	10	
		$\frac{5}{7}$, or .714
600	15	
		$\frac{7}{5}$, or 1.4
400	20	
		$\frac{9}{3}$, or 3
200	25	

b. There are several ways to explain why elasticity is greater at higher prices on a linear curve. At higher prices, a given price change will result in a smaller percentage price change. The smaller resulting denominator of the elasticity ratio leads to a larger overall ratio. Similarly, as prices rise, quantities fall, thereby implying greater percentage quantity changes for a given absolute quantity change, and a larger numerator. Alternatively, the sizes of total revenue changes first increase and then decrease as price is lowered throughout a linear demand curve, thus implying declining elasticity.

8-3. a. Using averages in the elasticity equation, the income elasticity of demand for VCRs is $0.6666 \div 0.2857 = 2.33$. It is income-elastic.

b. It is presumably a luxury good.

8-5. The problem is with the denominator, percentage change in P. Because the initial price was zero, any increase in price is of infinite percentage. However, if we take the average elasticity over a segment, there will be no problem. P will become the average of P_1 ($=0$) and P_2 ($=10$), or $(P_1 + P_2)/2 = 5$.

8-7. a. $E_p = 5.8$

b. Demand is price-inelastic.

c. $E_s = 1.067$

d. Supply is price-elastic (but only slightly so).

8-9. In each case, "before" is before the development of an acceptable substitute for the good in question, and "after" is after the development of that substitute. For example, between 1840 and 1880, the railroad emerged as a good substitute for canal transportation. In general, the better the substitutes for a good, the greater the price elasticity of demand for that good. Thus in each case we would expect the price elasticity of demand to be higher after the emergence of the substitute.

Chapter 9
The Financial Environment of Business

9-1. A corporation would need the largest dollar amount of financing, and a sole proprietorship would need the least amount. Corporations tend to be large firms with greater requirements for capital. Financing would be required to purchase the capital. Conversely, sole proprietorships tend to be small firms with smaller capital requirements. Therefore a small firm would require less financing.

9-3. The taxation of corporate dividends applies only when profits are paid out to shareholders, and thus it encourages firms to finance expansion by reinvesting earnings rather than issuing new stocks and bonds. Exempting $10,000 in dividends from federal taxes amounts to a reduction in taxes levied on profits paid to shareholders in the form of dividends. As a result, corporations will be encouraged to engage in less reinvestment and instead to finance more of their expansion through a combination of additional stock and bond financing.

Chapter 10
The Firm: Cost and Output Determination

10-1. The opportunity cost of continuing to possess the van is being ignored. For example, if the van could be sold without much problem for $10,000 and you could earn 10 percent per year by investing that $10,000 in something else, the opportunity cost of keeping the van is $1,000 per year.

10-3. a. $1
       b. 5 cents
       c. $1
       d. 10 cents
       e. It is rising.
       f. When the marginal product of labour is rising, the marginal cost of output falls; when the marginal product of labour is falling, the marginal cost of output rises.

10-5. The long-run average costs represent the points that give the least unit cost of producing any given rate of output. The concept is important when one must decide which scale of operations to adopt. Such a decision usually takes the form of deciding what size plant to construct.

10-7. a.

Output	AVC
0	$ 0
5	20
10	18
20	11
40	8

b. The marginal cost is $40 when increasing output from 10 to 20 units and $100 when increasing from 20 to 40.

c.

Output	ATC
0	$ 0
5	60
10	38
20	21
40	13

10-9.

Units of Labour	Total Product	Marginal Product	Average Product
6	120	–	20
7	147	27	21
8	170	23	21.25
9	180	10	20

Chapter 11
Perfect Competition

11-1.

Output (units)	Fixed Cost	AFC	Variable Cost	AVC	Total Cost	ATC	MC
1	$100	$100.00	$ 40	$40	$140	$140.00	$40
2	100	50.00	70	35	170	85.00	30
3	100	33.33	120	40	220	73.33	50
4	100	25.00	180	45	280	70.00	60
5	100	20.00	250	50	350	70.00	70
6	100	16.67	330	55	430	71.67	80

a. The price would have to drop below $35 before the firm would shut down in the short run.

b. $70 is the short-run break-even point for the firm. The output at this price would be 5 units per period.

c. At a price of $76, the firm would produce 5 units and earn a profit of $30 ($6 per unit over 5 units).

11-3. The industry demand curve is negatively sloped; it is relevant insofar as its interaction with the industry supply curve (EMC) determines the product price. The demand the individual firm faces, however, is infinitely elastic (horizontal) at the current market price.

11-5.   a. $100
        b. $100
        c. $100
        d. $100

11-7. For simplicity, assume that your friend computed her "profit" the way many small businesses do: She ignored the opportunity cost of her time and her money. Instead of operating the car wash, she could have earned $25,000 at the collection agency plus $12,000 ($200,000 × 6 percent) on her savings. Thus the opportunity cost to her of operating the car wash was $37,000. Subtracting this amount from the $40,000 yields $3,000, which is her actual profit, over and above opportunity costs. You would tell her she really isn't making such great profits.

Chapter 12
Monopoly

12-1.   a. The rectangle that shows total costs under ATC_1 is $0WCQ$. Total revenue is shown by $0XBQ$. This monopolist is in an economic profit situation. MC=MR is the output at which profit—the difference between total cost and total revenue—is maximized.

b. With ATC_2, the rectangle showing total costs is $0XBQ$. The same rectangle, $0XBQ$, gives total revenue. This monopolist is breaking even. MC=MR shows the only quantity that does not cause losses.

c. Under ATC_3, total costs are represented by rectangle $0YAQ$, total revenue by $0XBQ$. Here the monopolist is operating at an economic loss, which is minimized by producing where MC=MR.

12-3. Four conditions are necessary: (1) market power, (2) ability to separate markets at a reasonable cost, (3) differing price elasticities of demand, and (4) ability to prevent resale.

12-5. If E_p is numerically greater than 1 (elastic), marginal revenue is positive; a decrease in price will result in more total revenues. If E_p is numerically equal to 1 (unit-elastic), marginal revenue is 0; a change in price will not affect total revenues at all. If E_p is numerically less than 1 (inelastic), marginal revenue is negative; a decrease in price will result in less total revenues.

12-7. a.

Price	Quantity Demanded	Total Revenue	Marginal Revenue	Total Cost	Marginal Cost	Profit or Loss
$20	0	$ 0	—	$ 4	—	$24
16	1	16	$ 16	10	$ 6	6
12	2	24	8	14	4	10
10	3	30	6	20	6	10
7	4	28	22	28	8	0
4	5	20	28	40	12	−20
0	6	0	220	54	14	−54

b. The firm would operate at a loss if it produced 0, 5, or 6 units.

c. The firm would break even at a rate of output of 4 units.

d. The firm would maximize its profits by producing either 2 or 3 units. At either of those two outputs, it would be earning a profit of $10.

12-9. a. TR=$10,000, $16,000, $18,000, $16,000, $10,000, $3,000

b. MR=$6,000, $2,000, -$2,000, -$6,000, -$7,000

c. 3,000 units

d. A profit-maximizing firm always sets MR=MC, and at any output level greater than 3,000, MR is negative. Naturally, MC can never be negative, thus ensuring that output levels where MR is negative are impossible for a profit-maximizing firm.

Chapter 13
Monopolistic Competition, Oligopoly, and Strategic Behaviour

13-1. The marginal revenue of this ad campaign is $1,000. There was an addition of 40 cars per week at $25 per car. To determine whether profits have risen, we would have to know how much additional cost was incurred in the tuning of these cars, as well as the cost of the advertisement itself.

13-3. a. Approximately 64 percent ($525 million ÷ $825 million)

b. The ratio would rise as the industry is more narrowly defined and fall as it is more broadly defined. Because an "industry" is arbitrarily defined, concentration ratios may be misleading.

13-5. The kink arises from the assumptions of the model. It is assumed that if any one firm raises its price, none of the others will follow. Consequently, a maverick firm's price increase will result in a drastic decrease in its total revenue. Conversely, the model assumes that any price decrease will be matched by all rivals. For this reason, the quantity demanded will probably not increase enough to cover increased costs. And profit will probably be less. Under these assumptions, it is in no individual firm's interest to "rock the boat."

13-7. The advertising campaign must increase weekly ticket revenues by at least $1,000 per week or it will be discontinued. This will require an additional 200 movie viewers each week.

13-9. The payoff matrix looks like this:

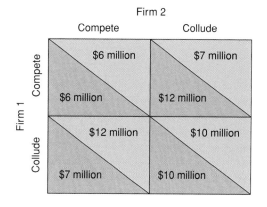

This situation parallels that of the prisoners' dilemma in that it is in the firms' collective interest to collude but in their individual interests to compete. If the possibility for collusion is a one-time-only arrangement, we have exactly the circumstances of the classic prisoners' dilemma, in which the dominant strategy is to compete, resulting in profits of $6 million for each firm. (This sounds good until you remember that each is *losing* $4 million relative to the joint maximum possible with collusion!) If this is a repeating game and if each firm can observe the behaviour of its rival, it may be possible for the firms to overcome their dilemma and reach the joint maximum—for example, by employing the "tit-for-tat" strategy discussed in the text.

Chapter 14
Regulation and Competition Policy

14-1. a. Quantity produced would be Q_b, and price would be P_c.
  b. Losses would equal the rectangle P_bBCP_c.

14-3. There will still be political pressure from Parliament if you enforce new regulations that dramatically increase the costs and hence the prices of products. Thus you can't simply do anything you feel like concerning new rules in the workplace. Since you must consider costs, you might want to estimate the impact each new rule has on the unit cost of each product affected. You would compare the total costs thus incurred because of the new rule with the estimated benefits to the community in terms of higher levels of worker safety and health.

14-5. Regulation typically brings benefits (lower prices) that are widely dispersed in small amounts over many people. But the costs of regulation—in this case, regulation of the hot springs price—are highly concentrated; indeed the hot springs owner bears all of the costs. The hot springs owner will no doubt oppose any regulation vigorously, while consumers will have only very weak incentives to press for it. Hence such regulation is unlikely.

Chapter 15
Labour Demand and Supply

15-1.

Quantity of Labour	Total Product per Week	MPP	MRP
1	250	250	$500
2	450	200	400
3	600	150	300
4	700	100	200
5	750	50	100
6	750	0	0

a. Demand schedule for labour:

Weekly Wage	Labourers Demanded per Week
$500	1
400	2
300	3
200	4
100	5

b. $100 each
c. Four

15-3. a. 15 million worker-hours per time period
  b. 10 million per time period
  c. Buyers can get all the labour they want at W_1; labourers can't sell all they want to sell at W_1.
  d. Because a surplus of labour exists, the unemployed will offer to work for less, and industry wage rates will fall toward W_e.

15-5. Suppose that the demand for the output product is highly elastic. Even a relatively small increase in the price of the input factor, which correspondingly raises the price of the output product, will cause a large decrease in the quantity of output demanded and therefore in the employment of the input.

15-7. The MRP of labour is $40 per worker-day ($3,040 less $3,000, divided by a change in labour input of one worker-day). The maximum wage that would still make it worthwhile to hire this additional employee would be $39.99 per day. If the going market wage is above that figure, you will not expand output.

15-9. Imposing limitations such as these implicitly reduces the ability of employers to compete for your services. Thus you can expect to receive a lower wage and to work in a less desirable job.

Chapter 16
Unions and Labour Market Monopoly Power

16-1.   a.   Marginal revenue product
      b. S
      c. Q_m
      d. W_m

16-3. Some examples would be BC Packers in Prince Rupert, BC; General Motors in Oshawa, ON.; and many textile companies in towns in Quebec. As long as your example is one of an employer that is dominant in its local labour market selling in fairly competitive markets, you are correct.

16-5. No, you should not. The MRP when you employ 31 people is $89.50 ($99.50 in revenue from selling the twenty-first unit, less $10 forgone in selling the first 20 units for 50 cents less than originally). The MFC is $91 ($61 to attract the twenty-first employee to your firm, plus the additional $1 per day to each of the original 20 employees). Because MFC exceeds MRP, you should not expand output.

16-7. Because the union acts in the interests of its members and the competitive wage is lower than the highest wage the union can obtain for its members.

Chapter 17
Rent, Interest, and Profits

17-1. The statement is false. Although there may be a substantial portion of rent in the revenues from these museums, we would have to assume that the museums are absolutely cost-free to keep in their current use in order to make the statement

that all revenues are economic rent. The most obvious expenses of keeping the museums operating are the costs of maintenance: cleaning, lighting, and other overhead costs. But these may be minor compared to the opportunity cost involved in keeping the museum *as a museum*. The buildings might make ideal government office buildings. They may be on land that would be extremely valuable if sold on the private real estate market. If there are any such alternative uses, the value of these uses must be subtracted from the current revenues in order to arrive at the true level of economic rent. Forgoing these alternative opportunities is as much a cost of operating the museum as the monthly utility bill.

17-3. The statement is false. Because a firm utilizes an input only to the point that the input's MRP is equal to its price, and marginal product is declining, it follows that all the intramarginal (up-to-the-marginal) units are producing more value than they are being paid. This differential is used to compensate for other factor inputs. The residual, if any, would be profits.

17-5.   a.   9 percent
      b.   The equilibrium interest rate will increase.
      c.   5 percent

17-7. In each case, the asset that qualifies the borrower for a lower interest rate is better collateral (or security) for the lender, and thus reduces both the chances of default and the lender's losses in the event that default does occur.

17-9. They would be reduced but not necessarily eliminated (because, for example, economic profits due to entry restrictions might still persist).

Chapter 18
Income and Poverty

18-1. Men might invest more in human capital; women might receive less and a lower-quality education and/or training; women in the workforce may take periods out of the workforce in order to raise children and thus accumulate less experience than men; discrimination may exist.

18-3. Productivity and equality

18-5. Such a program would drastically reduce efficiency. It would eliminate individuals' incentives to maximize the economic value of resources because they would receive no reward for doing so. It would also eliminate their incentive to minimize production costs because there would be no penalty for failing to do so.

Chapter 19
Environmental Economics

19-1.

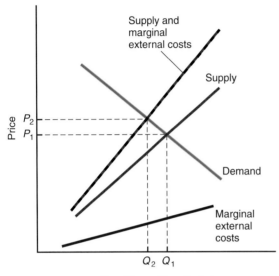

Quantity per Time Period

When the external costs are added to the supply curve (which is itself the sum of marginal costs of the industry), the total (private plus public) marginal costs of production are above the private supply schedule. At quantity Q_1 in the graph, marginal costs to society are greater than the value attached to the marginal unit. The demand curve is below the social supply curve. To bring marginal cost and marginal benefit back into line, thus promoting an economically efficient allocation of resources, quantity would have to be reduced to Q_2 and price raised to P_2.

19-3. a. The price of polluting should be set according to the marginal economic damage imposed by polluters; this means that similar quantities of pollution will cost polluters different prices in different parts of the country; pollution will be more costly in Toronto than in a small town in Saskatchewan.

b. Firms that find it cheaper to treat will do so; firms that find it cheaper to pay to pollute will pollute.

c. Yes, some firms will be forced to shut down due to increased costs; this is efficient, as the true costs to society of their operations were not paid by them and their customers; they were able to remain in business only by imposing costs on third parties.

d. This might be good because now the people who are using the resources will be forced to pay for them instead of imposing costs on others. Those who are not using these products were, in effect, subsidizing lower prices to those who were. This new solution seems fairer and is certainly efficient.

19-5. Everyone owns them and nobody owns them. Consequently, there is no incentive for any user to be concerned with the future value of the resource in question. This is perhaps most clearly observable in the behaviour of fishing boat owners. The goal of each boat owner is to harvest fish as long as marginal private cost is less than the going price of such fish. The opportunity cost of depleting the stock of fish does not affect the decisions of the proprietor. In light of the nonownership of the fish, any single boat operator would be foolish to behave otherwise.

19-7.

Annual Units of Pollution	a. Marginal Benefits	b. Marginal Costs
0	–	–
1	$ 30	$150
2	40	100
3	80	80
4	120	60
5	160	20

c. The net gain is (430-150) – 80 = 200.

d. The net gain is 430 – 410 = 20.

e. The optimal level is between 2 and 3 units, or where marginal benefit equals marginal cost.

19-9. The economically efficient amount of pollution occurs at a level at which the marginal costs of reducing it further would just exceed any benefits from that reduction. If pollution is reduced below this point, we would be better off with more pollution. The government might directly require firms or individuals to generate too little pollution (for example, through inappropriate environmental regulations), or it might establish pollution fees, fines, or taxes that overstate the damages done by the pollution and thus induce firms or individuals to reduce pollution too much.

Chapter 20
Development: Economic Growth Around the World

20-1. The following countries may be considered developing countries: Burkina Faso, Bangladesh, Afghanistan, India, and China; there are many others. The following are considered industrially advanced countries: Canada, Australia, Germany, France, and the United States; there are many others.

20-3. Initially, there is an agricultural stage where most of the population is involved in agriculture. Many developing countries are still in this stage. Then comes the manufacturing stage. Industry dominates the economy, and gains from the division of labour lead to rapid increases in output. In the final stage, the service sector becomes prominent in the economy. Canada and other industrially advanced countries are in this stage.

20-5. Economic development depends greatly on individuals who are able to perceive and take advantage of opportunities. Immigrants who possessed attributes such as these started Canada on the road to our present affluence. In general, voluntary exchange is mutually beneficial. If the potential immigrants are willing and able to offer their services at prices (wages) that existing residents are willing to pay, and to purchase the goods and services offered for sale by existing residents, the immigrants' arrival is likely to benefit existing residents as well as themselves.

20-7. It is important to remember that all resources are owned by human beings, and that in general there is an optimal (wealth-maximizing) mix of land, labour, and capital. So even though population growth (relative to growth in capital or land) would be expected to lower wages, it would also be expected to raise the earnings of capital and land. On balance, if the population growth moved the country closer to the optimal mix of land, labour, and capital, the added income accruing to the owners of land and capital would more than offset the reduced earnings of labour, producing an overall rise in per capita income.

Chapter 21
Cybernomics

21-1. You could do what the makers of the popular game "Doom" did: You could offer a more complete version of your word processing program for a fee. You could use the e-mail addresses of everyone who downloaded your free program to form the basis of a new marketing campaign to sell related items, such as self-improvement CD-ROMs. You could, of course, sell everyone a new, updated version of your program every year for some low price, such as $15.

ANSWERS TO CRITICAL ANALYSIS QUESTIONS

Chapter 1
The Nature of Economics

Issues and Applications: How Relevant Is Love in a Marriage Contract?

1. There is no difference between what economists and most people would predict about a good marriage. Economists assume that people act rationally, that is, they will not make decisions which leave them worse off. Marriage to a partner one does not love will probably not make a person happy. Therefore economists would expect to see marriage between people who love each other. Most people would expect to see the same.

2. If divorce is impossible, then people will spend a very long time (relative to the time spent when divorce is possible) looking for a spouse. Since the marriage is to last forever, the potential benefit is large. Thus people will incur relatively large "courting" costs looking for a mate before committing to marriage.

Chapter 2
Scarcity and the World of Trade-Offs

Issues and Applications: The Cost of Crime

1. Opportunity cost is such an important concept in analysing government programs to prevent crime because it highlights the trade-offs involved in crime prevention. A sum like $1 billion may not seem too much to eradicate crime in Toronto or Montreal, for example. But because our resources are limited, when that billion is converted into the hospitals and colleges and art galleries that would now be out of our reach, the trade-off becomes clear. It is not necessarily the dollars we spend on crime prevention that we need to count; we need to count the alternatives which we cannot now afford.

2. The opportunity cost of policing would rise as we added more resources to crime prevention. Picture a production possibilities curve representing all government services on the one hand and policing on the other. It would have the typical bowed out shape of the PPC in Figure 2.2 as we transferred less suitable

resources out of other government services and into policing. Not everyone would be able to do such a physical, dangerous job efficiently!

Chapter 3
Demand and Supply

Issues and Applications: How the Prices of Hockey Cards Have Responded to Changes in Supply and Demand

1. If the hockey players' lockout had actually dampened demand for hockey cards, the 1996 demand would have been weaker, and the demand curve would have shifted out less than shown in both parts of Figure 3.13. Prices for typical cards would be lower than P_2 in part (a) and P_4 in part (b).

2. The expansion of the National Hockey League into more American cities provides hockey card producers with new opportunities for producing hockey cards today. *Ceteris paribus*, the supply curve for 1998-99 hockey cards in a graph similar to part (b) would be further to the right, reflecting a greater supply of cards of the now larger number of players. However, the number of hockey cards produced in the 1979-80 and 1989-90 seasons would not change, and the supply of those cards would remain as pictured.

Chapter 4
Extensions of Demand and Supply Analysis

Issues and Applications: Grunge Meets Greed

1. Ticketmaster would not require a service charge as high as $50 because there would probably be little demand for tickets at that inflated price. A firm can only ask for a price as high as demanders will bear and, as we know, the quantity demanded of any good decreases as the price rises. Even if some fans would be willing to pay an additional $50 for a Pearl Jam ticket, it is unlikely that Ticketmaster could fill a venue with fans. In that case, Ticketmaster's revenues would be less than if it charged a lower service fee.

2. If the government restricted Ticketmaster to a $2 service charge on a $50 ticket, for example, the price to the customer would be $52 rather than the $60 it would be with a $10 charge. Look at Figure 4.4. At a price of $52, the demand for tickets would exceed the supply as it does at price P_1 and a shortage of tickets would occur. Some fans might purchase $52 tickets, and sell them to more devoted fans for $60 or even more. Without more information on the demand for rock concert tickets, we cannot say exactly how high a price, like P_2, scalpers would get.

Chapter 5
The Public Sector

Issues and Applications: Should We Switch to a Flat Tax?

1. Employees at Revenue Canada might well be against a flat-tax system. Advocates of a flat tax claim that one of the benefits would be a significantly downsized Revenue Canada, implying that many Revenue Canada employees might lose their jobs. We know from Chapter 1 that the rationality assumption tells us that people usually don't make decisions that reduce their well-being. It is likely that Revenue Canada employees would want to keep their jobs to maintain their well-being, and would thus oppose a flat-tax system.

2. A flat-tax system is more efficient than a progressive tax system because the method of calculation of tax owing is much simpler: there is only one calculation to make, rather than the many calculations required in a progressive system. There would be efficiencies realized by taxpayers who could complete their tax returns easily, and by Revenue Canada employees who could check the calculation as simply. The opportunity cost of the yearly tax return would fall, leaving resources free to pursue more productive activities.

Chapter 6
Economies in Transition

Issues and Applications: The Peruvian Transition from No Ownership to Clear Title

1. If suitcase farmers were given clear ownership rights to their land, they would have an incentive to settle down and produce a legal crop. With private owner-

ship comes the incentive to improve the land, since the profits from tilling it clearly belong to the owner.

2. It is not really possible to have wealth without property rights. If there are no property rights, who owns the wealth? What barriers are there to prohibit others from seizing your wealth, if it is not clearly defined as your property? Property rights—that is the right to own something exclusively—are necessary for the collection and retention of articles that make up wealth.

Chapter 7
Consumer Choice

Issues and Applications: Contingent Valuation: Pricing the "Priceless"

1. Opinion polls ask people to value something they are not purchasing. It is easy for an individual to put a $500 value on the use of a park; it is unlikely that same individual would pay $500 to use it. Demand curves show real willingness to pay for a quantity of a specific good or service.

2. Individuals normally express their perceived level of satisfaction by purchasing or not purchasing the good or service in question. If the individual values a product more than the price, that individual will purchase the product.

Chapter 8
Demand and Supply Elasticity

Issues and Applications: Productivity Improvements and Farm Incomes

1. Instead of increasing their productivity which increased the supply of wheat, farmers would have been better off trying to increase the demand for their wheat. Recall from Chapter 3 that factors which increase demand include tastes or preferences. An advertising campaign stressing the health benefits of bread might have helped, although we'll discover in Chapter 11 that collective action by farmers would have been difficult. Farmers could also have switched their land at least partly out of wheat and into some other crop with good demand but scant supply. This would have had the added benefit of reducing the supply and raising farm revenues from wheat.

2. If farmers had faced an elastic demand for wheat,

they would not have felt the same need to increase productivity. While incomes would have fallen to pre-war levels when demand fell off, any increase in supply with its attendant price decrease would result in increased revenues. Farmers would not need to increase productivity (shift out supply) as much to return to their war-time level of income.

Chapter 9
The Financial Environment of Business

Issues and Applications: Small Business Financing

1. The BDB and venture capital funds are not edging out the commercial banks by financing small businesses. Typically, sole proprietorships have difficulty convincing big lenders to finance them because they have little collateral and they lack the ongoing life of a corporation. The BDB and venture capital funds stepped into a void thereby assisting small business with financing requirements.

2. To circumvent adverse selection problems, the BDB requires applicants to open the books of their business for examination. The BDB could also require, among other things, extensive business plans and personal guarantees of loans. To circumvent moral hazard problems, the BDB could require frequent financial reports and unannounced inspections of the business by bank officers.

Chapter 10
The Firm: Output and Cost Determination

Issues and Applications: Wireless Communications

1. Recall that when additional units of a variable factor are added to a fixed factor, eventually the additional output resulting from the extra variable factor will diminish. In this case, the transmission towers are the fixed factor. The number of communication units accessing the wireless technology is the variable factor. Diminishing marginal returns might set in as the number of telephone calls in any one area becomes so great that transmission slows or the signal weakens. This happens now with cellular telephones—sometimes you cannot get a "line" to call out on; all the "circuits" are busy.

2. The long run for any firm is that amount of time it takes to change the scale of its operations. For the

wireless cable firms, the scale would be determined by the number of transmission towers it erects. Therefore the long run for a wireless cable firm would be that period of time it takes to erect, or to dismantle, transmission towers.

Chapter 11
Perfect Competition

Issues and Applications: Future Shop Versus the Traditional Record Retailers

1. No, the retail record market will not remain perfectly competitive. One of the characteristics of perfect competition is that there are a large number of small firms. Each time a Future Shop enters the market it drives out many more small record sellers. Gradually the market will become one of a few firms, the subject of Chapter 13.

2. The retail record business would probably be a constant cost industry. The major inputs are labour and "records" (CDs, tapes). Labour would come from a large pool of retail clerks. It is unlikely that the record business's growing demand for them would be significant enough to lead to rising wages. (We will learn more about this in Chapter 15.) The CDs come from recording companies. They are relatively inexpensive to produce and can be easily turned out in very large quantities. Unless the retail record industry expanded at a remarkably fast pace, the price of its major inputs would be unlikely to rise significantly.

Chapter 12
Monopoly

Issues and Applications: The Right to Develop Drugs Based on Genetic Data

1. It is not necessarily "bad" for the economy that SmithKline is charging a price greater than marginal cost for its discoveries. Research is expensive and SmithKline's discoveries have great potential value for society. Charging a price greater than marginal cost allows SmithKline to finance its research.

2. SmithKline does not have a pure monopoly with respect to genetic data. It has competitors—Roche Holding and Glaxo Holdings to mention just two. Nevertheless, given SmithKline's success, you could say it has an effective monopoly over the data.

Chapter 13
Monopolistic Competition, Oligopoly, and Strategic Behaviour

Issues and Applications: Game Theory: Opening Up the Brewing Industry

1. This game is a negative-sum game. Although the microbrewery gains $15 million, Labatt and Molson together lose $16 million.

2. Labatt and Molson could use other entry deterring strategies. They could reduce the price of their beer to average total cost. They would not earn economic profits, but the competing breweries would no longer have an incentive to enter the industry. Labatt and Molson could also introduce switching costs. For example, they could offer frequent flyer miles so customers have a vested interest in staying with one company. In fact, Molson offers Air Miles with the purchase of 15-can cases of its Canadian brand.

Chapter 14
Regulation and Anti-Competition Policy

Issues and Applications: Competition Policy for Non-economic Concerns?

1. There is certainly an argument for growing concentration of print ownership due to economies of scale. The work of reporters, for example, can be used in an increasing number of newspapers, thus reducing the unit cost per reporter. Newsprint can be bought in increasing amounts, possibly reducing the average cost of paper. Similarly, other supplies can be purchased in larger lots. One printing press might be used for more than one paper, if, for example, one paper in a particular locality was a morning paper and the other an evening paper. This would reduce the average cost of the printing press.

2. One reason the Competition Tribunal does not try to measure editorial diversity is that it would be almost impossible to do so in our economy. If all our newspapers and television and radio stations were owned by the same person who was dictating editorial content, then it would be clear that diversity did not exist. But within newspaper chains, there is often a certain amount of editorial independence. How would regulators tell what is an acceptable amount of diversity or too little? We have no current way of measuring this.

Chapter 15
Labour Demand and Supply

Issues and Applications: Are Immigrants Pushing Down Canadian Wages?

1. When immigrants come to Canada they become part of the consuming public. Their demand for goods and services, *ceteris paribus*, increases the domestic demand and prices rise. The rise in output prices increases the affected firms' marginal revenues, and hence their marginal revenue products. Through this mechanism, the demand for labour increases. The final effect on the wage is indeterminate, except that it will be higher than if there were no demand increase at all.

2. In the absence of immigration, Canada's labour force would shrink. With a smaller supply of labour, wages would rise, but the quantity of output would decline unless there were major productivity increases. It is likely that Canada's level of material wealth would decline with a declining population.

Chapter 16
Unions and Labour Market Monopoly Power

Issues and Applications: Pro Sports Means Big Bucks

1. A monopoly is an output market with one producer. A monopsony is an input market with one employer. A bilateral monopoly is an input market with one employer and one employee association.

2. One argument to justify subsidizing professional sports would be the revenues that the sport brings to the city from sports fans coming to see games. Out-of-town fans would eat in restaurants, stay in hotels, and shop, in addition to seeing the games. Tax revenues from these purchases would repay over the long term the short-term subsidy provided during the building of the stadium or arena.

Chapter 17
Rent, Interest, and Profits

Issues and Applications: A Million-Dollar Jackpot Doesn't Make a Millionaire

1. It does cost Canadian lottery foundations more to pay out in lump sums than if they were paying in instalments. Instead of paying in a lump sum, the lottery foundation could invest the unpaid portion of the jackpot and earn a market return on it. The opportunity cost of paying out in a lump sum is the forgone interest the foundation could have earned.

2. People play the lottery because they are willing to bet a very small part of their wealth on a very small chance that they will win a large sum of money. This explains the recent success of casinos in Canada. The odds of winning in a casino are larger than the odds of winning a lottery, but the payoff in absolute dollar terms is much lower. However, people find it exciting to take a chance on the roll of the dice, the turn of a card, or the numbers coming out of the lottery cage as long as not too much has been bet. Also someone wins and you cannot win (i.e., the expected return is zero) if you don't play.

Chapter 18
Income and Poverty

Issues and Applications: Eradicating Child Poverty

1. The new integrated child benefits plan will probably not end child poverty in Canada although it will likely improve the material conditions of many poor children. There are too few resources to be allocated to this plan to bring all children up to income equality. Since poverty is measured on a relative scale, some children will always be at the low end of the scale and will be classified as poor.

2. There are two main reasons implementing the critics' plan might be unsuccessful. First, putting money into improving economic conditions might not work. The money could be misplaced, it could provide a one-time improvement which doesn't continue over the long run, or it could be insufficient to make noticeable improvements in the economy. Second, people who are currently on social assistance may not necessarily get the jobs created by economic improvement. A physically challenged unemployed person may not qualify for the job. The jobs created may not be close to a centre of poverty, so that those who need the jobs would be able to get to work.

Chapter 19
Environmental Economics

Issues and Applications: Technology to the Rescue of Dwindling Fish Stocks

1. In the Canadian west a century ago, ranchers branded their cattle. Each rancher had a unique brand which was burned onto the cattle's hides. When herds intermingled, ranchers could sort out which cattle belonged to which rancher. In this way, they circumvented the common property problem.

2. One of the most obvious is to do what New Zealand did—set a catch limit, and sell or issue rights to a certain percentage of the catch. This is similar to the way provincial governments issue licences for game animals that allow a certain number of animals to be taken by a hunter. Another way would be to restrict the number of fishing licences available for fishers. So far as deep sea fishing outside territorial waters is concerned, mechanisms for enforcing catch limits are virtually non-existent. As long as a vessel is in international waters, it may engage in fishing. International regulatory bodies that include all countries do not exist.

Chapter 20
Development: Economic Growth Around the World

Issues and Applications: Can PCs Bridge the Gap Between Less Advanced and More Advanced Economies?

1. Latecomers adopt new technology more quickly than established economies because they have fewer resources invested in old technology. Businesses and governments in established economies which have invested millions of dollars in a computer system are

reluctant to invest more millions every time innovation produces a better product—even though the relative price of the new system is falling. However, when businesses and governments in developing economies invest in new technology they are more likely to be adding to, rather than replacing, their existing technology.

2. For technological innovation to spread rapidly in a country, businesses and consumers must have quick and inexpensive access to the technology. An economy which is closed typically applies either import quotas or high import tariffs to products entering the country. If these trade barriers apply to new technology, then businesses and consumers have neither quick nor inexpensive access to it, and the innovations will not spread.

Chapter 21
Cybernomics

Issues and Applications: Cyberpiracy

1. The firm that produces the CDs will not retain its monopoly if the bootlegging is widespread. However, if the bootlegging is confined to one country, then the firm may be able to retain its monopoly in other countries in which it sells.

2. Illicit copying of computer programs, while illegal, may not always be bad for the owner of the copyright. If people who copy the program like the way the program operates, they may wish to purchase more programs written by the same person. In other words, one copied program could lead to several purchased programs.

GLOSSARY

Absolute advantage The ability to produce a good or service at an "absolutely" lower cost, usually measured in units of labour or resource input required to produce one unit of the good or service.

Accounting profit Total revenues minus total explicit costs.

Adverse selection The circumstance that arises in financial markets when borrowers who are the worst credit risks are the ones most likely to seek loans.

Age-earnings cycle The regular earnings profile of an individual throughout that person's lifetime. The age-earnings cycle usually starts with a low income, builds gradually to a peak at around age 50, and then gradually curves down until it approaches zero at retirement.

Aggregates Total amounts or quantities; aggregate demand, for example, is total planned expenditures throughout a nation.

Anticombines legislation Laws that restrict the formation of monopolies and regulate certain anti-competitive business practices.

Asymmetric information Information possessed by one side of a transaction but not the other. The side with more information will be at an advantage.

Average fixed costs Total fixed costs divided by the number of units produced.

Average physical product Total product divided by the variable input.

Average tax rate The total tax payment divided by total income. It is the proportion of total income paid in taxes.

Average total costs Total costs divided by the number of units produced; sometimes called *average per-unit total costs*.

Average variable costs Total variable costs divided by the number of units produced.

Best response function The manner in which one oligopolist reacts to a change in price, output, or quality made by another oligopolist in the industry.

Bilateral monopoly A market structure consisting of a monopolist and a monopsonist.

Black market A market in which goods are traded at prices above their legal maximum prices or in which illegal goods are sold.

Bond A legal claim against a firm, usually entitling the owner of the bond to receive a fixed annual coupon payment, plus a lump-sum payment at the bond's maturity date. Bonds are issued in return for funds lent to the firm.

Bureaucrats Nonelected government officials who are responsible for the day-to-day operation of government and the observance of its regulations and laws.

Capital gain The positive difference between the purchase price and the sale price of an asset. If a share of stock is bought for $5 and then sold for $15, the capital gain is $10.

Capital loss The negative difference between the purchase price and the sale price of an asset.

Capitalism An economic system in which individuals own productive resources; these individuals can use the resources in whatever manner they choose, subject to common protective legal restrictions.

Capture hypothesis A theory of regulatory behaviour that predicts that the regulators will eventually be captured by the special interests of the industry being regulated.

Ceteris paribus **assumption** The assumption that nothing changes except the factor or factors being studied.

Collateral An asset pledged to guarantee the repayment of a loan.

Collective bargaining Bargaining between the management of a company, or a group of companies, and the management of a union, or a group of unions, for the purpose of setting a mutually agreeable contract on wages, fringe benefits, and working conditions for all employees in all the unions involved.

Collective decision making How voters, politicians, and other interested parties act and how these actions influence nonmarket decisions.

Common property Property that is owned by everyone and therefore by no one. Air and water are examples of common property resources.

Communism In its purest form, an economic system in which the state has disappeared and individuals contribute to the economy according to their productivity and are given income according to their needs.

Comparable-worth doctrine The belief that women should receive the same wages as men if the levels of skill and responsibility in their jobs are equivalent.

Comparative advantage The ability to produce a good or service at a lower opportunity cost compared to other producers.

Complements Two goods are complements if both are used together for consumption or enjoyment—for example, coffee and cream. The more you buy of one, the more you buy of the other. For complements, a change in the price of one causes an opposite shift in the demand for the other.

Concentration ratio The percentage of all sales contributed by the leading four or leading eight firms in an industry; sometimes called the *industry concentration ratio*.

Conglomerate merger The joining of two firms from unrelated industries.

Constant returns to scale No change in long-run average costs when output increases.

Constant-cost industry An industry whose total output can be increased without an increase in long-run per-unit costs; an industry whose long-run supply curve is horizontal.

Consumer optimum A choice of a set of goods and services that maximizes the level of satisfaction for each consumer, subject to limited income.

Consumption The use of goods and services for personal satisfaction.

Cooperative game A game in which the players explicitly collude to make themselves better off. As applied to firms, it involves companies colluding in order to make higher than competitive rates of return.

Corporation A legal entity that may conduct business in its own name just as an individual does; the owners of a corporation, called shareholders, own shares of the firm's profits and enjoy the protection of limited liability.

Cost-of-service regulation Regulation based on allowing prices to reflect only the actual cost of production and no monopoly profits.

Craft unions Labour unions composed of workers who engage in a particular trade or skill, such as shoemaking, printing, or baking.

Creative response Behaviour on the part of a firm that allows it to comply with the letter of the law but violate the spirit, significantly lessening the law's effects.

Cross elasticity of demand (E_{xy}) The percentage change in the demand for one good (holding its price constant) divided by the percentage change in the price of a related good.

Cybernomics The application of economic analysis to human and technological activities related to the use of the Internet in all of its forms.

Decreasing-cost industry An industry in which an increase in output leads to a reduction in long-run per-unit costs, such that the long-run industry supply curve slopes downward.

Demand A schedule of how much of a good or service people will purchase at any price during a specified time period, other things being constant.

Demand curve A graphical representation of the demand schedule; a negatively sloped line showing the inverse relationship between the price and the quantity demanded (other things being equal).

Demerit good A good that has been deemed socially undesirable through the political process. Cigarettes are an example.

Deregulation The elimination or phasing out of regulations on economic activity.

Derived demand Input factor demand derived from demand for the final product being produced.

Diminishing marginal utility The prin-

ciple that as more of any good or service is consumed, its extra benefit declines. Otherwise stated, increases in total utility from the consumption of a good or service become smaller and smaller as more is consumed during a given time period.

Discounting The method by which the present value of a future sum or a future stream of sums is obtained.

Diseconomies of scale Increases in long-run average costs that occur as output increases.

Distribution of income The way income is allocated among the population.

Dividends Portion of a corporation's profits paid to its owners (shareholders).

Division of labour The segregation of a resource into different specific tasks; for example, one automobile worker puts on bumpers, another doors, and so on.

Dominant strategies Strategies that always yield the highest benefit. Regardless of what other players do, a dominant strategy will yield the most benefit for the player using it.

e-commerce The use of the Internet in any manner that allows buyers and sellers to find each other. It can involve business selling directly to other businesses or business selling to retail customers. Both goods and services are involved in e-commerce.

Economic goods Goods that are scarce.

Economic profits Total revenues minus total opportunity costs of all inputs used, or the total of all implicit and explicit costs. *Can also be viewed as* the difference between total revenues and the opportunity cost of all factors of production.

Economic rent A payment for the use of any resource over and above its opportunity cost.

Economic system The institutional means through which resources are used to satisfy human wants.

Economics The study of how people allocate their limited resources to satisfy their unlimited wants.

Economies of scale Decreases in long-run average costs resulting from increases in output.

Efficiency The case in which a given level of inputs is used to produce the maximum output possible. Alternatively, the situation in which a given output is

produced at minimum cost.

Efficiency wages Wages set above competitive levels to increase labour productivity and profits by enhancing the efficiency of the firm through lower turnover, ease of attracting higher-quality workers, and better efforts by workers.

Effluent fee A charge to a polluter that gives the right to discharge into the air or water a certain amount of pollution. Also called a *pollution tax*.

Elastic demand A demand relationship in which a given percentage change in price will result in a larger percentage change in quantity demanded. Total expenditures and price changes are inversely related in the elastic region of the demand curve.

Empirical Relying on real-world data in evaluating the usefulness of a model.

Entrepreneurship The factor of production involving human resources that perform the functions of raising capital, organizing, managing, assembling other factors of production, and making basic business policy decisions. The entrepreneur is a risk taker.

Entry deterrence strategy Any strategy undertaken by firms in an industry, either individually or together, with the intent or effect of raising the cost of entry into the industry by a new firm.

Equilibrium The situation when quantity supplied equals quantity demanded at a particular price.

Exclusion principle The principle that no one can be excluded from the benefits of a public good, even if that person hasn't paid for it.

Explicit costs Costs that business managers must take account of because they must be paid; examples are wages, taxes, and rent.

Externality A situation in which a private cost diverges from a social cost; a situation in which the costs of an action are not fully borne by the two parties engaged in exchange or by an individual engaging in a scarce-resource-using activity. (Also applies to benefits.) A consequence of an economic activity that spills over to affect third parties. Pollution is an externality.

Featherbedding Any practice that forces employers to use more labour than they would otherwise, or to use existing labour in an inefficient manner.

Financial capital Money used to purchase capital goods such as buildings and equipment.

Firm A business organization that employs resources to produce goods or services for profit. A firm normally owns and operates at least one plant in order to produce.

Fixed costs Costs that do not vary with output. Fixed costs include such things as rent on a building. These costs are fixed for a certain period of time; in the long run, they are variable.

Free-rider problem A problem that arises when individuals presume that others will pay for public goods so that, individually, they can escape paying for their portion without causing a reduction in production.

Game theory A way of describing the various possible outcomes in any situation involving two or more interacting individuals when those individuals are aware of the interactive nature of their situation and plan accordingly. The plans made by these individuals are known as game strategies.

Goods All things from which individuals derive satisfaction or happiness.

Government, or political, goods Goods (and services) provided by the public sector; they can be either private or public goods.

Horizontal merger The joining of firms that are producing or selling a similar product.

Human capital The accumulated training and education of workers.

Implicit costs Expenses that managers do not have to pay out of pocket and hence do not normally explicitly calculate, such as the opportunity cost of factors of production that are owned; examples are owner-provided capital and owner-provided labour.

Import quota A physical supply restriction on imports of a particular good, such as sugar. Foreign exporters are unable to sell in Canada more than the quantity specified in the import quota.

Incentive-compatible contract A loan contract under which a significant amount of the borrower's assets are at risk, providing an incentive for the borrower to look after the lender's interests.

Incentive structure The motivational rewards and costs that individuals face in any given situation. Each economic system has its own incentive structure. The incentive structure is different under a system of private property than under a system of government-owned property, for example.

Incentives Things that encourage us to engage in a particular activity.

Income elasticity of demand (E_i) The percentage change in demand for any good, holding its price constant, divided by the percentage change in income; the responsiveness of demand to changes in income, holding the good's relative price constant.

Income in kind Income received in the form of goods and services, such as health care; to be contrasted with money income, which is simply income in dollars, or general purchasing power, that can be used to buy *any* goods and services.

Increasing-cost industry An industry in which an increase in industry output is accompanied by an increase in long-run per-unit costs, such that the long-run industry supply curve slopes upward.

Industrial unions Labour unions that consist of workers from a particular industry, such as automobile manufacturing or steel manufacturing.

Industrially advanced countries (IACs) Canada, Japan, the United States, and the countries of Western Europe, all of which have market economies based on a large skilled labour force and a large technically advanced stock of capital goods.

Industry supply curve The locus of points showing the minimum prices at which given quantities will be forthcoming; also called the *market supply curve.*

Inefficient point Any point below the production possibilities curve at which resources are being used inefficiently.

Inelastic demand A demand relationship in which a given percentage change in price will result in a less than proportionate percentage change in the quantity demanded. Total expenditures and price are directly related in the inelastic region of the demand curve.

Inferior goods Goods for which demand falls as income rises.

Inside information Information that is not available to the general public about what is happening in a corporation.

Insider-outsider theory A theory of labour markets in which workers who are already employed have an influence on wage bargaining in such a way that outsiders who are willing to work for lower real wages cannot get a job.

Intelligent shopping agents Computer programs that an individual or business user of the Internet can instruct to carry out a specific task such as looking for the lowest-priced car of a particular make and model. The agent then searches the Internet (usually just the World Wide Web) and may even purchase the product when the best price has been found.

Interest The payment for current rather than future command over resources; the cost of obtaining credit. Also, the return paid to owners of capital.

Labour Productive contributions of humans who work, involving both mental and physical activities.

Labour market signalling The process by which a potential worker's acquisition of credentials, such as a degree, is used by the employer to predict future productivity.

Labour unions Worker organizations that seek to secure economic improvements for their members; they also seek to improve safety, health, and other benefits (such as job security) for their members.

Laissez-faire French for "leave [it] alone"; applied to an economic system in which the government minimizes its interference with the economy.

Land The natural resources that are available from nature. Land as a resource includes location, original fertility and mineral deposits, topography, climate, water, and vegetation.

Law of demand The observation that there is a negative, or inverse, relationship between the price of any good or service and the quantity demanded, holding other factors constant.

Law of diminishing (marginal) returns The observation that after some point, successive equal-sized increases in a variable factor of production, such as labour, added to fixed factors of production, will result in smaller increases in output.

Law of increasing relative cost The observation that the opportunity cost of additional units of a good generally increases as society attempts to produce more of that good. This accounts for the bowed-out shape of the production possibilities curve.

Law of supply The observation that the higher the price of a good, the more of that good sellers will make available over a specified time period, other things being equal.

Least-cost combination The level of input use that produces a given level of output at minimum cost.

Lemons problem The situation in which consumers, who do not know details about the quality of a product, are willing to pay no more than the price of a low-quality product, even if a higher-quality product at a higher price exists.

Limited liability A legal concept whereby the responsibility, or liability, of the owners of a corporation is limited to the value of the shares in the firm that they own.

Limit-pricing model A model that hypothesizes that a group of colluding sellers will set the highest common price that they believe they can charge without new firms seeking to enter that industry in search of relatively high profits.

Long run The time period in which all factors of production can be varied.

Long-run average cost curve The locus of points representing the minimum unit cost of producing any given rate of output, given current technology and resource prices.

Long-run industry supply curve A market supply curve showing the relationship between price and quantities forthcoming after firms have been allowed the time to enter into or exit from an industry, depending on whether there have been positive or negative economic profits.

Lorenz curve A geometric representation of the distribution of income. A Lorenz curve that is perfectly straight represents complete income equality. The more bowed a Lorenz curve, the more unequally income is distributed.

Macroeconomics The study of the behaviour of the economy as a whole, including such economy-wide phenomena as changes in unemployment, the general price level, and national income.

Majority rule A collective decision-making system in which group decisions are made on the basis of 50.1 percent of the vote. In other words, whatever more than half of the electorate votes for, the entire electorate has to accept.

Marginal cost pricing A system of pricing in which the price charged is equal to the opportunity cost to society of producing one more unit of the good or service in question. The opportunity cost is the marginal cost to society.

Marginal costs The change in total costs due to a one-unit change in production rate.

Marginal factor cost (MFC) The cost of using an additional unit of an input. For example, if a firm can hire all the workers it wants at the going wage rate, the marginal factor cost of labour is the wage rate.

Marginal physical product The physical output that is due to the addition of one more unit of a variable factor of production; the change in total product occurring when a variable input is increased and all other inputs are held constant; also called *marginal productivity* or *marginal return*.

Marginal physical product (MPP) of labour The change in output resulting from the addition of one more worker. The MPP of the worker equals the change in total output accounted for by hiring the worker, holding all other factors of production constant.

Marginal revenue The change in total revenues resulting from a change in output (and sale) of one unit of the product in question.

Marginal revenue product (MRP) The marginal physical product (MPP) times marginal revenue. The MRP gives the additional revenue obtained from a one-unit change in labour input.

Marginal tax rate The change in the tax payment divided by the change in income, or the percentage of additional dollars that must be paid in taxes. The marginal tax rate is applied to the highest tax bracket of taxable income reached.

Marginal utility The change in total utility due to a one-unit change in the quantity of a good or service consumed.

Market All of the arrangements that individuals have for exchanging with one another. Thus we can speak of the labour market, the automobile market, and the credit market.

Market clearing, or equilibrium, price The price that clears the market, at which quantity demanded equals quantity supplied; the price where the demand curve intersects the supply curve.

Market demand The demand of all consumers in the marketplace for a particular good or service. The summing at each price of the quantity demanded by each individual.

Market failure A situation in which an unrestrained market economy leads to too few or too many resources going to a specific economic activity.

Merit good A good that has been deemed socially desirable through the political process. Museums are an example.

Microeconomics The study of decision making undertaken by individuals (or households) and by firms.

Minimum efficient scale (MES) The lowest rate of output per unit time at which long-run average costs for a particular firm are at a minimum.

Minimum wage A wage floor, legislated by government, setting the lowest hourly rate that firms may legally pay workers.

Mixed economy An economic system in which decisions about how resources should be used are made partly by the private sector and partly by the government, or the public sector.

Models, or theories Simplified representations of the real world used as the basis for predictions or explanations.

Money price The price that we observe today, expressed in today's dollars. Also called the *absolute, nominal,* or *current price.*

Monopolist A single supplier that comprises its entire industry for a good or service for which there is no close substitute.

Monopolistic competition A market situation in which a large number of firms produce similar but not identical products. Entry into the industry is relatively easy.

Monopoly A firm that has great control over the price of a good. In the extreme case, a monopoly is the only seller of a good or service.

Monopsonist A single buyer.

Monopsonistic exploitation Exploitation due to monopsony power. It leads to a price for the variable input that is less than its marginal revenue product. Monopsonistic exploitation is the difference between marginal revenue product and the wage rate.

Moral hazard A problem that occurs because of asymmetric information *after* a transaction occurs. In financial markets, a person to whom money has been lent may indulge in more risky behaviour, thereby increasing the probability of default on the debt.

Natural monopoly A monopoly that arises from the peculiar production characteristics in an industry. It usually arises when there are large economies of scale relative to the industry's demand such that one firm can produce at a lower average cost than can be achieved by multiple firms.

Negative-sum game A game in which players as a group lose at the end of the game.

Nominal rate of interest The market rate of interest expressed in today's dollars.

Noncooperative game A game in which the players neither negotiate nor collude in any way. As applied to firms in an industry, this is the common situation in which there are relatively few firms and each has some ability to change price.

Nonprice rationing devices All methods used to ration scarce goods that are price-controlled. Whenever the price system is not allowed to work, nonprice rationing devices will evolve to ration the affected goods and services.

Normal goods Goods for which demand rises as income rises. Most goods are considered normal.

Normal rate of return The amount that must be paid to an investor to induce investment in a business; also known as the *opportunity cost of capital*.

Normative economics Analysis involving value judgments about economic policies; relates to whether things are good or bad. A statement of *what ought to be*.

Oligopoly A market situation in which there are very few sellers. Each seller knows that the other sellers will react to its changes in prices and quantities.

Opportunistic behaviour Actions that ignore the possible long-run benefits of cooperation and focus solely on short-run gains.

Opportunity cost The highest-valued, next-best alternative that must be sacrificed to attain something or to satisfy a want.

Opportunity cost of capital The normal rate of return, or the available return on the next-best alternative investment. Economists consider this a cost of production, and it is included in our cost examples.

Optimal quantity of pollution The level of pollution for which the marginal benefit of one additional unit of clean air just equals the marginal cost of that additional unit of clean air.

Partnership A business owned by two or more co-owners, or partners, who share the responsibilities and the profits of the firm and are individually liable for all of the debts of the partnership.

Payoff matrix A matrix of outcomes, or consequences, of the strategies available to the players in a game.

Perfect competition A market structure in which the decisions of individual buyers and sellers have no effect on market price.

Perfectly competitive firm A firm which is such a small part of the total industry that it cannot affect the price of the product it sells.

Perfectly elastic demand A demand that has the characteristic that even the slightest increase in price will lead to zero quantity demanded.

Perfectly elastic supply A supply characterized by a reduction in quantity supplied to zero when there is the slightest decrease in price.

Perfectly inelastic demand A demand that exhibits zero responsiveness to price changes; no matter what the price is, the quantity demanded remains the same.

Perfectly inelastic supply A supply for which quantity supplied remains constant, no matter what happens to price.

Physical capital All manufactured resources, including buildings, equipment, machines, and improvements to land that is used for production.

Planning curve The long-run average cost curve.

Planning horizon The long run, during which all inputs are variable.

Plant size The physical size of the facto-

ries that a firm owns and operates to produce its output. Plant size can be defined by floor area, by maximum physical capacity, and by other physical measures.

Positive economics Analysis that is strictly limited to making either purely descriptive statements or scientific predictions; for example, "If *A*, then *B*." A statement of *what is*.

Positive-sum game A game in which players as a group are better off at the end of the game.

Present value The value of a future amount expressed in today's dollars; the most that someone would pay today to receive a certain sum at some point in the future.

Price ceiling A legal maximum price that may be charged for a particular good or service.

Price controls Government-mandated minimum or maximum prices that may be charged for goods and services.

Price differentiation Establishing different prices for similar products to reflect differences in marginal cost in providing those commodities to different groups of buyers.

Price discrimination Selling a given product at more than one price, with the price difference being unrelated to differences in cost.

Price elasticity of demand (E_p) The responsiveness of the quantity demanded of a commodity to changes in its price; defined as the percentage change in quantity demanded divided by the percentage change in price.

Price elasticity of supply (E_s) The responsiveness of the quantity supplied of a commodity to a change in its price; the percentage change in quantity supplied divided by the percentage change in price.

Price floor A legal minimum price below which a good or service may not be sold. Legal minimum wages are an example.

Price leadership A practice in many oligopolistic industries in which the largest firm publishes its price list ahead of its competitors, who then match those announced prices. Also called *parallel pricing*.

Price searcher A firm that must determine the price-output combination that maximizes profit because it faces a downward-sloping demand curve.

Price system An economic system in which relative prices are constantly changing to reflect changes in supply and demand for different commodities. The prices of those commodities are signals to everyone within the system as to what is relatively scarce and what is relatively abundant.

Price taker A competitive firm that must take the price of its product as given because the firm cannot influence its price.

Price war A pricing campaign designed to drive competing firms out of a market by repeatedly cutting prices.

Primary market A financial market in which newly issued securities are bought and sold.

Principal-agent problem The conflict of interest that occurs when agents—managers of firms—pursue their own objectives to the detriment of the goals of the firms' principals, or owners.

Principle of rival consumption The recognition that individuals are rivals in consuming private goods because one person's consumption reduces the amount available for others to consume.

Principle of substitution The principle that consumers and producers shift away from goods and resources that become relatively higher priced in favour of goods and resources that are now relatively lower priced.

Prisoners' dilemma A famous strategic game in which two prisoners have a choice between confessing and not confessing to a crime. If neither confesses, they serve a minimum sentence. If both confess, they serve a maximum sentence. If one confesses and the other doesn't, the one who confesses goes free. The dominant strategy is always to confess.

Private costs Costs borne solely by the individuals who incur them. Also called *internal costs.*

Private goods Goods that can be consumed by only one individual at a time. Private goods are subject to the principle of rival consumption.

Private property rights Exclusive rights of ownership that allow the use, transfer, and exchange of property.

Privatization The sale or transfer of state-owned property and businesses to the private sector, in part or in whole.

Also refers to *contracting out*—letting private business take over government-provided services such as garbage collection.

Product differentiation The distinguishing of products by brand name, colour, and other minor attributes. Product differentiation occurs in other than perfectly competitive markets in which products are, in theory, homogeneous, such as wheat or corn.

Production Any activity that results in the conversion of resources into products that can be used in consumption.

Production function The relationship between inputs and output. A production function is a technological, not an economic, relationship.

Production possibilities curve (PPC) A curve representing all possible combinations of total output that could be produced assuming (1) a fixed amount of productive resources of a given quality, and (2) the efficient use of those resources.

Profit-maximizing rate of production The rate of production that maximizes total profits, or the difference between total revenues and total costs; also, the rate of production at which marginal revenue equals marginal cost.

Progressive taxation A tax system in which as income increases, a higher percentage of the additional income is taxed. The marginal tax rate exceeds the average tax rate as income rises.

Property rights The rights of an owner to use and to exchange property.

Proportional rule A decision-making system in which actions are based on the proportion of the "votes" cast and are in proportion to them. In a market system, if 10 percent of the "dollar votes" are cast for blue cars, 10 percent of the output will be blue cars.

Proportional taxation A tax system in which regardless of an individual's income, the tax bill comprises exactly the same proportion. Also called a *flat-rate tax.*

Protocol The data formatting system that permits computers to access each other and communicate.

Public goods Goods to which the principle of rival consumption does not apply; they can be jointly consumed by many individuals simultaneously at no addi-

tional cost and with no reduction in quality or quantity.

Purchasing power The value of money for buying goods and services. If your money income stays the same but the price of one good that you are buying goes up, your effective purchasing power falls and vice versa.

Quota A set amount of output (less than the equilibrium amount) which farmers can supply to marketing boards for sale.

Random walk theory The theory that there are no predictable trends in security prices that can be used to "get rich quick."

Rate of discount The rate of interest used to discount future sums back to present value.

Rate-of-return regulation Regulation that seeks to keep the rate of return in the industry at a competitive level by not allowing excessive prices to be charged.

Rationality assumption The assumption that people do not intentionally make decisions that would leave them worse off.

Real-income effect The change in people's purchasing power that occurs when, other things being constant, the price of one good that they purchase changes. When that price goes up, real income, or purchasing power, falls, and when that price goes down, real income increases.

Real rate of interest The nominal rate of interest minus the anticipated rate of inflation.

Recycling The reuse of raw materials derived from manufactured products.

Regressive taxation A tax system in which as more dollars are earned, the percentage of tax paid on them falls. The marginal tax rate is less than the average tax rate as income rises.

Reinvestment Profits (or depreciation reserves) used to purchase new capital equipment.

Relative price The price of a commodity expressed in terms of another commodity.

Rent control The placement of price ceilings on rents.

Resource allocation The assignment of resources to specific uses by determining what will be produced, how it will be produced, and for whom it will be produced.

Resources Things used to produce other things to satisfy people's wants.

Retained earnings Earnings that a corporation saves, or retains, for investment in other productive activities; earnings that are not distributed to stockholders.

Scarcity A situation in which the ingredients for producing the things that people desire are insufficient to satisfy all wants.

Secondary market A financial market in which previously issued securities are bought and sold.

Separation of ownership and control The situation that exists in corporations in which the owners (shareholders) are not the people who control the operation of the corporation (managers). The goals of these two groups are often different.

Services Mental or physical labour or help purchased by consumers. Examples are the assistance of doctors, lawyers, dentists, repair personnel, housecleaners, educators, retailers, and wholesalers; things purchased or used by consumers that do not have physical characteristics.

Share of stock A legal claim to a share of a corporation's future profits; if it is *common stock,* it incorporates certain voting rights regarding major policy decisions of the corporation; if it is *preferred stock,* its owners are accorded preferential treatment in the payment of dividends.

Share-the-gains, share-the-pains theory A theory of regulatory behaviour in which the regulators must take account of the demands of three groups: legislators, who established and who oversee the regulatory agency; members of the regulated industry; and consumers of the regulated industry's products or services.

Short run The time period when at least one input, such as plant size, cannot be changed.

Short-run break-even price The price at which a firm's total revenues equal its total costs. At the break-even price, the firm is just making a normal rate of return on its capital investment. (It is covering its explicit and implicit costs.)

Short-run shutdown price The price that just covers average variable costs. It occurs just below the intersection of the marginal cost curve and the average variable cost curve.

Shortage A situation in which quantity demanded is greater than quantity supplied at a price below the market clearing price.

Signals Compact ways of conveying to economic decision makers information needed to make decisions. A true signal not only conveys information but also provides the incentive to react appropriately. Economic profits and economic losses are such signals.

Social costs The full costs borne by society whenever a resource use occurs. Social costs can be measured by adding private, or internal, costs to external costs.

Socialism An economic system in which the state owns the major share of productive resources except labour. Socialism also usually involves the redistribution of income.

Sole proprietorship A business owned by one individual who makes the business decisions, receives all the profits, and is legally responsible for all the debts of the firm.

Specialization The division of productive activities among persons and regions so that no one individual or area is totally self-sufficient. An individual may specialize, for example, in law or medicine. A nation may specialize in the production of lobsters, computers, or cameras.

Strategic dependence A situation in which one firm's actions with respect to price, quality, advertising, and related changes may be strategically countered by the reactions of one or more other firms in the industry. Such dependence can exist only when there are a limited number of major firms in an industry.

Strategy Any rule that is used to make a choice, such as "Always pick heads"; any potential choice that can be made by players in a game.

Strikebreakers Temporary or permanent workers hired by a company to replace union members who are on strike.

Subsidy A negative tax; a payment to a producer from the government, usually in the form of a cash grant.

Substitutes Two goods are substitutes when either one can be used to satisfy a similar want—for example, coffee and tea. The more you buy of one, the less you buy of the other. For substitutes, the change in the price of one causes demand for the other to shift in the same direction as the price change.

Substitution effect The tendency of people to substitute cheaper commodities for more expensive commodities.

Supply A schedule showing the relationship between price and quantity supplied for a specified period of time, other things being equal.

Supply curve The graphical representation of the supply schedule; a line (curve) showing the supply schedule, which generally slopes upward (has a positive slope), other things being equal.

Surplus A situation in which quantity supplied is greater than quantity demanded at a price above the market clearing price.

Tariffs Taxes on imported goods.

Tax bracket A specified interval of income to which a specific and unique marginal tax rate is applied.

Tax incidence The distribution of tax burdens among various groups in society.

Technology Society's pool of applied knowledge concerning how goods and services can be produced.

Terms of exchange The terms under which trading takes place. Usually the terms of exchange are equal to the price at which a good is traded.

Theory of contestable markets A hypothesis concerning pricing behaviour that holds that even though there are only a few firms in an industry, they are forced to price their products more or less competitively because of the ease of entry by outsiders. The key aspect of a contestable market is relatively costless entry into and exit from the industry.

Theory of public choice The study of collective decision making.

Third parties Parties who are not directly involved in a given activity or transaction.

Tit-for-tat strategic behaviour In game theory, cooperation that continues so long as the other players continue to cooperate.

Total costs The sum of total fixed costs and total variable costs.

Total revenues The price per unit times the total quantity sold.

Transaction costs All costs associated with making, reaching, and enforcing agreements, including the informational costs of finding out price and quality, service record, and durability of a product, plus the cost of contracting and enforcing that contract.

Transfer payments Money payments made by governments to individuals for which in return no services or goods are concurrently rendered. Examples are welfare, old age security payments, and Employment Insurance benefits.

Transfers in kind Payments that are in the form of actual goods and services, such as public education, low-cost public housing, and health care, and for which in return no goods or services are rendered concurrently.

Unit elasticity of demand A demand relationship in which the quantity demanded changes exactly in proportion to the change in price. Total expenditures are invariant to price changes in the unit-elastic region of the demand curve.

Unlimited liability A legal concept whereby the personal assets of the owner of a firm can be seized to pay off the firm's debts.

Util A representative unit by which utility is measured.

Utility The want-satisfying power of a good or service.

Utility analysis The analysis of consumer decision making based on utility maximization.

Variable costs Costs that vary with the rate of production. They include wages paid to workers and purchases of materials.

Vertical merger The joining of a firm with another to which it sells an output or from which it buys an input.

Voluntary exchange An act of trading, done on a voluntary basis, in which both parties to the trade are subjectively better off after the exchange.

Wants What people would buy if their incomes were unlimited.

Zero-sum game A game in which any gains within the group are exactly offset by equal losses by the end of the game.

INDEX